AI Game
Programming
Wisdom

AI Game
Programming
Wisdom

Edited by Steve Rabin

CHARLES RIVER MEDIA, INC.

Hingham, Massachusetts

Publisher: Jenifer Niles
Production: Publishers' Design and Production Services, Inc.
Cover Design: The Printed Image
Cover Images: Valve Software, Lionhead Studios, Stainless Steel Studios, Steve Rabin

CHARLES RIVER MEDIA, INC.
10 Downer Avenue
Hingham, Massachusetts 02043
781-740-0400
781-740-8816 (FAX)
info@charlesriver.com
www.charlesriver.com

This book is printed on acid-free paper.

Steve Rabin. AI Game Programming Wisdom.
ISBN: 1-58450-077-8

Library of Congress Cataloging-in-Publication Data
Rabin, Steve.
    AI Game Programming Wisdom / Steve Rabin.
        p.   cm.
    ISBN 1-58450-077-8 (hardcover with CD-ROM : alk. paper)
    1. Computer games—Design.   2. Computer games—Programming.
3. Computer graphics.   I. Title.
    QA76.76.C672 R33 2002
    794.8'154469—dc21

                                                            2001008585

Printed in the United States of America
03 7 6 5 4 3 2

Contents

Preface

Steve Rabin

On behalf of over 45 authors, welcome to *AI Game Programming Wisdom*! It is my great honor to deliver more than 70 articles containing the insight, knowledge, and wisdom that only comes through genuine experience and hard work. The authors have candidly revealed their mistakes and triumphs with the sincere hope that *you* will benefit and continue to push the field of game AI forward.

This book is a testament that artificial intelligence (AI) in games is serious business, and is no longer an afterthought in game development. Never before has so much valuable information on game AI been assembled in one place. Information strives to be free, even with the minefield of NDAs and the competitive, secret nature of game development. This book is but a first step toward serious cooperation and collaboration between game AI professionals.

Imperfect, Yet Impressive

Writing game AI is one of the most challenging tasks a programmer can undertake. Intelligence, by its very nature, is difficult to describe. Encapsulating it into a shipping product is that much harder. So, while it is destined to fall short of ideal expectations, people have slaved toward making it as perfect as possible. The techniques in this book are a result of this crazy process; the process of taking something incredibly difficult, enforcing time, money, manpower, and processing limits, and pushing to see what can be achieved. Of course, it is not perfect … but nonetheless, it is very impressive. Prepare to be impressed as you comb through and tackle the articles within.

This book is like a toolbox filled with wrenches, hammers, drill bits, and duct tape. You never know what you are going to need for a particular job. However, be sure to explore this book thoroughly, because if you don't know what tools you have, you might try to remove that nail with a welding torch; and your coworkers won't want to be around when you do.

The Encompassing Nature of Game AI

When I first started putting this book together, I was surprised to receive some rather strong criticism as to what shouldn't be considered game AI. Some individuals objected to including topics such as pathfinding or scripting in this book, suggesting that these topics aren't very interesting problems with respect to intelligence. While these are valid opinions, I've always held a much more inclusive stance regarding game AI. I've been influenced from two distinct sources.

First, it seems that game AI should be anything that a game AI programmer will have to program in order to make the game characters appear intelligent. So, while topics such as basic AI architectures and learning are critical, so are topics like pathfinding, scripting, and animation selection. The AI in a game must not only think, but also must sense its environment and act convincingly within it.

Second, when a consumer plays a game and the characters in the game look stupid, the consumer blames the AI. Whether the characters can't aim properly, move naturally, or maintain a rudimentary awareness of the situation, it is the AI that becomes suspect. There is no doubt in the consumer's mind as to what constitutes game AI. The characters must *appear* as if they know what they are doing, whether it's walking around an obstacle, participating in simple chitchat, or deciding when to retreat.

The articles chosen for this book reflect this encompassing view of AI. Squeezed into this volume, you'll find the topics that an AI game programmer has to deal with on a daily basis. There are plenty of books on pure AI topics, but this is one of the few books that witnesses the merging of contemporary AI with all of the messy practicalities of video games.

Learning: The Next Big Thing

With confidence, I can say that the next big thing in game AI is *learning*. I make that statement based on four factors. First, the very successful game *Black & White* featured learning techniques as a core component of gameplay, and proved that learning is a legitimate and practical technology for mainstream games. Second, after working on the first two *Game Programming Gems* books in 1999 and 2000, I can attest that very few proposals submitted for the AI section dealt with learning. Conversely, a very large number of learning and adaptation articles were submitted and accepted for this book (written during 2001). Clearly, many game developers have recently been pursuing and researching learning techniques. Third, recent polls of AI game developers show that learning leads almost 2:1 over every other category as the "next big thing" (www.gameai.com). Lastly, job advertisements for AI game programmers have been appearing that stress learning and adaptation as job requirements. The following quote is an excerpt from a job advertisement for Microsoft:

> *The Sports and Racing Games group is looking for a developer with a passion to create cutting-edge artificial intelligence systems. These systems will not merely react to the game player's input; they will anticipate and adapt. Games will no longer rest on the shelf because they have become too easy to beat.*

Therefore, with these four data points, learning will undoubtedly make a significant difference in game AI in the following years. In preparation for this new push, the *Learning* part of this book presents 10 articles and roughly 90 pages of material dedicated to learning. First, John Manslow will explain how learning and adaptation fit into your game design. Then, Richard Evans, Jonty Barnes, and Jason Hutchens will help you get up to speed on their achievements and aspirations with *Black & White*. Meanwhile, Fri Mommersteeg and François Dominic Laramée will explain several techniques for recognizing and predicting player patterns—essential to anticipating the player. With the help of several other authors, the *Learning* part will definitely help you stay on the cutting edge of game AI.

Building This Book

Putting together a book like this is an amazing process. By understanding that process, I believe it helps to put these articles in perspective.

This book began as an offshoot of the *Game Programming Gems* series. During the time that I was involved with the first two books in the series, I realized that there were dozens and dozens of great AI articles that would never get printed because of space limitations. Game AI truly deserved a book of its own.

After consulting Charles River Media and taking the pulse of other game AI developers at the 2001 Game Developers Conference, I realized that this book was ready to become a reality. There were many people interested in both reading such a book as well as writing for it. Once the project was given the green light, I created a Web site and began to track down authors.

In the pursuit of authors, I left no stone unturned. I scoured the Web for the names of AI game developers and sent out hundreds of personal invitations for people to submit proposals. I combed through every Proceedings from the Game Developer Conference and hunted down names of people who had previously written for *Game Developer* magazine. I flew to E3 in May of 2001 and spoke with dozens of companies and developers, spreading the word. Lastly, I posted the call for proposals on game programming mailing lists and numerous Web sites, including the infamous www.fat-babies.com (where you go to read the dirt on the game industry).

This hunt for game AI professionals paid off. I was flooded with over 170 amazing proposals from people who wanted to write for the book. Of those proposals, I carefully sifted and created the final selection that you now hold in your hands.

Once proposals were accepted, authors had two months to write their articles and code their demos. At the end of two months, an intensive peer review period began, in which each author reviewed at least three other papers. The feedback from fellow authors was tremendous, and proved to substantially raise the quality of each paper.

After the articles were revised from peer review, it was my turn to take a crack at them. Paper by paper, I spent the next three months reading every sentence in every paper. On average, each paper was edited back and forth three to four times between myself and each author. The goal was to make sure that you, the reader, is never misled, confused, or lost. Next, copyeditors painstakingly reviewed each paper again to correct remaining grammar, style, and formatting issues. Finally, the page proofs were returned to the authors for final corrections and approval. Then the book was off to the presses.

It is my sincere hope that this extensive selection and review process has created a book that you can routinely look to for guidance and inspiration. Take this book as a roadmap of what has successfully worked in the past, and use it to create even better systems in the future. With any luck, hopefully you will be writing about your own acheivements in a future *AI Game Programming Wisdom* book.

www.AIWisdom.com

As part of my commitment to supporting the game AI community, I'd like to announce the creation of a new Web site: www.AIWisdom.com. This Web site will track and catalog game AI articles, like the ones found in this book, the *Game Programming Gems* series of books, *Game Developer* magazine, the Proceedings of the annual Game Developers Conference, the Web, and many other sources. This site will allow you to view titles of articles along with abstracts, by topic, genre, source, or date published. Make it the first stop when you're looking for practical game AI solutions and insight. This Web site will also serve as the place to go for corrections to this book, as well as announcements for opportunities to write for future volumes.

Acknowledgments

A book like this requires the talents of many, many people. First, I would like to thank the authors who really made this book shine. Each article, overflowing with wisdom, is what makes this book so incredibly valuable. I owe a great deal to their hard work and their willingness to share their knowledge with fellow game developers.

I would also like to thank Jenifer Niles and Dave Pallai at Charles River Media for their encouragement and support in making this book a reality. I had always felt that there should be a book like this, and they were an integral part in making it happen.

This book would not exist if it were not for the vision of Mark DeLoura in bringing the *Game Programming Gems* series into existence. When Mark first told me about the book he was working on, I knew it was going to be important—and I knew I wanted to be a part of it. Thankfully, he allowed me to contribute a good chunk of my knowledge to it, thus paving the way for me to be a section editor in *Game Programming Gems 2* and eventually creating this book.

Several people dedicated their spare time to ensure the quality of many of the articles. I would like to thank Jim Boer, Miguel Gomez, Justin Heyes-Jones, and Tom Kent for their assistance.

Most importantly, I would like to thank my family. This includes my ever-loving wife, Leslie, and my two children, Aaron and Allison, who have had to endure months of recruiting, coordinating, and editing work as I managed to get this book completed on time in a span of six months. I couldn't have done it without their support and patience. Finally, I would like to thank my parents, Barry and Diane, whose encouragement has given me the confidence to take on tough challenges.

—Steve Rabin

About the Cover Images

The four images on the cover represent several game AI achievements from the authors of this book. While the images are not meant to imply that the games exist on the CD, they stand as a tribute to the hard work of the respective authors.

Top-Left Image: *Half-Life*

Valve Software's *Half-Life* was generally regarded by the gaming public as a ground-breaking game in terms of AI. In his article *Strategic and Tactical Reasoning with Waypoints*, Lars Lidén from Valve Software describes some advanced AI techniques that allow the AI to reason about the strategic importance of various locations in a game.

Top-Right Image: *Black & White*

Lionhead Studios' groundbreaking game *Black & White* showed the gaming world that learning AIs could be successfully integrated into a compelling and enthralling game. Three of the engineers who helped bring *Black & White* into existence share their knowledge and insight from this innovative game with no less than four amazing articles.

Bottom-Left Image: *Empire Earth*

Stainless Steel Studios' *Empire Earth* is an immense RTS game that required the talents of three full-time AI engineers. Each has written about his experience, bringing seven articles filled with wisdom on topics such as architecting an RTS AI, building a generic pathfinding engine, advanced A* optimizations, and military combat formations.

Bottom-Right Image: *Flocking Demo*

The schooling fish in this demo by Steve Rabin shows off some standard flocking techniques originally proposed by Craig Reynolds. The fascinating realization about flocking is that simple rules applied individually by each fish result in complex emergent behavior of the group as a whole. Lessons learned from this demo were contributed to article 9.6, "Simulating Real Animal Behavior" by Sandeep Kharkar. In addition, see article 4.6, "Simple Swarms as an Alternative to Flocking," by Tom Scutt.

Author Bios

Joe Adzima—Motocentric, Inc.

joe_adzima@yahoo.com

Joe currently works for Motocentric in Boulder, Colorado. Prior to his current assignment, Joe created the AI for the racing titles *Midtown Madness I & II*, and *Midnight Club Street Racing*. Joe holds a B.S. in mechanical engineering from the University of Florida, and has been programming for the games industry for the past six years. Prior to the games industry, Joe had a nine-year career in the defense industry designing creative AI solutions for military applications. When he's not behind the computer, he spends his time caring for his family, and hiking in the Rocky Mountains.

Bob Alexander—Stormfront Studios

balexand@earthlink.net

Bob Alexander has been programming since 1980. A few years after receiving his degree in computer science at U. C. Irvine in 1988, he worked for one of the four original AI companies, Inference Corporation. Bob has been working in the games industry for eight years. His most recent release is *NBA2K* on the Dreamcast, where he co-wrote the AI. He is currently programming the AI on an upcoming boat combat game called *Blood Wake* for Microsoft's XBox launch.

Thor Alexander—Hard Coded Games

thor@hardcodedgames.com

Thor Alexander has spent the last 10 years working to bring believable autonomous characters to the game industry. Recently, he founded Hard Coded Games in Austin, Texas to bring state-of-the-art AI and machine learning to online games. Previously, Thor held senior AI programming positions at Electronic Arts and Xatrix Entertainment, and was a founding member of Asgard Interactive and Harbinger Technologies.

Greg Alt—Surreal Software

galt@eskimo.com

Greg Alt (www.eskimo.com/~galt) has been in the games industry for six years, developing for the PC and PlayStation 2, although he really got started with games in the fifth grade by writing *Mars Mission* for the TRS-80 Model I. He is currently working for Surreal Software as an AI programmer, extending the AI system for the PlayStation 2 sequel to *Drakan: Order of the Flame*, and designing and implementing a new AI system for two other upcoming PlayStation 2 games. He has also worked on *Drakan* by Surreal Software, and *StixWorld* by PsychoHazard Software. He has a master of science degree in computer science from the University of Utah.

Jonty Barnes—Lionhead Studios

jbarnes@lionhead.com

Jonty Barnes is a founding member of Lionhead Studios and was a lead programmer on *Black & White*. The later part of the project saw his concentration on the gesture enhanced interface, and leading the implementation of the scripting language and story. Jonty entered the games industry in 1991 working at Bullfrog Productions. Before completing a degree in computer systems engineering at university, he worked on seven published titles, including the original *Dungeon Keeper* where he wrote the AI for the creatures. Jonty is currently leading Lionhead's next project that takes the *Black & White* world further.

Lee Berger—Turbine Entertainment Software

lberger@roy.org

Lee Berger currently works for Turbine Entertainment Software where he helped in the creation of *Asheron's Call*. After *Asheron's Call* shipped, Lee has focused his energies in the design and implementation of a distributed scripting language that will be used in all of Turbine's future massively multiplayer online games.

Gari Biasillo—Electronic Arts Canada

gbiasillo@ea.com, gbiasillo@shaw.ca

Gari Biasillo has over 16 years of experience in the video game industry with over 15 published titles under his belt. He began to program when the Commodore 64 and ZX Spectrum were at the peak of technology. In 1985, at the age of 14, his first game was released; two years later, he joined Interceptor Micros, one of Britain's founding video game companies. During his tenure, Gari has been programming in various areas of expertise, including AI, sound drivers, rendering, and physics. His current role at Electronic Arts Canada is the lead rendering programmer on *NHL*.

Bruce Blumberg—M.I.T. Synthetic Characters Group

bruce@media.mit.edu

The goal of Bruce Blumberg's group, Synthetic Characters, is to build a system that can robustly learn the kinds of things animals learn easily, that behaves with the everyday commonsense that animals display, and that evokes the same feelings of companionship and understanding that animals such as dogs invoke in us. Professor Blumberg has been a lecturer for the SIGGRAPH course on Artificial Life for Graphics, Animation, and Virtual Reality from 1996 to 1998; a lecturer in the SIGGRAPH 2000 course on Smarter Animated Agents; and a lecturer in the ALIFE for Games tutorial at the Game Developers Conference in 2000 and 2001. He was also on the jury for the Enhanced Realities venue of SIGGRAPH '98, and the Millennium Motel venue of SIGGRAPH '99. Blumberg and his group have been responsible for a number of interactive installations at SIGGRAPH, including ALIVE 1993, 1995; Swamped, 1998; (void *): A Cast of Characters, 1999. Other installations include sheep|dog: Trial By Eire, at the opening of the Media Lab, Europe, July 2000; and sand:stone, Digital Salon 1999. Blumberg received his doctorate from the Media Lab, studying under Professor Pattie Maes. He came to the Media Lab from NeXT Inc, where he was one of the original employees, and prior to NeXT was the product manager for the original Apple LaserWriter. He has a S.M. from MIT's Sloan School and a B.A. from Amherst College.

Mark Brockington—BioWare Corp.

markb@bioware.com

Mark Brockington has a Ph.D. in computing science from the University of Alberta. Mark is a lead research scientist at BioWare Corp., where he has worked for the last four years. Mark worked on the multiplayer code for the *Baldur's Gate* series, and is the lead AI/networking programmer for *Neverwinter Nights*.

Timothy Cain—Troika Games

cain@troikagames.com

Timothy Cain started working in the games industry in 1982, programming a bridge card game for Electronic Arts while he was in high school. After completing a master's degree in computer science at the University of California at Irvine, Tim returned to the industry in 1992. He made several games at Interplay, including the award-winning RPG *Fallout*, and juggled the roles of programmer, designer, and producer. In 1998, Tim co-founded his own company, Troika Games, which is currently making the RPG *Arcanum*. Tim has also taught undergraduate courses in computer game design at UCI.

Phil Carlisle—Team17 Software Ltd.

pc@team17.com

Phil has been game programming for about 20 years after getting access to a friend's Atari home computer. He spent many years in pursuit of a career as an architect, but later decided to switch from architecture to game programming. After completing a

BSc Hons degree in network and distributed systems at Leeds Metropolitan University, he began working for Team17 software, where he has spent the last five years working on various games, including *Worms 2* and *Worms Armageddon*. He has been involved with all types of game programming from graphics to networking, and everything between, but is now focussing on gameplay and character interaction (AI).

Alex J. Champandard—Artificial Intelligence Depot

alex@ai-depot.com

Alex has been interested in cognition and the theory of the mind from a young age, notably taking a philosophy module during his French baccalaureate. He has spent three years studying at the University of York, a course focused on the major fields of AI, graduating as a bachelor of science. Over the years, Alex has had a keen passion for the demo-scene, and has actively contributed to the graphics community via several articles and columns on flipCode. He has also worked on *Malice*: Argonaut's soon to be released XBox title where, among other things, he devised a modular agent-based flocking particle system. Alex is now doing post-graduate work with top researchers on behavior learning within a real-time noisy environment, a theory that he has applied to creating an FPS bot in his spare time. He is also the founder of the Artificial Intelligence Depot (http://ai-depot.com/), an ambitious site dedicated to the fascinating field of AI.

Chris Charla—Digital Eclipse Software Inc.

chrisc@digitaleclipse.com

Chris Charla joined Digital Eclipse as production manager early in 2001, where his job has him focusing on almost anything but managing production, including developing game designs, concepts, and proposals; creating AI; and working with development teams on design issues. Prior to Digital Eclipse, he worked at Imagine Media in a number of roles, including editor-in-chief of *Next Generation* and *Official Dreamcast Magazine*, and launch editor of IGN.com. He's been playing and making games since the Apple II days. He tries not to look at his career as a reaction to his parents not buying him an Atari 2600.

Mike Christian—Paradigm Entertainment

mikec@pe-i.com

Mike created the AI for *F1 World Grand Prix* and *Looney Tunes: Duck Dodges*, both for the Nintendo 64. Experience from those projects went into a toolkit being used to create character AI for two action titles for the latest consoles. He has been programming for over 16 years, with six of them in the game industry. He is currently the lead for an action title to be released on PlayStation 2 and XBox.

Mark Darrah—BioWare Corp.

markd@bioware.com

Mark Darrah has a B.Sc. in computing science from the University of Alberta. Mark is a lead programmer at BioWare Corp., where he has worked for the last four years. Mark has worked on all the games in the *Baldur's Gate* series, and was lead programmer on *Tales of the Sword Coast*, *Baldur's Gate 2*, and *Throne of Bhaal*.

Chad Dawson—Stainless Steel Studios

cd1f@yahoo.com

Chad is currently grinding away on *Empire Earth* at Stainless Steel Studios along with fellow AI programmers Dan Higgins and Bob Scott. Previously, he designed and programmed the neural network simulation package "PDP++" with the PDP Research Group at the Center for the Neural Basis of Cognition at Carnegie Mellon University. While at Carnegie Mellon, Chad obtained a B.S. in mathematics and computer science specializing in artificial intelligence and robotics. He later earned a master's degree in human computer interaction from Carnegie Mellon while focusing his studies on interactive entertainment. He has also served for eight years as a Signal Corps Officer in the United States Army and Army Reserve.

Richard Evans—Lionhead Studios

revans@lionhead.com

Richard is head of AI at Lionhead Studios, where he recently finished work on the highly acclaimed *Black & White*. He studied philosophy at King's, Cambridge and went on to take a master's degree in AI at Edinburgh. After spending a number of years tinkering with novel AI techniques in his bedroom, he eventually emerged and was happy to shelter under the Umbrella of Coolness that is Lionhead Studios. Richard and his wife Tiffany have produced a child, Barnaby Morgan Evans, who they scrutinize intensely, to try to figure out how he learns.

John Hancock—LucasArts Entertainment Co.

Jhancock@lucasarts.com

John Hancock has a Ph.D. in robotics from Carnegie Mellon University where he worked on vision and navigation algorithms for robotic cars. He has six years of AI programming experience, including two years in the games industry. While at Activision, he wrote the tactical and weapon AI for *Star Trek: Armada*. He joined LucasArts in May 2000, where he is currently developing the AI for *Star Wars: Obi-Wan* for the XBox. A designer at heart, John got his start in games by developing add-on levels for Bungie's *Marathon Infinity* to procrastinate writing his doctoral thesis.

Vernon Harmon—LucasArts Entertainment Co.

vharmon@lucasarts.com

Vernon Harmon received a bachelor's degree in mathematics and computer science from Carnegie Mellon University. He then worked within the Soar community at CMU for a few years before transitioning into the games industry. During his six-plus years in the industry, he has done AI programming, lead programming, designing, and writing, and has worked on RPGs, RTSs, FPSs, turn-based strategy games, and adventure games. In November 2000, he accepted a position at LucasArts to oversee the AI for *Star Wars: Galactic Battlegrounds*. He is interested in machine learning and speech processing, as well as music, education, soccer, and all things creative.

Daniel Higgins—Stainless Steel Studios

webmaster@programming.org

Dan is a proud member of *Empire Earth's* AI team, which consists of the talented Bob "The Bug Basher" Scott, and the amazing Chad Dawson. His background is in writing high-performance search engines for the *History Channel, A&E Channel*, and the *Biography Channel*. At a previous job, Dan did some COM integration architecture programming, but will only recall the details of it after a few stiff drinks and a lot of tears. In *Empire Earth*, Dan was responsible for the pathfinding, terrain analysis, computer player military, and animal AI. He is a computer science graduate of Frostburg State University in Maryland, and has a borderline maniacal passion for C++, games, STL, and optimization.

Jason Hutchens—Amristar

hutch@amristar.com.au

Jason Hutchens is an Australian engineer perhaps best known as the author of Mega-HAL, a mildly popular conversation simulator. From 1999 to 2000, Jason worked at Lionhead Studios on *Black & White*. Until recently, he was chief scientist at Artificial Intelligence, a private research company based in Israel, working on a project to create a baby machine that could grow up to pass the Turing Test. Since 1996, Jason has entered the Loebner Prize in AI, an instantiation of the Turing Test. He won in 1996 and has been unable to repeat the performance since. Whether or not this is indicative of improvements in the field is left to the reader as an exercise. Jason is currently a director of Amristar, an Australian IT innovation company with its eyes on the computer entertainment industry.

Damian Isla—M.I.T. Synthetic Characters Group

naimad@media.mit.edu

Damian Isla is a graduate student with the M.I.T. electrical engineering and computer science department and the Synthetic Characters Group of the M.I.T. Media Lab under Bruce Blumberg. His research focuses on brain architecture, synthetic perception, models of short-term memory and attention, and spatial reasoning. His thesis, "The Virtual Hippocampus" describes models for environment learning, navigation, and object permanence that together constitute a simulated creature's spatial sense. As a graduate student, he has worked on a number of AI-based projects that have been exhibited at GDC 2000, the opening of the Media Lab Europe in Dublin, and E3 2001. Recently, he gave a talk at GDC 2001 entitled "CreatureSmarts: The Art and Architecture of a Virtual Brain."

Before coming to the lab, Damian was an undergraduate at M.I.T. receiving a bachelor's degree in electrical engineering and computer science in 1999. He has worked with Marvin Minsky's Society of Mind Group, also at the Media Lab, and with the Virtual Worlds Group of Microsoft Research.

Sandeep Kharkar—Microsoft

eltoro_the_deep@hotmail.com

Sandeep Kharkar has a bachelor's degree in computer engineering from India and a master's degree in computer science from Utah State University. Throughout his education he scoffed at AI, calling it "fool's gold," and stuck with parallel processing as his line of interest. However, he has realized the folly of his ways and is a hard code AI follower now. He has published papers in various fields including parallel processing, software engineering, and game architecture. He has been programming professionally for seven years and has programmed mostly games, but also compilers, video phones, and agricultural data analysis tools! His AI credits include three hunting simulations for Sierra and the Golfer AI, and the birds and bees for *Links 2001*. He is currently working on camera AI for *Amped: Freestyle Snowboarding* an upcoming XBox title.

Kristin King

kaking@eskimo.com

Kristin King (www.eskimo.com/~kaking) has worked as a technical writer for seven years. She's been published in several Microsoft Windows Resource Kits and the magazine *NetWare Connection*, and her work has won awards from the Society for Technical Communication. She wrote the story for *StixWorld*, a game by PsychoHazard Software. She is also a published fiction writer, with an M.F.A. from the University of Washington, and the recipient of a Pushcart Prize. In her spare time, she likes to juggle and kayak.

Neil Kirby—Bell Labs

nak@lucent.com

Neil Kirby is a member of the technical staff at Bell Laboratories, the R&D arm of Lucent Technologies. He is currently exploring .NET technologies for use in operations and support systems. His previous assignments included a wide range of software development activities, as well as building speech recognition software and teaching at the university level. Neil holds a master's degree in computer science from The Ohio State University. In his spare time, he designs multiplayer, tactical combat computer games. He especially enjoys writing programs for computer opponents that play well without cheating. He has spoken on a wide variety of topics at the Computer Game Developers Conferences since 1991. He lives with his spouse and son in central Ohio.

François Dominic Laramée

francoislaramee@videotron.ca

François Dominic Laramée has plagued the game industry for almost a decade, during which he finagled his way into a variety of short-lived jobs as studio head, producer, designer, and programmer until he ran out of luck and had to become a freelancer. He single-handedly destroyed over 20 titles released on half a dozen platforms, has waylaid thousands of readers with his articles, and somehow managed to con two different universities into granting him graduate degrees. Visit his mediocre Web site, http://pages.infinit.net/idjy, at your own risk.

Lars Lidén—Valve Software

lars@valvesoftware.com

Lars has had a long-time interest in computational intelligence and computer games. After receiving a Ph.D. in cognitive and neural systems from Boston University, he found the perfect merge of the two by joining the games industry as an artificial intelligence specialist. His introduction to the games industry was at Presto studios, where he designed their AI engine from the bottom up. Currently, he is developing synthetic characters and working on the second-generation AI engine for Valve.

John Manslow—Neural Technologies Ltd.

john@jmanslow.fsnet.co.uk

John graduated from the University of Northumbria (UK) in 1994 with a first class honours degree in microelectronic engineering, specializing in the design of hardware neural networks. After a brief period of contractual work at the university's communications research group, he joined Neural Computer Sciences, where he developed an object-oriented neural network library. In 1996, John enrolled for a Ph.D. with the

University of Southampton's image, speech, and intelligent systems research group, applying AI to the analysis of satellite imagery. Upon completion of his Ph.D., John joined Codemasters Software Company Limited in the role of AI research and development programmer, and worked on several projects aimed at introducing learning into games. In early 2001, John moved to Neural Technologies Limited, where he uses advanced AI in the detection of telecommunications fraud. Current interests include the application of AI in games and the evolution of artificial organisms. John has over eight years of experience working with AI and contributed an article on neural networks to the book *Game Programming Gems 2*.

James Matthews—Generation5

jmatthews@generation5.org

James Matthews is a director and the chief editor of Generation5.org, one of the Internet's largest artificial intelligence Web sites. His work with Generation5 has introduced him to many different areas of AI—gaming and robotics being his two favorite. He is currently working for a degree in artificial intelligence and philosophy at the University of Leeds, UK. Outside of AI, James has a passion for Japan and Ibanez guitars.

Alex McLean—Pivotal Games

alex@pivotalgames.com

Alex first started programming in assembly language on the Sinclair ZX81, Atari 8-bit, and Commodore 64. Later came 16-bit systems that started a still present interest in the real-time demo-coding scene. He graduated from Edinburgh University with a joint honors degree in artificial intelligence and computer science in 1994. His dissertation involved genetic algorithms and artificial evolution, with the resulting working system forgoing the University's Sun workstations in favor of 68000 assembly and a Commodore Amiga! Rather than start on a Ph.D., Alex entered the games industry as a software engineer at MicroProse and later went on to be head of software engineering at Eidos' Pumpkin Studios. While there, he was lead PC programmer for the 3D real-time strategy title, *Warzone 2100*. As a co-founder and technical director of Pivotal Games, Alex is currently working on the graphics and AI for their first release, the action-strategy *Desert Storm*.

Mike Mika—Digital Eclipse Software Inc.

mikem@digitaleclipse.com

Mike Mika is the creative director for Digital Eclipse Software, Inc., and has been developing games professionally for nearly six years. His love for game development goes much farther back, to the early days of Apple II and Commodore 64. His most recent programming work can be seen in Disney's *Alice in Wonderland*, Disney's

Tarzan, Little Nicky, Klax, and *NFL Blitz* for the Game Boy Color. His role as creative director puts him into the designer's chair, helping programmers and artists realize their talent across a variety of platforms, applying his nearly 20 years of programming experience to the test. His next round of work will be seen on the PS2, Nintendo GameCube, and Game Boy Advance.

Fri Mommersteeg—Eindhoven University of Technology, Netherlands

frimommersteeg@hotmail.com

Fri Mommersteeg is a 21-year-old graduate student of the computer science department at Eindhoven University of Technology. Besides his study, he did jobs ranging from software tester and Web developer to tools programmer and software analyst. He has worked part-time in the e-commerce business, and assisted during practicals for first-year students. He managed to do all this while attending colleges at a fair pace, and has received a scholarship for being an excellent student. His wish is to apply his theoretical knowledge in game programming, and realize his true dream: becoming a game developer!

John O'Brien—Red Storm Entertainment

jobrien@nc.rr.com

John O'Brien spent five years wandering in the wilderness working on operating systems and databases while designing game AI architectures for fun before discovering he could get paid to do his hobby. He has been doing AI work in the games industry for four years, publishing three titles with Red Storm Entertainment. John spoke about Team AI at the 2001 Game Developer's Conference. He has a degree in computer science from Drew University.

Jeff Orkin—Monolith Productions

jorkin@blarg.net

In his five years in the game industry, Jeff has developed AI and animation systems for two titles at Sierra Studios and is currently working on AI and animation systems for the sequel to *The Operative: No One Lives Forever* at Monolith Productions. Jeff holds a degree in computer science from Tufts University, and a minor in computer animation from The School of the Museum of Fine Arts, Boston. He is currently completing a master's degree in computer science at the University of Washington. His personal Web site is www.jorkin.com.

Marco Pinter—Badass Games

marco@badass.com

Marco Pinter launched into the multimedia arena in the early 1990s by creating a popular Windows-based digital video editing package. He later founded and ran development house Digital Media International (a.k.a. Addictive Media) for several years. Pinter has acted as producer and/or lead programmer on a wide variety of titles published by Mattel Media, Activision, Disney Imagineering, and others. Pinter received his M.S. in computer science from the University of California, concentrating in artificial intelligence. He currently specializes in AI for games, working with hybrid techniques in genetic algorithms, artificial life, neural networks, and advanced pathfinding. He has published in *Game Developer* magazine and *The McGraw Hill Handbook of Multimedia*, and has spoken at the GDC and AGDC.

Falko Poiker—Relic Entertainment

falko_3@hotmail.com

Falko Poiker started his foray into computer game AI by creating the computer player for Relic's *Homeworld*. Prior to this, Falko earned a BASc in engineering at Simon Fraser University and worked at various engineering companies, including Motorola Canada Inc. and Dornier Aerospace GmbH in Germany. While working on *Homeworld 2* at Relic, Falko worked closely with designers in their quest to script compelling levels for the game using *Homeworld's* proprietary scripting language KAS (Kick Ass Scripting). He also scripted his own single-player levels and programmed opponent AI. No longer with Relic, Falko is currently travelling through Europe.

Steve Rabin—Nintendo of America, Inc.

steve@aiwisdom.com, steve_rabin@hotmail.com

Steve Rabin is a 10-year video game industry veteran working at Nintendo of America. He's written AI for three published games and was a contributing author for *Game Programming Gems 1, 2, & 3*, as well as the AI section editor for *Game Programming Gems 2*. He has previously spoken on AI at the Game Developers Conference and holds a degree in computer engineering from the University of Washington, where he specialized in robotics.

John Reynolds—Creative Asylum Ltd.

john@creative-asylum.com

John has been programming computer games since 1983, taking time out to earn a degree in applied computing from Manchester Metropolitan University. He now works for Creative Asylum, in the UK, and recent projects include *Rally Champi-*

onship and *Pac-Man: Adventures in Time*. John is also a columnist for the games industry magazine *Develop*.

Bob Scott—Stainless Steel Studios

bob@stainlesssteelstudios.com

Bob is currently developing the AI for *Empire Earth* at Stainless Steel Studios, along with Dan Higgins and Chad Dawson (also contributing authors). While his games industry experience is a mere five years, he has been programming for nearly 20 years, a good portion of that dealing with robotic control systems. He holds a degree in computer science with a focus on AI from the University of California at Santa Cruz. He has programming credits in several titles from Red Orb Entertainment, and is looking forward to adding *Empire Earth* to that growing list.

Tom Scutt—Gatehouse Games Ltd.

tom@gatehousegames.com

Tom Scutt obtained a degree in philosophy and cognitive studies at University of Sussex before completing a Ph.D. in AI (controlling autonomous robots using biologically realistic neural networks) at the University of Southampton. He then worked for seven years as a lecturer in AI at the University of Nottingham and published more than a dozen papers on a variety of subjects, including neural networks, autonomous robotics, language acquisition, cricket phonotaxis, and the philosophy of mind. Four years ago, he left academia to begin working as an AI programmer at Core Design Ltd., and was responsible for the AI programming in the last three *Tomb Raider* games. In 2001, he left Core Design to form Gatehouse Games, where he is currently working on a multiplayer role-playing game for the handheld market.

P. J. Snavely—Acclaim Entertainment

psnavely@acclaim.com

P. J. Snavely is a five-year veteran of both PC and console baseball games. His work with baseball AI has appeared in five different baseball titles, the latest and greatest being *All-Star Baseball 2002*. After a three-year stint at Stormfront Studios where he worked on the *Tony La Russa* baseball series, P. J. was the lead programmer on *All-Star Baseball*, and is currently the producer for *All-Star Baseball 2003*. He received a degree in computer engineering from the University of South Carolina, and completed some graduate work involving middle-game chess positions and game logic. His interests include baseball, football, basketball, fantasy sports, foosball, and being the commissioner of any league he can start.

Noah Stein—Vision Scape Interactive

noah@acm.org

Noah Stein has been programming since the advent of the Atari 800. His first credit appeared on *DeluxePaint ST* written by Artistech Development. Noah entered the games industry full-time in 1993 after studying computer engineering at U.C. San Diego. After an early focus on 2D graphics and AI, he has set his current focus on 3D graphics, software architectures, and tools pipelines.

Smith Surasmith—Angel Studios

ssurasmith@angelstudios.com

Smith Surasmith has been in the video game industry for five years. He has worked for Activision and is currently with Angel Studios. He has worked on six published projects, with one on the way. Of these, he has written or is currently writing AI for *Heavy Gear* and *Smuggler's Run*, and *Smuggler's Run 2*. He holds a degree in computer science from Brown University.

Paul Tozour—Ion Storm Austin

gehn29@yahoo.com

Paul Tozour is currently the AI developer for *Thief 3* at Ion Storm Austin. He previously developed the combat AI ("bots") for Microsoft's highly acclaimed *MechWarrior 4: Vengeance*. Paul has been in the industry for approximately seven years and has been credited with programming and design work on a real-time strategy title published by Red Orb Entertainment.

William van der Sterren—CGF-AI

william.van.der.sterren@cgf-ai.com

William van der Sterren is owner and developer at CGF-AI (www.cgf-ai.com), a small company providing AI solutions for tactical games and simulations. William contributed a chapter on "Terrain Analysis for 3D Action Games" to the *Game Programming Gems II* book, and spoke on the same subject at the 2001 Game Developers Conference. William also holds a senior scientist position at the Philips Electronics Research labs, and has master degrees in both computer science (Twente University) and technical design (Eindhoven University of Technology).

Tom Vykruta—Surreal Software

pharcyde000@hotmail.com

In 1995, Tom Vykruta broke into the industry as a lead programmer on an unreleased *Quake* mod where he worked with talented developers who shortly thereafter became employed by Valve, Id, Raven, Ion., and GlyphX. Next came freelance work (Six Flags theme parks, etc.) and ground-up development of a critically acclaimed *Quake 2* keyframe sequencer, *Demented 2*, published alongside *WorldCraft*. A week after high school graduation, Tom was offered a job with *Surreal* and chose it in favor of higher education. With *Drakan* under his belt, Tom is now a PS2 technology programmer working on *Drakan 2*. During the last two years, Tom has also been actively developing a 3DMMORPG *Traveler's Quest* in his spare time.

Steven Woodcock—Wyrd Wyrks

ferretman@gameai.com

Steven Woodcock's background in game AI comes from 18 years of ballistic missile defense work building massive real-time war-games and simulators. He did a stint in the consumer arena, and then returned to the defense world to help develop the AI for the national missile defense system. He maintains a Web page dedicated to game AI at www.gameai.com, and is the author of a number of papers and publications on the subject. He now pursues game AI through a variety of contract work, helps moderate the Game AI round tables at the Game Developers Conference, and has had the honor of serving as contributor to and technical editor for several books and magazines in the field. Steve lives in gorgeous Colorado Springs at the foot of Pikes Peak with his lovely wyfe (sic) Colleen, an indeterminate number of pet ferrets, and one neurotic red basenji. Hobbies include hiking, shooting, writing, and working on old GMC trucks (go figure).

Michael Zarozinski—Louder Than A Bomb! Software

MichaelZ@LouderThanABomb.com

Michael owns and operates Louder Than A Bomb! Software, a company that builds software to help put artificial intelligence theory into practice. He was a contributing author to *Game Programming Gems 2* and has worked as an AI consultant in the video game industry. Michael's life-long interest in artificial intelligence resulted in an *ELIZA* clone written for the TI994/A and many brushes with electrocution while building robots from old vacuum tube radios. You can read more about Michael—perhaps more than you need to know—at www.LouderThanABomb.com/ about_us.htm. In his spare time, Michael maintains his own little piece of cyberspace: aiGuru.com. There, you'll find information on all things AI along with his rants and/ or raves on AI and non AI-related subjects. He can be reached at MichaelZ@ LouderThanABomb.com.

GENERAL WISDOM

1.1

The Evolution of Game AI

Paul Tozour—Ion Storm Austin
gehn29@yahoo.com

The field of game artificial intelligence (AI) has existed since the dawn of video games in the 1970s. Its origins were humble, and the public perception of game AI is deeply colored by the simplistic games of the 1970s and 1980s. Even today, game AI is haunted by the ghosts of *Pac-Man's* Inky, Pinky, Blinky, and Clyde. Until very recently, the video game industry itself has done all too little to change this perception.

However, a revolution has been brewing. The past few years have witnessed game AIs vastly richer and more entertaining than the simplistic AIs of the past. As 3D rendering hardware improves and the skyrocketing quality of game graphics rapidly approaches the point of diminishing returns, AI has increasingly become one of the critical factors in a game's success, deciding which games become bestsellers and determining the fate of more than a few game studios. In recent years, game AI has been quietly transformed from the redheaded stepchild of gaming to the shining star of the industry.

The game AI revolution is at hand.

A Little Bit of History

At the dawn of gaming, AIs were designed primarily for coin-operated arcade games, and were carefully designed to ensure that the player kept feeding quarters into the machine. Seminal games such as *Pong, Pac-Man, Space Invaders, Donkey Kong,* and *Joust* used a handful of very simple rules and scripted sequences of actions combined with some random decision-making to make their behavior less predictable.

Chess has long been a mainstay of academic AI research, so it's no surprise that chess games such as *Chessmaster 2000* [SofTool86] featured very impressive AI opponents. These approaches were invariably based on game tree search [Svarovsky00].

Strategy games were among the earliest pioneers in game AI. This isn't surprising, as strategy games can't get very far on graphics alone and require good AI to even be playable. Strategy game AI is particularly challenging, as it requires sophisticated unit-level AI as well as extraordinarily complex tactical and strategic computer player AI. A number of turn-based strategy games, most notably MicroProse's *Civilization* [MicroProse91] and *Civilization 2,* come to mind as early standouts, despite their use of cheating to assist the computer player at higher difficulty settings.

Even more impressive is the quality of many recent real-time strategy game AIs. *WarCraft II* [Blizzard95] featured one of the first highly competent and entertaining "RTS" AIs, and *Age of Empires 2: The Age of Kings* [Ensemble99] features the most challenging RTS AI opponents to date. Such excellent RTS AIs are particularly impressive in light of the difficult real-time performance requirements that an RTS AI faces, such as the need to perform pathfinding for potentially hundreds of units at a time.

In the first-person shooter field, Valve Software's *Half-Life* [Valve98] has received high praise for its excellent tactical AI. The bots of Epic Games' *Unreal: Tournament* [Epic99] are well known for their scalability and tactical excellence. Looking Glass Studios' *Thief: The Dark Project* [LGS98], the seminal "first-person sneaker," stands out for its careful modeling of AIs' sensory capabilities and its use of graduated alert levels to give the player important feedback about the internal state of the AIs. Sierra Studios' *SWAT 3: Close Quarters Battle* [Sierra99] did a remarkable job of demonstrating humanlike animation and interaction, and took great advantage of randomized AI behavior parameters to ensure that the game is different each time you play it.

"Sim" games, such as the venerable *SimCity* [Maxis89], were the first to prove the potential of artificial life ("A-Life") approaches. *The Sims* [Maxis00] is particularly worth noting for the depth of personality of its AI agents. This spectacularly popular game beautifully demonstrates the potential of fuzzy-state machines (FuSMs) and A-Life technologies.

Another early contender in the A-Life category was the *Creatures* series, originating with *Creatures* in 1996 [CyberLife96]. *Creatures* goes to great lengths to simulate the psychology and physiology of the "Norns" that populate the game, including "Digital DNA" that is unique to each creature.

"God games" such as the seminal hits *Populous* [Bullfrog89] and *Dungeon Keeper* [Bullfrog97] combined aspects of sim games and A-Life approaches with real-time strategy elements. Their evolution is apparent in the ultimate god game, Lionhead Studios' recent *Black & White* [Lionhead01]. *Black & White* features what is undoubtedly one of the most impressive game AIs to date—some of which is described in this book. Although it's certainly not the first game to use machine learning technologies, it's undoubtedly the most successful use of AI learning approaches yet seen in a computer game.

It's important to note that *Black & White* was very carefully designed in a way that allows the AI to shine—the game is entirely built around the concept of teaching and training your "creature." This core paradigm effectively focuses the player's attention on the AI's development in a way that's impossible in most other games.

Behind the Revolution

A key factor in the success of recent game AI has been the simple fact that developers are finally taking it seriously. Far too often, AI has been a last-minute rush job, implemented in the final two or three months of development by overcaffeinated programmers with dark circles under their eyes and thousands of other high-priority tasks to complete.

Hardware constraints have also been a big roadblock to game AI. Graphics rendering has traditionally been a huge CPU hog, leaving little time or memory for the AI. Some AI problems, such as pathfinding, can't be solved without significant processor resources. Console games in particular have had a difficult time with AI, given the painfully tight memory and performance requirements of console hardware until recent years.

A number of the early failures and inadequacies of game AI also arose from an insufficient appreciation of the nature of game AI on the part of the development team itself—what is sometimes referred to as a "magic bullet" attitude. This usually manifests itself in the form of an underappreciation of the challenges of AI development—"we'll just use a scripting language"—or an inadequate understanding of how to apply AI techniques to the task at hand—"we'll just use a big neural network."

Recent years have witnessed the rise of the dedicated AI programmer, solely devoted to AI from Day One of the project. This has, by and large, been a smashing success. In many cases, even programmers with no previous AI experience have been able to produce high-quality game AI. AI development doesn't necessarily require a lot of arcane knowledge or blazing insights into the nature of human cognition. Quite often, all it takes is a down-to-earth attitude, a little creativity, and enough time to do the job right.

Mainstream AI

The field of academic artificial intelligence consists of an enormous variety of different fields and subdisciplines, many of them starkly ideologically opposed to one another. To avoid any of the potentially negative connotations that some readers might associate with the term "academic," we will refer to this field as *mainstream AI*.

We cannot hope to understand game AI without also understanding something of the much broader field of artificial intelligence. A reasonable history of the evolution of the AI field is outside the scope of this article; nevertheless, this part of the book enumerates a handful of mainstream AI techniques—specifically, those that we consider most relevant to present and future game AI. See [AI95] for an introduction to nearly all of these techniques.

- **Expert systems** attempt to capture and exploit the knowledge of a human expert within a given domain. An expert system represents the expert's expertise within a knowledge base, and performs automated reasoning on the knowledge base in response to a query. Such a system can produce similar answers to those that the human expert would have provided.

- **Case-based reasoning** techniques attempt to analyze a set of inputs by comparing them to a database of known, possibly historical, sets of inputs and the most advisable outputs in those situations. The approach was inspired by the human tendency to apprehend novel situations by comparing them to the most similar situations one has experienced in the past.

- **Finite-state machines** are simple, rule-based systems in which a finite number of "states" are connected in a directed graph by "transitions" between states. The finite-state machine occupies exactly one state at any moment.

- **Production systems** are comprised of a database of rules. Each rule consists of an arbitrarily complex conditional statement, plus some number of actions that should be performed if the conditional statement is satisfied. Production rule systems are essentially lists of "if-then" statements, with various conflict resolution mechanisms available in the event that more than one rule is satisfied simultaneously.

- **Decision trees** are similar to complex conditionals in "if-then" statements. DTs make a decision based on a set of inputs by starting at the root of the tree and, at each node, selecting a child node based on the value of one input. Algorithms such as ID3 and C4.5 can automatically construct decision trees from sample data.

- **Search methods** are concerned with discovering a sequence of actions or states within a graph that satisfy some goal—either reaching a specified "goal state" or simply maximizing some value based on the reachable states.

- **Planning systems** and **scheduling systems** are an extension of search methods that emphasize the subproblem of finding the best (simplest) sequence of actions that one can perform to achieve a particular result over time, given an initial state of the world and a precise definition of the consequences of each possible action.

- **First-order logic** extends propositional logic with several additional features to allow it to reason about an AI agent within an environment. The world consists of "objects" with individual identities and "properties" that distinguish them from other objects, and various "relations" that hold between those objects and properties.

- The **situation calculus** employs first-order logic to calculate how an AI agent should act in a given situation. The situation calculus uses automated reasoning to determine the course of action that will produce the most desirable changes to the world state.

- **Multi-agent systems** approaches focus on how intelligent behavior can naturally arise as an emergent property of the interaction between multiple competing and cooperating agents.

- **Artificial life** (or **A-Life**) refers to multi-agent systems that attempt to apply some of the universal properties of living systems to AI agents in virtual worlds.

- **Flocking** is a subcategory of A-Life that focuses on techniques for coordinated movement such that AI agents maneuver in remarkably lifelike herds and flocks.

- **Robotics** deals with the problem of allowing machines to function interactively in the real world. Robotics is one of the oldest, best-known, and most successful fields of artificial intelligence, and has recently begun to undergo a renaissance because of the explosion of available computing power. Robotics is generally divided into separate tasks of "control systems" (output) and "sensory systems" (input).

- **Genetic algorithms** and **genetic programming** are undoubtedly some of the most fascinating fields of AI (and it's great fun to bring them up whenever you find yourself in an argument with creationists). These techniques attempt to imitate the process of evolution directly, performing selection and interbreeding with randomized crossover and mutation operations on populations of programs, algorithms, or sets of parameters. Genetic algorithms and genetic programming have achieved some truly remarkable results in recent years [Koza99], beautifully disproving the ubiquitous public misconception that a computer "can only do what we program it to do."
- **Neural networks** are a class of machine learning techniques based on the architecture of neural interconnections in animal brains and nervous systems. Neural networks operate by repeatedly adjusting the internal numeric parameters (or weights) between interconnected components of the network, allowing them to learn an optimal or near-optimal response for a wide variety of different classes of learning tasks.
- **Fuzzy logic** uses real-valued numbers to represent degrees of membership in a number of sets—as opposed to the Boolean (true or false) values of traditional logic. Fuzzy logic techniques allow for more expressive reasoning and are capable of much more richness and subtlety than traditional logic.
- **Belief networks**, and the specific subfield of **Bayesian inference**, provide tools for modeling the underlying causal relationships between different phenomena, and use probability theory to deal with uncertainty and incomplete knowledge of the world. They also provide tools for making inferences about the state of the world and determining the likely effects of various possible actions.

Game AIs have taken advantage of nearly all of these techniques at one point or another, with varying degrees of success.

Ironically, it is the simplest techniques—finite-state machines, decision trees, and production rule systems—that have most often proven their worth. Faced with tight schedules and minimal resources, the game AI community has eagerly embraced rules-based systems as the easiest type of AI to create, understand, and debug.

Expert systems share some common ground with game AI in the sense that many game AIs attempt to play the game as an expert human player would. Although a game AI's knowledge base is usually not represented as formally as that of an expert system, the end result is the same: an imitation of an expert player's style.

Many board game AIs, such as chess and backgammon, have used game trees and game tree search with enormous success. Backgammon AIs now compete at the level of the best human players [Snowie01]. Chess AI famously proved its prowess with the bitter defeat of chess grandmaster Garry Kasparov by a massive supercomputer named "Deep Blue" [IBM97]. Other games, such as *Go*, have not yet reached the level of human masters, but are quickly narrowing the gap [Go01].

Unfortunately, the complexities of modern video game environments and game mechanics make it impossible to use the brute-force game tree approach used by systems such as Deep Blue. Other search techniques are commonly used for game AI navigation and pathfinding, however. The A* search algorithm in particular deserves special mention as the reigning king of AI pathfinding in every game genre (see [Stout00], [Rabin00] for an excellent introduction to A*, as well as [Matthews02] in this book).

Game AI also shares an enormous amount in common with robotics. The significant challenges that robots face in attempting to perceive and comprehend the "real world" is dramatically different from the easily accessible virtual worlds that game AIs inhabit, so the sensory side of robotics is not terribly applicable to game AI. However, the control-side techniques are very useful for game AI agents that need to intelligently maneuver around the environment and interact with the player, the game world, and other AI agents. Game AI agent pathfinding and navigation share an enormous amount in common with the navigation problems faced by mobile robots.

Artificial life techniques, multi-agent systems approaches, and flocking have all found a welcome home in game AI. Games such as *The Sims* and *SimCity* have indisputably proven the usefulness and entertainment value of A-Life techniques, and a number of successful titles use flocking techniques for some of their movement AI.

Planning techniques have also met with some success. The planning systems developed in mainstream AI are designed for far more complex planning problems than the situations that game AI agents face, but this will undoubtedly change as modern game designs continue to evolve to ever higher levels of sophistication.

Fuzzy logic has proven a popular technique in many game AI circles. However, formal first-order logic and the situation calculus have yet to find wide acceptance in games. This is most likely due to the difficulty of using the situation calculus in the performance-constrained environments of real-time games and the challenges of adequately representing a game world in the language of logical formalisms.

Belief networks are not yet commonly used in games. However, they are particularly well suited to a surprising number of game AI subproblems [Tozour02].

The Problem of Machine Learning

In light of this enormous body of academic research, it's understandable that the game AI field sometimes seems to have a bit of an inferiority complex. Nowhere is this more true than with regard to machine learning techniques.

> *It's beginning to sound like a worn record from year to year, but once again, game developers at GDC 2001 described their game AI as not being in the same province as academic technologies such as neural networks and genetic algorithms. Game developers continue to use simple rules-based finite- and fuzzy-state machines for nearly all their AI needs [Woodcock01].*

There are very good reasons for this apparent intransigence. Machine learning approaches have had a decidedly mixed history in game AI. Many of the early attempts at machine learning resulted in unplayable games or AIs that learned poorly, if at all. For all its potential benefits, learning, particularly when applied inappropriately, can be a disaster. There are several reasons for this:

- Machine learning (ML) systems can learn the wrong lessons. If the AI learns from the human player's play style, an incompetent player can easily miseducate the AI.
- ML techniques can be difficult to tune and tweak to achieve the desired results. Learning systems require a "fitness function" to judge their success and tell them how well they have learned. Creating a challenging and competent computer player is one thing, but how do you program a fitness function for "fun?"
- Some machine learning technologies—neural networks in particular—are heinously difficult to modify, test, or debug.
- Finally, there are many genres where in-game learning just doesn't make much sense. In most action games and hack-and-slash role-playing games, the AI opponents seldom live long enough to look you in the eye, much less learn anything.

Besides these issues, it's fair to say that a large part of the problem has sprung from the industry's own failure to apply learning approaches correctly. Developers have often attempted to use learning to develop an AI to a basic level of competence that it could have attained more quickly and easily with traditional rules-based AI approaches. This is counterproductive. Machine learning approaches are most useful and appropriate in situations where the AI entities actually need to learn something.

Recent games such as *Black & White* prove beyond any doubt that learning approaches are useful and entertaining and can add significant value to a game's AI. Learning approaches are powerful tools and can shine when used in the right context. The key, as *Black & White* aptly demonstrates, is to use learning as one carefully considered component within a multilayered system that uses a number of other techniques for the many AI subtasks that don't benefit from machine learning.

We Come in Pursuit of Fun

Much of the disparity between game AI and mainstream AI stems from a difference in goals. Academic AI pursues extraordinarily difficult problems such as imitating human cognition and understanding natural language. But game AI is all about *fun*.

At the end of the day, we are still a business. You have a customer who paid $40 for your game, and he or she expects to be entertained. In many game genres—action games in particular—it's surprisingly easy to develop an AI that will consistently trounce the player without breaking a sweat. This is "intelligent" from that AI's perspective, but it's not what our customers bought the game for. Deep Blue beat Kasparov in chess, but it never tried to entertain its opponent—an assertion Kasparov himself can surely confirm.

In a sense, it's a shame that game AI is called "AI" at all. The term does as much to obscure the nature of our endeavors as it does to illuminate it. If it weren't too late to change it, a better name might be "agent design" or "behavioral modeling." The word *intelligence* is so fraught with ambiguity that it might be better to avoid it completely.

The misapprehension of intelligence has caused innumerable problems throughout the evolution of game AI. Our field requires us to design agents that produce appropriate behaviors in a given context, but the adaptability of humanlike "intelligence" is not always necessary to produce the appropriate behaviors, nor is it always desirable.

Intelligence Is Context-Dependent

The term "IQ" illustrates the problem beautifully. The human brain is an extraordinary, massively interconnected network of both specialized and general-purpose cognitive tools evolved over billions of years to advance the human species in a vast number of different and challenging environments. To slap a single number on this grand and sublime artifact of evolution can only blind us to its actual character.

The notion of IQ is eerily similar to the peculiar Western notion of the "Great Chain of Being" [Descartes1641]. Rather than viewing life as a complex and multifaceted evolutionary phylogeny in which different organisms evolve within different environments featuring different selective pressures, the "Great Chain of Being" collapses all this into a linear ranking. All living organisms are sorted into a universal pecking order according to their degree of "perfection," with God at the end of the chain.

An article on IQ in a recent issue of *Psychology Today* [PT01] caught my eye:

> *In 1986, a colleague and I published a study of men who frequented the racetracks daily. Some were excellent handicappers, while others were not. What distinguished experts from nonexperts was the use of a complex mental algorithm that converted racing data taken from the racing programs sold at the track. The use of the algorithm was unrelated to the men's IQ scores, however. Some experts were dockworkers with IQs in the low 80s, but they reasoned far more complexly at the track than all nonexperts—even those with IQs in the upper 120s.*
>
> *In fact, experts were always better at reasoning complexly than nonexperts, regardless of their IQ scores. But the same experts who could reason so well at the track were often abysmal at reasoning outside the track— about, say, their retirement pensions or their social relationships.*

This quote gives us a good perspective on what game AI is all about. What we need is not a generalized "intelligence," but *context-dependent expertise*.

Game AI is a vast panorama of specialized subproblems, including pathfinding, steering, flocking, unit deployment, tactical analysis, strategic planning, resource allocation, weapon handling, target selection, group coordination, simulated perception, situation analysis, spatial reasoning, and context-dependent animation, to name a few.

Each game is its own unique "evolutionary context," so to speak, and a game's AI must be evolved within that context. The most successful game AIs have arisen when the developers clearly identified the specific subproblems they needed to solve and created solutions exquisitely well tuned to solve those problems in that specific game.

This is not to say that generalized, humanlike cognitive skills are unimportant, but we must avoid the temptation to grab for answers before we fully understand the questions. Stop and ask yourself: *What behaviors does the AI actually need to exhibit in this game, and under what circumstances does it need to produce those behaviors?* What gameplay mechanics will make our customer happy, and how does our AI need to support them? Once we've decided what we want our AIs to do and when we want them to do it, we can then determine what AI tools we truly require to approach those problems.

In order to attain "context-dependent expertise," we must first become experts ourselves. No developer can create a competent game AI unless he is competent enough to play the game himself and judge another player's skill. Once you have developed your own skill set, you can then attempt to figure out the cognitive mechanisms behind your own play style and the actual decision-making processes that you use when faced with a given situation in the game.

If we can reverse-engineer our own cognitive algorithms—if we can clearly describe our own "racetrack algorithm"—then it becomes relatively simple to create an AI that imitates our own decision-making processes and plays the game as we do.

Evolution

The title of this article—"The Evolution of Game AI"— is used in two ways. First, it describes the evolution of AI in games as a whole since the birth of the video game. Second, and more importantly, it describes the evolution of the AI within a given game over the course of its development. Week after week, milestone after milestone, the AI develops new, increasingly sophisticated behaviors, and its technologies constantly evolve to better fit the game that it inhabits.

Every game is different, and every AI depends on the game's design. It's very easy for game designers to make seemingly minor decisions that can dramatically affect the way the AI needs to operate.

This is why there is no "magic bullet." There is no substitute for fully understanding the problem at hand. We cannot develop great game AI without addressing all of the problems that each AI agent faces within the game. We must always care more about the quality of our AI than the technologies under the hood. The challenge is to develop AIs that are experts at challenging and entertaining the player in a specific game.

AI Is Context-Dependent

So, where do we go from here? How will game AI grow and evolve into the future?

Some developers have taken a cue from the success of licensed "game engines" such as *Quake* and *Unreal* and have attempted to create generalized AI "engines" that can be used in *any* game [Soar01][ACE01]. In this author's opinion, such attempts are unlikely to be successful. As noted earlier, a game's AI is exquisitely dependent on the design of the game it inhabits, and to gloss over the context of the specific game is to "throw the baby out with the bath water." Any AI engine broad enough to be used in any game will not be specific enough to solve the difficult AI challenges of a particular game.

Instead, this author believes that game AI will evolve according to genre. Although the term "genre" might seem overly narrow at times, it does a good job of distinguishing the separate evolutionary pathways on which game AI has evolved and will likely continue to evolve in the future. The AIs of hockey games, real-time strategy games, first-person shooters, basketball games, turn-based strategy games, and first-person "sneakers" each face unique AI challenges. These dramatic differences make it remarkably difficult to share AI technologies between games in different genres in any useful way.

It seems likely that the most successful products in these genres will build on their past successes, continuing and evolving their AI systems as the game designs themselves grow ever more sophisticated.

A Broader Perspective

As we have seen, the rich and colorful field of academic artificial intelligence has an enormous amount to offer game AI. Over time, game AI and academic AI will inevitably draw closer. However, the plethora of AI technologies available—and the difficulty of applying them correctly—has made it difficult for game AI to take advantage of what the research has to offer. As Marvin Minsky [Minsky92] writes:

> *Many students like to ask, "Is it better to represent knowledge with Neural Nets, Logical Deduction, Semantic Networks, Frames, Scripts, Rule-Based Systems or Natural Language?" My teaching method is to try to get them to ask a different kind of question. "First decide what kinds of reasoning might be best for each different kind of problem—and then find out which combination of representations might work well in each case."*
>
> *[...] My opinion is that we can make versatile AI machines only by using several different kinds of representations in the same system! This is because no single method works well for all problems; each is good for certain tasks, but not for others. Also, different kinds of problems need different kinds of reasoning.*

As the game AI field evolves, we will undoubtedly gain a far deeper understanding of how best to select and apply the cornucopia of academic AI techniques at our disposal to the multitude of game AI subproblems we face. However, given the remarkable success of game AI in recent years, we shouldn't be at all surprised to find that the academic community has much to learn from us as well.

However, for game AI to really evolve, we need to broaden our perspective of game AI beyond the AI field. Although I have a Computer Science degree (1994), the time spent directing and acting in stage plays has been more useful for game AI work than anything learned for my degree. Several researchers, most notably [Laurel93], have also explored the application of dramatic techniques to interactive entertainment.

The field of evolutionary psychology in particular has an enormous amount to offer game AI. Game AI development is itself an experiment in evolutionary psychology—it is literally evolving the psychology of game entities.

Every gamer has experienced the initial thrill and eventual drudgery of being attacked by hordes of mindless opponents incapable of fundamental tactics such as retreating, dodging, hiding, feinting, making threat displays, negotiating with the enemy, cooperating with one another, or even taking cover.

What's disappointing about this sad state of affairs is not simply that we don't imitate nature—that was never the point, after all. What's unfortunate is that we so often choose only the dullest colors from the brilliant palette of natural behaviors to draw from—behaviors that can truly make our games more entertaining. Even the most simple-minded of nature's creatures will avoid combat if possible. Real animals size up an opponent, retreat when necessary, or make a grandiose display of size or strength in the hope of convincing the enemy to back down or pick a weaker target. Animals sneak up on their prey, attempt to distract them from the rest of the herd, and employ complex group tactics to ambush or mislead their foes. We have much to learn from *The Discovery Channel*.

AI as Game Design

Many of AI's most important contributions to games are likely to arise from the symbiosis between game design and AI. In order for this symbiosis to occur, we need to ensure that we, as AI developers, continually grow in our understanding of the techniques and principles of game design. We also need to work relentlessly to educate our teams—and our game designers in particular—about the tremendous potential of AI to improve our games. Better, richer, deeper AI continually opens up more game design possibilities, and these design improvements in turn open up new opportunities for AI. Game AI can and should be considered a natural extension of game design.

For AI to reach its full potential, game design must evolve beyond its all-too-common obsession with designer-controlled narrative and linear gameplay. It's *not* about the story: it's about the gameplay. AI-centric games such as *The Sims, Black & White*, and *Thief: The Dark Project* point the way to a future in which the interaction of human and artificial minds becomes a primary thread in a richly woven tapestry of game mechanics.

The Future of Game AI

If there's ever been a time for wide-eyed optimism, this is it. Game AI has never before had so much opportunity to excel, so many resources at its disposal, so many sources of inspiration to draw from, or so much popularity among the general public.

Game AI sits at a broad crossroads of evolutionary psychology, drama, academic AI, game programming, and game design. As the industry grows and evolves, we are in a unique position to combine the fruits of all of these fields and disciplines into an extraordinary new discipline. We stand poised at the edge of revolution, ready to help push the world of gaming into its rightful place as the great art form of the 21st century. This book represents one of the very first steps in that direction.

References and Additional Reading

[Ace01] *ACE: the Autonomous Character Engine*, BioGraphic Technologies. See www.biographictech.com/.

[AI95] Russell, Stuart J. and Norvig, Peter, *Artificial Intelligence: A Modern Approach*, Prentice Hall, 1995.

[Blizzard95] *WarCraft II: Tides of Darkness*, Blizzard Entertainment, 1995. See www .blizzard.com/.

[Bullfrog89] *Populous*, Bullfrog/Electronic Arts, 1989. See www.bullfrog.com/.

[Bullfrog97] *Dungeon Keeper*, Bullfrog/Electronic Arts, 1997. See www.bullfrog .com/.

[CyberLife96] *Creatures*, CyberLife Technologies/Millennium Interactive/Warner Brothers Interactive Entertainment, 1996. See www.creaturelabs.com/.

[Descartes1641] Descartes, Rene, *Meditations on First Philosophy*, 1641. See http://philos.wright.edu/DesCartes/MedE.html.

[Ensemble99] *Age of Empires II: The Age of Kings*, Ensemble Studios/Microsoft, 1999. See www.ensemblestudios.com/aoeii/index.shtml.

[Gems00] Ed. DeLoura, Mark. *Game Programming Gems*, Charles River Media, 2000.

[Go01] Homepage of The Intelligent Go Foundation, www.intelligentgo.org/.

[IBM97] Deep Blue, www.research.ibm.com/deepblue/home/html/b.html.

[Koza99] Koza, John R.; Bennett, Forrest H. III; Keane, Martin; Andre, David. *Genetic Programming III: Darwinian Invention and Problem Solving*, Morgan Kaufmann, 1999.

[Laurel93] Laurel, Brenda, *Computers as Theatre*, Addison-Wesley, 1993.

[Lionhead01] *Black & White*, Lionhead Studios/Electronic Arts, 2001. See www .bwgame.com/.

[LGS98] *Thief: The Dark Project*, Looking Glass Studios/Eidos Interactive, 1998. See www.eidosinteractive.com/.

[Matthews02] Matthews, James, "Basic A* Pathfinding Made Simple," *AI Game Programming Wisdom*, Charles River Media, 2002.

[Maxis89] *SimCity*, Maxis/Brøderbund, 1989. See www.simcity.com/.

[Maxis00] *The Sims*, Maxis/Electronic Arts, 2000. See www.thesims.com/.

[MicroProse91] *Sid Meier's Civilization*, MicroProse, 1991

[Minsky92] Minsky, Marvin. *Future of AI Technology*. See www.ai.mit.edu/people/ minsky/papers/CausalDiversity.html.

[PT01] *Psychology Today*. Sussex Publishers Inc., August 2001.

[Rabin00] Rabin, Steve, "A* Aesthetic Optimizations," and "A* Speed Optimizations," See [Gems00].

[Sierra99] *SWAT 3: Close Quarters Battle*. Sierra Studios, 1999. See www.sierrastudios.com/games/swat3/.

[Snowie01] *Snowie*, Oasya SA. See www.oasya.com/.

[Soar01] Soar, http://ai.eecs.umich.edu/soar/.

[SofTool86] *Chessmaster 2000*, Software Toolworks, 1986.

[Stout00] Stout, Bryan, "The Basics of A* for Path Planning," See [Gems00].

[Svarovsky00] Svarovsky, Jan, "Game Trees," See [Gems00].

[Tozour02] Tozour, Paul, "An Introduction to Bayesian Networks and Reasoning Under Uncertainty," from *AI Game Programming Wisdom*, Charles River Media, 2002.

[Valve98] *Half-Life*, Valve Software, Inc./Sierra, 1998. See www.sierrastudios.com/games/half-life/.

[Woodcock01] Woodcock, Steven, "Game AI: The State of the Industry 2000-2001: It's Not Just Art, It's Engineering," *Game Developer* magazine, August 2001.

1.2

The Illusion of Intelligence

Bob Scott—Stainless Steel Studios
bob@stainlesssteelstudios.com

Computer-controlled characters exist to give the single-player aspect of a game more depth and playability. The vast majority of people still do not play online against other humans. Thus, to provide an interesting experience to these players, we as game developers must create worthy, humanlike competitors. Our success at this venture can greatly influence the popularity and sales of a game.

At this point in time, we can't create actual intelligence in our games; the best we can do is to create the "illusion of intelligence." This article gives you a number of ideas on how to do this while avoiding the "illusion of stupidity."

Scope

This article is meant to cover the high-level decisions that govern how a computer player will play the game. For example, a real-time strategy (RTS) player might decide to play a game that focuses on combat with archers and siege weapons. A first-person shooter (FPS) player might decide to concentrate on using a rocket-launcher to improve his skill with that weapon.

There are more complicated behaviors as well—the archer/siege weapon RTS player has to decide how to implement that strategy, perhaps by creating walls around the town, advancing through the epochs quickly, or making alliances with neighboring players. As AI developers, we attempt to mimic these behaviors. Indeed, for many games, we are doing nothing short of attempting to create the illusion of a human player.

Hallmarks of a Human Player

Since the computer player is viewed as a replacement for human players, let's examine what the expectation is when playing with and against other humans.

Predictability and Unpredictability

Human players are known for doing unpredictable things. In an RTS, this might mean attacking a much stronger force for the purposes of distraction. In a sports simulation, it might mean calling a play that doesn't make sense in context, like a pass play from the ½-yard line in football.

Conversely, many human players are predictable in certain ways. FPS players might have a preferred route through their favorite map. RTS players might have a scripted buildup phase that you can count on. Football simulation players (and some real teams) like to throw the ball.

Note the obvious conflict between these—human players can be both predictable *and* unpredictable. In some cases, this can happen within the same game. In other cases, a human player might be unpredictable across multiple game sessions, but predictable within a single game. When playing an RTS, you might tend to plan a certain strategy at the beginning of a game and base all of your decisions on that. For example, you might decide that you want to base all of your attacks on airplanes, so everything you do will be directed toward that strategy. If your opponent can figure out that tactic, you can be beaten.

Developing an AI to mimic this is difficult. There needs to be enough randomness in the overall goal so that replay is interesting, but there also needs to be enough predictability that the human player can figure out that strategy some of the time and counter it. In addition, you need to be able to determine what the human player's strategy is to effectively counter it and provide a challenging experience.

Support

Often, a human player might select a computer player to act as an ally, either against human opponents or other computer opponents. Most support duties are not that hard to handle—defending your allies' towns as well as your own, taking part in large-scale attacks, and so forth.

As an aside, the most difficult aspect of the support role is communication with the human player. Using simple commands activated by button clicks will minimize the complexity in communication.

Surprise

Once all of these are in place, the final icing on the cake is surprise. You should strive to provide as many surprises as you can. Players will notice an AI that performs an admirable job of playing the game, but they will *talk about* an AI that surprises them. Surprises come in many forms and are specific to different genres. In an RTS game, behaviors such as pincer attacks, misinformation, harassment, and ambushes provide surprise. In an FPS, surprises might include ambushes, suppression fire, flanking maneuvers, and team support.

Finally, there is a class of surprises that is very hard to emulate, sometimes referred to as "believable stupidity." On the face of things, these actions look bad, but are something that a human player might try to do. In a role-playing game (RPG), this might include use of an ultra powerful spell that inadvertently hurts the spell caster.

These behaviors can provide comic relief in a game. As these behaviors are very hard to get right, and can easily be overdone, they should be kept to a minimum.

Winning, Losing, and Losing Well

An important thing to remember is that the human game player is *playing* the game. In the frenzy to develop a game, this fact can be easily overlooked. Think for a moment about what your plans are when you sit down to play a game. It's likely that you want to be entertained. It's also likely that you are using the game to role-play some kind of character that you can't be in real life. In games where "winning" is possible, it's likely that you *want to win*.

Let's look at that a little closer. We could separate our game audience into two groups. First is the player who just wants to win easily. The second group is the player who wants to win half the time and lose half the time. They usually want the battle to appear nearly hopeless until the end when they turn the tide of battle and prove their superiority.

An AI that wins (or loses) most of the time is fairly easy to develop. Most games can vary the number and quality of opponents to affect the desired end. In an RTS, for example, army size and rock-paper-scissors adjustments can mean the difference between victory and defeat. In an FPS or sports simulation, accuracy and speed of opponents can be adjusted. The real issue in these cases is the believability of the opponent. Huge armies early in the game in an RTS are not possible without obvious cheating. Massive waves of enemies in an FPS tend to point to a lack of attention to AI.

As we come to the middle ground again, we realize that the required effect can be achieved by closely tuning the opponents' behavior. Varying the quality of response over the course of the battle can be a good way to influence the close victory for the human player, as long as the variations are believable. In an RTS, poorer target selection combined with slower reload times is one nice way to vary difficulty. The key is close monitoring of the battles and overall game status to keep computer players on an even level with the human players. Ensuring equivalent force strength can stabilize the balance of power.

The difficulty setting is usually used to determine whether the AI always loses or attempts to give the human player a challenge. In some types of games, the computer players can change their response based on the number of wins or losses. These games strive to always provide the middle ground, but usually overshoot the extremes.

Whichever response you choose, make sure that the adjustments you make to the computer player are believable. That believability is defined by the parameters of the game. In an RTS game, intelligent target selection is expected. In an FPS, inhuman accuracy and the ability to predict where a human player will be is not expected. In a football simulation, 100-yard touchdown passes should be completely avoided.

Emergent Behavior

Emergent behavior is that which cannot be predicted through analysis at any level simpler than that of the system as a whole...Emergent behavior, by definition, is what's left after everything else has been explained [Dyson97].

We can use emergent behavior (EB) to give the illusion of intelligence to a game AI. In fact, in many cases, occurrences of EB can even provide the illusion to the developers themselves! At one point during the testing of *Empire Earth*, one computer player attempted to expand to an area on the other side of an enemy's town. As his citizens were attempting to break through, a massive attack force came in and kept the enemy busy while the citizens got through. This was not programmed in—the attack just happened to coincide with the expansion attempt due to the adjustment of timers governing both behaviors.

Unfortunately, it is very hard to purposely create EB; rather, one needs to create an architecture in which EB can occur. Architectures that support high-level commands, goal-based decisions, and timer-based decisions will often result in emergent behavior [Scott02]. Script-based approaches to AI will generally not exhibit EB [Tozour02]. In general, the developer needs to ensure that decisions take place in somewhat random orders to encourage EB.

Cheating

All AI developers will face the question of cheating at some point during development. There are purists who insist the AI should never cheat—they should have exactly the same inputs available to them as a human player. Most game players would say that they don't want an AI that cheats. Those same players also say that they would like an AI that is challenging. Interestingly, several games that support user-created AI files have a thriving community of people specifically writing cheating AIs, ostensibly to extend the life of the game.

Many objections to AI cheating come down to an argument that the AI will have an unfair advantage against the human player. In fact, the computer is at a severe disadvantage since it cannot improvise. At best, a computer player can choose from as many strategies as the developers have time to teach it. Once the human player knows them all, the computer ceases to be a challenge. We might eventually be able to develop an AI that can think the way humans do, but until then, the human player will always have this advantage.

It is worth noting that if asked whether they would prefer a brain-dead AI or one that cheats, most players would prefer the latter *as long as the cheating is not obvious*. Many forms of cheating are not obvious to the player and are not even considered cheating. Performing terrain analysis on a random map before it's explored is a form of cheating, but one that most players are willing to forgive if it improves the performance of the game.

The developer needs to also keep in mind that players and developers have different definitions of cheating. If the AI does something that is similar to what the human does, but the AI is more precise, more efficient or faster at it, the player might think the AI is cheating. While developing *Empire Earth*, we had a standing order that whenever anyone playing against the computer saw something that they considered a cheat, they were to report it. We could then discuss the issue and perhaps tone it down, or eliminate it to improve the experience.

Conclusion

The key qualities of any game AI should be that it is *fun* and *challenging*.

The fun factor can be achieved by enabling emergent behavior and providing surprise in a game where the player might not otherwise expect it. Remember that you're developing a *game*—it's supposed to be fun!

Providing a challenge must apply to as broad an audience as possible, from complete novices to those who play online tournaments.

References

[Dyson97] Dyson, George B., *Darwin Among the Machines: The Evolution of Global Intelligence*, Perseus Book Group, p 9, 1997.

[Scott02] Scott, Bob, "Architecting a Game AI," *AI Game Programming Wisdom*, Charles River Media, 2002.

[Tozour02] Tozour, Paul, "The Perils of AI Scripting," *AI Game Programming Wisdom*, Charles River Media, 2002.

Solving the Right Problem

Neil Kirby—Lucent Technologies Bell Laboratories

nak@lucent.com

One of the more fascinating observations from the Game Developers Conference (GDC) AI round tables was that solving a *different* problem from the one thought to be at hand could result in a superior solution [Kirby00]. This article gives two such examples and then examines the process. In looking at this process, emphasis is placed on what developers can do to get to a different—and better—problem to solve.

Some of the actions you can take might be part of your programming practice already; they are good programming techniques and are well known. However, the others usually are not defined as programming related and might be new. They can be thought of as "cross-training" for your brain, and they can be learned and practiced.

Solving a Different Problem Might Be More Effective

An Example from the GDC 2000 AI Round Tables

One participant in the AI roundtables gave us the following example. His company wanted to implement speech recognition in its adventure game. If all of the NPCs (non-player characters – those controlled by the computer) can talk to the player, it would only be natural for the player to talk to the NPCs. The NPCs would have to understand what the user said, figure out what the user meant, and then react in a way that showed the user that he was understood. However, speech recognition is a large mountain of a problem to solve. It can be done, but it takes a great deal of machine resources and it is difficult to do well. Hiding behind the mountain of speech recognition is the somewhat bigger mountain of a problem known as natural language processing (NLP). Speech recognition can be thought of as taking dictation and transcribing the text; NLP is taking that text and making sense of it. Both have problems.

For speech recognition problems, consider the following example strings:

"Little Red Riding Hood"
"Ladle Rat Rotten Hut"

There are accents in the United States where the first string is pronounced in a way that sounds to other speakers like the second. Both use real words spelled properly, and a simple speech recognition engine might return either of them.

For NLP problems, consider the words *pissed* and *plowed*. In the slang of the United States the two words have one set of meanings (*angry* and *drunk*, respectively). In England, they have rather different meanings (*drunk*, and an impolite reference to sex, respectively). When people make these types of mistakes, they are usually thought to be funny. When computers—especially games—make them, they are thought to be stupid.

Inroads have been made in both areas. Speech recognition products that run on PCs have been affordable for a few years; current products and prices can be found easily on the Web at sites such as amazon.com [Amazon01]. Text-based adventure games and Web sites such as *Ask Jeeves* show good progress at NLP. However, taken together, the problems were too big for this person's computer game. The internationalization issues alone would have been daunting had both problems been solved.

Therefore, they solved a different problem. Their research showed that large motion gestures are universal across human cultures. For example, the "I don't know" shrug is the same the world over. Small gestures should be avoided because they are not universal. While some of the differences are small but unfortunately noticeable, such as which finger a person starts with to count on their fingers, other small gestures differ shockingly from culture to culture. However, while small gestures vary, large gestures are consistent. By adding large gestures to the repertoire of NPC behaviors, the game was made much more engaging—the actual problem that speech recognition was supposed to solve. They found that the problem of doing large motion gestures, a problem different from speech input, solved the real problem better.

Another Example: The Sims

Getting autonomous units to behave intelligently has plagued many a game programmer. Getting a unit to identify or locate things that let it efficiently achieve its goals is a hard bit of work. The previous two sentences are not identical problems. Neither is the second a restatement of the first in terms more specific to a game genre—it just seems that way to people who have written such AI. Almost always, this is couched in terms of how real units interact with the real world. The units figure out what they want to look for, and they search the world space (and their memory) to try to find them. *Where can I get something to eat? What is a good ambush point?* Answering these questions solves the problem at hand.

Will Wright, in *The Sims*, solved the real problem (intelligent behavior) by turning the second one (identifying and locating) around. What he called "smart terrain" made it far easier for the Sims to get what they needed. Smart terrain is the idea that objects on the terrain broadcast what they offer to any Sims that might be passing by [Doornbos01]. The Sims do not identify these objects on the terrain; they instead listen to what the terrain is telling them. The attractiveness of the objects that meet the current needs of a Sim cause the Sim to move toward them. For example, a refrigerator might broadcast the fact that it can satisfy the "hunger" need. If a Sim is getting hungry and walks within the influence of the refrigerator, the Sim might decide to fulfill his hunger need with that object.

First Principles: What Is the Real Problem We Are Trying to Solve?

The real answer is that we are trying to entertain someone who has about US $50 or less and some sort of computing device. Therefore, when faced with a difficult AI problem in our games, we can flip the problem over as, "Can I solve a different problem and get a result that is equally or more entertaining?" In the example of speech input, the real problem solved was, "Can we make the game more engaging?" They avoided the speech problem by concentrating on the *problem it was supposed to solve* and solving it in a different way. In the Sims example, the real problem of having units behave intelligently was not solved by making the units smarter, but by making the terrain smarter.

In logic terms, think of having an entertaining AI in the game as problem A. Problem A is usually not a very narrow problem. So, we think of a narrower problem, which we can call problem B, which solves problem A. Then we solve problem B. The downfall with this perfectly workable method is that there might be a problem C (or D, or E…) that also solves problem A and was never thought of.

A	(the real problem)
B	(another problem that is easier to think about)
B → A	(*B* solves *A*; *many developers stop here*)
C	(yet another problem that is easier to think about than *A*)
C → A	(*C* also solves *A*)

Game AI Developers Have Been Doing This All Along

The fact that "cheating" by the AI is even an option clearly demonstrates that game AI developers have always been changing the problem they are trying to solve. In a lecture at the 1996 Computer Game Developers Conference (CGDC), Steve Meretzky gave an example from an adventure game [Meretzky96]. There were two chests on opposite ends of the game world. One held the key to the other. In a causal world, the contents of the chests would be deterministic, and half of the time the player would go to the wrong chest first. In the more entertaining world of the game, the first chest the player came to was always the one with the key. It might seem like a hack, but it was better at solving the entertainment problem than a more "realistic" solution.

How Do You Find the Better Problem?

Coming up with the better problem requires that you are willing to look for multiple solutions. It is also a creative process, since it requires going beyond the normal solution space. All of this improves with practice. Some of it takes time as well.

Start Early in the Process, but Continue Looking

Starting early will not, in and of itself, guarantee that you will find better problems to solve, but starting late almost certainly will prevent it. *The precious resource is time*; specifically, the amount of time you have to think about implementing your solution before starting work. An even more precious resource is the amount of time you have to think about what you might implement *instead*. It is worth noting that "Idea Time" is one of the 10 measures used in the *Situational Outlook Questionnaire* (SOQ) and its predecessor, the *Creative Climate Questionnaire* (CCQ), both of which are used "to effectively discern climates that either encourage or discourage creativity and the ability to initiate change" [Isaksen99].

Even after the design phase, looking for alternative problems that solve the smaller problems at hand can bear fruit. Practicing with the "small stuff" makes you more likely to be able to have the "Aha!" experience with the "big stuff" [Kirby91].

Get the Hooks in Early

A common theme from the GDC AI round tables was that AI programmers were often hindered from implementing an optimal AI because the "hooks" required by the AI code were not present in the game engine. If the AI code cannot access certain information because of architectural limitations, then doors are closed to particular solutions. The AI programmer needs to ensure that access to information will be considered in the early phases of game design, architecture, and software design. Coming up with the better problem to solve is useless if it cannot be solved within the game engine.

Multiple Solutions to Every Problem

One data point does not show trends, and it is hard to do "good, better, best," with only a single solution available. Coming up with a second way to solve a problem should be easier than the first, assuming you have time to do that much thinking. With one solution potentially in the bag, the pressure to come up with another solution is more manageable. There is still pressure, which is important for people who cannot think without it. That pressure is that if you do not come up with alternative ideas, you will be forced to implement your first one, and that idea might be a lot more work than you care to do. Even if all you ever come up with are two or three solutions each time, *the habit is important*. "The need to be efficient seems to foster an environment that retards creativity by limiting exploration" [Edwards01].

Michael Abrash, at his 1996 CGDC talk, pointed out that it took the id Software team a year of trying things before they settled on their final approach to the graphics engine for *Quake I* [Abrash96]. He also mentioned that the actual coding time of that final solution was approximately one month's worth of effort. They did not stop until they found the right solution to the problem at hand. While this might serve as an upper bound on how hard to look for alternative solutions, it should also provide clear encouragement: industry leaders do this. Abrash emphasized this more explicitly a year later, "So why even bother mentioning this? Partly to show that not every interesting idea pans out; I tend to discuss those that pan out, and it's instructive to point out that many ideas don't. That doesn't mean you shouldn't try promising ideas, though. First, some do, and you'll never know which unless you try. Second, an idea that doesn't work out in one case can still be filed away for another case… The more approaches you try, the larger your toolkit and the broader your understanding will be when you tackle your next project" [Abrash97].

Multiple solutions can be thought of as insurance policies against oversight, but often those multiple solutions are solutions to the same problem. The habit of coming up with them operationalizes the idea that there is always more than one way to solve a problem. It is close but not quite the same as coming up with multiple different problems to solve.

Thinking Out-of-the-Box

Getting to the better problem usually requires thinking outside the normal solution spaces. What would someone who doesn't have a clue do? What do the children think? Young children, when asked to solve a problem that is beyond their ability, will still attempt it, usually by some rather off-the-wall solution sometimes relying on a few revisions to reality. In a similar manner, an astute person asked about problems not in his field will often put together not-quite-possible solutions because he does not know the rules or limits. This is where you want your thought space to be in the early stages. Since we are writing entertainment products, and not air traffic control software for the Federal Aviation Administration, we might be allowed to bend reality so that the off-the-wall, not-quite-in-this-universe solutions actually work.

You might not always have access to the right people outside your field against whom to bounce ideas. One way to help *you* to think outside of your box is to barge in on some other boxes. For a while, at least, your thinking will tend to ignore the conventional limits because you do not know what they are or have not come to accept them. Take up the study of other things that involve creative problem solving. There is a well-known phenomenon in graduate programs [Brand87]. Students in one area are seduced by interesting problems in another, and they bring skills and abilities (and a lack of knowledge of what is known to be impossible) from other disciplines to bear on the problems and they sometimes solve them. While you are exploring other people's boxes, pay close attention to their out-of-the-box solutions.

There are an infinite variety of other things available to study. In "Design Plunder," Will Wright suggests, "architecture, chair design, Japanese gardens, biology, toys, psychology, comics, sociology, epidemiology and more" [Wright01]. An armload of books, selected randomly from the nonfiction section of a local library, ought to yield at least a few interesting topics to study. Whether it is chairs, architecture, motorcycles, or medieval siege machinery, all it has to be is refreshing and require thoughtful reflection. You will know you are on the right track when your thinking leads you to ponder, "How did they . . . ?" and "How would I . . . ?" and "There's got to be a better way. . . ."

Creativity Needs Practice

Out-of-the-box thinking and creativity are closely related. Athletes train more often than they compete, and their training activities are often different from what they do in competition. Finding the better solution relies heavily on creative abilities that might not be heavily exercised during coding. That is not to say that coding requires no creativity, but that skill and discipline are at the forefront for the long coding phase of a project.

It doesn't matter if you are not "good" at a creative activity. You do not have to be "good" at pushups before they strengthen your arms. You do have to *do them* to get them to strengthen your arms, and so it is with creative activities: you have to do them to exercise those parts of your brain. Those creative activities that easily integrate with daily life are best because, as with athletic exercise programs, those that intrude on a busy schedule are not likely to get done.

Since the activity you are "cross-training" for is problem solving, the best creative activities are those that present some challenges where creativity is employed to overcome them. If the activity you select poses no challenges, or poses challenges that you can never overcome, it will probably be less effective at giving your creativity a good workout. If you hold a Ph.D. in the area of your selected creative activity, it might not have much challenge anymore. If all of your leftovers are covered with green and blue fuzzy growths, the challenge of creating a pleasant meal from them is probably too difficult to overcome.

Just as there are many other "boxes" to look into to practice out-of-the-box thinking, there is an infinite number of creative things you can do. Photography, painting, drawing, making music, making an interesting new meal out of the leftovers in your refrigerator, chain-sawing your firewood into totem pole figures, using a cheap propane torch and spool of tin solder to convert the metal objects in your recycling bin into sculpture, or dashing off a quick bit of haiku poetry are all creative activities that can get you into the habit of being creative. There are probably people with creative interests just like yours out on the Web. Google.com gave 6690 hits on "torch sculpture art," 325,000 hits on "haiku," and 2760 on "chainsaw sculpture," so there surely is something creative that fits you out there.

Creativity—
So very ephemeral
Yet so critical

The preceding haiku was dashed off in about 30 seconds, within the classically appropriate period of time, "while the ink in your brush is still wet." It is not perfect since it does not easily suggest a season of the year, although "ephemeral," has mild connotations of autumn and falling leaves. It has the right number of syllables (5,7, and 5, respectively) for each line. We mention the time it took only to illustrate that creative activities can be fit into even the most hectic of periods; they need not be grand productions to be effective. In fact, if they are simple enough to be easily integrated into everyday life, there is a much greater chance that they will be practiced regularly.

The illustrative haiku was not intentionally imperfect, but it provides a better example because it is. The output of your creative activities need not have great intrinsic value, and for many people, it is better if they do not. Many of the activities mentioned previously were selected because their outputs are ephemeral. Firewood totem figures burn slightly better than the bark-covered limbs from which they were carved. Metal sculptures from the recycling bin still recycle. The memory stick in your digital camera, full of valiant, if imperfect efforts, is a few button presses away from being empty, ready for the next challenge. The exquisite meal made from last week's leftovers is but an inspiring memory. Out on your hard drive, yesterday's haiku will be overwritten by today's haiku, less than 10 milliseconds after the disk commands are issued. Since no one else has to see it, you can try anything you can think of—the journey is more important than the destination.

Not only do creative activities keep your creative abilities in good shape for the critical time at the beginning of your next project, they can keep you from going crazy during the hard slog of your current one. There is a lot to be said for dashing off biting, sarcastic haikus about the stupidities of work (or romantic ones for your significant other's birthday). And even steel bends to your will when you have a lighted torch in hand—something your code might not do.

Conclusion

Part of coming up with a better problem to solve is the simple discipline of using good programming and project management habits. These include looking for alternative solutions and taking the time to give the initial phases of design proper thought. Beyond that is the intentional practice of nonprogramming activities to "cross-train" your brain. Finding out-of-the-box solutions is a skill that can be learned and can be practiced. Corporate America has demanded it of its staff, and thus of their trainers and consultants [Epstein96]. This is also true of purely creative activities. They can be learned and practiced, too. It is up to you to do them. If, "the truth is out there," then so are better problems to solve.

References

[Abrash96] Abrash, Michael, "The Quake Graphics Engine," in lecture, Computer Game Developers Conference, 1996.

[Abrash97] Abrash, Michael, "Quake: A Post-Mortem and a Glimpse into the Future," *1997 Computer Game Developers Conference Proceedings*, CGDC, 1997.

[Amazon01] amazon.com, www.amazon.com, Software > Categories > Utilities > Voice Recognition, accessed August 2001.

[Brand87] Brand, Stewart, *The Media Lab: Inventing the Future at M.I.T.*, Viking Penguin, 1987.

[Doornbos01] Doornbos, Jamie, "Those Darn Sims: What Makes Them Tick?" in lecture, Game Developers Conference, 2001.

[Edwards01] Edwards, Steven, "The Technology Paradox: Efficiency versus Creativity," *Creativity Research Journal*, Volume: 13 Number: 2, Lawrence Erlbaum Associates, Inc., 2001.

[Epstein96] Epstein, Robert, *Creativity Games for Trainers: A Handbook of Group Activities for Jumpstarting Workplace Creativity*, McGraw-Hill, 1996.

[Isaksen99] Isaksen, Scott G.; Lauer, Kenneth J.; Ekvall, Goran; "Situational Outlook Questionnaire: A measure of the climate for creativity and change." *Psychological Reports*, No. 85, 1999.

[Kirby00] Kirby, Neil, "GDC 2000 AI Round Table Moderators Report," Game Developers Conference, www.gameai.com, 2000.

[Kirby91] Kirby, Neil, "Intelligent Behavior Without AI: An Evolutionary Approach," *Proceedings of the 1991 Computer Game Developers Conference*, CGDC, 1991.

[Meretzky96] Meretzky, Steve, "A Story Wrapped Inside a Puzzle Wrapped Inside an Enigma: Designing Adventure Games," in lecture, Computer Game Developers Conference, 1996.

[Wright01] Wright, Will, "Design Plunder," in lecture, Game Developers Conference, CMP, 2001.

12 Tips from the Trenches

Jeff Orkin—Monolith Productions

jorkin@blarg.net

The following tips are things that game AI programmers have learned from experience. Seasoned game AI programmers might find most of these tips to be obvious, but those new to the field can use this list as a head start and learn from our mistakes. Although some of these tips apply to software development in general, they are especially pertinent to developing AI systems, which are often delicate systems that evolve significantly over the course of a game's development.

1. Do Your Homework

There is no such thing as a "one size fits all" AI system. Different techniques are appropriate for different situations. The right solution depends on a number of factors:

- **The emphasis of the AI in the game**: Is smooth pathfinding a priority, or is learning and expressing emotions more important?
- **The schedule and budget for engineering the AI**: How much time and manpower is available for AI development?
- **The team make-up**: How many programmers and designers are on the team? What are the experience levels of the team members?

It is important to determine the needs of your game, and the capabilities of your development team. Use these as guidelines to choose where to focus the AI development effort. Once a focus has been determined, research what has been done first. Choose approaches that might work for your situation, and develop new code where necessary as the schedule allows. Good sources for research include this book, *Game Developer* magazine, the *Game Programming Gems* book series, the Game Developers Conference, and academic societies such as the Association for Computing Machinery (ACM).

2. Keep It Simple

Game AI programmers should live by the K.I.S.S. plan, and Keep It Simple Stupid! AI systems typically have many parameters and many code branches. They can quickly get complex and out of control. Ideally, AI systems should allow designers and programmers to do complex things with simple parts; parts that are easy to comprehend, reuse, debug, and maintain. Simple parts have a better chance of surviving the inevitable code changes required as the game design evolves. Furthermore, simple parts will be more maintainable by other people if the code should change hands, or live on to other projects.

Imagine you are tasked with creating a finite-state machine for agents in an action game. The agents are in a passive state when the player is not in sight, and in a combative state once the player comes close enough. The previous statement could be translated into code literally, into an Idle state and an Attack state. If the agents are to have any variety to their behavior, these states will quickly get bloated with complex code. A better approach would be to create a lot of simple, general-purpose, reusable states. For example, instead of Attack there could be states for Chase, FireWeapon, Retreat, and CallReinforcements. Some of these small states might be reusable in other situations. All of them are simple enough to diagnose should a problem arise. An ally could use the Chase state to follow the player in a cooperative situation. Chase could be replaced with a more general GoTo state that simply walks or runs an agent to some specified position. Tip #6 goes into more detail on state reuse through hierarchies.

3. Try It Out on Paper First

Step 1 is to come up with the next great AI system. Step 2 is not implementation! On paper, write an outline of the code, a rough draft of some sample data files, and some sketches of scenarios an agent might encounter (programmer art will suffice). Present this draft to the designers who will be creating content with the new AI system. Once the system design has made it through this review process, many of the oversights will be resolved before any code is written. This will allow for a smoother implementation, and will provide a more robust system. Keep these scenario sketches for use as documentation of how the system works, and review and update them as the system changes. Designers can reference the sketches to learn to use the AI system more effectively.

4. Precompute Navigation

Writing code to enable an agent to navigate around a 3D environment is a difficult problem for academics. The problem is much easier to solve for game developers, because we are allowed to cheat! While it is mathematically possible to calculate paths around the surrounding geometry, it can be computationally expensive. Instead, use precomputed pathfinding data that is invisible to the player, and allows agents to cheaply navigate wherever they need to go.

At a low level, physics systems calculate collisions by checking for intersections between a ray, box, or sphere with the rest of the geometry of the world. It is expensive to calculate the player's collisions, and the cost is compounded with each agent that is also checking collisions, or casting rays to plan a path.

Rather than testing collisions as an agent moves from one point to another, the agent can use navigational hint information that is invisible to the player. A tool can generate the hint information automatically, or designers can place hints by hand. Various techniques can be used to create these hints:

- Designers can paint floor geometry with colors or textures that signify blocked areas, or levels of movement preference.
- Designers can place line segments to be used as preset paths for agents to follow from one place to another [Adzima00].
- Designers can place boxes in such a way that there is always at least one box with a clear line of sight to another.
- Designers can create geometry to define areas in which agents can freely move about without checking for collisions with the world.
- A tool can analyze the level data and use some criteria to determine which polygons can be walked on. These polygons can be used to generate a navigational mesh [Tozour02a].

Undoubtedly, there are many other techniques as well, but the important point is that the agent uses complex pathfinding and the physics systems as little as possible. Refer to article 4.5, "Navigating Doors, Elevators, Ledges, and Other Obstacles," [Hancock02] in this book for more information on navigational hints placed by designers.

5. Put the Smarts in the World, Not in the AI

It is impossible to write an AI system that can handle every situation, and the task only grows during the development of a game. A better solution is to write simple AI systems that let agents choose desirable destinations, and navigate to them. Once they arrive at a destination, objects and locations in the game world can give the agent specific instructions of what they can or should do. The instructions might be given in the form of messages or scripts.

For example, an agent might know that it is hungry. This agent can search for objects in the world that announce themselves as edible, and navigate to the closest one. Once the agent arrives, the object runs a script that tells the agent whether to play an animation of picking an apple from a tree, opening a refrigerator, or using a vending machine. The agent appears to be very intelligent, when really it knows very little and is simply following instructions.

Another big benefit of putting the intelligence into the world is that it makes the AI infinitely extensible. New animations or scripts can make the agent do new things without any change to the code for the underlying AI systems themselves. This technique has been generously exploited by the game *The Sims*, as proven by the hundreds of objects available for download from the Web.

6. Give Every Action a Timeout and a Fallback

Nothing looks worse for AI than an agent that repeatedly does the wrong thing. No one will notice an agent that takes a left when it should have taken a right, but everyone will notice an agent that continues trying to run into a wall forever. Every AI system should check for success conditions within a reasonable amount of time. If these conditions are not met, the AI should give up and try something else. At a minimum, an agent can fall back to interesting idle animations that express the agent's confusion or frustration. If enough processing power is available, the agent can reevaluate its situation and formulate a new plan.

7. Use a Hierarchy of States

A finite-state machine (FSM) is a common mechanism for controlling the behavior of agents in a game. If states are designed in a simple, general-purpose, reusable fashion, each state can be reused in a variety of situations. Putting states into a hierarchy facilitates the reuse of simple lower-level states. Higher-level states can deal with big-picture decision-making and planning, leaving the specifics to lower-level states.

Imagine a game with an *Indiana Jones* style puzzle, in which the player must traverse a tiled floor marked with a grid of symbols. If the player steps on the wrong tile, the environment gets more dangerous, with fire shooting from cracks in the floor and enemies becoming more ferocious. As the player steps on the correct tiles, enemies calm down and the floor cools. The same enemy creatures might appear elsewhere in the game, but they have unique behavior while the player is solving the tile puzzle.

States for moving and attacking can be substates of a higher-level state governing the behavior of the enemies while the player is solving the tile puzzle. These movement and combat states can be used elsewhere in the game, as substates of a different parent state. The hierarchy of states creates a state machine that is unique to the behavior of the enemies while the player is in the tile puzzle, and keeps the code for the lower-level states clear of branches checking the player's current progress in any specific part of the game.

8. Do Not Let Agents Interfere with the Crucial Storytelling Events

Agents should be aware of game events that are important to telling the story. When the player is conversing, listening to dialog, or solving a piece of a puzzle, agents should know to back off and not get in the way. If the player needs to fend off enemies while the story is unfolding, he or she might miss something.

While one possibility is to make storytelling sequences noninteractive, the game will be much more immersive if the player still has control as the story is being told. A simple mechanism such as a Boolean flag on the player can signal agents to keep their distance when necessary.

9. Keep Agents Aware of the Global State of the World

Believable worlds and characters are what make games immersive. Agents should remember what has happened to them, and be aware of what has happened to others over the course of the game. They can then change their behavior and dialog accordingly, to convince the player that they are really living beings with thoughts and feelings.

Global flags and data about the player's progress might suffice for giving the illusion that agents are aware of changes to the world around them. It might be more impressive if the player witnesses agents passing information to each other. This requires each agent to keep some model of the state of the world. In this book, article 8.6, "A Dynamic Reputation System Based on Event Knowledge," [Alt02] details how to get the AI to remember events and form opinions of the player.

Even more impressive is the ability of agents to learn through observation, trial, and error. Agents can employ decision-tree learning techniques to make sense out of their observations [Evans01], [Quinlan93].

10. Create Variety through the Data, Not through the Code

A variety of enemy behaviors keeps games interesting. Creating many different behaviors in code requires many AI programmers, and removes the designers' control over game play and play balancing. Instead, the code should provide one or a handful of basic behavior types that are infinitely customizable through data [Rabin00].

Any behavior can be programmed, but it takes time. Every new line of code adds another potential bug and increases compilation time. More important is the fact that the agents' behavior is in the hands of programmers, when ultimately behavior is a product of collaboration between the programmers and the designers. The iterative process of refining code based on designer feedback can eat up a lot of unanticipated time.

If the AI systems take a data-driven approach, and expose as many of the variables as possible, every line of code can pay off repeatedly. Expose an agent's velocity, awareness, demeanor, field of view, available FSM states, inventory, and everything else. The development team might find that the AI systems can do things that were never anticipated. There is, however, a potential downside to exposing so much to the designers. Designers might find themselves overwhelmed and confused when presented with a plethora of mysterious variables. It is important to provide good defaults and documentation for every variable. Educate the designers about the system in order to find the balance between risk and flexibility. Game development teams are filled with creative people. The more of them who can experiment with the AI, the better the game will be. Good game AI is the result of a cooperative effort between programmers and designers.

Scripting languages take data-driven design a step further. Beyond exposing variables, scripting languages also expose logic. This might sound dangerous, but a language can be designed to be simple enough to minimize the risks, yet still give designers the ability to specify how to respond to game events [Huebner97]. Scripting languages can be extremely powerful tools, providing AI systems with infinite variety. A language can be a double-edged sword, however. Putting a lot of control over the AI into the designers' hands can inspire creativity, but putting too much control into scripts can increase risks of bugs and make setting up AI an overwhelming task. Refer to article 10.6, "The Perils of AI Scripting," [Tozour02b] for some precautions on the perils of scripting languages.

11. Make the Data Easily Accessible to Designers

Creating interesting AI and achieving good play balancing requires a great deal of experimentation. Designers should be able to tweak every value while the game runs, to fine-tune the AI. Statistics and formulas should be exposed through data files and/or scripts, rather than embedded in code. User interfaces can be used to exercise control over the interaction.

A user interface for formulas can allow designers to fill-in-the-blanks with appropriate values. Even state machines can be exposed, possibly through a visual decision-tree editor that allows for intuitive modeling of behavior. Designers are much more likely to tweak AI by making selections in drop-down boxes than by editing text files. The more the AI is tweaked, the better it will be.

12. Factor Stat Formulas into AI

Agents' attributes and abilities are often defined by statistics. This is particularly true of role-playing games (RPGs) such as *Diablo* and *Baldur's Gate*. Decisions in RPGs are based on the stats of characters. This concept should be taken as far as possible. Stat formulas should factor into every aspect of an agent's behavior, including how fast it travels, how intelligently it navigates, what attacks and defenses it chooses, and how it uses the world around it.

As more stats are factored into the AI, the stats of the player's character will start to hold more meaning. Agility can affect how much distance an agent covers when it moves, and how fast it animates. There can be spells that decrease agility, thus making enemies more sluggish. Stats for magic can affect the size of spells that characters conjure. The player will easily be able to see how his or her character's stats compare to other characters', making character improvements more rewarding.

Reuse, Don't Reinvent

With these tips in hand, you can leapfrog many of the AI programming stumbling blocks, and move onto solving more interesting problems. Instead of reinventing the wheel and trying to optimize 3D navigation, learn from the experience of others

[Rollings00]. Cheat with precomputed pathfinding hints. Put the smarts in the world. Create variety through data. Treat these tips and this book as your personal team of consultants, and use existing solutions where possible. Spend your newfound free time working on agents that learn, cooperate with other agents, and express emotions convincingly [Evans01]. Make a game that stands out and takes AI to the next level.

References

[Adzima00] Adzima, Joe, "Using AI to Bring Open City Racing to Life," *Game Developer* magazine, Volume 7, Number 12, 2000.

[Alt02] Alt, Gregg, and King, Kristin, "A Dynamic Reputation System Based on Event Knowledge," *AI Game Programming Wisdom*, Charles River Media, 2002.

[Evans01] Evans, Richard, "The Future of AI in Games: A Personal View," *Game Developer* magazine, Volume 8, Number 8, 2001.

[Hancock02] Hancock, John, "Navigating Doors, Elevators, Ledges, and Other Obstacles," *AI Game Programming Wisdom*, Charles River Media, 2002.

[Huebner97] Huebner, Robert, "Adding Languages to Game Engines," *Game Developer* magazine, Volume 4, Number 6, 1997.

[Quinlan93] Quinlan, J. R., *C4.5: Programs for Machine Learning*, Morgan Kaufmann, 1993.

[Rabin00] Rabin, Steve, "The Magic of Data-Driven Design," *Game Programming Gems*, Charles River Media, 2000.

[Rollings00] Rollings, Andrew, Morris, Dave, *Game Architecture and Design*, The Coriolis Group, 2000.

[Tozour02a] Tozour, Paul, "Building a Near-Optimal Navigational Mesh," *AI Game Programming Wisdom*, Charles River Media, 2002.

[Tozour02b] Tozour, Paul, "The Perils of AI Scripting," *AI Game Programming Wisdom*, Charles River Media, 2002.

USEFUL TECHNIQUES
AND
SPECIALIZED SYSTEMS

Building an AI Diagnostic Toolset

Paul Tozour—Ion Storm Austin

gehn29@yahoo.com

If you ever visit the offices of Ion Storm Austin, listen carefully and you might hear an odd thumping noise on the windows. Investigate more closely and you'll notice a colorful blue bird wandering back and forth along the ledge. He slams his beak into the window for several minutes before moving further down the ledge to torture the unfortunate soul in the next office.

Game AI characters are all too similar. Countless times when developing AI, you will find yourself staring at the screen, shaking your head, wondering how on earth your character ended up doing the insanely stupid thing it just did—or why it failed to do what it knew it was supposed to do.

At times, the AI seems all too much like a human child in its ability to torment and confound its creator, and AI development can seem more like a diaper-level parenting task than anything resembling clean, professional software development. Our ambitions for a "lifelike" AI are fulfilled in the worst possible way.

In the case of the bird, there's no doubt that the little blue guy sees his own reflection and thinks it's a competing alpha male. He never questions for a moment how his image can peck right back at him with such perfect timing.

This is the unfortunate result of combining a seemingly innocuous new technology—reflective windows—with a species whose evolution failed to prepare it for the difficult challenge of self-recognition.

Cracking Open the Cranium

Whenever you don't understand the reasons for your AIs' behavior, you need a way to crack open the cranium and figure out the problem quickly and easily. Behavioral flaws are inevitable, and more often than not, the difference between success and failure comes from being able to diagnose and correct those flaws as quickly and easily as possible.

As programmers, we have the power to build immensely powerful diagnostic tools that will give us full control over the systems we develop. The right set of tools will make tinkering and guesswork unnecessary. This article describes techniques for building a powerful and full-featured AI diagnostic toolset. The color plates in the middle of this book provide additional examples of some of the AI diagnostic tools described in this article.

AI diagnostic tools aren't a substitute for a debugger, and a debugger can never replace good diagnostics. A good debugger is indispensable, but even the best debugger isn't sufficient to test and debug game AI. A debugger gives you depth but not breadth—it lets you view the entire state of the system at any moment, but it's not very good at showing you how specific variables change over time. You need to be able to play the game and quickly determine how different combinations of stimuli affect the resulting behaviors. Many AI data structures also have a natural visual representation, and it's far easier to provide this representation in its natural format than to attempt to interpret the data from stack dumps and variable watch windows in the debugger. Many of the visualizations referenced in this paper can be seen in Color Plates 4 through 11.

It's also critical to keep in mind that many people other than yourself will be dealing with your AI on a day-to-day basis. Quite often, many of these individuals—particularly the testers and level designers—lack the degree of technical sophistication required to understand and troubleshoot the AI systems without additional assistance.

If you provide powerful, customized tools to indicate what's going on inside your AIs' heads, you can allow your team to learn about the AI on their own. Your diagnostics provide your team with valuable insights about how the AI works "under the hood." The level of understanding that becomes possible with your tools will help your team develop a shared AI vocabulary, and this can dramatically elevate the level of the dialogue between the AI developers and the design team.

Building Flexible Diagnostics

Most of the utilities described in this article operate on specific sets of AI entities, so it's useful to have a way to specify on which AIs the utilities will operate. For example, the user could specify that subsequent commands will apply to all AIs in the game, all AIs of a specific type or alignment, or AIs that have been specially tagged in the game's editor. For action games and other single-avatar games, the user might be able to specify the nearest AI to the player, or the AI the user is currently aiming at, as the recipient of the command. For strategy games and other games in which you can select specific units, the user could specify that the command applies to the set of currently selected AIs.

The best user interface for this type of AI toolset is an extensible in-game menu system. It's very useful to be able to provide descriptive menu item text that describes what action a specific menu option will perform when you click on it. This is particularly helpful for designers and other team members who would prefer to be able to use your tools without having to continually look up arcane console commands in the documentation.

Unfortunately, many game debugging systems are limited to simple text entry consoles or shortcut key combinations specified in initialization files. In this case, you will need to provide documentation on all the available commands to the team to use your AI tools—or, better yet, build a menu system yourself.

Many game development systems also provide a way to log text to output files or debugger output windows. This functionality can be useful at times, but it is fundamentally noninteractive and is often little better than stepping through your code in the debugger. This article focuses on interactive tools and tools that specifically lend themselves to graphical representations.

AI Commands

We can divide our AI tools into two broad categories: *commands* that change the state of the system, and *diagnostics* that allow us to view any part of the system without modifying it.

This section suggests a number of commands that might be useful or appropriate for your particular game and your specific AI architecture. This list is intended only as a starting point—naturally, your game might require special diagnostic tools unique to the particular game or the specific AI architecture you're developing.

- **Destroy**. Destroys some number of AI-controlled units.
- **Invulnerable**. Makes some number of units invulnerable. In many cases, it's also useful to be able to make the player invulnerable as well.
- **Stop movement**. Makes selected AI units unable to move.
- **Freeze**. Completely halts the selected units' AI.
- **Blind**. Disables all visual input for selected AIs.
- **Deaf**. Disables all audio input for selected AIs.
- **Insensate**. Makes selected AIs completely oblivious to all sensory inputs.
- **Duplicate**. Clones the selected AI entities.
- **Forget**. Makes AIs forget their current target and lose all knowledge they possess.
- **Reset**. Completely resets the selected AIs and returns them to their starting state.
- **Modify State**. Modifies the internal state of the selected AIs—for example, by forcing the AI to execute a specific behavior or combat tactic, or by setting the current "state" of an AI's finite-state machine.
- **Set Target**. Set an AI's current combat target to a specific game entity.
- **Change Game Speed**. Allows the user to speed up, slow down, or pause the game.
- **Teleport to Location**. Moves the user's viewport to any location in the game world.
- **Teleport to AI**. Similar to teleport. Switches the user's perspective to that of any of the AI agents in the game. A drop-down menu of all the AIs currently present in the game can also be quite useful if the game doesn't have too many AI units.
- **Follow**. Makes the user's viewport continuously follow and monitor a specific AI.

- **Switch player control**. Allows the user to take control of another player. For example, this would allow the user to assume control of an opposing team in a sports game or take over an AI unit in an action game.
- **Spawn objects**. It's often useful to be able to dynamically spawn new items, either to use them in the game or to give AIs an opportunity to use them.

AI Diagnostic Tools

This section provides a short list of diagnostic tools that can be used to view the internal state of your AIs and the specific pieces of knowledge at their disposal.

Nearly all of these diagnostics are incredibly simple to implement, and the time they save in testing, tweaking, and debugging will make up for their development time several times over. The main tools required to build these diagnostics are a simple 3D line-drawing primitive and a way to draw arbitrary text onscreen.

It's generally a good idea to make all of the following diagnostics completely independent of one another. You can store a list of which diagnostics are currently enabled, perhaps as a linked list of integer IDs or a set of bit flags that can be set within a single integer, and use this to determine which diagnostics are currently turned on.

Also, note that unlike the AI commands listed in the previous section, diagnostic tools tend to be highly useful within the game's editing tools as well as within the game itself. A game will usually share a large amount of code in common with its editor anyway, so it makes sense that wherever possible, we should make our diagnostic tools available within both contexts.

- **Unit identification**: Display the text name and/or numeric object ID of each selected AI entity.
- **Unit statistics**: Diagnostics can display the type or species of each selected entity, its current hit points and armor level, the entity's current world-space coordinates, and the value of any additional properties associated with the entity, such as the contents of its inventory, what weapons it possesses, its current skill settings, and so on.
- **Unit AI state**: Diagnostics can easily display the state of any given AI subsystem. If you're developing an AI based on a finite-state machine, for example, it's helpful to display the current state of an AI at any given moment. If you're using a fuzzy-state machine, you can display the numeric weight of each state in real time (assuming your fuzzy-state machine is small enough to fit on the screen). If you're using a decision-tree learning algorithm, display the contents of the current decision tree.
- **View search space**: Any game that features AI pathfinding will typically have some precomputed data structure(s) to represent the search space within the game world. For example, many 3D games use a navigation mesh to represent the connectivity of the walkable surfaces in the world (see [Snook00]). It's critically important to be able to view these data structures within the game.

- **View pathfinding search**: Whenever your AIs perform a search, it's helpful to be able to view the specific locations the algorithm searched. Provide support to show the nodes the search looked at, the state (free/blocked) of each node, the order in which the nodes were searched, and the computed path cost values at each node. Consider additional options to allow the user to slow the search to one iteration per frame so that you can watch it explore the search space in slow motion.

- **View computed movement path**: A set of connected lines can be used to indicate the path that a specific AI intends to follow.

- **View Pre-smoothed path**: In some cases, an A* search algorithm will first calculate an initial path, and then perform an iterative procedure to smooth out the path. In this case, it's useful to be able to see the shape of the path before smoothing occurred.

- **View embedded tactical information**: Many combat-oriented games will pre-process each level and embed tactical information to give the AIs a sense of the spatial significance of different areas, such as predetermined "way points" and "cover points" (see [van der Sterren01]).

- **View past locations**: Each AI can save a list of locations it has visited in the past. This diagnostic draws connected lines indicating the locations an AI has visited in the past, which can be very useful for determining how an AI reached its current location, or even which AI it is. If memory is an issue and the game has many units, it's trivial to put a cap on the number of locations saved.

- **View current target**: Draws an arrow from each selected AI to its current intended target in combat.

- **View designer-specified patrol paths**: Level designers often need to specify canned AI paths, patrols, or formations that the AIs will use in their levels. As you will typically need to provide editing tools in your game editing system to allow the designers to specify these paths and formations, it then becomes trivial to supply the same functionality in the game itself.

- **View formation leader**: Draw an arrow from each AI in a formation to the AI it's currently following.

- **View sensory knowledge**: In order to tweak AIs' sensory capabilities, we need diagnostics to show us what they notice at any given moment. For example, we can draw a line from each AI to any suspicious stimuli it notices, and use the color of the line to indicate the intensity of the stimulus or the specific sensory subsystem (visual, audio, tactile, etc.) that noticed the stimulus.

- **View animation and audio commands issued**: AIs will typically communicate with the lower-level animation and audio subsystems for a particular AI entity by creating and issuing discrete "play sound" and "play audio" commands. Diagnostics can allow you to view these commands as they are issued.

- **View current animations**: Consider providing support to display the current animations a character is playing and any appropriate parameters. This can be particularly useful when attempting to identify multiple animations being played back simultaneously by a hierarchical animation system [Orkin02]. It can also help debug your game's inverse-kinematics (IK) systems.

- **View player commands**: Similarly, in games in which each player controls multiple AI units (such as strategy games and many sports games), an AI player will typically communicate with the AI entities it controls by issuing discrete player commands. It's helpful to be able to view these commands as they are issued to the player's units.

- **Show strategic and tactical data structures**: Many games with a heavy tactical and/or strategic element require AI players that can perform strategic and tactical reasoning using data structures such as influence maps, functional asset trees, and dependency graphs (see [Tozour01]). Providing visual representations of these data structures is key to your ability to debug them and observe their behavior in real time.

- **Show fire arcs considered**: A ranged combat AI system will typically consider some number of points to shoot at on or near an enemy unit (possibly the player). It will then typically use line testing to determine which of these potential target points are feasible. A few diagnostic lines in the game can show you which target locations the AI is considering, and which lines it has discovered to be blocked.

- **Show tracers**: When a game includes projectile weapons, it's often useful to be able to view the actual paths the projectiles followed. This is a big help when debugging fast-moving projectiles (such as bullets), and it's invaluable when attempting to pinpoint the differences between the trajectory the AI thought the projectile would follow and the actual trajectory that the physics system ultimately produced.

Fixing the Problem Faster

When a sink breaks, any self-respecting plumber will open the cabinets under the sink and look at the pipes.

Game programmers, on the other hand, prefer to stand around and hypothesize about why the sink might have broken, tinker endlessly with the faucet, and occasionally convince themselves that the sink is hopeless and install a brand new sink.

Don't do that.

References and Additional Reading

[Orkin02] Orkin, Jeff, "Realistic Character Behavior with Prioritized, Categorized Animation," *AI Game Programming Wisdom*, Ed. Steve Rabin, Charles River Media, 2002.

[Snook00] Snook, Greg, "Simplified 3D Movement and Pathfinding Using Navigation Meshes," *Game Programming Gems*, Ed. Mark DeLoura, Charles River Media, 2000.

[Tozour01] Tozour, Paul, "Influence Mapping" and "Strategic Assessment Techniques," *Game Programming Gems 2,* Ed. Mark DeLoura, Charles River Media, 2001.

[van der Sterren01] van der Sterren, William, "Terrain Reasoning for 3D Action Games," *Game Programming Gems 2*, Ed. Mark DeLoura, Charles River Media, 2001.

A General-Purpose Trigger System

Jeff Orkin—Monolith Productions

jorkin@blarg.net

A trigger system serves two main purposes in a game: it keeps track of events in the game world that agents can respond to, and it minimizes the amount of processing agents need to do to respond to these events. The benefit of a centralized trigger system is that triggers can be culled by priority and proximity before delivering them to agents. This way, each individual agent only processes the highest-priority triggers within its vicinity.

A trigger can be any stimulus that a game designer wants an agent to respond to [Nilsson98], [Russell95]. In an action game, triggers might be anything audible or visible that affects the behavior of agents, such as gunfire, explosions, nearby enemies, or dead bodies. Triggers might also emanate from inanimate objects that agents need to know about, such as levers and control panels. Triggers can be generated from a variety of sources, including game code, scripts, console commands, and animation key frames. Agents can specify which types of triggers are of interest to them.

Benefits of Centralization

The alternative to a centralized trigger system is polling for events. There are several disadvantages to polling. Polling requires each agent to query the world to find events of interest. For example, if an agent is interested in responding to enemy gunfire, it needs to iterate through all of the other characters in the world, and query them for their last weapon-firing information. This requires each agent to store extra history data about anything that might interest others. Since each agent needs to query every other agent, the agents perform a $O(n^2)$ search even to find out that no one fired a weapon recently. If any agent goes inactive to reduce the CPU load, that agent cannot respond to triggers and will not even notice a rocket whizzing right by him.

In a centralized system, triggers are registered when events occur. Each cycle, the system iterates once through a list of all agents. For each agent, the system uses a series of tests to determine if the agent is interested in any currently existing triggers. If none of the triggers are of interest to an agent, that agent does not need to do any processing at all. In addition, the system has opportunities to cull out triggers by trigger-type and proximity.

Culling can be especially effective when combined with grouping, as we discuss at the end of this article. Existing triggers are sorted by priority, so that agents can respond to the most important thing at any instant. If an enemy is standing in front of an agent, the agent really does not care about footstep sounds in the distance. The centralized system is also more general, reusable, and extensible than polling, because a new trigger type can be added to the system without writing any specific code to handle the new type.

Defining a Trigger

A trigger is defined by a bit-flag enum for its type, and a set of variables describing its parameters. This `TriggerRecordStruct` defines an instance of a trigger.

```
struct TriggerRecordStruct
{
    EnumTriggerType    eTriggerType;
    unsigned long      nTriggerID;
    unsigned long      idSource;
    Vector             vPos;
    float              fRadius;
    unsigned long      nTimeStamp;
    unsigned long      nExpirationTime;
    bool               bDynamicSourcePos;
    ...
};
```

The trigger types are enumerated as bit-flags. Each agent has a member variable that defines triggers of interest by combining bit-flags for trigger types into one unsigned long. Trigger types for an action game might look like this:

```
enum EnumTriggerType
{
    kTrig_None       = 0,
    kTrig_Explosion  = (1 << 0),
    kTrig_EnemyNear  = (1 << 1),
    kTrig_Gunfire    = (1 << 2),
    ...
};
```

Combining bit-flags allows an agent to specify what to pay attention to, and what to ignore. An agent may toggle flags on and off during the course of the game to temporarily ignore or focus on certain trigger types. A blind agent that only responds to sound would set his trigger flags to the bitwise-Or of audio triggers, and omit anything visual, like this:

```
dwTriggerFlags = kTrig_Explosion | kTrig_Gunfire;
```

The trigger ID is a unique identifier assigned by the trigger system at the time the trigger is registered. This ID allows a trigger to be referenced later, which we discuss later in this article in regard to removing a trigger.

The source ID is the ID of the game object that created the trigger. The source might be a character that fired a weapon, or a landmine that exploded. The agent that responds to a trigger might need to know who generated it so that it can return fire, or run directly away from the source of an explosion.

Each trigger has a position and radius in the world. An agent will only react to a trigger if it is within the trigger's radius. Many triggers are static, but some might continue to move through the world. If the bDynamicSourcePos flag is set to true, this specifies that the trigger is moving and needs its position to be reset every cycle. This flag allows a moving target to register one trigger, instead of registering a new trigger every time it moves. An example might be an EnemyNear trigger, which is intended to alert an agent that an enemy is in its proximity. This trigger's position needs to track the position of its source.

Triggers exist for some specified amount of time. Each trigger is stamped with the time it was created, and the time it should be deleted from the world. In the code provided, time is measured in milliseconds returned by the Windows multimedia timer's timeGetTime() function. An expiration time of zero means that the trigger exists forever, or until it is removed from the system by something other than timing out. For example, if agents are supposed to pull a lever when they come near it, the lever can register a trigger that never expires. When the lever is pulled, the stimulus can be removed from the system.

The Trigger System

The trigger system itself is a class that stores records for existing triggers, and provides methods for registering, removing, and updating triggers.

```
class CTriggerSystem
{
public :
    CTriggerSystem();
    ~CTriggerSystem();

    unsigned long RegisterTrigger( EnumTriggerType _eTriggerType,
        unsigned long _nPriority, unsigned long _idSource,
        const Vector& _vPos, float _fRadius, float _fDuration,
        bool _bDynamicSourcePos);

    void RemoveTrigger(unsigned long nTriggerID);
    void Update();

private :
    TRIGGER_MAP m_mapTriggerMap;
    bool m_bTriggerCriticalSection;
};
```

Existing triggers are stored in an STL multimap [Musser01], sorted by priority.

```
typedef std::multimap<unsigned short, TriggerRecordStruct*,
                 std::greater<unsigned short> > TRIGGER_MAP;
```

Rather than using the default `less<unsigned short>` comparison function, the `greater<unsigned short>` comparison function is specified so that the highest-priority triggers will be listed first. A multimap is used to allow duplicate keys, meaning triggers with the same priority.

Registering a Trigger

Triggers are added to the trigger system by calling `RegisterTrigger()`. `RegisterTrigger()` creates a new trigger and sets its parameters to the specified values. Rather than passing all of the values as parameters, predefined trigger types could be stored in resource files, and a reference to a structure could be passed instead.

```
unsigned long CTriggerSystem::RegisterTrigger(
    EnumTriggerType _eTriggerType, unsigned long _nPriority,
    unsigned long _idSource, const Vector& _vPos, float _fRadius,
    float _fDuration, bool _bDynamicSourcePos )
{
    // Create a trigger record, and fill it in.
    TriggerRecordStruct* pTriggerRecord =
    new TriggerRecordStruct( _eTriggerType, _idSource, _vPos,
                        _fRadius, _fDuration, _b
                           DynamicSourcePos);

    // Trigger records are sorted by priority.
    m_mapTriggerMap.insert( TRIGGER_MAP::value_type(_nPriority,
                        pTriggerRecord) );

    // Return the unique identifier for this trigger.
    return pTriggerRecord->nTriggerID;
}
```

The function returns a unique trigger ID to the caller. This ID can be stored, and used to refer back to this trigger instance. In particular, the ID can be used to remove the trigger.

Removing a Trigger

At times, it might be necessary or desirable to remove an existing trigger from the world. If the source of a trigger dies, the trigger might have no meaning. Some triggers might be toggled active and inactive. A lever that has been pulled might no longer be of any use to agents. A character might be able to disguise himself to temporarily stop emanating the EnemyNear trigger. In all of these cases, the existing trigger can be removed from the system by calling `RemoveTrigger()`.

```
void CTriggerSystem::RemoveTrigger( unsigned long nTriggerID )
{
    TRIGGER_MAP::iterator it = _mapTriggerMap.begin();
    while( it != m_mapTriggerMap.end() ) {
        if( it->second->nTriggerID == nTriggerID ) {
            delete(it->second);
            return;
        }
        else ++it;
    }
}
```

Updating the Trigger System

The heart of the trigger system is the Update() function. Update removes expired triggers, refreshes dynamic positioning triggers, and notifies agents of triggers that are relevant to them.

```
void CTriggerSystem::Update()
{
    CAgent* pAgent = NULL;
    float fDistance = 0.f;

    TriggerRecordStruct* pRec;
    TRIGGER_MAP::iterator it;
    unsigned long nCurTime = timeGetTime();

    // Delete expired trigger records. For records that are not
    // expired, update position if the dynamic flag is set.
    it = m_mapTriggerMap.begin();
    while( it != m_mapTriggerMap.end() )
    {
        pRecord = it->second;
        if( (pRec->nExpirationTime != 0) &&
            (pRec->nExpirationTime < nCurTime) )
        {
            delete(pRec);
            it = m_mapTriggerMap.erase(it);
        } else {
            // Update pos if dynamic flag is set. Reset time-stamp.
            if( pRec->bDynamicSourcePos == true )
            {
                UpdatePos(pRec->vPos);
                pRec->nTimeStamp = nCurTime;
            }
            ++it;
        }
    }

    // Trigger Agents.
    for( unsigned long i=0; i<g_nNumAgents; ++I )
    {
        pAgent = g_pAgentList[i];

        // Check if it's time for Agent to update.
```

```
if( nCurTime > pAgent->GetNextTriggerUpdate() )
{
    pAgent->SetNextTriggerUpdate(nCurTime);

    // Loop thru existing trigger records.
    for( it = m_mapTriggerMap.begin();
         it != m_mapTriggerMap.end(); ++it )
    {
        pRec = it->second;

        // Does Agent respond to trigger?
        if( !(pRec->eTriggerType & pAgent->GetTriggerFlags()) )
            continue;

        // Is source the Agent itself?
        if(pRec->idSource == i)
            continue;

        // Check radius.
        fDistance = DIST(pRec->vPos, pAgent->GetPosition());
        if( fDistance > pRec->fRadius) )
            continue;

    // HandleTrigger returns true if the
    // Agent responded to the trigger.
    if( pAgent->HandleTrig(pRec) )
    {
        // Listen to highest priority trig at any instant.
            break;
    }
    }
    }
}
}
```

First, Update() iterates through the existing triggers. If a trigger's expiration time has passed, the trigger is deleted. Otherwise, if the trigger has a dynamic source position, its position and timestamp are reset, essentially making a new trigger.

Next, Update() iterates through all of the agents in the world and notifies them of relevant triggers. This loop consists of a number of if statements, providing early outs before more expensive checks. The first early out is based on an agent's update time. Each agent has an update rate, which prevents it from updating every frame. A reasonable update rate might be 15 times per second. Update times should be staggered among agents, so that agents with the same rate do not all update on the same cycles.

For agents that are ready to update during the current cycle, Update() iterates through the existing triggers. Each trigger's type is checked against the agent's flags for trigger types of interest. The agent will only do further checks on triggers of interest.

If the agent is interested in a trigger, and the source of the trigger is not the agent itself, the final and most expensive check, the distance check, is made.

If a trigger passes all of the tests for an agent, the agent's HandleTrig() function is called to handle the trigger. HandleTrig() might do additional calculations and tests to determine if the agent is going to respond to this trigger. The agent returns true or false to let Update() know if it is going to respond to the trigger. An agent can only respond to one trigger at any instant, so if the agent returns true, it will stop checking additional triggers. If the agent returns false, the loop continues to allow the agent to respond to other triggers. The agent records the trigger's timestamp to ensure that it handles each trigger only once, and only handles triggers more recent than the last. The triggers are sorted by priority, so the agent will respond to the highest-priority trigger at any instant.

There is an assumption behind the decision to respond to only one trigger: the trigger puts the agent into some state of a finite-state machine. This state governs how the agent will respond to the game event represented by the trigger. By responding to the highest-priority trigger, the agent is behaving in the most appropriate manner given the current situation. If a different system is in place for the agent, and it is necessary to respond to multiple triggers at the same instant, the agent can return false in order to continue peaking at lower-priority triggers. In any case, triggers should have a duration longer than one cycle. This way, an agent can choose to respond to lower-priority triggers after handling the highest priority.

Processing a Grouping Hierarchy of Agents

Agents can be grouped to maximize the benefits of the trigger system's culling. If there is a large number of agents in the world, it might be inefficient to check each individual agent against the list of existing triggers. Instead, triggers can be checked against groups of agents. The trigger system can be adapted to handle groups, with a few minor modifications.

Agents can be grouped by a variety of criteria, including their world position, update rate, race, or faction. The trigger system can test these groups recursively. If the system determines that a group is interested in an existing trigger, it can then test each member of the group. The members of a group can also be groups, creating a multi-level hierarchy. For instance, agents might be grouped by race, and then subgrouped by world position. Grouping allows many agents to ignore a trigger through a single test. Agents can efficiently ignore triggers on the other side of the world. Neutral agents who ignore most triggers can minimize their processing.

In terms of implementation, the class for a group of agents can be derived from the class for an individual agent. As agents are added to the group, the group's member variables are set to reflect the combined attributes of all members of the group. For example, the group's flags for triggers of interest are set to the combination of flags from all agents in the group. If a group has two members—one who is interested in explosions, and another who is interested in the location of the enemy—the flags for the group would be set like this:

```
PGroup->SetTriggerFlags( pAgent0->GetTriggerFlags() |
                         pAgent1->GetTriggerFlags() );
```

```
// The above is equivalent to this.
dwTriggerFlags = kTrig_Explosion | kTrig_EnemyNear;
```

The group's position can be handled in a similar fashion. The position of the group is set to the average of the positions of all members of the group. The group needs one additional variable for its radius, which is set to encompass all of the positions of group members. The trigger system's distance check can be modified to check a radius around an agent or group of agents against the radius around the trigger. When the radii intersect, `HandleTrig()` is called.

The trigger system's `Update()` function can be modified to take a pointer to a list of agents, rather than using the global list of agents. `Update()` is first called to check a list of groups of agents. `HandleTrig()` for the group can then call `Update()` again, passing in the group's list of agents. Repeat this process to recurse from the group level to the individual agents.

Triggering the Possibilities

Once a basic trigger system is in place, the possibilities for the game's AI are endless. Triggers can be used to alert agents of gunfire and explosions. An agent with low health can use a dynamically positioned trigger to signal the need for help to allies. Agents can even detect what the player has interacted with via triggers attached to interactive objects in the game world, such as doors.

Imagine this scenario: the player fires his gun to open a locked door. The gun registers a trigger for the gunfire sound, which triggers a nearby agent. The agent walks to the location of the sound, and notices the player. The player is visible to the enemy through a dynamically positioned trigger for the character's visibility. The agent chases the player by following the position of the dynamic trigger. The player kills the agent, who registers a permanent trigger for his body's visibility. Another agent walks by and responds to the body's trigger. He becomes suspicious and turns on flags to check for additional triggers including footprints. Sure enough, the player has left a trail of triggers registered at the positions of his bloody footprints. As the agent follows the player's footprints, he comes across an alarm button. The alarm emanates a permanent trigger, registered when the alarm was created. This trigger causes the agent to walk over to the button and sound the alarm, triggering other agents to search for the player.

This is only a sampling of how the trigger system can be used to create exciting gameplay. The possibilities are only limited by the designer's imagination.

References

[Musser01] Musser, David R.; Derge, Gillmer J.; Saini, Atul, *STL Tutorial and Reference Guide: C++ Programming with the Standard Template Library 2nd Ed.*, Addison-Wesley Publishing Co., 2001.

[Nilsson98] Nillson, Nils J., *Artificial Intelligence: A New Synthesis*, Morgan Kaufman Publishers, Inc., 1998.

[Russell95] Russell, Stuart, Norvig, Peter, *Artificial Intelligence, A Modern Approach*, Prentice Hall, 1995.

2.3

A Data-Driven Architecture for Animation Selection

Jeff Orkin—Monolith Productions

jorkin@blarg.net

In addition to navigation and planning, a common task for AI systems in games is to determine which animations a character should play. Navigation and planning systems carry out their decisions by animating the character. Innovations in animation technology, such as skeletal animation and motion capture, facilitate sharing animation across multiple characters. The time and resources saved by sharing animation allows for the creation of a much wider variety of animations. Rather than simply playing a "Run" animation, a character might now play a specific "RunWithSword," "InjuredRun," or "AngryRun" animation. As the number of animations grows, so does the complexity of the code controlling which animation to play in a specific situation.

A character might choose the appropriate animation to play under certain conditions. The conditions might include factors such as the character's mood, state of health, or what the character is carrying [Rose98]. This article describes a technique for animation selection in the context of a fantasy role-playing game (RPG), in which characters play different animations depending on the type of weapon they are carrying. The technique applies equally well to action, adventure, and other game genres. "Attack" animations are not the only ones to change depending on the weapon. A character carrying a heavy sword might lumber as he walks, while a character carrying a staff might use the staff as a walking stick.

The Action Table is a simple, data-driven approach to animation selection that keeps the complexity out of the code [Rabin00]. With the use of the Action Table, the code stays clean and maintainable, and artists are empowered with the ability to control the animation selections. This article describes the implementation of the Action Table, and goes on to describe how this technique can be extended to handle randomization and dynamic animation lists.

The Brute-Force Approach

The brute-force approach of using if-else statements, or switch statements, will successfully select an animation based on some condition, but it has a number of problems. The code might look like this:

```
if ( m_curWeaponType == kWeap_Sword )
{
        PlayAnim ( m_szSwordWalk );
}
else if ( m_curWeaponType == kWeap_Bow )
{
        PlayAnim ( m_szBowWalk );
}
...
```

The code is simple enough to read and understand, but as the number of weapon types increases, so will the code. Similar code will be required for each animated action, causing further bloat. With the addition of features such as randomization of animation, the code will become needlessly complex and unmaintainable. Furthermore, every time an artist wants to add a new weapon type or action, he or she will need the help of a programmer. Programmers can become bottlenecks to creativity. If artists are empowered with the ability to experiment, the game is sure to look and play better.

The Action Table: A Clean, Data-Driven Solution

ON THE CD

The Action Table puts all of the decision-making into the data, leaving the code clean and maintainable. Only the lookup mechanism is in code. The full code listings for a basic and optimized version of the Action Table can be found on the CD that accompanies this book. The C++ class for the Action Table has one function and one member variable. Other than auxiliary functions like Read() and Write(), the only member function is GetAnimation(), which takes two query parameters, enums for the condition and the action, and returns an animation filename.

```
const char* GetAnimation( EnumAnimCondition eAnimCond,
                          EnumAction eAction );
```

Any time the character wants to select an animation appropriate for its current weapon and action, it calls just one line of code. For example, if a character with a two-handed sword wants to attack, it calls:

```
PlayAnim ( m_ActionTable->GetAnimation( kACond_TwoHandedSword,
                                        kAct_Attack ) );
```

In the case of a fantasy RPG, the conditions are the types of weapons a character can carry, and the actions are things a character can do. These enum lists can grow over the course of the game's development. The enums might look like this:

```
enum EnumAnimCondition {
        kACond_Invalid = -1,
        kACond_Default =  0,
        kACond_OneHandedSword,
        kACond_TwoHandedSword,
```

```
                    kACond_Bow,
                    kACond_Staff,
                    ...
        };

        enum EnumAction {
                    kAct_Invalid = -1,
                    kAct_Default =  0,
                    kAct_Idle,
                    kAct_Walk,
                    kAct_Run,
                    kAct_Attack,
                    kAct_React,
                    kAct_OpenDoor,
                    ...
        };
```

Removing the Programmer Bottleneck

Programmers can provide the artists with a large vocabulary of enums for possible conditions and actions, and add more upon request. Artists are free to modify a data file to assign animations to the actions, without programmer assistance. Ideally, they could interact with the file through a GUI application that eliminates the risk of syntax or data entry errors. The data file should require at least one default animation per action that the character might perform. The artists have the freedom to add variations for different conditions. The data file might look something like this:

```
Default
            Default         default.anm
            Idle            default_idle.anm
            Walk            default_walk.anm
            ...
        OneHandedSword
            Idle            1hs_twirl.anm
        TwoHandedSword
            Idle            2hs_sharped.anm
            Walk            2hs_lumber.anm
        ...
```

How It Works

The Action Table's GetAnimation() query function works by looking up the animation in a set of nested STL maps. The single member variable of the Action Table is a map, sorted by the condition. The map's key is the EnumAnimCondition, and the value is another STL map, sorted by the action. The key to the second map is the EnumAction, and the value is the string for the animation filename. The typedefs for the maps look like this:

```
typedef std::map<EnumAction, char*> ACTION_ANIM_MAP;
    typedef std::map<EnumAnimCondition, ACTION_ANIM_MAP>
    CONDITION_ACTION_MAP;
```

The specifics of the implementation can be easily changed if necessary. Rather than a string filename, the second map could store some other kind of identifier for the animation resource. Any sorted list data structure could be substituted for STL. It is notable, though, that STL maps are particularly efficient, with 16 bytes of overhead per element and $O(log\ N)$ search times through a red-black tree [Isensee99].

Sorted lists might seem overly complex, when a simple two-dimensional array would suffice. An array with conditions on one axis, and actions on the other would allow immediate lookups. However, sorted lists are preferable for two main reasons. First, the Action Table does not require a character to have a specific animation for every action under every condition. A character might fall back to a default action animation if a specific one is not provided. For instance, a character might play the same "Drown" animation if he is carrying anything other than a staff. The second reason is that each character type has its own Action Table, which might have only a subset of the entire list of possible conditions or actions. An enemy barbarian might have animations for "Idle," "Walk," "Run," "Attack," and "React," while an ambient pig might only have "Idle," "Walk," and "React." If every character's Action Table was an array covering all possibilities, sparse arrays would waste space. In addition, STL maps provide existing code that can be used to easily implement enhancements to the Action Table, described later in this article.

The Action Table's member variable is a `CONDITION_ACTION_MAP`. When `GetAnimation()` is called, it first calls `find()` on the `CONDITION_ACTION_MAP` to find the `ACTION_ANIM_MAP` that corresponds to the character's weapon type.

Next, it calls `find()` on the ACTION_ANIM_MAP to find the animation resource that corresponds to the character's action, and returns the resource filename. If it is unable to find a matching action, it tries to fall back to a default animation for the specified action.

```
const char* CActionTable::GetAnimation( EnumAnimCondition
    eAnimCond, EnumAction eAction )
{
        CONDITION_ACTION_MAP::iterator ca_it;
        ACTION_ANIM_MAP::iterator aa_it;
        ca_it = m_condActionMap.find( eAnimCond );

        // Get list of actions for this animation condition.
        if( ca_it != m_condActionMap.end() )
        {
                ACTION_ANIM_MAP* pActionAnimMap = &( ca_it->second );
                ActionAnimInfoStruct* pAnimInfoStruct = NULL;

                aa_it = pActionAnimMap->find( eAction );
                szAnimFileName = aa_it->second;
                return szAnimFileName;
        }

        // No animation was found for the specified eAnimCond
        // and eAction, so see if a default animation exists.
```

```
            if( eAnimCond != kACond_Default )
            {
                    return GetAnimation( kACond_Default, eAction );
            }

            return NULL;
        }
```

Adapting the Action Table

The Action Table as described is particularly well suited to animation systems that allow partial-body animations. Partial-body animations allow a character to perform multiple actions at once. For example, a character can continue walking with its lower body while its upper body animates an attack or reaction.

There are various ways the Action Table could be adapted to suit an animation system that only allows full-body animations. In a full-body animation system, there might need to be another level of branching, to allow actions to be animated depending on the character's movement or posture. For example, there might be separate animations for attacking while walking, and attacking while standing still.

One approach could be to pack two enums into the key for the second map. Rather than keying off only the EnumAction, the first 16 bits could be the EnumAction, and the second 16 bits could be the EnumPosture. Another approach could be to key off a custom struct holding several enums for action, posture, movement, and anything else. STL maps allow users to supply their own custom comparison functions for unique data types like the struct described previously.

Enhancement: Randomization

Randomization is a common requirement of an animation system for a game. Characters typically have several idles, attacks, and reacts, so they look more lifelike and less robotic as they animate. The Action Table can easily handle randomization by changing the ACTION_ANIM_MAP from an STL map to a multimap.

For the most part, STL multimaps are identical to maps. The difference is that multimaps allow for duplicate keys. This means that the data can contain several different animations for the same action and condition. The multimap provides a count() function to find out how many values share a key, and a find() function that returns the first iterator corresponding to the specified key. Here is an example of counting how many animations match an EnumAction, and randomly choosing one of them:

```
// Get number of animations listed for this action.
long nCount = pActionAnimMap->count( eAction );

// Pick a random index.
long nIndex = Rand( nCount );
aa_it = pActionAnimMap->find( eAction );
for( long i=0; i<nIndex; ++i, ++aa_it );
```

```
szAnimFileName = aa_it->second;
return szAnimFileName;
```

Enhancement: Action Descriptor

When randomizing animations, it might be useful to be able to determine which animation was randomly selected. For example, depending on which attack animation was chosen, there might be a different sound effect or different amount of damage inflicted. An additional enum for the Action Descriptor can provide the needed information.

```
enum EnumActionDescriptor {
        kADesc_Invalid = -1,
        kADesc_None   =  0,
        kADesc_Swing,
        kADesc_Jab,
    };
```

The ACTION_ANIM_MAP can be modified to use a struct as the value instead of a character string. The struct contains the character string filename, and accompanying Action Descriptor.

```
struct ActionAnimInfoStruct
    {
        char szAnimFileName[MAX_PATH];
        EnumActionDescriptor eActionDesc;
    };
    typedef std::multimap<EnumAction,
    ActionAnimInfoStruct> ACTION_ANIM_MAP;
```

Finally, GetAnimation() can be modified to take a third parameter; a pointer to an Action Descriptor.

```
const char* GetAnimation(EnumAnimCondition eAnimCond,
        EnumAction eAction, EnumActionDescriptor* peActionDesc);
```

Now, when GetAnimation() is called, the caller can pass in an EnumActionDescriptor to be filled in after GetAnimation() randomly selects an animation. The caller can then determine if the Attack action was specifically a swing or a jab. Putting it all together, the new randomization code looks like this:

```
// Get number of animations listed for this action.
    long nCount = pActionAnimMap->count( eAction );

    // Pick a random index.
    long nIndex = Rand( nCount );
    aa_it = pActionAnimMap->find( eAction );
    for( long i=0; i<nIndex; ++i, ++aa_it );
    pAnimInfoStruct = &( aa_it->second );

    if( peActionDesc != NULL )
```

```
{
    *peActionDesc = pAnimInfoStruct->eActionDesc;
}
return pAnimInfoStruct->szAnimFileName;
```

Enhancement: Dynamic Animation Lists

Often, games reward players for continued gameplay by unlocking special capabilities as the game progresses. The Action Table can be easily modified to allow the animation list to grow over the course of the game. Rather than randomly selecting an animation out of the entire list of animations that correspond to an Action, there can be a variable controlling the maximum number to randomize between. GetAnimation() can have one more parameter for the maximum random number:

```
const char* GetAnimation( EnumAnimCondition eAnimCond,
                          EnumAction eAction,
                          EnumActionDescriptor* peActionDesc,
                          long nRandMax );
```

The nRandMax variable can then be factored into the randomized index selection. This variable could be an index, or a percentage of the animation list. In the code presented here, it is an index:

```
// Get number of animations listed for this action.
long nCount = pActionAnimMap->count( eAction );
long nMax = min ( nCount, nRandMax );

// Pick a random index.
long nIndex = Rand( nMax );
```

As the game progresses, the nRandMax variable passed into the function can increase. In an RPG, a larger nRandMax could be passed into GetAnimation() to unlock attacks that require more skill as the character's agility increases. Attack animations in the data would then need to sorted, listing the lowest skill level attacks first.

Optimization

An optimization can be made that eliminates the need for the second STL map. Since there probably are not enough Actions or Conditions to fill two bytes, the Action and Condition can be combined into a single 4-byte key for a multimap of animations.

```
#define CREATE_KEY(condition, action) (condition << 16) | action

    typedef std::multimap<unsigned long,
    ActionAnimInfoStruct> CONDITION_ACTION_MAP;
```

CREATE_KEY creates an unsigned long multimap key from the Condition and Action enum. The final version of GetAnimation() using a single multimap looks like this:

```
const char* CActionTable::GetAnimation(
EnumAnimCondition eAnimCond, EnumAction eAction,
EnumActionDescriptor* peActionDesc )
{
    unsigned long key = CREATE_KEY( eAnimCond, eAction );

    CONDITION_ACTION_MAP::iterator ca_it;
    ca_it = m_condActionMap.find( key );

    // Get list of actions for this animation condition.
    if( ca_it != m_condActionMap.end() )
    {
        ActionAnimInfoStruct* pAnimInfoStruct = NULL;

        // Get number of animations listed for this action.
        long nCount = m_condActionMap.count( key );

        // Pick randomly from a list of animations
        // for this action
        long nIndex = Rand( nCount );
        for( long i=0; i<nIndex; ++i, ++ca_it );

        pAnimInfoStruct = &( ca_it->second );

        if( peActionDesc != NULL )
        {
            *peActionDesc = pAnimInfoStruct->eActionDesc;
        }
        return pAnimInfoStruct->szAnimFileName;
    }

    // No animation was found for the specified eAnimCond and
    // eAction, so see if a default animation exists.
    if( eAnimCond != kACond_Default )
    {
        return GetAnimation( kACond_Default, eAction,
                             peActionDesc );
    }

    return NULL;
}
```

Expressing AI with Animation

Animation is the means of expressing what a character is thinking. In order to create convincing behavior in artificial beings, everything that a character animates should express its current frame of mind. Whether a character is walking, climbing, idling, or attacking, the animation for the action should reflect the character's emotions, state of health, and physical interactions with objects in the world. The Action Table is a mechanism that simplifies the task of customizing animations to match a character's current situation.

References

[Isensee99] Isensee, Pete, "Embracing the C++ STL: Why Angle Brackets Are Good for You," www.tantalon.com/pete/roadtrip99.zip, 1999.

[Rabin00] Rabin, Steve, "The Magic of Data-Driven Design," *Game Programming Gems*, Charles River Media, 2000.

[Rose98] Rose, Charles; Cohen, Michael; Bodenheimer, Bobby, "Verbs and Adverbs: Multidimensional Motion Interpolation," *IEEE Computer Graphics and Applications*, Volume 19, Number 5, 1998.

2.4

Realistic Character Behavior with Prioritized, Categorized Animation

Jeff Orkin—Monolith Productions

jorkin@blarg.net

Skeletal animation systems allow AI programmers to create realistic behavior for characters by playing multiple, layered animations simultaneously. With current skeletal animation technology, there is no reason to limit characters to only playing full-body, lower-body, or upper-body animations. Today's characters can move any part of their body independently, just like a live person or animal. A character should be able to fire her gun with one hand while running, as she furrows her brow, grits her teeth, and lets her hair blow in the wind! The challenge, however, is trying to manage these independent layers of animation.

Using a separate animation controller for each part of the body will quickly lead to overly complex code, and a confusion of interdependencies. A better solution is a layered, prioritized animation system in which the layers are categorized by the regions of the body that they affect. This article describes the implementation of such a system, in which animations are stored in a sorted list of a single animation controller.

Prioritization and Categorization

A system of prioritized, categorized animations centralizes code for starting and stopping animations. This centralized system eliminates the need for doing any checks before playing a new animation. The animation controller uses the category of the animation to determine the sorting order, and uses the priority to determine when to stop previous animations.

The first step is to mark each animation with its priority and category. Then, store the priority as an integer starting at zero for the lowest priority, and increment to a chosen upper limit. The category can be a bit-flag enum, describing the region of the body that the animation affects. Ideally, an animator should set the priority and category at the time the animation is exported from the authoring software. If this is not possible, the animation can be wrapped in a data file that specifies the priority and category, and references the actual animation data.

For priorities, choose standardized ranges that make sense for a particular game. For example, set the priority for all idle animations to 0, walks to 5, attacks to 10, reacts to 20, and deaths to 100. This ensures that characters will behave consistently.

Use bit-flags for the category enum so that specific parts of the body can be combined into more general regions of the body. For example, a lower-body animation includes animation for both legs and a tail. The enum might look like this:

```
enum EnumAnimCategory {
    kACat_Invalid    = (0 << 0),
    kACat_LeftLeg    = (1 << 0),
    kACat_RightLeg   = (1 << 1),
    kACat_Tail       = (1 << 2),
    kACat_LowerBody  = kACat_LeftLeg | kACat_RightLeg
                       | kACat_Tail,
    kACat_Torso      = (1 << 8),
    kACat_RightArm   = (1 << 9),
    kACat_LeftArm    = (1 << 10),
    kACat_Head       = (1 << 11),
    kACat_UpperBody  = kACat_Torso | kACat_RightArm
                       | kACat_LeftArm | kACat_Head,
    kACat_FullBody   = 0xffffffff,
};
```

The exported animation data should correspond to the category. If an animation is categorized as upper body, the exported animation should only contain bone animation data for bones from the waist up. Alternatively, if a bone weighting system is in place, all bones can be exported, but bones below the waist should have a weight of zero.

The Animation Controller Class

The animation controller class has one important member variable, and one core function for requesting to play an animation. The variable is an STL map of animation instances, sorted by category. An animation instance is a struct that stores a reference to an animation resource file, and any specific instance data such as the current frame.

```
struct AnimFileStruct {
    char            szFileName[MAX_NAME];
    unsigned long   nPriority;
    EnumAnimCategory eCategory;
    ...
};

struct AnimInstanceStruct {
    AnimFileStruct*  pAnimFileStruct;
    ...
};

typedef std::map<unsigned long, AnimInstanceStruct,
std::greater<unsigned long> > ANIM_INSTANCE_MAP;
```

The core function of the controller is PlayAnim(). This function takes an AnimFileStruct as a requested animation to play, and compares it against all of the animations currently playing. The requested animation's category and priority is used to determine if it should be allowed to play, and if any of the animations currently playing should be stopped.

```
bool PlayAnim( AnimFileStruct* pRequestedAnim );
```

After each call to PlayAnim(), the animation controller is left with a list of the animations currently playing. Every update, the character iterates through this list, and applies the animations to its bones. The animations are sorted from more general categories to more specific categories, so that animations will be applied to the skeleton in the correct order. For example, first a full-body walk will be applied to the entire body, and then a left-arm animation of the character firing her gun will override the bones of the left arm.

Assumptions about the Animation System

There are some assumptions about the animation system that must be true in order for the animation controller's list to produce the correct results. Each frame of animation must be stored as a list of bone rotations. Rotations for all animations are stored relative to the same default pose. When an animation is applied to a bone, it overrides any rotation applied by previous animations [Watt92].

Note that animations in the list are overriding prior animations, rather than doing any type of additive blending. In most cases, this is the desired result. Blending an arm swaying from a walk animation with the extended arm of a gun-firing animation would produce a strange mixture of the two arm movements. Blending during transitions between animations, however, is desirable, and is described later in this article.

How It Works

The PlayAnim() function is the heart of the animation controller. This is where the controller compares a requested animation to a list of currently playing animations. Through a series of tests, the controller determines if the requested animation can play, and if any animations in its list need to be stopped. Complete code for PlayAnim() is presented at the end of this section. The rest of the code for the animation controller class can be found on the CD that accompanies this book.

ON THE CD

PlayAnim() takes a pointer to the AnimFileStruct for a requested animation as an argument. The function iterates through its map of animation instances, comparing the category and priority of each instance to the values found in the requested animation's AnimFileStruct.

First, PlayAnim() checks if the same animation is already playing. If so, the request is declined.

Next, `PlayAnim()` checks if the category of the requested animation clashes with the category of an animation that is already playing. If any of the same bits are set in both the category of the requested animation and the category of an animation that is playing, these animations apply to at least some of the same bones. For example, an upper-body animation and a right-arm animation would clash.

If the categories clash, and the categories are the same, the animation with the highest priority wins. If the requested animation has the highest priority, the animation that is currently playing is erased from the list of animations. If the requested animation does not have the highest priority, it is rejected.

If the requested animation has a higher priority and its category encompasses that of an animation that is currently playing, the animation currently playing is erased from the list of animations. For example, a full-body animation encompasses a lower-body animation.

Finally, if the requested animation did not fail any of the previous tests, it is added to the list of currently playing animations. The STL map will take care of inserting it in the correct place in the list according to its category. The function then returns success or failure.

```cpp
bool CAnimController::PlayAnim( AnimFileStruct* pRequestAnim )
{
    bool bPlayAnim = true;

    ANIM_INSTANCE_MAP::iterator it;
    for( it = m_mapAnimInstances.begin();
    it != m_mapAnimInstances.end(); ++it )
    {
        EnumAnimCategory ePlayingCategory =
        (EnumAnimCategory)it->first;
        AnimFileStruct* pPlayingAnim =
        it->second.pAnimFileStruct;

        // Check if animation is already playing
        if( pRequestAnim == pPlayingAnim )
        {
            bPlayAnim = false;
            break;
        }

        // Check if categories clash.
        else if( ePlayingCategory & pRequestAnim->eCategory )
        {
            unsigned long nPlayingPriority =
            pPlayingAnim->nPriority;

            // If an animation of the same or lower
            // priority, and the exact same category is
            // playing, stop the currently playing
            // animation. The requested animation will
            // replace it.
```

```
                        if(ePlayingCategory == pRequestAnim-
                          >eCategory)
                        {
                             if( nPlayingPriority >
                             pRequestAnim->nPriority )
                             {
                                  bPlayAnim = false;
                                  break;
                             }
                             else {
                                  m_mapAnimInstances.erase( it );
                             }
                             break;
                        }

                        // If requested animation has a higher
                        // priority, and encompasses the currently
                        // playing animation, stop the currently
                        // playing animation.
                        // For example, UpperBody encompasses LeftArm.
                        if( ((unsigned long)ePlayingCategory <
                        (unsigned long)pRequestAnim->eCategory)
                        && (nPlayingPriority <
                        pRequestAnim->nPriority) )
                        {
                             m_mapAnimInstances.erase(it);
                             break;
                        }
                   }
              }

              // No conflicts were found, so play the
              // requested animation.
              if( bPlayAnim )
              {
                   m_mapAnimInstances.insert(
                   ANIM_INSTANCE_MAP::value_type(
                   (unsigned long)(pRequestAnim->eCategory),
                   AnimInstanceStruct(pRequestAnim) ) );
              }

              return bPlayAnim;
         }
```

Blended Transitions with Bone Caching

It is important to blend between animations as they transition from one to the next. Blending keeps the character's motions smooth and natural, instead of choppy and robotic. It might seem difficult to smoothly blend between animations when any number of animations can be playing on individual parts of the body. The key is to cache the bone rotations at the time a transition needs to start.

Bone caching is a simple technique that requires very little modification to existing data structures for a skeleton. Rather than storing a single quaternion per bone for the current rotation, the skeleton stores an array of quaternions. The array does not have to be very big—a cache of three or five bone rotations should suffice.

The skeleton can use the cache to gradually transition into any new animation. When a new animation starts, the current bone cache index is incremented. This leaves the skeleton with a snapshot of all of its previous bone rotations, without ever having to copy any data. The new animation can then refer to the cached snapshot during its first few frames, as it gradually blends in a decreasing amount of the cached rotations. The code to apply an animation with a transition might look something like this:

```
Quaternion q;
for( long i = 0; i < nBoneCount; ++i )
{
    // Use spherical linear interpolation to rotate the bone
    // some amount between frame1 and frame2, depending on
    // the elapsed time.
    q.Slerp( frame1_bones[i], frame2_bones[i], fTime );

    // Check if a snapshot was cached to transition
    // from. The fTransitionTime decreases as the
    // transition completes.
    if( (transitionCacheIndex != kInvalidBoneCacheIndex)
        && (transitionCacheIndex != curCacheIndex) )
    {
        // Do a spherical linear interpolation between
        // the cached rotation and the new rotation.
        q.Slerp( pBone[i].GetRot( transitionCacheIndex ),
        q, fTransitionTime );
    }

    pBone[i].SetRot( q, curCacheIndex );
}
```

For more information about quaternions and spherical linear interpolation, see [Shankel00].

Opening the Door to Realistic Behavior

A prioritized, categorized animation system opens the door to creating realistic character behavior. Characters can now fluidly move from one activity to another and perform multiple actions at once. This removes many obstacles that would otherwise limit the AI systems. Attack animations can be layered over animation for standing, walking, running, or jumping. Facial expressions can be layered over any other animation [Lander99]. Animations for reacting to damage can be layered over the appropriate parts of the body. Each layer brings the character behavior one step closer to the infinitely layered behavior of an actual, living being.

References

[Lander99] Lander, Jeff, "Flex Your Facial Animation Muscles," *Game Developer* magazine, Volume 6, Number 7, 1999.

[Shankel00] Shankel, Jason, "Interpolating Quaternions," *Game Programming Gems*, Charles River Media, 2000.

[Watt92] Watt, Alan; Watt, Mark, *Advanced Animation and Rendering Techniques*, ACM Press, 1992.

Designing a GUI Tool to Aid in the Development of Finite-State Machines

Phil Carlisle—Team17 Software Ltd.

pc@team17.com

Typically, when a designer wants to explain the working of an object's AI in a game, the first thing he does is reach for a pen and paper and draw a flowchart or state diagram. For designers with no programming knowledge, it can be difficult to explain to programmers exactly the intent of the AI design.

This article proposes a method of streamlining the AI design and development process through the implementation of a GUI-based tool. The tool introduces the use of a modeling concept (much like UML) that is usable by designers, but can also be translated into working C++ code for final implementation by programmers.

This article covers the concepts and implementation of a graphical tool for diagramming finite-state machines (FSMs) specifically for games. It works through the initial design of the GUI components and how they match the data structures in the game. It then describes the workflow that the tool will enable. Finally, it describes the code generation process (an important part of the tool that translates the diagrams into useful skeleton code) and how the final output could be incorporated into the AI and game architectures.

The Basic Components

When representing the AI of an object based on finite-state machines, there are a few classes of objects that need to be graphically modeled. Here we examine the main class types and how they connected and interact with the model.

Machine

The "machine" class is the container for all parts of a particular state machine. This is essentially the wrapper that interfaces between the program and the state machine itself (as we will see later, it helps to have a container for the state machine). The machine class keeps the current state variable, the default state information, holds lists of inputs, outputs, conditions, and states, and provides interface functions for use in conditions that access data external to the state machine.

State

The next class required is the state. In our tool, we represent a state as a rectangular box with slightly rounded corners. In order to support hierarchical FSMs, we can incorporate substate boxes, which are basically smaller state boxes entirely enclosed by another state box. Any state box that contains substate boxes is called a *super state* box.

Transition

The next class of objects we represent is the transition from one state to another. We represent this as a line with a center circle (representing the condition) that connects two or more state boxes. As part of the process of making the tool easier to use, we must incorporate logic that will automatically separate and prevent lines from crossing each other where possible.

Transitions are the class of objects that drive the system. They control the flow of execution by setting the "current active state" of the state machine through use of a conditional. Transitions can be one-to-many; in other words, you can have one state connected to the input side of a transition, and many states connected to the output side of a transition based on the type of condition used in the transition.

Condition

Conditions are a model of the transition from one state to another. Typically, the condition has input, normally a variable or function, that, when true, signals the change from one "current active state" to another. It also has one or more outputs, corresponding to the new state to be transitioned to when the condition is met. Conditions are required in order for a transition to be valid. The default transition line with no condition circle would not generate a valid transition at code generation time.

Typical conditions are:

- Boolean
- Equality
- Range
- Greater Than
- Less Than
- Contains

Input and Event

Inputs are exactly that, inputs of data into the state machine. Typically, inputs can be thought of as variables that can be modified either internally to the state machine or externally by the application. Inputs allow the state machine to react to changes in its environment. Typical inputs are simple types such as integers, floating-point values,

Boolean values, and so forth. However, inputs can also be function calls. Events are inputs that are fed into the machine from another source, the difference between an input and an event being that inputs are available to the machine all the time, while an event is simply a notification that a value has changed. Inputs are displayed in our model by a square box. Inputs are indicated in a transition by having a connection between the transition and the input box.

Action

An action is simply a block of code that is executed. An action can occur because of a transition or as part of a current state. For example, we might want to alert another object that the transition occurred; for example, a guard alerting other AI guards when he sees a player. Actions are also held in states to define the code that is executed while the state is current. Curly braces enclosing a capital "A," for example, {A}, represent actions (Figure 2.5.1).

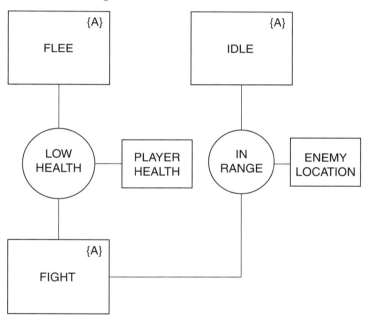

FIGURE 2.5.1 *A typical simple state machine, showing a range-based condition choosing between the initial state and a fight-or-flight reaction state. Also shown are actions inside states and how the enemy location event is modeled.*

Modeling a Simple Object

Let's look at modeling a simple state machine as an example of how to use the specific components. In this example, we have a state machine for a fictional creature, as shown in Figure 2.5.2.

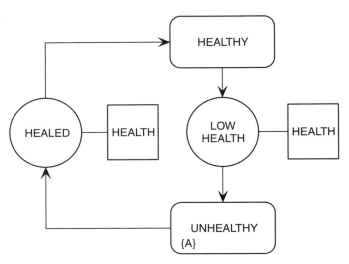

FIGURE 2.5.2   *A simple creature's behavior model.*

This state machine is concerned with the creature's state of health. The default state is to be healthy. During execution of the program, the "HEALTH" variable would drop below a given value; for example, an update causes the creature to incur damage, causing the "LOW HEALTH" condition to become valid. This, in turn, causes the transition from the default healthy state to the unhealthy state. In this creature's model, the way it regains health is by eating food. The action of eating food is performed while the model is in the unhealthy state, and is represented in the diagram by the {A} in the unhealthy state box. In a more complex model, this might be extended to sleeping or drinking a health potion. Note the condition attached to the healthy-to-unhealthy transition.

Each state machine (referred to in this article as a *model*) begins in the GUI as a blank page with a single "default" state. This is simply an empty model that does nothing. In order to extend the model into something useful, the designer would simply place components from a toolbox of the component types into the blank page, and connect them to the other components with transition lines. In Figure 2.5.2, the default state for the creature is to be healthy. In the healthy state, the creature does nothing. We then add another state to the model in Figure 2.5.2, which we call "unhealthy," and a transition. The condition attached to the transition checks for a threshold value in the "health" input in order for the transition to occur, at which point we start having a model for the creature that actually does something; in this case, transition from healthy to unhealthy.

Normally, in a model, each state would have an action or list of actions that are performed when the state machine is in that state. As an example, in Figure 2.5.2, the healthy state might have an action that causes the creature to emit a happy sound effect. The unhealthy state might have an action that causes the creature to emit a pleading sound effect, indicating to the player that it requires food. So, our model now actually has an effect in the game; when a creature becomes unhealthy, it changes its sound to indicate its plight.

Converting the Model to Code

One of the main goals for using a modeling tool such as this is to increase the productivity of the AI designer. In order to achieve this goal, a method of rendering the modeled state machine into code is required.

In order for the state machine code to be easily integrated into another object, a container class is used, which is the machine class described previously. An object simply adds a member variable of the derived machine class instance and interfaces with that member variable.

At code generation time, the design for the given machine is converted to .h and .cpp files via a relatively simple process. Initially, a class derived from the base "Machine" class is declared and its header file created. The base machine class contains lists of states, transitions, actions, and so forth.

Then, the constructor of the machine-derived class is written to the .cpp file. The constructor instantiates all of the contained model elements. Each item is added using an add member of the parent object. For instance, super states and transitions are added to the machine container because they have no parent. Substates are added to their parent state, and actions are added to whatever object to which they are attached. Any component that requires references or pointers to other components to operate, in order to avoid circular references, is instantiated last and added to the machine container class after the other components so that any references to other object instances are valid. A typical example would be a "target state" pointer required by the transition class so that it can set the "currently active" state in the machine class.

Actions are special case objects, in that they actually represent code, so they do not require conversion. Actions are typically either script or C++ code, depending on the nature of the project. Typically, the script entered in an action object would simply be written out to a script file, which could then be referenced when integrating the model into the application. Actions are typically just stored as a reference in their containing component, usually a state or a transition, via a script name or other identifier.

Here is an example constructor for the model presented in Figure 2.5.1:

```
CreatureMachine::CreatureMachine()
{
    // add all variables to the variable list
    AddVariable("Health",VAR_INTEGER,&m_Health);
    AddVariable("EnemyLocation",VAR_POSITION,&m_Enemy;

    // now add conditions (may reference variables)
    AddCondition("InRange",LESSTHAN,"EnemyLocation",100);
```

```
AddCondition("LowHealth",LESSTHAN,"Health", 50);

// now add all the actions (may be referenced by the // states)
AddAction("IdleAction");
AddAction("FightAction");
AddAction("FleeAction");

// now add all the states
AddState("Idle","IdleAction");
AddState("Fight","FightAction");
AddState("Flee","FleeAction");
// now add all the transitions (may reference states
// and variables)
// transitions syntax : <condition-name> <start state>
// <end state>
AddTransition("In Range","Idle","Fight");
AddTransition("Low Health","Fight","Flee");
};
```

This code uses a number of Add setup functions to add various components into the state machine. Typically, the components are referenced by name for lookup purposes. However, for efficiency's sake, references to other components are added as references or pointers via an Add member function of the component base class.

Integrating the Generated Code

The execution of the given state machine is quite straightforward. An update member of the machine-derived instance is called. This in turn calls an update member on each of the transitions it contains.

The update member of the transition class checks any conditions it contains to see if the condition is true; if it is, a change in state occurs by calling a member function of the machine class to set the new "currently active" state. The currently active state is then updated, which might cause actions (either code or script) to be executed.

An important point to note is that there has to be some interface between the machine container and its surrounding code, since the machine might be part of a "player" class and hence would need access to "player" related variables, such as health, speed, and so forth. The player reading its attributes from variables stored in the state machine would be optimal for this purpose. However, sometimes it is useful to incorporate a state machine into an existing class, which might already contain its own data structures. One way of accomplishing this is to have a two-way mapping between an external variable and a named input in the state machine container.

For instance, assume we are integrating a state machine into an existing class called player and we need to access a variable in this class called m_Health, which is an integer value. The following pseudo-code would allow the player class to add the health variable to the state machine instance.

```
MyStateMachine Machine;
Machine.AddVariable("Health",VAR_INTEGER,&m_Health);
```

This would add the address of the `m_Health` member variable into a keyed list of input variables. Then, to allow the state machine to access the value, it simply reads the value of the integer returned by the corresponding key lookup. When an input component is created with the name of a key in the keyed list, any later call to `AddVariable` with the same key name would replace the pointer to the data type stored in the input component. Effectively, an input component can alter the value of a variable, which is stored in another class via a keyed variable name lookup.

Conclusion

Tools are an important part of game creation, and having a good usable tool dedicated to a specific purpose can greatly increase a game's chance of success. What is described here is a tool that if implemented should increase the productivity of an AI designer or programmer in much the same manner that a dedicated level-building and design tool can help a level designer. The ability to take a model from the design stage into the production stage is more efficient than separate design and production. With the greater part of the process being automated, it should be less prone to errors or misinterpretation.

References

There are seemingly very few references to game applications of GUI systems for state machine design; however, there are many regarding state machine design using GUI interfaces for other industries such as process control. The basic elements of a state machine editor are likely to be very similar in any GUI interface; hence, these references are still of value.

Web References

Grace, a Java tool used to create graph editors (such as state machine editors).
www .doclsf.de/grace/about.html
Active HDL, an example of process control using GUI state machine editing.
www.aldec.com/support/application_notes/knowledgebase/an0003_design_entry
.htm
Stateflow: A GUI-based tool for FSM creation that interacts with Matlab.
www.uvigo.es/servicios/atic/seinv/manuais/matlab/toolbox/stateflow/ug/sf_intro
.html

2.6

The Beauty of Response Curves

Bob Alexander

balexand@earthlink.net

Every once in a while we run across techniques that turn out to be another Swiss Army Knife of programming. A classic example is the dot product. The dot product is a beautiful mathematical construct. Its implementation is simple, but it has a surprising number of uses.

This article discusses another of these incredibly useful tools: the *Response Curve*. The Response Curve consists of an array of bucket edge values. These edge values are used to map an incoming value to an output, by finding the edge-bound bucket that contains the incoming value, and interpolating across the bucket edges to produce an output result.

The Response Curve is simple in its implementation, but its uses are infinite. It allows the programmer to map an incoming value to an output heuristically rather than mathematically. This is because the samples in the curve can be any imaginable one-to-one mapping. We will see some examples of this later in the article.

Background

The Response Curve consists of a series of edge values. These edge values bound buckets and are stored as a simple array, as shown in Figure 2.6.1. The number of buckets is always one less than the number of samples.

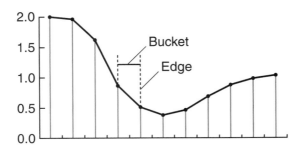

FIGURE 2.6.1 *Basic Response Curve.*

The shape of the curve is defined by the samples. This shape can be as smooth or as rough as desired by simply varying the number of samples across the input range. Since only one copy of a given curve needs to exist in memory, the difference between sample count is purely a matter of what produces the best curve for the context in which it is used. Memory should not be a concern.

Implementation

The implementation of the Response Curve consists of an array of bucket edges values, a range minimum, a bucket size, and a bucket count. The minimum range value defines the input value that corresponds to the edge value of the first bucket. The bucket size (d_b) is the magnitude of the input value spread across the bucket, and the bucket count is simply one less than the sample count (Equation 2.6.1).

$$d_b = \frac{i_{max} - i_{min}}{n_{samples} - 1} \tag{2.6.1}$$

The bucket index (i_b) is found by using Equation 2.6.2. If the bucket index is less than zero, we clamp by returning the first sample. If the index is greater than or equal to the bucket count, we return the last sample.

$$i_b = Floor\left(\frac{v - i_{min}}{n_{buckets}}\right) \tag{2.6.2}$$

Once we have the bucket index, we can calculate the relative distance (t) across the bucket using Equation 2.6.3.

$$t = \frac{\left[(v - i_{min}) - i_b d_b\right]}{d_b} \tag{2.6.3}$$

Finally, to calculate our return value, we use the relative bucket distance to interpolate across the bucket using Equation 2.6.4.

$$v' = \left[(1 - t) \cdot Samples_{i_b}\right] + \left(y \cdot Samples_{i_b + 1}\right) \tag{2.6.4}$$

One important thing to note is that the implementation described here clamps the input values prior to bucket calculation. This means that the output values will always be in the range defined by the bucket edge values, preventing the output from exceeding the range of expected values.

Examples of Use

In implementing fuzzy systems, we need to have functions that determine the degree of membership an object has in a given set.

Heuristic Components

For example, we might want to determine to what extent an infantry soldier belongs to the set of things that want to attack another enemy unit. This membership amount can then be used to either trip a threshold decision point to attack the unit, or just increase the tendency to head toward or aim in that direction. These are often referred to as heuristic functions.

As is often the case in a heuristic function, weighing other subcomponents together often derives the degree of membership in the overall heuristic set. Simple weight values could be applied to each subcomponent. However, when exception conditions arise, they need to be written into the function to handle them. These types of exception conditions can lead to less fluidity (and adaptability) in the degree calculation. By using the Response Curve, we can get around the problem.

For example, two of the things we might want to consider in the preceding attack heuristic are the health of the unit and the distance from the enemy to some defendable position. For the most part, we would want the unit to avoid attacking when its health is low; that is, until the enemy gets too close. To simplify things, we'll assume the output heuristic range is [0,1]. The two curves could then be represented as shown in Figure 2.6.2.

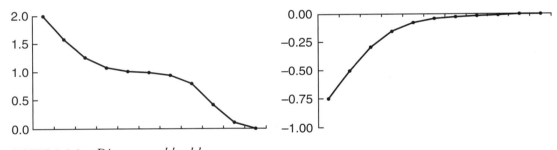

FIGURE 2.6.2   *Distance and health curves.*

Although, with some effort, a mathematical expression could be found to estimate the curves shown in Figure 2.6.2, that expression would have to be recalculated for any change to the curve. Moreover, we might find that there is no inexpensive way to adequately estimate the function. Instead, if we use Response Curves, not only can we handle the exception, but tweaking is simple and it's very cheap to calculate.

Application of these curves is just as simple. First, take the enemy distance from the target and divide it by some maximum engagement distance. Plug that value into the first curve to get a value in the range [0,2]. Then, take the unit's health and divide it by its maximum health. Plug that value into the second curve to get another value in the range [−1,0]. Adding the two values together gives a number in the range [−0.75,2], where at zero and below, we definitely do not want to attack, and at one or above, we definitely do want to attack.

We can see that Response Curves are truly indispensable for implementing nice, fluid heuristics. Exceptions are handled simply. Instead of fighting with the math for representing the thought process, we can approach the implementation of the heuristic, well, heuristically.

Targeting Errors

Another interesting application of the Response Curve is the determination of a targeting miss by an AI unit. One problem with using a straight random offset is that the shot spread is unnatural. This is especially true if the spread is meant to simulate the wavering of the gunner's hands—people just don't waver that fast.

By using a Response Curve and some oscillating function such as a Sine wave, we can implement a smoothly random swirl where we have direct control over the probability of hits. In addition, we can control where we miss and where we hit.

Consider the graphs in Figure 2.6.3. These represent two possible targeting curves.

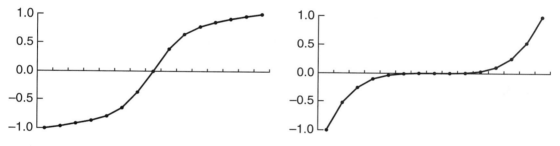

FIGURE 2.6.3 *Bad aim versus good aim Response Curves.*

In the first curve, the gunner is shooting away from the center of the target most of the time, while in the second graph, the gunner will hit the target most of the time. We can shape these curves in whatever way we want to get the desired spread. In fact, one possible shape can be used to implement targeting error against the player that adds more excitement in a first- or third-person game. Consider the curves in Figure 2.6.4.

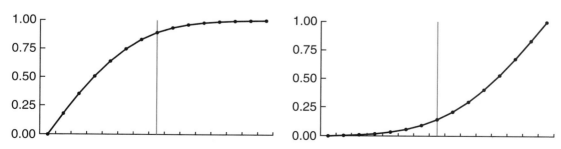

FIGURE 2.6.4 *Bad aim versus good aim player leading Response Curves.*

If we model the right side of the curve toward the front of the player, the missed shots will always be in front of the player rather than behind. This way, the player sees all of the missed shots and the action feels more exciting.

Improvements

One variation on the curve described here is to store edge normals (first-order derivatives) in addition to the edge values. This would allow for smoother curves with less data. However, whether this is an actual improvement depends on if you are trying to save memory or CPU, since interpolation would cost more CPU. On the other hand, satisfactory results can be achieved by simply increasing the granularity of the samples.

A very useful tool in generating and maintaining samples is a spreadsheet program such as Microsoft Excel. Actually, any program with an easy way of graphing the data is useful. The real beauty of using a spreadsheet program is the ability to use formulas. These can make initial curve generation very easy. Some programs, such as Excel, even allow editing of the samples by manipulating points in the graph by dragging them around with the mouse. This makes working with Response Curves a very natural task.

Conclusion

Once this is implemented as part of the AI programmer's toolset, it will find its way into almost every aspect of the AI. Many problems having to do with fuzzy set construction are simplified. Exception cases simply become extensions of a continuous function implemented in a Response Curve. The possibilities are endless.

References

[Cox98] Cox, Earl, "Fuzziness and Uncertainty," *The Fuzzy Systems Handbook*, Academic Press, 1998.

[Mendel00] Mendel, Jerry, "Membership Functions and Uncertainty," *Uncertain Rule-Based Fuzzy Logic Systems*, Prentice-Hall, 2000.

2.7

Simple and Efficient Line-of-Sight for 3D Landscapes

Tom Vykruta—Surreal Software

pharcyde000@hotmail.com

ON THE CD

Conventional algorithms dealing with grid-based 3D landscapes can quickly grow into unmanageable conglomerations that are difficult to debug. Fortunately, a clean, all-purpose remedy for this very situation exists. A wrapper class (source code included on the CD) allows an algorithm to make key assumptions about the ray and grid configuration. Eight logic paths simplify into one. Furthermore, the wrapper class works on such an abstract level that logic in the algorithm does not need to change.

Let's take the most basic example, rasterizing a 2D line. Eight distinct scenarios exist that at some abstract level must be handled separately. These eight cases can be visualized as subsets of lines that fall into the eight sectors of a circle. An efficient algorithm must be aware of three distinct traits:

- Is the X- or Y-axis major?
- Is dx positive or negative?
- Is dy positive or negative?

The easiest of the eight sectors to work in, or the *ideal slope*, lies between 0 and 45 degrees. If you limit yourself to this scenario, you can make two key assumptions when writing your algorithm:

- X will always increase by positive one.
- Y will always increase by some precomputed positive number.

A special transformation matrix takes any arbitrary ray and "transforms" it into a virtual grid. In the virtual grid, the ray has an ideal slope where the aforementioned rules are always true. All calculations are performed in this virtual grid space, and the output is run through a transform function that yields the *real space* (untransformed) coordinates. It is a breeze to write and debug algorithms when you are limited to the one case, and another benefit is that the CPU overhead of using the matrix is minimal. Handling all eight cases implicitly costs valuable time in writing and debugging, and the algorithm will be far less optimal.

Ideal Sector Transform Matrix

The underlying concept behind the matrix is very basic. The transformation is essentially a rotation of a point around the origin such that it ends in the ideal sector (0–45 degree range, indicated by the shaded area in Figure 2.7.1).

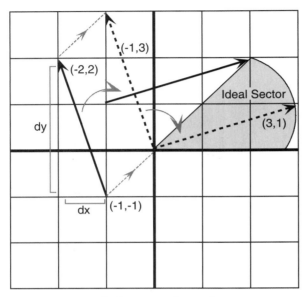

FIGURE 2.7.1   *Ideal sector and transformation.*

Each of the eight sectors possesses a unique combination of three binary traits. The relationship is described as $2^{(dimensions + 1)}$ = *number of sectors*. In 2D, this equates to $2^3 = 8$, and this article will not go beyond 2D. The traits are described by the following conditionals: *dx > 0, dy > 0, dx > dy*. Only in the ideal sector, all three are true. Logic dictates that if an operation is performed on a ray belonging to foreign sector, such that the operation will mutate the ray's three foreign sector traits to match those of the ideal sector, the ray will relocate to the ideal sector. Performing the same three operations in reverse returns the ray to its exact original state within the original foreign sector. A 3x1 Boolean matrix reflects these traits. To initialize the matrix, these three traits are stored. If the third trait is true, the first two matrix elements are swapped. The internal matrix structure looks like this:

Matrix Initialization: [dx < 0] [dy < 0] [ABS(dx) < ABS(dy)]

Given a ray from (–1, –1) to (–2, 2), initialization of the matrix requires a relative vector. The relative vector for those two points is (–1, 3). Referring to the three traits and the relative vector, the initialized matrix looks like this:

[false] [true] [true]

Given the preceding matrix and subsequent transformation function, the *real* coordinates (–1, –1) and (–2, 2), transform to *virtual* coordinates of (–1, 1) and (2, 2). The relative vector of the virtual coordinates has an ideal slope of (3, 1). The transformation function is surprisingly simple:

```
void TransformToVirtualGridSpace(x, y)
{
if (matrix[2]) // dx < dy
    swap(x, y);
    if (matrix[0]) // dx < 0
        x = -x;
    if (matrix[1]) // dy < 0
        y = -y;
}
```

Transforming back to real space involves the same three operations, but in reverse order. This transformation isn't limited to absolute coordinates. It works equally with a relative vector, because a relative vector is essentially an absolute point relative to (0, 0). Transforming (0, 0) is unnecessary because it belongs to all sectors and therefore is unaffected by the transform.

Offset Transformation

One piece of the puzzle remains. Let us assume that the landscape stores data such as visibility and friction for each *element*, or set of two polygon triangles, surrounded by four adjacent vertices (indicated by the shaded squares in Figure 2.7.2).

To access this data structure, we must index into an array using the coordinates of the bottom-left corner of the element. However, "bottom left" in virtual space is not equivalent to "bottom left" in real space.

Let's examine a realistic scenario. An algorithm is stepping along the grid, and at some point detects a collision (indicated by a hollow dot in Figures 2.7.1 and 2.7.2). To resolve the collision, element-specific information is required. The *offset* from the bottom-left corner of the element to the vertex that the algorithm is touching appears to be (1, 0) (indicated by a dotted arrow). In real space, this is not correct. Because the element index will reference an array in real space, we indeed need the real space

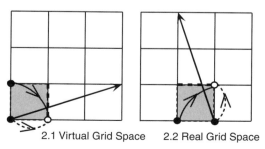

2.1 Virtual Grid Space   2.2 Real Grid Space

FIGURE 2.7.2 *Offset transformation.*

solution. The real solution is (1, 1) indicated by the solid arrow. A new transformation algorithm is required for this.

Passing the apparent virtual offset of (1, 0) into the new transformation function should return the actual real offset of (1, 1). Look closely at the list of eight matrix configurations with offset inputs and offset outputs in Table 2.7.1. The highlighted row indicates the configuration as seen in Figure 2.7.2. Adding the output offset of (1, 1) from our virtual point of (1, 0) results in the real "bottom left" point in virtual space.

Table 2.7.1 Converting Offsets Based on Matrix Configuration

Input	Matrix				Output	
X	Y	[dx < 0]	[dy < 0]	[dx < dy]	X	Y
1	0	0	0	0	1	0
1	0	0	1	0	1	1
1	0	1	0	1	0	0
1	0	1	1	1	1	0
1	0	1	1	0	0	1
1	0	1	0	0	0	0
1	0	0	1	1	1	1
1	0	0	0	1	0	1

The standard transform function will not work because the offset vector is not an absolute point relative to the ray's orientation, but rather an offset relative to the center of a transformed element. Instead, the offset can be thought of as a two-dimensional binary value. Three operations generate the correct transform: an *XOR*, or binary flip in each axis, and potentially a swap. Notice the resemblance to the first transformation function. The new transform function looks like this:

```
void TransformOffsetToRealSpace(x, y)
{
    x ^= matrix[0];
    y ^= matrix[1];
    if (matrix[2] == TRUE)
        swap(x,y);
}
```

Now that we've established how to efficiently navigate back and forth between real and virtual space, let's apply this technique to a real-world scenario.

Ray-Landscape Collision

Many outdoor 3D engines exploit some derivation of a grid-based landscape. For academic purposes, a single rectangular grid is used in the following example. However, this technique cleanly extends to support a complex hierarchy of intersecting height

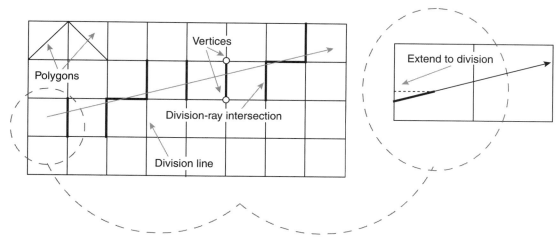

FIGURE 2.7.3 *Ray-grid collision.*

fields, with scalable level of detail. Figure 2.7.3 illustrates a top-down view of an ideal
ray intersecting with a grid:

A brute-force *LOS*, or line-of-sight algorithm, blindly performs a series of expensive ray-polygon intersections. The key behind a lightning-fast collision system is to
minimize the number of ray-polygon intersection tests, and only check the height of
the ray as it passes over each *division line* (connection between two adjacent vertices).
The algorithm is simple to write, thanks to the transformation matrix. The computational cost is also minimal, because the actual collision check consists of a float compare, comparing the height of the ray against the height of the two land vertices that
make up the division line.

The first step in performing this collision check is transforming the ray into virtual grid space. Next, if the ray doesn't already lie on a division line, it must be
extended backward to the nearest division line. It is important to extend backward,
and not forward, as a collision could occur in the very first element. Because of the
ideal sector assumptions, this extend will always be along the negative X-axis. The
endpoint must also be extended, forward this time. Figure 2.7.3 illustrates the extend.

Now that the ray is aligned to the grid, the first height compare is performed to
find whether the ray initially lies above or below the first set of vertices. It is assumed
that no collision has occurred yet. The algorithm steps along the ray at z-element
sized X intervals, using a pseudo-Bresenheim line algorithm, checking the height of
the line against the height of the two vertices that make up each intersecting division.
The intersecting divisions are indicated by dark lines in Figure 2.7.3. If the ray's relative height changes sign, a potential collision has occurred and a full-blown polygon-
ray intersection with the two triangles of that element is performed. In Figure 2.7.4,
the ray's relative height changes from "above" to "below" at vertex 6; therefore, division 5-6 will be checked as a potential collision.

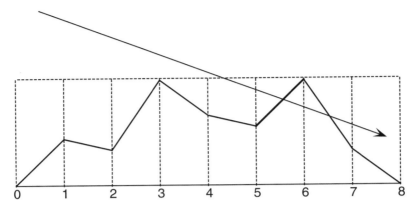

FIGURE 2.7.4   *XY profile of ray-grid collision in Figure 2.7.3.*

Optimizations

The preceding application is a simple, practical use of the transformation matrix. In a real-world scenario, a collision system can be further simplified by implementing higher-level, more trivial rejections. For example, the landscape could be broken up into several smaller chunks, each with its own precomputed world-aligned bounding box (ABB). The algorithm will collide with these ABBs, reject the nonintersecting ABB chunks, and sort the intersecting ones by distance along ray to intersection point with ABB, front to back. Large segments of landscape will potentially be rejected without even colliding with the polygonal geometry if the ray doesn't intersect that ABB chunk.

In flight games, the chunk rejection yields a tremendous increase in speed, because an airplane generally performs a very vertical LOS, where a majority of the ray lies far above landscape geometry. The more expensive LOS collision with the actual geometry is minimal because of the front-back sort. The collision will occur with one of the first few ABBs, and due to the front-back sort, the rest can safely be ignored. To further optimize, another approach is breaking up the collision ray into several chunks. This type of optimization is too specific to use in general, and should be fine-tuned to its environment.

Conclusion

Algorithms dealing with the landscape grid geometry will benefit tremendously from the virtual grid transform. Simplifying pathfinding code, for example, leads to some obvious benefits as well as some not so obvious ones. The more obvious benefits include less code, which equates to more optimal code generated both by human and compiler. Fewer bugs are likely to fall through the cracks, and a cleaner debugging environment is available for those bugs that do fall through. A programmer not familiar with your code will understand it more clearly, and maintain it more cleanly. Finally, as an unexpected benefit, the optimized, streamlined code becomes more suitable for layering on complex behaviors with minimal increase in code size. What once was too risky and time consuming is now a trivial and practical solution.

Fast LOS might not be a requirement for your project, but while a slow LOS limits other features that rely on it, a fast one opens up new possibilities for those features. Combining the discussed techniques will lead to lightning-fast LOS. These techniques are by no means limited to landscape. Combining object ABBs with the landscape ABB soup is a fast, clean approach to an all-purpose LOS system.

There are no DLLs to link or SDKs to surrender to. Any project, during any stage of development, can benefit. The simplistic, elegant, unintrusive nature of the ideas and algorithms discussed here is the real gem.

2.8

An Open-Source Fuzzy Logic Library

Michael Zarozinski—Louder Than A Bomb! Software

MichaelZ@LouderThanABomb.com

Fuzzy logic can make game AI "subtle… complex… lightning fast at runtime" [O'Brien96] and enable AI "to perform some remarkably human factoring" [Morris99]. In one form or another, fuzzy logic makes its way into most games. However, it often does not go beyond complex *if-then-else* statements because of the complexities involved in creating a fuzzy logic system from scratch.

The Free Fuzzy Logic Library (FFLL) is an open-source fuzzy logic class library and API that is optimized for speed-critical applications, such as video games. This article is a brief overview of FFLL and some of its features that are relevant to game developers.

As an open-source project, FFLL might evolve rapidly. This fact combined with the space considerations for this book requires that this article focus on FFLL's features rather than go into fuzzy logic theory or the details of the code and API.

ON THE CD

The source code for FFLL can be found on the CD and on the FFLL homepage [FFLL01]. At the time of this printing, FFLL does not have support for the more esoteric aspect of fuzzy set theory such as alpha-cuts and lesser-known composition and inference methods. Check the FFLL homepage to see when new features are added.

FFLL Open-Source License

ON THE CD

FFLL is published under the BSD open-source license. This allows for the free use and redistribution of binaries and/or source code, including the use of the source code in proprietary products. While this license does not *require* that you contribute any modifications, enhancements, bug fixes, and so forth back to the project, you are strongly encouraged to do so, helping to make FFLL a better library. The full text of this license can be found on the CD and at http://ffll.sourceforge.net/license.txt.

IEC Fuzzy Control Programming Standard

While not widely known, the International Electrotechnical Commission (IEC) has published a standard for Fuzzy Control Programming (IEC 61131-7). Unfortunately, this standard is not freely available and must be purchased (see www.iec.ch or www.ansi.org). However, the Draft 1.0 version from 1997 is available, and there doesn't appear to be any significant differences between the draft and the final versions [IEC97].

The IEC 61131-7 standard specifies a Fuzzy Control Language (FCL) that can be used to describe fuzzy logic models. FFLL is able to load files that adhere to this standard.

Terminology

The lexicon in fuzzy logic is often confusing, despite the existence of the IEC standard. The following is a list of terms used in this article along with some of their aliases used in other fuzzy logic literature.

- **Variable**: A fuzzy variable is a concept such as "temperature," "distance," or "health." Also referred to as Fuzzy Linguistic Variable (FLV).
- **Set**: In traditional logic, sets are "crisp"; either you belong 100 percent to a set or you do not. A set of tall people might consist of all people over six feet tall; anyone less than six feet is "short" (or more appropriately, "not tall"). Fuzzy logic allows sets to be "fuzzy," so anyone over six feet tall might have 100-percent membership in the "tall" set, but might also have 20-percent membership in the "medium height" set. Also referred to as term or fuzzy subset.
- **Rules**: These are the *if-then* components of the fuzzy system. Also referred to collectively as a Fuzzy Associative Matrix (FAM).
- **MIN**: The Minimum operation is the same as the logical "AND" operation; it takes the lesser of two or more values.
- **MAX**: The Maximum operation is the same as the logical "OR" operation; it takes the greater of two or more values.
- **PROD**: The Product operation multiplies two or more values together.
- **Degree of Membership (DOM)**: A value between zero (no membership) and one (full membership) that represents a crisp value's membership in a fuzzy set. Also referred to as degree of support, activation, or degree of truth.
- **Inference**: The process of evaluating which rules are active, combining the DOMs of the input sets that make up that rule, and producing a single DOM for the output set activated by that rule. Typical inference methods are MIN, MAX, and PROD. Also referred to as aggregation.
- **Composition**: The process of combining multiple DOMs (from the inference step) for an output set into one DOM. Typical composition methods are MIN, MAX, and PROD. Also referred to as accumulation.
- **Crisp Value**: A precise numerical value such as 2, −3, or 7.34.
- **Membership Function**: A function that expresses to which degree an element of a set belongs to a given fuzzy set.
- **Fuzzification**: The conversion of a numerical (crisp) value into DOM values for the sets in a variable.
- **Defuzzification**: The process of converting a set (or sets) into a crisp value.

FFLL Features

While there is no substitute for looking through the code, this section highlights some of the features of FFLL.

Class Hierarchy

The following chart shows the class hierarchy of FFLL:

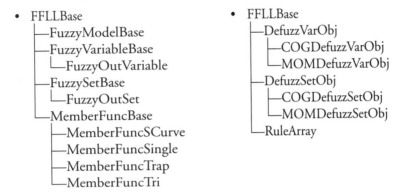

- FFLLBase
  - FuzzyModelBase
  - FuzzyVariableBase
    - FuzzyOutVariable
  - FuzzySetBase
    - FuzzyOutSet
  - MemberFuncBase
    - MemberFuncSCurve
    - MemberFuncSingle
    - MemberFuncTrap
    - MemberFuncTri

- FFLLBase
  - DefuzzVarObj
    - COGDefuzzVarObj
    - MOMDefuzzVarObj
  - DefuzzSetObj
    - COGDefuzzSetObj
    - MOMDefuzzSetObj
  - RuleArray

Membership Functions

Fuzzy variables contain sets, and each set has a membership function associated with it. The membership function defines the set's shape and is used to "fuzzify" the *x* values of the variable by associating a DOM with an *x* value. While the most common membership function used in fuzzy systems is a triangle [Kilr/Yuan95], FFLL provides support for *Triangles*, *Trapezoids*, *S-Curves*, and *Singletons* as shown in Figure 2.8.1.

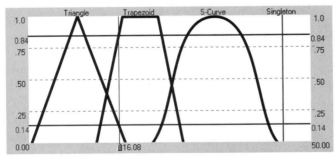

FIGURE 2.8.1   *A variable showing the four membership function types available in FFLL.*

It is worth noting that the *S-Curve* membership function is not limited to bell-shaped curves, and can represent fairly complex curves as shown in Figure 2.8.2.

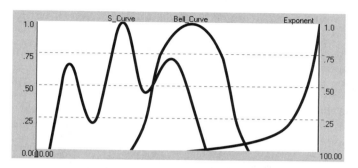

FIGURE 2.8.2 *Some of the complex* S-Curves *possible in FFLL.*

In Search of Speed

FFLL was designed to be fast; therefore, lookup tables are used wherever possible, sacrificing some memory for the sake of speed.

Each set's membership function contains a lookup table used to speed the "fuzzification" process. This lookup table is the values array in the MemberFuncBase class, which contains FuzzyVariableBase::x_array_count elements. Each array element holds a DOM value that is between zero and FuzzyVariableBase::dom_array_max_idx. Values of 100 or 200 for x_array_count provide good results; the larger the value of x_array_count, the larger the memory footprint of the model.

The variable's X-axis values must be mapped to the values array. The value of x_array_count determines how many X-axis values are represented by each element in to the values array. For example, if a variable's X-axis had a range of 0 to 50 (as in Figure 2.8.1) and x_array_count was 100, each index in the values array would represent 0.5 *x* values (50/100). If x_array_count is changed to 50, each "step" would be 1 *x* value (50/50). Think of the value of x_array_count as the "sample frequency" of the membership function; the more samples, the smoother the curve.

To determine the DOM of a variable's *x* value, it is converted to an index into the values array by the FuzzyVariableBase::convert_value_to_idx() function. Each set in a variable has its values array checked at that index to get the set's DOM.

Figure 2.8.1 shows a variable with four sets and an input value of 16.08, which has a DOM of 0.14 for the *Triangle* set and a DOM of 0.84 for the *Trapezoid* set. The other sets in that variable have a value of zero for that index in the values array.

One-Dimensional Rules Array

FFLL stores rules in a one-dimensional array. This avoids the complexities of dynamically allocating a multi-dimensional array in C/C++ when the number of dimensions is not known beforehand.

To speed access to the array elements and avoid potentially costly multiplications typical during array accesses, the offsets into the array are precalculated and stored in the `rule_index` variable of the `FuzzySetBase` class. These values are added together to get the final array index.

For example, in a 3x3x3 system (three input variables, each with three sets) there would be 27 total rules. The `rule_index` values would be:

Variable 0:	Variable 1:	Variable 2:
set 0: 0	set 0: 0	set 0: 0
set 1: 9	set 1: 3	set 1: 1
set 2: 18	set 2: 6	set 2: 2

To get the rule index corresponding to `rules[2][1][1]`, the offset for the third element in the set array for Variable 0 is found, which is 18. This process continues for each dimension in the array, adding each value to end up with the equation: 18 + 3 + 1 = 22—which is the 22nd element in the one-dimensional rules array. This means that only (N–1) additions are required every time the rule index for an N dimensional array is calculated.

Defuzzification

To eliminate extra calculations, FFLL does not calculate the defuzzified output value until it is requested. For example, if a model has four input variables and the output value is calculated every time an input value changed, three unnecessary output calculations would occur.

The Center of Gravity defuzzification method makes heavy use of lookup tables, while the Mean of Maximum method simply stores a single value per output set. See `COGDefuzzVarObj` and `MOMDefuzzVarObj`, respectively, for each method's details.

Model/Child Relationship

One or more "objects" can use a FFLL model at the same time. These "objects" are referred to as children of the FFLL model. For example, a racing game might use one model, and each AI controlled car would be a child of the model. Any child-specific information, such as input and output values, are part of the child. The API encapsulates this information to ease coding.

Multithread Support

Since all the classes in FFLL hold information (such as the rules) that is shared among children, and each child maintains its own input values, each child can safely be in a separate thread. Note that at the time of this printing, the children themselves are not thread-safe.

Unicode Support

All strings in the FFLL library use the wide character data type `wchar_t`. This provides the ability to use FFLL in double-byte languages, and avoids using Microsoft-specific macros such as TCHAR that produce different code dependent on the values defined during compilation [MSDN01].

Loading a Model

FFLL can load files in the Fuzzy Control Language (FCL) as defined in the IEC 61131-7 International Standard for Fuzzy Control Programming. See Listing 2.8.1 for an example of a FCL file.

Viewing a Model

ON THE CD

Creating and debugging a fuzzy model is a difficult task if you can't visualize what the fuzzy variables and sets look like. While FFLL does not provide any built-in viewing capabilities, the FCL format is supported by Louder Than A Bomb!'s Spark! fuzzy logic editor. A free version of this program, called Spark! Viewer, is available on the CD and on the Web [Louder01].

Exported Symbols

FFLL can be used as a class library and/or through an API. For class library use, the FFLL_API macro determines how classes are exported (if the code is compiled as a DLL) using the "standard" programming method of conditional compilation:

```
#ifdef _STATIC_LIB
#define FFLL_API
#else
#ifdef FFLL_EXPORTS
#define FFLL_API __declspec(dllexport)
#else
#define FFLL_API __declspec(dllimport)
#endif
#endif // not _STATIC_LIB
```

If FFLL_EXPORTS is defined, most of the classes will be exported, allowing developers to access the classes directly and bypass the API functions. These classes are exported using __declspec(dllexport), a method of exporting that is not supported by all compilers/linkers. If you define _STATIC_LIB, no importing or exporting of classes is performed.

The FFLL API functions are exported using extern "C" and a .def file. This is the most generic method and avoids any name mangling/decoration. The .def file also allows explicitly assigning ordinal values to functions, which avoids version conflicts as new API functions are added to FFLL.

Linking to a DLL can be difficult if you're using a compiler other than the one the DLL was built with. Check your compiler's documentation and/or the FFLL homepage for tips on linking with the FFLL library.

FFLL API

As this article is not intended to be the FFLL documentation, only the API functions that are used in the sample program (Listing 2.8.2) are listed with a brief description of each. For full documentation, see the FFLL homepage [API01].

Why an API?

You might be wondering, "why bother with an API to FFLL when programmers can access the classes directly—why add *more* code to FFLL?" The API is for developers who want to use the precompiled DLL and/or do not want to import the classes into their application. If you are using a compiler other than the one a DLL was built with, there might be several confusing steps to import the library correctly.

Unicode Support

Any function that requires strings as parameters will have both an ASCII and wide-character version. If _UNICODE is defined when you compile your application, the wide-character version is called; otherwise, the ASCII version is called.

API Functions

Table 2.8.1 lists the FFLL API functions used in Listing 2.8.2. For the full API documentation, see the FFLL homepage [API01].

Table 2.8.1 Several FFLL API Functions Used in Listing 2.8.2

ffll_new_model	
Purpose:	Creates a model object that contains the fuzzy logic model.
Parameters:	None
Returns:	int: The index of the model created, or −1 if error.

ffll_load_fcl_file	
Purpose:	Creates a fuzzy model from a file in the IEC 61131-7 Fuzzy Control Language (FCL) format.
Parameters:	model_idx—index of the model to load the file into.
	path—path and name of the file to load.
Returns:	int: The index of the model loaded if success, or −1 if error.

ffll_new_child	
Purpose:	Creates a child for the model.
Parameters:	model_idx—index of the model to create the child for.
Returns:	int: The index of the child if success, or −1 if error.

Table 2.8.1 (*Continued*)

ffll_set_value

Purpose:	Sets the value for an input variable in a child.
Parameters:	model_idx—index of the model the child belongs to.
	child_idx—index of the child to set the value for.
	var_idx—index of the variable to set the value for.
	value—value to set the variable to.
Returns:	int: Zero if success, or –1 if error.

ffll_get_output_value

Purpose:	Gets the defuzzified output value for a child.
Parameters:	model_idx—index of the model the child belongs to.
	child_idx—index of the child to get the output value for.
Returns:	float: The defuzzified value for the child; if no rules fired, FLT_MIN is returned.

A FFLL Example

While it is possible to build an entire fuzzy logic model using FFLL's exported classes, in practice it is best to create fuzzy logic models using the FCL language.

A detailed explanation of the FCL is not practical in this article due to space and copyright restrictions. The interested reader can find details on FCL on the Web [IEC97] and in the FFLL code.

Listing 2.8.1 is an FCL file that creates a fuzzy model to calculate the *aggressiveness* of an AI-controlled character based on its health and its enemy's health. The model has two input variables, *Our_Health* and *Enemy_Health*, and one output variable, *Aggressiveness*. Note that the sets that comprise the conditional part of the rules (specified in the RULEBLOCK section) are ANDed together in the order that the variables they belong to are declared in the FCL file.

Listing 2.8.1 Fuzzy Control Language (FCL) example file.

```
FUNCTION_BLOCK

VAR_INPUT
    Our_Health      REAL; (* RANGE(0 .. 100) *)
    Enemy_Health    REAL; (* RANGE(0 .. 100) *)
END_VAR

VAR_OUTPUT
    Aggressiveness  REAL; (* RANGE(0 .. 4) *)
END_VAR

FUZZIFY Our_Health
```

```
        TERM Near_Death := (0, 0) (0, 1) (50, 0) ;
        TERM Good := (14, 0) (50, 1) (83, 0) ;
        TERM Excellent := (50, 0) (100, 1) (100, 0) ;
    END_FUZZIFY

    FUZZIFY Enemy_Health
        TERM Near_Death := (0, 0) (0, 1) (50, 0) ;
        TERM Good := (14, 0) (50, 1) (83, 0) ;
        TERM Excellent := (50, 0) (100, 1) (100, 0) ;
    END_FUZZIFY

    FUZZIFY Aggressiveness
        TERM Run_Away := 1 ;
        TERM Fight_Defensively := 2 ;
        TERM All_Out_Attack := 3 ;
    END_FUZZIFY

    DEFUZZIFY valve
        METHOD: MoM;
    END_DEFUZZIFY

    RULEBLOCK first
        AND:MIN;
        ACCUM:MAX;
        RULE 0: IF Good AND Good THEN Fight_Defensively;
        RULE 1: IF Good AND Excellent THEN Fight_Defensively;
        RULE 2: IF Good AND Near_Death THEN All_Out_Attack;
        RULE 3: IF Excellent AND Good THEN All_Out_Attack;
        RULE 4: IF Excellent AND Excellent THEN Fight_Defensively;
        RULE 5: IF Excellent AND Near_Death THEN All_Out_Attack;
        RULE 6: IF Near_Death AND Good THEN Run_Away;
        RULE 7: IF Near_Death AND Excellent THEN Run_Away;
        RULE 8: IF Near_Death AND Near_Death THEN Fight_Defensively;
    END_RULEBLOCK

    END_FUNCTION_BLOCK
```

This model's two input variables (*Our_Health* and *Enemy_Health*) are graphically shown in Figure 2.8.3. The output variable for this model is *Aggressiveness* (Figure

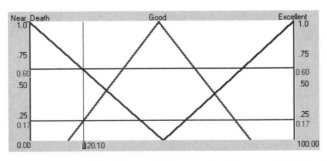

FIGURE 2.8.3   *Health variables specified in the FCL file in Listing 2.8.1 with an input value of 20.10.*

2.8.4) and contains singleton output sets. Singletons are used with the Mean of Maximum defuzzification method to output a discrete value that can easily be interpreted by the calling program (Listing 2.8.2).

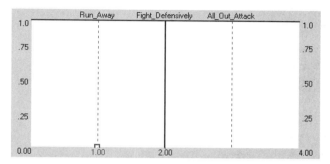

FIGURE 2.8.4 *Aggressiveness output variable specified in the FCL file in Listing 2.8.1.*

ON THE CD

Listing 2.8.2 is a program that loads the FCL model shown in Listing 2.8.1, accepts input from the user, and displays the system's output value. The program can be found on the CD.

Listing 2.8.2 Demo FFLL program.

```
#include "FFLLAPI.h" // FFLL API
#include <iostream.h>// for i/o functions

#define OUR_HEALTH    0 // our health is 1st variable
#define ENEMY_HEALTH  1 // enemy health is 2nd variable

int main(int argc, char* argv[])
{
    float our_health, enemy_health; // values for input variables
    char  option; // var for selection of what user wants to do

    cout.setf(ios::fixed);
    cout.precision(2); // only display 2 decimal places

    // create and load the model
    int model = ffll_new_model();

    int ret_val = ffll_load_fcl_file(model, "..\\aiwisdom.fcl");

    if (ret_val < 0)
        {
        cout << "Error Opening aiwisdom.fcl";
        return 0;
        }

    // create a child for the model...
```

```
    int child = ffll_new_child(model);

while (1)
    {
    cout << "SELECT AN OPTION:\n\tS - set values\n\tQ - quit";
    cout << endl;
    cin >> option;

    if (option == 'Q' || option == 'q')
        break;

    if (option == 'S' || option == 's')
        {
        cout << "Our Health: " ;
        cin >> our_health;
        cout << "Enemy's Health: "  ;
        cin >> enemy_health;
        cout << "Aggressiveness: ";

        // set input variables...
        ffll_set_value(model, child, OUR_HEALTH, our_health);
        ffll_set_value(model, child, ENEMY_HEALTH, enemy_health);

        // get and display the output value
        int output = ffll_get_output_value(model, child);

        switch(output)
            {
            case (1):
                cout << "Run Away!";
                break;

            case (2):
                cout << "Fight Defensively";
                break;

            case (3):
                cout << "All Out Attack!";
                break;

            } // end switch

        cout << endl;
        } // end if option = 's'

    } // end while(1)

return 0;

} // end main()
```

The following shows some sample output from the program in Listing 2.8.2:

Our Health: 25
Enemy's Health: 75

Aggressiveness: Run Away!
Our Health: 75
Enemy's Health: 25
Aggressiveness: All-Out Attack!

Conclusion

Fuzzy logic can be a powerful tool in an AI programmer's arsenal. It can add depth and unpredictability to your game AI—much to the dismay of the QA department.

FFLL provides a solid base of code that you are free to enhance, extend, and improve. Whether used for rapid prototyping or as a component in an AI engine, FFLL can save significant time and money.

Finally, please consider contributing any modifications you make to FFLL to the project so it can evolve and others can benefit from your contributions.

References

[API01] Available online at http://ffll.sourceforge.net/api/, September 2001.
[FFLL01] Available online at http://ffll.sourceforge.net/, September 2001.
[IEC97] International Electrotechnical Commission IEC 61131 Draft 1.0, available online at www.fuzzytech.com/binaries/ieccd1.pdf, September, 2001.
[Kilr/Yuan95] Kilr, George J., Yuan, Bo, *Fuzzy Sets and Fuzzy Logic: Theory and Applications*, Prentice Hall, p. 13, 1995.
[Louder01] Available online at www.LouderThanABomb.com, September 2001.
[Morris99] Morris, Daniel, "Neural-Net AI and Fuzzy Logic," *PC Gamer*, July 1999, p. 82.
[MSDN01] "Generic-Text Mappings in TCHAR.H," available online at http://msdn.microsoft.com/library/default.asp?url=/library/en-us/vccore98/html/_core_generic.2d.text_mappings_in_tchar..h.asp, September 2001.
[O'Brien96] O'Brien, Larry, "Fuzzy Logic in Games," *Game Developer* magazine, April/May 1996, p. 53.

PATHFINDING WITH A*

3.1

Basic A* Pathfinding Made Simple

James Matthews—Generation5

jmatthews@generation5.org

The A* algorithm has been the source of much confusion and mystery within the game programming community. While the goals and basic theory of A* are relatively simple to understand, the implementation of the algorithm can be a nightmare to realize. This article will hopefully clarify the theory *and* the implementation of the A* algorithm. We will look first at the basics of A* as they apply to two-dimensional maps, and then study a C++ class that implements the algorithm.

An Overview

The A* (pronounced *a-star*) algorithm will find a path between two points on a map. While many different pathing algorithms exist, A* will find the shortest path, if one exists, and will do so relatively quickly—which is what sets it apart from the others. There are *many* flavors of A*, but they all build around the basic algorithm presented here.

A* is a *directed* algorithm, meaning it doesn't blindly search for a path (like a rat in a maze), but instead assesses the best direction to explore, sometimes backtracking to try alternative means. This is what makes the A* algorithm so flexible.

Terms

Before we delve into A*'s particulars, we should define a few terms.

A **map** (or **graph**) is the space that A* is using to find a path between two positions. This doesn't necessarily have to be a map in the literal sense of the meaning. The map could be comprised of squares or hexagons, be a three-dimensional area, or even a spatial representation of game trees. The important thing to understand is that the map is the area within which A* works.

Nodes are the structures that represent positions on the map. However, the map will be in a data structure independent of the nodes. The nodes store information critical to the A* algorithm as well as positional information; thus, nodes act as a bookkeeping device to store the progress of the pathfinding search. It is important to remember that two or more nodes can correspond to the same position on the map.

The **distance** (or **heuristic**) is used to determine the "suitability" of the node being explored. We will use the term *distance*, since this article will primarily be dealing with applying A* to traditional two-dimensional maps.

The **cost** of a node is probably the hardest term to define—an analogy is probably best. When traveling large distances, various factors are taken into account (time, energy, money, or scenery) that affect whether a certain path is to be taken. Possible paths between the start and goal nodes will have associated costs, and it is the job of A* to minimize these costs. Note that there are no set algorithms or equations to determine the distance and cost of a node; they are *completely* application-dependent.

The A* Algorithm

We will now venture into the theory surrounding the A* algorithm. A* traverses the map by creating nodes that correspond to the various positions it explores. Remember that these nodes are for recording the progress of the search. In addition to holding the map location, each of these nodes has three main attributes commonly called *f, g,* and *h*, sometimes referred to as the *fitness, goal,* and *heuristic* values, respectively. The following describes each in more detail:

- *g* is the cost to get from the starting node to this node. Many different paths go from the start node to this map location, but this node represents a single path to it.
- *h* is the estimated cost to get from this node to the goal. In this setting, *h* stands for *heuristic* and means *educated guess*, since we don't really know the cost (that's why we're looking for a path).
- *f* is the sum of *g* and *h*. *f* represents our best guess for the cost of this path going through this node. The lower the value of *f*, the better we *think* the path is.

At this point, you might ask why we are measuring some distances and guessing at other distances. The purpose of *f, g,* and *h* is to quantify how promising a path is up to this node. Component *g* is something we can calculate perfectly. It is the cost required to get to this current node. Since we've explored all nodes that led to this one, we know the value of *g* exactly. However, component *h* is a completely different beast. Since we don't know how much farther it is to the goal from this node, we are forced to guess. The better our guess, the closer *f* is to the true value, and the quicker A* finds the goal with little wasted effort.

Additionally, A* maintains two lists, an *Open* list and a *Closed* list. The Open list consists of nodes that *have not* been explored, whereas the Closed list consists of all nodes that *have* been explored. A node is considered "explored" if the algorithm has looked at every node connected to this one, calculated their *f, g* and *h* values, and placed them on the Open list to be explored in the future.

Open and Closed lists are required because nodes are not unique. For example, if you start at (0,0) and move to (0,1), it is perfectly valid to move back to (0,0). You must, therefore, keep track of what nodes have been explored and created—this is what the Open and Closed lists are for. As mentioned earlier, nodes simply mark the state and progress of the search.

In pathing, this distinction becomes important because there can be many different ways to navigate to the same point. For example, if a pathway branches into two but converges again later, the algorithm must determine which branch to take.

The Algorithm

Now let us look at A* broken down into pseudo-code.

1. Let P = the starting point.
2. Assign f, g and h values to P.
3. Add P to the Open list. At this point, P is the only node on the Open list.
4. Let B = the best node from the Open list (best node has the lowest f-value).
   a. If B is the goal node, then quit—a path has been found.
   b. If the Open list is empty, then quit—a path cannot be found.
5. Let C = a valid node connected to B.
   a. Assign f, g, and h values to C.
   b. Check whether C is on the Open or Closed list.
      i. If so, check whether the new path is more efficient (lower f-value).
         1. If so, update the path.
      ii. Else, add C to the Open list.
   c. Repeat step 5 for all valid children of B.
6. Move B from the Open list to the Closed list and repeat from step 4.

A Simple Example

Certain steps within the algorithm might not make immediate sense (such as *5bi*), but for the moment, a very simple step-through should clarify most of the algorithm. Look at the example map shown in Figure 3.1.1.

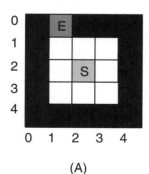
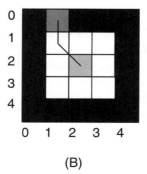

(A)   (B)

FIGURE 3.1.1 *A) Very simple map. B) Path solution.*

The center point is the starting position (S), and the offset gray point is the end position (E). The values f, g, and h are simple to assign for the starting point. Value g is zero since there is no cost associated with the first node. Value h is calculated differently for each application, but for map-based problems, something simple like the combined cost of the horizontal and vertical differences (called the Manhattan Distance) is sufficient, since this is a reasonable guess for the remaining cost. Therefore, if (dx,dy) is the destination point and (sx,sy) is the starting point:

$$h = |\ dx\text{-}sx\ | + |\ dy\text{-}sy\ |$$

For our problem, (sx,sy) is (2,2) and (dx,dy) is (1,0), so h is calculated as follows:

$$h = |\ 1\text{--}2\ | + |\ 0\text{--}2\ |$$
$$h = 1 + 2 = 3$$

Since h is 3 and g is 0, then f, which is the sum of g and h, equals 3. Generating the children is simple since all children are valid (all eight adjacent cells can be traveled to) and all are new nodes to be added to the Open list. The g-value for each child node will be 1, since g is the cost of getting to the parent (0) plus the cost of moving a position on the map (in this case, one tile). The h-value will be different for each node, but it is easy to see that $(1,1)$ will have the lowest score since it is the closest to our goal node. Therefore, $(1,1)$ is the best child node and will be the next to be explored.

Node $(1,1)$ has four valid children: $(1,0)$ $(1,2)$ $(2,1)$ and $(2,2)$. Now we have to determine which nodes are on the Open or Closed lists, and which are new nodes. Node $(2,2)$ is on the Closed list. It was our original starting point, and all its children have been opened up. Nodes $(1,2)$ and $(2,1)$ are on the Open list since their children have yet to be explored (and are children of $(2,2)$), and, finally, $(1,0)$ is a new node.

After assigning f, g, and h values to the nodes, it is evident that $(1,0)$ will have the best score, and upon the next iteration of the A* algorithm, it is discovered that $(1,0)$ is the goal node.

CAStar—A C++ Class for the A* Algorithm

CAStar is an example C++ class that implements the A* algorithm. It is a little more complex than a standard class, since it allows the programmer to supply his own cost and validity functions, as well as a variety of callback function pointers. We will not look at all of the class member functions; instead, we will focus on the node data structure and two important member functions. These two member functions, LinkChild and UpdateParents, handle most aspects of A*.

First, let us look at the node data structure:

```
class _asNode {
    public:
    _asNode(int, int);
    int f,g,h;
    int x,y;
    int numchildren;
```

```
        int number;

        _asNode *parent;
        _asNode *next;
        _asNode *children[8];
        void    *dataptr;
    };
```

ON THE CD

The node data structure implemented as a mini-class to aid member variable initialization (see the source files on the CD-ROM). The member variables are self-explanatory: f, g, and h values, x and y variables for positional information, numchildren to track the number of children, and number, a unique identifier for each map position.

Following, we have a pointer to the parent of the node. The pointer labeled next is used in the Open and Closed lists (implemented as linked-lists). We then have an array of pointers to the children (pathfinding on a grid requires an array size of eight). The final variable is a void pointer that the programmers can use to associate some form of data with the node.

CAStar::LinkChild

LinkChild takes two pointers to _asNode structures. One denotes the parent node (node), and the other is a temporary node (temp) that only has its x and y variables initialized. LinkChild implements steps *5a* and *5b* of the original pseudo-code.

```
void CAStar::LinkChild(_asNode *node, _asNode *temp)
{
  int x = temp->x;
  int y = temp->y;
  int g = node->g +
          udFunc(udCost, node, temp, 0, m_pCBData);
  int num = Coord2Num(x,y);
```

First, we retrieve the coordinate information from temp. Notice how we calculate *g* by using the parent's *g-value* and then calling the user-defined cost function, udCost. The last line generates the unique identifier for our node position.

```
    _asNode *check = NULL;

    if (check = CheckList(m_pOpen, num)) {
       node->children[node->numchildren++] = check;

       if (g < check->g) {
          check->parent = node;
          check->g = g;
          check->f = g + check->h;
       }
    } else if (check = CheckList(m_pClosed, num)) {
       node->children[node->numchildren++] = check;

       if (g < check->g) {
```

```
            check->parent = node;
            check->g = g;
            check->f = g + check->h;

            UpdateParents(check);
        }
    }
```

If you refer back to our pseudo-code, you will see that we must first check whether the node exists on either the Open or Closed lists. CheckList takes a pointer to a list head and a unique identifier to search for; if it finds the identifier, it returns the pointer of the node with which it is associated.

If it is found on the Open list, we add it to the array of node's children. We then check whether the g calculated from the new node is smaller than check's g. Remember that although check and temp correspond to the same position on the map, the paths by which they were reached can be *very* different.

If the node is found on the Closed list, we add it to node's children. We do a similar check to see whether the *g-value* is lower. If it is, then we have to change not only the current parent pointer, but also *all* connected nodes to update their f, g, h values and possibly their parent pointers, too. We will look at the function that performs this after we finish with LinkChild.

```
        else {
            _asNode *newnode = new _asNode(x,y);
            newnode->parent = node;
            newnode->g = g;
            newnode->h = abs(x-m_iDX) + abs(y-m_iDY);
            newnode->f = newnode->g + newnode->h;
            newnode->number = Coord2Num(x,y);

            AddToOpen(newnode);

            node->children[node->numchildren++] = newnode;
        }
    }
```

Finally, if it is neither on the Open or Closed list, we create a new node and assign the f, g, and h values. We then add it to the Open list before updating its parent's child pointer array.

CAStar::UpdateParents

UpdateParents takes a node as its single parameter and propagates the necessary changes up the A* tree. This implements step *5bi1* of our algorithm!

```
    void CAStar::UpdateParents(_asNode *node)
    {
        int g = node->g, c = node->numchildren;

        _asNode *kid = NULL;
```

```
for (int i=0;i<c;i++) {
   kid = node->children[i];
   if (g+1 < kid->g) {
      kid->g = g+1;
      kid->f = kid->g + kid->h;
      kid->parent = node;

      Push(kid);
   }
}
```

This is the first half of the algorithm. It is fairly easy to see *what* the algorithm does. The question is, *why* does it do it? Remember that node's *g*-value was updated before the call to UpdateParents. Therefore, we check all children to see whether we can improve on their *g*-value as well. Since we have to propagate the changes back, any updated node is placed on a stack to be recalled in the latter half of the algorithm.

```
_asNode *parent;
while (m_pStack) {
   parent = Pop();
   c = parent->numchildren;
   for (int i=0;i<c;i++) {
      kid = parent->children[i];

      if (parent->g+1 < kid->g) {
         kid->g = parent->g +
          udFunc(udCost, parent, kid, 0, m_pCBData);
         kid->f = kid->g + kid->h;
         kid->parent = parent;

         Push(kid);
      }
   }
}
```

The rest of the algorithm is basically the same as the first half, but instead of using node's values, we are popping nodes off the stack. Again, if we update a node, we must push it back onto the stack to continue the propagation.

Utilizing CAStar

As mentioned, CAStar is expandable and can be easily adapted to other applications. The main advantage of CAStar is that the programmer supplies the cost and validity functions. This means that CAStar is almost ready to go for any 2D map problems.

The programmer supplies the cost and validity functions, as well as two optional notification functions by passing function pointers of the following prototype:

```
typedef int(*_asFunc)(_asNode *, _asNode *, int, void *);
```

The first two parameters are the parent and child nodes. The integer is a function-specific data item (used in callback functions), and the final pointer is the m_pCBData (cost and validity functions) or m_pNCData (notification functions) as defined by the programmer. See the A* Explorer source code and documentation on the CD-ROM for examples on how to use these features effectively.

ON THE CD

A* Explorer

A* Explorer is a Windows program that utilizes CAStar and allows the user to explore many aspects of the A* algorithm. For example, if you would like to look at how A* solves the simple map given at the beginning of this chapter in Figure 3.1.1, do the following:

ON THE CD

1. Run A* Explorer off of the book's CD.
2. Select "File, Open," and find *very_simple.ase* in A* Explorer's directory.
3. Use the Step function (F10) to step through each iteration of A*. Look at the Open and Closed lists, as well as the A* tree itself.

Alternatively, if you would like to see how relative costing (as described in the next section) affects A*'s final path, open *relative_cost.ase* and run the A* algorithm (F9). Now, select "Relative Costing" within the "Pathing" menu and re-run A*. Notice how the path changes.

A* Explorer has a huge number of features that we don't have room to cover here, so take a look at the online help for a complete breakdown of the features, including breakpoint and conditions, map drawing, and understanding the A* tree.

Ideas and Expansions

The A* algorithm is great because it is highly extensible and will often bend around your problem easily. The key to getting A* to work optimally lies within the cost and heuristic functions. These functions can also yield more realistic behavior if tuned properly. As a simple example, if a node's altitude determines the cost of its position, the cost function could favor traversing children of equal altitude (relative costing) as opposed to minimizing the cost (Figure 3.1.2).

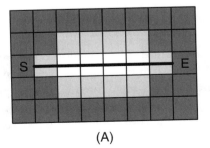
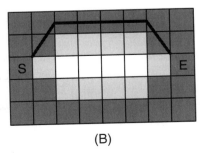

(A)   (B)

FIGURE 3.1.2 *A) Path generated by normal costing, and B) relative costing.*

This is a good example of how altering the cost function yields more realistic behavior (in certain scenarios). By adapting the distance and child generation functions, it is easy to stretch A* to non-map specific problems. Other ideas for enthusiastic readers to explore include hexagonal or three-dimensional map support, optimizing the algorithm, and experimenting with different cost and distance functions.

Of course, one of the best places to look for additional ideas and expansions to A* lies within the other articles of this book and the *Game Programming Gems* series of books!

Conclusion

A* is a difficult algorithm to fully understand. On paper, it looks simple, when looking at someone else's code, it *still* looks simple—but understanding it completely can be a daunting task. Hopefully, after reading this chapter, you will understand how A* works, its potential applications, and ideas on expanding and improving it. Use CAStar and A* Explorer to help further your experience and knowledge of A*.

A* Resources on the Internet

Generation5:	www.generation5.org/
The Game AI Page:	www.gameai.com/
Flipcode:	www.flipcode.com/

3.2

Generic A* Pathfinding

Dan Higgins—Stainless Steel Studios, Inc.

webmaster@programming.org

After dedicating months, or years, to optimizing a pathfinding engine, wouldn't it be great to use this fast code in other places besides pathfinding? A good pathfinding engine can be used for many more purposes than just moving units around the world. In the real-time strategy game *Empire Earth*, we used the pathfinding engine for tasks such as terrain analysis, choke-point detection, AI military route planning, weather creation/movement, AI wall building, animal migration routes, and of course, unit pathfinding.

What Can a Generic A* Machine Do?

Typically, pathfinding is used to find a navigation route from a starting point to an ending point. This route is generally a small subset of the world that was searched during the pathfinding process. Instead of just "finding a path," an A* machine can be used to find the negative of a path. It sounds strange, but suppose you want all tiles except the path found, or in the case of a flood-fill (my favorite use of the A* machine), you simply want all the nodes that were searched.

As an example, imagine that given a tree, we want to gather all the trees that are connected to it so we can form a forest. This means not just adjacent trees, but all trees adjacent to each other that are somehow connected to this one tree. To do this, put an imaginary unit on this tree, and make a rule that this unit can only walk on trees, so to get to its destination, it can only move on tiles with trees. Now, just like dangling a carrot in front of a donkey to get it moving, give the unit an impossible goal so that they start pathfinding. They will try hard to get there, and in doing so, will flood the forest to find the path. This means, they will touch every connected tree before declaring that the path is impossible to achieve.

After the path, your Open list should be empty and your Closed list will have all the nodes searched. If you only allow valid nodes to enter your A* lists, then the entire Closed list is the forest. If you allow invalid nodes on your lists, then you'll need to traverse your Closed list and determine which nodes have trees on them. We recommend that you do not add invalid nodes to your A* lists, as they serve to only increase search time. For more information on why this is important and how to cache closed boundary nodes, see article 3.4, "How to Achieve Lightning-Fast A*" [Higgins02].

114

The A* Machine

Creating an A* machine is much like custom building a computer. The computer comes with a power supply, motherboard, and case, but among other things, is missing the CPU, memory, and graphics card. Like an empty computer, the A* machine comes with the core A* algorithm code, but needs a storage class to hold all its data, a goal class to tell it what to do and where to go, and a map to supply it with something to search.

The Storage

The A* machine needs a storage class to hold its A* node traversal data, and house the traditional open and closed A* lists. It can also return the cheapest node on any of the lists. The storage container that you choose will make the largest performance difference in your A* processing. For example, during terrain analysis in *Empire Earth*, we use a very fast, but memory expensive, storage container because when we are done with terrain analysis, all that memory is returned to the operating system. If we didn't, and used the standard, memory-efficient A* storage, terrain analysis would take minutes to perform. Instead, with the fast storage container [Higgins02], it only takes a few seconds to process the entire map multiple times.

Another variation on the storage container we used in terrain analysis was to always return the top Open list node without searching for the cheapest node to process next. This is ideal for flood-fill tasks such as forest detection, since tile costs will mean nothing, and the A* engine acts only as a highly optimized flood-fill tool.

The Goal

The goal class determines what really happens in the A* engine. The goal contains data such as the unit, the source, the destination, the distance methods, and the essential TileIsOpen and GetTileCost methods. The wonderful part about a generic goal class is that it holds whatever is appropriate for the current A* task. For example, the forest-processing goal contains a forest ID counter, the primary type of tree found in the forest, and its main continent. This means that a unit's pathfinding goal is quite different from the forest goal outside of having a few boilerplate methods that all goal classes are forced to implement.

Required methods:

- SetNodeStorage: This method tells the goal about the storage container.
- ShouldPause: This method will return true if it's time to pause the A* engine. This would be used if you are using time-sliced pathfinding.
- DistanceToGoal: The distance function used in A*.
- GetIsPathFinished: This will return true when we have reached our goal, hit the pathfinding performance cap, or run out of nodes to process.
- TileIsOpen: One of the two main ingredients in any pathfinding engine. This returns true if this tile is passable.

- `GetTileCost`: This is the other important method in any pathfinding engine. It returns a cost for walking on this tile.
- `ShouldReEvaluateNode`: This is used for pathfinding smoothing. If you re-process nodes during your path, this determines if path smoothing on this node should be done.

The Map

The map is the search space for A*. It could be the map of your world, or it could be an array. This is handy for reusing your A* to handle any 2D array of values. For example, to detect choke points, an array can be filled with choke-point flags. Then, the A* machine can run through them and collect them into a group of points. Once you have collected these points, the possibilities are endless. For example, you could use those points to make convex hulls, or to create areas for a high-level pathfinding system.

In order to make the A* machine use a generic map component, we need to wrap the array, map, or any other search space we will be using in a class that supports a few standard methods:

Map wrapper class methods:

- `GetTile(X, Y)`: This goes to the map and asks for the value at a given X, Y.
- `GetMaxXTiles`, `GetMaxYTiles`: These are used for sizing things inside our storage container.

The Engine

The A* engine portion is pretty simple, and is the heart of the A* process.

An A* engine's heart would look something like Listing 3.2.1.

Listing 3.2.1 Excerpt from `AStarMachine<TGoal,` `TStorage, TMap>`'s run method.

```
// Infinite loop. The goal will tell us when we are done.
for(;;)
{
    // used for time-slicing
    this->mRevolutions++;

    // get the best choice so far
    this->mCurrentNode = this->RemoveCheapestOpenNode();

    // if == true, then its likely that we are not at the
    // goal and we have no more nodes to search through
    if(this->mGoal.GetIsPathFinished(this->mCurrentNode))
        break;

    // for all 8 neighbor tiles, examine them by checking
    // their TileOpen status, and putting them on the
    // appropriate A* lists. (code not shown)
```

```
        // add this node to closed list now
        this->AddNodeToClosedList(this->mCurrentNode);

        // Should we pause? (used in time-slicing)
        if(this->mGoal.ShouldPause(this->mCurrentRevolutions))
            break;

        // if == true, this means we have exceeded our max
        // pathfinding revolutions and should give up.
        if(this->mGoal.ShouldGiveUp(this->mRevolutions))
            break;

        // used for time-slicing
        this->mCurrentRevolutions++;
    }
```

Exploiting Templates

Templates are essential to making the A* machine reusable and fast. Certainly, you can gain reusability by using base classes and virtual functions, but this architecture achieves reusability and great speed by using templates. Since virtual functions are most useful when you call a method through a base class pointer, we can skip that overhead because with templates, we can specify a specific class name as a template argument and bind directly to the most derived classes.

A good example of this is the distance function. We could make our distance function virtual, but for a Manhattan distance function (abs(inSourceX - inDestinationX) + abs(inSourceY-inDestinationY)), why add the assembly overhead of a virtual function when it can be made generic and inlined by using templates?

The Dark Side of Templates

As amazing as templates are, they do have some downsides. While many compilers are modernizing, template performance can vary widely depending on your compiler. In addition, templates often make you write code completely in a header file, which can make "edit and continue code" impossible, and a simple change to the header might cause a full rebuild of your code. Templates can also cause some code bloat, although this depends on a number of factors. Overall, in many architectures including the A* machine, the positives outweigh the negatives.

There are two tricks that help when architecting with templates. First, use template-free base classes to make using these template classes easy to contain. For example, suppose you're going to have a pathfinding queue of A* machines. A pathfinding system would use this queue to determine which of the many path searches and flood-fills it should work on next. Unless all the A* machines use the same template arguments, you'll need an A* base class. The following is an example of some methods that might be found in an A* base class:

```
class AStarBase
{
    // normal stuff including the virtual destructor
    virtual AStarGoalBase* GetGoalBase(void) = 0;
    virtual void GetPath(vector<Waypoint>& outPath) = 0;
    virtual void RunAStar(void)  = 0;
    virtual void SetBailoutCap(long inMaxRevolutions);

    // etc.
};
```

Second, use templates to ensure function names. Don't be afraid to call methods on your template pieces. For example, in the A* machine, the map template piece needs a GetTile(X,Y) method on it. This means that to use an array as a map, it needs to be wrapped in a class that supplies those methods. Thus, by calling methods on template pieces, it forces these template pieces to comply with certain expectations set by the template class.

Putting the Pieces Together

The A* machine is made up of several pieces, and in fact, derives from some of its template arguments. To understand how these pieces fit together, let's examine our forest processor A* machine. An example of the A* class hierarchy used for a forest processor is shown in Figure 3.2.1.

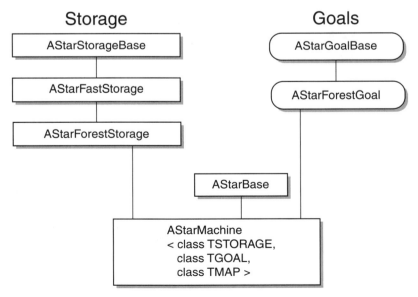

FIGURE 3.2.1 *Object model of an A* machine customized for forest creation.*

The A* machine class uses the storage container template argument as one of its base classes.

This class definition is:

```
template<class TSTORAGE, class TGOAL, class TMAP>
class AStarMachine : public AStarBase, public TSTORAGE
```

To create the forest A* machine, we combine the storage, goal and map classes, and use it like:

```
// typedef for clarity in code example.
typedef AStarForestStorage ASTARSForest;
typedef AStarForestGoal ASTARGForest;
AStarMachine<ASTARSForest, ASTARGForest, Map> theMachine;

// set the source and destination
theMachine.SetSource(theSourcePoint);
theMachine.SetDestination(theDestinationPoint);

// run it!
theMachine.RunAStar();
```

Modifier Goals

A powerful concept that we used in *Empire Earth* was modifier goals. A modifier goal is a small class that supports two methods, `GetTileCost` and `TileIsOpen`. During pathfinding, if a pathfinder had a pointer to a modifier goal class inside it, it would check the modifier's methods rather than the normal `TileIsOpen` and `GetTileCost` methods.

This can sound odd, because normally it's easier to just derive from a pathfinder, and overload the calls to `GetTileCost` and `TileIsOpen`. The main problem arises when you want to have many unique pathfinders, but you also want to have your pathfinders' memory pooled. It can be expensive to pool all the unique pathfinders, since they all will be unique declarations of the class.

You could work around this by making the storage class a pointer instead of part of the inheritance chain. You would also want to replace some of the inline template class methods calls with virtual function calls, but that would throw away some of the speed increases and not be something we generally want. On the bright side, modifier goals bridge this gap by giving us the reusability power, without making us sacrifice the power of having memory-pooled pathfinders.

The code inside the pathfinding goal that accesses the modifier goals looks like the following. Note: `U2Dpoint<T>` is a templatized 2D point class.

```
long GetTileCost( U2Dpoint<long>& inFrom, U2Dpoint<long>& inTo )
{
    // Modifier goals keep us from having more pathfinder
    // classes when all we need is a 2 method modifier
    if (this->mModifierGoal == NULL)
```

```
        return this->InternalGetTileCost(inFrom,inTo);
    else
        return this->mModiferGoal->GetTileCost(inFrom,inTo);
}
```

The `TileIsOpen` method is almost identical to the `GetTileCost` method, which operates as a simple gate that either processes the function internally, or hands it off to the modifier goal. Unfortunately, because the `ModiferGoal` is a base class pointer, we will incur a virtual function hit when we call modifier goals. This is generally acceptable, since most of the time, modifier goals are not used, and the A* machine only uses two of its methods. An example of when we would use a modifier goal would be pathfinding for submarines.

```
    // This is used to modify the pathfinder,
    // making it slightly slower, but saves memory.
    class PathModifierSubmarine : public PathModifierGoalBase
    {
    public:
        virtual long GetTileCost( U2Dpoint<long>& inFrom,
                                  U2Dpoint<long>& inTo);

        virtual bool TileIsOpen( Tile* inTile, U2Dpoint<long>& inPoint);
    };
```

As unusual as they seem, modifier goals can make life much easier. For example, when writing a weather storm creation, the A* engine was used with a simple modifier goal that controlled the shape and size of the storm pattern. In a very short amount of time, we were able to modify the pathfinder to do something unique without writing a lot of code, or recompiling a header file.

What Would Edgar Chicken Do?

Remember:

- **Reuse that A*.** Instead of writing a pathfinding engine, write a generic A* engine. This way it can be used for much more than just pathfinding. It would be a shame to not take advantage of the months or years of optimization work.
- **Templatize your engine.** Use templates to get speed and reusability. Don't be intimidated by templates, they are amazing tools. Check your compiler to see how it well it deals with templates.
- **Learn from STL (Standard Template Library).** STL is part of the C++ ANSI Standard, and it's well designed, fast, easy to use, and promotes reusability. There are some great books available that will help you to understand and appreciate STL's design [Stroustrup97], [Myers01].

- **Optimize storage.** Use different types of storage classes to trade memory for performance. Customize storage to fit the specific task.
- **Customize goal classes.** Use different types of goal classes. The goal classes should be extremely specific to the current task.
- **Use different maps.** Don't be afraid to use different maps with the A* engine. The A* engine can pathfind across arrays, or other maplike structures. You can even expand your A* algorithm to use "adjacent nodes" as on a graph instead of just tiles. An A* graph machine really deserves a full article in itself, but is a very powerful concept.
- **Modify and conquer.** Modifier goals will make life simpler. Once the A* engine is written, you can do most of your work from modifier goals. Using modifier goals allows you to easily implement a memory-pool of templated pathfinders, while still keeping the pathfinders generic. It can almost be seen as runtime method modification.
- **Exploit A*.** Once you have an A* engine written, you'll be able to quickly and easily handle many complicated tasks. Be creative with it, and push it to the limits of reasonable use. You'll probably be happy that you did.

References

[Higgins02] Higgins, Daniel F., "How to Achieve Lightning-Fast A*," *AI Game Programming Wisdom,* 2002.

[Myers01] Myers, Scott, *Effective STL: 50 Specific Ways to Improve Your Use of the Standard Template Library,* Addison-Wesley Publishing Co., June 2001.

[Patel01] Patel, Amit J., "Amit's Game Programming Information," available online at www-cs-students.stanford.edu/~amitp/gameprog.html, 2001.

[Rabin00] Rabin, Steve, "A* Speed Optimizations," *Game Programming Gems,* Charles River Media, 2000.

[Stroustrup97] Stroustrup, Bjarne, *The C++ Programming Language,* Addison-Wesley Publishing Co., July 1997.

3.3

Pathfinding Design Architecture

Dan Higgins—Stainless Steel Studios, Inc.

webmaster@programming.org

Question: Why did the chicken cross the road?
Answer: Because the path was terrible.

Or, at least that's what the people playing your game are going to think. Regardless of how good your pathfinding is, people are always going to complain about it, so one way to sleep soundly at night is to make your pathfinding almost perfect.

Unfortunately, great pathfinding can be tough to do without using most of the CPU. Even if you have a fast A* or pathfinding engine, there are still barriers you'll need to cross in order to maintain a good frame rate and find great paths.

In this article, we describe some of the techniques used in *Empire Earth* to ensure that hundreds of units could simultaneously pathfind across the world without bogging down the system. These techniques focus primarily on how to split paths up over time and still keep the user believing that the paths are computed instantaneously. So, while you won't find the answer to, "Why did the chicken cross the road?" in this article, perhaps after reading this, you will be closer to solving the question of "How did the chicken cross the road?"

What You'll Need for the Trip

This chapter assumes that you have a solid understanding of A* [Rabin00], [Patel01] and an A* or pathfinding engine [Higgins02a]. It's not important that your A* engine be fast or slow, since the techniques in this chapter should help any type of A* engine.

Here is a quick reference card. Some terms you'll need are:

- **A* machine**: This is the generic A* engine described in article 3.2, "Generic A* Pathfinding" [Higgins02a].

- **Unit**: This is the person, creature, entity, or anything else that one would wish to pathfind from one point to another.
- **Node**: This refers to the A* node, which encompasses the following information: position, cost of the node, cost to the destination, and so forth.
- **Pathfinding revolution**: This is a single iteration through the A* engine's main loop. In short, it's a single push through the following: grab the cheapest node, examine all eight neighbors, and put the node on the closed list loop [Higgins02a].
- **Out-of-sync**: When a networked game goes out-of-sync, it means that the game ceases to be the same on both machines. This could mean that a unit dies on one machine while surviving on another—a major problem for multi-player games.

The Road to Cross

The first of many hurdles to cross is to prevent the game from freezing every time we path some units across the screen. This "game freeze" can be considered the plague of pathfinders. It's a game killer, and is one of the most significant problems we will need to solve until we all have 5-trilliahertz computers with googles of memory.

It makes sense that if a unit needs to move to the other side of the world, and the A* algorithm ends up searching through thousands of nodes to find a successful path, the game would cease to function while this process happened. A technique that handles this problem is to split the paths up over time. This will ensure that no matter how many units in the game are pathfinding, the frame rate won't be crippled.

Time-sliced pathfinding sounds like it would only work for a static map, but this is not the case; it works well for both static and dynamic maps. In the real-time strategy game *Empire Earth*, we use time-sliced pathfinding to path across giant maps that were constantly changing and supported thousands of units.

You might think that a dynamic map would change too much to make time-sliced pathfinding a viable solution. Dynamic maps might have gates or doors that are suddenly locked, buildings collapsing into a roadway, or traffic jams blocking a choke point. By the time the path was completed, the map could have changed, and you would have to start all over again. However, there is no need to worry since the same mechanisms that detect and handle collisions will work for time-sliced pathfinding.

It's not all tea and biscuits, though; it does take a slightly more complex architecture to support time-sliced pathfinding. *Empire Earth* was able to use time-sliced pathfinding by using a three-step path architecture that consisted of a quick path, a full path, and finally, a splice path.

The Quick Path

Quick paths are designed to get a unit moving. When a player gives a unit an order, he expects the unit to respond quickly rather than sit and think for a while. Quick paths use a high speed, short-distance pathfinder [Higgins02b] to move the unit anywhere from 3 to 15 tiles. The main objective of this path is to buy us time to compute the real path in the background.

For example, let's suppose Edgar Chicken wants to path around this body of water (Figure 3.3.1). When his path request is generated, we immediately do a quick path. For now, let's say that we want to stop after 10 revolutions since that could reasonably produce a path of five tiles in length. When the pathfinder hits its 10-revolution limit, it picks the closest point to the destination as its ending point.

We see that a five-tile path is generated (each tile is indicated by a dash in Figure 3.3.1) and Edgar Chicken begins moving down the path toward the destination. It's important to note that not all quick paths are straight lines; they are simply paths that bail out early and get as close to the destination as possible. It just so happens that this path is a straight line. Once the path is generated, the quick path can retire to a life of luxury and shift the responsibility to the next stage of the pathfinding process, the full path.

The Full Path

The "full path" is the real deal. This is the path that gets processed over time and could search thousands, or even millions, of A* nodes to find the correct path. It's the workhorse of the pathfinding engine and silently churns away in our pathfinding queue (more on that later), while the unit moves toward the goal along its quick path.

Life will be much easier if you follow one rule in your A* engine implementation: Once a tile is determined to be open or blocked, it will keep that state for the duration

FIGURE 3.3.1 *The quick path is a short burst path that gets the unit moving in the general direction of the destination.*

of the path. This caching of tile open/blocked status serves two purposes. First, our pathfinding will be more CPU friendly, since we will do fewer potentially expensive calls to determine if a tile is blocked. Second, it keeps the pathfinder from generating confused or broken paths. More information on how to cache these nodes can be found in [Higgins02b].

If you decide not to cache the results, be aware that you will have a few problems to handle, such as potential dead-end paths (A* list chains with invalid ending nodes), or a pathfinder that spins its wheels because just as it's about to finish the path, it finds that it has to rethink it. Cache your nodes; you'll be happy you did.

To begin the full path, and to guarantee a fully connected path, we need to start the full path from the *destination* of the quick path. We then put the full path on the pathfinding queue (more on this later) and let it work. When the full path finishes, the result of the entire path (quick path + full path) will look like Figure 3.3.2.

The Splice Path

Now that we have a complete path that was generated mainly in the background and goes from our source to our destination successfully, we are ready to call it a night and go home. Wait a minute, though, the path in Figure 3.3.2 is pretty ugly. Our unit will have to walk backward on its path, and will look like it took a wrong turn. Most players will find this kind of path unacceptable, and will complain. So, unless you are planning to create online pathfinding support groups to comfort unhappy gamers, you had better fix this hideous path.

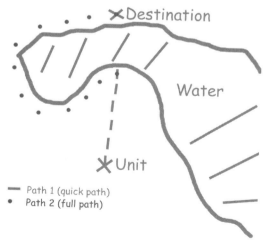

FIGURE 3.3.2 *The full path is the longest leg of the path and goes from the destination of the quick path to the true endpoint of the path.*

Ok, ok, so it's the quick path's fault. It got as close to the goal as it could before handing off the task to the "full pathfinder." Fortunately, we can avoid the players getting a negative perception of the path by using a third high-speed path called the *splice path*.

It's the job of the splice path to correct the errors made by the quick path, and convince the player that we knew the right path all along. This path will be instantaneous and uses the same high-speed pathfinder used by the "quick path."

So that we can brush away the path blemishes, the splice path needs to start from the units' current position, and select a point along our "full path" as the path's destination. The decision of which "full path" point to intercept is something you will want to tweak when tuning your pathfinding engine. For example, you might want to choose a point that is eight waypoints along the path, or instead, walk the current path until some distance has been reached. It's a magic number that you will need to experiment with. This magic number is a common example of the "looks versus performance" issue that pathfinders constantly battle with.

While tuning this number, keep in mind that the farther along the path you decide to intercept, the more likely it is that any errors will be corrected. Naturally, pathfinding out farther doesn't guarantee fun in the sun, since the farther out one paths, the more CPU will be used. The good news is that a happy balance between game performance and player experience is easily achievable—it just takes work to find it.

The outcome of the splice path creates a path that appears to the player to be a direct path around the lake (Figure 3.3.3). This means we are entering the final step of our pathfinding process, the extra-waypoint removal.

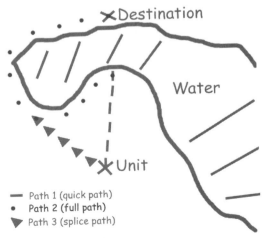

FIGURE 3.3.3 *The splice path goes from the unit's current position to a point along the "full path." Its purpose is to hide any potential errors made by the quick path.*

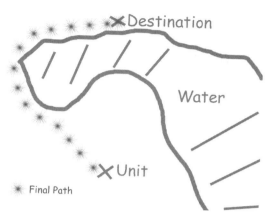

FIGURE 3.3.4 *This is the final path the unit will take to its destination. The path should appear to the user to be one complete path instead of three.*

Since the splice path took a shortcut, we have to prune away all those path points that are no longer needed so at the conclusion of the three-step path process and point pruning, we have a nice attractive path as shows in Figure 3.3.4. The players should now give you a big smile and clap their hands, but they won't. Just be happy that they don't mention pathfinding. If they don't mention it too much, it means you did an outstanding job. I suppose this is why pathfinding is considered high art, since it's all about the player's impressions of it.

Priority Paths

What happens if a unit gets to the end of its quick path before the full path is finished computing? Generally, this is not a happy time, because it means that either the quick path was not long enough to let the full path complete its computation, or that there are lots of units in the game that are currently pathfinding, thus giving less CPU time to each path.

Whatever the reason is, we need to make the unit's "full path" finish. In order to make this happen without dragging the system down, a good technique is to do a priority path. The priority path takes the unit out of the pathfinding queue, sets its max revolutions cap a little bit higher than what it currently is, and then finishes the path.

The method DoPriorityPath from a path manager class would look something like this:

```
PathManager::DoPriorityPath(Unit* inUnit)
{
    // find the pathfinder for this unit.
    Pathfinder* thePath = this->FindPathfinder(inUnit);
```

```
// If we have a node, finish the path right away!
if(thePath != NULL)
{
    // Tell it not to pause.
    thePath->SetPauseCount(-1);

    // let's artificially cap the path so that they
    // don't bring down the CPU.
    thePath->AddToMaxRevolutions(250);

    // go-pher-it..
    thePath->RunAStar();

    // Process the completed path.
    this->ProcessFinishedPath(thePath);

    // Remove this unit's path
    // which includes erasing it from our queue
    this->RemovePath(inUnit);
}
}
```

In *Empire Earth*, we found that the majority of priority paths happen when a unit is on a tile that is as close as it can get to an unreachable destination. This means the moment it paths, the quick path ends right away since it's as close as it can get, and we are faced with an immediate priority path.

Managing the Paths

Now that we know the process of constructing a complete path by combining three paths, we need to examine the process of how these paths are managed. To do this, we should try to hide the details of pathfinding by masking them within a path manager.

There are many important things that the path manager will need to be responsible for, some of which are methods like `DoPriorityPath`, `FindSplicePath`, `FindQuickPath`, and `PostPathProcess`. In addition, it's a great place to hold memory pools of pathfinders, stats about the pathfinding of the game, and, of course, our path queue.

When you make a game with computer players, it's scary that these computer player units could wall themselves in, or get stuck forever trying to path somewhere and drag down system performance. In *Empire Earth*, we kept track of all computer player units' pathfinding. If a computer player unit tried to path from the same source tile to the same destination tile more than 10 times in the span of 30 seconds, we would kill that unit. This seemed to work quite well, and while it weakens the computer player opponent, it's all about player perception—it doesn't matter how good your computer player is if the game runs at two frames per second. Fortunately, by the end of *Empire Earth's* development, we found this situation rarely ever arises, but it's great insurance.

The real heart of the path manager is the path queue. It's where paths go when they are in the "full path" stage so that they have the potential to get processed every game tick. This pathfinding queue is the key to ensuring predictable performance when pathfinding units.

If you want to tune your pathfinding (and we hope you will), you need some system of measurement. The key ingredient to a path-tuning recipe is path revolutions. If you measure the number of revolutions the A* engine has processed, you can control how much flooding the A* algorithm does, how it moves through your path queues, and many more things. Each revolution is a single iteration through the typical A* loop, which consists primarily of:

1. Get the cheapest node.
2. Look at its neighbors (generally eight).
3. Put the node on the closed list.

Why not use time to measure performance? Time would be great if this was a single-player game, but in a multi-player situation, it's fraught with out-of-sync potential. A path might take far less CPU time on player one's brand new XRoyalsRoyce 5000 than on player two's ZXSlothPowered 100. If you measure performance in pathfinding revolutions, you are guaranteed that while player one might compute the path faster than player two, they will both finish on the same game tick, thus not causing the game to go out-of-sync.

The Path Manager Update

Each update of the path manager consists of performing X number of overall revolutions per game tick. It needs to use some type of time-slicing technique to split the number up among the pathfinders in the queue. A few ways to divide the max revolutions per tick among the pathfinders are:

- **Equal time**: Divide the revolutions by the number of paths in the queue. This will ensure that all pathfinding engines get an equal amount of processing time each tick. The downside is that as with all equal-slice schemes, sometimes the pathfinders that really need the extra time don't get it.
- **Progressive**: Start each pathfinder with a low number of max revolutions per tick. Each time through the queue, this number should get larger, so the longer the path seems to be taking, the more time we spend in the queue computing it. Make sure you cap it so it doesn't starve out the other pathfinders. This scheme was used for *Empire Earth*, and it produced the best results.
- **Biased**: In order to get quick paths for the user, you can bias them to get more time compared to other creatures that aren't as critical. Depending on your game, you could classify different factions or units or even use a unit's "human versus computer player" ownership as a means of getting different proportions of pathfinding time.

If you're really interested in different time-slicing schemes, we recommend picking up an operating systems book, such as *Operating System Concepts, 6th Edition,* [Silberschatz01].

An example of the path manager's update follows:

```
// Note: Using Revs as short for Revolutions
// to conserve code space here
// While we have paths to process and haven't
// exceeded our pathfinding revolutions-per-tick cap...
while(this->mPathsQueue.size() &&
        theRevsCompleted < kMaxRevsPerGameTick)
{
        // Get the first pathfinder
        // impl note: mPathsQueue is an STL deque
        thePath = this->mPathsQueue.front();

        // Run, Run, Run!
        thePath->RunAStar();

        // How many revolutions so far?
        theRevsCompleted += thePath->GetRevsThisRun();

        // If we aren't still working, then we are done!
        if (!thePath->GetIsStillWorking())
        {
                // Post processing
                this->ProcessFinishedPath(thePath);
        }
        else
        {
                // Is it less than the max revolutions allowed?
                if(thePath->GetRevsPerRun() < kMaxRevsPerRun)
                {
                        // Set its revolution cap X more
                        // each time so the more often it moves
                        // through the queue, the more it
                        // processes each time.
                        theRevsPerRun = thePath->GetRevsPerRun();
                        thePath->SetRevsPerRun(theRevsPerRun + 1);
                }

                // Take it off the front of the queue
                // and put it on the rear of the queue.
                this->mPathsQueue.push_back(thePath);
        }

        // Remove it from the front.
        this->mPathsQueue.pop_front();
}
```

What Would Edgar Chicken Do?

Remember:

- **Quick path**: Do this to get the unit moving. Use a small, high-speed pathfinder with an early bail-out revolutions cap. The distance of the quick path should be proportional to how busy the path manager's queue is.
- **Full path**: When the instantaneous quick path is complete, path from the end of the quick path to the real destination by splitting it over time and putting the path on the path manager's queue.
- **Priority path**: If a unit finishes walking its quick path before the full path is finished, elevate the path revolutions slightly for the full path, and finish it or bail out. Then, remove it from the pathfinding queue since you're as close as you are going to get.
- **Splice path**: Once the quick path and full path are completed, do another instantaneous, high-speed path from the unit's current position some point further down the complete path (quick path + full path). This will smooth out any errors the quick path made by removing the unit's need for backtracking on its path. Make the splice path look ahead equal to or farther than the quick path's distance. This will make sure you don't have to backtrack because of too short a splice path.
- **Path manager performance tuning**: Use revolutions to balance performance. This makes the game performance consistent, regardless of how many units are pathfinding.
- **Max revolutions per tick**: Use a progressive-revolution or biased scheme for managing which paths get processed each game tick.
- **Tune in**: When you tune the numbers for your splice path and quick path, if you find you're often doing priority paths, then your splice paths aren't long enough. If you backtrack a lot, your splice paths probably aren't long enough, or you need to do a higher-level path scheme first, such as hierarchical pathfinding [Rabin00].

Regardless of how fast your A* engine is, you can probably benefit from using some good, home-cooked, time-sliced pathfinding techniques in your pathfinding architecture.

Thanks to Richard Woolford for the use of Edgar Chicken. (No chickens were harmed in the writing of this article.)

References

[Higgins02a] Higgins, Daniel F., "Generic Pathfinding," *AI Game Programming Wisdom,* 2002.

[Higgins02b] Higgins, Daniel F., "How to Achieve Lightning-Fast A*," *AI Game Programming Wisdom,* 2002.

[Patel00] Patel, Amit J. "Amit's Game Programming Information," available online at www-cs-students.stanford.edu/~amitp/gameprog.html, 2000.

[Silberschatz01] Silberschatz, A.; Galvin, P. B.; and Gagne, G., *Operating System Concepts, 6th Edition*, John Wiley & Sons, 2001.

[Rabin00] Rabin, Steve, "A* Speed Optimizations," *Game Programming Gems*, Charles River Media, 2000.

3.4

How to Achieve
Lightning-Fast A*

Dan Higgins—Stainless Steel Studios, Inc.

webmaster@programming.org

Excluding performance limitations, an A* engine [Higgins02a] that cannot find the achievable path solution, when one is available, is a broken pathfinder. Generally, once we move beyond the bugs of the A* engine, we quickly hit the real problem of pathfinding: performance. Implementing an A* engine that can generate a successful path under real-world time constraints is a beast in itself, the taming of which requires creativity, development time, and, most of all, optimization.

This article details some useful A* optimization tricks and highlights some of the successful strategies discovered when implementing the pathfinding engine for *Empire Earth*. It doesn't focus on the all-important high-level optimization tricks. Instead, we are going into the depths of the pathfinder to see what makes it tick, and to speed it up. Before reading further, you should have a solid understanding of the A* algorithm [Mathews02], [Rabin00].

No "Assembly" Required

Anyone who has purchased a gas grill, or even a desk from a local office-supply store, knows the pain of assembly. None of the optimizations listed in this article require assembly programming. In fact, no assembly code was used for *Empire Earth's* pathfinding engine, and we were quite happy with the performance results. That's not to say that assembly wouldn't have helped, but by the end of the game's development, pathfinding wasn't near the top 20 performance spikes of the game.

Know Thy Tools

Optimization tools are vital for pathfinding development. Without them, it's difficult to gauge the improvement made by a particular optimization. Indeed, it's not uncommon for an optimization to yield opposite results, and instead slow the pathfinding.

There are many tools on the market for profiling code and performance. In *Empire Earth*, we used Intel's VTune along with in-code timers to optimize pathfinding.

"Egads!" you say. Yes, in-code timers aren't without their drawbacks. They can slow processing slightly, and can be somewhat inaccurate, mostly because of multi-threading. With that said, we found timers to be the number-one tool to gauge the pathfinding performance. In *Empire Earth*, we used about 80 percent in-code timers with an essential 20 percent VTune feedback to speed up the code.

Basically, there is no one tool that's going to be the best for optimizing. The timers showed us performance under real-world conditions, but didn't show us branch prediction slowdowns, common cache misses, and expensive source lines. VTune did an excellent job of showing us these issues, as well as gauging overall pathfinding performance progress throughout the *Empire Earth* project. In the beginning and even the middle of our pathfinding optimizations, VTune reported pathfinding spikes that towered over all other performance spikes in the game. By the conclusion of the optimizations, we had to dig deep inside the VTune data in order to find the pathfinding performance. It was also a great tool for helping us develop a roadmap of where we should focus our low-level optimization time.

Timers are great for seeing approximately how long your paths are going to take. They are also tools that can be displayed on the screen, so you can check performance at any time. While they are not 100-percent accurate because other threads might be doing a lot of work and slowing the pathfinding thread, it's still a realistic measurement of improvement. We would run the same path repeatedly while optimizing and watching the time for the path computation fall.

It's vital that you use performance tools, and use whatever gets the job done. You should use your intuition, and then double-check yourself with products such as Intel VTune, and Numega's True Time. Many developers run at the mention of using intuition when optimizing, but it's a good place to start. Make sure you don't just rely on your intuition to optimize. Even if you were a psychic, it would be a big mistake to not double-check your results with a performance-measuring program.

Algorithm Optimizations

This article is mainly about useful, low-level C++ optimizations for A*, but it would be silly to not mention two of the biggest optimizations that aren't C++ related. You should also read the other A* articles in this book for great ideas on other A* optimizations beyond C++.

Pathfind Less

This sounds obvious, but reducing the number of paths, and more importantly, the number of A* revolutions done during the game, can be one of the greatest optimizations. It's crucial that pathfinding not rely on low-level optimizations alone. Whether you do a high-level pathfinding scheme, redefine your search space, bound the amount of A* node flooding, or perform group pathfinding, the "reduce the usage" technique is a great overall way to do some high-level optimization.

Flood Insurance

Watch for the flooding. The A* algorithm floods areas of the map while trying to get to the desired goal, so it's important to measure the amount of flooding the algorithm is doing. Controlling the A* flood is handled by tuning the `TileCost` and `Distance` functions to achieve the right balance of looks, performance, and flooding. Like the typical "memory versus CPU" struggle we programmers commonly face, pathfinding faces a "looks versus performance" struggle. There have been times where one tile would be shaved off in a long path, but it would triple the amount of CPU processing to pull it off. It's a tricky problem, and one that requires careful consideration. If you want that path to look just a little bit neater, is it worth doubling the performance cost?

The way to track flooding (besides showing the number of revolutions) is to draw the search routines on the map. Being able to watch the progress and final outcome of your pathfinding is a must-have debugging tool. It is essential that your graphics team help support this type of onscreen visual support. Otherwise, it's difficult to understand the pathfinder's behavior from numbers alone.

An example of flood tracking is shown in Figure 3.4.1. Notice the dark area on the map. When the pathfinder finishes a path, it loops through all the Open and Closed list nodes, and temporarily darkens the map tiles by changing their terrain. From this picture, you can see how half of the world is darker because the pathfinder

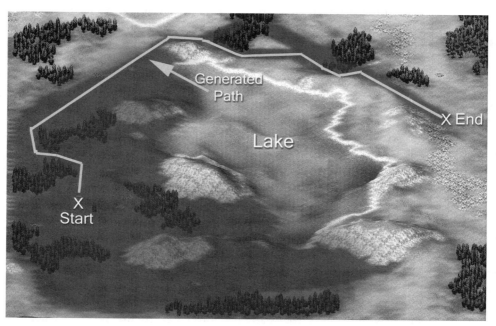

FIGURE 3.4.1 *A complete path with the dark areas of the map indicating the nodes our A* machine examined during the path.*

searched these tiles. That means the path was costly to compute because the lake in the middle of the map blocks the path and causes almost half of the map to be searched until A* can find a way around the lake.

Normally, this would mean that random maps would need to change so that the number of obstacles like this would be minimized. It's never a good day when a programmer has to tell designers that they need to limit their creativity because of the technology.

One of our goals for the pathfinding engine was to not let pathfinding limit the designers' map. Besides dealing with map size in relation to memory constraints, we wanted designers to make the most enjoyable random maps they could without having to worry about the pathfinding friendliness of them. This is one of the many reasons optimization is so important for pathfinding. We're happy to say that pathfinding never became an issue with random map generation.

C++ Is Mightier than the Sword

The main performance bottleneck that we need to conquer for A* to be fast is inside its storage system.

The AStarNode class houses the pathfinding information for a tile that is used by the A* engine. While most of the time STL is the right choice for data structures, this is a situation where the specialized A* Node list can benefit from *not* using STL, and instead manage its own linked list structures. It will be vital since at some point, you might want the option to do tricks with the linked-list nodes, and every microsecond you can shave off in pathfinding is beneficial.

```cpp
// A Star Node
struct AStarNode
{
    inline AStarNode(long inX = 0, long inY = 0)
    : mX(inX),mY(inY),mTotalCost(0), mCostOfNode(0),
      mCostToDestination(0),mParent(NULL),mNext(NULL),
      mListParent(NULL) { }

    AStarNode* mParent;       // who opened me?
    AStarNode* mNext;         // Next in my list
    AStarNode* mListParent;   // my list Parent
    long mTotalCost;          // f
    long mCostOfNode;         // g
    long mCostToDestination;  // h (estimate)
    long mX;                  // Tile X
    long mY;                  // Tile Y
};
```

The first thing to do is to pool all those A* nodes. Unless you're under very tight memory constraints, why waste precious CPU fetching memory when you're going to need it again during the next path?

An overall strategy for how much to pool could be difficult to come up with, since it needs to be so game specific. One of the memory-pooling estimation techniques we used was to figure out what the average "bad case" scenario was for the game. You don't want to waste memory with lots of nodes that never get used, but on the other hand, you don't want to make it so small that 50 percent of the time, you're reaching outside your memory pool.

A good place to start is to make a template memory pool class and have it keep statistics. At the shutdown of every game, it would dump memory pool statistics from all over the game. A sample output is:

MemoryPool< class SomeClass >: Stats are:

Requests: 97555
Deletions: 97555
Peak usage: 890
NormalNews: 0
NormalDelete: 0

This output tells you that we hit this pool hard and often, since there were over 97,000 requisitions of memory. It also tells us that the peak usage isn't that high, so the pool doesn't have to be that big. On something that is hit this often, it's probably a good idea to have it larger than the normal "peak usage" so that we don't have to dip into the "normal new and delete" area very often.

Unless you are writing for a platform with very limited memory, implementing a memory pool of `AstarNode structures` and memory pooling a fleet of pathfinders will save a lot of time that would otherwise be wasted in memory management. Explore what possibilities you have in terms of memory pooling. If you are working in a small and fixed memory environment, there might not be much you can do with pooling.

Start Your Engines!

The first performance issue to resolve is that of caching. Often, we need to know the state of an A* node, such as which list it's on, or if its been marked as a blocking tile. It's crucial that information like this be easily and quickly accessible. If we don't come up with a fast lookup system and instead rely on linear searches, we should just sell off the users' extra CPU because apparently we don't need it!

An easy solution to this that really pays off is to have an array of 1-byte flags that store state information and can be retrieved by a simple array lookup. Each flag in the array should be 1 byte per tile, and the array should be the size of the maximum search space (or map).

While there are many things one could put into the flags array, you only need five states:

- **Clear**: This node is unexamined and could be blocking or not blocking, and is guaranteed to not be on any of our A* lists.
- **Passable**: This node is passable for A*. If this is set, we know we have examined this node already and we do *not* have the "'blocked" state.

- **Blocked**: This node is blocked for A*. If this is set, we know we have examined this node already and we do *not* have the "'passable'" state.
- **Open**: This node is on the Open list and is *not* on the Closed list.
- **Closed**: This node is on the Closed list and is *not* on the Open list.

```
typedef unsigned char AStarNodeStatusFlags;
enum
{
    kClear    = 0x00, //empty, unexamined.
    KPassable = 0x01, //examined, node is not blocked
    KBlocked  = 0x02, //examined, node is blocked
    KOpen     = 0x04, //node is on the open list
    KClosed   = 0x08  //node is on the closed list
};
```

Using bit wise AND/OR operations on our flags array, we can quickly see if we have yet to visit a node, or if a node is blocked, open, closed, or passable.

Methods on the A* storage class that use these flags include:

```
// Gets the flag from the array
inline AStarNodeStatusFlags* GetFlag(long inX, long inY)
{ //add your own ASSERT check to ensure no array overruns.
  return this->mFlags + ((inX * this->mArrayMax) + inY); }

// returns true if the node is closed
inline bool GetIsClosed(AStarNodeStatusFlags* inFlag) const
{ return ((*inFlag & kClosed) != kClear); }

// clears the 'passable status' flag
inline void ClearPassableFlag(AStarNodeStatusFlags* inFlag)
{ *inFlag &= ~kPassable; }

// sets the 'open status' flag
inline void SetOpenFlag(AStarNodeStatusFlags* inFlag)
{ *inFlag |= kOpen; }
```

Using the flags in creative ways will go a long way in making the A* engine run well. A good use of the open/closed status is that whenever you need to retrieve a node, you can check the flag to see which list to search so that you don't need to search both lists for the node. Therefore, if you have a FindNodeInOpenList method, the first thing to do inside it is to check the flags array to see if the node is even on the Open list, and thus warrants searching for. If you're sweating the initialization of this array, don't panic; it's solved in the *Beating Memset* section later in this article.

"Egad!" you exclaim? Not enough memory for your maps? Unless you're writing for a console or smaller, there is a solution. You don't have to fit the entire map into your search space. Instead, you can use a sliding window system similar to Figure 3.4.2. Consider that the max search space you can afford to search is 62,500 tiles at one time. Make your array 250 × 250, and center your unit or start position in the center of the area. You will have to convert all game XY coordinates into this sliding

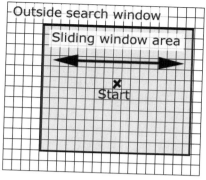

FIGURE 3.4.2 *A sliding window that is the virtual "XY map" used by the A* machine. This enables the A* machine to use smaller flag arrays.*

windows coordinate system in the `GetFlag` array call, but otherwise, things should work normally. If you need to search an area more than say, 300,000 tiles at once, you probably need to break up your path into a higher-level path first.

Breaking through the Lists Barrier

What really hurts in an A* implementation is searching through the lists of nodes. If we can break through the lists barrier, we'll be well on our way to warp-speed pathfinding.

Breaking the Open and Closed Lists

A good technique to increase the list performance is to make the Open and Closed lists hash tables. Depending on how you tune your hash function, you can end up with a table of equally balanced hash-table buckets, thus trimming down the search lists to something much more manageable. This technique makes long-distance pathfinding much easier on the CPU.

Here is an example method that uses the hash table. This method adds a node to the Closed list hash table and set its closed status flag. It's called from the A* engine whenever we close a node.

```
AStarStorage::AddNodeToClosedList(AStarNode* inNode)
{
    // Generate a hash code.
    long theHash = this->Hash(inNode->mX, inNode->mY);

    // Drop it into that list, and setup list pointers.
    if(this->mClosedLists[theHash] != NULL)
        this->mClosedLists[theHash]->mListParent = inNode;

    // the current bucket head is now our next node.
    inNode->mNext = this->mClosedLists[theHash];

    // This is now the head of this bucket's list.
    this->mClosedLists[theHash] = inNode;
```

```
    // set the closed node flag
    this->SetClosedFlag(this->GetFlag(inNode->mX, inNode->mY));
}
```

It's important to carefully tune both the size of your hash table and your hash function to achieve optimum performance. These two, if tuned well, can create a relatively even distribution throughout the hash table.

Never assume that just because you have a hash table, performance is better.

Over the long course of pathfinding optimization, we were constantly reminded how tweaking a number in certain functions could backfire, and make pathfinding twice as expensive. So, the rule is, have a reliable test suite of saved games, and every time you adjust a number, run through the tests again to see what impact it will have in a variety of situations.

We found that 53 was a good hash-table size, which helped give us a remarkably even distribution throughout the table and yet wasn't too large to make complete iteration expensive. The distribution element of the hash table depends much more on your hash function, so spend some time making that as good as possible.

Be a Cheapskate

When writing an A* engine, there are normally two options on how to store the Open list. The first method, which is preferred by most A* authors, is to have the Open list be a sorted heap structure that allows for fast removal, but slower insertion. The second method is to have an unsorted list where insertion is fast, but removal is slow.

After experimenting with different sorted structures, we found that we had better overall performance if we went with the unsorted Open list and got the fast insertions, $O(1)$, at the cost of slow removals, $O(n)$. The main reason for this was that we had a 1:8 ratio of removal operations to insertion operations. A typical iteration through the pathfinding loop would always remove one node from the Open list, but had the potential to do eight insertions. This was significant because we "reinsert" nodes back onto the Open list during pathfinding if we find a cheaper parent for the node. We do the reinsertion step because it will smooth the ending path; however, it has the unfortunate cost of doing more insertions into the Open list.

Even though we went with the unsorted list technique, the performance was still unimpressive, and when it came time to optimize the Open list spike, we had to look for alternative storage techniques. We figured the perfect situation for getting the cheapest node would be to grab the top node without having to worry about searching for it, much like what the sorted heap option offers. The downside is that in order to do this, we must have some sorted list structure. Sounds great, but in doing so we needed to eliminate the hit of sorted inserts that kept us from that design in the first place. The answer was in the marriage of the two ideas, which lead to the creation of the *cheap list*.

The cheap list is a list of about 15 nodes that are the cheapest on the Open list. When the A* engine calls the `RemoveLeastCostNodeInOpenList` method, all we do is remove the top node in the cheap list. If our cheap list is empty, then we refill it with 15 new entries.

To fill the cheap list, we make a single pass through the entire Open list and store the 15 cheapest nodes. This way, we don't have to do any node searching until at least 15 revolutions later.

In addition, whenever we add a node to the Open list, we first do a check to see if the node is cheap enough to be in the cheap list by checking the node on the end of the cheap list. If it costs more than the cheap list end node, the new node goes onto the top of the general Open list. Otherwise, we do the "sorted insert" into a list that is roughly 15 nodes deep.

This means that sometimes the list grows more than 15 long, which is ok, since we don't incur a cost when pulling from the cheap list when its not empty. We only get the performance hit when the cheap list empties and we make our run through the Open list to refill it.

We found that 15 was a good number to use for the size of the cheap list. It kept the sorted insert time low, and provided enough cached nodes so that we didn't get the list-refilling performance hit very often.

This doesn't mean we can always avoid doing insertions into the Open list during the normal A* neighbor checks. If a node was already on the Open list, and there was a new (and cheaper) cost for it, then we would do a fast check to see if it was cheaper than the end of the cheap list. If not, we left it (or moved it) into the general Open list. Otherwise, we would have to do a fast reinsertion into the cheap list. Even if we found that we couldn't avoid doing this reinsertion, that's ok since it's a fast process with a sorted insert into a very short list.

A further enhancement list would be to limit the cheap list to 15 nodes so that if we did an insertion into the cheap list, which was 15 deep already, we could pop the end of the cheap list and put it back on the top of the general (and unsorted) Open list. This means we would never be inserting into a list more than 15 deep, thus keeping the sorted insertion time more predictable.

This "cheap list" might sound rather strange, but it worked remarkably well. The `RemoveLeastCostNodeInOpenList` spike was obliterated without making the method `AddNodeToOpenList` become a spike. Huzzah! The two ideas put together came out with an ideal situation in which neither method was a speed hit. It gave wings to our long-distance pathfinders and enabled them to run fast and furious across our worlds.

Fast Storage

In *Empire Earth*, all of the quick paths, splice paths, and terrain analysis (see [Higgins02b]) use a fast-storage system that used more memory but had blazing speed. Because the added memory is expensive, we had only one fast-storage pathfinder for the entire game, and would not do any time-slicing within it. It was used for any instantaneous paths that needed to be generated.

It achieved the speed by eliminating all the node searches except for the cheap list updates. We did this by deriving from `AStarStorage`, and like the flags array, there is an array the size of the map, which is 4 bytes instead of 1 byte, per tile. It was an array of pointers to nodes so that there was no need to do any linear searches.

If you don't want to incur a pointer per-tile memory hit, you could use an STL map, set, hash_map, or hash_set to do fast lookups. We didn't implement this scheme, so we can't judge its performance. It's certainly not going to be as fast as an array lookup, and will come with a CPU cost for insertion/lookups that might not be worthwhile, but it's something worth exploring.

This did not mean we removed all the other A* lists, we simply used this in addition to them. We derived from the normal A* implementation and overloaded some of its methods. Since the A* machine uses templates, we were able to inline most methods without having to make anything virtual.

The following is an example of some of the FastStorage methods that were overloaded:

```
inline void AddNodeToOpenList(AStarNode* inNode)
{ // call base class version.
  AStarStorage::AddNodeToOpenList(inNode);
  // Add it to our own node sliding window array.
  this->AddNodeToNodeTable(inNode->mX, inNode->mY, inNode);
}

inline AStarNode* FindNodeInClosedList(long inX, long inY)
{ // the flags array will tell us if we should return it
    if(this->GetIsClosed(this->GetFlagForTile(inX,inY))
        return this->GetNodeFromNodeTable(inX, inY);
    else
        return NULL;
}
```

Beating Memset

The fast storage suffers from one major performance issue, the function memset, which is used to clear the pooled nodes before reuse of the pooled pathfinder. It was the final obstacle in the months of triumph and turmoil of pathfinding optimization. It was the last VTune spike in pathfinding, and seemed impossible to defeat. How could we beat memset? Should we write an assembly version?

After long speculation, we discovered that this spike could be crushed by using a dirty rectangle scheme. Since most of the A* machines are memory- pooled, and there is only one `FastStorage` based pathfinder, there is no need to clear the entire flags/Nodes array each time we path. Instead, during pathfinding, we expand a rectangle to encompass the area of the map we have searched, and clear only that area with memset.

The flags/nodes array is not a typical 2D array; it is a one-dimensional array that is laid end to end to simulate a 2D array.

The following is an excerpt from the `FastStorage`'s `ResetPathfinder` method. (Note: 1. `theBox` is a 2D integer rectangle that represents the bounds of what we searched LAST path with this pathfinder. In a sense, what is DIRTY. 2. theBoxes' Left is the lowest X and Top returns is the lowest Y coordinate. 3. theBoxes' Right is the highest X and Bottom is the highest Y.)

```
// Get the X offset where we will begin to memset from.
theXOffset = ((theBox.GetLeft() * mMaxX)+ theBox.GetTop());

// Get the amount we will need to clear.
theAmountToClear = (((theBox.GetRight() * mMaxX) +
                 theBox.GetBottom()) - theXOffset);

// memset NODE array using the Xoffset and AmountToClear
::memset(this->mNodes + theXOffset, NULL,
        theAmountToClear * sizeof(AStarNode*));

// Reset the flags array using the same dirty rectangle
::memset(this->mFlags + theXOffset, kClear,
        theAmountToClear * sizeof(AStarNodeStatusFlags));
```

You should have a debug-only method that iterates the entire map and makes sure that each array slot is initialized correctly. It will make your life much easier to know that the arrays are always clean each time you pathfind without getting a release mode speed hit.

What Would Edgar Chicken Do?

Remember!

- Optimizing is everything for the pathfinder.
- Read all the articles about A* in this book.
- High-level optimizations are more powerful than low-level optimizations, but pathfinding should incorporate both high- and low-level optimizations. Make the game's units pathfind less, control the A* algorithms flooding, and trade looks for performance unless you can afford the CPU.
- An A* engine is as good as the debugging tools you have.
  Develop tools to track floods, performance times, revolutions, and so forth. Use VTune, hand-timers, True Time, and any other performance tool you are comfortable using. If you don't have any or aren't comfortable with any performance monitoring tools, there is no better motivation than tuning pathfinding to become acquainted with some. Do *not* rely solely on your intuition for optimization, but also be sure you don't forget to use it.

- Pool, pool, pool that memory. If you are not severely limited on memory usage, you're throwing CPU out the window if you don't do some type of pooling. Use limits on your pools to handle typical situations, thus reducing the potential that you'll be hogging memory that won't be used.
- Don't use STL for your list structures. While STL is amazing, pathfinding warrants a hand-written linked-list and hash-table system.
- Make a flags array to indicate the state of each node. If the array is 1 byte per tile, it's well worth the memory for the incredible lookup speed and optimization tricks it can enable.
- If you can't afford the memory to dedicate to a flags array, try using a sliding window system and use as much memory as you can afford.
- Transform those Open and Closed lists into hash tables, and make sure to play with the hash function and size of the table to get the best distribution and performance.
- Use a cheap list to eliminate the sorted-insert spike, or the "search for the cheapest node on the Open list" spike.
- Write a fast storage class that has an array of pointers to nodes for ultra-fast node searches. This is more memory intensive, so only have one unless you can afford the memory.
- Long-distance pathfinders could use an STL map, set, hash_map, hash_set to store all nodes for fast lookups. Experiment with this; it may or may not be a benefit to your pathfinder.
- Beat memset with a dirty rectangle scheme. This applies to pooled pathfinders, and always do a complete clear the first time you use the pathfinder.
- Think "how can I pathfind less," or better yet, "how can I reliably pathfind across this giant space by doing short paths?"

At the end of our pathfinding optimizations, we were really happy with *Empire Earth's* pathfinding performance. We could path hundreds of units from one side of the world to the other without bringing the user experience down, and we've yet to see a case in which they didn't path successfully to their destination if it was reachable. All of these are the result of optimizations; the faster the pathfinder, the farther we can path out, which means a higher success rate for paths.

Finally, our last two pieces of advice are obvious. First, read everything you can from people who have pathfinding experience. You might learn what to do, and, as importantly, what *not* to do. The second is to look to your teammates for help. Teamwork at Stainless Steel Studios was a major factor in increasing performance of pathfinding, and we couldn't have done it without them. Bravo to them!

Thanks to Richard Woolford for the use of Edgar Chicken. (No chickens were harmed in the writing of this article.)

References

[Higgins02a] Higgins, Daniel F., "Generic A* Pathfinding," *AI Game Programming Wisdom*, Charles River Media, 2002.

[Higgins02b] Higgins, Daniel F., "Pathfinding Design Architecture," *AI Game Programming Wisdom*, Charles River Media, 2002.

[Matthews02] Matthews, James, "Basic A* Pathfinding Made Simple," *AI Game Programming Wisdom*, Charles River Media, 2002.

[Rabin00] Rabin, Steve, "A* Speed Optimizations," *Game Programming Gems*, Charles River Media, 2000.

[Patel00] Patel, Amit J., "Amit's Game Programming Information," available online at www-cs-students.stanford.edu/~amitp/gameprog.html, 2000.

3.5

Practical Optimizations for A* Path Generation

Timothy Cain—Troika Games

cain@troikagames.com

The A* algorithm is probably the most widely used path algorithm in games, but it suffers from classic time-space limitations. In its pure form, A* can use a great deal of memory and take a long time to execute. In fact, its worst-case scenario occurs when looking for a path when none are available, which is quite common in many games. Most articles on A* deal with improving the estimate heuristic or with storing and searching the Open and Closed lists more efficiently. Instead, this article examines methods of restricting A* to make it faster and more responsive to changing map conditions.

Such A* restrictions take the form of artificially constricting the search space, using partial solutions, or short-circuiting the algorithm altogether. For each restriction, the situations in which these optimizations will prove most useful are discussed. These optimizations allowed the efficient use of A* in *Arcanum*, a real-time roleplaying game with a large number of player-controlled and computer-controlled agents.

When referring to internal workings of the A* algorithm, the terms from [Stout00] will be used. For example, the list of unexamined nodes will be called the Open list, and the heuristic cost estimate will be referred to as CostToGoal. This article assumes an intimate knowledge of the basic A* pathfinding algorithm, and [Matthews02] in this book is an excellent introduction.

Iterative Deepening

A powerful optimization to apply to A* is iterative deepening, which is a method of imposing an artificial limit on the search algorithm. This limit can be anything that reduces the total search space of the algorithm. Iterative deepening for A* means to call the algorithm repeatedly, starting with a small limit on the central loop iterations, maximum path length, or maximum memory used. If a call to A* fails to find a path, iterative deepening gradually relaxes the limit in subsequent calls until the search succeeds or the limit reaches its maximum value. This method uses less memory for most calls because the artificial limit causes fewer nodes to be examined. Iterative deepening also speeds up the detection of almost-straight paths and improves performance in environments where other agents can temporarily block paths.

Iterative deepening can be easily added to A* by adding an extra parameter that acts as a limit for that call. This parametric limit can be the number of iterations of the central A* loop to allow, or the maximum amount of memory to use, or the maximum path length to allow. If the initial call to A* fails to find a path, then subsequent calls can increase this limit by a small amount. By starting with a small limit, iterative deepening forces A* to use less memory on the first few calls in its series of failed calls, meaning that it will reach failure condition more quickly in each of those calls.

In situations in which an almost straight-line path exists, such as a path with one tree in the way (Figure 3.5.1), a call to A* with a small limit will still find the path. The search algorithm just has to try a few locations on either side of the tree before it finds the correct path. By keeping the limit small, A* will avoid using (and therefore initializing) a large memory space of nodes.

The true power of this optimization comes from the observation that the subsequent calls to A* *do not need to be made immediately*. If the initial call fails, a small delay can be added before a subsequent call is made. This delay provides other game functions a chance for processing time, and smoothes the game's apparent performance. The extra time also allows any mobile blocking objects a chance to clear out of the way, which is a common cause for pathing failure in games.

For example, imagine that several agents attempt to enter a room through a single door. As soon as the first agent steps into the doorway (Figure 3.5.2), he blocks this path for the other agents, and they will spend a great deal of time fruitlessly searching for other paths that do not exist (which, as stated previously, is the worst-case scenario

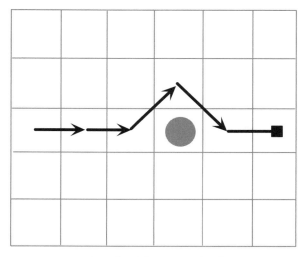

FIGURE 3.5.1 *A path with one tree in the way.*

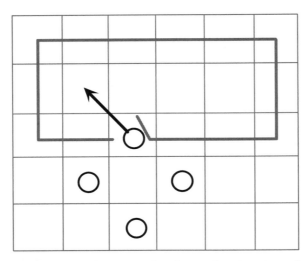

FIGURE 3.5.2 *A room with only one door into it, and several people trying to enter.*

for A*). By using iterative deepening, the blocked agents will make calls to A* with small limiting values that do not consume much search time. Before those limits can be increased too much in subsequent calls, the path will again become clear and another agent can enter the room through the door.

Iterative deepening is not always useful. When no path is possible, iterative deepening will actually *increase* the amount of time spent pathfinding. However, it is helpful in any game in which changing terrain conditions can cause paths to become blocked or unblocked over time. These changing conditions could be mobile blocking objects such as creatures that temporarily block paths as they move. They could also be immobile objects that change their blocking status, such as a force field that flickers on and off, allowing agents to pass through sporadically. In these cases, iterative deepening helps A* avoid spending too much processing time looking for paths that are temporarily blocked.

For more information on iterative deepening and its advantages and disadvantages as a general search method, see [Nilsson98].

Closing Blocked Nodes Immediately

When removing the least-cost node from the open list and examining its successors, one of the child nodes might be impassable. For example, the child could be a blocked node and no movement is possible through it. Whatever the reason, you can add the child node to the Closed list immediately. This operation will prevent high (actually, infinite) cost nodes from being appended to the Open list. In addition, depending on how the Open list is stored, this operation could speed up subsequent removals from the Open list by keeping the Open list smaller.

This optimization might seem obvious, but many implementations of A* use a simple formula to generate all successors of a particular node rather than just the unblocked ones. An example would be a grid where we return the eight surrounding nodes and rely on the traversal cost function to assign high costs to blocked nodes so that they are not selected by the removal function of the Open list. In a search space where many nodes can be blocked, this method results in many blocked nodes being added to the Open list. Depending on the implementation of the Open list, a large list will cause more work, and also cause extra time to be spent in either the insertion or the subsequent removal from the list.

Closing Off Multiple Paths Simultaneously

An often overlooked aspect of paths is *how* they are used by the game can be used to constrain *how* A* looks for them. For many games, the cost metric is the total length of the path, and A* searches for the shortest path. If the game cannot make use of paths longer than X steps (due to memory or animation limitations), then A* can ignore any node N whose TotalCost (which is CostFromStart + CostToGoal) exceeds X. Since the heuristic estimate CostToGoal is always an underestimate (to guarantee an optimal path), any path made with node N is guaranteed to be longer than X steps. Therefore, A* can abandon examining this node, and add it to the Closed list

Alternatively, A* can avoid generating these high-cost nodes altogether. When generating successor nodes, A* knows the cost of the parent node and can simply not generate any successors that have exceeded the required cost. This method avoids having to add nodes to the Closed list.

Additionally, as soon as the next popped node from the Open list has a TotalCost that exceeds X, A* can stop searching immediately and return failure. Since the popped node is guaranteed to have the lowest TotalCost of any node yet examined, A* now knows that the game cannot use any of the paths containing nodes on its Open list. In effect, A* has closed off every remaining path that can be formed from nodes in its Open list without having to examine any of them.

This optimization works well with other cost metrics besides path length. For example, the cost metric might be some form of terrain-based action cost in which the agent must spend some of his action points to move through that terrain type. Each agent might have a fixed number of action points to spend on each turn (or per second), and the game can pass in the agent's maximum available action points to A*. When TotalCost exceeds this maximum, the node can be added to the Closed list. Moreover, when the next popped node from the Open list exceeds this maximum, A* can immediately return failure.

Returning Partial Paths

If A* fails to find a path to the destination, either because none exists or because it reaches an imposed limit, it can usually return a partial path. This partial path can be the path with the smallest TotalCost, or the path with the minimum CostToGoal estimate on its final node. The former path is a fragment of the estimated shortest path to the destination, while the latter path gets the agent as close to its destination as possible without actually getting there.

The game can use these partial paths, along with iterative deepening, to make its computer-controlled agents more responsive. Each agent can call A* with a small parametric limit, and if a partial path is returned, the agent can begin to move along this path immediately. He can move along the path until reaching its end and then call A* again, or he can continue to call A* after each step with a slightly larger parametric value. The agent eventually will either find a path to the destination or come to rest at a location close to the destination. In either case, the agent will appear to be doing something, instead of just standing there and slowing the game with repeatedly failing calls to A*.

Partial paths can even provide the semblance of humanlike thinking to computer-controlled agents. They might begin to run one way, then appear to "change their minds," and head off in a new direction. Instead of appearing to have a godlike knowledge of their surroundings, they will explore their environment, even if that means going down blind alleys and backtracking. In some games, this behavior might be desirable.

Caching Failed Searches

As stated, the worst-case scenario for A* is searching for a path between two locations when no such path exists. By caching failed start-destination pairs, repeated calls to A* can avoid unnecessary work. This optimization is especially helpful in situations in which a computer-controlled agent is "stuck" and is making repeated calls to A* to get to his destination. After the first call fails, no additional search must be performed.

If mobile objects can block movement, then the entire cache should be cleared whenever a mobile object changes its location. While this might seem restrictive, in many situations in which game slow-down would be most noticeable, such as during combat, most agents do not change their location after initially moving (usually to the player's vicinity).

Similarly, a change to a blocking condition in any tile should cause the cache to be flushed. However, in any case, keeping the cache small is a good thing, since it must be checked before each call to A*. The benefit of the cache would be lost if it takes longer to search it than to actually perform an A* search.

Limiting Time Spent in A*

Another method to prevent slow-downs in real-time games is to limit the amount of time A* can spend searching for paths. One way to do this is to keep track of elapsed time during each iteration of an A* search; in other words, at each pop off the Open list. The search is aborted if the total time exceeds a preset value (but the search can possibly return a partial path to be used). This method will reduce game pauses due to long searches, but might prevent long paths from ever being discovered, especially on slower machines.

Alternatively, the time spent for each completed search can be totaled, and when this total exceeds a value, no more searches are allowed for a set period of time. This method allows long paths to be discovered, but might delay other agents from moving until searches are again allowed. Again, on slower machines, agents will be delayed more often. Depending on the nature of your game, one or both of these restrictions might be necessary to achieve good performance.

Both of these restrictions are useful in single-player games or in multi-player games in which the server generates the paths. However, in multi-player games in which each client can generate paths, restricting time can cause the various clients to become out-of-sync with each other. Instead, the algorithm should limit the total number of iterations of the central A* loop. See [Higgins02] for more details.

Offering Waypoints to Player-Controlled Agents

Humans are very good at seeing paths, so a human player can assist any pathing algorithm by selecting intermediate points, or waypoints, along a potential route. Instead of finding one long path, A* must find several shorter paths that connect to form a long path. Given the nature of the A* algorithm, the sum of several shorter path calculations is usually smaller than the longer path calculation.

In addition, using waypoints can make the game feel more responsive. Since the shorter path segments take less time for A* to discover, the player-controlled agent can begin moving to the first waypoint almost immediately. While that agent is moving, the paths to the subsequent waypoints can be calculated and stored. One caveat, however: any change to a blocking condition on these stored waypoint paths will require that path to be recalculated.

Avoiding A* Altogether

Always be on the lookout for situations in which you should *not* immediately use A*. As suggested in [Rabin00], first use a cheaper path algorithm, such as testing the straight-line path, to see if a simple path is available. Such simple paths are frequently available, and using the cheaper algorithm avoids the overhead involved in setting up A*.

Another way to avoid frequently calling A* for computer-controlled agents is to set up their waypoints to take advantage of straight-line pathing (in fact, your map tool could *enforce* this requirement on preset waypoints). For example, the left agent in Figure 3.5.3 needs to use A* to walk to his four waypoints, but the right agent in Figure 3.5.3 can use a straight-line path algorithm.

Another option is to not find a path at all. If neither the start nor the destination point is visible to the human player, you can always move a computer-controlled agent directly to the destination point without the human player being aware of your

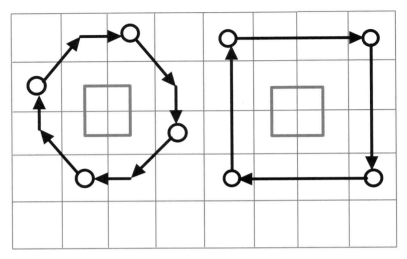

FIGURE 3.5.3 *A* (left) versus straight-line (right).*

transgression. This "optimization" is completely unnoticeable when employed on distant agents where the player would not see them moving along any part of their path.

Conclusion

Pathfinding in games is often an inefficient process, and using A* can be a computational time sink. By restricting how and when A* can search for paths, and by making good use of partial paths, a game can often reduce the time spent pathfinding by a significant amount.

References

[Higgins02] Higgins, Daniel, "Pathfinding Design Architecture," *AI Game Programming Wisdom*, Charles River Media, 2002.

[Matthews02] Matthews, James, "Basic A* Pathfinding Made Simple," *AI Game Programming Wisdom*, Charles River Media, 2002.

[Nilsson98] Nilsson, Nils J., *Artificial Intelligence: A New Synthesis*, Morgan Kaufmann Publishers, 1998.

[Rabin00] Rabin, Steve, "A* Speed Optimizations," *Game Programming Gems*, pp. 272–287. Charles River Media, 2000.

[Stout00] Stout, Bryan, "The Basics of A* for Path Planning," *Game Programming Gems*, pp. 254–263. Charles River Media, 2000.

PATHFINDING AND MOVEMENT

Simple, Cheap Pathfinding

Mike Mika and Chris Charla—
Digital Eclipse
mikem@digitaleclipse.com,
chrisc@digitaleclipse.com

As computing power in video game consoles and PCs has improved, artificial intelligence in games has advanced leaps and bounds over the primitive efforts seen in early games such as *Defender*, or Atari's *Adventure*. Today's game machines have CPU power that puts to shame even many university setups of 10 or 15 years ago, and AI schemes are rapidly rising to the level enabled by this technology. At the same time, the rise of gaming on limited computing devices, such as hand-held organizers and cell phones, and the continuing popularity of low-powered hand-held gaming systems (namely the Game Boy Color and Game Boy Advance) means that the demand for light-weight, tricky AI continues.

There are several cases in which using a lightweight AI method is appropriate. First, it might be the only thing you *can* use, especially if you're coding for the tight confines of a cell phone or Game Boy. Second, even on more robust hardware, light AI schemes can be applied to many (or in the case of our scheme, hundreds of) different creatures or objects simultaneously. Finally, we've probably all been guilty of over-engineering a solution to a problem. Sometimes it's better to start with the simplest possible solution, and then build up from there, rather than starting with something more complicated. Our scheme, which simulates a four-sensored, or whiskered robot, is about as simple as it gets! It is, computationally, incredibly cheap, yet generates surprisingly lifelike results. We have used it successfully in a number of published games for the Game Boy Color (including *NFL Blitz*, *Disney's Tarzan*, and *Alice in Wonderland*), as well as in several in-development works for mobile devices.

Weighted Nodes

This technique for pathfinding and movement relies on *weighted nodes*. We surround each object with an array of sensors that check for elements of repulsion and attraction. At its simplest, we work with a five-node object: one in the center, and one in each of the cardinal directions. The analogue is to a (theoretical) animal with four long whiskers extending beyond its body, or to a robot that has four sensors extending in each of the cardinal directions, and a single, magic, omnidirectional drive wheel located at the center. Even with a simple five-node object, the movement generated is surprisingly natural. With the appropriate sprite/graphic, this behavior can be very convincing using only a small amount of code.

The way the system works is essentially identical to the way whiskers work in a mammal. Each whisker—or sensor—on the "robot," when it senses anything but empty space, increases its value. The higher the value, the more it pushes the bot. For example, when the "east" sensor has a value higher than the "west" sensor, the bot begins to move westward.

Combining the bot with various attractors and repulsors—either an inherent bias in one direction (constantly decreasing the west bias on the bot, for instance) or a location (wall) or mobile object (other bot, player character, etc.)—we find that the bot quickly develops convincing behavior.

One of the reasons this behavior is convincing is that it is anticipatory: As the bot moves closer to a repulsor object (or a repulsor object moves closer to the bot) and the weight on the node increases, the bot naturally begins to move away. The sensors have a radius of detection, and the sensors themselves are located an arbitrary distance from the center node. This essentially gives the bot the apparent capability of visual comprehension: rather than bumping off an object, the bot appears to see it, and moves away, slowly at first, and then more quickly as the weight on the "whisker" grows.

This is a pretty common-sense system for programmers, but it is rarely used. Many games employ accelerators that are applied to the X- or Y-axis of a character. The problem with this technique is that it is often very easy to sneak up on a bot if you move diagonally toward the center node. With our scheme, it is very hard to do this. Another advantage to "whiskers" is that a bot will fall to an idle state when all sensors are off. In many other methods, bots are always running to or away from a target, or the program needs to check distance between the bot and its target and enter an idle state when out of a certain range. This works, but it requires more code than strictly necessary—a major factor when trying to cram code and art assets onto a 4MB cart, or a <100K cell-phone program!

The Key Routine

ON THE CD

The following text and code refers to the sample program and code included on the companion CD. Each sensor in this version can detect collision within a certain pixel radius. For this demonstration, the per-pixel detection is overkill, since this type of sensor will most likely rely on a higher-level collision mechanism. Regardless, it still works and demonstrates, even with overkill, how little processing is necessary for the behavior. The definition of sradius is the pixel sensitivity of the sensor, whereas distance is how far from the center point of the object the sensors are placed. The value repel is the amount of push the sensors exhibit when triggered, while bots is the number of bots to use in the example.

```
#define sradius         24    /*Sensor Radius*/
#define distance        8     /*Sensor offset from Bot*/
#define repel           .08   /*Sensor repel strength*/
#define bots            32    /*Number of Bots*/
```

For the *westbias.exe*, we adjusted westbias with a value of push, say, .08. This trips the sensor continually in that direction, causing the bots to rush across the screen. For actual applications, it's recommended that you switch to a more dynamic value, perhaps changing bias based on an onscreen attractor.

```
/*Bias, used to push bot in desired direction*/
#define northbias       0
#define southbias       0
#define eastbias        0
#define westbias        .08
```

The core routine is very simple. In our example, we simply check all four sensors per bot and adjust our push, or weight, per sensor. It is that simple. As you can see from the following code, we simply check for pixels other than the designated background, and adjust push accordingly. The more pixels in the sensitivity zone, the greater the push; this creates an organic behavior pattern.

```
for (c=0;c<bots;c++)        /* Update Array of Bots */
{

    for (x=0;x<sradius;x++)  /* Check West sensor on Bot */
    {
        for (y=0;y<sradius;y++)
            if (getpixel(vfb,BotPosx[c]-distance+x,BotPosy[c]+y))
                w_west[c]=w_west[c]+repel;
    }
    for (x=0;x<sradius;x++) /* Check East sensor on Bot */
    {
        for (y=0;y<sradius;y++)
            if (getpixel(vfb,BotPosx[c]+distance+x,BotPosy[c]+y))
                w_east[c]=w_east[c]+repel;
    }
    for (x=0;x<sradius;x++) /* Check North sensor on Bot */
    {
      for (y=0;y<sradius;y++)
            if (getpixel(vfb,BotPosx[c]+x,BotPosy[c]+y-distance))
                w_north[c]=w_north[c]+repel;
    }
    for (x=0;x<sradius;x++) /* Check South sensor on Bot */
    {
        for (y=0;y<sradius;y++)
            if (getpixel(vfb,BotPosx[c]+x,BotPosy[c]+y+distance))
                w_south[c]=w_south[c]+repel;
    }
```

Once we check each sensor for the current bot, we then apply the modified push variables before addressing the next bot.

```
/* Modify Bot position with Sensor data */
   BotPosx[c] = BotPosx[c]+(w_west[c]-w_east[c]);
   BotPosy[c] = BotPosy[c]+(w_north[c]-w_south[c]);
```

To keep our Bots from running in fear forever, we decelerate the weights, eroding the accelerator.

```
w_east[c] = w_east[c] *.9;  /* Sensor bias erosion - decelerate */
   w_west[c] = w_west[c] *.9;
   w_north[c] = w_north[c] *.9;
   w_south[c] = w_south[c] *.9;
```

Once that is done, we apply the bias values.

```
w_west[c] = w_west[c]+westbias; /* Trick sensor with a bias */
   w_east[c] = w_east[c]+eastbias;
   w_north[c] = w_north[c]+northbias;
   w_south[c] = w_south[c]+southbias;
}
```

That's it! In fact, the system is so simple and easy that we've found that even after explaining it to coworkers, they sometimes overcomplicate it, because it seems that it "can't be that easy." But it is!

Sample Programs

ON THE CD

Included on the CD are two very basic sample programs that demonstrate aspects of the control scheme. In the first, *example.exe*, there are a large number of bots. They are repulsed by the cursor, each other, and the walls. (In this example, they're actually repelled by anything that isn't the background color.) You can draw walls with the left mouse button and erase them with the right mouse button. Try corralling the sample across the bridge, drawing new obstacles, and erasing the current ones.

In the second example program, *westbias.exe*, each bot has been given a West bias, which forces the bot East. Try erasing the current background and replacing it with a more realistic "obstacle course."

The sample programs contain tons (well, 32) of bots in a small, nonscrolling space. This is to demonstrate the robustness of the system. You might want to lower the number of bots and recompile (note: the sample programs require the freeware Allegro graphics libraries) so you can pay closer attention to one or two bots at a time. You can also alter the radius of detection, and the sensors' distance from the center node. Finally, in these samples, we have shown repulsors only. Adding attractors (or, as we like to think of them, negative repulsors) is trivial.

Advantages

There are several advantages to this scheme, over more traditional or complicated approaches. As noted earlier, it generates very lifelike results. More than that, it is very efficient. Each node is not only a sensor, but also a pushing device. In one routine, each node both senses a repulsor and responds, rather than sensing and then relying on another routine to actually act on input.

After setup, each bot essentially requires only four if-then statements per frame update. Given the power even in a low-end system such as the Sony PlayStation One, this makes the bot object-avoidance behavior essentially computationally free! Further, even on very limited systems like the original black-and-white Game Boy, with its 4-Mhz 8-bit Z80-like processor, managing 20+ bots per frame (at 60 FPS) is easy without taxing the system.

Extensions and Applications

There are numerous extensions possible using this scheme. Not demonstrated in the sample programs, but obvious, are adding attractor or repulsor values to player characters or NPCs. Maybe the easiest true extension to the concept is simply adding more "whiskers." Going with five or six radial whiskers adds greater complexity to the behavior with only a very slight computational increase. Altering the collision detection to be polygonal, rather than per-pixel, is another logical step.

While the scheme was designed for 2D use, adding up and down sensors makes it an effective 3D solution for some problems. One experimental use we have considered is putting sensors on key points of a 3D humanoid figure. This would enable a computationally cheap way for the figure to, say, duck its head out of the way if a rock were thrown at it, without moving the whole body, or even turn its shoulder to avoid hitting another figure walking down a hall. We think that this type of ground-up solution, combined with a smart IK model, could lend itself to some surprisingly realistic motion.

Applications

As mentioned earlier, we've used this routine successfully on Game Boy to drive everything from running backs and tackles in a football game (*NFL Blitz* for the Game Boy) to smart chase routines in platformers (*Alice in Wonderland* and *Disney's Tarzan*). Maybe the most obvious application for games on more-powerful platforms is to use this routine to control hundreds of characters simultaneously, either herds of enemies, or incidental NPCs.

Although using more robust AI schemes is essential as games move forward, we feel there will always be room for cheap, tricky solutions—and not just for limited computing devices. Using a scheme similar to the one outlined here could add abundant "life" to a game, and greatly enhance the experience for the end user.

Exploring Small AI

Probably the best thing anyone interested in small AI can do is build a robot using a BASIC Stamp microcontroller from Parallax, Inc. (www.parallax.com), or a BASICX controller (www.basicx.com). The BASIC Stamp 1 can only hold 75 commands, but it's possible to create a robot with it that has very interesting behaviors. Because of the need to keep hobbyist robot kits cheap, they are very underpowered.

Once you experiment and get good results from a hobbyist robot kit, you'll probably find that you have learned many new techniques that can be applied to game AI. Parallax sells two good kits, and more can be found from Lynxmotion (www.lynxmotion.com) or Mondo-Tronics (www.robotstore.com). There are numerous robot simulators (like the one at http://rossum.sourceforge.net/index.html) available online as well.

Further Reading

[Horn87] Horn, Delton T., Smart Apples: *Thirty-One Artificial Intelligence Experiments for the Apple II*, McGraw-Hill Professional Book Group, 1987. Good basic primer for small AI apps on small machines.

[Wesson01] Wesson, Richard, "Path Finding Via 'Ant Races' (a flood-fill algorithm)," 2001. Available at: //www.gameai.com/antraces.html.

[Zobrist69] Zobrist, A. L., "A model of visual organization for the game of GO," AFIPS. Conf. Proc., 1969, 34, 103–112: Demonstrates a really simple approach to looking at a map.

4.2

Preprocessed Solution for Open Terrain Navigation

Smith Surasmith—Angel Studios

ssurasmith@angelstudios.com

Open terrain navigation is a common AI problem associated with modern video games. Games in genres such as real-time strategy, driving, and combat simulations have human players and agents competing in open terrain levels. Agents must maneuver around obstacles and move between locations without getting lost, bumping into things, or getting stuck.

Many game programming books discuss various solutions for open terrain navigation. The solutions they provide, such as A*, are usually runtime solutions. Because video game applications are demanding on computational hardware, a game often preprocesses as much as it can in order to reduce the runtime load on the CPU. This article discusses the issues involved with preprocessing the pathfinding portion of navigation, and provides a method for its implementation.

Overview of Navigational Approaches

There are three parts in putting together a navigational solution. The first is to partition the terrain in order to create data that is searchable. There are many partitioning schemes, such as *rectangular grid*, *quadtree*, *convex polygons*, *points of visibility*, and *generalized cylinders* [Stout00]. All of these techniques reduce the contiguous space of the terrain to a discrete space that search routines can interpret. A search space contains a number of nodes and edges. Each node represents a section of the environment, and each edge represents a path between a pair of nodes.

The second part is to create heuristic and cost tests for each unique traversal condition. Heuristic tests evaluate how well nodes match navigational goals. Cost tests evaluate the penalty of the paths to those goals. Different search algorithms might employ one or both types of tests. The purpose of conducting a search is to find the node that best matches the navigational goal, and to plan the path with lowest cost of traversal to that node. Characteristics of the terrain and the traversal needs of each agent contribute to the different heuristic and cost test conditions.

The last part is to employ the appropriate search algorithm in order to provide the best possible path solutions for navigation while remaining complementary to its host application. Providing the best possible path solution entails that the search algorithm use appropriate heuristic and cost tests. It must provide solutions for traversal from any location to any other location in the environment. The resulting path solution must be traversable by the agent for which the search is intended. Being complementary to the host application means that the algorithm must not exceed memory or CPU time allowed by the application.

Preprocessed Navigation

Runtime searches are demanding on system resources. A partitioned terrain can create a search space with hundreds or thousands of nodes. Each node represents a location in the world. A runtime algorithm checks many of these nodes each time it makes a search. The application allocates memory to store nodes that have been checked and those that have not been checked for each search, and there might be many searches occurring at the same time. Game programmers partition terrain to create as few nodes as possible. They optimize data structures and memory management to speed the accessing of data and the testing of costs and heuristics. They also use runtime searches judiciously, and use less time-consuming navigational methods when a search is unnecessary [Rabin00].

The idea behind a preprocessed navigation is to create a table of all the possible path solutions needed for navigation. The purpose for creating such a table is to reduce the runtime process dedicated to searching. Creating a solution table reduces the order of complexity for doing a search for the lowest cost path between any two nodes to $O(1)$. The application is able to spend less time on navigation and able to have more time to do other things.

Game developers already know they can create navigational data as assets that they can load and use at runtime without further processing. The partition data of the terrain, connectivity information, and game data embedded into the partition data are all part of the navigational data that can be preprocessed. They can now preprocess searches for path solutions as well. The problem for creating a solution for the lowest cost path between every node in the search space is called an *all-pairs shortest path* problem [Aho83].

The all-pairs shortest path is a common algorithm problem, and its solution is at the heart of the development of a preprocessed navigational solution. This article applies the algorithm for solving this problem to video games. The following sections discuss the issues involved in creating the all-pairs shortest path solution table, how to use the table at runtime, and some key optimizations to reduce the memory footprint for storing the solution table.

Analysis of Requirements

In order to preprocess path solutions effectively, a developer needs to have a clear understanding of the relationship between the game's requirements and characteristics of the environment. An analysis of the terrain gives clues to the partitioning approach and the amount of data required. An analysis of the game gives details as to how many unique solution sets the game will need, and determines what the heuristic and cost functions are. The developer needs this information to make decisions about the trade-offs between data complexity, resource efficiency, and completeness of the solutions.

Terrain Analysis

An appropriate partitioning scheme is the first step in creating an accurate representation of the terrain. Because representing every coordinate of the open terrain in a graph is not possible, the partition scheme must represent the terrain in only the features that matter to navigation. By representing as little of the terrain as necessary, the partition data can remain small. The size of the solution table depends on the number of nodes in the partition data. More nodes and edges provide greater detail, but also increase the size of the solution *exponentially*.

Although there are many ways of partitioning the terrain, this article will use the partitioning scheme known as "points of visibility" as an example [Rabin00]. This partitioning scheme is akin to a roadmap. Each point is like a city. The road connecting two nearby cities represents the visibility between the two cities. Cities are connected to other nearby cities over the entire map to form a large network. A traveler moves from one area to another by first finding the closest cities to the start and destination areas, then by following the roads connecting them. The network graph is the data structure representing this partitioning scheme. *Nodes* represent key points in the terrain just as cities do on a map. *Edges* are the roads connecting pairs of nodes. An agent is assumed to be able to traverse between any two nodes along the corridor defined by an edge. When traversing from one point to another, the start and destination nodes are called *end nodes,* and the series of roads that connect them is called the *path solution.*

A preprocessed solution can only take into account the terrain's static geographical features. The partition graph might contain paths around obstacles that do not change over the course of the game at runtime, such as large impasses like mountain ranges, bodies of water, cliffs, rifts, or smaller obstacles like nondestructible architecture. The graph cannot take into account obstacles that might move or change during runtime. Agents can use the solution for the partition graph only to navigate around static features of the terrain. They must use additional methods to avoid moving obstacles, or to take advantage of changing landscape. Figure 4.2.1 shows a directional graph that is created around static terrain features.

Game Analysis

Along with analyzing the terrain environment, an analysis of the game is necessary in order to formulate cost and heuristic functions that the application will use to generate the path solutions for the game. Game requirements can create needs for different searches and solutions. Because each solution table can take up a lot of memory, multiple solution tables have the potential to take up more memory than is available for

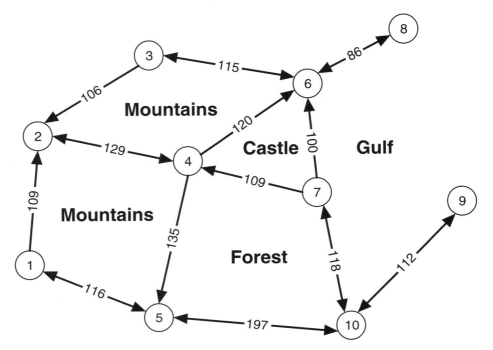

FIGURE 4.2.1 *The points of visibility graph shows nodes and edges of the partitioned terrain.*

the application. Therefore, minimizing the size and number of tables are important objectives in implementing a preprocessed solution.

A search algorithm uses cost functions to determine the path solutions between nodes. Therefore, using different cost functions might produce different tables of path solutions. In order to minimize the number of solution tables, the number of cost functions should remain small. Care must be taken to create cost functions that many agents can share, and to get rid of cost functions that produce solution tables with the same path solutions.

Between any given pair of nodes, each solution table provides only one path, and the path is guaranteed to have the lowest cost. If a game requires agents to use different paths between any given pair of locations, they must use a different method to determine a new path. This might mean creating a different table using different cost calculations, or some other method that is not discussed in this article.

When navigating over the terrain, agents use real-world positions. These positions are not represented by the network graph. In order to find a path between two positions in the world, agents need to determine which nodes match the start and destination positions. They do this by testing the nodes for their heuristics. For example, to find a node closest to the destination location in the world, for each node, a distance test between the node and the location yields the heuristic for that node.

The node whose distance is smallest from the destination is the node that matches the location. A solution table does not provide the heuristic costs for nodes; it only provides path solutions based on the cost of traversal between the end nodes. Heuristic tests are part of the runtime calculation to determine the end nodes. The end nodes determine the entry for looking up a path from the solution table.

Constructing the Solution Table

The creation of the solution table for all-pair shortest paths allows the game to push the node-searching portion of pathfinding from runtime to preprocessing. Once the analyses of game requirements are made, construction of the solution table can begin.

The process for constructing the solution table requires the integration of four components. The first component is the partition information. The partition information contains the data structure defining the nodes and edges. This is used to create cost functions, and will also be used during runtime for heuristic testing. The second component is the connectivity information. This component is created from the partition information. It uses a cost function to assign the cost values for edges. Then, this information is used for pathfinding between all pairs of nodes in order to create the solution table. The third is a search algorithm to process the paths between each pair of nodes. The final component is the data structure to store all the paths making up the solution table.

The Connectivity Information

The table in Figure 4.2.2 represents the connectivity represented by the graph shown in Figure 4.2.1. The table shows the cost between adjacent nodes represented

	1	2	3	4	5	6	7	8	9	10
1	0	109	na	na	116	na	na	na	na	na
2	na	0	na	129	na	na	na	na	na	na
3	na	106	0	na	na	115	na	na	na	na
4	na	129	na	0	135	120	na	na	na	na
5	116	na	na	na	0	na	na	na	na	197
6	na	na	115	na	na	0	na	86	na	na
7	na	na	na	109	na	100	0	na	na	118
8	na	na	na	na	na	86	na	0	na	na
9	na	na	na	na	na	na	na	na	0	112
10	na	na	na	na	197	na	118	na	112	0

FIGURE 4.2.2 *This cost table represents the graph in Figure 4.2.1.*

in the graph. Values have a minimum bound of zero, which is the lowest cost to travel between the connected nodes. The cost to traverse for a node to itself is zero.

The Search Algorithm

The all-pairs shortest paths search depends only on evaluating the cost of the path between each node pair. Heuristic cost estimates are not applicable because we know exactly where the nodes are and can calculate the cost between them. The common algorithms used to solve this type of problem are Dijkstra's algorithm and Floyd's algorithm.

Floyd's algorithm solves the all-pairs shortest paths problem directly, while Dijkstra's algorithm, normally used as a solution for *single-source shortest paths* problem, can be made to iterate through every pair of nodes. In cases in which the numbers of edges are much less than the square of the nodes, Dijkstra's algorithm performs better [Aho83]. This article will use Dijkstra's algorithm to illustrate the main points. Dijkstra's algorithm is easy to implement, and there are many resources explaining the algorithm [Aho83].

The Solution Table

The solution table holds the preprocessed navigation data. Fundamentally, the all-pairs shortest paths problem is $O(N^3)$ time complexity. If the size were also $O(N^3)$ complexity, the solution table would require too much memory. For a graph with N number of nodes, there are $N \times N$ pairs of nodes. If each pair requires a path through all nodes, each path will be of length N. The final table will then require N^3 number of entries. For as few as 100 nodes, the resulting table will require 1,000,000 entries.

Fortunately, the solution table only requires, at the most, N^2 number of entries. This is true because each node pair only needs to contain one value. Each value represents the next node in the solution path leading to the destination node. Therefore, the solution table implicitly distributes all the path solutions over the entire table. The N^2 solution table is shown in Figure 4.2.3.

Generating the Solution Table

The algorithm used to create the solution table involves very few steps. It goes through every node pair and uses Dijkstra's algorithm to search for the path solution. With each solution, it builds the solution table. The pseudo-code that follows shows a straightforward implementation. More efficient implementations are possible.

Dijkstra's algorithm finds the lowest cost path between two nodes by repeatedly spanning along the adjacent nodes with the lowest summed cost until the destination node is found. It first sets the start node as the current node with a traversal cost of zero. It marks the current node as traversed. Then, from the current node, it lists all of the adjacent nodes that have not been traversed. Each node on the list contains the sum of the cost since the start node, and the previous node along the path. From the list, it chooses the node with the lowest cost, sets it as the current node, and con-

Destination

Start

	1	2	3	4	5	6	7	8	9	10
1	1	2	2	2	5	2	5	2	5	5
2	4	2	4	4	4	4	4	4	4	4
3	2	2	3	2	2	2	2	2	2	2
4	5	2	6	4	5	6	5	6	5	5
5	1	1	10	1	5	10	10	10	10	10
6	3	3	3	3	3	6	3	8	3	3
7	4	6	6	4	4	6	7	6	4	4
8	6	6	6	6	6	6	6	8	6	6
9	10	10	10	10	10	10	10	10	9	10
10	5	7	7	7	5	7	7	7	9	10

FIGURE 4.2.3 *Solution table created from the connectivity data in Figure 4.2.2.*

tinues checking the new current node's list of adjacent nodes. When the algorithm encounters the destination node, it stops and returns the list with the path solution.

The algorithm for generating the solution table is as follows:

```
void CreateSolutionTable( void )
{
    for( each start node )
    {
        for( each end node )
        {
            if( start == end )
                solution[start][end] = end;
            else
            {
                list = Dijkstra( start, end );
                if( list )
                {   // found path
                    first = FindFirstNodeInPath( list );
                    solution[start][end] = first;
                }
                else
                {   // not reachable
                    solution[start][end] = -1;
                }
            }
        }
    }
}
```

From looking at the solution table and in the pseudo-code, notice that when a path is found, only the first adjacent node in the solution path is recorded. Even though Dijkstra's algorithm found the complete path, the only important part to save is the very first step toward the destination. Also notice from the pseudo-code that if a path does not exist between the node pair, then the value of the entry is assigned −1.

Once the solution table is created, as shown in Figure 4.2.3, finding the shortest path between any two nodes is simple. The rows are the start nodes and the columns are the destination nodes. Each value in the table is the node to travel to next. For example, to find a path from node 2 to node 8, follow these steps:

1. Find the value at row 2 and column 8. The value is 4. Therefore, the path starts at node 2 and travels first to node 4.
2. Find the value at row 4 and column 8. The value is 6. Therefore, the path continues from node 4 to node 6.
3. Find the value at row 6 and column 8. The value is node 8. Therefore, the path completes the navigation from node 6 to node 8, which is the destination. The shortest path from the start node to the destination node is (2 to 4 to 6 to 8). Verify this by looking back at Figure 4.2.1.

Runtime Application

At runtime, the application has all of the data it needs about nodes, edges, and paths loaded. The application can use the loaded data to perform pathfinding. This section discusses the costs incurred during runtime.

Memory and CPU Time Consumption

The solution does incur some runtime costs on the hardware. The most obvious is memory costs. The application has to load up information on all the nodes, such as location or other relevant runtime information. If there is information about the edges, such as information affecting how an agent traverses an edge, then the application loads that information also. Finally, the application has to load the necessary solution tables. For N number of nodes and M number of edges, there are an N^2 number of entries in each solution table. The size of the data loaded for the pre-processed solution is $O(N+M+N^2)$. Runtime solutions also have to load data for nodes and edges. The only difference between the runtime and the preprocessed solution is the loading of the solution tables.

The time cost for navigation is small. The biggest cost comes from finding the closest node in the network from a unique location in the world. At the very worst, each agent traverses every node to find the start node and again for the end node. For P number of agents, the time complexity for this process is $O(P*N)$. Specialized data structures can help reduce the number of heuristic tests made on the nodes. For example, using grids to sort the nodes can provide a quick way to find the end nodes associated with any two positions on the terrain. Instead of testing every node in the graph, finding the endpoints requires only two quick tests to see which grid coordinates contain the locations, and a few tests to find the closest nodes to each location.

The sorting of the nodes can reduce the search for the end nodes to constant time and reduce the previous complexity to $O(P)$.

When there is not enough memory, the application can compress the solution tables. However, this is a trade-off. The application reduces the size of the solution tables in order to gain back some memory, but loses the constant lookup time for path solutions. Compressing the table to reduce memory consumption will most likely incur increased time complexity in retrieving values from the table. The complexity can vary depending on the type of compression used.

Optimizations and Extensions

The main issue involved with preprocessing pathfinding is the amount of memory consumed by the solution data. There are many optimization techniques that can help reduce memory consumption. Techniques that reduce the complexity of the partition data are applicable to both runtime and preprocessed pathfinding. These techniques work on the general problem of terrain partitioning. They indirectly affect the size of the solution data. Other techniques, such as compression, directly reduce the size of the solution data. There are many optimization techniques, but here are a few.

The first optimization technique is to reduce the actual number of nodes representing the terrain. Partitioning the terrain only in the area that is being used at runtime is a good first step. There is no need to create a graph for the entire expanse of the environment if only a small portion of the terrain is used in any given mission level. Using the same amount of nodes in a smaller area to increase the level of detail is better than spreading out the nodes over a larger area that might not be entirely used.

Using hierarchical pathfinding [Rabin00] is also valuable in reducing the size of the solution. A coarse partition can represent an overall view of the terrain. The area within each partition can then represent a distinct region with its own partition and solution data. For example, in Figure 4.2.1, the edges connect each node around the mountains, forest, castle, and gulf. Each node can represent a region that is divided by the terrain. Each node can have a more detailed partition data and solution associated with it. Pathfinding within a region only uses the data associated with the area, and pathfinding between different regions uses the higher-level data along with the lower-level data associated with each of the two regions. Creating a hierarchy of graphs produces a set of solution tables that takes up less memory than using the same number of nodes over one graph. For example, a graph with 1000 nodes produces a solution table with 1,000,000 entries. If the 1000 nodes were broken down into 10 groups of 100 nodes, there would be 10 tables with 10,000 entries, making 100,000 entries, and including the connection between the 10 different groups, the final total is 100,100 entries, which is just above 10 percent of the original design size.

Another optimization technique is to compress the solution table. In Figure 4.2.3, the row for node 9 gives a good example of how compression could reduce greatly the amount of memory consumption by the solution table. For the most part, each node only contains a few connections with other nodes to form the adjacency list. The smaller the number of adjacency lists for each node means greater repetition across the rows. Node 9 for instance, must always traverse through node 10 to get to any other node in the graph.

Run-length encoding of the row is a reasonable technique and will compress [10, 10, 10, 10, 10, 10, 10, 10, 9, 10] to [8,10,1,9,1,10] by listing repeating values. Since patterns do not cross over different rows, it is only wise to compress each row individually. However, you should be aware that a compressed table will slow the lookup of values, since data must be decompressed on-the-fly. There are many other compression techniques available, but as compression ratios increase, decompression time will generally rise.

Conclusion

Preprocessing navigation is a good solution to navigating open terrain when terrain conditions remain unchanged throughout the runtime sections of the game, and when multiple classes of agents are able to share solution tables. Techniques used to optimize runtime searches such as A* can also be used to optimize the preprocessed solution. For the former, the application gains processing speed; for the latter, it gains memory. The solution table allows runtime lookups of lowest cost paths between node pairs, and has trivial impact on processing time as opposed to a runtime search. The method gives instant path solutions between every node defined in the search space. For games in which the navigation lends itself to well-defined paths, and platform requirements are strict, this asset-driven technique is a solid performer.

However, no one solution is useful all the time. Navigating open terrain requires a mix of different techniques. Use local collision avoidance techniques for nearby areas and to avoid moving objects not taken into account by the solution data. Use preprocessed data for longer distances. Use runtime pathfinding where necessary. Using multiple techniques that complement each other yields better results than any one technique alone.

References

[Aho83] Aho, Alfred V.; Hopcroft, John E.; Ullman, Jeffrey D., *Data Structures and Algorithms*, Addison-Wesley Publishing Company, 1983.

[Rabin00] Rabin, Steve, "A* Speed Optimizations," *Game Programming Gems*, Charles River Media, 2000.

[Snook00] Snook, Greg, "Simplified 3D Movement and Pathfinding Using Navigational Meshes," *Game Programming Gems*, Charles River Media, 2000.

[Stout00] Stout, Bryan, "The Basics of A* for Path Planning," *Game Programming Gems*, Charles River Media, 2000.

4.3

Building a Near-Optimal Navigation Mesh

Paul Tozour—Ion Storm Austin

gehn29@yahoo.com

Ask any game AI developer about pathfinding, and you're likely to get an earful about A* ("A-Star"). The A* algorithm is the unquestioned champion of game AI pathfinding, and several articles in this volume and the *Game Programming Gems* books ([Stout00], [Rabin00]) describe techniques for getting the most out of A*.

However, the core pathfinding algorithm is only a small piece of the puzzle, and it's actually not the most important. The trick is in the way you use the algorithm. A* is already so good that you'd have a hard time speeding it up by optimizing it much further, and you'd be hard-pressed to find a better algorithm, since A* is provably optimal.

The single best way to improve the performance of your A* search—and the quality of the paths that your search generates—is by optimizing the underlying *search space*.

In any game environment, AI characters need to use an underlying data structure—a search space representation—to plan a path to any given destination. Finding the most appropriate data structure to represent the search space for your game world is absolutely critical to achieving realistic-looking movement and acceptable pathfinding performance. A simpler search space will mean that A* has less work to do, and less work will allow the algorithm to run faster.

If the representation of the search space doesn't closely match the geometry of the game world, your movement and pathfinding systems will have to jump through hoops to make the movement look intelligent and natural. If your representation is overly complex, this will impose an unnecessary performance barrier that no amount of pathfinder optimization will be able to overcome.

The Navigation Mesh

One of the most powerful techniques for AI pathfinding in 3D worlds is the *navigation mesh* (a.k.a. "NavMesh") approach (the robotics field refers to these as *meadow maps*) [Murphy 00]. A NavMesh is a set of convex polygons that describe the "walkable" surface of a 3D environment. It is a simple, highly intuitive "floor plan" that AI characters can use for navigation and pathfinding in the game world.

[Snook00] introduces the concept of a navigation mesh and some standard techniques for NavMesh movement and pathfinding. This article focuses on techniques for constructing a good navigation mesh in the first place, with an emphasis on creating navigation meshes that are highly simplified and make it easy for the pathfinding system to find good paths quickly.

The navigation meshes we create are suitable for nearly any type of 3D game environment, as long as the game world doesn't change too dramatically during the course of gameplay. We will also consider several useful optimization techniques for speeding up the NavMesh generation process.

As we proceed, bear in mind that a navigation mesh, like any other type of precomputed pathfinding data structure, doesn't handle *dynamic obstacles*—that is, obstacles that can move during the course of the game, such as crates and other AI characters. The NavMesh only knows about the static parts of the game world, so you will need a separate layer of pathfinding to deal with dynamic obstacles. A visualization of this is shown in Color Plate 8.

Goals

This article describes algorithms that will automatically build a NavMesh that is as close to optimal as possible. For our purposes, "optimality" means:

- **Completeness**. The navigation mesh should cover every surface that any AI in our game could reasonably be expected to walk on.
- **Simplicity**. The NavMesh construction code should attempt to cover the surfaces of the game world with something reasonably close to the fewest possible number of polygons.
- **Consistency**. Navigation mesh construction should not use any random numbers. It should give us exactly the same output for two identical levels.
- **Excellent runtime performance**. We seek a clean, simple data structure that can be very quickly queried by the pathfinding system. This data structure should provide much faster pathfinding than would be possible by querying the raw geometry.
- **Full automation**. The NavMesh construction process must be completely automated. A designer should be able to load a level and press a button, and our code will automatically generate a NavMesh from the raw geometry. Some readers might be interested in providing tools for designers to tweak navigation meshes to their liking. This is a reasonable and achievable goal, but it is outside the scope of this article.
- **Reasonable build-time performance**. Since designers will rebuild the NavMesh on a regular basis as they develop their levels, constructing the navigation mesh should take no more than a few minutes for the largest possible game world.
- **Robust handling of degeneracy**. The NavMesh must be able to deal with degenerate input data. This includes input polygons with fewer than three vertices, polygons of 0 circumference, polygons with one significant edge of size 0,

or polygons that appear adjacent but whose vertices do not actually quite match up.

- **Robustness in the face of additional intersecting geometry**. We must be able to deal with the presence of additional geometry that arbitrarily intersects our existing geometry. For example, we might have a floor composed of a single rectangular polygon that is intersected by a complex, high-polygon, immovable object standing in the middle of the room. The NavMesh will need to be able to handle the existence of this object and automatically "subtract" it from the rectangular floor polygon.

Color Plates 4 and 5 show two examples of 3D levels with an optimized NavMesh superimposed on it. Each convex polygon (with an 'X' in the center) is a node of the navigation mesh.

The Points of Visibility Approach

There's another popular approach to pathfinding in 3D environments. We will refer to this technique as the *path lattice* or *points of visibility* approach. I briefly describe it here to better illustrate the benefits of the navigation mesh.

A path lattice approach begins with a number of points scattered throughout the game world. These are the initial "path nodes." Usually, these are manually placed in the level by the level designer himself. The game world editor will then test the lines between all of the path nodes placed in a given level to determine whether it's possible to walk in a straight line from any path node to any other. For any "unblocked" lines between nodes, it creates an "edge" between those nodes. The game's pathfinder can use this resulting network to find a path from any node to any other (assuming such a path exists).

Figure 4.3.1 illustrates how both approaches would handle a Texas-shaped room. The first image shows a lattice with arbitrarily placed path nodes. The second shows a NavMesh with nine nodes covering the walkable surface of the room.

In practice, the path lattice approach has some severe limitations.

First is the problem of *path node placement*. Most path lattice systems rely on level designers to place path nodes in the missions and levels they create. With large levels, this can create an enormous amount of additional work for the level design team, adding significant productivity overhead for every new level a designer creates. It also introduces a significant potential source of errors, since the AI movement system must now depend on the level designers in order to achieve basic competence.

Some games feature systems that automatically place path nodes in a level. However, these are rare and are seldom able to achieve the results that a human can achieve by placing the path nodes manually.

Second is the problem of *limited representation*. The path lattice only contains data indicating which locations in the game world are directly connected to which other locations. Once you attempt to move to a location that doesn't have a path node

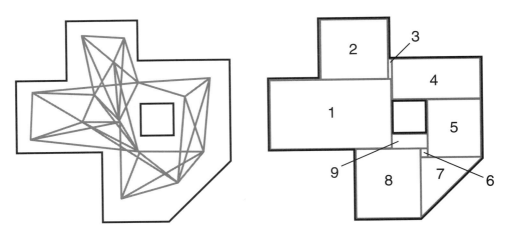

FIGURE 4.3.1 *Path lattice versus a NavMesh.*

nearby, the lattice is essentially useless. It has no way of knowing where the walls are. It's incapable of realizing that there's a big pillar standing in the middle of three path nodes connected in a triangle. And the moment you encounter a dynamic obstacle—such as a crate or another AI character—your path lattice becomes useless, and you must query the game world directly.

The main limitation of the path lattice approach is that it frequently generates low-quality movement paths. Two AIs running from A to B will typically follow the exact same path, leading to a perception that the AI is "on rails." If the designer places the path nodes in the wrong way, or if the AIs end up moving in a way that the designer didn't anticipate, this can lead to abnormal movement, such as characters "zigzagging" for no apparent reason.

The path lattice approach also suffers from serious problems with combinatorial explosion. Because the preprocessor must test every path node against every other path node in the game world to determine which path lines are viable, it is an N^2 problem. In other words, if you have 1000 path nodes in your level, the system will need to test $999 \times 1000 = 999,000$ paths.

Clearly, this can lead to very long level build times with large levels. The problem is exacerbated by the fact that you usually need to insert more path nodes to make the AI movement look better, and this puts path quality at odds with performance.

Building a Navigation Mesh

Greg Snook's original article on navigation meshes [Snook00] recommends building the navigation mesh from triangles. This is not strictly necessary. Any type of convex polygons will work quite nicely. As we'll see, quadrilaterals, and rectangles in particular, will frequently offer a more compact and convenient representation.

It's also very easy to convert any convex polygon into triangles if necessary. One easy way to do this is to simply find the polygon's center point by averaging the X, Y, and Z components of the vertices, and then draw a line from the center to each vertex.

You might be wondering why it's necessary for the polygons to be convex. Convexity is the only way we can guarantee that an AI can move in a single straight line from any point in the polygon to any other. A navigation mesh path consists of a list of adjacent nodes to travel on. Convexity allows us to guarantee that with a valid path, an AI agent can simply walk in a straight line from each node to the next one on the list.

Finding Convex Polygons

The problem of finding the simplest set of convex polygons to cover a given area is referred to in computational geometry as the *optimal convex partition* problem. The best known algorithm to solve this problem is $O(n^3 \log n)$ [Keil85], which our mathematics-to-programming pocket dictionary translates as "very, very slow."

The algorithm presented here is due to Hertel and Mehlhorn (see [O'Rourke94]). Although the Hertel-Mehlhorn algorithm doesn't guarantee that we end up with the absolute minimum number of polygons covering the floor surface, it's guaranteed to give us no more than four times the minimum number, which should be good enough. It's also very fast; with the appropriate data structures, it can be performed in linear time.

The Hertel-Mehlhorn algorithm can be summarized as follows:

1. Begin with a triangulation of the floor surface.
2. Remove a nonessential edge between a pair of convex polygons.
3. Repeat until we can no longer perform step 2.

We begin the process by looking at the raw geometry of the game world. We can query the game's engine for the polygons that make up all of the surfaces of a level—floors, walls, ceilings, and so on. Typically, this data will be a huge list of triangles, although if it's convex polygons, that's a nice added bonus and saves us some work.

Now we need to select the "walkable" surfaces. Assuming that our AI characters can't walk on walls or ceilings, we can simply iterate over all of the polygons in the level and determine which ones face upward. Each polygon in the level should include a *normal* value; that is, a vector that points in a direction perpendicular to the polygon. We only want polygons whose normals point more or less upwards; that is, surfaces that are more or less flat. We can measure the angle between a polygon's normal and a vertical line, and if the angle is greater than a certain "maximum angle" threshold, the surface is too steep to walk on.

As we add the level's polygons to the navigation mesh, it's a good idea to store each polygon's normal as well. We'll need to keep this data around to optimize the mesh properly. Our NavMesh pathfinding system might need to use the normals in the game as well. For example, our game might feature jagged terrain, and storing the normals would allow our game AI agents to know which surfaces are too steep for them to climb.

Merging Neighbor Nodes

Now we have a big navigation mesh. If we wanted, we could use this directly, without optimizing it further, but chances are we want to compact the NavMesh further to lower our memory requirements and speed up the NavMesh pathfinding process.

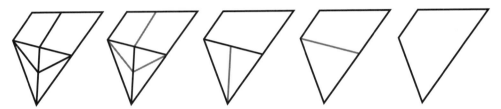

FIGURE 4.3.2 *Merging polygons into a single convex polygon.*

Now we apply the Hertel-Mehlhorn algorithm, which simply tells us to merge pairs of adjacent convex polygons into single, larger convex polygons. Figure 4.3.2 gives an example of how we can merge six nodes into a single node by repeated merging. By continuously repeating this process until there are no more nodes left to merge, we can dramatically reduce the number of polygons in our mesh.

Merging works as follows.

1. Find a pair of adjacent nodes (i.e., two nodes that share an edge between them) whose normals are nearly identical (i.e., their surfaces face the same direction).
2. Check to see if both nodes share the same two points along their shared edge. If the two endpoints of those edges aren't the same, we can't merge these nodes.
3. Attempt to eliminate the edge and merge the remaining vertices into a single convex polygon. If you can't make a convex polygon, the nodes can't be merged. If you can, delete both of the existing nodes and replace them with the new node.

Step 3 requires a bit more explanation. In order to merge two polygons A and B to form polygon C, we begin by pointing at the clockwise-most shared vertex in the A's vertex list. In other words, we look at the two vertices shared between A and B, and find the furthest vertex in clockwise order in A.

We then add all of A's vertices to C's vertex list. We now look at the last vertex added to A; this should be the other vertex shared between A and B. We locate this vertex in B's vertex list and add all of B's vertices beginning with this vertex.

Now we simplify the remaining polygon by eliminating any unnecessary vertices. A vertex is deemed unnecessary if it's redundant (i.e., the vertex is identical to the vertex immediately before it or after it in the vertex list), or if it's unnecessary to maintain the shape of the polygon (i.e., if we look at the line between the previous vertex and the next vertex and the current vertex lies somewhere on that line).

3 → 2 Merging

However, there's still plenty of room for improvement. Take a look at Figure 4.3.3. If you inspect your NavMesh closely, you'll notice that there are a couple of places in the NavMesh that share this pattern, where two polygons adjoin a third polygon and the first two polygons each share one of their sides with the third.

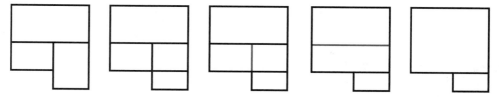

FIGURE 4.3.3 *Converting three convex polygons into two convex polygons.*

An algorithm we refer to as "3 → 2 merging" will allow us to merge these three nodes together into two much simpler polygons, as shown in the rightmost image.

Note that this technique doesn't only work with four-sided polygons. Figure 4.3.3 uses quadrilaterals only for the sake of simplicity. Figure 4.3.4 shows a triangle and two quadrilaterals merged into one triangle and one quad. The image on the left is the original geometry; the image on the right is after surgery.

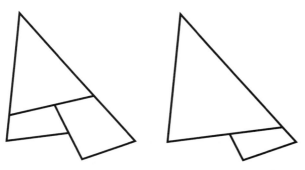

FIGURE 4.3.4 *Merging of mixed shapes.*

$3 \rightarrow 2$ merging is a difficult process, but it's well worth the effort. The algorithm works as follows. Note that we should only attempt the $3 \rightarrow 2$ merge process after we have already completed the basic adjacent-polygon merge process previously described.

1. Identify two adjacent nodes that share exactly one vertex between them. We'll call these nodes A and B. These are equivalent to the bottom two quads in the first image in Figure 4.3.3. The fact that these nodes still exist as separate polygons after the basic merge step proves that they cannot be merged together on their own, because, otherwise, the merge step would have merged them already.

2. Identify a single node adjacent to both of those original nodes, if one exists. This would be the large top node in the first image in Figure 4.3.3. We'll call this node C.

3. Determine if A and B both have one edge that runs parallel to an edge on C, and ensure that the endpoints of these parallel edges share one point in common so that they could be merged into a single line. If either node doesn't share a parallel adjacent edge, it means that this set of nodes is not a candidate for a $3 \rightarrow 2$ merge. This is equivalent to the vertical edges along the sides of the first image in Figure 4.3.3.

4. We begin the actual merge process by first discovering a point that is shared by A and B and is on an edge in C (Figure 4.3.5).

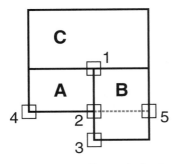

FIGURE 4.3.5 *Example for $3 \rightarrow 2$ merging.*

To avoid confusion with the names of the polygons, we'll use numbers to refer to vertices, and we'll call this point 1.

Note that node C will not actually contain point 1; the point merely lies along one of C's edges.

5. We now determine which of A and B holds the vertex we wish to use for splitting—this is vertex 2 in Figure 4.3.5. We note that A and B each has two

vertices one edge away from vertex 1. However, in each case, one of these vertices is shared with C. We take the two remaining vertices (vertices 2 and 3 in our example), and whichever is closest to vertex 1 must be the right one—in this case, vertex 2. Again, note that vertex 2 is not actually a vertex in B; it merely lies along one of B's edges.

6. Now we consider tracing a line from 2 to 5. In order to do this, however, we need to figure out exactly where point 5 is. We begin by noting that there are two vertices one edge away from vertex 2: 1 and 4. Since it can't be 1, it must be 4. We then extend the line from 4 to 2 off into infinity in the direction of vertex 2. We attempt to determine where it intersects another edge of B (i.e., where it intersects B along any line but the line between 1 and 3).

If there's no intersection, then these nodes aren't a candidate for a $3 \rightarrow 2$ merge, and we should try again with another set of nodes. If we do find a point, we call this point 5 and proceed.

7. We now split B into two separate nodes by dividing it along the line from 2 to 5. We'll call these subnodes B_1 and B_2, where B_1 is the top node (the node that contains vertex 1). To perform this split, we iterate over the list of B's vertices and insert each of points 5 and 2 into the vertex list *twice* in the appropriate position in the list. We can then search through this list and split it into two new vertex lists.

A simple example will demonstrate how to perform this split. If we call B's original vertices V_1, V_2, V_3, and V_4, and we call the new vertices X and Y, then we can insert the new vertices as shown in the second row of Table 4.3.1. Once we've added the vertices, we can iterate through the list to form the first subnode's vertex. Any time we hit X, we skip over all vertices in between until we hit the second Y (or skip over to the second X if we encounter a Y first). We then copy these vertices to the vertex list for our first subnode and delete them from the original list. Whatever vertices remain in the list will form the second subnode.

8. We now merge B_1 with node A using the merge procedure described in the previous section. We'll call this new node AB.

Table 4.3.1 Transforming (V_1, V_2, V_3, V_4) into (X, V_2, V_3, Y) and (V_1, X, Y, V_4).

Original Vertex List	V_1			V_2	V_3			V_4
With New Vertices	V_1	X	X	V_2	V_3	Y	Y	V_4
Vertex List 1	V_1	X					Y	V_4
Vertex List 2			X	V_2	V_3	Y		

9. We can use the same merge procedure to merge node AB with C to form ABC. We have now reduced the three nodes A, B, and C to two nodes, ABC and B_2.

Now that the process is finished, we can perform another Hertel-Mehlhorn merge step on the NavMesh as a whole. The node pairs that remain after the $3 \rightarrow 2$ merge (as in Figures 4.3.3 and 4.3.4) might now be candidates for merging with their neighbors where they were previously unable to merge.

Culling Trivial Nodes

At this point, our NavMesh is pretty close to optimal.

However, we can still take it a bit further. If you look closely at your navigation mesh, you'll notice that there are many tiny nodes still remaining in the mesh that are much too small to be useful. Small as they are, they still require as much memory as a larger node, because we still need several bytes to store the coordinates of each vertex in the node's vertex list plus the node's normal.

If we cull out these tiny nodes, we will not only vastly reduce the memory requirements of our NavMesh, we'll also improve runtime performance, since our pathfinder will no longer have to include these useless little nodes in an A* search.

Once your NavMesh has been generated, you can simply iterate through all of the NavMesh nodes and determine the surface area of each. Then, determine a good threshold for the minimum surface area, so that if any node's area is below that threshold, you consider it too small to be useful and remove it from the NavMesh.

Handling Superimposed Geometry

Now comes the tough part.

In many cases, you'll have extra geometry to deal with. For example, imagine that a level designer places a large, immobile treasure chest in the middle of a room. This is a single high-polygon object. The floor, however, is part of a binary-search partition (BSP) data structure, and it remains a single rectangle despite the treasure chest in the middle.

This means that we need to do the work ourselves—we need to manually subtract the treasure chest from the floor surface for the NavMesh to be valid.

The problem seems difficult at first, but there's a simple solution. We can use *recursive subdivision* to divide any NavMesh node into smaller nodes. If we took the subdivision to infinity (which we won't), we'd eventually end up with an infinite number of infinitely small subnodes, and every subnode would be either totally covered by the object (the treasure chest in our example) or totally outside the object.

Recursive subdivision simply means splitting the polygon into some number of smaller polygons. There will be exactly as many new subpolygons as there are vertices in the original polygon. Note that the resulting subpolygons will always be four-sided.

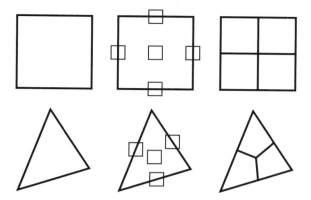

FIGURE 4.3.6 *Subdividing triangles and quadrilaterals.*

The following algorithm demonstrates how to subdivide a polygon using this technique. Figure 4.3.6 demonstrates subdivision for a square and a triangle.

1. Determine the center of the polygon by averaging the X, Y, and Z components of the polygon's vertices.
2. Find the midpoint of each of the polygon's edges.
3. Add new polygons by using the center and two midpoints along with each of the node's original vertices. First, add the center vertex to the new polygon's vertex list, then the first midpoint, then the original polygon vertex, and then the second midpoint.

Now that we know how to subdivide a NavMesh node, let's show how to use this process to subtract an obstacle from the NavMesh.

We begin by subdividing each NavMesh node that intersects the object. For each subnode generated from that original node, we either keep the subnode around (if it doesn't intersect the obstacle at all), throw it out (if it's totally inside the obstacle), or subdivide it again (recursively) if it's partly inside and partly outside the obstacle.

Once we reach a minimum polygon size, we will throw out the subnode instead of subdividing it further. This stops us from subdividing infinitely, and also gives us a threshold value that we can use to determine how close the NavMesh should approach a given obstacle.

The following pseudo-code shows how this algorithm works.

```
function Subdivide(Polygon p, Obstacle o)
{
    if p is totally inside o { delete p and return }
    if p is totally outside o { return }

    // we now know p is partly inside and partly outside o
    if the surface area of p is below a minimum threshold
    { delete p and return }
```

```
// we now subdivide and call this function recursively
// for each new node
create new sub-polygons from p (one poly per vertex)
for each sub-polygon
{ Subdivide(the sub-polygon,o) }
}
```

Re-Merging After Subdivision

Here's the cool part. After we're done subdividing, you'll notice that there's a lot of geometric sawdust left around. The subdivision process leaves a ton of little polygons lying around. How do we clean up the mess?

The answer is simple: we just use the adjacent-polygon-merging algorithm we demonstrated earlier in the article. Another quick sweep with the polygon-merging code will munge the NavMesh back to a near-optimal state.

This is the reason we used the algorithm for subdividing based on a node's center rather than subdividing one line at a time, as is usually done. The polygon-merging step will work particularly well with the smaller nodes generated from this process.

For example, imagine that we subdivided the square shown in Figure 4.3.6 and found that the two subsquares on the right side of the original square were the only ones that intersected the obstacle. The merging step will now recombine the two squares on the left into a single tall rectangle.

Better yet, if the subsquares on the right were only partly intersecting the obstacle, then the smaller subsquares of *those* squares might still be around, and they might be able to merge back into this rectangle after we do a little more merging on them. Figure 4.3.7 shows this little miracle of nature in action. The first two images show two steps of subdivision, after which the rightmost nodes are eliminated. The next five images show one way that the six remaining nodes can be re-merged into a single node.

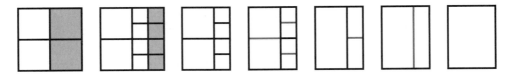

FIGURE 4.3.7 *Subdividing and re-merging a quadrilateral.*

Memory Optimizations

At the beginning of this article, we emphasized that you should store every NavMesh node's normal vector. However, it usually requires at least 12 bytes (three 4-byte floating-point values) to store a normal. If we end up with 20,000 nodes in our NavMesh—not an unreasonable number—it will cost us around 240K just to store the normals.

There are two good ways to optimize this. One is for each node to store a pointer to its normal instead of the normal itself. This pointer should be NULL if the normal is perfectly vertical. Assuming that we're dealing with human architecture rather than rugged terrain, 99 percent of our nodes will have normals that point upward, so we'll reduce our memory requirements to around 4 bytes per node.

The other option is to store all of the normals for all of the nodes in the NavMesh in a buffer, and allow each node to store a 2-byte index to its normal vector. This is an easy way to shave almost 200K off the 20,000-node mesh in our previous example.

Another good way to reduce our memory requirements is by pooling vertices. Many of our NavMesh nodes will share vertices, so rather than storing vertices directly, we can store all of the vertices in the entire mesh in a single vertex pool. Our NavMesh nodes can then keep track of the indices of their vertices in the vertex pool rather than storing the vertices themselves. This will save us the cost of a vertex (12 bytes) in any situation in which two nodes share a single vertex.

However, be warned that this is unlikely to give us significant memory savings unless there are enough shared vertices in the mesh to save us the cost of all of the additional 2- or 4-byte indices that a node must now store.

Build Optimizations

You might notice that we're missing a few important practical details. Some of the steps in our NavMesh construction process, such as the adjacent-node merging step and the $3 \rightarrow 2$ merge, require us to figure out which nodes are adjacent to one another.

Clearly, we need a good data structure to allow us to quickly determine adjacency. If we have to search every node in the NavMesh against every other to discover pairs of adjacent nodes, the time required to construct a NavMesh will get way out of hand.

A good way to solve this problem is to use an augmented version of the vertex-pooling technique described in the previous section. In addition to the vertex itself, all we need to do is store a list of pointers to all the NavMesh nodes that include this vertex in their vertex list. Every time we add a new vertex to the vertex pool, we also store a pointer to the node that added the vertex.

If we try to add a second vertex that's identical to a vertex already in the pool, we instead add a pointer to the second node to the original vertex's list. This is similar to reference-counting, except that we track every single node that refers to a given vertex.

After we create the initial navigation mesh, we can quickly scan through the vertex pool to find adjacent nodes. By definition, any vertex with two or more nodes in its list is shared by two or more NavMesh nodes, and the pointers tell us which nodes they are.

Note that this doesn't necessarily make things better. After all, we're going to end up manipulating the vertex pool by adding and removing lots of vertices during the NavMesh construction process. If we have to do a linear search through the vertex list every time we want to add a new vertex to find out if the vertex is unique, this will slow our build process dramatically.

The answer, as usual, is to use a hash table. Hashing all of the vertices in the pool will allow us to look up any given vertex almost instantly. If you're not already familiar with hash tables, consult your nearest data structures and algorithms book.

One caveat: the real world often contains degenerate vertices. That is, the raw geometry of our level will often contain two vertices that appear to be in the same location, but are in fact a slight distance from one another, so our hashing function will treat them as different vertices. A good solution is to sort the initial vertices (sorting by each vertex's X or Y coordinate), iterate through this sorted list to discover vertices that are sufficiently close together, and merge the nearby vertices into a single vertex.

Designer Control

This article emphasizes a fully automated approach to NavMesh generation. However, there are some cases where it's necessary to give designers a higher level of control over the NavMesh generation. In particular, designers will often want to remove certain parts of the game world from the NavMesh so AIs can't walk on them.

There are two main ways to approach this problem. One is to flag specific source polygons, textures, or materials so they never become part of the NavMesh. The second is to allow designers to place invisible "volumes" that specify areas that should not be integrated into the NavMesh.

In general, though, this functionality is less important than one would think. Surfaces such as window sills and railings will typically be small enough that the small-node culling process will automatically eliminate them from the NavMesh. Surfaces such as kitchen counters will be part of the NavMesh, but a good pathfinder should naturally know not to use them to navigate across the kitchen.

Extending the NavMesh

The techniques presented here are a good start, but many types of game environments present special pathfinding challenges that the NavMesh can't handle without additional features. A game world might feature ladders or other surfaces that need to be climbed, rivers and other bodies of water that require AIs to swim across them, gaps and chasms that the AIs must be able to jump over, and moving geometry such as elevators.

The key to tackling such challenges is to add the concept of "links" between NavMesh nodes. A link is a connection between two NavMesh nodes. All of the links we have discussed so far are *adjacent* links; that is, links between nodes that are immediately adjacent and share an edge in common. We can extend the concept of links by adding special types of links such as *jump links*, *ladder links*, and so on.

Although the process of creating NavMesh links is beyond the scope of this article, it should be easy to see that with a little extra work you can extend this system to automatically detect where the various flavors of links should be placed, and insert them into the NavMesh appropriately.

References and Additional Reading

[Keil85] Keil, J. M., "Decomposing a Polygon into Simpler Components," *SIAM Journal on Computing*, 1985.

[Murphy00] Murphy, Robin R. *Introduction to AI Robotics*, MIT Press, 2000.

[O'Rourke94] O'Rourke, Joseph, *Computational Geometry in C, Second Edition*, Cambridge University Press, 1994.

[Rabin00] Rabin, Steve, "A* Speed Optimizations," *Game Programming Gems*, Ed. Mark DeLoura, Charles River Media, 2000.

[Snook00] Snook, Greg, "Simplified 3D Movement and Pathfinding Using Navigation Meshes," *Game Programming Gems*, Ed. Mark DeLoura, Charles River Media, 2000.

4.4

Realistic Turning between Waypoints

Marco Pinter—Badass Games

marco@badass.com

Pathfinding is perhaps the most critical core component of game AI systems, and while huge volumes have been written, it remains a significant challenge with each new game produced. One of the greater challenges is achieving realistic-looking turning between waypoints, in a fashion that is efficient to calculate and remains true to game physics. In this article, we present a method of quickly calculating a geometrically correct path from one waypoint to the next, and discuss a variety of methods for simulating or achieving consistency with game physics.

Not many years ago, most games were created so that the game agents (vehicles, characters, etc.) followed their computed A* path precisely. This meant that at each waypoint, the character would abruptly turn to a new direction in an entirely unrealistic and visually unsettling way (Figure 4.4.1a). Recently, most games have incorporated sophisticated approaches to address this problem. A common, quick fix is to apply a spline across all the waypoints in a path [Rabin00]. Although the spline solution smoothes existing waypoint paths, it does not take into account any of the geometry, physics, or other attributes, like turning radius, that can be crucial for particular agents.

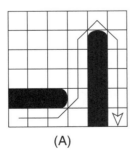
(A)

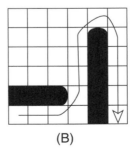
(B)

FIGURE 4.4.1 *Traveling between waypoints, straight-line and curved.*

For fast objects like cars, trucks, or planes, and for slower agents studied closely, physical realism is a priority. In order to address this, we use a geometric approach that takes an agent's turning radius into account (Figure 4.4.1b).

Turning radius is a fairly straightforward concept: it is simply the radius of the smallest circle that can be made if the agent turns as "hard" as it can. Anyone who has been caught behind an 18-wheel truck at a stoplight knows that larger vehicles tend to have much wider turning radii than smaller vehicles. (Game agents that do not have a fixed turning radius are addressed later in the article.)

Using the Turning Radius

If an agent with a fixed turning radius starts at a particular position and orientation, and wants to get to a destination, there are only one or two optimal routes. Either (a) the agent turns right, driving in a clockwise circle until directly facing the destination, or (b) turns left, driving in a counter-clockwise circle until directly facing the destination, and then proceeds straight from there (Figure 4.4.2). In certain cases, (a) and (b) can be the same distance; in which case, either choice will do.

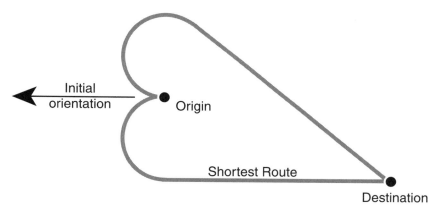

FIGURE 4.4.2 *Two shortest options for getting to the destination with a fixed turning radius.*

There are some simple geometric relationships that make it possible to calculate these routes (Figure 4.4.3).

Note that the agent drives around a virtual circle during the initial, curved portion of the route. The agent may drive almost halfway around the circle, or only a few degrees, depending on the initial orientation versus the angle to the destination. Note that point P is the center of that circle, point Q is the point at which the agent departs from the circle (and starts going straight), and *d* is the length of the straight-line segment.

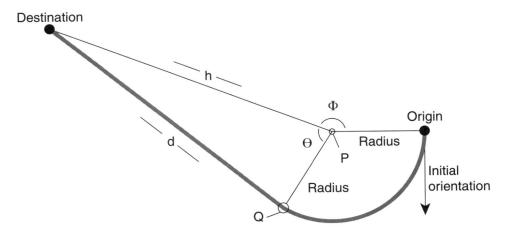

FIGURE 4.4.3 *Geometric relationships of turning radius.*

One important caveat: The techniques here assume that you have already implemented some form of line-of-sight smoothing, to remove unnecessary intermediate waypoints along straight lines. Many of the references provide simple methods of doing this.

Listing 4.4.1 demonstrates how to determine the parameters of the route. Note that the code in Listing 4.4.1 should be called twice, both with bTurnRight==true and with bTurnRight==false. Afterward, the total route lengths (curveLength + d) should be compared, and the shorter one (either bTurnRight or !bTurnRight) chosen. Note that the computation is based on a pure Cartesian coordinate system, where y values increase in an upward direction, as opposed to the screen system, where y values increase in a downward direction. This will not change the results, but it does mean that when bTurnRight is true, it will actually appear to be turning left on the screen. Finally, while not implemented in the code samples here, all computations based on angles should be translated to radians in the 0 to 2π range of values.

Listing 4.4.1 Determining the fastest route between two waypoints.

```
// CalculateSegment:  Determine the fastest route between two waypoints
// Input parameters:  origin, orientStart, bTurnRight, radius
// Output parameters: P, Q, curveLength, d, angleStart, orientFinal

// Calculate location of P (distance r from Origin, and
//   center of the turning circle)
// (Turning right from the origin means that P is located
//   90 degrees clockwise from the initial orientation;
//   Turning left means the reverse.)

if (bTurnRight)
```

```
        angleToP = orientStart - PI_VAL / 2.0;
else
        angleToP = orientStart + PI_VAL / 2.0;

P.x = origin.x + radius * cos(angleToP);
P.y = origin.y + radius * sin(angleToP);

// Calculate distance from P to Destination.
dx = dest.x - P.x;
dy = dest.y - P.y;
h = sqrt(dx*dx + dy*dy);

// If the destination is inside the circle,
//   we can't reach it.
if (h < r)
   return false;

// Calculate the length of 'd' based on the other two sides
//   of the right triangle, and theta as well.
d = sqrt(h*h - radius*radius);
theta = acos(radius / h);

// Calculate angle phi from arctangent relationship
phi = atan2(dy, dx);

// Determine point Q from position P and angle
angleFinal = (bTurnRight ? phi + theta : phi - theta);
Q.x = P.x + radius * cos(angleFinal);
Q.y = P.y + radius * sin(angleFinal);

// Calculate final values needed:
//   Total distance of curve; and final orientation
angleStart = angleToP + PI_VAL / 2;
totalCurve = bTurnRight ? angleStart - angleFinal
                        : angleFinal - angleStart;
curveLength = totalCurve * radius;
orientFinal = bTurnRight ? angleFinal - PI_VAL/2
                        : angleFinal + PI_VAL/2;

return true;
```

Listing 4.4.2 demonstrates how to determine the precise position and orientation of the agent at any point in time. Note that this system is completely time-independent; therefore, while some other systems require moving agents at discrete time intervals, here we can operate without any such restrictions.

Listing 4.4.2 Determining position and orientation at a given time interval.

```
// CalcPosition: Determine current position based on
//    pre-calculated path between waypoints.
// Input Parameters:  speed, elapsed, radius, P, Q,
//         curveLength, bTurnRight, angleStart, orientFinal
```

```
// Output parameters: orientation, curPos

// Compute the total distance covered in the path so far
dist = speed * elapsed;
// If the agent is still in the curved portion...
if (dist < curveLength)
{
    // Find the angle on the arc where the agent is
    theta = angleStart
            + (bTurnRight ? -1.0 : 1.0) * dist / radius;

    // Determine the current position and orientation
    curPos.x = P.x + radius * cos(theta);
    curPos.y = P.y + radius * sin(theta);
    orientation = bTurnRight ? theta - PI_VAL / 2
                             : theta + PI_VAL / 2);
}
// If the agent is on the linear portion
else
{
    // Find the distance we've moved along the straight line
    distNow = dist - curveLength;
    // Find the current position and orientation
    curPos.x = Q.x + distNow * cos(orientFinal);
    curPos.y = Q.y + distNow * sin(orientFinal);
    orientation = orientFinal;
}
```

Using this solution coupled with other smoothing solutions, there are times when the curving of an agent's path causes it to partially overlap a wall or blocker (Figure 4.4.4). In most games, this is a relatively unnoticeable effect to the end user, and it is sufficient to ignore the issue. Other solutions involve forcing a fluid turning radius (see next section), or, if the agent is capable of backing up, effecting a three-point turn.

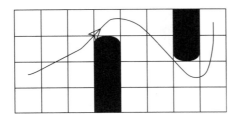

FIGURE 4.4.4 *The blocker-overlap problem.*

Another method of reducing this problem, using the general technique described here, is to use some basic predictive analysis to leave the agent at a more realistic orientation at each waypoint. The basic notion is to give the agent some limited intelligence so that, rather than blindly heading for each waypoint and then turning toward the following one, it knows which way it will have to turn as it approaches a waypoint, and starts the turn in advance. [Pinter01b] describes a geometric method of waypoint route calculation that allows you to specify both an initial and final orientation.

Fluid Turning Radius

Not all vehicles have a fixed turning radius, and of course, not all game agents travel in vehicles. So, how do we define a turning radius for a vehicle like a tank, which can turn in place, or for people and animals, which can also make tight corners or turn in place? It turns out that all agents with a fluid turning radius have one thing in common: they can move one set of wheels or legs faster than the other, and even move one set backward while the other moves forward. (You can try this at home. To turn counter-clockwise in place, you will automatically step back with your left foot and forward with your right foot until you are faced the correct way.)

The problem for the agent is that turning in such a fashion over a tighter radius requires slowing down. We assume the agent will choose to travel at its optimal speed whenever possible, and only when required to turn in a tighter radius will it slow down to achieve that. This is actually a very effective way of dealing with the blocker-overlap problem discussed in the previous section. Now, whenever an agent's curved route would take it too far over a blocked tile, it can instead recalculate the route with a tighter turning radius. In general, there is a linear relationship between speed and turning radius, so it's fairly simple to determine the amount of deceleration required to make a turn. Then, after the turn is complete, we assume the agent will accelerate again to its optimal speed.

Implementing the preceding algorithm in the simplest fashion can still leave a visible problem. It will sometimes result in agents performing instantaneous accelerations or decelerations, which is not physically possible. The easiest way to address this is to slightly "fudge" the physics, and allow the agent to decelerate over a shorter period of time during the start of its tight turn. This will be unnoticeable to the player, but might not be acceptable if precise physics are required. An alternate solution is to always plan one route ahead, and if the next route requires a slower speed, perform a deceleration during the end of the current route. If you are implementing the predictive analysis discussed in the previous section, the two code segments can be combined.

Conclusion

In this article, we provided a method for achieving more realistic and accurate turning for traveling from one waypoint to the next in a predetermined path. We also presented a variety of techniques for dealing with problems such as blocker-overlap, fluid turning radius, and realistic deceleration. It should be clear that when deciding how to implement waypoint-to-waypoint movement, as when deciding on an overall pathfinding implementation, the particular details depend heavily on the specific requirements of the game being built. Often it is beneficial to merge a variety of different techniques to achieve the desired results in your particular game.

References

[Pinter01a] Pinter, Marco, "Toward More Realistic Pathfinding," *Game Developer* magazine, April 2001.

[Pinter01b] Pinter, Marco, "Toward More Realistic Pathfinding," available online at www.gamasutra.com/features/20010314/pinter_01.htm, *Gamasutra.com*, 2001.

[Pottinger99] Pottinger, Dave C., "Coordinated Unit Movement," *Game Developer* magazine, Volume 6, Number 1, January 1999.

[Rabin00] Rabin, Steve, "A* Aesthetic Optimizations," *Game Programming Gems*, Charles River Media, 2000.

4.5

Navigating Doors, Elevators, Ledges, and Other Obstacles

John Hancock—LucasArts Entertainment Co.

jhancock@lucasarts.com

Good navigation is critical in creating intelligent, believable game characters. Mistakes can shatter the illusion of intelligence that game programmers and designers strive to create. On the other hand, versatile navigation evidenced by an AI character running to an elevator to get away from the player can increase character believability significantly, and can be entertaining as well.

This article discusses how to make your game characters generate and execute paths that include obstacles such as doors, elevators, switches, jumps, and ledge hangs. We focus on correctness, ease of use, and efficiency. Since runtime analysis of a 3D game world is expensive, the key to versatile navigation is to store additional information in the navigation map.

Generating the Path Planning Graph

The first step in creating a path planning system is generating the map data for the path search. A grid representation is often used when character movement is limited to an essentially two-dimensional surface. However, in a 3D game in which characters need to move both on the ground and vertically, a graph approach is more appropriate since it is generally more efficient in memory and CPU usage. Generating a graph requires additional code and/or manual labor.

A graph consists of *nodes* defining locations in the world and *links* between nearby nodes. The entire graph of nodes and links is a *nodemap*. A path is just a series of contiguous links in the nodemap. In this definition, links are unidirectional since some character actions (like jumps) might only be required in one direction. Thus, there are generally two links between adjacent nodes, one in each direction.

Some graph-based path planners do not explicitly represent the amount of free space around nodes or links. This can lead to one of two problems. If characters are forced to move exactly along the infinitely narrow links in the graph, they will appear unnatural or robotic. On the other hand, if characters are allowed to stray from the path, they might hit obstacles or fall from a cliff. These problems lead us to the first modification of our nodemap.

Nodes are given a finite radius, and links are defined such that the width matches the diameter of each node endpoint and varies linearly between (Figure 4.5.1). Node radii are set such that none of the adjoining links intersect geometry or hang over empty space. A radius at each node is a data-efficient means to represent free space around the node and along the link. Radii convey space in 2D horizontal space.

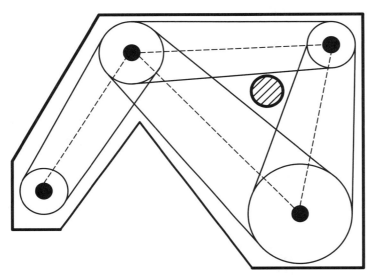

FIGURE 4.5.1 *This illustrates a top-down view of an oddly shaped room with a single pillar (indicated by the shaded area) with a nodemap consisting of four nodes (indicated by solid circles) and four links. Nodes have finite radii that determine the boundaries of the links between the nodes (indicated by thin lines). Node radii can provide a computationally and data-efficient means of representing the free space in an area.*

Unless annotated otherwise, vertical clearance appropriate for any character is implied—nodes are cylinders, not spheres. Representing free space in this way lets an AI know how far it can stray from the link axis, or whether it has already strayed. It is simple to determine whether a point P is inside the link by finding the closest point on the link axis Q and comparing the distance and the local link width at Q.

The path planning graph can be automatically generated as in standard path planning techniques, such as Voronoi diagrams and visibility graphs [Latombe91], or it can be manually generated. Regardless of how the map is initially generated, it is important that it can be edited for each 3D environment. By separating path planning into an editable data component plus an algorithm component rather than algorithm alone, it is possible to fix some troublesome pathfinding locations by changing or annotating the local graph rather than changing the algorithm. An algorithmic change might solve one problem, but cause another elsewhere. The flexibility provided by the nodemap can be especially important at the end of a project, when a global algorithm change will force the Quality Assurance team to retest every level of your game.

One way of generating a nodemap is to have a player or the level designer run a character around the world with the game engine automatically generating a node at the character's location whenever the character is more than a given distance from any other node (four to eight meters works well depending on the environment). Using this method, the engine should generate links automatically to nearby visible nodes using line-of-sight testing, and set node radii so that links do not intersect world geometry. Some links created in this manner might not be traversable and must be removed by the level designer.

The nodemap editor should also allow the designer to override the node radii calculated by the engine. While this does not generate optimal maps in terms of efficiently representing space, it does give the level designer the ability to control path appearance along major routes. A mouse click or keypress can be used to force the creation of a node where the character is standing to mark an important location.

Annotating the Nodemap

The next step in versatile navigation is to annotate the nodemap. Both nodes and links should be labeled with information relevant to navigation. Using data labels to aid the path planner and executor can improve both the efficiency and readability of the code. Runtime geometry detection and analysis is expensive in complicated 3D worlds. Labels allow geometry detection to be used only when needed, such as when a character is required to jump and grab a ledge. The extra map data also allows special code to be written for path execution on different types of links, and to apply different rules for determining success or failure in path execution. To keep the memory footprint as small as possible, many of the labels can be stored in a series of bitfield flags.

Nodes can be named for use as destinations for scripted events, labeled as strategic locations for sniping or ambushing the player, or as switch or elevator locations. In the case of elevator locations, the floor number must also be stored along with a handle to the elevator. Nodes also store information about the state of the character when the node was created. For example, one bit in the flag bitfield represents whether the character was hanging from a ledge when the node was created. Another flag represents whether the character had to crouch.

Links are labeled with information relevant to traversing that link. If a switch-activated door is present, the name or a handle to it must be stored. Doors that open automatically for characters do not need to be labeled. Links where it would be especially hazardous to travel outside of the link boundaries (such as those running along a cliff) are also flagged. More flags are used if traversing the link requires a character to jump.

If system memory is tight, it is not a good idea to allocate memory for all label types for all nodes and links, since only a small fraction of nodes and links receive labels. In this case, labels can be stored separately in a hash table, or a label structure can be allocated dynamically only for those nodemap elements that need it.

Goal-Based Path Planning and Execution

Path planning and execution is a complicated problem. A little organization can go a long way toward making your programming easier. Treating path execution as goal satisfaction provides a natural object-oriented structure to the problem. Using goals as the basis for your path execution will make your code easier to read, write, maintain, and debug. For purposes of this article, path execution goals have the following attributes:

- Goals are responsible for determining their own success or failure.
- Goals provide an Update() function that is called each timestep when the goal is being executed.
- Goals can create their own subgoals, which are stored in a queue.
- Subgoals are created only when the parent goal is first executed, not first created, following principles of *lazy evaluation.* Lazy evaluation techniques defer computation until the results are needed [Meyers96].
- Subgoals are executed one at a time, in order.
- While any subgoals are present, the parent goal sends no control input to its game object.
- When a subgoal succeeds, it is removed from the queue.
- When a subgoal reports a failure, the parent goal can replan or report failure to its parent.

The highest-level goal in path planning is Goal_GotoPosition where the position can be on or off the nodemap. When Goal_GotoPosition executes, if the destination is far enough away, it generates a subgoal Goal_GotoNode with the node closest to the destination as its argument.

Goal_GotoNode requests a search (use A* or your favorite algorithm) to find a path consisting of a series of nodemap links that connect the starting position to its destination node. A function GenerateGoalsFromPath() takes that path and creates path execution goals that are added to the goal queue. For simple paths in the absence of path smoothing, the function generates a Goal_FollowLink for each link in the path. Goal_FollowLink handles the traversal of a single link.

Path smoothing using line-of-sight testing can replace several contiguous Goal_FollowLinks with a single Goal_GotoNode that performs no planning (a constructor option in Goal_GotoNode can force a direct path). Only links that have no annotations are removed through path smoothing.

Goal_FollowLink can handle multiple types of links, including jumps over chasms, jumps over walls, and links along cliffs. Depending on the labels applied to the nodemap, it will execute different functions. For ordinary links, characters need only face the goal position and walk toward it. If the link was labeled as running along a cliff, Goal_FollowLink uses control algorithms designed to always keep the character within the link boundaries, at the cost of appearing more robotic.

Another link type requires the character to jump over a chasm. In this case, at each update cycle, the AI performs a *line check* against the world geometry to test the ground in front of it. The line check performs collision detection on a specified line segment. When the line check fails to hit anything, it signifies that the AI is near the cliff edge, and the AI begins its jump. For a jump up or over a wall, the AI performs a line check to detect the wall in front of it, and begins its jump when it is close enough. A link that connects two ledge grab nodes instructs the character to move right or left along the ledge while hanging from it.

Both Goal_FollowLink and Goal_GotoNode are designed to detect failures. If the character is stuck for an extended period or has deviated significantly from the desired route, such as if the character has been pushed from a ledge, the goal can report a failure to its parent, or replan. It is also possible for goal failure or success to adjust the cost of a link or node in the nodemap so that it might be avoided or favored on future path plans. This ability can be important in dynamic environments in which a moved object might block a previously valid link.

Doors and Elevators

Some nodemap links pass through doors or elevators. GenerateGoalsFromPath() must handle these links differently, since they might require deviations from the path in order to operate the switches that will activate the door or elevator. Working backward from the end of the path provided by the A* search, a Goal_FollowLink is created for each ordinary link in the path and inserted at the front of the goal queue. As soon as a door or elevator link is encountered, the appropriate Goal_GoThroughDoor or Goal_RideElevator is created, and the remaining links in the path (those in front of the door or elevator) are thrown out.

The path execution goals we've defined so far make using doors and elevators fairly simple. Goal_GoThroughDoor handles everything necessary to get to the opposite side of a door by using some of our existing goals (code provided on the companion CD). The goal first queries the door to find a switch that is reachable from the AI's present location. A door can have a switch on either side of it, so we have to be sure we choose the correct one. This involves using the results from a connected component extraction described later. Once that switch is determined, the goal can begin its work. Given the situation illustrated in Figure 4.5.2, Goal_GoThroughDoor divides its work among three subgoals:

ON THE CD

```
Goal_GoThroughDoor( DoorLink )
{
    Goal_HitSwitch( DoorSwitch )    //hit switch to open door
    Goal_GotoNode( DoorEntry )      //go to node in front of door
    Goal_FollowLink( DoorLink )     //pass through door
}
```

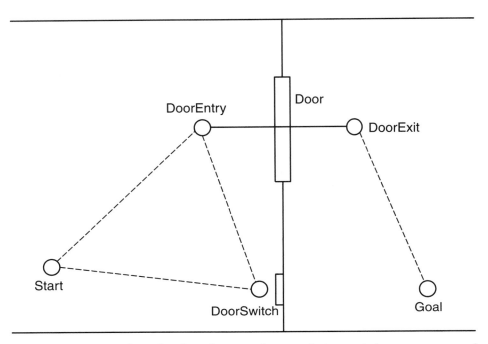

FIGURE 4.5.2 *To get through a door that must be opened via a switch* (DoorSwitch), *the character must first hit the switch, then move to the* DoorEntry *node, and then travel along the link that passes through the door to the* DoorExit *node. Circles indicate node locations. A dotted line between nodes indicates that a path exists between the nodes, but the path could consist of many links.*

DoorLink is the link that passes through the door and connects the nodes labeled DoorEntry and DoorExit. Note that we cannot replace the last two subgoals with a single goal Goal_GotoNode(DoorExit), because this would cause infinite recursion since it would simply generate another Goal_GoThroughDoor goal.

The subgoal Goal_HitSwitch can itself be broken into three tasks:

```
Goal_HitSwitch( Switch )
{
    Goal_GotoNode( GetSwitchLocation( Switch ) )
    Goal_TurnTowards( Switch )
    PushButton( Switch )
}
```

GetSwitchLocation() looks up the node location of the switch in an associative array, such as an STL map, created when the nodemap is loaded. PushButton() is just a function call (not a goal) that sends a message to the switch to activate it.

Let us assume that there are two links between the start position and the door switch, and three between the DoorExit node and the goal. After a few update cycles, once we have started executing `Goal_HitSwitch` and its subgoal `Goal_GotoNode`, our complete recursive goal queue would be:

```
Goal_GotoNode
  Goal_GoThroughDoor( DoorLink )
    Goal_HitSwitch( DoorSwitch )
      Goal_GotoNode( GetSwitchLocation( DoorSwitch ) )
        Goal_FollowLink
        Goal_FollowLink
      Goal_TurnTowards( DoorSwitch )
    Goal_GotoNode( DoorEntry ) //not yet expanded
    Goal_FollowLink( DoorLink )
  Goal_FollowLink
  Goal_FollowLink
  Goal_FollowLink
```

Indentation represents the nesting level of the goals. Note that `Goal_GotoNode` `(DoorEntry)` has not yet been expanded, according to our lazy evaluation rule about goal execution. Lazy evaluation improves efficiency, since it is possible the character will die or will have to replan before it begins execution of that goal.

`Goal_GoThroughDoor` can be used to navigate similar obstacles as well, including force fields and retractable bridges. A force field has an open and closed state just like a door, while a retractable bridge might be treated analogously to a door in which the extended state is the same as the door open state, and the retracted state is the same as the door closed state.

Elevators (or similar transport mechanisms such as trains) are handled similarly, with the exception that `GenerateGoalsFromPath()` collapses multiple contiguous links along the same elevator into a single `Goal_RideElevator` (see code on the CD). `Goal_RideElevator` divides its work into four tasks:

```
Goal_RideElevator
{
    Goal_HitSwitch( CallSwitch )    //hit the call switch
    Goal_GotoNode( EntryNode )      //go to node outside elevator
    Goal_FollowLink( EntryLink )    //enter the elevator
    PushButton( InternalSwitch )    //push the button (and wait)
}
```

Like the door example, we need to find the correct switch to call the elevator. To find it, we make use of the connected components information discussed in the next section.

Connected Component Extraction

For A*, the most expensive search is for the path that doesn't exist. When no path exists, A* will perform an exhaustive search. To avoid these inefficient searches, it is a good idea to run a connected component extraction algorithm on the graph at startup. The algorithm labels every node with a component number. If two nodes have the same component number, then a path exists between them. This changes an exhaustive search to a constant time, or *O(1)* operation to determine that no path exists.

ON THE CD

Although this is a standard algorithm, the possibility of one-way links and different character abilities adds some complications (see "ExtractRegions.cpp" included on the CD). The definition of "connected" needs to change. If some characters can jump, but not others, it is useful to know whether a given character with known abilities can reach node A from node B, without a search. To solve the problem, we run the basic connected component extraction algorithm [Latombe91] multiple times with a different definition of "connected" each time, so that each node gets labeled with multiple component numbers, one for each version of "connectedness" we care about. We run one version that uses any connection, a second that breaks connections at jumps, a third that breaks connections at elevators, and a fourth that breaks connections at doors.

The component number based on connections broken at doors can be used in the Goal_GoThroughDoor to determine which switch to use to operate the door. The AI chooses the switch that has the same component number as the node on its side of the door. There are two limitations in this method. The first occurs if the correct switch is separated from the door by yet another door, in which case no switches will be deemed accessible. The second occurs if there is a way around the door that would result in both sides of the door being in the same connected component, in which case the system cannot decide between switches on either side of the door. The game designer must decide whether these limitations are acceptable. If unacceptable, the limitations could be overcome by additional nodemap annotation.

Component numbers are not allowed to cross one-way links, since if node A has the same component number as node B, it says A is reachable from B, and vice versa. A one-way link violates this reciprocity. Instead, whenever a one-way link is encountered during the connection component extraction, it is saved to a list. The list is then used to generate a matrix of Boolean values that says which regions are reachable from one another. Note that there is a global connection matrix and a region type per node for each definition of connectedness (see PathNode::PathExists() in "NodeAnd-Link.cpp" on the CD for an example of how to put it all together).

ON THE CD

Conclusion

The keys to the intelligent navigation approach presented in this article are the annotated nodemap and goal-based path execution. The modified connected component extraction algorithm allows the system to efficiently determine whether a path exists for any given character between two nodes.

The nodemap provides a very flexible tool for adjusting character behavior on a per-node or per-link basis. For the approach to work, however, you need good editing tools and people who take the work seriously. If the input is sloppy, the results will be too. When constructed carefully, however, the annotated nodemap can allow your AI characters to do remarkable things. It can also improve your code readability and efficiency. In short, it's a good way to cheat. We hope you will find ways to cheat with it that we never considered.

Goal-based approaches and recursion are very powerful tools, and the queue-based system makes it trivial to manage those goals. Goals are also a natural fit with hierarchical pathfinding techniques. Given the right basic goals, it took very little additional code to add the ability to use doors and elevators. Once you add these tools to your AI toolbox, we doubt you will give them up.

References

[Latombe91] Latombe, Jean-Claude, *Robot Motion Planning*, Kluwer Academic Publishers, 1991.

[Meyers96] Meyers, Scott, *More Effective C++*, Addison-Wesley Publishing Company, 1996.

4.6

Simple Swarms as an Alternative to Flocking

Tom Scutt—Gatehouse Games Ltd.

tom@gatehousegames.com

Craig Reynolds' flocking algorithms have been well documented and are highly successful at producing natural-looking movement in groups of agents. However, the algorithms can be computationally expensive, especially where there are a large number of agents or a complex environment to detect against. For this reason, they are not always suited to real-time applications such as video games.

This article details a much simpler algorithm for producing natural-looking movement in large swarms of creatures involving tens or hundreds of agents. Although this algorithm cannot guarantee separation of creatures within the swarm, the overall impression of organic movement is very convincing.

Issues with Flocking

The flocking algorithms described by Craig Reynolds [Reynolds87], [Woodcock00] describe how a group of agents can be made to move in a naturalistic fashion using the simple steering behaviors of *separation*, *alignment*, and *cohesion*. Separation makes the agent steer to avoid getting too close to its near neighbors; alignment makes the agent steer so as to match its heading to the average heading of its near neighbors; and cohesion makes the agent steer toward the average position of its near neighbors. The emergent behavior of a group of agents using these rules is to move in a fashion similar to a flock of birds or a shoal of fish. With the addition of a fourth rule (*avoidance*, which makes the agent steer away from a nearby nonflock object), agents can steer around obstacles in the environment and move so as to avoid enemies.

Flocking algorithms are perfect for simulating the naturalistic behavior of small to medium numbers of creatures, especially in games in which the behavior of those creatures is a major focus of the gameplay (e.g., Nintendo GameCube's *Pikmin*). However, as the number of creatures increases, conventional flocking algorithms become increasingly expensive. Every agent in a flock has to check against every other agent in the flock to see if it is close enough to influence it, resulting in $\frac{1}{2}(n^2)$ separate distance calculations (providing intermediate results are stored in an interaction array) for a flock of size n. Then, the effects of separation, alignment, and cohesion must be calculated for each agent for each of its near neighbors. Again, because these influences are reciprocal, storing intermediate results can halve the number of calculations.

There is also the issue of how the flock is to interact with the environment. Although multiple obstacles can be set up and dealt with using the avoidance rule, this introduces the associated problem that an increase in the number of obstacles leads to an exponential increase in the number of calculations. It is clear that flocking is a computationally intensive task in which large numbers of agents are involved. It can also be difficult to organize global control over a flock, especially if one is to stick to the original spirit of Reynolds' algorithm.

Simple Swarms

The swarming algorithm presented in this article is intended for situations in which there are tens or hundreds of agents involved in the swarm; in other words, situations in which flocking calculations would normally prove prohibitive. It provides a computationally efficient method for moving large numbers of agents in a manner that gives the swarm an "organic" feel, and allows for an easy global control system. However, it is not intended for situations in which it is a key part of the game that the creatures should behave exactly like fish or birds. The algorithm makes no attempt at avoiding collision or even interpenetration between swarm members. It is intended for very large numbers of small, fast-moving agents such as rats, spiders, or cockroaches. The algorithm given in the example code in Listing 4.6.1 is intended for land-based creatures that can climb walls, but it is easy to adapt the algorithm for flying or swimming creatures such as bats, wasps, or piranhas.

It is assumed throughout that the target of the swarm is the player-controlled character, but there is, of course, no reason why this must be the case. For background swarms, the target could simply be a point moved through the environment. It could also be part of the gameplay that the player has to transfer the swarm to another target (this could be a method to remove an otherwise impassable enemy and the swarm itself).

Initialization

The easiest way to introduce agents is simply to bring them into existence off-camera. The swarming algorithm will produce variations in heading and position, but it is not problematic to give the agents some randomness to begin with.

However, it is in some ways a waste to trigger the swarm off-camera. There are many ways in which the introduction of the swarm can be made into a dramatic set-piece. Dropping creatures from the ceiling onto the player, spraying them from a hole in the wall, or having a cascade of creatures over the lip of a pit (preferably one occupied by the player) are all ways in which you can make the most of the swarm's entrance. Swarms can also be introduced by "exploding" them into an area when a container is destroyed (e.g., a crate) or opened (e.g., a coffin).

Each agent's `timer` should be given an initial small random value. This means that when the swarm disperses, it will do so gradually rather than *en masse*.

Movement

The update algorithm for each agent can be summarized as follows:

The agent is considered to be in one of two zones depending on whether `abs(dx)` `+ abs(dz)` is less than `SWARM_RANGE`.

If the agent is in the outer zone (i.e., distant from the target), then small variations in speed and direction usually keep the agents separated. If the heading of the agent strays too far from the target (e.g., the player), then it is brought back into line.

Once the agent is in the inner zone, its speed and heading are set by two interdependent formulae—its heading is dependent on its speed, and its speed is dependent on its heading. This leads to the agents swirling around the target point, although the exact nature of the movement is dependent on the parameters used in the speed and heading formulae.

On top of this basic movement algorithm there is very simple collision handling, and code to deal with climbing up walls and falling. Clearly, this is for situations in which the agents are representing creatures that have these sorts of capabilities. The collision routines are very simple because we might be dealing with hundreds of agents. Obviously, if there are not going to be many agents, or processor time is not at a premium, then these routines could be made more complex.

The Algorithm

For each active agent, store its current position, and then update its x and z position according to its speed and heading (y-rotation), and its y position by adding its fall speed. Change the agent's fall speed due to gravity. Calculate the difference between the agent's position and the target's position to give delta values for x, y, and z. Next, work out the *relative* angle (`angle`) of the target to the agent (`atan(dz,dx)` − `agent->yrot`). If the agent is fleeing from the target (because its `timer` is greater than a specified value), negate this `angle`. If the player is within a certain distance of the agent (use a proper distance check, or a simple collision box to save time), damage the player.

If the agent is not falling, then its steering and heading are adjusted as follows depending on whether it is in the inner or outer zone (e.g., if `(abs(dz) + abs(dx) >` `SWARM_RANGE)`, it is in the outer zone).

Outer zone: Increment the agent's speed if it is less than its maximum. The maximum speed should vary from agent to agent. If the agent is heading in roughly the right direction (`abs(angle) < AGENT_LOCK_ANGLE`), give the agent's y-rotation a small amount of waver; otherwise, change its y-rotation rapidly toward the correct heading.

Inner zone: Change the agent's y-rotation depending on its speed, and change its speed depending on its angle. The exact nature of the formulae for these changes determines the look of the swarm's movement around its target. As an example:

```
if (agent->speed & 0x1)
agent->yrot += SWIRL_ANGLE;
else
        agent->yrot -= SWIRL_ANGLE;
agent->speed = 48 - (abs(angle) >> 10);
```

This concludes the basic swarm steering code. However, it will also be necessary to carry out simple collision detection with the environment and get the agents to bounce off or climb walls, and to fall if they drop from a high place. The details of this will depend a great deal on the way in which the game world is represented, but an example is given in the code at the end of this chapter (Listing 4.6.1).

Termination

It is unlikely that players will be able to shoot individual agents in the swarm. Apart from the length of time this would take (and the unfeasibility of the task), it is likely to wreak havoc with the targeting algorithm to have to check hundreds of potential targets. In the version of the algorithm given here, agents are made inactive when their timer reaches a predetermined value or if they are falling too fast (this stops agents dropping "through" a level). However, depending on the creatures that are being represented, there are many other situations in which you might want to destroy the creature (by making it inactive) or cause it to flee by setting its timer to an appropriate value. For instance, a swarm of bees might be destroyed if it comes within range of a flaming torch held by the player, or the swarm might flee if the player becomes completely submerged in water.

Conclusion

As stated earlier, although Reynolds' flocking algorithms are perfect for small numbers of creatures, steering behaviors can become very expensive when the flock is large and the environment is complex. This article detailed a practical alternative for situations in which hundreds of agents need to be controlled. Swarms can be used in a variety of ways: for background effects, for nuisance value or as part of a puzzle, or simply as a deadly enemy. For pure dramatic effect, there are few things to compare with the appearance of a swarm of hundreds of separate entities behaving in an organic and very threatening manner.

Example Code

Listing 4.6.1 Swarm update. (Code reproduced by kind permission of Core Design Ltd.)

```
void UpdateAgents()
{
    AGENT_STRUCT    *agent;
    long    h, i, angle, dx, dy, dz, oldx, oldy, oldz;

    agent = &agents[0];

    for (i=0;i<MAX_AGENTS;i++,agent++)
    {
        //for each agent, check to see if it's active
        if (agent->active)
        {
            //remember its current position
            oldx = agent->xpos;
            oldy = agent->ypos;
            oldz = agent->zpos;

            //update x and z pos depending on y-rotation and speed
            agent->xpos += agent->speed * SIN(agent->yrot);
            agent->zpos += agent->speed * COS(agent->yrot);

            //update y depending on fallspeed
            agent->ypos += agent->fallspeed;

            //update fallspeed by adding gravity
            agent->fallspeed += GRAVITY;

            //calculate the difference between the agent's
            //position and the target position
            dz = target->zpos - agent->zpos;
            dy = target->ypos - agent->ypos;
            dx = target->xpos - agent->xpos;

            //work out the *relative* angle of the target to the agent
            //if it's time for the agent to flee, reverse the angle
            //It's a good idea to initialize agents with the timer
            //set to a small random value. That way, the swarm will
            //gradually disperse over time.
            if (agent->timer < (AGENT_LIFE_TIME - AGENT_FLEE_TIME))
                angle = ATAN(dz, dx) - agent->yrot;
            else
                angle = agent->yrot - ATAN(dz, dx);

            //It wasn't done here, but one could influence
            //the swarm depending on the way the player is facing.
            //One could also extrapolate player movement to set up the
            //player's likely future position as the target

            //Hit the player if within range
```

```
//(using your favored collision method)
//Here: a simple collision box.
if (abs(dz) < AGENT_HIT_RANGE && abs(dy) < AGENT_HIT_RANGE
   && abs(dx) < AGENT_HIT_RANGE)
   {target->hp-=AGENT_DAMAGE;}

if (!agent->falling)
// steer because not the agent is not falling
{
//if the target is outside your set range,
//go (roughly) towards it
   if (abs(dz) + abs(dx) > SWARM_RANGE)
   {
   //increase speed to the maximum for this creature
   //give each creature a slightly different maximum
   //(done here by & the index with 0x1f)

      if (agent->speed < 24 + (i & 0x1f))
         agent->speed++;

      if (abs(angle) < AGENT_LOCK_ANGLE)
      {
         //vary the steering each cycle — more organic
         agent->yrot += (global_counter - i) << 3;
      }
      else if (angle < 0)
         agent->yrot -= AGENT_TURN_SPEED<<1;
      else
         agent->yrot += AGENT_TURN_SPEED<<1;
   }
   else
   //if the target is roughly within a short range,
   //swirl around it
   {
      if (agent->speed & 0x1)
         agent->yrot += AGENT_TURN_SPEED;
      else
         agent->yrot -= AGENT_TURN_SPEED;

      //play around with the numbers in this next line
      //to get a variety of different behaviors
      agent->speed = 48 - (abs(angle) >> 10);

   }
}
//end of steering

h = FloorHeight(agent->x_pos,agent->y_pos,agent->z_pos);
if (h < agent->ypos — AGENT_MAX_STEP)
//If the agent's new position would be much higher
//than its current position, bounce it off the wall
//by resetting its position and changing its angle
{
   //if the agent hits a wall while it's fleeing,
   //deactivate it. This looks fine with small creatures
```

```
    if (agent->timer > (AGENT_LIFE_TIME - AGENT_FLEE_TIME))
        agent->active = 0;

    if (angle > 0)
        agent->yrot += 180_DEGREES;
    else
        agent->yrot -= 180_DEGREES;
    agent->xpos = oldx;
    agent->ypos = oldy;
    agent->zpos = oldz;
    agent->fallspeed = 0;
}
//If the agent's new position would take it onto a
//block of climbable height, angle its body upward,
//reset its x and z position and move it upwards
else if (h < agent->ypos - AGENT_IGNORE_STEP)
{
    fx->pos.x_rot = AGENT_CLIMB_ANGLE;
    fx->pos.x_pos = oldx;
    fx->pos.y_pos = oldy - AGENT_CLIMB_SPEED;
    fx->pos.z_pos = oldz;
    fx->fallspeed = 0;
}
else if (agent->ypos > h)
//the agent is below the floor surface, so move it up to
//the floor, reset its fallspeed and set falling to 0.
//This happens every cycle the agent isn't in the air
//(as we always try to change the y-pos due to gravity)
{
    agent->ypos = h;
    agent->fallspeed = 0;
    agent->falling = 0;
}

if (agent->fallspeed < AGENT_MAX_FALLSPEED &&
    agent->timer < AGENT_LIFE_TIME)
//tilt things as they fall
    agent->xrot = -(agent->fallspeed << 6);
else
//if they fall too fast or time's run out, kill them
    next_agent = agent->active = 0;

    agent->timer++;

        }
      }
    }
```

References

[Reynolds87] Reynolds, C. W., "Flocks, Herds and Schools: A Distributed Behavioral Model," *Computer Graphics*, 21(4), SIGGRAPH '87 Proceedings, pp. 25–34, 1987.

[Woodcock00] Woodcock, Steven, "Flocking: A Simple Technique for Simulating Group Behavior," Game Programming Gems, Charles River Media, pp. 305–318, 2000.

TACTICAL ISSUES AND INTELLIGENT GROUP MOVEMENT

Strategic and Tactical Reasoning with Waypoints

Lars Lidén—Valve Software

lars@valvesoftware.com

For the behavior of computer-controlled characters to become more sophisticated, efficient algorithms are required for generating intelligent tactical decisions. Non-player characters (or NPCs) commonly use waypoints for navigation through their virtual world. This article will demonstrate how preprocessing the relationships between these waypoints can be used to dynamically generate combat tactics for NPCs in a first-person shooter or action adventure game. By precalculating and storing tactical information about the relationship between waypoints in a bit string class, NPCs can quickly find valuable tactical positions and exploit their environment.

Beyond Pathfinding

It is common practice in 3D games for level designers to place waypoints in their levels for NPCs to navigate the environment [Lidén00]. These waypoints serve as nodes in a node-graph that represents all the ways in which an NPC can navigate through the world. Connections between nodes in the node-graph are either generated automatically in a preprocessing step, or placed manually by a level designer. Pathfinding algorithms such as A* are then used to generate routes through the node-graph [Stout00].

As the waypoints used for navigation inherently contain information about the relationship between positions in the world, they can be exploited to efficiently calculate information about the strategic value of particular world locations [Lidén01] and [vanderSterren01]. A closer look at a node-graph reveals that in addition to pathfinding information, it also contains data about the approachability of each waypoint, whether a waypoint is a dead end, and even if a waypoint is the sole approach to a particular region. Furthermore, with a little extra work, the node-graph can be used to generate static visibility information between nodes. Precalculating whether one waypoint has line-of-sight to another allows for fast runtime evaluation of map locations.

Fast Map Analysis

For the real-time evaluation of a map to be effective, an economical method for assessing the danger and strategic value of each location in the map must be employed. This is of particular importance when an NPC has to contend with multiple enemies, as any assessment must take the visibility and location of each enemy into account. The computational cost of such a method must not become prohibitive as the number of nodes and enemies increases.

An effective technique is to store connectivity and visibility information in a *bit string* class that consists of a string of bits of arbitrary length with operators for Boolean operations such as *<and>*, *<or>*, and *<not>*. For a node-graph N_n, consisting of n nodes, connectivity is represented by a set of n bit strings, C_n, in which the length of each bit string corresponds to the number of nodes in the node-graph, and each bit represents the connectivity from node n to every other node in the node-graph.

Network visibility is represented by a set of bit strings, Λ_n, in which the length of each bit string corresponds to the number of nodes in the node-graph, and each bit represents the visibility from node n to every other node in the node-graph. If β (E_i, t) is a function that returns the nearest waypoint for enemy i at time t, then the visibility of an enemy i is given by the bit string:

$$V_{it} = \Lambda_{\beta(E_i, t,)} \tag{5.1.1}$$

Each bit in the bit string represents whether each waypoint is visible to enemy, i. For notational simplification, the time component will not be included in subsequent equations, as it is understood that formulas apply to a specific time.

Using Visibility

The most straightforward use of visibility is to determine which locations are potentially *safe*, and those that are likely to be *dangerous*. For an NPC with a set of k enemies E_k, the set of dangerous waypoints is determined by *<or>*ing the visibility bit strings for each enemy's nearest waypoint:

$$V = \sum_{j=0}^{j=k} V_j \tag{5.1.2}$$

V is then the set of waypoints from which the NPC might have a line-of-sight (LOS) to shoot at an enemy. To determine LOS, each enemy must still be checked explicitly, as visibility bit strings tell us only about the visibility of each enemy's nearest waypoint, not their actual positions.

Safe nodes are given by the inverse, $\bar{V}$. These nodes are good candidates for safe locations to which an NPC can flee or reload safely (Figure 5.1.1).

Safe Pathfinding

Another straightforward use of visibility information is to find safe paths for an NPC to traverse the environment. Most pathfinding algorithms use a cost function to determine the shortest path through the node-graph [Stout96]. If a penalty is added to transitions that pass through nodes that are designated as not being safe, the

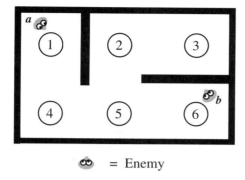

$$
\begin{array}{c}
\text{Node} \\
\begin{array}{cccccc}
1 & 2 & 3 & 4 & 5 & 6
\end{array}
\end{array}
$$

	Node 1	2	3	4	5	6
(a) $V_1 =$	1	0	0	1	0	0
$V_2 =$	0	1	1	0	1	0
$V_3 =$	0	1	1	0	0	0
$V_4 =$	1	0	0	1	1	1
$V_5 =$	0	1	0	1	1	1
(b) $V_6 =$	0	0	0	1	1	1

�= Enemy

DANGER NODES:

$V = V_a \cup V_b = 1 \ \ 0 \ \ 0 \ \ 1 \ \ 1 \ \ 1$

Nodes 1, 4, 5 and 6 are dangerous

SAFE NODES:

$\overline{V} = 0 \ \ 1 \ \ 1 \ \ 0 \ \ 0 \ \ 0$

Nodes 2 and 3 are safe

FIGURE 5.1.1 *Dangerous and safe nodes.*

pathfinding algorithm will be biased toward finding safe paths for the NPC. Depending on the size of the penalty given to dangerous waypoints, the NPC can be made to favor either: (1) safe paths when they aren't particularly longer than a regular path, or (2) safe paths at any cost, even when they take the NPC well out of its way.

Intelligent Attack Positioning

Although an all-out frontal assault can have its place, it isn't always the most intelligent form of attack. The set of dangerous waypoints, **V**, can give us locations from which an NPC can attack its enemies; it does nothing to protect the NPC from attack. A more sophisticated strategy would be to find a location from which the NPC can attack a particular enemy that also protects it from simultaneous attack by other enemies. Fortunately, determining such locations is straightforward and can be computed quickly.

As before, the set of potential waypoints from which a particular enemy, E_a, can be attacked is given by the set of nodes that are visible to that enemy (Figure 5.1.2 step 1):

$$V_a = \Lambda_{\beta(E_a)} \tag{5.1.3}$$

Nodes that are visible to the NPC's other enemies are determined by <*or*>ing their individual visibilities (Figure 5.1.2 step 2):

$$V_{\bar{a}} = \prod_{j=0}^{j=k} V_j, j \neq a \tag{5.1.4}$$

These waypoints are then eliminated from the set of potential attack positions, by taking the intersection with its inverse; namely, the set of waypoints that are safe from the other enemies, $\overline{V}_{\bar{a}}$ (Figure 5.1.2 step 3):

$$V'_a = V_a \prod \overline{V}_{\bar{a}} \tag{5.1.5}$$

The result is a set of locations from which a particular enemy can be attacked that are safe from all other enemies.

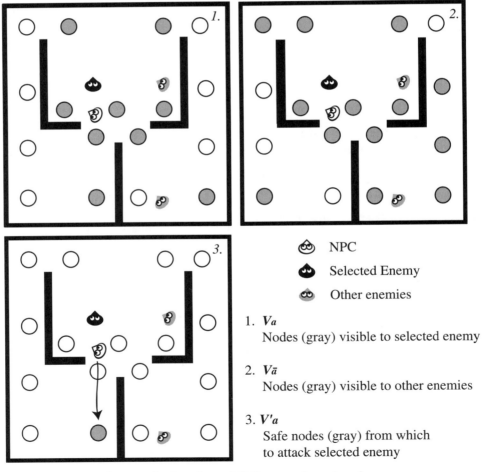

FIGURE 5.1.2 *Finding a safe place for an NPC to attack a selected enemy.*

Taking It Further

So, we have a quick way to find candidate locations from which to attack a particular enemy that is also safe from other enemies. What are some other strategies that an intelligent opponent might employ? It would be nice if our attack location had safety nearby in case our NPC needed to reload or the selected enemy suddenly launched a rocket in our NPC's direction. Fortunately, this is an easy qualification to add. From Equation 5.1.2, the set of all safe nodes is given by $\overline{V}$. Furthermore, from the node-graph, we know the connectivity of each of the candidate attack nodes, namely C_a. Therefore nodes in V'_a should be eliminated if:

$$C_a I \overline{V} = 0 \qquad\qquad (5.1.6)$$

The remaining locations have LOS to the selected enemy, are protected from other enemies, and have nearby locations to take cover from all enemies.

Flanking

Another interesting combat behavior is that of flanking. Flanking takes both the position and facing direction of an enemy into account, the goal being to surprise an enemy by attacking from behind. The procedure for finding potential flanking attack locations is virtually identical to that of finding normal attack locations. The only difference being that before eliminating nodes that are visible to other enemies (Equation 5.1.5), the set of potential attack locations, V_a should be culled to remove waypoints that the selected enemy is facing.

Once a flanking waypoint has been selected, if the pathfinding algorithm has been weighted to use safe waypoints, the NPC will look for a path that is out of sight of the selected enemy. The resulting behavior will be that of the NPC sneaking around behind to attack its enemy.

Static Waypoint Analysis

Unless cheating is employed, it's likely that an NPC doesn't have perfect knowledge about the locations of each of its enemies. Additionally, an NPC might want to place itself in a strategic location before enemies arrive. Consequently, in addition to finding tactical positions for a set of enemy locations during runtime, it is also useful to characterize each waypoint's strategic value in a static environment. Such characterization can be done in a preprocessing step before the game is played.

As we have seen, in quantifying a location's strategic value, visibility is perhaps the most important factor. Highly visible locations are dangerous, as they can be attacked from many positions. One can readily identify such locations by looking at visibility between nodes in the node-graph. The danger of each node can be characterized by giving it a weight based on the number of other nodes in the graph that have visibility to that node (Figure 5.1.3 step 1). If the weights are used to adjust the pathfinding cost function, the NPC will prefer to take paths that are less likely to be visible to an enemy.

Although nodes with low visibility are safe, they don't have a great deal of attack potential. Those with high visibility have the advantage that they can attack many positions. Ideally, we want a location that is safe, but has the greatest attack potential. Such locations can readily be determined from the node-graph by selecting nodes that have high visibility whose neighbors have low visibility (Figure 5.1.3 step 2).

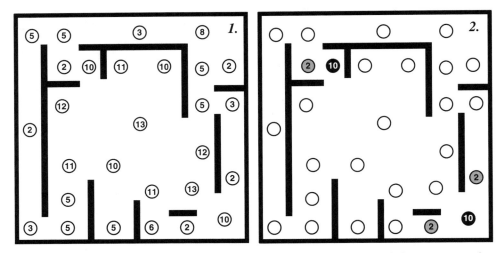

FIGURE 5.1.3 *Static waypoint analysis. 1. Nodes marked for their visibility count. Nodes in protected areas such as hallways automatically get a low weighting, while those in exposed areas get a high rating. 2. Sniper locations (marked in black) have high exposure and are attached to regions with low exposure (marked in gray).*

Pinch Points and Squad Tactics

Observation of human players reveals that experienced FPS players anticipate the actions of their opponents [Laird00]. For example, if an enemy enters a room with a single exit, rather than follow the enemy into the room, an experienced player will wait just around the corner, setting up an ambush at the exit point.

One can readily precalculate such tactical pinch-points by analyzing the node-graph (Figure 5.1.4 step 1).

For each node, **N** in the node-graph with only two neighbors:

- Temporarily eliminate node, **N**, from the graph, call its neighbors as **A** and **B**.
- If both **A** and **B** are connected to large regions, **N** is not a pinch point; try another **N**.
- Attempt to find a path between **A** and **B**.
- If path exists, **N** is not a pinch point; try another **N**.
- Call the node connected to the larger region, **O** (for outside).
- Call the node connected to the smaller region, **I** (for inside).

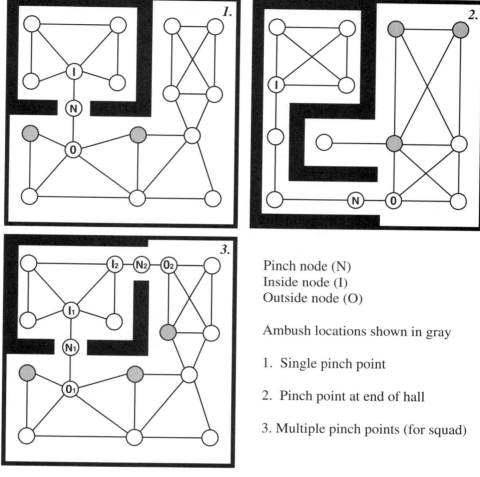

Pinch node (N)
Inside node (I)
Outside node (O)

Ambush locations shown in gray

1. Single pinch point

2. Pinch point at end of hall

3. Multiple pinch points (for squad)

FIGURE 5.1.4 *Finding places to ambush an enemy.*

To find potential ambush locations for **N**, we need a waypoint that has LOS to **O** and not **N**. This is simply:

$$A = V_O \, \mathbf{I} \, \overline{V}_N \tag{5.1.7}$$

When an enemy enters the region gated by node **I**, and NPC can set up an ambush at any of the nodes in the set **A**.

Things are slightly more complicated when detecting pinch points at the end of hallways. To include such cases, the following step must be added (Figure 5.1.4 step 2):

- If **O**'s neighbor has only one other neighbor in addition to **N**:
  —Move **N** to **O**.

—Move **O** to the other neighbor of the old **O**.
—Repeat until **O** has only one neighbor.

Squad Tactics

Regions with more than one exit can still qualify as having valid pinch points for NPCs that organize into squads, as each exit from a region can be guarded by a different NPC in the squad. For a squad with two members (Figure 5.1.4 step 3):

For each node, N_1 in the node-graph with only two neighbors:

- Temporarily eliminate node, N_1, from the graph; call its neighbors as **A** and **B**.
- If **A** and **B** are connected to large regions, N_1 is not a pinch point; try another N_1.
- Attempt to find a path between **A** and **B**.
- While generating the path if a node with only two neighbors is found:
  —Temporarily eliminate it and call it N_2.
  —Attempt to find a path between **A** and **B**.
- If path exists, not a pinch point, try another N_1.
- Call the nodes connected to the larger regions, O_1 and O_2 (for outside).

The ambush points for the two members of the squad are:

$$A_1 = V_{O_1} \mathbf{I} \, \overline{V}_{N_1} \quad \text{and} \quad A_2 = V_{O_2} \mathbf{I} \, \overline{V}_{N_2} \tag{5.1.8}$$

This can easily be generalized for squads of any size.

Limitations and Advanced Issues

There are a couple of caveats to the methods discussed here. Although use of a bit string class to store visibility and calculate tactical positions keeps the memory and computational costs down, for exceptionally large node-graphs, the size of bit strings could get prohibitively large. Each node stores one bit for every other node in the network, for a total of [*# of nodes*]^2 bits stored in memory. Each <and> and <or> operation requires [*# of nodes* / *sizeof (int)*] bitwise operations. The size of bit strings can be reduced by eliminating visibility and connectivity data for nodes in widely separated regions of world space that have no chance of having visibility or direct connectivity. Rather than representing the world as one large node-graph, a hierarchy of networks can be employed. Using node-graph hierarchies rather than a single large node-graph also has other unrelated advantages, including faster pathfinding [Rabin00].

A second limitation is that the effectiveness of precalculated tactical information relies to some degree on a level designer placing nodes in proper positions. If, for example, a level designer neglects to place nodes at a second exit to a region, the preprocessing step might incorrectly assume that a pinch point exists when in actuality there is a second exit that is usable by the player. With experience, level designers can learn proper node positioning. Additional research on the automatic generation of node placement by the computer might eliminate the need to rely on level designers for intelligent node placement.

There are several other issues to consider that are beyond the scope of this article. Here, it was assumed that all connections were bidirectional. In many situations, connections (such as jumps) are unidirectional. The determination of pinch points will be slightly different for unidirectional connections, and movement in both directions must be checked.

In many games, it is possible for a player or an NPC to gain cover by ducking behind obstacles. In such cases, a single location might serve as both a cover location and a position from which to attack. Such locations can be exploited by annotating the relevant waypoints. This can be done either manually by a level designer, or done as part of the preprocessing computations by the computer.

Conclusions

Computer-controlled characters commonly use waypoints for navigation of the world. This article demonstrated how existing waypoints can be used to automatically generate combat tactics for computer-controlled characters in a first-person shooter or action adventure game. The techniques might be applicable to other genres, but have yet to be tested in these arenas.

A level designer who is familiar with the behavior of NPCs and their ability to navigate, usually places waypoints in key locations in an environment. Tactical information about locations in the environment can be efficiently calculated from this implicit data and exploited by NPCs. Storing data in a bit string class allows for an economical method for calculating tactical information whose computational cost remains reasonable for large numbers of nodes and enemies.

Precalculated visibility information can provide a rough approximation of the danger of particular areas in a given map and locations from which an NPC can mount an intelligent attack. With waypoint visibility information, it is relatively straightforward to establish a line-of-sight to an enemy, automatically generate flanking locations, sniping locations, and to detect "pinch locations" where an enemy can be ambushed.

References

[Laird00] Laird, John, "It Knows What You're Going to Do: Adding Anticipation to a Quakebot," *Artificial Intelligence and Interactive Entertainment: Papers from the 2000 AAAI Spring Symposium*, Technical Report SS-00-02, 41–50, 2000.

[Lidén00] Lidén, Lars, "The Integration of Autonomous and Scripted Behavior through Task Management," *Artificial Intelligence and Interactive Entertainment: Papers from the 2000 AAAI Spring Symposium*, Technical Report SS-00-02, 51–55, 2000.

[Lidén01] Lidén, Lars, "Using Nodes to Develop Strategies for Combat with Multiple Enemies," *Artificial Intelligence and Interactive Entertainment: Papers from the 2001 AAAI Spring Symposium*, Technical Report SS-01-02, 2000.

[Rabin00] Rabin, S., "A* Speed Optimizations," *Game Programming Gems*, Charles River Media, 2000.

[Stout00] Stout, W. B., "The Basics of A* for Path Planning," *Game Programming Gems*, Charles River Media, 2000.

[Stout96] Stout, W. B., "Smart Moves: Intelligent Path-Finding," *Game Developer* magazine, October 1996.

[vanderSterren01]: van der Sterren, W., "Terrain Reasoning for 3D Action Games," *Game Programming Gems 2*, Charles River Media, 2001.

5.2

Recognizing Strategic Dispositions: Engaging the Enemy

Steven Woodcock—Wyrd Wyrks

ferretman@gameai.com

This article focuses on a problem common to many strategic war games: determining how one might engage the enemy. While this might seem straightforward enough to the player ("hey, they're over *there*, so I just need to move *this* and *this*), the computer AIs don't have the advantage of billions of years of biological evolution and have a bit harder time accomplishing this. Further, the AI must approach the enemy *intelligently*, rather than haphazardly trickling units toward the opposition (as we have all seen some games do).

This article outlines a variety of approaches loosely called *strategic dispositions* that are intended to help the budding turn-based or real-time strategy game developer build an AI that will work well at the strategic level. We discuss a variety of analytical techniques in the context of a strategic war game to assess the strong and weak points of the enemy, and then select the best location for an attack. Along the way, we'll cover one way to handle defensive moves as well (since in the larger context, that's merely a "strategic move to the rear"). We'll build on the basic *influence map* [Tozour01a] approach, and then add other techniques as enhancements to the basic approach to help the AI make better strategic movement decisions.

Influence Maps

Tozour outlines the fundamentals of influence maps in his article, and many of the considerations the developer will face in building them. A basic, finalized 2D influence map might look rather like Figure 5.2.1.

In this influence map, we've generalized the influence of each unit across the map (ignoring terrain for the moment), cutting each unit's influence by one-half for each square it moved away from the unit. We rounded down where there were any fractions. Squares that have a value of "0" are clearly under nobody's direct control and

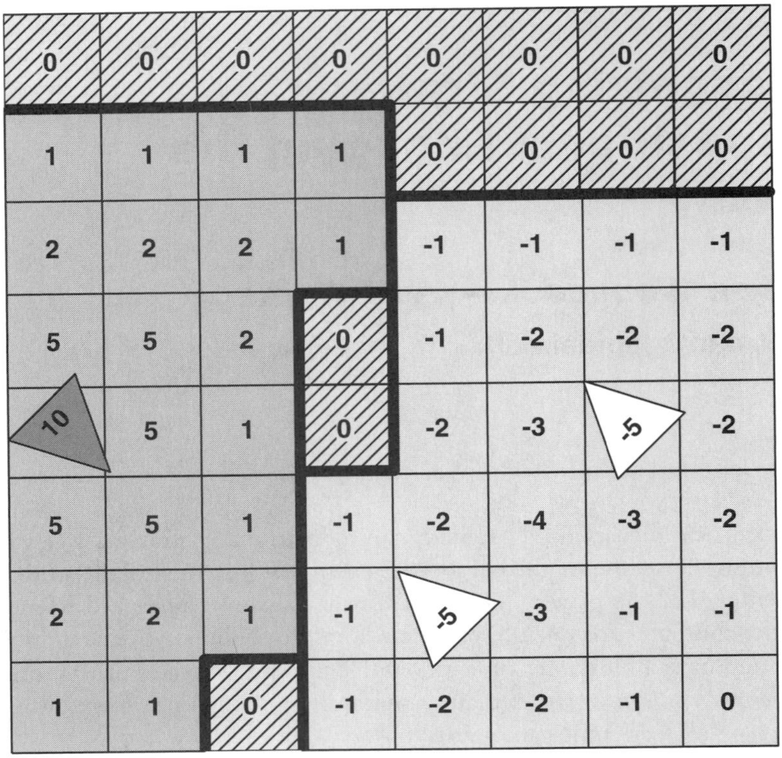

FIGURE 5.2.1 *A basic influence map showing a basic two-on-one engagement.*

are indicated with a crosshatch, while others are marked with a darker or lighter gray depending on the side that "owns" them. The "border" between the various units is indicated with a heavy black line. Any square surrounded entirely by zeros (in the upper right-hand corner of our example) are clearly "no man's land" and beyond the control of anybody. Note that the values flip from positive to negative as we travel toward the enemy units, indicating a reversal of control. Looking at the map from the black unit's point of view (on the left), the "front" is clearly comprised of the "0" value squares plus those squares in which influence flips from positive to negative.

If this were a one-on-one game of some kind, we might stop right here, select the enemy unit most vulnerable (due to damage or other factors we might use), and pick a path to the target. In this case, all things being equal, we'd probably go after the white unit on the lower right; he's closer, if nothing else, and we've already "pushed" his zone of control (i.e., the negative numbers) in pretty close to him. The overall "gradient" between our unit's influence and his is lower (10 to –1 versus 10 to –3).

Categorizing the Enemy

However, for most strategy games (whether real-time or turn-based doesn't really matter), we're more likely to have a situation resembling Figure 5.2.2. This map shows several units (black and white) with overlapping influences. There are seven white units numbered 1 through 7 scattered across the right side of the map, while six black units numbered 11 through 66 occupy a slightly tighter grouping on the upper left. Crosshatching and the heavy black lines still indicate the boundary between each side. For the purposes of discussion, we'll assume that the influence map has already taken into account things such as range, terrain, and so forth, and that every unit has a basic "strength" of five points. The "center of mass" of the black units is indicated by the reverse crosshatched square in the upper left.

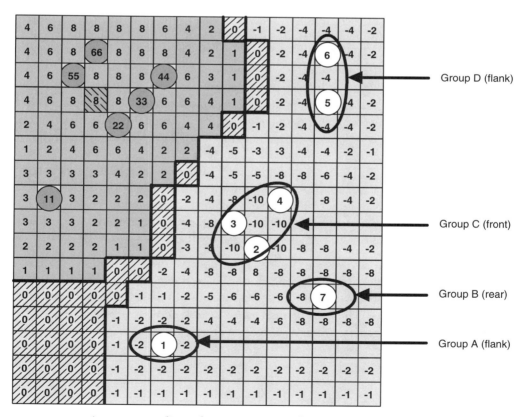

FIGURE 5.2.2 *A more complicated engagement with several units.*

One approach to using this information to help the AI make strategic decisions is to identify the enemy's front, flanks, and rear. We can then have our AI attack in the enemy's weakest areas. If we were to take the job of the AI for the black units and examine the white units, we can see some obvious groupings on how we might identify various groups.

Algorithmically we might use something along the lines of the following to make these formation identifications:

1. Determine the *center of mass* of our units (i.e., the approximate location with the highest value as determined by the influence map).
2. For every enemy unit we can see:
   a. Select the unit that has the greatest "gradient" of influences between the center of mass of our units and his. We arbitrarily call that the *front*. There can be only one front.
   b. If a given unit is within two squares of a unit belonging to the designated front, add it to the front as well.
   c. If a given unit is further than two squares from the front and has a gradient of influences less than that leading from the center of mass of our units to the front, it is designated as a *flank* unit. There can be several flanks.
   d. If a given unit is within two squares of a unit belonging to a designated flank, add it to the flank as well.
   e. If the shortest path to a given unit from our center of mass runs through a square belonging or adjacent to a unit delegated to the front, that unit is designated as part of the enemy's *rear*. There can be more than one rear.
   f. If a given unit is within two squares of a unit belonging to an area designated as the rear, add it to the rear as well.
3. Any unit that isn't allocated to one of the preceding groups (front, flank, or rear) is treated independently and can be considered an *individual* unit. There can be any number of individuals.

Note that anytime we classify a given enemy unit, we should move on to the next unit. Typically, one doesn't assign a unit to both flank and rear, for example.

This approach should lead to an allocation of white units corresponding to that in Figure 5.2.2. The rules themselves are flexible enough to be tweaked for the precise needs of the game, and can vary by side or an individual commander's "personality."

Engaging the Enemy

Doing It "By the Book"

The approach described previously does a reasonable job of identifying where the enemy is and what areas he controls versus what areas the player controls. It also provides a starting point for grouping the enemy into various categories of threat, and begins to suggest various approaches to engaging them at a strategic level. Other texts [Snook00, Pottinger00] have described how we might find paths toward the enemy and do some strategic planning [Tozour01b] against them.

One way of instructing units in strategic engagements is to use the tried-and-true methods developed by various armies over the centuries. If we are designing a game in which Napoleonic-era strategies make sense, we can proceed from that point. Most of the armies of Europe had a basic "strategy manual" that told each general exactly what to do once the enemy's front, flanks, rear, and so forth had been identified [Chandler01]. Moreover, since most nations of the era had differing rules of engagement, you automatically get AIs that "feel different"—an important facet for most strategic games.

There is a danger, however, in that using these approaches might lead to a somewhat predictable AI if the human is familiar with what the nationality of the AI is "supposed" to do. There are various ways around this. Two of the most popular are to provide each AI commander with his own personality that modifies his behavior somewhat, and to have the AI randomly choose from more than one reasonable strategy. Combined, the player only knows that what is happening is reasonable but (hopefully) unexpected.

Making Your Own Rules

If we're building, say, a futuristic real-time strategic (RTS) game, we've got more work to do to build an AI worthy of the name. The old rules don't really apply much as the settings are generally just too different. While we could simply direct, say, the white units to attack the nearest enemy they see (something seemingly common in many RTS games), we'd ideally like to put a bit more thought into it than that.

Identifying weak points in the enemy's disposition seems to be a natural approach. Looking again at the situation from the perspective of the black units, there are enemies that are relatively isolated (such as White 1 in the lower center of the map). However, that same unit is also a relatively long distance from the bulk of our forces (the center of mass indicated by the hashed square in the upper left), and engaging it would tend to expose *our* flank.

One solution might be to build some type of algorithm to help us with this decision. For Figure 5.2.2, for example, we might build an algorithm that compares the strength of the attackers, the observed strength of the defenders, the influence map gradient between the two, and the distance between them.

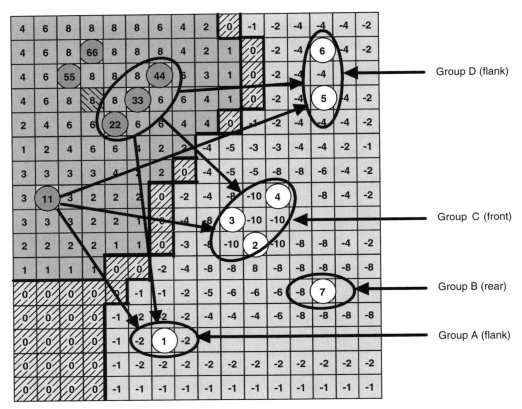

FIGURE 5.2.3 *An analysis of options.*

```
Option Value = (Attack — Defense) / (Distance * Gradient)
```

(Note that this is just for the purposes of illustration, kept simple for the purposes of this article. We're not trying to emulate any particular human behavior.)

This would generate a variety of options that the AI can then choose from based on its personality, random numbers, and so forth. Such an algorithm might give us a list of options looking something like Figure 5.2.3.

In Figure 5.2.3, we've analyzed the relative strengths, positions, and movement costs for black units 11 through 44. We've decided to leave units 55 and 66 in reserve for the moment, since they're in our rear and presumably exist mostly to counter breakthroughs or to add a decisive extra blow to any attack. We now have a total of six options available to us:

- Units 22, 33, and 44 have three options available:
  —*Option 1* to attack white Group D (a flank; value 0.08)
  —*Option 2* to attack white Group C (his front; value 0.0)
  —*Option 3* to attack white Group A (another flank; value 0.16)
- Unit 11 also has three options available:
  —*Option 4* to attack Group D (value –0.07)
  —*Option 5* to attack Group C (value –0.13)
  —*Option 6* to attack Group A (value 0.0)

If one were to apply an alpha-beta tree [Svarovsky00] to these options, a combination of *Option 1* and *Option 6* would fall out. Clearly, black unit 11 ought to engage Group A, while units 22, 33, and 44 seek to engage Group D.

What do we do with units 55 and 66? After making the preceding decisions for the units 11 through 44, we might subsequently decide to move units 55 and 66 toward Group C a bit in order to provide better flanking and to discourage that group from interfering with either attack. This move is "uphill" toward the center of mass of our units, a good rule of thumb for repositioning reserve units in general. Note that we've had to make two passes through the AI to assign units 55 and 66; our design deliberately kept them in reserve until after we'd assigned the units closer to the "front."

It should be stressed again that the precise option one might choose—indeed, the calculation of the options themselves—is really highly game dependent. The algorithm provided isn't very sophisticated and doesn't take a variety of potentially important factors into account. It's intended more as an example of what can be rather than as an ironclad suggestion, although it *will* work for a variety of strategic game applications.

Maximizing Points of Contact

Assuming your design allows for it, another approach might be to try to maximize the "points of contact" between your units and the enemy, while (ideally) minimizing *his* potential points of contact with *your* units. This is how many games are played, actually—as the player, you're continually trying to put more of your firepower against the enemy units while minimizing how much he can put against you. That's a classic way to achieve local superiority; in fact, a prelude to any number of future maneuvers. Take a look at Figure 5.2.4.

Here we've taken the situation outlined earlier and examined the situation from the point of view of the white units. We've employed an algorithm that attempts to compute the maximum number of "contact points" we might create by moving our units toward the black units, and came up with the following options:

- *Option 1:* Group A engages black unit 11 (one contact point).
- *Option 2:* Group C engages black unit 11 (three contact points).

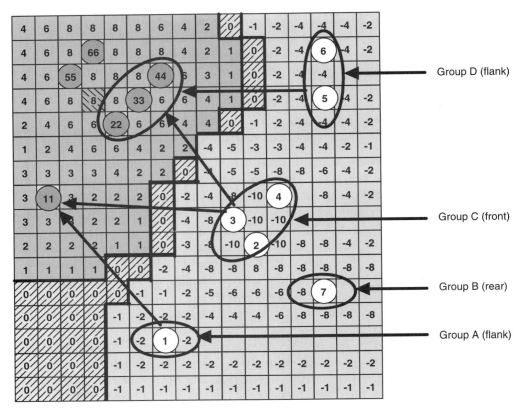

FIGURE 5.2.4 *Maximizing contact points.*

- *Option 3:* Group C engages black units 22, 33, and 44 (nine contact points).
- *Option 4:* Group D engages black units 22, 33, and 44 (six contact points).

Note that we haven't bothered to figure out combat strengths and whatnot, which ought to be a filter applied at this stage for most games. Assuming all was equal (as is the case in our example), another simple alpha-beta tree would probably result in our choosing a combination of options 1, 3, and 4, as these combined make for the largest number of contact points (16 total). Group B would probably be instructed to either move up closer to the fight for later allocation, or (depending how far out our algorithm looked) might join Group A against its objective. Further, the black units don't have much in the way of potential for creating their own contact points in response, since the only "unengaged" units he should have are in the rear, assuming our plans are successful.

Note too that we've tended to instruct the white units to move "uphill," toward the greatest areas of influence of the black units. This is intentional and is generally seen in

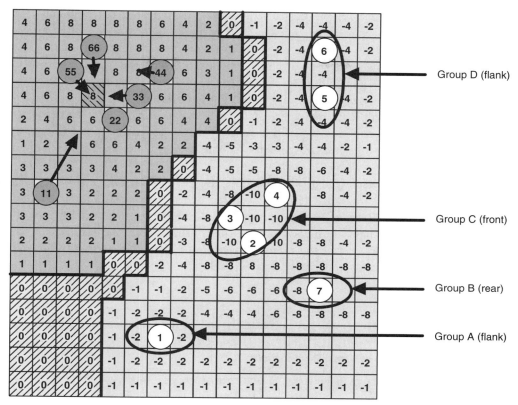

FIGURE 5.2.5 *Minimizing contact points.*

cases where the individual units have relatively equivalent firepower and have relatively equivalent influences. This motion uphill tends to maximize contact points over time, which is what we're after using this approach.

Minimizing Points of Contact—On the Defensive

One strategic decision our AIs might have to face is how to allocate forces while fighting on the defensive. It's all well and good to be deciding how to attack the enemy, but we've all seen AIs that did well on the offense but fell apart when on the defense. We'll probably want to figure out some reasonable ways to retreat from a battle and preserve our forces for a more favorable engagement later.

Figure 5.2.5 shows one such approach.

Here we've basically implemented the inverse of the method just described. Rather than trying to maximize our contact with the enemy, we can flip the algorithm around to *minimize* our contacts. This will naturally pull our units "away" from the enemy and group them together into naturally defensive clusters, from which we might be able to mount local attacks and delay action in future turns.

Note how we've done this by moving units toward the "high" points on our influence map and generally *away* from the influence of the white units. This naturally will increase their overlapping defensive values and (the next time we evaluate the influence map) will result in a tighter, more cohesive formation. This is the opposite of the situation described in Figure 5.2.4, in which we moved the greatest number of units *away* from our center of mass and "uphill" toward the black unit's highest area of influence.

Again, exactly what each unit does also depends on the capabilities of each unit, movement limitations, terrain considerations, and so forth. Much of that will be automatically driven out by a properly set up influence map, or perhaps an independent terrain-based influence map can be consulted after the basic options are generated. Remember that the example presented is greatly simplified, since every game will handle units, movement, terrain, and so forth differently.

Conclusion

Several ways one might improve on the suggestions are presented here.

Improvements and Drawbacks

The influence map built in the first section could easily include more detail—terrain considerations, partially damaged units, and so forth. Terrain analysis [Pottinger00] can also be used to great effect in conjunction with this, since it will drive out unusual terrain considerations (such as bridges, choke points, etc.) that can greatly influence the construction of each side's influence map(s). Choke points or bridges will stand out as highly concentrated influences surrounded by negative or enemy influence; those patterns can be identified and tagged by the AI as indicating important areas of the map. One must be careful not to make such a complex influence map that useful information is swamped by minutia, however, and there are CPU restrictions to consider as a part of map generation.

The "no man's land" between the two sides as outlined in Figure 5.2.2 (the zero-valued squares and adjacent squares that suddenly flip from positive to negative) isn't very wide. Moreover, it might not be as accurate as we'd like in terms of who controls what pieces of the map. That matters because that thin strip is a quick way to identify the likelihood of a given side seizing control of important objectives—it's important to get it right if it's to be meaningful. An influence that's pushed out far from our units shows that we have at least local superiority of firepower. There are many ways to compute a better influence map. One obvious way is to overlay the map with a finer grid, although the downside to that is, of course, greater CPU usage to generate the influence map. Another option is to change the values we assign to the influences of each unit or our formula for how quickly they drop off. This type of change would be highly game specific, however; our only suggestions here are a.) to experiment much, and b.) make everything easily changeable via an AI script if your game design supports such a thing.

The algorithms presented in the second section are fairly basic and don't do much to make qualitative comparisons between the units, nor apply qualitative assessments to what course of action is finally chosen. The developer would probably want to expand on these or substitute his own based on his game's needs and the amount of CPU he has available. As with most AI problems, the more complex the algorithm, the more CPU resources will have to be devoted to solving the problem, comparing results, and so forth. Fortunately, this is rapidly becoming a thing of the past [Woodcock01] as more CPU power becomes available to the AI in the natural course of hardware evolution.

Maximizing or minimizing contact points has a lot of value, but must be handled carefully. Maximization must include some other value judgments in the decision-making process (i.e., I *really* ought to capture *that* square because it's a bridge). An AI that only attempts to maximize contact points inevitably leads to huge long lines of units arrayed against each other in a WWI-style slugfest. By contrast, an unrestricted attempt to minimize contact points will inevitably lead to situations in which the AI groups its units into defensive circles, rather like the wagon trains of the Old West— lots of overlapping firepower there, but not much defense of anything besides your neighbor. Your AI won't gain many objectives or protect objectives important to the player unless their clusters just happened to overlap one.

What You Do Depends on the Game

The most important thing to remember is that what you do depends on the game. You want your AIs to be intelligent and react to the other side's moves, and yet you don't want them to "thrash" units between two or more reasonable options—you want them to actually make a *choice* and stick with it for as long as it is reasonable. Swapping between two states is called *state thrashing* and should be avoided at all cost, since it makes even the smartest strategic AI look very, very dumb.

References

[Chandler01] Chandler, David, *The Art of Warfare on Land,* Penguin USA, 2001.

[Pottinger00] Pottinger, Dave, "Terrain Analysis in Realtime Strategy Games," Proceedings, Game Developers Conference, available online at www.gdconf.com/archives/proceedings/2000/pottinger.doc, 2000.

[Snook00] Snook, Greg, "Simplified 3D Movement and Pathfinding Using Navigation Meshes," *Game Programming Gems*, Charles River Media, 2000.

[Svarovsky00] Svarovsky, Jan, "Game Trees," *Game Programming Gems*, Charles River Media, 2000.

[Tozour01a] Tozour, Paul, "Influence Mapping," *Game Programming Gems 2*, Charles River Media, 2001.

[Tozour01b] Tozour, Paul, "Strategic Assessment Techniques," *Game Programming Gems 2*, Charles River Media, 2001.

[Woodcock01] Woodcock, Steve, "Previous Game AI Poll Results," available online at www.gameai.com/oldpolls.html#RESOURCES2001, 2001.

Squad Tactics: Team AI and Emergent Maneuvers

William van der Sterren—CGF-AI

william.van.der.sterren@cgf-ai.com

"I'm taking fire. Need backup!" Bullets are hitting the low wall that provides barely enough cover for the soldier. "No can do," a nearby squad member replies. On the left, the call for "Medic!" has become softer and infrequent. Then, finally, the squad's machine gun starts spitting out its curtain of protection. "Move up! I'll cover you," the machine gunner calls.

When the AI operates in squads, it can do a lot for a tactical combat game: the squad's behavior and communications create a more realistic atmosphere. Squads fighting against the player will challenge his tactical capabilities, and squads fighting with the player might offer him a commander role.

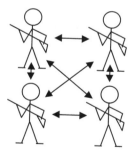

de-centralized approach: squad members exchange requests and intentions

intelligence distributed equally over squad members

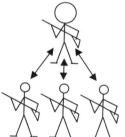

centralized approach: squad leader receives info, issues commands

leader has to know more, privates need to know less

FIGURE 5.3.1 *Decentralized squad organization versus a centralized squad organization.*

It is easy to answer *why* squad AI should be part of a combat game. However, it is not so easy to answer *how* to add squad AI to that game! There are many approaches to realize (part of) the required squad behavior, but none of these is complete or perfect.

This article and the next discuss two ways of realizing squad AI and squad tactics (Figure 5.3.1). This article presents a decentralized approach to squad AI: interactions between squad members, rather than a single squad leader, determine the squad behavior. And from this interaction, squad maneuvers emerge. This approach is attractive because it is a simple extension of individual AI, and because it can be easily combined with level-specific scripting. However, this approach is weak at maneuvers requiring autonomy or tight coordination.

The next article discusses a centralized approach to squad AI, with a single squad-level AI making most of the decisions. That squad-level AI autonomously plans and directs complex team maneuvers. However, that squad-level AI has trouble dealing with the strengths and needs of individual squad members.

This article briefly defines the key concepts of squad AI and squad tactics. It discusses the decentralized design, and its elements. Two examples are used to illustrate how this design enables squad tactics: a squad attack, and an ambush. Based on the example, this article discusses the strengths and weaknesses of the decentralized design, and some workarounds for the weaknesses.

For clarity and brevity, the squad here is assumed to consist of infantry soldiers, but the ideas presented also apply to many other small combat formations (tank platoons, trolls, naval vessels, giant robots, and so forth).

Squads and Leadership Style

A squad is a small team, consisting of up to a dozen members, with its own goals. The squad tries to accomplish its goals through coordinated actions of its members, even under adverse conditions. Casualties and regroupings cause variations in the squad's structure. Moreover, nearby operating friendly squads might interfere with the squad's operations.

Squads typically have a leader. In some cases, this leader is very visible and has a different role than the other squad members. In other cases, such as in room-clearing actions, the leader acts like any other squad member: the success of the action is primarily due to training, rather than the leader.

The squad selects and executes certain maneuvers to accomplish its goals. Such a maneuver provides each squad member with a role and task. A squad maneuver can be tightly or loosely coordinated. In a tightly coordinated maneuver, squad members rely on detailed repeatedly rehearsed drills, and continuously exchange information to synchronize and adjust their actions. Much of the synchronization is done through quick, nonverbal communication, such as predefined hand signals.

In a loosely coordinated maneuver, squad members synchronize their actions less often, or just with part of the squad. The squad relies less on well-known standard procedures, and needs larger (verbal) communications to synchronize the actions.

In designing squad AI, these concepts play an important role.

Squad AI through Cooperating Members

One approach to squad AI is the decentralized approach, in which the squad members coordinate their actions without the need for an AI squad leader. This approach is attractive for various reasons:

- It simply is an extension of the individual AI.
- It robustly handles many situations.
- It deals well with a variety of capabilities within the team.
- It can easily be combined with scripted squad member actions.

This combination of properties makes the decentralized approach an attractive choice for games that have the player to fight through levels of manually positioned teams of opponents. *Half-Life* [Half-Life98] collected a lot of fame for applying such an approach.

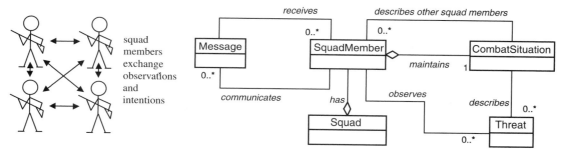

FIGURE 5.3.2 *The concept behind the decentralized squad AI (sketch and UML class diagram).*

The design of the decentralized approach is shown in Figure 5.3.2 (a UML class diagram [Fowler01]). The squad consists of AI members who all publish the following information to nearby squad members:

- Their intentions ("I'm moving to position <x,y,z>," "I'm firing from <x,y,z> in direction <pitch, yaw> at threat at <x,y,z>," "I'm going to reload").
- Their observations ("threat seen at <x,y,z>," "grenade tossed toward <x,y,z>)."

To select the most appropriate action to perform, each AI member takes into account the situation of his teammates and the threats known to the team, in addition to his own state. The required changes to the individual AI's periodic think method are illustrated in Listing 5.3.1.

There are no radical changes required to turn an individual AI into a cooperating squad member AI. Of course, many of the changes are found under the hood, but this way of implementing squad AI enables you to extend your individual AI rather than having to start from scratch.

Listing 5.3.1 The differences in AI think "loops" for solo AI and squad member AI.

```
void SoloAI::Think() {
  CombatSituation* sit = GetSituation();
  sit->Observe();


  for each available action {
    if( action.IsApplicable(sit) )
    {
      determine value of action in
        sit;
      if better than best action,
        make best action
    }
  }

  execute best action();
}
```

```
void SquadMemberAI::Think() {
  CombatSituation* sit = GetSituation();
  sit->Observe();
  sit->ProcessTeamIntentions();
  sit->ProcessTeamObservations();
  for each available action {
    if( action.IsApplicable(sit) )
    {
      determine value of action in
        sit;
      if better than best action,
        make best action
    }
  }
  nearbySqdMembers->AnnounceAction();
  execute best action();
}
```

Where Is the Squad Behavior?

However, if the squad member AI is not much different from the solo AI, and if this approach does not use a squad leader, where then do we find any squad behavior, let alone squad tactics?

In this decentralized approach, we find the squad behavior in the interactions of the squad members, rather than in their individual actions. That is because we use *emergent behavior.*

Emergent behavior (or self-organizing behavior) is functionality originating from the interactions of elements, rather than from their individual actions. The emergent behavior is generated from lower-level, simpler behavior [Reynolds87].

The tactical behavior of our squad should emerge from the interaction of the squad members. More specifically, it should emerge from the exchanged observations and intentions, and how this information is used in planning and executing individual squad member actions. The resulting behavior should be more than the sum of the individual squad member behaviors. This emergence of squad behavior is best explained with the example in the next section.

Emergent Fire-and-Maneuver Behavior

Let's assume that our solo AI features some simple combat behavior: it either fires at a threat, or moves via the shortest path to a better position to fire again. By moving, the AI is able to close in on threats, and prevents the threat to get a stable aim on him.

That solo AI decides to move (Move_Up) when it lacks a threat to engage, or when it has been at the same spot for a certain time. The solo AI will fire during the Engage_Threat state, unless it runs out of threats or out of time. This behavior is illustrated as a finite state machine in Figure 5.3.3.

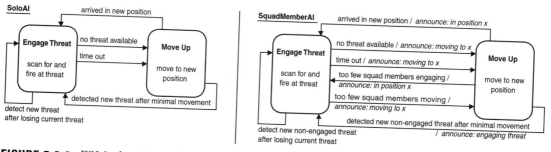

FIGURE 5.3.3 *FSMs describing the behavior of a solo AI (left) and squad member AI (right).*

The squad member AI does things a little different. First (in SquadMemberAI:: Think()), it announces its important intentions and decisions, so nearby squad members can use that to their advantage. Second, it determines the most appropriate action based on both his internal state and the perceived intentions and observations of his nearby squad members. (We will see in more detail how squad members communicate later in this article.)

When engaging a threat, the squad member AI will also decide to move up if it notices too many fellow squad members being static and engaging threats. When the squad member spots a threat it knows to be already engaged by fellow squad members, the squad member will not stop to engage it.

These changes to the individual AI lead to the fire-and-maneuver behavior scenario described in Figure 5.3.4. The emerging fire-and-maneuver behavior originates from the interactions between our simple squad member AIs. These interactions are easily translated to audible communications, making the squad behavior become more expressive and real.

Furthermore, this approach is robust against squad members becoming casualties. No matter which squad member is taken out, none of the other squad members will cease alternating firing and moving, although the time-out (engaging or being in a position for too long) might start playing a bigger role.

The approach is also sufficiently flexible to deal with squad members having different or special capabilities: one squad member might move slower, or be able to clear mines without the other squad members having to know or understand.

However, is this all there is to squad tactics? No! This decentralized approach to squad AI is just a solid base from which to work. It is easily extended with increasingly realistic tactics, as we will see in the next example.

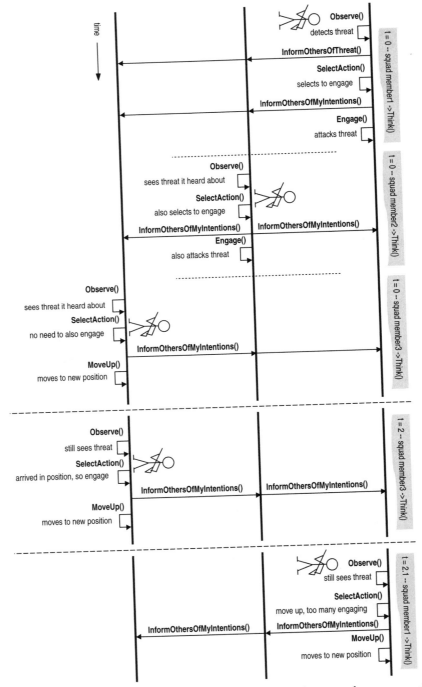

FIGURE 5.3.4 *Sequence diagram, describing the interaction between three cooperating squad members.*

Squad Assault: Tactical Enhancements

Imagine the following situation: A small four-man patrol, consisting of a patrol leader, a rifleman, a machine gunner, and a sniper, runs into an enemy position, and launches an attack (Figure 5.3.5).

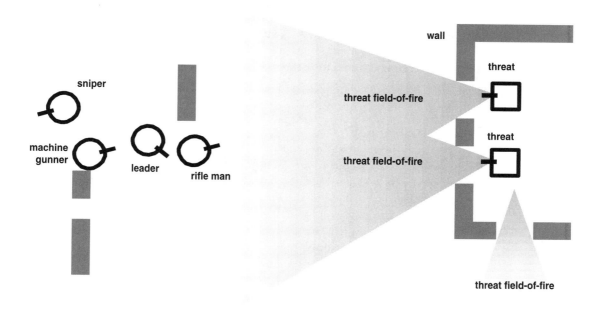

FIGURE 5.3.5 *Example of a four-man patrol arriving in a hostile situation.*

Now, we want our squad to do more than just fire and move: the squad is to employ proper tactical behavior, including:

- Stay close to cover.
- Prevent blocking other team members' lines-of-fire.
- Take weapon capabilities into account.
- Maintain team cohesion; in particular, stay within audible range and preferably maintain a line-of-sight to other squad members (analogous to the "flocking" rules for separation, cohesion, and avoidance).
- Spread out, and prevent becoming a bunched-up target.
- Stay aware of enemy positions and movement; thus, try to keep a line-of-sight on the enemy and his surroundings.

We can deal with these requirements in a straightforward way if we extend

- The squad member's mental picture (the `CombatSituation` class).
- The messages exchanged between the squad members.

- To include additional tactical information about the other squad members and their positions, capabilities, and actions.

  We also need to process this extra information, which is done using:

- A "next position to move to" algorithm, picking the tactically most suitable destination.
- Squad member subclasses (leader, rifleman, machine gunner, and sniper) defining the parameters for their specific behavior.

The Squad Member's Mental Picture

To move and engage according to the tactical requirements, a squad member should maintain the following situation (in the CombatSituation class):

- For each squad member:
  —Current position and activity of squad member.
  —Claimed destination position (and optionally, the path to the destination).
  —Line-of-fire (often a cone, originating at the squad member position, and with a radius determined by his aiming and the weapon's characteristics).
- For each opponent:
  —Last known position, and state.
  —Estimated current position(s).
  —Squad members engaging this opponent.
  —Squad members able to observe this opponent.
  —Line-of-fire.
- For other hazards and threats (fires, incoming hand grenades, etc.):
  —Known/estimated position.
  —Damage radius.

Communication among Squad Members: the Messages

The messages exchanged between the squad members convey the intentions and observation of these squad members. The messages should contain all the information needed by the receiving squad member to update his mental picture. The messages listed in Table 5.3.1 are typically needed.

Table 5.3.1 Squad Member Messages to Communicate Observations and Intentions

Intention	Parameters	Observation	Parameters
Moving to pos	Path	Threat spotted	Threat pos
Arrived in pos	Destination	Threat down	Threat pos
Frag (grenade) out	Frag destination	Threat moving	Threat old + new pos
Engaging threat	Threat pos, line of fire	Teammate down	member name

Each message also includes the identification of the sender. Upon receiving the message, the squad member updates his CombatSituation accordingly.

Depending on the squad coordination style, you might need to introduce additional messages for tighter synchronization.

Why use messages to pass squad member state information around, when this information is also available by inspecting SquadMemberAI objects directly? Well, passing state information via messages often is more attractive because:

- You can model communication latency by briefly queuing the messages.
- You can present the message in the game using animations or sound.
- You can filter out messages to the player to prevent overloading him.
- The squad member will send messages to dead squad members it assumes still to be alive, adding to realism (and preventing "perfect knowledge").
- You can use scripted entities to direct one or more squad members by having the scripted entities send messages to these squad members.
- You can accommodate human squad members, whose state information is largely unavailable, but for whom the AI can emulate messages with observations and intentions.

Picking a Tactically Sound Next Position

Acting tactically requires being in the right spot. For a squad member involved in our maneuver, this right spot depends on his personal capabilities and needs, on the needs of his squad members, and on the positions of the enemy (see Figure 5.3.6 next page).

In the maneuver, squad members employ brief moves, taking just a few seconds. Therefore, if each squad member repeatedly moves to the "tactically best nearby position," given the positions of all squad members and threats, some tactically sound maneuvering is likely to emerge.

Each squad member uses an evaluation function to pick the most suitable spot from all nearby spots. This function evaluates many tactical aspects of each position, based on the squad member's state and preferences, known squad claims on positions, and the threats. This is done as shown in Listing 5.3.2.

Listing 5.3.2 Algorithms for picking a next position and evaluating each position.

```
// SquadMemberAI::PickNextPosition
for( spot=nearbyspots.begin(); position!=nearbyspots.end(); ++spot ) {
  if( IsClaimedByFellowSquadMember(*spot) )
    continue;
  value = GetManeuverValueForNextPosition(*spot);
  if( value > highestvalue ) {
    mostsuitablespot = *spot;
    highestvalue= value;
  }
}
float SquadMemberAI::GetManeuverValueForNextPosition(spot)
```

```
{
  return    m_BunchPenalty         * ProjDistToBuddiesAsSeenFromThreat(spot)
          + m_BlockedPenalty       * BlockedLineOfFireBySqdMembers(spot)
          + m_BlockingPenalty      * BlockingLineOfFireOfSqdMembers(spot)
          + m_NeedForCover         * DistanceToNearestFreeCoverSpot(spot)
          + m_NeedForContact       * NumberOfLinesOfSightToBuddies(spot)
          + m_NeedCohesion         * ProperDistanceToBuddies(spot)
          + m_NeedForIntel         * NumberOfLinesOfSightToThreats(spot)
          + m_NeedToAvoidCorpses   * DistanceToDeadBuddies(spot)
          + m_NeedForClosingIn     * MinimumDistanceToThreats(spot)
          // below are non-reactive
          + m_NeedForStrongSpot    * AverageTacticalValueOfSpot(spot)
          + m_FormationPenalty     * DistanceFromFormationSlot(spot);
}
```

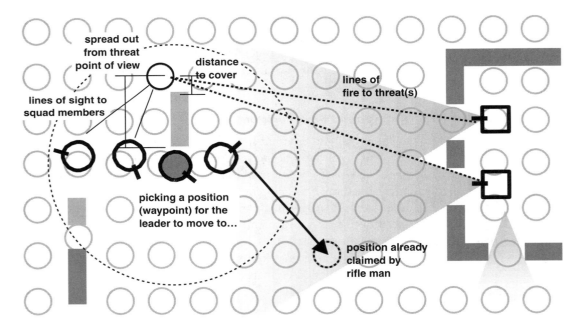

FIGURE 5.3.6 *The leader evaluating positions and picking one (center, top) to move to.*

The evaluation function is robust: it will return a spot to move to in all types of situations and terrain, as long as sufficient maneuver space is available.

Note that most of the "best next position" evaluation criteria are reactive: these criteria are largely determined by the behavior of the threat and other squad members. This reactivity typically leads to varied behavior when the battle is repeated.

However, this reactivity does not provide good results in the absence of threats. In such a situation, the squad should occupy sound tactical locations that in general provide a good fighting position against any threat. The squad can do so by avoiding any spot that limits the ability to attack, such as ladders, deep water, or elevators. More sophisticated approaches are also possible: see article 5.1 by Lars Lidén, "Strategic and Tactical Reasoning with Waypoints," and [vanderSterren01].

Additionally, the squad member can try to maintain its position in the squad's formation (and pay a penalty for spots away from that position).

Personalizing the Squad Member Behavior

Different squad members have different preferences for a position to move to. These differences are due to the squad member's capabilities, the state of the squad member and his equipment, and the circumstances.

Riflemen behave different from machine gunners and snipers: riflemen move quick and often, and are expected to close in with the enemy. Machine gunners, on the other hand, will be slowed by their load, and prefer delivering support fire from a rather static position. Machine gunners will not move very often, and consequently need a position providing sufficient concealment and cover. A sniper will not close in, but engage the enemy from a distance. Having a clear view and some cover is important for the sniper.

The squad member's state also influences the position preferences: cover is more preferred when the squad member is wounded, or has to reload.

The presence of threats and friendly forces influences how the squad member moves: a large number of friendly forces and few threats cause aggressive and audacious moves, whereas the reverse situation results in more cautious position choices.

The algorithm in Listing 5.3.2 uses the member characteristics and state to select a next position. For example, a sniper will have a weak tendency to close in with the enemy (attribute m_NeedForClosingIn) and a strong penalty for blocking squad lines-of-fire (a large negative value for m_BlockingPenalty).

Problems and Workarounds

A few problems are lurking beneath the surface of this fire and maneuver procedure. Especially in an obstacle rich environment, it is possible for squad members to choose moves and paths that conflict.

For example, one squad member might block the only path to a destination of another squad member, or two squad members might bump into each other, both trying to go the other direction via the same spot.

By taking into account the claimed path positions in the evaluation function (Listing 5.3.2), it is possible to prevent these conflicts to some extent: a squad member will not select a position on a path temporarily claimed by another squad member. Then again, in combat, things do go wrong, and the AI should be prepared to deal with exceptions.

To resolve these conflicts, a priority system can be used [Gibson01]. The squad member priority determines who of the two (or more) squad members will have to give way or pick another destination. Such a priority can be based on the time to destination (shorter time to destination results in higher priority), the urgency of the squad member, or the strength of his weapon.

In some terrain conditions, squad members might fail to close in with the enemy. For example, if there is a canal between the squad and the enemy, squad members might fail to make it across the canal. The range in which the squad members search for new positions might be smaller than the width of the canal, so the squad members fail to pick spots across the canal. In addition, the squad members will refuse to pick a spot in the canal itself, because these are not good positions to attack from or to find cover.

This problem can be overcome by having the squad members occasionally use a larger range to pick positions from. The use of a larger range, although computationally more expensive, has the added advantage of increasing the chances of a squad member attempting to flank the enemy. Randomly searching in a larger range also leads to more varied behavior.

Another problem is silly movements: movements that do not make sense in combat, but simply result from the AI's need to periodically move around (in this algorithm). Especially when a large squad is operating in close quarters with insufficient movement space for the whole squad, this might happen.

Again, each squad member AI itself can test for these conditions, and reduce its need to move. Alternatively, introducing an explicit squad (leader) AI with a corresponding overview of the situation may be a better approach. You'll find more on squad level AI in article 5.4, "Squad Tactics: Planned Maneuvers."

Waiting in Ambush: Pros and Cons

The pros and cons of this emergent squad AI will be illustrated using another example (or rather, a counter-example, since it primarily highlights the cons). Our squad is to perform an L-shaped ambush from a position near the edge of the woods. To execute this ambush, our squad needs to be able to:

- Wait until the enemy moves into the kill zone, after which the squad is to aggressively attack the enemy.
- Pull back to a predefined rally point shortly after engaging the threats.
- Return fire, leave the ambush, and pull back to the rally point when discovered (and engaged) by the enemy before it reaches the kill zone (Figure 5.3.7).

This decentralized approach to squad AI deals well with half of these ambush requirements. First, each of the squad members will return fire when being attacked, without relying on instructions from a team leader (who might have become the first casualty). It will not be easy for the enemy to take out the ambush from a distance.

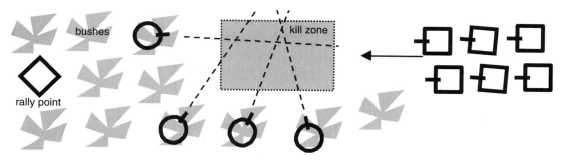

FIGURE 5.3.7 *Executing an L-shaped ambush: waiting for the enemy to enter the kill zone.*

Second, this AI is easily enhanced to include a strong preference for being near the rally point. As a result, the squad members (at least, those who survive) will fire and maneuver toward the rally point. To enable this behavior, the level designer should be given access to such an optional, editable squad member "property."

By implementing a squad member aggression level that depends on the number of nearby team members, and on the number of threats it is engaging, we can get the squad to briefly engage the enemy, and fall back when taking casualties.

However, our decentralized approach has trouble dealing with the other ambush requirements. Most important, a squad organization based on cooperation rather than an explicit leader will have serious trouble reaching a decision and executing it unanimously. For our ambush, this means that our squad is not organized to collectively hold fire until the threats reach the kill zone. We would have to introduce a "sleep" state, and wake up the squad either when receiving hostile fire, or when hostile forces activate a trigger positioned at the kill zone.

Additionally, the squad lacks autonomy. Whereas the squad does consist of autonomous members, nobody has been tasked to think for the squad. If the enemy moves toward the kill zone, but decides to pull back before reaching it, nobody in the squad will bother to assault. Due to the same lack of autonomy, the squad would never initiate the L-shape ambush itself.

It is up to level designers to invent the ambush and position the squad.

Conclusions

Squad behavior might already emerge when squad members share their individual observations and intentions, and base their decisions on their individual state and the perceived states of nearby squad members.

The squad member AI presented here is a simple extension of standard individual AI, but results in squad behavior that is reactive, varied, and robust: squad members participate in squad maneuvers from their individual situation, needs, and strengths.

The squad members use messages to share intentions and observations. Because of the message-based communication, the squad has little trouble accommodating scripted team members.

Together with good placement, this emergent squad AI approach is well suited to provide challenging squad behavior in single-player games.

If your squad AI is expected to act autonomously, you will need to use an explicit squad AI, dealing with squad-level reasoning and decisions. Even in that case, the message-based cooperation between fairly autonomous squad members is an important ingredient. The next article addresses this squad level reasoning in more detail.

References and Other Inspirations

[Fowler01] Fowler, Martin, Scott, Kendal, *UML Distilled: A Brief Guide to the Standard Object Modeling Language*, 2nd ed., Addison-Wesley, 2000, free tutorials available at www.celigent.com/omg/umlrtf/tutorials.htm.

[Gibson01] Gibson, Clark, O'Brien, John, *The Basics of Team AI*, Game Developer Conference, available online from www.gdconf.com/archives/proceedings/2001/o'brien.ppt, 2001.

[Reynolds87] Reynolds, C. W., *Flocks, Herds, and Schools: A Distributed Behavioral Model*, Computer Graphics 21 (SIGGRAPH '87 Proceedings) related material available online at www.red3D.com/cwr/boids/, 1987.

[vanderSterren01] van der Sterren, William, "Terrain Analysis for 3D Action Games," *Proceedings*, Game Developers Conference 2001, paper and presentation available from www.cgf-ai.com, 2001.

[Half-Life98] Half-Life SDK2.1, Valve Software www.fileplanet.com/index.asp?section=0&file=44991.

[NOLF01] No One Lives Forever SDK, Monolith www.noonelivesforever.com/downloads.

For more inspiration, have a look at the emergent squad AI implementations available on the Internet, as part of game mod developers SDKs (do read the accompanying license agreement first!):

5.4

Squad Tactics: Planned Maneuvers

William van der Sterren—CGF-AI

william.van.der.sterren@cgf-ai.com

The military rely on two important elements to achieve their objectives in dangerous, chaotic, and confusing circumstances: leaders and well-rehearsed procedures. Without a leader thinking for the squad as a whole, that squad is unable to quickly assess its situation and decide on the best course of action, such as a group retreat. Without relying on a small number of well-known procedures, the squad will waste time exploring options and resolving confusion.

The same holds for squad AI we develop: left on their own, the squad members might be able to defend themselves, or overwhelm a defense in a simple attack (as is illustrated in the previous article). However, it takes squad-level AI to assess the situation for the squad as a whole, and choose the best action. When executing the maneuver, the squad-level AI will be able to detect problems, and either resolve them or abort the maneuver for another one.

This article discusses squad-level AI and reasoning. First, we look at how squad-level AI and individual AI interact (and sometimes conflict). Then, we discuss how to assess the squad's situation and pick a course of action. Based on an example (pulling back our squad while laying down cover and suppression fire to slow down the enemy), we discuss the planning and execution of such a maneuver. We conclude with a number of pros and cons of squad-level AI.

While far from a complete overview of squad-level AI, this article assists you in identifying the challenges of squad-level AI. It provides a number of combat-proven solutions, while building on the emergent squad AI discussed in the previous chapter. For clarity and brevity, the squad again is assumed to consist of infantry soldiers, but the ideas apply well to other small combat formations.

Squad AI and Individual AI

Splitting the squad's AI in two parts, squad-level AI and individual AI, offers a number of benefits. It separates concerns, thereby significantly reducing the amount of problems that each type of AI has to cope with. It allows us to change and specialize each kind of AI independently from another.

Additionally, by doing a number of computations just once for the entire squad, rather than for each squad member, we might be able to reduce the demand on the CPU (later in this article is an example).

The relation between the `Squad` and `SquadMember` is illustrated in Figure 5.4.1. The `Squad` consists of a number of `SquadMembers`. The `Squad` maintains a squad-level situation based on observations received from the `SquadMembers`, and `Commands` it issued to the `SquadMembers`. The squad-level situation is different from the `SquadMember`'s individual situation (`MemberSituation`), as will become clear in the next section. You might want to compare this with the class diagram of the emergent squad member AI (Figure 5.3.2 in the previous chapter).

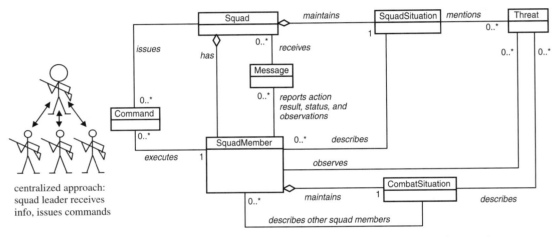

FIGURE 5.4.1 *The relation between Squad and SquadMember (as a UML class diagram).*

The `Squad` coordinates the `SquadMember` actions into an effective maneuver by assigning goals and tasks to these `SquadMembers` using `Commands`. While essential for coordinating the `Squad`, these `Commands` also cause problems in the design of the AI and in the resulting behavior. Some of the `Commands` issued will conflict with the `SquadMember`'s objectives, or be inappropriate for the situation (`MemberSituation`) at hand.

Authoritarian Command Style

The Authoritarian style has the `SquadMember` always obey and execute the command (because there is no "I" in team). This style results in rapidly responding `SquadMembers` and tightly coordinated maneuvers. It also enables the `Squad` to sacrifice (or risk) one `SquadMember` for "larger" squad-level purposes: reducing danger to the other `SquadMembers`, or meeting a `Squad` objective (through a suicide attack).

However, this style performs badly when the `SquadMember`'s situation is inconsistent with the `Squad` level view. For example, a `SquadMember` ordered to defend a front-line will have serious problems with a lonely enemy sniper at his rear. Dealing with that sniper conflicts with his orders, but at the Squad level, the sniper is just an easily overlooked detail. The Squad might not send a command to deal with the sniper.

Coaching Command Style

Another extreme style is the Squad acting as coach for the SquadMembers. The squad just issues tasks to the SquadMembers. The Squad relies on the SquadMember to execute the task to its best abilities, when the SquadMember sees fit. The SquadMember informs the Squad when it is not capable of executing the task. This feedback enables the Squad to reassign that task to another member.

Obviously, the SquadMember confronted with the dilemma of a sniper at his rear and a front to defend will simply engage the largest threat of the two, and inform the Squad of his temporary incapability to defend the front, or of the sniper present in the rear. However, with a group of individually operating SquadMembers, it will be tough for the Squad to execute any maneuver with speed and momentum: SquadMembers are easily distracted by details having little to do with the Squad's mission, such as picking up a better weapon lying nearby.

Picking the Best Command Style

While there is no such thing as the optimal command style, you will go a long way addressing your squad requirements by a smart mix of the two styles discussed here. Enhance the authoritarian style with early feedback from the SquadMember when it is not capable of executing the command. Annotate each command with the value of its execution to get more attention as coach. Explicitly communicate the rules-of-engagement for each squad member, based on the situation. For example, you can leave a lot of initiative to individuals when regrouping the squad, but you will need immediate and guaranteed compliance when executing a door-breaching-room-clearing drill.

Assessing the Squad's Situation

The squad-level view of the situation enables the AI to select and plan the best course of action for the squad as a whole. This "squad situation" also serves to monitor and evaluate the execution of the current course of action. Like any view of interpretation, it will be incomplete or incorrect at times.

The squad situation is not just the combination of the situations reported by the squad members. It has a different time horizon: squad maneuvers typically take longer than the solo AI plans and actions; consequently the squad situation should include more "predicted future."

The ingredients representing the squad situation largely depend on the courses of action available to the squad, and the potential threats and risks.

In general, situations in squad-level battles are not as clear cut as in sports games. Positions are not as predictable and easy to recognize as a 3-5-2 formation (in soccer) or 4-3 zone defense (in football). This is because of the complex and sometimes even dynamic terrain, the varying team sizes due to casualties, and the large variations in member capabilities with respect to movement, observation, weapons, and armor.

Nevertheless, there are several tools available to build a useful picture of the squad's situation. For example, influence maps provide the AI with a picture of the locations occupied and threatened (influenced) by friendly and hostile forces.

Influence maps are a good representation of the current and nearby future situation if the game hosts many units, if units can easily fire in any direction, and if the combat model is attrition based. (Influence maps are discussed in article 5.5, "Recognizing Strategic Dispositions: Engaging the Enemy," and in [Tozour01].) If the game features few units, limited fields of fire, and single-shot kills, influence maps might not be a good enough approximation. In that case, you might want to manually pick the ingredients that sketch a good picture of the situation. This is illustrated in Figure 5.4.2.

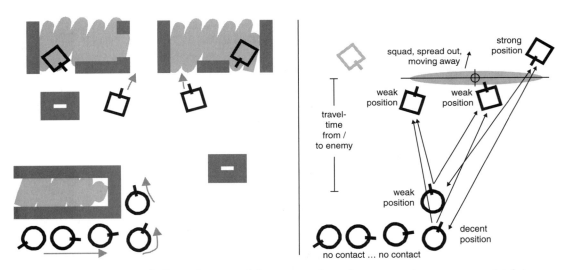

FIGURE 5.4.2 *Situation (left), and extracted features used to select appropriate maneuver (right).*

A small squad of five is turning the corner, and spots a number of hostiles. Two of the friendly squad members see (just) three hostiles (of the four present), and have a line-of-fire to all three. Only one of the hostiles has a direct line-of-fire to two members of the friendly squad.

This situation can be expressed in a number of abstract features, which in turn can be used to select the most appropriate maneuver. This situation can be interpreted as follows (ignoring the threat that has not been spotted yet):

The hostile force has its center near the middle threat, is well spread out (as seen from the friendly squad), and, on average is moving away from the squad. The travel time from the squad to the hostile positions equals that of the reverse trip (which would not be the case if the enemy were in a hard-to-reach high spot from which it could jump down).

Two of the hostiles have a weak position, being out in the open with little cover nearby. The third hostile, in the building, does have a strong position. One of the two squad members with a line-of-sight to the hostiles is also in a weak position, whereas the other has some cover nearby.

As seen by the squad, the force ratio is 5 to 3, with a line-of-fire ratio of 2 to 1. The friendly positions are about as good as those of the enemy. In addition, it takes the squad as much time to close in with the enemy as it would take the enemy to close in with the squad. The range of the engagement is small.

With this more general description of the situation, in terms of force ratio, line-of-fire ratio, and so forth, we can define rules for selecting the appropriate maneuver, as covered in the next section.

However, in your game, you will need more ingredients to construct a useful squad-level view of the situation. If other teams are near and available for help, their presence needs to be taken into account. Historic data such as a threat being spotted to move to a certain building some 10 seconds ago can be used. Even experience, such as the tendency of the enemy to defend a certain position in strength during previous games, might be included.

Picking the Appropriate Maneuver

Now that our squad AI has turned observations, historic data, and experience into a picture of the situation, it needs to determine the best maneuver for that situation. To do so, the squad AI keeps track of the maneuvers permissible, evaluates the fitness of each of these maneuvers for the situation, and picks the maneuver with the highest fitness.

First, we look at evaluating the maneuver's fitness. It then will become clear why the squad also needs to keep track of permissible maneuvers.

One way to evaluate the fitness of a maneuver is using fuzzy rules that express the situation in which the maneuver is applicable. For example, if the pullback maneuver is best selected when our squad is the weaker force, has relatively few lines-of-fire, occupies a weaker position, and the enemy is close by, this could be expressed as:

```
fitness(pullback) =
    weaker(force ratio) ∩ weaker(line-of-fire ratio)
  ∩ weaker(position quality) ∩ equalorworse(close-in time)
  ∩ mediumorshorter(range)
```

A maneuver might be applicable in multiple situations. In that case, there would be additional rules for that maneuver. The maneuver's fitness then is the highest fitness returned by the maneuver's rules.

These fuzzy rules are a handy means to define maneuver selection criteria because they closely resemble the conditions and rules-of-thumb that we use ourselves. That close resemblance makes it easy to come up with new and better rules for employing a maneuver, and facilitates tuning and debugging.

So, why is it necessary for the squad to keep track of permissible maneuvers? If the squad's view of the situation is correct and complete, the highest-scoring maneuver would always be the one to pick. However, the squad's view is typically not correct and complete: the maneuver being executed strongly affects the way the squad observes its surroundings, and consequently affects the squad's view.

Imagine that our outnumbered squad decides to pull back to a safe position 15 seconds away. The squad hopefully breaks contact with the enemy in the first five seconds, and spends the next 10 seconds completing the maneuver and reaching the safe position. Due to breaking contact, the squad will lose touch with the enemy. And soon, our squad is likely to "see" a situation with few, if any, enemies.

It now is possible for the squad to reassess the situation, erroneously preferring other maneuvers over completing the pullback maneuver. The squad might even decide to turn and attack the last few enemies that it has not yet forgotten about. In that case, it probably would choose to pull back again soon. Obviously, we don't want our squad to oscillate between maneuvers.

A good way to prevent most of these oscillations is to restrict transitions between maneuvers by means of a state machine. For example, the state machine illustrated in Figure 5.4.3 would prevent our squad from attacking before it completed its pullback maneuver. Alternatively, you could have the squad AI cheat and provide it with perfect information.

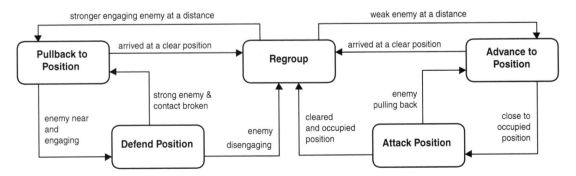

FIGURE 5.4.3 *A state machine defining the valid sequences of maneuvers to prevent oscillation.*

Although not illustrated here, the squad's objectives, tasks, and rules-of-engagement (as set up in the hierarchy) play an important role in selecting the best maneuver to execute.

Case: Bounding Overwatch Pullback

It is easier to explain how the squad executes a maneuver if we use an example: a bounding overwatch pullback maneuver. In this maneuver, the member farthest from the destination moves toward the destination, bypassing all his teammates, while his teammates lay down suppression fire to delay the pursuing enemy. After being passed by, it is the next farthest teammate's turn to pull back. He then lays down cover fire for a few seconds and moves to the front of the formation (Figure 5.4.4).

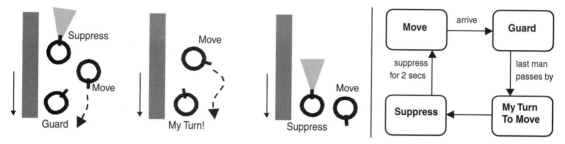

FIGURE 5.4.4 *The tail squad member's behavior when moving back, and the corresponding FSM.*

The path used to pull back should be a good combination and compromise of short travel time, cover, concealment from pursuing enemies, and sufficient space to maneuver (leapfrog beyond a teammate).

Searching for such a path is not cheap (CPU-wise), nor is it guaranteed that a good enough path exists. These constraints make this maneuver a squad-level issue: the squad member AI, with or without interaction, would not be able to efficiently select and execute such a maneuver (Figure 5.4.5).

FIGURE 5.4.5 *A pullback path, cover fire locations, and two bounding moves in progress.*

Maneuver Classes

Our squad will have a repertoire of maneuvers, and execute only one at a time. Although the maneuvers vary significantly (regrouping a team, or laying in ambush is quite different from pulling back), they interact with the squad through a few general interfaces. Therefore, the maneuver is best implemented as a separate class, according to the OO design pattern "Strategy" [Gamma94]. This design is illustrated in Figure 5.4.6. The Maneuver class will have access to most of the squad's state.

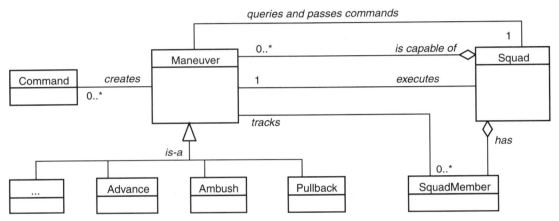

FIGURE 5.4.6 *The relations between squad, maneuvers, and commands (as a UML class diagram).*

As illustrated in Figure 5.4.4, in the pullback maneuver each SquadMember goes through a number of states that are specific for that maneuver. That same Squad-Member probably will go through different states when clearing a room, or leaving a helicopter.

Rather than trying to combine all these states into a single SquadMember state machine, we will get a cleaner and easier-to-manage design if the Maneuver itself tracks the SquadMember and its state within the Maneuver.

Performing the Maneuver

A maneuver is executed in several stages: first the maneuver is prepared, which includes planning and issuing the initial commands to the squad members. For the pullback maneuver, that involves constructing the path, determining the ordering of the squad members, and sending them to their first positions.

Then, during the main stage, the progress of the maneuver is monitored. Each SquadMember that arrives at its position informs the Squad. The Maneuver then provides the SquadMember with a new Command (such as "hold position until SquadMember x passes by").

At any time, the execution of this pullback maneuver might run into problems: for example, if one of the squad members falls from a ledge and can only reach the destination via a completely new path, the squad as a whole might decide to pull back along that new path. In such a case, the squad goes through maneuver preparation again before continuing (Figure 5.4.7).

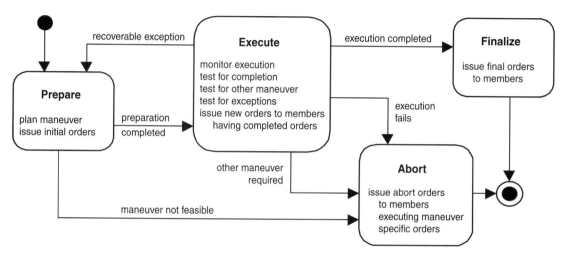

FIGURE 5.4.7 *The various stages in performing a maneuver (as a UML state chart).*

When execution of the maneuver fails, or when the SquadSituation calls for some other Maneuver, the Maneuver should be aborted. It might be necessary to issue "abort" commands to some SquadMembers to stop them from continuing with activities unique to the Maneuver being aborted.

Similarly, if the Maneuver is completed, special orders might be necessary to ready the SquadMembers for subsequent Maneuvers.

Preparing the Pullback Maneuver

To prepare the bounding overwatch pullback maneuver, the squad needs a good and safe destination, and an appropriate path for the squad to pull back along. The squad might locate that safe destination, for example, using an influence map.

But how does the squad create a path that is suitable for our pullback maneuver (and looks like the one in Figure 5.4.5)? Such a path provides cover and concealment from pursuing threats. That path also provides sufficient space for a SquadMember to leapfrog past his fellow SquadMembers toward his next position.

The path being illustrated is also one of the quicker ways to get to the destination: we do not want the enemy to get there before our Squad does. Finally, the path should preferably consist of positions that allow for decent fighting positions against any unforeseen threats: nearby cover, freedom of movement, and absence of obstacles such as ladders, doors, and deep water.

A tactical pathfinding problem like this simply calls for the Swiss Army Knife of pathfinding: A*. A* easily handles custom cost functions that are more complex than just distance or travel time [Reece00].

To construct a path according to our pullback requirements, the maneuver can use a cost function to evaluate the next node on the path, such as:

```
float CostsForNextNode(node next, const vector<node>& pathsegment)
  const
{
  float traveltimecosts, lackofcovercosts, nobypasscosts, unsafecosts;
  traveltimecosts  = TravelTime(pathsegment.back(), next);
  lackofcovercosts = NumberOfNodesAbleToFireAtNode(pathsegment, next);
  nobypasscosts    = LackOfByPassAtNodeToNode(pathsegment.back(), next);
  unsafecosts      = TacticallyBadPosition(next);
  return  kDuration  * traveltimecosts + kCover * lackofcovercosts
        + kAmpleSpace * nobypasscosts  + kSafe  * unsafecosts;
}
```

This cost function differs from a standard A* cost function in the penalties (additional costs) for:

- Nodes that can be fired at from preceding nodes (which would be beneficiary to any pursuing threats).
- Nodes that provide insufficient space to bypass (actually, the penalty applies to the previous node when moving toward the next node, because only then is movement direction known).
- Nodes that are a bad position from which to fight.

The total costs for adding this "next" node to the path is a weighted mix of the travel time and these penalties.

Although we can enhance the A* cost function with a number of penalties, we typically cannot do the same with the A* heuristic: estimating whether the remaining part of the path will lack cover, or will lack space to bypass a squad member is not possible. Instead, we will have to make do with a traditional A* heuristic (such as the travel time for the linear distance to the destination).

In the presence of additional penalties, such a heuristic is pretty optimistic. As a result, this A* search probably explores more nodes and paths than a traditional shortest path search. Note also that the cost function checks for lines-of-fire, which does not come cheap in most in game engines. Thus, constructing such a path is best left to the squad, rather than done by each individual squad member.

When A* provides us with a path, that path might not be good enough. As long as the destination is reachable, A* will always return a path to that destination, even if all penalties apply. Therefore, the AI needs to check whether the path is good enough, or change the A* algorithm to stop after exceeding a certain cost limit. Such a cost limit, however, is not that easy to define.

If no suitable path can be found, the Maneuver should be aborted and the squad should choose an alternative maneuver. Perhaps the squad should pull back in another way (using an emergent fire-and-move maneuver, as discussed in the previous chapter), or stay and defend its current position.

If the pullback path is good enough for the squad's purposes, it is time to pick the positions where the squad members are to halt, turn, and provide suppression fire. A simple heuristic will do the job: iterate over the path toward the destination, and mark:

- Each position just before a bend in the path that blocks the line-of-fire from many preceding positions on the path, provided that:
  —This position features sufficient room for squad members to bypass it.
  —This position is a good position from which to fire.

The tactical justification of this heuristic is simple. If you are being pursued and you need to fire at your pursuers, the best spot is where you just need to turn the corner to have cover and be closer to your destination.

These spots alone might not result in bounds of comparable length. It might be necessary to mark a few additional bypassable fighting positions, and to remove some selected spots. In Figure 5.4.5, the black circles mark the spots where the squad members are to make their brief stand.

Executing the Pullback Maneuver

The Squad, the Pullback maneuver object, and the SquadMembers interact as illustrated in Figure 5.4.8 to execute the maneuver.

The Squad has selected the Pullback maneuver and prepares it, resulting in initial orders for its SquadMembers. The maneuver does not directly interact with the Squad-Member but passes the commands via the Squad. This allows the Squad to implement command passing in any way it chooses: briefly delay the command, use an explicit leader making the appropriate sounds and gestures, and so forth.

If the maneuver runs according to plan, the bulk of the work has already been done during the preparation. During the normal periodic Execute(), it suffices to check if the maneuver concludes, fails, or if any exceptions occur.

The Maneuver directs its SquadMembers by responding when they complete a task. In such a case, the SquadMember informs the Squad, who in turn informs the Maneuver. The Maneuver then looks up the SquadMember's role, expected state, and next state, and issues a corresponding command.

If a SquadMember fails to comply with a command and informs the Squad, the Maneuver might respond similarly (by issuing another command), or by aborting or restarting the maneuver.

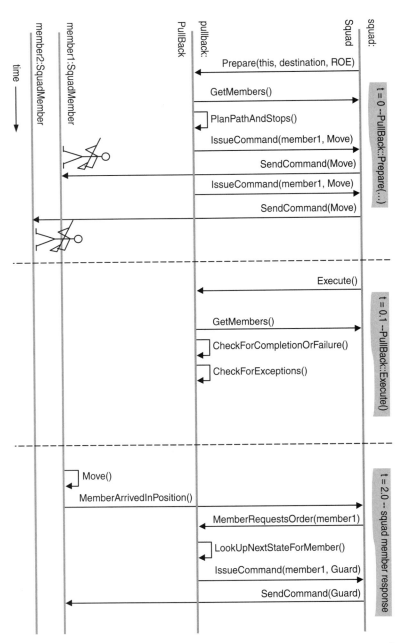

FIGURE 5.4.8 *Sequence chart of the interaction between Squad, Maneuver, and SquadMembers.*

When you start developing maneuvers for your squad, always start with simple ones, and keep them around. The squad AI will need them to fall back on, if complex maneuvers fail.

Conclusions

Game AI squads are able to autonomously select and execute "special forces" style maneuvers, even in the presence of complex 3D terrain. To build such a squad, you need skilled members: individual AI that is eager and reliable in executing orders and in communicating with its squad and squad members.

It also takes a leader: squad-level AI that is able to read the situation, to select the maneuver appropriate for the situation, and to direct the squad members. Together, squad-member AI and squad-level AI should produce a coordinated single effort to achieve the squad's objectives.

However, as in reality, building such a squad also takes a lot of training—read: development effort and experimentation time from you. This article, together with the previous one, should help you "train" your AI squads efficiently before they ship to fight their battles...

In contrast with the previous article, the squad AI presented here is centralized (one AI thinking for all of the team). Centralized solutions are good for synchronization and coordination, but have trouble handling variation. For example, in the pullback maneuver presented, no attention is given to the squad member's individual capabilities: would a sniper be able provide suppression fire? Should we give the machinegun a specific position?

Of course, these cases can be dealt with, but as exceptions, thereby introducing complexity and typically a good amount of code.

Please note that squad AI is a much larger issue than discussed in this article. Here, we ignored formations, strategic AI, scripts issuing directions to the squads, and lots of other things. Luckily, this article is amidst articles discussing these other issues.

References and Other Inspiration

[Gamma94] Gamma, Erich, et al., *Design Patterns*, Addison-Wesley, 1994.

[Gibson01] Gibson, Clark and O'Brien, John, "The Basics of Team AI," *Proceedings*, Game Developers Conference, 2001.

[Reece00] Reece, Doug, et al., "Tactical Movement Planning for Individual Combatants," *Proceedings of the 9th Conference on Computer Generated Forces and Behavioral Representation*, also available online at: www.sisostds.org/cgf-br/9th/, 2000.

[Tozour01] Tozour, Paul, "Influence Mapping," *Game Programming Gems 2*, Charles River Media, 2001.

A list of publications on tactical AI, with material originating from the game industry, defense industry, and academia, is maintained at www.cgf-ai.com.

5.5

Tactical Team AI Using a Command Hierarchy

John Reynolds—Creative Asylum

john@creative-asylum.com

Team-based AI is becoming an increasingly trendy selling point for first- and third-person action games. Often, this is limited to scripted sequences or simple "I need backup" requests. However, by using a hierarchy of decision-making, it is possible to create some very convincing teams that make decisions in real time.

The importance of the bot—that is, a computer-controlled non-player character (NPC)—has increased since the introduction of multi-player gaming. Playing with, or against, human opponents can really show the shortfalls of the computer players.

Many action games are now using teams as a fundamental part of their game design. Others have team-based elements for the multi-player games, such as capture the flag or cooperative death-match games. Providing the player with teammates and opponents who are comparable to humans is a tough challenge. However, approaching the task as a human team would is a good start.

Hierarchy of Command

Every effective team needs a good command hierarchy. Decisions must be made at the top level and carried out effectively by the lower levels. Each level will have responsibilities, with lower levels being subordinate to the higher levels. The levels of command must also have effective communication, with orders being made in sufficient detail and information passed up the hierarchy so that decisions can be made in response to changing circumstances.

In order to clarify this concept, a metaphor-based on military ranks can be used. The *commander* makes the top-level, strategic decisions and issues orders to each *captain*. Each captain organizes his team to carry out the commander's orders. This might involve breaking the team down further, in which case the *sergeant* would look after the specifics of the subteam. Finally, there is the *soldier*. The soldier carries out the orders while looking out for information (Figure 5.5.1).

The soldier is what we would recognize as a bot, moving around the level and firing. The other ranks are purely conceptual, and are not seen directly. However, a more senior rank could be attached to a bot, provided it also takes on the role of soldier.

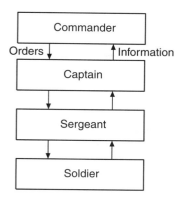

FIGURE 5.5.1 *Command hierarchy.*

However, this would allow the chain of command to be broken if the senior bot was to be killed, leaving the subordinate bots without orders until a soldier reports the loss of the captain. The commander would then assign a new captain.

To provide an example scenario, a soldier sees an opponent in room 5 and notifies the higher levels. The commander decides to allocate six soldiers to perform an outflanking maneuver using the two doors leading to room 5. The captain organizes the six soldiers into two teams, one for each door, of three soldiers each. A sergeant is allocated to each subteam to make sure they get to their assigned doors safely. Each sergeant commands his three soldiers to move carefully, covering their rear as they go.

The soldiers move around obstacles toward their destination, looking out for anything of interest to report as they go. All the soldiers are keeping the formation assigned to them by the sergeant. When all the soldiers are in position, at their assigned doors, the captain gives the command to attack room 5, indicating which direction to take when they enter. All six soldiers enter the room looking for the enemy and proceed around the room in their specified direction. Once the attack is completed, the captain informs the commander that the maneuver is complete.

Decision Support

A good set of decision support routines is an essential element for creating convincing AI. Decision support is needed at every level. All levels of command need to know a great deal about the environment where the soldiers and their opponents are. Some of the more complex functions are described next. Other, simpler, routines are outlined in Table 5.5.1.

```
bool CanReachWithoutRoom(int iAvoid, int iFrom, int iTo);
```

Can a solider travel from room iFrom to room iTo without passing through room iAvoid? This is used to determine which soldiers can reach the destination while avoiding the room where the opponent is suspected to be.

Table 5.5.1 Decision Support Routines

Function	Description
RoomDoorLeadsTo(Door)	Which room the door leads to.
EstimateToWaypoint(From, To)	Time estimate to get to waypoint.
NumDoors(Room)	How many doors does the room have?
NearestBot(Waypoint)	Finds the nearest bot to the given waypoint.
NumOrdered(Order)	Number of bots carrying out the specified order.
IsTeamInPosition()	Is the team in position and ready for new orders?

```
int RoomsMustCross(int iFrom, int iTo, int *piRoomList);
```

Fills the array pointed to by piRoomList with a list of rooms that a soldier *must* travel through when moving from room iFrom to room iTo. If a room can be bypassed, it is not included in the list. The function returns the number of rooms in the list. This is used to determine whether the opponent must travel through a room in order to reach a target.

```
int ExitsToRoom(int iFrom, int iTo, int *piDoorList);
```

Fills the array pointed to by piDoorList with a list of doors through which a solider might travel when moving from room iFrom to room iTo. The function returns the number of rooms in the list. This is used to determine which doors must be covered to prevent the opponent from entering a room.

```
int FindAvailableBots(int *piBotList, int iThreshold);
```

Modifies the list piBotList, which initially contains a list of soldiers to be considered, to include only those soldiers that are currently doing something less important than the value set by iThreshold. For example, attacking the opposition has a higher value than patrolling. Table 5.5.2 lists an example set of values

Table 5.5.2 Soldier Priority

Current Status	Priority
Patrolling	+8
Searching	+16
Moving to location	+24
Guarding	+32
Attacking	+48
In combat	+56
Rank of Sergeant	+2
Rank of Captain	+3
Health low	+1
Ammo low	+1

for different duties, ranks, or circumstances of a soldier. A soldier will start with a priority of zero and will add the priority value from the table according to its circumstances. These values allow soldiers to be chosen by their current status, and for soldiers of a certain rank or health to be omitted unless their status is of a lower priority.

Implementation

The decision support routines are the building blocks of the AI implementation. We can now look at how these blocks can be used to reach decisions, ways in which processing time can be kept to a minimum, some techniques for making individual soldiers behave convincingly, and some tips on debugging.

Choosing a Strategy

The commander will have a number of options whenever new information is presented. Figure 5.5.2 shows how decisions are made for a simple set of strategies. The strategies are chosen according to their effectiveness. The most effective strategy for the current situation will be considered first, and, if not suitable, drop down to less effective maneuvers. The example in Figure 5.5.2 could be implemented using a rule-based system. This way, more maneuvers could be added by expanding the set of rules.

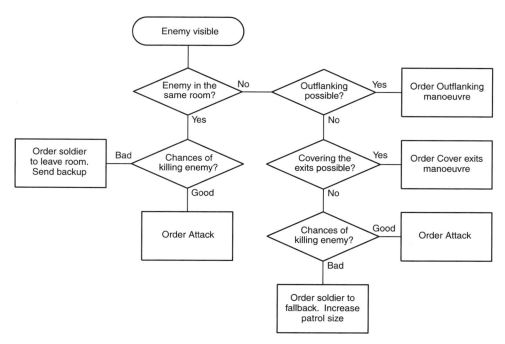

FIGURE 5.5.2 *Strategic decision-making.*

Adding a random element to the choice of strategy can reduce predictability as the player becomes more familiar with the game. This is good if the player is playing against the team of bots, as it will prevent the player from anticipating the strategy that will be adopted. However, if the player is a member of the team, predictability may well be beneficial, as the team would be behaving as the player would expect.

Randomizing the choice of strategy will also impact the game's level of difficulty, as the most effective strategy will not always be used. This would provide some variance to the challenge presented in each team-based attack.

Message Passing

The use of message passing is very effective when implementing team-based AI. Using messages to communicate between the different layers of the hierarchy is a very natural way of passing orders and information. It also has the added advantage of being very processor friendly: the higher levels only need to process data when some new information is received, and no one has to poll their superiors or subordinates to gather information.

A list of the *order messages* can be found in Tables 5.5.3, 5.5.4, and 5.5.5. The *information messages* sent by the captain are found in Table 5.5.6, and the *information messages* sent by the soldier are in Table 5.5.7.

Table 5.5.3 Commanders' Orders

Order	Parameters
Patrol	Roomlist
Search	Roomlist
Move To	Waypoint Number
Guard	Room Number, Door Number (optional)
Attack	Room Number
Defend	Room Number
Join Team	Captain ID
Leave Team	No parameter
Outflank	Room Number, Reachable Door List
Cover Exits	Room to prevent opponent from entering, Roomlist for search

Table 5.5.4 Captains' Orders

Order	Parameters
Guard	Door Number
Cover	Waypoint to stand at, Direction to cover
Attack	Waypoint list indicating route to follow
Search	Waypoint list indicating route to follow
Move to Room	Room Number, Door Number (optional)

Table 5.5.5 Sergeants' Orders

Order	Parameters
Follow	Bot Number
Cover Rear	Bot Number
Check Door	Door Number
Wait	Waypoint to wait at
Formation	Formation ID

Table 5.5.6 Captains' Information

Information	Parameters
Maneuver Complete	No parameters
Maneuver Not Possible	No parameters

Table 5.5.7 Soldiers' Information

Information	Parameters
In Position	No parameters
Search Complete	No parameters
Enemy Located	Enemy waypoint
Enemy Lost	Last seen at waypoint
Soldier Down	Bot ID
Low on Ammo	No parameters
Injured	No parameters

Data Sharing

Orders should contain as much data as will be useful for subordinate levels to carry out their tasks effectively. Tables 5.5.3, 5.5.4., and 5.5.5 list the orders given by the commander, captain, and sergeant, respectively, along with the parameters that provide the information useful to the subordinate levels. The data contained in the parameters should prevent any duplicate processing from having to be carried out.

Certain data, such as the last position where the opponent was seen, will be of interest to every level. This can be shared using globally accessible data to avoid lengthy messages being sent to multiple soldiers. However, global data can lead to problems when debugging and should be used with care. Global data should not be used to replace messages. The soldier should still report the change in data, even if the data is in a globally accessible place, just to keep the processing advantages of the message-based system.

Preprocessing

Some preprocessing must occur to calculate which areas are rooms and how they are connected. How this process works is dependent on the map data and so will not be discussed here. However, this static data might present some problems with deformable scenery. If the room and door data can be calculated quickly enough, then this could be done whenever some scenery is destroyed and a new entrance to a room is opened up. However, if the map data does not allow such fast processing, then the designer must be aware of the AI implications of scenery deformation.

Sergeant- and Soldier-Level AI

The importance of the AI for the individual bot, the soldier in the metaphor, should not be underestimated. This extends beyond aesthetically pleasing pathfinding routines and on to convincing the player that the soldier has some common sense, and has been to combat school. Even if an AI team is working well, the player will be very critical if the soldiers are moving in an unconvincing way or making some dubious low-level decisions. Some basic tactics are outlined next that might help provide a more convincing soldier and vary the gameplay a little.

Soldiers supporting each other during movement—be it in the form of bunny hopping, covering the rear, or just moving in formation—will provide a greater threat to the opponent and give a convincing feel to the team. This behavior should be organized by the sergeant.

Soldiers should not move past an open doorway without checking it to some degree. If soldiers are certain the room they are passing is safe, then they can just pass. They might also just give a glance if they are in a hurry or are fatigued. However, if the situation is tense, then soldiers might be more cautious. This is also true for moving around a corner. There are tactical ways to go round a corner, and these should be implemented as convincingly as possible.

The use of cover also contributes to the suspension of disbelief. This is not trivial to implement, particularly if there is more than one opponent. However, if soldiers are aware of their surroundings, they need to consider strategic options such as ambushes.

Soldiers should patrol the rooms they have been allocated in a logical order. This might be achieved using a simple algorithm based on the nearest room in the list and the time in which it was visited. This might be modified to provide some variance to the patrol route without having the soldier constantly crossing the map to get to the next room. This also avoids the problem of players memorizing the patrol route.

When several soldiers are simultaneously attacking a room through a single door, there are tactical methods of entry. Implementing some of these techniques will provide realism, challenge the opponent, and provide some variance to the attack.

Debugging

It is always hard to trace what is happening when a soldier does something stupid. By the time it has happened, several frames have gone by and the AI routines are working on something completely different. Fortunately, this implementation offers the programmer the opportunity to log the messages between the levels of command. This can be used to provide quite a natural dialogue between levels of command outlining all the information and decisions that have been made. This can be invaluable when tracing where the errant information has come from or which decision was at fault.

Outflanking Maneuver

To help explain the implementation, it is helpful to look at a couple of examples. The first is a simple outflanking maneuver (Figure 5.5.3).

If an opponent is suspected to be in a room that has more than one doorway, then the commander could give the order to outflank the opponent. This would involve the captain sending a group of soldiers to different doors and, when everyone is in place, giving the order to attack. This will present the opponent with a simultaneous threat and is therefore very effective.

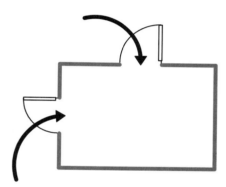

FIGURE 5.5.3 *Outflanking maneuver.*

Strategic Decision Process

The job of the strategic decision process is to check that the maneuver is both possible and appropriate. In this pseudo-code example, there must be at least two available soldiers and at least two accessible doors for this maneuver to be achievable. While the routine is checking the number of doors that are accessible, the door IDs are stored to prevent duplication of some of the processing when organizing the maneuver.

If the routine deems the maneuver achievable, then the available soldiers are ordered to join a team and a captain is chosen.

```
RoomSeen = Room where opponent has been seen
ReachableDoors = 0
if( NumDoors( RoomSeen ) < 2 )
    Abort maneuver. Not enough doors.
NumBots = FindAvailableBots( AvailableBotList, Threshold )
if( NumBots < 2 ) Abort maneuver. Not enough bots available.
```

```
for each door RoomDoor in room RoomSeen
    for each bot in AvailableBotList
        if( CanReachWithoutRoom( RoomSeen,
            RoomDoorLeadsTo( RoomDoor ), AvailableBot.Room ) )
        {
            ReachableDoors = ReachableDoors + 1
            Continue to next door. Do not process other bots.
        }

if( ReachableDoors < 2 )
    Abort maneuver. Unable to reach enough doors.
for each bot in AvailableBotList {
    Order them to join the team belonging to the first
    bot in the list. This makes the bot the Captain.
}
Order the first bot in AvailableBotList (the Captain) to outflank
    room RoomSeen.
```

One important criteria missing in this example is that of travelling distance. Each available soldier is considered when trying to find soldiers to cover a door, even if it means the soldier has to travel across the entire map. This would not work in an action game in which the opponents were continually on the move. The distance between the opponent and the door must be compared to the distance between each soldier and the door. If it would take significantly longer for the soldier to reach the door, then perhaps the maneuver should not be considered.

Maneuver Organization

The captain organizes the maneuver that has been approved at the strategic level. This pseudo-code sends the soldiers in the team to the door closest to where they are currently situated.

```
NumDoors = Number of doors commander says are reachable
DistanceToDoor[NUMBOTS]

for each bot (bot) in team {
    for each door (door) to be breached {
        Estimate = EstimateToWaypoint( bot.position, door.waypoint )
        if Estimate < DistanceToDoor[bot] {
            DistanceToDoor[bot] = Estimate
            ClosestDoor = door
        }
    }
    Order the bot to move to door ClosestDoor
}
```

This does not evenly spread the soldiers over the different doors. Therefore, some extra code should be created to count the number of soldiers at each door and adjust the numbers accordingly. If this is necessary, it is probably best to change the destination of the soldiers that are travelling the farthest. This means soldiers that are close to a door will get there quickly to cover it.

As each soldier reaches his assigned door, he will return an `InPosition` message to the captain. At each message, the captain should call the `IsTeamInPosition` function. If the team is in position, then an attack order can be given and the maneuver will be complete.

Covering Exits Maneuver

This example describes a complex maneuver requiring the use of many decision support routines, and contains the risk of being aborted by the captain.

If an opponent is known to be in a room, then the commander might consider it tactically useful to guard all the exits from the room and order other soldiers into the area. Because there might be several ways out of a room, a number of exits might need to be watched. However, assuming this is possible, it is a good way of holding the opponent in a small area until backup arrives. When backup does arrive, the captain will order the team to search the rooms one by one until the opponent is found, while other members of the team maintain their guard on all the possible exits (Figure 5.5.4).

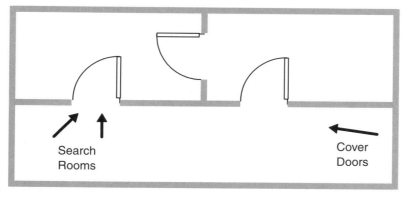

FIGURE 5.5.4 *Covering exits maneuver.*

Strategic Decision Process

The strategic decision process will try to determine whether the maneuver is possible and advantageous by checking whether the opponent must cross a specified room (`SuggestedRoom`) in order to get from their room (`RoomSeen`) to a target, (`TargetRoom`). The `SuggestedRoom` will usually be the room from where the opponent was seen.

Provided the opponent must cross the room, and there are enough soldiers to cover the exits and search the rooms, the soldiers will be organized into a team and a captain allocated. The captain will then be ordered to organize the maneuver.

```
RoomList      //Filled by RoomsMustCross function.
MustCrossRoom = false
RoomSeen      //Room where opponent was last seen.
NumExits      //Set by the ExitsToRoom function.
DoorList      //Filled by the ExitsToRoom function.
TargetRoom    //Room where opponent must reach to complete a goal.
AvailableBotList   //List of bots available for this maneuver.
NumAvailableBots   //The number of bots available for this maneuver.

RoomsMustCross(RoomSeen, TargetRoom, RoomList)
for each room(Room) in RoomList {
    if(RoomList.Room = SuggestedRoom)
        MustCrossRoom = true
}
if MustCrossRoom = false
    Abort maneuver as the opponent could by-pass the room
NumExits = ExitsToRoom(RoomSeen, Room, DoorList)

if NumAvailableBots < NumExits {
    Abort maneuver as there are not enough soldiers. This
    is a very rough guess, however.
}
for each bot in AvailableBotList {
    Order them to join the team belonging to the first
    bot in the list. This makes the bot the Captain.
}
Order the first bot in AvailableBotList (the Captain) to cover the
    exits from room RoomSeen.
```

As with the outflanking maneuver, the time it takes for the soldiers to get to the room is important, and considering this when planning the maneuver might be beneficial.

The number of rooms that must be searched might also be taken into consideration. If the opponent is being trapped in half of the map, then it might be unwise to send a team into such a large area to search for him.

`TargetRoom` represents a known location where the opponent needs to reach. This might be the exit to the level, or an area where hostages are being held, for example. There might also be more than one target room in a level, in which case, the `RoomsMustCross` function would have to be modified to take into consideration several target rooms.

Maneuver Organization

Organizing the covering exits maneuver is straightforward, but the processes used are a little more complex.

1. Find how many soldiers are needed to cover exits. One soldier might be able to cover several exits if placed in the right position; however, two or more might be necessary. If there are not enough soldiers to cover the exits and assault the rooms, then the captain must report that the maneuver is not possible. Ideally, there would be two or more soldiers to search the rooms.

2. Order the soldiers that are to cover the exits to get into their designated positions.
3. Decide on the first room to search. This is one with the lowest number of internal doors and is reachable from the current room.
4. Order the soldiers to move to the reachable doors of the first room.

When all the soldiers are in position, a *search* order should be sent. The soldiers will search the first room and report back any findings. If the opponent is not found, then a search command should be given for the next room. This would continue until the opponent has been found or all the rooms have been searched.

Conclusion

Using a command hierarchy is a simple and effective solution to coordinating bots in real time. Using a message-based system reduces the processing overhead by allowing the sharing of data and only processing options when new information has been given.

Intelligent teams make very powerful allies and enemies. This raises some issues of gameplay. A player will become quickly bored if his allies are too accomplished and could finish the game unaided. Similarly, if the opposition is so effective that the player stands no chance of winning, then frustration will soon set in. Balancing the playability so the bots are flawed enough to give the player a chance while still seeming natural will certainly be a challenge.

The possibilities presented by effective teamwork are limited only by the imagination. This article only presents a simple team-based system. Creating ambushes, laying suppressing fire, or flushing out the opposition are just some of the possibilities. However, whichever strategies are implemented, teamwork will certainly provide an interesting twist to the action genres.

References

[Gibson01] Gibson, Clark, and O'Brien, John, "The Basics of Team AI," *Game Developers Conference Proceedings*, pp.323–331, 2001, also available online at www.gdconf.com/archives/proceedings/2001/o'brien.ppt.
[Pottinger99a] Pottinger, Dave C., "Coordinated Unit Movement," *Game Developer* magazine, pp.42–51, January 1999, also available online at www.gamasutra.com/features/game_design/19990122/movement_01.htm.
[Pottinger99b] Pottinger, Dave C., "Implementing Coordinated Movement," *Game Developer* magazine, pp.48–58, February 1999, also available online at www.gamasutra.com/features/19990129/implementing_01.htm.
[Rabin00] Rabin, Steve, "A* Aesthetic Optimizations," *Game Programming Gems*, pp.272–287, Charles River Media, 2000.

A good list of references on the use of AI in military strategy can be found online at www-leav.army.mil/nsc/warsim/reason/links/index.htm.

5.6

Formations

Chad Dawson—Stainless Steel Studios

cd1f@yahoo.com

Mankind learned early on that fighting as a group can be much more effective than fighting alone. It wasn't long before early wolf-pack hunting strategies evolved into organized formations of war that could turn the tide of battle. Today, formations are expected for any type of cohesive group movement. From squad-based first-person shooters to sport sims to real-time strategy games, anytime that a group is moving or working together it is expected to do so in an orderly, intelligent fashion. In this article, we will explore some of the important factors to consider when implementing formations in your game.

Eye Candy versus Gameplay

Moving armies around in formation is fun to do and great to watch. When the soldiers (hereafter referred to as "units") march in time and line up perfectly, the player experiences a great sense of control and order. However, when the battle heats up, the real question becomes, "Are these formations going to pay off, or are they merely a frivolous parade?" If you are designing a parade simulator, this might be an easy decision, but it's likely that you need the formations to contribute to the gameplay and have some impact on the outcome of the battle. In the following sections, we will look at how types of formations, directional facing, and formation movement can affect gameplay and help determine the best implementation.

Types of Formations

Some of the most commonly seen formations are shown in Figure 5.6.1. Many of these have historical significance and are used in modern military operations [Army01]. Aviation expands on these basic formations with 3D formations such as the Echelon, in which varying altitude can also come into play. While the examples in this section will adhere to a 2D implementation, it should be straightforward to extend into 3D if required.

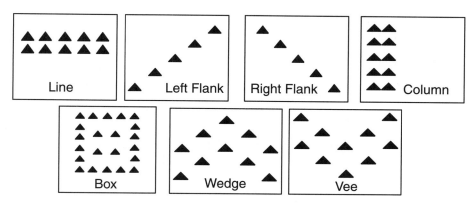

FIGURE 5.6.1 *Common formations.*

Is Facing Important?

The direction each member is facing in a formation can be critical if a unit can only react in that direction. This might be due to a limited line-of-sight or movement restrictions that prevent the unit from quickly turning around. In some formations such as the Line and Column, all members of the formation usually face in the same direction. The Box and Circle formations might have units all facing outward (for defense) or inward (for attacking). The Wedge, Vee, and Flank formations gain much of their usefulness from the overlapping fields of fire of each member. Even the line formation can be modified into a staggered line to prevent friendly fire and project more firepower in the facing direction (Figure 5.6.2).

FIGURE 5.6.2 *Line-of-fire and unit facing considerations.*

The preceding examples can be represented as a vector of individual `Formation-Position` structures organized into a containing `Formation` structure. The offsets in the formation positions can be relative to the center of the formation or the first (lead) position in the formation.

```
struct FormationPosition
{
    float   mXoffset;   // horizontal offset
    float   mYoffset;   // vertical offset
```

```
      float   mDirection; // the facing angle
}

struct Formation
{
    vector<FormationPosition> mPositions;
}
```

In some situations, it might be more appropriate for the positions and facing directions to be relative to the previous position rather than the center or lead. One example would be a dynamic column in which each unit faced outward left or right mirroring how the unit in front of him was facing.

Who's on First?

So, you know where you want the formation to be and which direction the formation should face. The next challenge is determining which units will go to which formation position. If the units are already in formation, then the choice might be as simple as keeping them in the same formation slot. Often, the units will be scattered about or the mix and number of units will have changed to such an extent that some choices will have to be made to reassign formation positions.

Mixed Unit Type Ordering

It is common to create a formation out of a heterogeneous mix of units with varying abilities. Some of the units might be able to fire long range. Others might be stronger or faster. Some of the units might be injured or otherwise incapacitated. By considering these attributes, a formation can be ordered in such a way as to maximize its combat effectiveness. Typically, weaker and longer-range units are positioned in the back of a line formation or in the center of a box formation (Figure 5.6.3). Faster units might be placed on the flanks of the formation so that they have increased freedom of movement when engaging the enemy.

Closest Position

Other situations call for a formation to form quickly without reshuffling. If a line formation's facing direction is reversed, should it invert, or should the units just change formation slots and turn around (Figure 5.6.4)? If the units are slow or cannot move around each other easily, then turning around and moving to the closest formation position would be the best choice. This is especially applicable if the unit mix is homogenous and the mixed unit type ordering described earlier is less important.

Calculating the absolute best match of units to positions, based on shortest distance, can be computationally expensive. The naïve implementation is $O(N!)$. The solution is to use a cheaper approximate calculation. First, sort the units based on their minimum distance to the closest position. Then, iterate through the sorted list of units and assign each unit the closest unused position.

FIGURE 5.6.3 *Mixed unit formation ordering in* Empire Earth. *Also shown in Color Plate 3.*

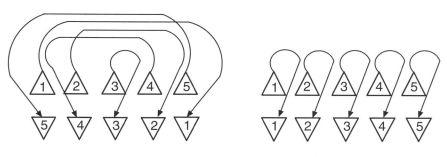

Maintaining Position Ordering   Choosing Closest Position

FIGURE 5.6.4 *Pathing and collision considerations.*

Unit Mobility

For performance reasons, most pathing engines do not factor in a unit's direction when computing a path (see Pinter[02] for a directional pathing implementation). If your game attempts to model realistic physics with varying angular and linear velocities, the straight-line distance is not necessarily the best measure of the time it will take to reach a destination. If a unit is told to move to a location just behind its current position, and the unit's physics only allow it to move forward, then it might take a good while for the unit to turn around and reach that point, then turn around again and face the way it started. Often, the fastest destination position for a unit is one that is in the direction it is currently facing. (For some excellent solutions to formation movement with realistic vehicular movement restrictions, see [VanVerth00].)

With multiple units all trying to do the same thing, the likelihood of crossed paths and the resultant collision resolution can significantly delay getting into formation. If a group of units is moving a long distance to their formation, then it is advantageous to choose formation positions that reduce the number of crossed paths. If we sort the units along a vector from the center of their starting positions to the center of the destination formation, we can establish parallel paths that can help reduce unit collisions (Figure 5.6.5). If necessary, we can sort again on the shorter perpendicular

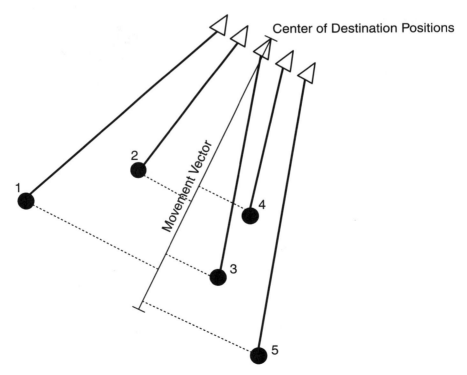

FIGURE 5.6.5 *Unit positions sorted by distance to movement vector.*

vector to establish positioning in unit ranks. This can also help avoid the leapfrogging of units from the back ranks to the front ranks.

Arrival Time

The technique in Figure 5.6.5 assumes a relatively clear path from the origin to the destination. If obstacles block the units, they might each have to take a circuitous route to reach the destination. The result could be units reaching the formation in the wrong order or at an indeterminate position. In this case, a useful strategy would be to have all of the units path to the center of the formation. The first unit to arrive at the destination would initially occupy the center formation position. When the second unit arrives, it could either push the first unit to another open position or take an open position for itself. The choice of how the positions are dynamically filled depends, of course, on the formation in question and the mobility of the units at the destination.

Spacing Distance

The Phalanx formation was historically powerful due to the tight spacing of the infantry to provide a defensive wall of shields. This was also its weakness, since the tight spacing reduced the formation's maneuverability. Spacing variations, either fixed or user scalable, can provide additional gameplay control. If units vary in size, the off-set positions would need to be scaled accordingly so that both large and small units can create formations with the desired spacing. With a mixed group of units, the spacing can be scaled to the size of the largest unit, or alternatively, the units could be split into ranks of similarly sized units with each rank scaled accordingly.

Ranks

A line formation would not typically stretch on forever as more units were added to the formation. At some breaking point, a second line would be formed behind the first. Extending our Formation structure, we can set up an offset for the next rank. When all of the original FormationPosition structures have been filled, a new rank can be created at the specified offset from the current one.

```
struct Formation
{
    float mRankOffsetX;
    float mRankOffsetY;
    vector<FormationPosition> mPositions;
}
```

Playbook

Some formations might call for specific units in specific positions. The offensive line in American football is a formation with assigned positions for the center, quarter-back, and other players. The starting setup in the game of chess also has assigned positions for each of the unique pieces. In these cases, the mixed unit ordering described earlier is not specific enough, and restrictions must be placed on which units can fill a slot. If no unit matches those restrictions, the slot might be skipped, leaving an intentional hole in the formation.

Moving Out

The examples we have explored so far have looked at fixed formations. This might be acceptable for setting up a defense when waiting for the enemy. However, when attacking or moving across the game field, additional issues need to be addressed. In the following section, we explore when to rally in formation, pathing integration, and formation integrity.

When Do the Units Fall-In to Formation?

In the previous section, we examined how each of the destination formation positions might be chosen for the selected units. Figure 5.6.5 shows units pathing toward the formation destination, but how far forward should that path be? If it is desirable for the units to be in formation during the entire course of movement, then the units should gather into formation as quickly as possible at the center of their starting locations. From there, the units would then path to the destination formation. Depending on the initial locations of the units, this starting formation might delay the movement or cause some units to backtrack as they head toward the starting formation positions (Figure 5.6.6).

An alternative would be to create the initial formation just ahead of the unit nearest the destination. This would reduce back pathing to the formation. Unfortunately, the lead unit with a short path might have to wait a considerable time until the other units reach the formation. This might give the impression to the player that nothing is happening. Regardless, this might be the best choice of rallying locations for a coordinated attack along the movement direction.

A third choice involves units pathing directly to their final destination formation. This has the advantages of faster movement and no delays. As the units get closer to the destination, their positions increasingly resemble the intended formation. Along the way, however, the benefits of the formation are not as effective, as the spacing between the units might be much greater than the other options—although, this might be the best choice for a quick retreat.

Which rallying option you choose depends on the type of game you are developing and the desired behavior. It might be reasonable to give the player some control over which type of formation move he or she performs. Allowing the player to queue multiple linked formation movements can provide the flexibility needed to handle many situations.

Group Pathing and Movement

Once a formation is specified for a group, the unit positions are chosen, and the destination locations are specified, the game's pathing engine must compute the exact

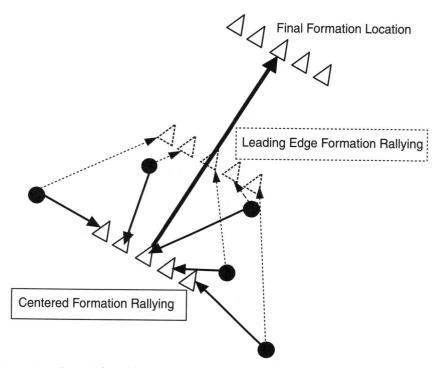

Final Formation Location

Leading Edge Formation Rallying

Centered Formation Rallying

FIGURE 5.6.6 *Centered and leading-edge formation rallying.*

paths for the units. Some of the pathing complexity might be reduced if the pathing engine can make use of the group and formation information. Since the units will be traveling together, it is often possible for them to share a path to the destination. If formation integrity is desired, the resulting path must be wide enough to allow the breadth of the formation to pass through. In the previous examples, a path could be calculated for the lead unit (the one closest to the destination), and then the other units could apply their formation offsets to that path to determine their individual paths. (See [Pottinger99a] and [Pottinger99b] for some excellent suggestions for control of group movement.)

Alternatively, the trailing units could employ a flocking behavior to guide their movement. By integrating the formation position offsets and spacing distances into the standard flocking guidance functions, the units should move behind the lead unit in roughly the intended formation. (See Woodcock[01] for more information on a flocking movement implementation.)

When mixed units are moving as a group, variations in unit movement and turning speeds can break the formation integrity. One solution is to have all units move at the speed of the slowest unit. While this will tend to keep the formation together (assuming they started together and were facing the same direction), it might result in visual artifacts as the faster units run in slow motion. Instead, a capped adaptive speed can be used to speed up slower units and slow down faster units to a certain extent, when it is determined that they are out of formation. If all else fails, the leading units can stop and wait for the trailing units to catch up.

Reacting to Obstacles and Combat

While it is desirable for units in moving formations to stay together, there might be unavoidable situations in which formation integrity cannot be maintained. A common case is that of the choke point. A choke point is a location on the game field that is narrower than the formation's width. In this case, some of the units must break formation while other units pass through the choke point. When the formation breaks, the units out of formation have a few choices: they can wait in place until the first units in the formation pass through the choke point, or they can seek an alternative path. Waiting in place often helps preserves proximity integrity, since at least they are waiting together.

Choosing an alternate path is also a consideration when an unexpected obstacle blocks a formation's path. In this case, it is useful to break the formation into subformations and route them around either side of the obstacle. If the formation is already organized into ranks, it can be split from front to back along the rank borders. If it is a mixed formation, it is desirable to split the formation in such a way that the relative distribution of unit types is the same. If one of the alternate paths is longer than the other, it might make sense to split the formation based on unit speed so that both subformations arrive at the destination at the same time.

Spotting an enemy unit to attack or reacting to an ambush might also necessitate a break in formation. Formation units might spread out to avoid area damage, or converge to chase down an enemy unit. If the formation is hit from the side or rear, the formation might need to wheel around to face the attack. If the formation is on a scouting patrol, the best reaction might be just to continue movement as before. Your game might have user-selectable unit stances (aggressive or cautious, for example) that dictate which response is appropriate. Implementing a state flag on the formation group to indicate why the formation was broken can be useful when making decisions whether an individual unit should stay in formation or react to combat.

After the obstacle has been circumvented, the choke point squeezed through, and the combat resolved, the formation must be regrouped. We can use the same method at this point as we used to assemble the formation originally. Decisions concerning the group integrity, initial formation location, and movement considerations are similar to before. If units were lost in combat, the formation will need to reassign positions to account for the smaller number of members. For many situations, simply refilling the positions using factors described earlier and thus shrinking the formation will be adequate. If key positions are required or empty slots are preferred, then the FormationPosition structure can be extended to contain importance weightings or skip flags as needed.

Conclusion

Formations are a great addition to any game that uses coordinated unit movement. A simple collection of offset positions can be extended with facing directions, scaling factors, ranks, and position restrictions to handle a wide range of formation types and variations. Depending on the desired gameplay, unit positions within formations can be assigned through weighting unit attributes, relative facings, and destination distance calculations. Loose formation integrity during movement is the key to successful group movement from the initial movement order through reactions to obstacles, choke points, and combat. With the information provided, you should have a head start on implementing a formation system and integrating it into the pathing engine and physics simulation systems of your game.

References

[Army01] Army, United States, "Field Manual 7-8 Infantry Rifle Platoon and Squad," U.S. Army Infantry School, 2001. www.adtdl.army.mil/cgi-bin/atdl.dll/fm/7-8/ch2.htm#s3

[Pinter02] Pinter, Marco, "Realistic Turning between Waypoints," *AI Game Programming Wisdom*, Charles River Media, 2002.

[Pottinger99a] Pottinger, Dave C., "Coordinated Unit Movement," *Game Developer* magazine, January, 1999. www.gamasutra.com/features/19990122/movement_01.htm

[Pottinger99b] Pottinger, Dave C., "Implementing Coordinated Unit Movement," *Game Developer* magazine, February, 1999. Also available online at www.gamasutra.com/features/19990129/implementing_01.htm.

[VanVerth00] Van Verth, Jim, "Formation-Based Pathfinding with Real-World Vehicles," Game Developers Conference Proceedings, 2000.

[Woodcock01] Woodcock, Steven, "Flocking with Teeth: Predators and Prey," *Game Programming Gems 2*, Charles River Media, 2001.

GENERAL PURPOSE ARCHITECTURES

6.1

Architecting a Game AI

Bob Scott—Stainless Steel Studios

bob@stainlesssteelstudios.com

The intent of this article is to give the fledgling AI developer a head start on what will likely be a long, difficult job. Developing an AI for a game is a major undertaking, and many new developers are somewhat stunned by the sheer amount of work that goes into it. We hope this will serve as a roadmap and a starting point from which to expand. We'll tend to be fairly general, in order to cover as many different genres as possible. The intricacies of specific genres are discussed within this book in more detail.

The List

The initial phase of designing a game AI is to decide what your AI *should* do and what it should *not do*. This last point is very important—you want to avoid anything that makes your AI seem, well, not intelligent. In developing the AI for *Empire Earth*, we had some definite ideas of the types of behavior that didn't work in previous RTS games.

This phase involves no coding. Ideally, you sit down with the development team and brainstorm. It's even better if you can include typical players of your type of game. Be aware that this phase can take quite a long time. On *Empire Earth*, we spent a good month or so developing our list, which eventually became a 20-to-30 page document of bullet points. Don't skimp on this—include *everything* you can think of. Even include the things that you know aren't possible (you never know what new technologies might become available, or your developers might have a breakthrough). Put it all in, and then prioritize it very generally—things that *must* be in, things that *should* be in, and things that you can live without (wish list items).

When we say include everything, we mean it. If you're developing a first-person shooter (FPS) and you wish your characters could interact with the player, put that in. If you want the characters in your golf simulation to occasionally get angry and throw their clubs into the nearest body of water, put that in. Really—go crazy during this period!

This is a good time to brainstorm ideas for development as well. You can talk about scripting, cheating, technologies—whatever comes to mind. The basic idea is to get as much information as you can early on. Staffing can also be discussed here. If you're lucky, you'll have a dedicated AI team that you can count on to be able to do the work. In most cases, you will start out with one person with the promise to add people later—make sure this happens! Of course, the requirements all depend on the type of game you're developing. Some might only require one AI person; others barely get by with three (*Empire Earth*, for example).

The last thing to mention in this section is that you want to do this as early in the project as you can. Tuning an AI requires play testing, and this requires lots of time. On EE, we started the AI nearly two years before release, and we were tuning it right up to the end.

Identifying Components

Once you've defined what your AI will do, the next step is to apply simple software engineering concepts to break the work into manageable pieces. Often, there might be a "natural" organization that is specific to your game type. For example, a squad-based game naturally breaks down into leaders, squads, and squad members. A role-playing game (RPG) might consist of friends, foes, and neutral players. An RTS would contain military leaders and economic leaders. A 4X game (eXplore, eXpand, eXploit, and eXterminate) would add a research arm.

Apply this concept recursively to each section until you get a sense that the pieces are of sufficiently small size that they can be easily developed. It is perfectly reasonable to leave large sections alone until later, as long as the interfaces between them are well defined. The only requirement at this level is that you provide enough pieces and connections to carry out the plan you developed in the previous section. Repeatedly go over those ideas and see if they fit your pieces—if they don't, add pieces or connections until they do.

This is an important step—it can be very difficult to add components once the interfaces are set and development is well advanced. Spend a little more time with the AI design document you came up with, and make sure as much of that document is covered by your components. This can be accomplished with little more than pen and paper, or a simple diagramming tool such as Visio.

Identifying Interfaces

The connections (interfaces) between your components will decide how easy it is to get things done. As an example—we have a component in *Empire Earth* that is responsible for getting new units trained. There is a method that allows the caller to specify that a unit should be trained as close as possible to a specific location. That method is responsible for ensuring that there are sufficient resources to train the unit and building the training buildings if so required. It might even need to signal other components to advance through new epochs in order to reach the point where the unit can be trained. This greatly simplifies the development of the military component, as it could just request units and not worry about the details.

Providing these high-level methods and interfaces between components also enables emergent behavior to occur. Coupled with variations in timing, unusual events can occur that were not planned for.

Of course, high-level interfaces are not enough, and occasionally very specific interfaces are required. These are often added after initial development.

Development

If you are blessed with multiple developers working on AI, it is natural to have people specialize. In this case, communication between the developers often mimics the interfaces in the design. Be sure to go over your components and identify dependencies between them. For example, an RTS game usually consists of a component responsible for training units—this component should probably be done fairly soon, since most other components will rely on it.

Behavior Modification

One of the easiest ways to tune an AI is by providing the ability for someone other than the developer (like an expert player) to adjust values that affect the behavior of the AI. In our experience, the more expert players who assist in tuning, the better. Use of a database or at least a text file is crucial here. Which you choose depends on whether you have database people around or an existing text file parser.

These behavior values can be hard values that specify exact quantities, or can be hints that provide a general value for the AI to work with. The more hard numbers are used, the more predictable the AI becomes, so we prefer using hints as much as possible. These also allow the AI to get close to a value without requiring it to match the value (something that might be hard or impossible to do). This has been a drawback to some games—the AI can get stuck trying to meet the requirements of a hard number to the detriment of other aspects of the AI.

Note that even some hard numbers can provide some unpredictability. One of the values we could tweak in *Empire Earth* was the density of towers. This was a hard value that specified how far apart towers were required to be, but there weren't any numbers that specified exactly where they should be put. Thus, while we could count on them not overlapping too much, we could never know exactly where they'd be placed. This contributed greatly to the unpredictability of the AI. Note that this density number was a better choice than a hard number such as "three tiles from the town center"—that would have made the AI more predictable.

We alluded to the fact that you might want people other than developers tuning these numbers. In fact, it's a requirement in any large AI project. Without providing these values for others to set and test, we would not have been able to finish feature development on the AI team. Additionally, it's hard to find a broad range of player experience among the members of the AI development team. Fortunately, there were plenty of other people inhouse with different experience levels.

Testing

This can be one of the most time-consuming areas of AI development. Most developers spend nearly as much time observing the AI behavior as they do actually coding. Being able to adjust the speed of the game and pit multiple computer players against each other, with the developer able to observe, is the best way of doing this.

The form that testing will take, as well as who will test it, depends largely on whether the AI is deterministic. A scripted AI can easily be tested to see if it follows the script by nearly anyone—no specialized knowledge is required. A nondeterministic AI is harder to test and quite often comes down to how the AI *feels*, which requires a judgment call by someone who has played with or against an AI before. This might be a developer or a good player; in fact, both should be employed, since there is quite a range of talent out there, and one player's hard AI is another's pushover.

Debugging aids are crucial during testing. On *Empire Earth*, we combine text-based overlay pages that convey status information from all of the components of the AI, as well as unit overlays that tell us what individual units are doing. The ability to switch ownership of players is useful as well—you can temporarily take control of one of the computer players and make a change to see how it reacts. Thus, the observer becomes a crucial part of the test. Paul Tozour's article in this book gives some good ideas on adding debugging info to your AI [Tozour02].

Performance Considerations

Although the amount of CPU available for AI has been consistently increasing, attention must be given to performance. Except for the simplest techniques, many methods require a lot of CPU time. Sometimes, there is no way to solve a problem without a brute-force (and therefore time-consuming) approach.

In this case, the best approach is to create an environment in which a task retains state between available updates, and use each update to perform a slice of the problem. These slices can be monitored and suspended when the available time runs out.

In games with multiple AI players, updates can be rotated among them. As long as the amount of time between updates is short enough, there should be no negative impact on the effectiveness of the AI. In games with multiple components, the components themselves can be updated at certain time intervals. These intervals can be adjusted to fit the required responsiveness of the component. For example, a resource-gathering component of an RTS AI can be set to update itself every 30 seconds as long as the unit AI takes care of details.

Tuning of the update frequencies is a tedious, iterative process. You need to make the frequency short enough to be effective, but long enough to avoid impacting the CPU. You also need to make sure you pick frequencies that don't overlap each other to avoid stacking updates that bog the game down visibly. Prime numbers help a lot in this case. More ideas for increasing the performance in your AI can be found in other sections of this book, and in the excellent *Game Programming Gems* books [Rabin01], [Dawson01].

Conclusions

Developing AI for a modern game *is* difficult and time consuming. Players demand intelligence in their games, and will complain endlessly if it doesn't exist. Players demand computer players that avoid "artificial stupidity." Players depend on computer players to hone their skills before taking on other human players.

If you plan well and use common sense, you can reduce this large task into many smaller tasks that can be done in a finite amount of time. In the end, you'll have a massive, well-tuned, intelligent, nearly human player that might earn the praise of your players!

References

[Dawson01] Dawson, Bruce, "Micro-Threads for Game Object AI," *Game Programming Gems 2*, Charles River Media, 2001.

[Rabin01] Rabin, Steve, "Strategies for Optimizing AI," *Game Programming Gems 2*, Charles River Media, 2001.

[Tozour02] Tozour, Paul, "Building an AI Diagnostic Toolset," *AI Game Programming Wisdom*, Charles River Media, 2002.

6.2

An Efficient AI Architecture Using Prioritized Task Categories

Alex W. McLean—Pivotal Games

alex@pivotalgames.com

Real-time games work on the assumption that once the code has passed through the front-end and entered the main game loop, it will run through this loop repeatedly until some exit condition arises. In order that the game runs at a frame rate that's considered acceptable, we need to ensure that one pass through this loop happens as quickly as possible. The elements of the loop will contain many diverse subsections: rendering, AI, collision detection, player input, and audio are just a few. Each of these tasks has a finite amount of time in which to execute, each is trying to do so as quickly as possible, and all of them must work together to give a rich, detailed gaming world.

This discussion concentrates on the AI component and, specifically, how to distribute it over time and make it fast for real-time games. We're going to describe a method of structuring the AI so that it can execute quickly and efficiently. Two benefits will be realized by doing this—the game will run more smoothly, and we'll be able to bring about more advanced AI.

The Requirements

In any well-designed game, a decision should be made about how much time will be available for the AI systems. Some games, particularly those that are turn-based or those in which the frame rate is largely irrelevant, have few time restrictions placed upon the AI—it simply doesn't matter how long it takes to execute. For real-time games, a more realistic scenario is that the developers will require the game to run at a specified frame rate, and that some portion of the frame time will be made available to the AI.

We need to ensure that we're using no more than this allocation, because if we do, we'll adversely affect the frame rate. This can be especially important on console platforms where a fast and *constant* frame rate is often an essential requirement. It might even be necessary for the platform's *technical requirements checklist* (TRC). Equally, it's in our interest to have the AI expand to make use of available resources. In other words, we should use *all* of the available time with any spare capacity being seen as offering opportunity.

The Approach

We're going to be looking at a *high-level* approach to achieving our goal. The basic framework should give us an AI architecture that's quick, efficient, and has sufficient scope and power to realize the necessary behaviors required by modern-day, cutting-edge games. The approach is not algorithmic or dependent on contrived data structures. Rather, it is a way of restructuring the typical AI loop found in many real-time games, so we are using the time and resources available to our best advantage. There are three main parts to the approach.

- **Separation**. We will split our individual AI components into two sets: those that might be considered *periodic* (require processing every so often), and those that are *constant* (require processing every frame). This component is aimed at processing the AI tasks with a degree of urgency that is appropriate to each task.
- **Distribution**. We need to distribute our workload over frames and have the load for any given frame automatically adjusted, on-the-fly, to ensure that we roughly use the same amount of processor time each frame. This component is aimed at distributing the periodic tasks, thus attempting to process the least amount of them per frame while still realizing acceptable results. Note that individual tasks are atomic and are not distributed over multiple frames—yet!
- **Exclusion**. Finally, we need to look at how much of our AI work is actually necessary for each frame. Often, it is the case that many aspects of a game's AI don't require processing at all for a particular frame. This can be left until last and is readily implemented once the previous two components are in place.

Application

In order to illustrate the approach, we'll use the example of a world that has a large number of characters moving about a complex environment. These entities can see, hear, and attack each other. The details and content of the necessary individual functions aren't going to be discussed here—just the methods of making the best use of these functions. A simple initial AI loop might look something like the following:

```
CGame::UpdateAI()
{
    CCharacter *pChar = GetFirstCharacter();
    while( pChar )
    {
        pChar->ProcessAI();
        pChar = pChar->GetNext();
    }
}
```

```
CCharacter::ProcessAI( void )
{
    ProcessVision();
    ProcessHearing();
    TrackTarget();
    UpdateMovement();
}
```

This code might accomplish the goal, but it's far from optimal. By taking this example and applying each of the previously mentioned steps, we'll make this loop use less processor time while still achieving the same goals.

Separation

There are many parts to a game AI, and not all of them must be called every frame. However, some parts must, and we need to split all of our AI into two sets. The set that an AI action falls into will dictate how frequently it will be called. The first, or *periodic*, set of actions for a given character will be called relatively infrequently, while the second, or *constant*, set will be called every frame. We will now clarify the distinction between the two sets.

- **Periodic AI.** This is processing in which it's not necessary to call an update every single frame. Both vision and hearing in the previous example might readily fall into this category for many games. We can often consider updating what a character can see or hear every so often as opposed to every frame. There is also a side effect to this technique, which for many games might even be considered appealing. Put simply, we occasionally *don't* want the AI to respond immediately to all inputs. The delay that results can often be viewed as a reaction time.

    Let's look at our example world again. It might be acceptable for a character to take a fraction of a second to notice a new character when it walks into view. This will happen automatically with a periodic update. The actual time that a character takes to notice another character will also vary. Sometimes, a character will see the other character immediately if it came into view just before its update. Sometimes, a character will take longer, with the maximum delay occurring when the new character became visible in the frame immediately following the viewer's update. Conversely, it takes the same type of interval to realize that the character's enemy has just run behind an obstacle.

    An artifact of this approach is that the characters continue to fire their weapon or look at an enemy for a short time after they disappear behind something. However, this leads to realistic behavior; the assailant sprays bullets down the wall of the building that its enemy has just run behind, and it takes a short while to see an enemy that just popped out from behind the scenery. Obviously, for many character actions, this type of latency might not be desirable and the decision of which set the action falls into must be made on a case-by-case basis.

- **Constant AI**. This is processing for which an update *must* be executed every frame. Obvious examples are movement update, character animation, and tracking a target. Often, it is the case that the constant AI component set is using information from the periodic AI set, and will continue to use that information until it is "refreshed" at the next periodic update. An example will clarify this. Consider again the character that is targeting an enemy. To aim the gun, the character must calculate an appropriate weapon orientation based on relative positions. For an update that gives smooth gun motion, we need these calculations to be included in this constant update set. The processing that decides which enemies can be seen (if any) can be left as periodic, and will be updated every so often. To the player, it is unlikely that these distinctions will be noticed and as previously mentioned, we sometimes get side effects that lead to satisfactory, or even desirable, behavior.

Distribution

The second component of this framework is to distribute our work over frames. We have our two separate sets and we've made the distinction of what actions fall into each. We must now bring about the update process that makes the distinction for flow of execution. The simplest way to do this, in terms of distribution, is to process a certain number of characters per frame, with the exact number being variable according to demand or some other requirement(s). Note that on any given frame, all characters will have their constant set processed, while only some will receive periodic updates.

We'll need some data that keeps track of the current AI character. At its simplest, this can just be a pointer to a character class (m_pPresentCharacter). Each time we process a character, we move on to the next one. We stop when we have processed all of the characters, or more likely, when we have processed a certain amount. When we have reached the end of the list and returned to the first character, we can look at how long it has been since we last visited this character. This gives us the time interval that occurs between the periodic updates of any given character.

The important thing to note is that in most applications using a periodic set, we're only going to be processing *some* of the characters each frame, not all of them. If the calculated interval is insufficient for our needs, then we must increase the number of characters that we process per frame for periodic AI updates. More interestingly, if our time falls under our required minimum interval, we have two choices. We can either process fewer characters per frame, or we can do more in the update for an individual character, leading to richer, or more advanced AI. Either way, we get what our original specification required, and the game has benefited.

Now that we have our tasks split into two sets, we are able to look at a newer version of our main AI loop. Before we do this, we need to consider a further improvement. We've decided that the best way to bring about a periodic update is to process fewer characters per frame. We can do this by starting out with a best guess of how many characters we want to process per frame, and record the interval that passes between the update of an individual character.

```
CGame::UpdateAI( void )
{
    CCharacter    *pChar;
    BOOL          bExit = FALSE;
    unsigned int CharsProcessed=0;

    pChar = GetFirstCharacter();

    /* CONSTANT */
    while( pChar )
    {
        pChar->ProcessConstantAI();
        pChar = pChar->GetNext();
    }

    /* PERIODIC */
    while( CharsProcessed < m_CharsPerFrame )
    {
        m_pPresentCharacter->ProcessPeriodicAI();
        CharsProcessed++;
        m_pPresentCharacter = m_pPresentCharacter->GetNextCyclic();
    }
}

CCharacter::ProcessConstantAI( void )
{
    TrackTarget();
    UpdateMovement();
}

CCharacter::ProcessPeriodicAI( void )
{
    ProcessVision();
    ProcessHearing();
}
```

We can alter the time interval between updates for a character by raising or lowering m_CharsPerFrame. If we set m_CharsPerFrame to the number of characters in the world, then we can even revert to the original, basic AI loop. By carefully managing the *time interval* that occurs between the update of behavior for any given character, we can ensure we achieve the twin goal of cutting down the work required per frame and realizing interesting, realistic behavior. It's important to note that care must be taken in managing this interval, since it will directly affect how the characters will behave in the world. Characters that are processed more often will react more quickly, and this will place constraints on the allowable domain of the interval since it will affect gameplay.

Two things should be observed in the code. First, additional code is required to ensure that we don't end up looping indefinitely or processing a character more than once, with the latter case being likely when we have fewer characters in our world than m_CharsPerFrame. Second, note that the GetNext() function in the original example has been replaced with GetNextCyclic() for the periodic update section.

This is because we must now loop back to the first game character, rather than just stopping at the end of the list.

As an illustration, perhaps we have a world in which there are 100 game characters. To process a periodic action such as vision for all these characters, every frame would use a good deal of available processing power. If we process a smaller number per frame, perhaps just 10, then we'd be doing far less work and, assuming even a relatively conservative frame rate of 20 frames a second, we'd still update any given individual character twice a second. In all probability, this wouldn't even be noticeable to the player, and we've already cut our vision work down to 10 percent of what it was before. This is a substantial saving and clearly illustrates how a simple technique can result in a huge reduction in workload. It should be clear that techniques such as these are every bit as valid as the low-level approach of optimizing a specific algorithm deep within an AI loop.

Exclusion

We've now split our AI set up into periodic and constant sets. We've distributed our workload over time, and have made this distribution adaptive. What's next? We've reduced the amount of work we're doing, but the final stage is to consider all the work that's required and see if some of it can be skipped completely.

A simple example is excluding the processing of characters that are too far away from the player. If they're too far away to see, then should we even worry about them at all for the periodic update? This can be a considerable saving and is always worth considering as an optimization. Of course, sometimes, characters might not be excluded; perhaps we want a character to walk to our location from afar in order to serve a gameplay/design purpose. This is fine and can be solved by marking that character as one that cannot be excluded by this particular optimization. It does not prohibit us from applying this improvement to other characters in which no such restriction is necessary.

Distance is just one criterion by which we can make the decision to disregard a character for processing. The actual mechanism that makes the decision will be very game specific, and in all probability, quite complex. Remember that we can afford to be fairly selective here in deciding what to exclude, since for all but the simplest games, this decision-making process will still be markedly less work than the whole AI loop for any given character. We therefore need a function that will evaluate an individual character, and decide whether it should be included in the periodic update. Many criteria for exclusion are possible:

- The character is too far away.
- The character has never been rendered, or is not presently on screen.
- The character hasn't been rendered recently.
- The character is dead—rather obvious, but often forgotten!
- The character is a designated "extra" or nonessential element of the game world, and should only be present when there is excess processing capability.

This list is largely governed by the game's genre and requirements, but these should be enough to illustrate the principles. Our previous code will change again to:

```
while( NumCharsProcessed < m_CharsPerFrame )
{
    if( FALSE == m_pPresentCharacter->CanBeExcludedFromUpdate() ) {
        m_pPresentCharacter->ProcessPeriodicAI();
        NumCharsProcessed++;
    }
    m_pPresentCharacter = m_pPresentCharacter->GetNextCyclic();
}
```

Restrictions

A final point is that this evaluation function will require certain data to be made available. In our example, in order to decide if the character is too far away from the player, we'll need to calculate certain information in the *constant* update function. This is important since, otherwise, a character could walk out of range, be excluded from processing, and never return since their distance would never be reevaluated, which is clearly undesirable. This would occur because we had mistakenly included functionality used to decide whether the character should be processed in a nonconstant set. We can't make a decision if a precondition hasn't been decided!

It's also the case that under certain special circumstances, we might still have to do the update even if the character satisfies some of the criteria for exclusion. For this reason, the ordering of the rules that dictate exclusion is very important. We cannot simply exclude a character if it is far away when it has been marked as being required by design or gameplay-critical. This decision-making process should be in a CanBeExcludedFromUpdate() function. A very simple example follows:

```
BOOL CCharacter::CanBeExcludedFromUpdate( void )
{
    if( TRUE == m_bCanNeverBeExcluded ) {
        return FALSE;
    }
    if( IsDead() ) {
        return TRUE;
    }
    if( m_DistanceToPlayer > CUTOFF_THRESHOLD ) {
        return TRUE;
    }
}
```

Conclusions

This discussion gives some idea of how to approach distributing the AI workload on either an existing AI loop, or how to structure the design of a planned one. Many more improvements can be made. The most obvious improvement is that we can go deeper and not only distribute the load of processing for all game entities, but also distribute the processing of an individual entity's action [Dawson01]. A common example is pathfinding. For complex 3D environments, we could perhaps split the work required for a pathfinding request over a number of frames.

When AI is distributed like this, we can spend more time processing other elements of the game. It requires time and effort to retrofit an approach like this, but it's reasonably simple to do and might readily be implemented in stages. Distribution of processor load and optimization in general is often a problem that should be tackled at a high level first. It's often the case that low-level optimization might not even be necessary if sufficient gains are made at a higher level [Abrash94], [Rabin01].

References

[Abrash94] Abrash, Michael, *The Zen Of Code Optimization*, The Coriolis Group, 1994.

[Bentley82] Bentley, Jon Louis, *Writing Efficient Programs*, Prentice Hall, 1982.

[Dawson01] Dawson, Bruce, "Micro-Threads for Game Object AI," *Game Programming Gems 2*, Charles River Media, 2001.

[Rabin01] Rabin, Steve, "Strategies for Optimizing AI," *Game Programming Gems 2*, Charles River Media, 2001.

[Rolf99] Pfeifer, Rolf, and Scheier, Christian, *Understanding Intelligence*, MIT Press, 1999.

6.3

An Architecture Based on Load Balancing

Bob Alexander
balexand@earthlink.net

In writing AI for games, we continually fight the CPU budget to get the most intelligence into our non-player characters (NPCs). We want them to be challenging and fun. However, smart AI requires processing power. We need CPU time to iterate over objects in the world and do heuristic analysis. We need to perform line-of-sight (LOS) checks. We need to do pathfinding. The list goes on and on, and we need to do them in a small percentage of the frame time. Too much work done in a frame, and the frame rate starts to suffer, which is completely unacceptable.

So, how do we do all of that work and not violate our CPU budget? Certainly, we can profile our code, and rewrite critical functions. However, when that still does not get us within our budget, what do we do then? We load balance our AI. We find the tasks in the system that are peaking too much per frame, and rewrite them so smaller parts of the task can be run over several frames. When we do that, we spread the CPU burden over multiple frames. Usually, we do this when the AI CPU budget has already been exceeded, and we are looking for ways of getting back on track. This kind of seek and destroy is done until we can run at a consistent frame rate.

As an alternative to the preceding scenario, this article suggests that instead of looking to load balancing as an optimization task, we approach every task in the AI with load balancing in mind. This article will describe a single-threaded task scheduling system that can be used as the core task processor of an AI architecture. This lets us tune the system more easily when the AI starts to push the envelope of the CPU time budget.

Background

In an ideally load-balanced system, the AI would always take the same amount of time each frame. Processing only a small portion of every task per frame would accomplish this. In fact, each portion would be small enough so that the total AI time is *exactly* within budget. Of course, we can't hit the ideal every time, but we can try.

In AI, though, we are lucky, since there are very few things in AI that need to be evaluated every frame. In fact, it could be argued that there is nothing in AI that needs to be evaluated every frame. This fact can be exploited to allow us to perform tasks that would otherwise be too costly. Moreover, by breaking up even well-behaved tasks, we could free up CPU time in order to implement AI that would otherwise not be possible.

For example, code that controls the driving of a car in a race does not need to evaluate its situation 60 times a second. Instead, if that behavior only did its evaluation 10 times a second, the player would probably not notice. However, we would have increased the performance of that behavior by 600 percent! That's great, but we have a problem. If we just run the driving behaviors every six frames, we would have no driving behavior CPU usage for five frames, but then the AI would spike on the sixth frame.

In order for this to work, we need to spread the tasks out. In the previous example, this could be done by looking at each car's driving update as a separate task. Then, instead of spiking on the sixth frame, we use nearly the same amount of CPU for all six frames. This is key in load balancing. There are many ways to spread tasks depending on the nature of the task, the game, and the context. Therefore, in addition to looking at an overall load-balanced architecture, we will also look at four examples of some standard task spreading.

Tasks

A task is defined as a periodic maintenance function that handles the update of a part of the system. This includes things such as behaviors, heuristic calculations, and bookkeeping. Although some algorithms are more difficult to break up, a task scheduling system using periodic maintenance functions is simple and robust—so, it's worth the effort.

Base Task Object

The base task object is comprised of a callback function to process the task and a time-of-execution value. The callback function will be called at the appropriate time, based on the time-of-execution value.

This is a base task object that can be subclassed to include more specific task-related information. A subclassed task needed for one of our example scheduling groups is described next.

Timed Task for Maximum Time Group

The timed task is a specialized subclass of the base task, which implements basic timing and profiling statistics. The variations on profiling are far greater than can be covered here, so we'll focus on the most basic functionality. This task subclass calculates an estimate of the time the task will take to execute on its next run. When scheduling tasks for the next frame, this time value is used to attempt to only schedule enough functions to fill the maximum time value.

One way of determining this time is to accumulate a running average of the execution time of the tasks. However, the task will most likely vary in its execution time.

If it varies dramatically, you might end up with spikes in the execution. Therefore, we could also store the largest execution time, or maintain a separate running average over the last few runs. Then, we could return a weighted-average of these values to produce a better estimate.

One other solution would be to implement the running of timed functions in the actual root update. (See the section *Improvements*.)

Scheduling Groups

Scheduling groups are a convenient way to think about scheduling. A scheduling group is a group of tasks along with some algorithm that dictates when each task should be processed.

Base Group Functionality

Three types are explained: the *spread group*, the *count group*, and the *maximum time group*.

Spread Group

The *spread group* is a group of tasks that will be spread out over a specified time period. Each task in the group will run once during that time period. In our driving AI described previously, the group would consist of all the driving AIs, and the specified time period would be one-tenth of a second.

To implement a spread group scheduler, we maintain a running time value. This value is used as the scheduling time for the next task to schedule. Each time the group scheduling function is run, it first increments the running time value to make sure it is greater than the current game time. Then, for each unscheduled task in the group, the current schedule time is set on the task and it is inserted into the schedule. After scheduling each task, the schedule time is incremented by the value dt / n. The dt value is the desired time delay between executions of a single task, and the n value is the number of tasks in the group (Figure 6.3.1).

Count Group

The count group simply runs a constant number of tasks each frame. Since the group scheduler runs each frame, the system will not run more than the specified number of tasks in each of those frames.

This group is ideal for tasks that are guaranteed to take a constant time to run. If the tasks vary too much, the AI might spike. For example, the game might require a task that periodically checks the distance an object has moved and flags it when it has moved outside an area. This is a simple constant time function, and would be well suited for this group.

Maximum Time Group

The maximum time group only schedules enough tasks for the next frame such that their total *expected* execution time does not exceed a maximum value. To do this, it

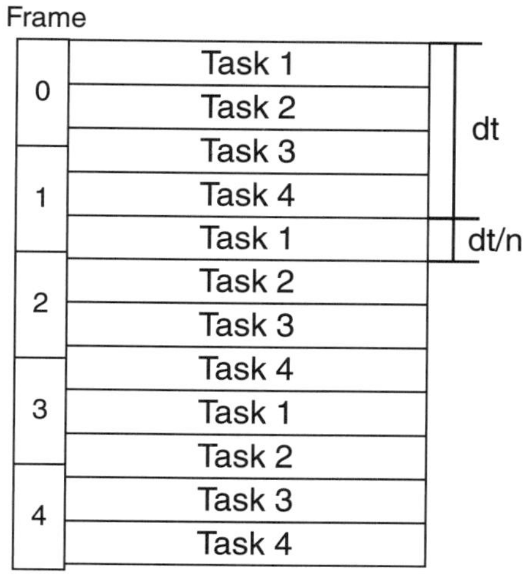

Frame

0	Task 1	
	Task 2	dt
	Task 3	
1	Task 4	
	Task 1	dt/n
2	Task 2	
	Task 3	
3	Task 4	
	Task 1	
	Task 2	
4	Task 3	
	Task 4	

FIGURE 6.3.1 *Task frame-base timeline.*

uses the estimated execution time as described previously in the section *Timed Task for Maximum Time Group.*

Any task that can vary widely in its execution time is a good candidate for this type of group. For example, LOS checks tend to be iterative algorithms with unpredictable termination conditions. Therefore, by using a maximum time group, we can put off some LOS checks for a frame, when one spikes enough to jeopardize our budget.

Root Update

The core of the root update is our task scheduling system, which consists of two stages. First, we execute all tasks that expire before the time of the current frame; then, we run all group scheduling methods to allow rescheduling of tasks. These two stages comprise the entire AI update and can be wrapped in a single function.

As tasks execute, they will spawn other tasks that will be registered with scheduling groups. When these groups run their rescheduling function, then these tasks will be set to execute.

Executing Tasks

The system maintains a time-ordered queue (a linked list of task objects containing their desired runtimes). The front of the queue is executed until its runtime is greater than the current time. Tasks are popped from the front of the queue and executed. This continues until the task at the front is scheduled for the next frame.

Profiling

One main advantage of this scheduling system is the ability to profile. By grouping tasks into groups of similar function, it is easier to track down areas of the AI that spike badly or require too much time. The following is useful information to gather and store:

- Total execution time of task executions within the group
- Total number of task executions within the group
- Maximum task execution time in the group
- The total executing time of the group in the last frame
- The number of tasks executed from the group in the last frame
- Maximum total group execution time per frame

In general, both groups and tasks can be transient, but for profiling, it is best that scheduling groups are static. Otherwise, the data needed for profiling all parts of the system will not be available for reporting.

Predictors

Task updates can be executed even less often through the use of a *value predictor*. Value predictors use numbers generated in the past to estimate, or predict, numbers in the future. Over large time spans, these predictions can be useless. However, for short time intervals between task executions, values calculated in those tasks will usually change very little. Using value predictors, we can simulate tasks running every frame, even though we are actually running them at a lower frequency.

Basic Value Predictor

The base predictor works by storing the timestamp of the last time the value was updated. In addition, first-order (Equation 6.3.1) and second-order (Equation 6.3.2) derivatives are estimated and stored.

$$v = \frac{dx}{dt} = \frac{x - x_0}{t - t_0} \tag{6.3.1}$$

$$a = \frac{dx}{dt^2} = \frac{v - v_0}{t - t_0} \tag{6.3.2}$$

Using these parameters, values in between the updates are adequately predicted. For more complicated situations, it might be desirable to add the storage of the third-order derivative as well.

Using Equation 6.3.3, we can estimate the future value. Although the prediction will be inaccurate the farther out in time we estimate, in a game, times between task executions are small. For values that don't vary dramatically in such small timeframes, the value predictor can be fairly accurate.

$$x' = x + vt + \frac{1}{2}at^2 \tag{6.3.3}$$

2D and 3D Predictors

The implementation of the single-value predictor can be extended to implementations of 2D and 3D vectors. In fact, these multidimensional predictors are great for tracking points in space that are expensive to calculate (e.g., projectile/target intersections points).

Limitations and Variations

There can be problems when large jumps occur in a single update cycle. This is especially problematic if the cycle is large enough. This can be mitigated through the use of value clamping.

There are two main types of value clamping. First, we can specify max range values for the predictor to ensure that all values returned by the prediction function will be within tolerance. Second, we can provide an option that allows us to clamp the predictor to a specific value. In the second case, this is done by setting v and a to zero.

One special case should also be noted: special consideration must be made the first time the value is set. For example, if you initialize the value to zero at startup, then the first time it is actually set, it might get set to some large value. The v and a estimates will most likely result in even larger predictions. This can be true even for short time intervals. The best solution is to make sure that the first time the value is set, v and a are still maintained at zero.

Improvements

For simplicity, the previous text described the task schedule as a time-ordered linked-list. In practice, this has proven to be a big hit on performance, since tasks must be inserted into the right spot in the list, taking $O(n)$ time.

A good alternative is to break the schedule into smaller time buckets. The size of the bucket should be at least as small as the time for each frame (e.g., one-sixtieth of a second). These buckets are then allocated in a ring buffer that is large enough to handle the farthest time delta between any scheduled task and the current frame time. For example, say a bucket represents a time chunk of one-sixtieth of a second. If the largest anticipated delay between the time of scheduling and time of execution were 10 seconds, the array would need to have 600 buckets.

Scheduling is changed from an $O(n)$ insertion sort to a constant time function. This is because we are executing entire buckets at a time, so no time sorting is required within the bucket.

Descheduling still requires an $O(m)$ search and delete, but m is the number of tasks within the bucket rather than the number of all functions in the schedule. It should also be noted that descheduling is rare; in most cases, the task will be removed from the bucket when the task is executed. Since the bucket execution code simply walks the task list in the bucket, the task is removed by popping it from the front of the bucket's task list.

One other advantage of this technique is the ability to profile expected task runs for future frames. This might allow us to shift tasks down the bucket ring to alleviate spiking.

Finally, we described a maximum time group, in which we attempt to run as many tasks in the group as we can until we have used up a maximum time value. Using the group scheduling system described in the article, we are forced to try to estimate the time for each task when it executes. However, if we handle the running of these tasks at the top level, we are able to actually time the functions as they are executed, and we would be much less likely to spike.

Conclusion

Imagine a system in which all tasks in AI are simply and automatically executed through a load-balancing system. Such a system forces the programmer to approach every solution with load balancing in mind. The programmer starts to think in terms of how tasks can be broken up and spaced over time. The result is a system that not only can be much more easily retuned for performance, but one that will be implemented more efficiently in the first place.

References

[Leopold01] Leopold, Claudia, "Coordination Models," *Parallel and Distributed Computing*, John Wiley & Sons, 2001.

[Wilkinson98] Wilkinson, Barry, and Allen, Michael, "Load Balancing and Termination Detection," *Parallel Programming*, Prentice Hall, 1998.

A Simple Inference Engine for a Rule-Based Architecture

Mike Christian—Paradigm Entertainment

mikec@pe-i.com

Rule-based systems have been around since the 1970s—practically forever in computer years. However, that doesn't mean they have outlived their usefulness in game AI. On the contrary, such a system can give your game AI some powerful capabilities and yet be very easy to implement. This article explains a simple approach to rule representation and how to implement an inference engine to process behaviors at a high-level of abstraction. The purpose of such a system is to make behaviors understandable and easy to manipulate.

Rules

The rules we will be using are of the if-then variety, similar to what we programmers see every day. *If* some expression, *then* do some code. In mainstream AI, these types of rules are often used in deduction systems in which the *if* pattern is known as the antecedent, and the *then* pattern is a consequent, a conclusion that is deduced from the *if* pattern [Winston92].

If	?x knows how to write code
then	?x is a programmer

Much has been written about this type of rule and the many types of systems that have been created to deal with them, even entire languages such as Prolog. However, this is not the type of rule that the system in this article deals with. This system works with a specific type of rule known as a *reaction rule*.

Reaction rules, which we shall simply refer to as *action* rules, are useful for getting your AI characters to behave. That is not to say that consequent rules are not useful, just that they are not the focus of this article.

Action rules in a game might look like the following.

If	?x	sees an enemy	then	?x	charge the enemy
If	?x	catches the enemy	then	?x	punch the enemy

| If | ?x | gets hurt | then | ?x | run home |
| If | ?x | gets mortally wounded | then | ?x | die |

As you can see, these rules are highly abstracted from what is really going on in the system. To "see" an enemy, a non-player character (NPC) might do something like check distance, line-of-sight, and viewing angle for enemies in the vicinity. The pseudo-code would look something like:

```
for all enemies in the vicinity
    is the enemy within my sight range?
        is the enemy within my viewing angle?
        if a line-of-sight ray can reach the enemy
            return true
return false
```

The real code would occupy more lines and would involve support functions for proximity testing, viewing angle calculations, and line-of-sight testing. As you can see, one could easily lose sight of the big picture, the behavior, when getting down to the nitty-gritty of the AI code for just one of the NPC functions. One of the purposes of the rule is to hide the details of what is going on in the AI support systems, and allow the developer to concentrate on the overall behavior. In fact, the antecedent and action portions of a rule can be functions:

If	?x	seesEnemy()	then	?x	chargeEnemy()
If	?x	catchesEnemy()	then	?x	punchEnemy()
If	?x	hurt()	then	?x	goHome()
If	?x	mortallyWounded()	then	?x	die()

where ?x would be a NPC and the functions could be methods of that NPC's class. The code could be in an update function called for every game update. If the antecedent function returned true, then the action function would be called and the action would be performed for that update. The code could look like:

```
void NPC::update()
{
    if ( seesEnemy() )        chargeEnemy();
    if ( catchesEnemy() )     punchEnemy();
    if ( tired() )            rest();
    if ( hurt() )             goHome();
    if ( mortallyWounded() )  die();
}
```

What we have in the previous code are rules that hide the complexity of the subsystems, the low-level systems that handle sound, motion, animation, and so forth. Rules of this type are okay, but this implementation brings to light some problems with rules. One of the problems is ordering. Which rule is the most important? Which is the least? You could rearrange them in order of importance and put `else` statements in front of the `ifs`. This would work, but what if you wanted to add a rule where when the NPC sees an enemy while wounded, he runs away? Then, ordering is not so clear; we need some sort of rule context. Code would have to be added for this case, maybe rules within rules. Making exceptions in code is okay, but then our rules start to look less like rules and more like regular code. Over time, this is likely to get worse as more rules are added and more special cases need to be coded to handle the problems of context. There is a better way.

Goals

Goals are a natural concept for NPC behavior and provide a context for rules and an intuitive vehicle for actions. Consider the following goals and rules for a cat-chasing dog.

GOAL (Wander)	IF (SeesCat)	GOTO (ChaseCat)
GOAL (ChaseCat)	IF (CatGetsAway)	GOTO (Wander)

Even without yet knowing how the goals and rules are implemented, you can still see what the behavior of our dog is. He wanders around until he sees a cat, and then he chases it. If the cat gets away, then he simply goes back to wandering around.

Goals can be thought of as states, like those found in a finite-state machine (FSM) [Dybsand00], [Rabin00]. In fact, the inference engine described in this article is actually an FSM in disguise, so you might prefer to use *state* instead of *goal* for your implementation. *Goal* as it is used in this system is meant to represent the purpose of the NPC for a given moment of time, in which the NPC may or may not actually reach the actual state implied in the name. In addition, as you will see later, the code supporting goals often contains states within the goals. Use of the term *goal* helps differentiate the higher-level state and its substates.

Goals in this system are directly tied to actions. In the preceding example, the actions are `Wander` and `ChaseCat`. Only one goal is processed at a time; consequently, only one action is performed at a time. Moreover, only the rules that belong to the currently processed goal are tested, thus providing context. Rules are processed in order, and the first one that has its condition met transfers control to a new goal. The `GOTO` keyword signifies the transfer concept.

An important note to make at this point is that goals don't entirely solve the problem of rule ordering; they only provide a context for sets of rules. The rules in a goal are processed in order of appearance in the rule list. More work can be done to enhance the rule ordering, such as using weights or implementing fuzzy rules as mentioned in the section *Enhancement: Scripting and Goal Construction Tool* at the end of this article.

There is one more important feature our goals can have and that is to be able to process goals within goals. This feature allows us to have contexts within contexts; in other words, subgoals. Consider the following:

GOAL (Idle)		
	IF (Refreshed)	GOSUB (Wander)
	IF (Tired)	GOSUB (Nap)
GOAL (Wander)		
	IF (SeesCat)	GOTO (ChaseCat)
GOAL (ChaseCat)		
	IF (CatGetsAway)	GOTO (Wander)
GOAL (Nap)		

We have added a new goal named Idle. It contains a Refreshed and a Tired rule. Notice the new GOSUB keyword. When a GOSUB rule is triggered, the inference engine transfers control to the referenced goal, but keeps processing the other rules in the current goal, all except for the rule that triggered the transfer. What this means for our dog is that when control transfers to the Wander goal, the Tired rule still gets tested. In addition, when control transfers to the Nap goal, the Refreshed rule still gets tested.

The Inference Engine

Now is a good time to stop and look at how goals are processed by the inference engine. Basically, the engine needs to be able to execute the current goal action and loop through each of the current goal's rules to see if any of them triggers control to a new goal. If a rule fires, then control is switched to a new goal. There is a bit more to the engine than that, but it will be explained as we go along.

The first thing we need to do is to make sure our inference engine can understand what goals and rules are. There are several ways to do this, from providing a scripting interface to custom rule-building tools to simply making functions calls in code. For the sake of clarity, this article implements the creation of goals and rules in code. However, we will use macros to represent them. The use of macros gives you the ability to see "behavior at a glance," since there is none of that messy code in the way. Macros can be hard to debug, so there is a trade-off. However, once the macros are solid, they can actually make rule construction less error prone.

One more thing before looking at the macros: a collection of rules and goals owned by an IEOwner object will be referred to as a "brain." This is mostly for ease of communications.

The macros developed for this article are:

IE_START (name)	Starts goal construction for the inference engine and gives the brain a name.
GOAL (action)	Specifies a goal and the action object.
IF (cond)	Specifies the first part of a rule and its conditional object.
GOTO (goal)	Specifies a goal to transfer total control to.
GOSUB (goal)	Specifies a goal to transfer control to, but keeps the rules of the current goal for processing by pushing the goal's rules on a stack.

RETURN   Signals that processing should return to the previous goal.
IE_END   Indicates the end of the goals and tells the inference
                    engine to link all the goals and rules.

ON THE CD

The macros work together to build a set of goals and rules, referred to as a brain, for any class derived from IEOwner (inference engine owner). The IE_START and IE_END macros encapsulate a method called makeBrain(). IE_START also creates a contained IE (inference engine) object. The other macros make various calls to the IE object to construct goals and rules. See the ieowner.h file on the source CD.

Every action, condition, and goal referenced by the macros are actually names of classes derived from a class called IEExec (inference engine executor). Do you remember in earlier examples that the if-then parts of the rules contained functions? The IEExec class is used instead. The class gives us a common interface for all the behavioral subcomponents. You could still use functions, but we find the class more useful because it can provide more than just updates for actions and conditions; it also provides initialization, start and finish methods, and provides the inference engine access to the owner of the IEExec object.

Once the macros have created a brain, then it is ready to be put to work inside the game update loop. This is done by calling an IEOwner's think method. The think method performs an update on the brain created by the macros. This update can be broken up into the following steps:

1. If starting a goal, then call the current goal start method.
2. If finishing a goal, then process the current goal finish() until it returns false. Then, make the next goal being transferred to the current goal and push it onto the goal stack.
3. For all goals on the stack:
   a. For all rules in this goal that have not been triggered:
      i. Call the update() for the rule.
      ii. If update() returns true, then...
         1. Set the goal it points to as the next goal, and set the current goal as finished.
         2. If the rule is a GOTO type, then pop the current goal off the stack.
         3. If the rule is a GOSUB type, then mark this rule as triggered so it won't be triggered again while the current goal is on the stack.
         4. Return and process no more rules.
4. Call the current goal's update().

To explain these steps, let's take our dog NPC and use a Nap goal as an example. Nap would be derived from IEExec and supports the methods init, start, update, and finish. When the Nap goal is first added to the inference engine, via the GOAL macro, an IEGoal is created that contains the exec (shorthand for an IEExec instance) and the Nap's init method is called. The init method sets a pointer to the owner (IEOwner) of the exec; in this case, our dog. Other tasks init might do is initialize nap-specific data for any of the subsystems such as a sleeping or yawning animation. Once Nap is initialized, it is ready to be used by the inference engine through the `think` method.

Step 1 of `think` gives a goal the opportunity to perform one or more passes to prepare for the main action in the goal's behavior by calling the `start` method. Usually, only one call to start is needed to prepare a goal for processing, but the ability exists to support multiple calls in multiple updates. The inference engine will continue calling `start` on subsequent updates as long as `start` returns false. Once `start` returns a true, that is the signal that it has succeeded and processing of the goal can proceed. In the case of the Nap goal, `start` begins an animation for the owner (the dog) to lie down. It also sets up an internal state to LieDown for the start of the Nap `update`.

Step 2 is the complement of step 1. When control has been transferred to a new goal, then the previous goal has the opportunity to "clean up" through the `finish` method. For example, say our dog was just starting to lie down for his nap, he spotted a cat, and control transferred to a chase goal. We would not want him to instantly snap out of the lying-down animation and start chasing the cat; we would want him to stand up first. The `finish` method for Nap could do this, before allowing control to transfer to chase, by returning false until the dog was standing up. Once `finish` returns true, then the inference engine knows it can continue the transfer.

The third step is the update of the main goal action through its `IEExec` for Nap. This update contains the bulk of the behavior for the goal. For Nap, this is the various substate changes for lying down, yawning, sleeping, getting up, yawning again, and stretching. Each substate contains code for making the subsystem calls for sound, motion, animation, and so forth. For this article, the substate changes are made through a switch statement, but could easily use a state machine. You could even use goals and rules for the middle layer. More will be explained about `IEExec` in a following section.

The last step processes the rules for all goals on the goal stack, ignoring any rules that have been triggered. Processing a rule means calling the rule exec's `update` method. If the update returns true, then the rule is "triggered" and control is transferred to the goal it refers to. If the rule is a `GOSUB` type, then the current goal is left on the stack so its rules will continue to be processed. This allows goal nesting, which can be a very useful feature for subgoal type of features. If the rule is a `GOTO` type, then the current goal is popped off the stack so its rules are no longer considered.

More about Execs

The `IEExec` class is the interface for objects that can execute goal actions or rule conditionals. In all fairness, most of the "real" AI work is done inside classes derived from `IEExec`. They form the middle layer of this system in which calls are made to low-level support systems for sound, motion, effects, animation, and so forth. For `IEExec` objects that are used to support goal actions, such as Nap, the update method contains all of the substate management for manipulating behavior for that goal. The inference engine does not care what goes on inside IEExec objects, but only cares that these objects supply it with the necessary functions to use them to process goals and rules.

All IEExec derived classes are required to supply an init, update, getOwner, and a getName method. The start, finish, and reset methods are optional. The most important method of this class is update. Both goal actions and rule conditionals call update. If update returns true for a rule conditional, then that rule is triggered. A goal action calls update to process the behavior for that goal.

ON THE CD

The init method is used to establish the owner of the exec object. Only execs of the same IEOwner type can be used to construct rules for that owner. This is important when considering how execs will know how to work with an IEOwner, and what specific data is available to them. To make IEExecs more useful, it is a good idea to generalize the types of IEOwners they work with. For the example on the CD-ROM, there is an IEOwner derived class called Character that provides an interface for all the subsystem support for all characters in the sample game. Therefore, any IEExec that has a Character as an owner can access these functions and associated data.

The methods start and finish are used only by goal action's execs. As mentioned earlier, a goal action often needs to prepare itself for the updates to follow. The start method will be called repeatedly until it returns false. The update method for the goal action will not be called, and the rules will not be evaluated until start() returns false, indicating that the goal has been initialized. The finish method is similar. When control is transferred away from a goal by a rule trigger, finish is called every update until it returns false. Control is not actually transferred until this occurs. This gives goals a chance to "clean up," to be in a state that makes sense before transferring control. Take the example of a man jumping over a ditch:

GOAL (JumpDitch)

                IF (SeesMonster)   GOTO (RunAway)

If our man saw the monster in mid-jump, we would not want him to start running in mid-air in the opposite direction. The finish method gives the JumpDitch exec a way to make sure the man lands on the ground before any other goal can take over.

Enhancement: Scripting and Goal Construction Tool

Goals and rules could easily be exposed to a scripting interface. The obvious advantage is that the basic behavior for AI could easily be rearranged without code changes

An alternative to a scripting interface is to build a specialized tool for constructing goals and rules. The advantage to such a tool is that, like a scripting interface, it allows for easy modifications to behavior. It also has the advantage of reducing error, as the tool would only allow you to select rule and goal objects that have been registered with the system.

Creating such a tool is not as difficult as it might sound. Interfaces are fairly easy to build with tools such as MFC or Visual Basic. The only trick is to come up with a scheme for encoding the data so that the runtime understands what the tool has created.

Enhancement: Data Packets

A scheme for representing data for use by IEExec objects could be very useful. For example, say you had a goal exec called GotoLocation. The exec needs to know what location. This could be represented by a data structure that contained coordinates of the location and any other information the logic needed. Then, what is needed is a method for attaching the data to the exec and a runtime-type mechanism so the exec can make sure that the data is the right type.

Enhancement: Multiple Antecedents

Antecedents are the *if* portion of rules. Multiple antecedents could be very useful and would not be too difficult to add to the system. For example, take the rule:

```
IF SeesEnemy GOTO ChaseEnemy.
```

Depending on the current goal at the time, you might want a rule like:

```
IF SeesEnemy AND Healthy AND Refreshed GOTO ChaseEnemy.
```

Enhancement: Fuzzy Rules

Rules could also have a fuzzy component to them (for information on fuzzy logic, see [McCuskey00]). Rule execs could return a fuzzy value instead of true or false; say, almost true or nearly false. This could work with multipart rules in which each *if* portion of the rule could have its fuzzy values added together. For example, take the rule:

IF SeesEnemy AND OnAlert THEN ChaseEnemy.

If an NPC only sort-of saw an enemy, like a shadow or movement out of the corner of his eye, then SeesEnemy might return a 0.4. If OnAlert returned a 0.0, then the rule would not trigger. However, if OnAlert was any higher, like if an alarm was going off, then it would push the total value over 0.5 and trigger the rule. Alternatively, all the rest of the rules could be tested to see which had the highest fuzzy value, and that one would be triggered.

Conclusion

A rule-based system as described in this article is conceptually easy and yet potentially powerful. It gives you the ability to understand and manipulate behaviors at a high abstraction level, that of goals, and is natural to how we humans think of game characters behaving. The system also forces its architect(s) to design each subcomponent in a standard and flexible way, via the IEExec interface.

Hopefully, this article has given you some insight as to how even simple mainstream AI concepts can make your system more empowered, and can be a springboard into learning much more.

On the CD-ROM

ON THE CD

The sample code for this article on the CD-ROM contains the complete inference engine, along with the rules for dog and cat interacting in a 2D world and with each other. The demo is a text-based program that prints out messages on what the NPCs are doing and how they are feeling. A fake animation and a 2D motion system are used to demonstrate how execs can interact with subsystems.

References

[Dybsand00] Dybsand, Eric, "A Finite-State Machine Class," *Game Programming Gems*, Charles River Media, 2000.

[McCuskey00] McCuskey, Mason, "Fuzzy Logic for Video Games," *Game Programming Gems*, Charles River Media, 2000.

[Rabin00] Rabin, Steve, "Designing a General Robust AI Engine," *Game Programming Gems*, Charles River Media, 2000.

[Winston92] Winston, Patrick Henry, *Artificial Intelligence*, Addison-Wesley, 1992.

6.5

Implementing a State Machine Language

Steve Rabin—Nintendo of America, Inc.

steve@aiwisdom.com, steve_rabin@hotmail.com

It is generally recognized that in game AI, state machines are the most used software pattern. This kind of popularity doesn't happen by accident. Rather, state machines are widely used because they possess some amazing qualities. They are simple to program, easy to comprehend, easy to debug, and completely general to any problem. They might not always provide the best solution, but few can deny that they get the job done with minimal risk to the project.

However, state machines have a darker side as well. Many programmers look at them with distrust since they tend to be constructed ad hoc with no consistent structure. They also tend to grow uncontrollably as the development cycle churns on. This poor structure, coupled with unbounded growth, makes many state machine implementations a maintenance nightmare.

With the current state of affairs, we have this great concept of a state machine, but it often is abused and tortured in actual implementation. This article presents a robust way to structure your state machines with a simple language. This State Machine Language will not only provide structure, but it will unleash some powerful concepts that will make programming games much easier. The next article, "Enhancing a State Machine Language through Messaging," will expand on this language with a powerful communication technique using messages. Keep in mind that each article has full source code on the accompanying CD. While this technique is built around C++, a similar C-only version appears in [Rabin00].

ON THE CD

Game Developer-Style State Machines

Just so that we're all on the same page, it's important to understand that when game developers speak of *state machines* or *finite-state machines*, they are only loosely referring to the traditional Computer Science definition. If you want to be strict about it, traditional finite-state machines are rather cumbersome, redundant, and not very useful for complicated systems. Therefore, game developers never actually use those strict definitions. Instead, they might have states within states, multiple state variables, randomness in state transitions, code executing every game tick within a state, and all kinds of things that violate the rigorous formalism of a proper finite-state machine.

However, it's this lax attitude that makes game programmers create state machines similar to the following:

```
void RunLogic( int *state )
{
    switch( *state )
    {
        case 0: //Wander
            Wander();
            if( SeeEnemy() ) {
                if( GetRandomChance() < 0.8 ) *state = 1;
                else *state = 2;
            }
            if( Dead() ) *state = 3;
            break;

        case 1: //Attack
            Attack();
            if( Dead() ) *state = 3;
            break;

        case 2: //RunAway
            RunAway();
            if( Dead() ) *state = 3;
            break;

        case 3: //Dead
            SlowlyRot();
            break;
    }
}
```

To a game developer, the preceding code is a legitimate state machine. It isn't pretty, but there are worse-looking state machine abominations. Consider a state machine that looks up state transitions in a table and is spread across multiple files. At least with the preceding code, you have good readability, a sense of wholeness, and a fighting chance of debugging it. These are all Really Good Things.

However, this ad hoc state machine code has some serious weaknesses.

- The state changes are poorly regulated.
- States are of type int and would be more robust and debuggable as enums.
- The omission of a single break keyword would cause hard-to-find bugs.
- Redundant logic appears in multiple states.
- No way to tell that a state has been entered for the first time.
- No way to monitor or log how the state machine has behaved over time.

So, what is a poor game programmer to do? The answer is to provide some structure, while retaining the positive qualities such as readability and ease of debugging. This can be accomplished with the following State Machine Language.

A State Machine Language

Our State Machine Language will only have six keywords in it. Amazingly, these keywords will be created with the help of macros so that our language is completely implemented inside C++. While an independent language is completely feasible, keeping it integrated with the native game code provides some huge advantages, such as retaining the ease of debugging and not wasting time writing parsing and support tools.

Here are the six macro keywords:

- `BeginStateMachine`
- `EndStateMachine`
- `State`
- `OnEnter`
- `OnExit`
- `OnUpdate`

Listing 6.5.1 shows an example of what a state machine looks like when constructed with these keywords. Note that it's very similar to the previous switch-based state machine; however, it conceals a very powerful control flow.

Listing 6.5.1 Example structure of the State Machine Language.

```
BeginStateMachine

    State( STATE_Wander )
        OnEnter
            // C or C++ code for state entry
        OnUpdate
            // C or C++ code executed every tick
        OnExit
            // C or C++ code for state clean-up

    State( STATE_Attack )
        OnEnter
            // C or C++ code for state entry

EndStateMachine
```

The execution of our state machine is straightforward. When it first starts up, it enters the first state (STATE_Wander) and executes the code under OnEnter. After that, the state machine receives update messages on every game tick and executes the code under OnUpdate in the current state. If the code triggers a state change, the OnExit code is automatically executed, the state is changed, and, finally, the OnEnter section of the new state is executed.

So far, it isn't clear how all this actually works, but the structure is now there to make consistent, readable, debuggable, and robust state machines.

Actual Implementation

The six macro keywords are as follows (OnEvent is a helper—it's not used directly):

```
#define BeginStateMachine    if(state < 0){if(0){
#define EndStateMachine      return(true);}}else{assert(0); \
                             return(false);}return(false);
#define State(a)             return(true);}}else if(a == state){if(0){
#define OnEvent(a)           return(true);}else if(a == event){
#define OnEnter              OnEvent(EVENT_Enter)
#define OnUpdate             OnEvent(EVENT_Update)
#define OnExit               OnEvent(EVENT_Exit)
```

After macro expansion, the state machine in Listing 6.5.1 is transformed into Listing 6.5.2. This should give you a better understanding of what actually is executed.

Listing 6.5.2 State machine after macro expansion.

```
if( state < 0 ) {                          //BeginStateMachine
    if( 0 ) {                              //
        return( true );                    //State()
    }                                      //
}                                          //
else if( STATE_Wander == state ) {         //
    if( 0 ) {                              //
        return( true );                    //OnEnter
    }                                      //
    else if( EVENT_Enter == event ) {      //
        //C or C++ code for state entry
        return( true );                    //OnUpdate
    }                                      //
    else if( EVENT_Update == event ) {     //
        //C or C++ code executed every tick
        return( true );                    //OnExit
    }                                      //
    else if( EVENT_Exit == event ) {       //
        //C or C++ code for state clean-up
        return( true );                    //State()
    }                                      //
}                                          //
else if( STATE_Attack == state ) {         //
    if( 0 ) {                              //
        return( true );                    //OnEnter
    }                                      //
    else if( EVENT_Enter == event ) {      //
        //C or C++ code for state entry
        return( true );                    //EndStateMachine
    }                                      //
}                                          //
```

```
else {                              //
   assert( 0 );                     //
   return( false );                 //
}                                   //
return( false );                    //
```

The macro expanded code in Listing 6.5.2 has some nice properties. First, the macros expand in a building-block fashion, allowing an arbitrary number of states with any combination of event responses. In fact, the building blocks are so versatile that a state machine consisting of only `BeginStateMachine` and `EndStateMachine` is completely legal and compiles. In order to achieve this nice building-block property, some seemingly useless `if(0)` statements are embedded within the macros to make everything work out correctly. Fortunately, most compilers will typically optimize these out.

A second great property is that a handled event returns a `true`, while an event that isn't handled returns a `false`. This provides an easy way to monitor how the state machine is or isn't handling events.

A third nice property is that you can't mess up the state machine by forgetting something like a `break` keyword. The keywords are simple enough that you can easily spot errors. Moreover, you don't need curly braces around any of your states or event responses, which tends to make the whole thing easier to read.

Behind the Scenes

As presented, this State Machine Language needs something to feed it the proper events, such as `OnEnter`, `OnUpdate`, and `OnExit`. The job of dispensing these events is performed by a small function inside the `StateMachine` class called `Process`, which is shown in Listing 6.5.3.

Listing 6.5.3 Support functions for the state machine.

```
void StateMachine::Process( StateMachineEvent event )
{
    //Sends the event to the state machine
    States( event, m_currentState );

    //Check for a state change and send new events
    int safetyCount = 10;
    while( m_stateChange && (—safetyCount >= 0) )
    {
        assert( safetyCount > 0 && "States are flip-flopping." );

        m_stateChange = false;

        //Let the last state clean-up
        States( EVENT_Exit, m_currentState );

        //Set the new state
```

```
            m_currentState = m_nextState;

            //Let the new state initialize
            States( EVENT_Enter, m_currentState );
        }
    }

    void StateMachine::SetState( unsigned int newState )
    {
        m_stateChange = true;
        m_nextState = newState;
    }
```

Listing 6.5.3 shows the simplicity of this State Machine Language. When the state machine is first initialized in the game, it calls the Process function with the argument EVENT_Enter. Then, every game tick the Process function is called with the argument EVENT_Update.

To trigger a state change in this language, the function SetState in Listing 6.5.3 is called from within the actual state machine. SetState queues a state change that is then handled by the while loop inside the Process function. Within the while loop, EVENT_Exit is sent to the current state so that it can execute any cleanup code. Then, the current state is officially changed and EVENT_Enter is finally sent to the new state.

The purpose of the while loop is to process all successive state changes within the current game tick. If for some reason the state machine was designed badly and flip-flops infinitely between states, the while loop will catch this bug and assert. This is another feature of the language that helps provide robustness.

Integrating this Solution

Having seen the State Machine Language, you might be wondering how is it actually integrated within a game. The infrastructure for the state machine is held within the base class StateMachine that enforces a single virtual function named States. For example, to create a robot state machine, a new class Robot can be derived from StateMachine as in the following code:

```
class Robot : public StateMachine
{
public:
    Robot( void ) {};
    ~Robot( void ) {};

private:
    virtual bool States( StateMachineEvent event, int state );
    // Put private robot specific variables here
};
```

The state machine for the robot is then put inside the States virtual function, as in the following code:

```
bool Robot::States( StateMachineEvent event, int state )
{
BeginStateMachine

    // Put any number of states and event responses.
    // Refer to the code on the CD for more examples.

EndStateMachine
}
```

Once you have your robot state machine, your game objects can instantiate it and run its logic. In addition, there is nothing that precludes an AI entity from owning several different state machines at a time, or swapping them in and out as needs change.

ON THE CD

You'll find the fully implemented State Machine Language on the CD-ROM. There isn't much code, so run it in the debugger and step through to examine how everything works. Before you run off and try to build your game around this simple state machine, consider the more complicated form of the State Machine Language, as presented in the next article. You will find both versions on the accompanying CD-ROM.

Conclusion

Some people will chide and scoff when using macros for a purpose such as this, but the benefits of such a design have to be considered. This State Machine Language provides some truly amazing features:

- Simple enforced structure
- Excellent readability
- Natural to debug
- Full power of C/C++ within the state machine
- Easy to add code for entering or exiting a state
- State changes are more formal and protected
- Error checking for flip-flopping state changes
- No need to spend months developing a custom language

While the benefits described so far are wonderful, the true power of this language is demonstrated in article 6.6, "Enhancing a State Machine Language through Messaging." In this article, several important features are added, including general messaging, generic timers, and global event and message responses over all states. These features might seem incremental, but instead take the language to a whole new level of sophistication and usefulness.

References

[Dybsand00] Dybsand, Eric, "A Finite State Machine Class," *Game Programming Gems*, Charles River Media, 2000.

[Rabin00] Rabin, Steve, "Designing a General Robust AI Engine," *Game Programming Gems*, Charles River Media, 2000.

6.6

Enhancing a State Machine Language through Messaging

Steve Rabin—Nintendo of America, Inc.

steve@aiwisdom.com, steve_rabin@hotmail.com

The previous article, "Implementing a State Machine Language," set the groundwork for a powerful language that can structure state machines in a simple, readable, and very debuggable format. In this article, that language will be expanded to encompass the problem of communication between AI game objects. This communication technique will revolutionize the State Machine Language by allowing complicated control flow and timers.

The Concept of Messages

At the core level, a message is a number or enumerated type. However, the key is that these numbers have a shared meaning among independent systems, thus providing a common interface in which events can be communicated. For example, we could define the following enumeration to be messages in our game.

```
enum MSG_Name { MSG_Attacked, MSG_Damaged, MSG_Healed, MSG_Poisoned };
```

The idea is that you can *send a message* to any game object or system in your game. For example, if a character strikes an enemy, the message `MSG_Attacked` could be sent to that enemy, and the enemy could respond appropriately to that message event. By having game objects communicate with messages, deep and responsive AI can be achieved fairly easily. Moreover, the technique of messages makes it easy to keep most behavior *event-driven*, which is important for efficiency reasons [Rabin01a].

Messages as Letters

If we think of a message as a letter (i.e., the kind delivered by a mail carrier), rather than just a number, we can make some significant advances. Consider the following sample message class:

```
class MSG_Object
{
public:
    MSG_Name m_Name;          //Message name (enumeration)
    float    m_Data;          //Extra data for the message
    objectID m_Sender;        //Object that sent the message
    objectID m_Receiver;      //Object that will get the message
    float    m_DeliveryTime;  //Time at which to send the message
};
```

The MSG_Object class shows what the letter analogy can achieve. If a game object wants to notify another game object of an event, it could fill in this message object and pass it to a general routing system. This routing system could then completely determine what to do with the message object, since all the important information is stored directly inside the object.

Message Timers

When a message object is self-contained and stores all the information needed for delivery, it can also store the time at which it should be delivered. With this simple concept, the routing system that receives these message objects can retain them until it's time to be delivered, effectively creating timers. These message timers are best used when a game object sends a message to itself, at a later time, to create an internal event timer.

For example, a game object might see an enemy just as it comes into sight, but there should be a slight delay before it runs away. The game object can achieve this by sending a message to itself to be delivered a half-second in the future. Thus, reaction times can easily be modeled using messages.

Messages as Events

Now that we have the complete concept of messages, we can incorporate them into the State Machine Language, as another kind of event: a message event. The following macro keyword will be added to the language:

```
#define OnMsg(a)    return(true);}else if(EVENT_Message==event && \
                    msg && a==msg->GetMsgName()){
```

With the capability to send and respond to messages, the State Machine Language becomes truly powerful. The following state machine shows an example of a game object that runs away when attacked:

```
BeginStateMachine

    State( STATE_Wander )
        OnMsg( MSG_Attacked )
            SetState( STATE_RunAway );

    State( STATE_RunAway )
        OnEnter
            //run away
```

```
EndStateMachine
```

The same state machine can be built to simulate a reaction time of 0.5 seconds before running away, as follows:

```
BeginStateMachine

    State( STATE_Wander )
        OnMsg( MSG_Attacked )
            SendDelayedMsgToMe( 0.5, MSG_TimeOut );
        OnMsg( MSG_TimeOut )
            SetState( STATE_RunAway );

    State( STATE_RunAway )
        OnEnter
            //run away

EndStateMachine
```

Scoping Messages

Scoping is the concept that something is only valid within a certain context. By defining a scope for messages, we can ensure that they won't be misinterpreted in the wrong context. For example, if a game object sends a message to itself in the future, it might want to scope the message so that it's only valid within that state. If the message gets delivered in the future and the game object is in a different state, then the message can be thrown away since it's not valid anymore.

Scoping messages becomes important when certain generic message names get overused. This inevitably will happen, and scoping creates a simple way to prevent many bugs. Consider the following code:

```
BeginStateMachine

    State( STATE_Wander )
        OnMsg( MSG_Attacked )
            SendDelayedMsgToMe( 0.5, MSG_TimeOut, SCOPE_TO_THIS_STATE );
        OnMsg( MSG_TimeOut )
            SetState( STATE_RunAway );

    State( STATE_RunAway )
        OnEnter
            SendDelayedMsgToMe( 7.0, MSG_TimeOut );
        OnMsg( MSG_TimeOut )
            SetState( STATE_Wander );

EndStateMachine
```

The previous state machine takes advantage of message scoping. If it didn't, multiple attack messages received in STATE_Wander could queue up timeout messages to be delivered in the future. The first timeout message would trigger the state change, while the rest would artificially cause the state STATE_RunAway to be exited prematurely. However, because of message scoping, the extraneous queued timeout messages are ignored once the state is no longer STATE_Wander.

Redundant Message Policy

The previous example showed how multiple delayed messages, all basically the same, could accumulate in the message router. Message scoping helped solve the symptoms, but the real problem is what to do with redundant messages.

The answer to redundant messages is to come up with a standard rule. There are three options if an identical message is already on the queue.

1. Ignore the new message.
2. Replace the old message with the new one.
3. Store the new message, letting redundant messages accumulate.

In practice, the best policy is #1: to ignore a new message if it already exists on the queue. The previous state machine gives a good reason for this. If policy #2 is used, redundant messages keep replacing older ones and the message might never get delivered because it keeps getting replaced. If policy #3 is used, redundant messages keep getting queued up, which was clearly not intended. Thus, policy #1 is closest to the desired behavior.

Global Event Responses

One of the worst things about state machines is the redundant code that appears in multiple states. For example, if every single state should respond to the message MSG_Dead, then a message response must be redundantly put in each of those states. Since redundant code is a recipe for disaster, this language provides a workaround.

The solution is to create the concept of *global event responses*. While normally event responses only get triggered for a particular state, these responses are active regardless of the current state. In this language, global event responses are placed at the top of the state machine before any of the states. The following state machine shows an example for how MSG_Dead can be a global event response, thus able to be triggered regardless of the current state.

```
BeginStateMachine

    OnMsg( MSG_Dead )
        // Global response - Triggered regardless of state
        SetState( STATE_Dead );

    State( STATE_Wander )
        OnEnter
            //Wander
```

```
State( STATE_RunAway )
    OnEnter
        //Run away

State( STATE_Dead )
    OnEnter
        //Die
    OnMsg( MSG_Dead )
        //Ignore msg — this overrides the global response

EndStateMachine
```

For the preceding state machine to work properly, the code that sends the state machine events must be modified. Normally, an event is sent to the state machine only once. With the concept of global event responses, it must first try sending an event to the current state, but if there is no response, then it must try sending the event to the unlabeled *global* state.

But how does it know if an event was handled by a particular state? If you look at the original macros for the State Machine Language, shown again in Listing 6.6.1, you'll see a bunch of return statements containing either true or false. Those return statements correctly report back if an event was handled. Therefore, if an event is sent to the state machine and false is returned, that same event is then resent to the implicit global state.

Listing 6.6.1 Macros for the State Machine Language

```
#define BeginStateMachine    if(state < 0){if(0){
#define EndStateMachine      return(true);}}else{assert(0); \
                             return(false);}}return(false);
#define State(a)             return(true);}}else if(a == state){if(0){
#define OnMsg(a)             return(true);}else if( EVENT_Message == \
                             event && msg && a == msg->GetMsgName()){
#define OnEvent(a)           return(true);}else if(a == event){
#define OnUpdate             OnEvent( EVENT_Update )
#define OnEnter              OnEvent( EVENT_Enter )
#define OnExit               OnEvent( EVENT_Exit )
```

When global event responses are allowed, it is even more critical to use the OnExit construct properly. OnExit allows you to execute special cleanup code when a state is exited. Since global event responses can potentially change any state at will, the OnExit response is the only guaranteed way to know if a state is going to transition so you can execute any cleanup work for the current state.

Interestingly, global event responses create a unique problem. What if you want a global event response to the message MSG_Dead in every state but STATE_Dead? The solution, as shown in the previous state machine, is to override the message response MSG_Dead within STATE_Dead. Since messages are sent first to the current state, you can override or consume the message before it can be sent to the global event responses.

As with any powerful construct, you need to exercise caution, since a global event response has the power to transition out of any state at any time. As each new state is added to an existing state machine, each global event response must be considered for the possible implications.

Recording Behavior for Debugging

The need for good debugging of state machines is critical. While keeping the state machine in native C/C++ code is a huge advantage, it doesn't help much when a dozen AI entities interact over a fraction of a second and a bug must be tracked down.

The solution is to be able to monitor and record every event that's handled and not handled by each state machine. Ideally, the game should keep a log of events from every game object's state machine, complete with timestamps. Then, the game could dump each of those logs out to a text file, allowing multiple game object logs to be compared in order to find out what went wrong.

Amazingly enough, this State Machine Language allows for completely transparent monitoring. The trick is to embed logging function calls within the macro keywords themselves. The resulting macros in Listing 6.6.2 aren't pretty, but they get the job done beautifully.

Listing 6.6.2 Macro keywords with embedded logging event functions.

```
#define BeginStateMachine    if(state < 0){char statename[64]= \
                             "STATE_Global";if(0){
#define EndStateMachine      return(true);}}else{assert(0); \
                             return(false);}}return(false);
#define State(a)             return(true);}}else if(a == state) \
                             {char statename[64] = #a;if(0){
#define OnMsg(a)             return(true);}else if(EVENT_Message == \
                             event && msg && a == msg->GetMsgName()){ \
                             g_debuglog.LogStateMachineEvent( \
                             m_Owner->GetID(),msg,statename,#a,true);
#define OnEvent(a)           return(true);}else if(a == event){ \
                             g_debuglog.LogStateMachineEvent( \
                             m_Owner->GetID(),msg,statename,#a,true);
#define OnUpdate             OnEvent( EVENT_Update )
#define OnEnter              OnEvent( EVENT_Enter )
#define OnExit               OnEvent( EVENT_Exit )
```

One of the neat tricks performed by these macros is that the event and message enumeration names are correctly logged in English, not by numbers, even though no translation strings were ever coded. By using the "#" operator in the macro, the enumeration names, like MSG_Attacked, get directly coded into the state machine as characters. This allows them to be printed out to the screen or dumped to a file in a meaningful way, instead of just as integers.

Code on the CD-ROM

ON THE CD

The example code on the CD-ROM demonstrates the State Machine Language with full messaging capabilities. The code has the minimal infrastructure required to implement all of the features described in this article. This infrastructure includes the state machine base class, a game object database, a message routing system, and a time class for keeping track of game time (needed for routing of delayed messages and timestamping of debug logs).

In the main function, partially shown in Listing 6.6.3, you'll find that it creates a single game entity, requests a unique ID for it, adds it to the game object database, gives it a state machine, and initializes the state machine. Once in the main game loop, only three things are done: mark off time for that tick, tell the game object's state machine to update itself (send an OnUpdate event), and let the message router deliver delayed messages that have expired.

Listing 6.6.3 Partial listing of the main function.

```
//Create game object
GameObject myGameObject( g_database.GetNewObjectID() );
g_database.Store( myGameObject );

//Give the game object a state machine
myGameObject.SetStateMachine( new Robot( &myGameObject ) );
myGameObject.GetStateMachine()->Initialize();

// Game Loop
while(1)
{
   g_time.MarkTimeThisTick();

   myGameObject.GetStateMachine()->Update();

   g_msgroute.DeliverDelayedMessages();
}
```

The purpose of the code on the CD-ROM is not to show off a great demo (in fact, it has no interesting output), but rather to act as a simple example that you can step through in the debugger to see how it works. The code demonstrates the state machine operating, sending delayed messages to itself, message scoping, and logging of all state machine events and state transitions.

Enhancements

ON THE CD

The following are two possible enhancements that can be made to the State Machine Language. Each can be easily integrated into the State Machine Language code that is supplied on the accompanying CD-ROM.

Switching State Machines

The unbounded growth of states is one of the main problems plaguing state machines. Global event responses reduced this problem greatly, but the real solution is to be disciplined and not let too many states exist within a single state machine. This can be achieved by dividing an AI's tasks into independent chunks that can each become a state machine. When an AI needs to change tasks, the entire state machine can be swapped out with a more appropriate one.

An example in which switching state machines makes sense is in an RTS. Since units in an RTS are given discrete orders, each order such as Patrol or Attack can be its own state machine. This application is described in detail in the article "An Architecture for RTS Command Queuing" in the book *Game Programming Gems 2* [Rabin01b].

Simultaneous State Machines

Another way to deal with limiting the size of state machines is to use several different state machines at the same time. For example, you can imagine an AI that has a master state machine to make global decisions and other state machines that deal with movement, gunnery, or conversations. Structured correctly, this is a powerful way to limit the complexity of individual state machines.

Summary of State Machine Advances

Even if you never use the State Machine Language as described, you should take away several important state machine advances that can make your games easier and more robust to code, provided you somehow incorporate the following ideas:

- State machines should be easy to read.
- State machines should be easy to debug.
- State machines should be easy to build and prototype.
- State machines should have a way to communicate with other game objects.
- State machines should have global event responses to reduce redundant code.
- State machines should have a way to set event timers.
- State machines should allow transparent monitoring and logging of all events and state transitions for debugging.
- States should allow execution of special code when first entered.
- States should allow execution of special code when exited.

Conclusion

The State Machine Language in this article is deceivingly simple, yet it embodies some very important software engineering principles that will keep your project from getting into trouble: simplicity, maintainability, robustness, and ease of debugging. There are fancier solutions to state machines, such as full-blown independent languages, but the sacrifices are steep in terms of development time and complexity [Tozour02], [Brockington02].

ON THE CD

Take a look at the code provided on the book's CD and experiment with the state machine constructs. The code is designed to be very clean and should be trivial to add to any game. With a little love, hopefully, this State Machine Language can become an integral part of your next big game.

References

[Brockington02] Brockington, Mark, and Darrah, Mark, "How Not To Implement a Basic Scripting Language," *AI Game Programming Wisdom*, Charles River Media, 2002.

[Rabin00] Rabin, Steve, "Designing a General Robust AI Engine," *Game Programming Gems*, Charles River Media, 2000.

[Rabin01a] Rabin, Steve, "Strategies for Optimizing AI," *Game Programming Gems 2*, Charles River Media, 2001.

[Rabin01b] Rabin, Steve, "An Architecture for RTS Command Queuing," *Game Programming Gems 2*, Charles River Media, 2001.

[Tozour02] Tozour, Paul, "The Perils of AI Scripting," *AI Game Programming Wisdom*, Charles River Media, 2002.

DECISION-MAKING ARCHITECTURE

7.1

Blackboard Architectures

Damian Isla and Bruce Blumberg
naimad@media.mit.edu, bruce@media.mit.edu

Any type of social system—whether a swarm of bees, a pack of wolves, a sports team, or an army—requires some coordination of action. Individuals need to take certain roles, and high-level goals need to be served by occasionally nonobvious, low-level, cooperative action. This is as true for groups of simulated agents in a computer game as it is for natural and social systems. As the number of agents in a system increases along with the number of potential roles for individual agents, controlling and coordinating their behavior becomes increasingly difficult.

The same types of problems are faced by those building virtual brains. If grandfather Minsky is to be believed, and the thing we call "mind" *is* a society of individually unintelligent agents [Minsky85], then some means has to be found to coordinate all those agents' divergent actions. Because sometimes, surely, two brain centers can want contradictory things.

The blackboard approach might be one possible means of handling this coordination. Although simple (practically trivial) to implement, the architecture has proven elegant and powerful enough to be useful for problems ranging from synthetic character control to natural language understanding and other reasoning problems. It was, in fact, as a technique for formal reasoning and problem-solving that blackboards were first conceived way back in the 1970s.

The blackboard architecture is built around a metaphor: the physical blackboard we all used at school was itself a problem-solving tool. We have all experienced crowding around a blackboard with a group of friends or colleagues to tackle a particularly nasty problem. In these cases, the blackboard was useful because it provided a shared space in which the problem could be broken down and incrementally solved.

Perhaps the group broke into smaller groups to solve different parts of the problem ("to prove the theorem, we need to prove lemma 1 and lemma 2 first"), or to attempt different high-level approaches ("I'm going to prove it by induction" versus "I'm going to use a proof through counter-example"). Despite this subgrouping (or *subgoaling*, to use the terminology of the blackboard literature), each group still had direct visual access to the work of the other groups, which aided in reconciling divergent tactics ("I see you're getting further with the proof through counter-example than I am with the induction, so I'm going to put it aside for now") and opportunistic problem-solving ("I couldn't help but notice that you're having trouble with that Taylor-series expansion. I just happen to be the world's foremost expert on Taylor series!").

The canonical blackboard architecture formalizes this metaphor. It is described in detail in the next section.

The Canonical Blackboard Architecture

While the definition of a blackboard is general enough to lend itself to numerous implementation strategies, there is a canonical architecture that most implementations fall under. This architecture is shown in Figure 7.1.1, and consists of:

- **Blackboard**: A publicly read/writeable information display. Typically, the blackboard contains a list of logical assertions upon which other components operate. Although it is possible to maintain the blackboard contents as a simple jumble of

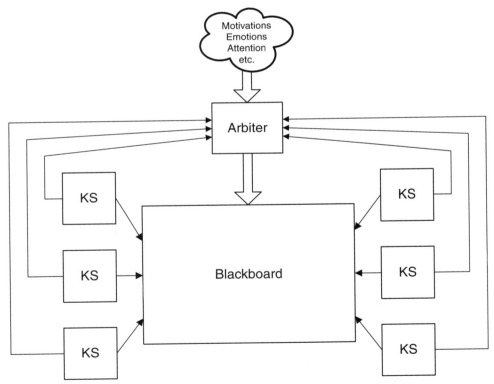

FIGURE 7.1.1   *The canonical blackboard architecture. A central blackboard is surrounded by Knowledge Sources (KSs) that compete for temporary control of the blackboard. The arbiter decides which relevant KS will be allowed to execute based on arbitrary control input.*

assertions, many systems impose a structure on the assertion space. Just as writing on a physical blackboard has a spatial location to it, methods can be found to organize the assertions on the virtual blackboard, so that external components need only explore specific areas of the blackboard for contents they are interested in. Some systems, for example, impose a hierarchy to the assertions, identifying some assertions as *data* (the initial input to the system) and other assertions as *goals*, with a specified number of intermediate levels. Some systems also annotate assertions with a credibility rating, indicating how likely the assertion is.

- **Knowledge sources (KSs)**: Flanking the blackboard are a series of components that are able to operate on the information that the blackboard contains. These are the "specialists" that will collaborate to solve the problem. Like all specialists, KSs only have very narrow regions of expertise, and so only know what to do in a very narrow set of circumstances. Usually, KSs are inactive, awaiting specific sets of preconditions to become true. A KS might also return a "willingness to run," or *relevance*, indicating its degree of applicability to the current contents of the blackboard. When KSs are found to be relevant, they can be executed, their actions modifying the contents of the blackboard. These modifications might take the form of new logical assertions, changes to existing assertions, or control signals to other KSs. Significantly, KSs are only allowed to communicate with one another through the blackboard.

- **Arbiter**: Given a single snapshot of the blackboard contents, it is possible that any number of KSs can indicate a nonzero relevance. It is the job of the arbiter to decide which of the relevant KSs to execute. This is a critical step, and constitutes the entirety of the control strategy for the entire blackboard system. In many of the earlier systems, the arbiter would pick a single "winning" KS—this was a means of ensuring that two contradictory actions were not taken in a single timestep (e.g., KS1 wants to replace assertion X with assertion Y, but KS2 wants to replace it with assertion Z). A trivial strategy for picking a single winner would simply be to pick the KS with the highest self-generated *relevance*. However, any number of strategies is possible, including ones that incorporate a focus of attention, a motivational state, an emotional state, a personality model, and so forth. An advanced arbiter might choose the KS based not only on immediate relevance (which is what the KS returns), but also on expected relevance to the overall goal, resulting in behavior that is both *data-driven* and *goal-driven* [Carver92].

On a single update, a list of relevant KSs is collected based on recent changes to the blackboard. This list is passed to the arbiter, which uses whatever methods it wants to choose a winning KS. This KS is then executed, causing further changes to the blackboard. For some problems, the new state is examined for *termination conditions* that would indicate that the problem is solved (i.e., that the blackboard contains the solution). If the termination conditions are not met, then the cycle is repeated.

Those familiar with classical AI techniques might at this point recognize the blackboard as a form of rule-chaining. There are a number of important characteristics that distinguish a rule-based system as a blackboard:

- Whereas many rule-based systems typically require a compact and uniform encoding of both trigger-conditions and actions in their rules, blackboards allow arbitrary code to be executed for both these parts. Where one KS (the blackboard rule-equivalent) might act solely based on the contents of the blackboard, another might pause execution and solicit input from the user, or perform any arbitrarily complex operation. A single KS could encapsulate an entire subsystem (as it will in the next section: *Blackboards for Intra-Agent Coordination*).
- Whereas classical rule-chaining systems allow only forward-chaining or only backward-chaining, blackboard systems impose few enough constraints to allow one, the other, or both at once.
- Related to the above, blackboards allow multiple concurrent *lines of reasoning*. There might be multiple strategies for solving a single problem, for example, and both might be investigated at the same time. Maintaining these lines of reasoning depends, of course, on the sophistication of the arbiter. Note that in principle, nothing prevents two contradictory assertions from being present in the blackboard at the same time. It is simply assumed that the structure of the blackboard will eventually reconcile the contradiction at a higher level, perhaps by discarding the assertion with the lower credibility.

Blackboards in many recent works have followed the general structure described previously, although in greatly abstracted form. Many of the constraints of the system have been lifted. For example, many times no arbiter is used, allowing any number of KSs to be executed at once.

One important trend is that blackboards are being used increasingly for control rather than for reasoning. Although the line between the two is often hazy, it might generally be considered that the weight of decision-making has been moved out of the blackboard and arbiter and into the KSs. As stated already, a single KS might encapsulate an entire subsystem that uses the blackboard simply as the medium through which it issues and receives instructions from other subsystems. The assertions of the blackboard in this case are actually *control signals*.

Despite these differences, two fundamental aspects of the blackboard remain:

- A KS needs not know (or needs not *constrain*) when and how the assertions or control signals it produces will be used.
- A KS needs not know (or needs not *heed*) the originator of the assertions or control signals it acts upon.

As an example of the first point, if the control signal constitutes a request for some action to be performed (or some state to be attained), the KS that issues it needs not care how or who satisfies the request, only that the request is in the end satisfied. As an example of the second, if the control signal constitutes an instruction to the KS, the KS needs not care where the request comes from, only that it is responsible for fulfilling it.

COLOR PLATE 1 A scene from the cinematic sequence introducing the "Lost Brother" challenge in the game *Black & White*. Referenced in article 10.5. Courtesy of Lionhead Studios.

COLOR PLATE 2 A happy young cow with a big appetite and a history of violent confrontation. From the game *Black and White*. Referenced in article 11.7. Courtesy of Lionhead Studios.

COLOR PLATE 3 An example of formations in *Empire Earth*. Referenced in article 5.6. Courtesy of Chad Dawson and Stainless Steel Studios.

COLOR PLATE 4 A part of a navigation mesh covering a staircase. Each convex polygon (with an "X" in the center) is a node of the navigation mesh. Referenced in articles 2.1 and 4.3. Courtesy of Paul Tozour and Ion Storm Austin.

COLOR PLATE 5 A part of a navigation mesh covering a balcony. Referenced in articles 2.1 and 4.3. Courtesy of Paul Tozour and Ion Storm Austin.

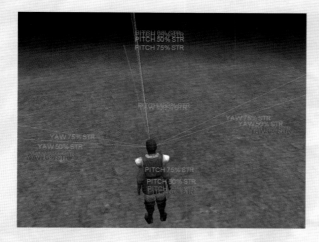

COLOR PLATE 6 Yaw and pitch lines. These lines indicate an AI's field of view (the maximum vertical and horizontal angles) and the degree to which the intensity of a visual stimulus changes depending on its angle from the direction the AI is looking. These diagnostics are available in both the level editor and the game itself. Referenced in article 2.1. Courtesy of Paul Tozour and Ion Storm Austin.

COLOR PLATE 7 Visual distance arcs. These arcs indicate how the intensity of a visual stimulus changes depending on its distance from the AI. These diagnostics are available in both the level editor and the game itself. Referenced in article 2.1. Courtesy of Paul Tozour and Ion Storm Austin.

COLOR PLATE 8 Pathfinding diagnostics. The green line segments show an AI's path on the navigation mesh, while the blue line segments illustrate the local path that the AI found around the barrels. Referenced in articles 2.1 and 4.3. Courtesy of Paul Tozour and Ion Storm Austin.

COLOR PLATE 9 Recent-path diagnostics. Each AI keeps track of the locations it has visited recently, up to some fixed maximum number of past locations. The line segments fade from red (most recent) to blue (least recent). This gives designers an easy way to figure out the path that a given AI followed to get to its current location. Referenced in article 2.1. Courtesy of Paul Tozour and Ion Storm Austin

COLOR PLATE 10 Patrol paths. This particular path illustrates the use of "choice points" that allow AIs to randomly select possible paths to follow (with probabilities set at 50/50 and 90/10), circular paths (in the lower-right corner), and an AI in formation (in center left). These diagnostics are available in both the level editor and the game itself. Referenced in article 2.1. Courtesy of Paul Tozour and Ion Storm Austin.

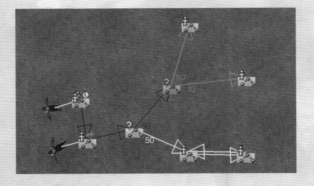

COLOR PLATE 11 AI behavior diagnostics. This display shows the AI's current "alertness thermometer" (red bar at the left), its name (top of white text in center), its current state stack (center three rows of white text), and its current audio occlusion level (blue bar at right)—that is, the extent to which its hearing is currently impeded by various sounds in its vicinity, making it more difficult for the AI to hear the player. Referenced in article 2.1. Courtesy of Paul Tozour and Ion Storm Austin.

In the next section, we will describe a system in which a blackboard is used as a device for coordinating the action of numerous subsystems within a single agent's "brain."

Blackboards for Intra-Agent Coordination

The C4 architecture is a behavior simulation architecture developed by the Synthetic Characters group of the MIT Media Lab, and has already been described in [Burke01] and [Isla01]. One of the central components of C4 is a blackboard that holds much of the state of the system.

Figure 7.1.2 compares two potential schemes for intersystem communication. In 7.1.2a, systems communicate directly, such that, for example, Working Memory passes its representations directly to the Action Selection system, and the Action

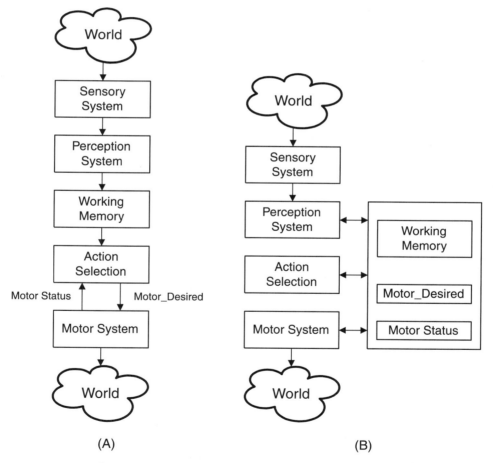

(A)   (B)

FIGURE 7.1.2   *Alternative architectures for C4. (A) Passes information directly between subsystems; (B) passes information via a blackboard.*

Selection System passes its instructions directly to the Motor System. In 7.1.2b, these signals are passed via a blackboard, such that, for example, the Action Selection System posts its instructions to the Motor_Desired slot of the blackboard, and the Motor System knows to find its instructions there. These two schemes might seem equivalent, and indeed they are, for this simple configuration.

The advantage of the blackboard structure becomes apparent when we attempt to extend the architecture. Figure 7.1.3 shows a more up-to-date configuration of C4. Note that several new systems have been added, ranging from the purely cosmetic (the LookAt motor subsystem) to the fundamental (such as the Attention System and the Navigation System).

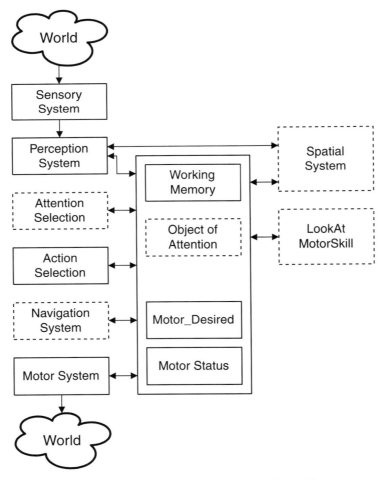

FIGURE 7.1.3   *C4++. New systems have been added. The complexity of the interconnections is kept to a minimum by simply connecting each system to the common blackboard.*

However, thanks to the blackboard architecture, these additions did not necessitate any changes to the other systems. This is especially important since not all creatures built with C4 will use all the systems (some creatures we build do not have a working memory, for example). In other cases, we might want systems to come online as the creature develops (a Sex-Drive System, it might be presumed, would only become active at puberty). The blackboard allows these changes to be made without any disruption of the data flow from the point of view of the other systems.

A typical interaction is the one that takes place between the Action Selection, Navigation, and Motor Systems. Action Selection issues motor signals intended for the Motor System; however, those signals can be intercepted and modified by the Navigation System. Action Selection might produce a request to perform a *Pick-up* on the object of attention. Although the animation representing the *Pick-up* action will ultimately be played out by the Motor System, the Navigation System might recognize that the act of picking up necessitates being near the object of attention. If the Navigation System detects that the agent is indeed near the object of attention, then it will leave the motor request alone, thus allowing the animation to be performed when the Motor System runs. If, however, the object of attention is far away, the Navigation will replace the request with its own request to *Walk with bearing theta*, in which theta is the angle toward the objects of attention. This will cause the agent to approach the appropriate object. When the agent reaches the object, the Navigation System will cease overriding the motor request (each system rewrites its request to the blackboard every time step). At this point, the Pick-up request will go through and the Motor System will perform the appropriate animation.

We might reference the two points at the end of the last section: the Action Selection system does not know what system is satisfying its motor request posting (although intended for the Motor System, it is the Navigation System that initially acts upon it), and the Motor System does not know where its instruction comes from. The blackboard architecture allows the Navigation System to be inserted cleanly between the Action Selection System and the Motor System without any modifications necessary to either of them. This is, of course, extremely useful from the point of view of a developer. The blackboard allows the brain architecture to be fluid, such that different configurations of subsystems can be experimented with (new systems added, others reordered, etc.) without disrupting any of the existing structure.

Although not strictly necessary, it can sometimes be useful for posters to the blackboard to identify themselves. In C4, this feature is used as a debugging tool to keep track of who writes to the blackboard and when. This can be used to produce a complete log of dataflow in the system, which is useful for identifying bugs.

Blackboards for Inter-Agent Coordination

Just as the blackboard can be used to coordinate the activity of multiple systems within a single brain, it can also be used to coordinate the activity of multiple agents. In the Improv animation scripting system [Perlin96], a simple world event blackboard is used to distribute information about actor states and actions. If one actor tells a joke, a *told-a-joke* token might be placed on the blackboard for the actors to react to. Some might laugh, others might roll their eyes in disapproval, depending on their personalities and their attitude toward the joke-teller.

BBWar

ON THE CD

Included on the CD is the Java source code for *BBWar*, a simple RTS-like game in which two computer-controlled teams battle each other for world domination. The goal for each one is to destroy all the cities of the other. The game is built around the blackboard architecture shown in Figure 7.1.4.

The "specialists" represented by the KSs have been taken very literally: KSs are individual military units that have special abilities. For example, *Soldiers* are the only types of units that can attack other units, but they wander around aimlessly (going after the

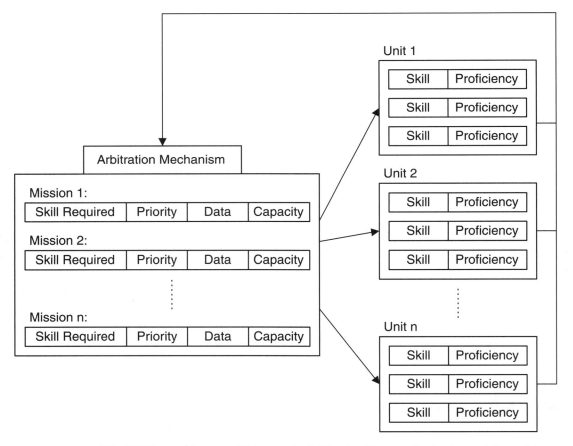

FIGURE 7.1.4 *The BBWar architecture. Units are individual military units (such as soldiers, cities, commanders, etc.) that compete for the missions posted in the blackboard.*

nearest enemy within a certain range) unless they are led by a *Commander*. The commanders, in turn, will attack specific enemy cities if instructed to do so by a *Colonel*.

Each unit is given a set of skills (the KS's *action*) that can be executed on demand. Each skill is also annotated by a proficiency indicating how good the unit is at performing the skill. Exactly how the skill is performed is left unspecified. High-level strategic units such as the Colonel might use global flow- or terrain-analysis to decide what areas of the opponent's territory to focus on. Lower-level commanders might make decisions on more local information. In either case, the results of most actions are new postings to the blackboard or modifications to existing ones.

The blackboard contents take the form of open *missions*. Each mission consists of a required skill name, a priority level, a capacity (how many units does the mission require?) and a piece of arbitrary data that, it is assumed, an appropriately skillful unit will be able to interpret as the mission parameters. While there is no explicit structure to the blackboard postings, it is assumed that units from different levels of the military hierarchy will pay attention to different types of postings. Commanders look for ATTACK_CITY missions, whereas soldiers might look for ATTACK_LOCATION missions.

Implementation

The blackboard itself is implemented as a hash table. This hash table maps string labels corresponding to skill names (e.g., ATTACK_CITY) to lists of open missions that call for that skill. Each timestep, each unit selects its current mission as follows:

```
ActionSelect(time, unit, blackboard)
Skills ← getSkills(unit)
For each element, c, of list skills
    List rel-list = blackboard.read(skills[c])
    rel_missions ← Concatenate(rel_missions, rel-list)

For each element, c, of rel_missions
relevances[c] = CalculatePriority(unit, rel_missions[c])

w_index = highest(relevances[])
if (relevances[w_index] > CalculatePriority(unit, curMission))
ApplyForMission(unit, rel_missions[w_index], relevances[w_index])
```

The ApplyForMission method attaches an "application" to the mission. Later, in the AllocateMission method (not shown here), the arbiter will go through the list of applications and pick the one(s) with the highest relevance. The units that supplied the *n* winning applications (where *n* is the mission's capacity) will be granted the mission. The CalculatePriority method is used to rate how important a possible mission is:

```
CalculatePriority(unit, mission)
priority ←
getPriority(mission) *
getProficiency(unit,skillRequired(mission)) /
(1.0 + DistanceFromTarget(unit, mission)/10.0)
```

The second line of this method applies a distance penalty, so that missions that are far away are of lower priority than nearby ones.

A single world update is very simple:

```
World_update(time)
For each element, c, of list units
actionSelect(time, units[c], blackboards[getTeam(units[c])])
For each element, c, of list blackboards
    AllocateMissions(blackboards[c])
For each element, c, of list units
    ActionExecute(units[c])
```

`AllocateMissions` examines the blackboard postings and approves of the top n applications for each mission. Each of the successful applicant units then change their `currentMission` to be the mission that they were just granted. The function `getTeam` returns the number of the team to which the unit belongs (i.e., one blackboard is used for each team in the simulation). `ActionExecute` prompts the unit to do whatever it needs to complete its mission.

Part of an action execution might well involve the creating of new postings for the blackboard. These missions can be produced and posted as follows:

```
mission β createMission(skill_required, capacity, [location], priority)
writeToBlackboard(blackboard, skill_required, mission)
```

Since the blackboard is really just a hash table, the second line in the previous code is tantamount to adding the mission as data to the hash table with `skill_required` as the key.

Table 7.1.1 summarizes the units currently implemented in *BBWar* and their capabilities.

Note that the city has many skills. While it cannot directly fulfill the missions that call for those skills, it can produce units that can fulfill them. Thus, the city is the factory for the team. Note also that it issues missions that it can itself fulfill. The missions are issued externally to take advantage of nearby units. If a large number of soldiers are necessary to defend the city, for example, the mission might be fulfilled by a combination of nearby soldiers, soldiers produced and transferred by neighboring cities, and soldiers produced locally. Similar opportunistic behavior results when a Commander leads a group of soldiers into battle. If some of the soldiers are lost, their numbers can be replenished by nearby soldiers performing less important missions and soldiers produced by nearby cities.

The behavior that results is:

- **Opportunistic**: Units react to nearby enemies and allies.
- **Cooperative**: Peer units work together to solve subproblems as they arise (for example, the problem of defending a city can be solved through the cooperation of numerous soldiers and cities).

Table 7.1.1 The Units and Their Capabilities

Unit	Skills	Action	Missions Produced
Colonel	None	None	One ATTACK_CITY for each enemy city.
Commander	ATTACK_CITY	Gathers a group of six soldiers, and attacks the city at the location specified	ATTACK_LOCATION with the location of the enemy. city.
Soldier	SHOOT ATTACK_LOCATION	Attack the nearest enemy. Move to the location specified, attacking any nearby enemies.	None.
Shield	SHIELD	Draws enemy fire away from the object it is shielding.	None.
City	ATTACK_CITY ATTACK_LOCATION SHIELD	Creates a commander. Creates a soldier. Creates a shield.	SHIELD and ATTACK_LOCATION (with its own position) when it is under attack.

- **Coordinated**: Instructions from higher-level units make sure that the actions of the lower-level units serve the overall goal of winning the war.

Note also the potential for extensibility. A group of soldiers thrown into a world will battle the enemy in a completely disorganized way. The introduction of a Commander, however, will immediately result in more coordinated behavior, since the soldiers will no longer simply shoot at the nearest enemy, but will be following mission orders for some higher-level goal, whatever that goal is. Similarly, nothing stops one from introducing new units with new, more intelligent capabilities into the world. As implemented, the game does not show much strategic intelligence. On the other hand, perhaps a *General* unit could be introduced to direct the actions of the team's Commanders in a more strategically informed way. These enhancements, once again, would not require any changes to the existing units.

Conclusions

The main source of the power of the blackboard is the fact that the architecture places such strict constraints on intercomponent communication. It is the demand that KSs communicate only through the blackboard—and that all communication take more or less the same superficial form—that results in behavior that is opportunistic, cooperative, coordinated, and extensible.

Blackboards are certainly not the answer to every problem, and in many cases, they are only the beginning of the solution. After all, the canonical architecture defined earlier is so general that some systems you have already built might qualify as blackboards. More than anything, the technique is a useful philosophical tool. They do not relieve you of the burden of coming up with a stable control strategy, and they do not relieve you of the tedious gameplay balancing that is necessary to ensure an enjoyable experience for the player. They do, however, provide a good framework around which to structure and think about these tasks.

References

[Burke01] Burke, R., D. Isla, M. Downie, Y. Ivanov, and B. Blumberg. "Creature-Smarts: The art and architecture of a virtual brain." In *The Proceedings of the Game Developers Conference,* San Jose, CA, March 2001.

[Carver92] Carver, N., and V. Lesser. "The Evolution of Blackboard Control Architectures." CMPSCI Technical Report 92-71. October 1992.

[Isla01] Isla, D., R. Burke, M. Downie, and B. Blumberg. "A layered brain architecture for synthetic creatures." In *The Proceedings of the International Joint Conference on Artificial Intelligence,* Seattle, WA, August 2001.

[Minsky85] M. Minsky, *The Society of Mind,* Simon & Schuster, 1985.

[Perlin96] Perlin, K., and A. Goldberg, "Improv: A system for scripting interactive actors in virtual worlds," *Computer Graphics* (SIGGRAPH '96 Proceedings) 1996: pp. 205–216.

7.2

Introduction to Bayesian Networks and Reasoning Under Uncertainty

Paul Tozour—Ion Storm Austin

gehn29@yahoo.com

Game AI agents exist within virtual worlds of our own design. Because of this, we have the power to grant them perfect knowledge of the world if we desire. However, there are many cases in which we would prefer to limit an AI agent's knowledge of the world and force it to perform humanlike reasoning in order to form a less accurate—but more interesting—assessment of its current situation.

Imagine a strategy game with a "fog of war" feature. The fog obscures a player's view in areas in which he has no influence. Imagine that a clever human player rushes his computer opponent repeatedly with small groups of tanks while secretly building a massive air force behind his base.

What sort of behavior should a computer opponent produce in this situation? If we only care about making our AI as challenging as possible, then the computer player should prepare for an invasion by air. Clearly, this constitutes "cheating," since the computer player has never seen the air force being constructed and has no way to know that it exists.

However, what we typically want is an AI that's more humanlike and more entertaining. The computer player should allow itself to be misled, and should reason that since it has only observed waves of tanks so far, it can expect to see even more waves of tanks.

The human player can now approach the game on a psychological level and attempt to turn the computer player's reasoning against it. The psychology of our AI player now becomes a critical component of the game mechanics, and by allowing it to be intentionally misled, we have given the human player powerful new tools for gameplay. In Ion Storm Austin designer lingo, it provides the user with powerful new "player verbs."

This article provides an introduction to probabilistic reasoning methods and Bayesian networks in particular. These techniques will allow our AIs to perform complex reasoning in a humanlike fashion. If nothing else, the literature ([Pearl87],

[Pearl01]) makes fascinating reading and provides a useful perspective on the underlying mechanics of human reasoning processes.

The techniques described here allow us to model the underlying causal (i.e., cause-and-effect) relationships between various phenomena and to describe this model in the form of a graph. Once we have constructed such a graph, we can use the axioms of probability theory to leverage it for a number of useful game AI tasks, such as predicting the likely outcome of a specific action, attempting to guess another player's current situation or frame of mind, or selecting an optimal behavior in a given situation.

Bayes' Rule

The foundation of probabilistic reasoning is Bayes' Theorem, which allows you to reverse the direction of any probabilistic statement. Let's say you want to know the chance that it rained yesterday if you suddenly find out that your lawn is wet. Bayes' Theorem allows us to calculate this probability from its inverse: the probability that your lawn would be wet if it had actually rained the day before. Bayes' Theorem is written as:

$$P(A|B) = P(B|A)P(A) / P(B)$$

$P(A|B)$ translates as "the probability of A given that what I know is B"—in this case, "the probability that it rained yesterday, given that your lawn is wet." The theorem allows us to rephrase this in terms of the probability of B given A ("$P(B|A)$") and the independent probabilities of A and B ("$P(A)$" and "$P(B)$"). These translate into:

$P(B|A)$ = the probability that the lawn would be wet, if it actually rained
          yesterday
$P(A)$ = the probability of rain, all other things being equal
$P(B)$ = the probability of your lawn being wet, all other things being equal

As we will see, the ability of Bayes' Rule to reverse the direction of a probabilistic statement is critical to our ability to perform humanlike reasoning in belief networks.

Bayesian Networks

If we can state some number of propositions and clearly define the causal relationships between them (in the form "A causes B"), we can arrange those propositions and their interrelationships in a graph structure. Once we have created this graph, we can use probabilistic reasoning to perform inference on the graph.

Imagine you get a call at work from a neighbor telling you that your burglar alarm is ringing. However, you happen to know that your alarm system is also sensitive to earthquakes. It might have been set off by an earthquake instead of a burglary.

Figure 7.2.1 shows a belief network based on those three propositions, demonstrating that "Burglary" and "Earthquake" can both cause "Alarm" to be true.

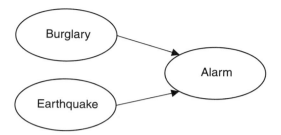

FIGURE 7.2.1 *A belief network.*

We begin by calculating the independent probabilities of an earthquake or a burglary occurring, all other things being equal. Assuming we live in a relatively safe part of California, we can guess at the following probabilities:

P(B) = Probability of Burglary	P(E) = Probability of Earthquake
.001	.002

We then determine the conditional probability of our alarm going off in the event of all possible permutations of earthquakes and burglaries—burglary only, earthquake only, both, or neither. Assume that by testing our alarm system in various ways—or reviewing historical data—we arrive at the probabilities shown in Table 7.2.1.

Table 7.2.1 Probabilities of an Alarm Going Off Given Certain Events

Burglary?	Earthquake?	Alarm?
TRUE	TRUE	.95
TRUE	FALSE	.94
FALSE	TRUE	.29
FALSE	FALSE	.001

Now we can take the numbers we arrived at for the prior probabilities for "earthquake" and "burglary" and plug them into the table. For each row in the table, we can multiply the prior probability of each of B and E by the resulting conditional probability of an alarm (the "Alarm?" column from Table 7.2.1) to determine the actual probability of the alarm being set off in each case. In other words, in each row, we calculate P(B) * P(E) * P(A|B,E).

Table 7.2.2 Computing the Actual Probabilities of a Burglary and/or an Earthquake

P(B)	P(E)	P(A|B,E)	P(A)	αP(A)
T=.001	T=.002	.95	0.000002	0.000795
T=.001	F=.998	.94	0.000938	0.372814
F=.999	T=.002	.29	0.000579	0.230127
F=.999	F=.998	.001	0.000997	0.396264
			0.002516	1

In Table 7.2.2, note the extra cell at the bottom of the "probability" column, with a value of 0.002516. This is derived by adding together all values of P(A) above it to determine the final probability of the alarm going off on any given day (0.25%).

The rightmost column shows the *normalized* probabilities; that is, the P(A) values adjusted so that they add up to 1. The "α" symbol in the expression αP(A) is the normalization constant; in this case, 0.002516 (i.e., 0.000938 / 0.002516 = 0.372814).

This tells us that if the alarm went off, and we don't know if there was a burglary or an earthquake, there's a 37% chance it was caused by a burglary, a 23% chance it was caused by an earthquake, a 39% chance it went off for no good reason, and a 0.0795% chance it was set off by a wacky simultaneous earthquake-and-burglary episode.

Suppose we now discover that there was in fact an earthquake near our house. We can now substitute 1 for P(E) being true and a 0 for P(E) being false. Note how the table changes dramatically, as reflected in Table 7.2.3.

Table 7.2.3 Determining the Probability of a Burglary when P(A) and P(E) Are Known

P(B)	P(E)	P(A|B,E)	P(A)	αP(A)
T=.001	T=1	.95	0.00095	0.003269
T=.001	F=0	.94	0	0
F=.999	T=1	.29	0.28971	0.996731
F=.999	F=0	.001	0	0
			0.29066	1

Table 7.2.3 tells us that there's now a 99.67% chance that the alarm was set off by the earthquake, and only a 0.33% chance that a burglary occurred at the same time.

Wherever there is a causal link of the form "A implies B" in our network, we need to specify a matrix that defines the probability of any given effect (any given value of B) given all possible causes (any possible value of A). The "Burglary / Earthquake / Alarm" chart in Table 7.2.1 is just such a matrix. In this case, each of our three propositions B, E, and A, can hold just one of two possible values, either true or false.

There are three basic types of inference we can perform using belief networks:

- **Causal inference** (a.k.a. "abduction" or "prediction"): Given that A implies B, and we know the value of A, we can compute the probability of B.
- **Diagnostic inference** (a.k.a. "induction"): Given that A implies B, and we know the value of B, we can compute the probability of A.
- **Intercausal inference** (i.e., "explaining away"): Given that A and B both imply C, and we know C, we can compute how a change in the probability of A will affect the probability of B, even though A and B were originally independent variables. The following section explains this in more detail.

"Explaining Away"

Part of what's so counterintuitive about probabilistic reasoning is that it depends highly on the order in which you discover certain things.

Suppose we have two independent variables A and B. Either of these can result in C being true. When we know that C is true, finding either A or B to be true makes the other *less* likely. A and B were initially independent variables, but this independence is revoked on account of their relationship with C. This seems counterintuitive at first, but it's easily demonstrated with a simple example.

Let's use the wet-lawn example we mentioned earlier. Our propositions are: **S** = your sprinkler was on this morning, **R** = it rained last night, and **W** = your lawn is wet.

Assume that there's a 1 in 3 chance of each of S and R being true. We can also assume S and R are independent of one another, since rain doesn't affect the sprinkler, or vice versa.

Take a look at Figure 7.7.2. Initially, there's a 33% chance of each of S and R (the sprinkler or the rain) being true, and a 5 in 9 (55%) chance that W is true (the lawn is wet).

If we discover that the lawn is in fact wet, we can now assert that there is a 3 in 5 (60%) chance of each of S and R being true. See Figure 7.2.2 to see why this must be the case.

The nine squares represent the possible actual states of the system, and finding that the lawn is wet convinces us that the true state of the system cannot occupy the four clear cells in the upper left, as these cells would mean the lawn was dry (because it didn't rain and the sprinkler was off). Therefore, the system must occupy one of the five cells along the right edge or the bottom of the grid (the cell in the bottom right corner represents the conjunction of both possibilities—i.e., it rained *and* your sprinkler was on).

Suddenly you get an e-mail from a friend. He tells you it rained yesterday. Discovering the actual value of R automatically changes the value of S. Finding that it rained makes it once again 33% likely that the sprinkler was on. The wetness of the lawn has been "explained away" by the rain. The probabilities now occupy only the rightmost column of Figure 7.2.2. Similarly, if your friend had told you it *didn't* rain, that would make the sprinkler hypothesis 100% probable, since nothing else could explain the wet lawn.

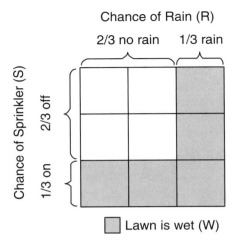

FIGURE 7.2.2   *The joint probability of rain (R) and sprinkler (S).*

Likewise, if you don't know whether it rained and you had instead discovered that the sprinkler was on, this would change your belief as to whether it rained.

Propagating Probabilities

We can construct arbitrarily large and complex graphs by assembling individual propositions and determining the proper causal relationships between those propositions. Once we have constructed such a graph, we can perform probabilistic inference on it using the axioms of probability theory, and Bayes' Rule in particular. A graph used in this fashion is referred to as a "belief network" or a "Bayesian network."

Unfortunately, the techniques for propagating probabilities through a Bayesian network are much too complex for the scope of this article. A future article might illustrate these techniques in the detail they deserve. In the meantime, the reader is referred to [Pearl87] and [Pearl01]. However, this section provides a conceptual overview of belief propagation and some details of its operation for interested readers.

Figure 7.2.3 gives an example of how propagation proceeds in a Bayes' net. Imagine that we have constructed a network as shown and we make an observation about the actual value of some proposition X. Now we want to figure out how the effect of that discovery influences the rest of the network.

Starting from the node labeled X, we can propagate both to X's parent node and its child node. Although we can propagate our probabilities asynchronously, as though our nodes were separate computers communicating to each other via the Internet, we know that the probabilities will be propagated along the links labeled "1" first, and then along the links labeled "2."

Note that because Bayes' Rule allows us to reverse the direction of a probabilistic statement, the direction of the arrows does not limit how we can propagate. We can

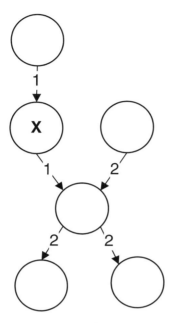

FIGURE 7.2.3   *Propagating influence through a sample Bayes' net.*

propagate probability backward just as easily as we can propagate forward, although we'll need to do the calculations differently in each case.

Within an individual node—representing a single proposition in our belief network—we have something that looks like Figure 7.2.4.

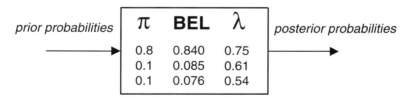

FIGURE 7.2.4   *Prior and posterior probabilities for a single belief node.*

Note that in this example, the node represents a belief with *three* possible values rather than the two-value (true/false) propositions we have been dealing with so far. For example, this node might represent our knowledge that exactly one of three prisoners is guilty of a crime and our current belief as to which of the three is the most likely culprit.

The inside of a belief node has three vectors: π, BEL, and λ.

π represents the sum of our *prior* beliefs that lead to this node. In this example, the π vector has pegged the prior assessments of our three prisoners' guilt at 80%, 10%, and 10%, respectively. This might come from other evidence presented in the courtroom, for example, indicating that the first prisoner is the likely culprit.

λ represents the sum of our *posterior* beliefs that emanate from this node. In this case, it might represent the results of a fingerprint test from the gun found at the crime scene. It places the probability of a match at 75%, 61%, and 54%, respectively, for each of our three prisoners.

BEL represents our actual belief in each of the prisoners' guilt. This is computed by multiplying the π and λ values together for each prisoner, and renormalizing the resulting vector to 1. In this case, we get initial values of (0.75 * 0.8 = <u>0.6</u>; 0.61 * 0.1 = <u>0.061</u>; and 0.54 * 0.1 = <u>0.054</u>). We add these together to get a value of 0.715, and we renormalize by dividing each of the original belief values by this number to compute final belief values (0.6 / 0.715 = <u>0.84</u>; 0.061 / 0.715 = <u>0.085</u>; 0.054 / 0.715 = <u>0.076</u>).

Probability propagation proceeds by passing the λ vector of each node forward to compute the π vector of each of the node's children, and passing the π vector of each node backward to compute the λ vector of each of the node's parents. The tricky part is dealing with the need to propagate from a single node to multiple parents or multiple children, the solutions to which are outside the bounds of this article.

An astute reader will ask, "how do we avoid circular propagation?" In other words, once we introduce a new observation, what keeps the resulting messages from propagating endlessly through the network?

The answer is that each new observation introduced to the system is tracked with a unique identifier, so that although the effects of each new observation are propagated throughout the entire network, we can ensure that wave of propagation for any new observation will only pass through each graph node exactly once. If we introduce an observation at the center of a network, for example, the resulting probability adjustments will propagate throughout the network and terminate at the endpoints.

To illustrate why this makes sense, imagine that you spread a rumor about Bob through your network of friends. Later, you hear the same rumor about Bob from Mary. If you find that Mary's rumor came from an independent source, your belief in the rumor should increase. If, on the other hand, you discover that Mary heard the rumor from somebody who heard it from you, your belief in the rumor should remain unchanged.

The ID-based tracking scheme is also useful for allowing us to track exactly how the network has reached its conclusions. When used properly, such a system can allow us to retrace our rationales and assemble detailed explanations for currently held beliefs.

Now let's look at how we can use these techniques in games.

Calculating Visibility and the Chance to Hit

A very simple example is calculating an AI's chance to notice an intruder or to score a hit in combat. These types of calculations will be based on a number of factors, such as the distance to the opponent, the opponent's speed and size, the AI's skills and sensory abilities, and the current visibility (including the current light level, the amount of fog obscuring the target, or the degree to which the target is hidden behind various obstacles).

We have a set of input variables, such as D = distance, V = visibility, S = target size, and so forth, which together will determine our chance to either see the target or hit it with a weapon. In both of these cases, our calculation depends on all of the factors being *true*—that is, P(I can hit given my current situation) = P(D = very close) $\land$ P(V = perfect visibility) $\land$ P(S = huge) $\land$ […]. If any of these factors is zero (for example, the target is too far from us), then our chance to see or hit the opponent should be zero.

This is equivalent to a single row in a probability matrix (as in our earthquake/ burglary charts earlier in the article) in which all of the inputs must be *true*. This permits us to simply multiply the initial factors together to determine the final probability.

Dependency Graphs

Most strategy games feature "tech trees" that describe the way a player's empire can develop new technologies and outline the requirements to attain any new technology.

Figure 7.2.5 illustrates a part of what a typical game's tech tree might look like.

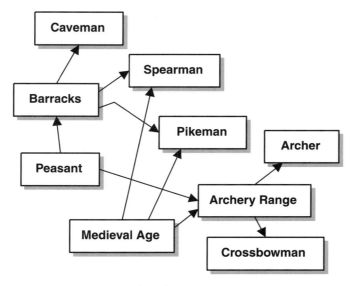

FIGURE 7.2.5   *A sample tech tree.*

In this example, the "Peasant" technology can single-handedly cause "Barracks" to exist. A technology such as "Archery Range" requires both the "Medieval Age" technology and a "Peasant" in order to be constructed.

There are a number of advantages we can gain immediately by taking advantage of the graphical nature of this data structure. Imagine we're developing a strategy game AI, and our AI player keeps track of its current knowledge of every player's tech tree, including one for itself [Tozour01]. We will refer to a tech tree used in this fashion as a "dependency graph."

- The dependency graph allows us to *build toward a goal.* The graph gives us an automatic foundation for developing complex plans. If we want to build Archers, we can simply search backward from "Archer" to determine that we must first reach the Medieval Age and then have our Peasants build an Archery Range.
- We can *estimate the accuracy of our surveillance of a given player* and *determine which opposing players require more surveillance.* A dependency graph with many unknown nodes, particularly as ancestors of nodes with known values, indicates that our knowledge of that player is incomplete. If we've seen an enemy's Crossbowmen but not his Archery Range, this tells us that we're missing some part of his empire and we need to increase our scouting and surveillance of that player.
- We can *identify weak spots in the opposing player's dependency graph* and *deliberately interfere with our enemies' building plans.* If we note that an opposing player possesses only a handful of Peasants, we might as well kill the Peasants before we proceed to his Barracks and Archery Range so that he cannot rebuild them.

However, this still doesn't give us as much information as we'd like. For a given game situation, we'd like to be able to plug in our current knowledge of every player and figure out what assumptions we should make about all of the technologies it could potentially attain. If we know that the enemy has a Pikeman, a Grand Magician, and a Krogoth, to what degree should we believe that he also possesses a Hydroponic Farm?

Surprisingly enough, we can translate this type of tech tree into a belief network with almost zero effort. All we need to do is assume that each node in the tech tree represents our belief that the player in question has attained that specific technology.

This allows us to instantiate our current knowledge about each player as beliefs in the network. We can then propagate these beliefs through the network to determine reasonable degrees of belief for all of the other technologies in the tech tree.

- We can *infer the existence or nonexistence of some technologies by the presence or absence of others.* If we see an enemy Pikeman, that enemy must have reached the Medieval Age and built at least one Barracks—and the Barracks probably still exists unless it was recently destroyed.
- We can use causal inference to determine *which dependencies an opposing player is likely to attain.* If a player has Peasants and has reached the Medieval Age, he is

likely to be able to create an Archery Range, and might very well have one already.

- We can *set bounds on the time required to reach a given dependency*. If we're certain that an opposing player hasn't reached the Medieval Age and has no Archery Ranges, we can add the absolute minimum times required to attain each of these two dependencies and assert that it will be at least that long before he can build Archers.

- We can *determine which dependencies a player is less likely to have attained* due to time or resource constraints. If a player can either reach the Medieval Age or build a Barracks in the first three minutes of the game, but not both, then noticing a Barracks within this time frame tells us that that player is not working on the Medieval Age. Therefore, we should prepare for attacks from Cavemen in the near future and not worry about attacks by Spearmen, Pikemen, Archers, or Crossbowmen from that player in the immediate future.

Detecting an Intruder

Another simple example is a "first-person sneaker" type of game. This is similar to a first-person shooter, except that the player must use stealth, cunning, and the occasional blunt instrument to the back of the head to avoid being killed or captured by the guards.

Our game designers have decided that if a guard becomes suspicious, and the player then leaves him alone for a while to cool down, the guard should eventually stop worrying about it, and should say something like "Ah, well … I guess it was just rats."

In this case, the guard himself is pretending to perform Bayesian inference—he is quite literally "explaining away" the evidence the player gave him!

The problem is that quite often, the player will present the guards with stimuli that are inconsistent with the "rats" hypothesis. If the player pelts the guard with arrows, throws a box against the side of his head, and drops the corpse of one of his kinsmen to the floor beside him, then a line like "I guess it was rats" obviously won't cut it.

Figure 7.2.6 shows a sample Bayes' net that can easily solve this problem. The nodes on the left represent some the various types of stimuli that the player can present, and the node on the right represents the possible conclusions that can result from those stimuli. All that is needed is a matrix of how the possible combinations of each of the four different types of possible stimuli will affect the guard's conclusion.

In this case, one need only ensure that any entries in the matrix that involve non-rat-related stimuli, such as "Dead Body" and "Hit By An Arrow," will totally discount "Rats" as a viable conclusion.

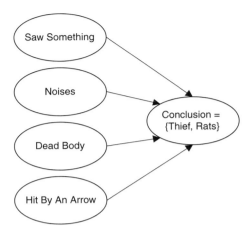

FIGURE 7.2.6   *A simple Bayes' net illustrating a guard's possible explanations for the evidence at hand.*

Similar Approaches

The probabilistic techniques presented here might seem vaguely similar to fuzzy logic in that they provide us with a means to perform reasoning using continuous variables; in other words, they allow us to use floating-point arithmetic instead of Boolean logic. However, as Pearl [Pearl87] points out, the two approaches have fundamentally different goals: fuzzy logic is about the degree of membership in a set, while probabilistic reasoning is about inferences regarding causation.

Bayesian techniques also share much in common with the Dempster-Shafer Theory [Laramée02]. Bayesian and D-S approaches perform reasoning in roughly similar ways.

However, the main limitation of both the Dempster-Shafer Theory and fuzzy logic relative to probabilistic reasoning is that both are built on traditional *monotonic logic*; that is, they state propositions that cannot change when new information is added to the system. The classic example is the "Tweety paradox:" "Most birds fly," "Most penguins do not fly," and "Penguins are birds." Our friend "Tweety" is both a penguin and a bird.

With systems built on monotonic logic, the fact that Tweety is a bird will make the result of the calculation highly dependent on the proportion of birds that can fly. If you inform such a system that 99.9% of birds can fly, the system will assert much more strongly that Tweety can actually fly. A system built on probability theory will not suffer from this problem, as it will base its conclusions primarily on the rule "penguins do not fly."

Whether or not the limitations of monotonicity will affect your AI depends on the specific architecture of your system. AI systems in games are unlikely to be complex enough to be seriously affected by this limitation. [Pearl87] provides more detail on the differences between monotonic and nonmonotonic reasoning, particularly with regards to the Dempster-Shafer Theory.

References and Additional Reading

[Laramée02] Laramée, François Dominic, "A Rule-based Architecture Using Dempster-Shafer Theory," *AI Game Programming Wisdom*, Ed. Steve Rabin, Charles River Media, 2002.

[Pearl87] Pearl, Judea, *Probabilistic Reasoning in Intelligent Systems: Networks of Plausible Inference*, Morgan Kaufman, 1987.

[Pearl01] Pearl, Judea, *Causality*, Cambridge University Press, 2001.

[Tozour01] Tozour, Paul, "Strategic Assessment Techniques," *Game Programming Gems 2*, Ed. Mark DeLoura, Charles River Media, 2001.

7.3

A Rule-Based Architecture Using the Dempster-Shafer Theory

François Dominic Laramée

francoislaramee@videotron.ca

Bayesian networks, as described in [Tozour02], use probability theory to make decisions based on uncertain information. This article describes an alternative method of reasoning, the Dempster-Shafer theory of belief (DST), which can be used in situations where the strict requirements of probability theory cannot be met, when ignorance must be modeled explicitly, or when evidence points towards a fuzzy set of possible events instead of a clear-cut answer.

To demonstrate how DST can be put to use in games, we will develop a simple application in which a baseball manager must decide whether he should replace his starting pitcher with a reliever based on multiple sources of conflicting evidence.

Foundations of the Dempster-Shafer Theory

The Limits of Bayesian Inference

(Note: Readers unfamiliar with Bayesian networks might want to skip to the next subsection.)

In real life situations, it is often difficult to fulfill the requirements of Bayes' rule of inference. [Russell95] states that sources of evidence can be combined using a manageable form of Bayesian updating only in situations in which the sources are either "conditionally independent" or linked by known conditional probabilities. Unfortunately, proving independence is often impossible, especially in systems like games where a large number of variables (i.e., units, time, weather, player input, etc.) influence each other in unpredictable ways. Computing reasonable estimates of conditional probabilities is hardly easier: a medical research specialist might be able to access the case histories of thousands of patients to calculate the odds that a certain type of mole might transform into skin cancer later in life, but game developers rarely have such a massive base of prior data with which to work.

As a result, developers are forced to make assumptions and approximations, usually based on hands-on experimentation with their games, when they design systems based on Bayesian inference. Sometimes, this is appropriate. When it is not, the conclusions derived by the AI might be wrong or unjustified. Given the fact that the number of conditional probabilities between variables that must be computed grows exponentially with the size of the world being modeled, Bayesian networks tend to break down at a surprisingly low level of complexity.

The Alternative: Belief Theory

To sidestep this problem, we will introduce the related but less restrictive concept of *belief*.

Consider the problem of estimating whether the Siberian Ice Cubes will win today's baseball game. You know that their season record so far is 60 wins and 40 losses, and that they have won 17 of 20 games when their ace pitcher "Snowy" Frozensky has started. However, you do not know whether he's scheduled to start today or not. You might want to base your estimate on one or more of the following concepts from belief theory:

- **Credibility** measures how much the evidence *explicitly supports* an assertion. In our case, given the team's record, the credibility of a win is 60%.
- **Plausibility** measures how much the evidence *fails to discredit* the assertion. Since we don't know for sure that Snowy isn't pitching, we might hope that he is, and given the team's record when he's on the mound, the plausibility of a win today is 85%.
- Actual **belief** is a subjective measure located somewhere between credibility and plausibility. Pessimistic estimates will be closer to credibility; optimistic ones, closer to plausibility. For simplicity's sake, we will usually define belief to be equal to credibility in this article.

More formal (and slightly different) definitions of these concepts can be found in [Kohlas95].

Dempster's Rule allows multiple sources of evidence to be combined so that they can support decision-making. A *hint*, or *piece of evidence*, describes belief in a (possibly fuzzy) assertion; for example, "we believe that the pitcher is either tired or nervous, with credibility 70%." A *source*, or *body of evidence*, regroups a number of related hints provided by the same witness(es) or other coherent process.

Beliefs and Uncertainty

At first glance, belief looks like probability and quacks like probability. Indeed, it is commonly represented by real numbers between 0 and 1, and it is estimated in similar fashion. However, the axioms governing belief are weaker than those of probability, and therefore easier to deal with. For example, while the sum of the probabilities of an event and its negation must be 1, the sum of the beliefs in an event and its negation might be less than 1, if there is insufficient evidence to support either conclusion.

For example, let us suppose that Paul's car crashes into David's in a parking lot, and that there are 10 witnesses to the accident, three of whom say that Paul is definitely to blame, while the other seven have no opinion. A probabilistic system trying to determine who should pay for the damage would be forced to split the 70% of inconclusive evidence according to some algorithm; say, 50-50:

P(Paul is to blame) = 0.3 + 0.5*0.7 = 0.65
P(David is to blame) = 0.5*0.7 = 0.35

However, is this justified? Maybe some of the witnesses who expressed no opinion believe that both drivers made reckless maneuvers. Maybe some tend to think that David made a false move, but they are not sure enough to say so. Or, perhaps some of them dislike Paul, and, while convinced that David is to blame, would never say so because their loyalties lie with David.

With belief theory, no such assumptions are made. Ignorance and uncertainty are represented explicitly by assigning belief to fuzzy events when needed. Indeed, where classic probability theory reasons on discrete events, belief systems deal with the *power set* of all possible events. When trying to decide between mutually exclusive events A, B, and C, a belief system would be able to accept evidence pointing to "A or B," "none at all," or "any of them without preference" just as easily as a Bayesian network would deal with P(A) or P(B).

In this case, the evidence provided by witnesses only justifies the following assertions:

Evidence(Paul is to blame) = 0.3
Evidence(Paul OR David is to blame) = 0.7

THEREFORE

Credibility(Paul is to blame) = 0.3
Plausibility(Paul is to blame) = 1.0
Credibility(David is to blame) = 0.0
Plausibility(David is to blame) = 0.7

This shows that there is insufficient evidence to blame anyone without a reasonable doubt. Where the probabilistic approach jumps to conclusions, DST waits for more compelling reasons to act.

Dempster's Rule

Computing beliefs from one source of evidence is all well and good, but sometimes the discrepancy between credibility and plausibility is too large to support meaningful conclusions. To make belief theory truly useful, we need a way to take advantage of the fact that multiple sources of information can confirm (or contradict) each other. This tool is called Dempster's Rule, and it is represented by the following equation:

$$Combined(N) = \frac{\displaystyle\sum_{X \cap Y = N} S_1(X) * S_2(Y)}{1 - \displaystyle\sum_{X \cap Y = \varnothing} S_1(X) * S_2(Y)} \qquad (7.3.1)$$

where X is a hint from the first body of evidence, Y is a hint from the second body of evidence, and $S_i(A)$ is the mass of belief associated with event A in source i.

Dempster's rule looks at the evidence provided by the sources and combines it in a way reminiscent of matrix multiplication:

- For each pair of hints (one taken from each source), see if they both support some event N. To do this, find the intersection N between the sets of events X and Y associated with both hints. If N is empty, the two hints contradict each other.
- Multiply the beliefs associated with the two hints, and add the product to the combined belief distribution for event N.
- To normalize the distribution, divide by a factor equal to 1 minus the products of the belief masses associated with contradictory hints.

If you examine the denominator carefully, you will notice that it becomes zero if all of the evidence provided by the first source points toward events that have nothing in common with those supported by the second source. Division by zero being illegal, Dempster's rule fails in this case. Intuitively, this makes sense: how can you draw meaningful conclusions when all of your evidence is contradictory? Still, you should exercise caution when dealing with wildly incompatible bodies of evidence, because the results become unstable when the denominator is too small.

Dempster's rule is associative and commutative, which means that it can be used to combine any number of sources in any order. This is a very desirable property, for obvious reasons. Our case study, for example, will feature four different sources of evidence.

Case Study: A Baseball Manager

Top of the eighth inning, a man on first, nobody out, and the game between the Siberian Ice Cubes and the Petawawa Black Flies is tied at 2. Snowy Frozensky has pitched a beauty so far, but he showed some signs of fatigue in the seventh inning, walking a couple of batters and surrendering an RBI double to the Flies' shortstop, a 145-pound player with a .211 career batting average. The Cubes' manager has little confidence in his middle reliever, Shaky Limpfingers Jr., but this is the last game of the year and it will decide who wins the pennant. . . .

The manager scratches his head. Gunner McLiner, the Flies' slugging first baseman, is on deck. The Cubes' owner, Shaky Limpfingers Sr., wants his boy to play; if McLiner drives Snowy's next pitch into the parking lot, the manager is going to be fired. Then again, if he pulls Snowy, he might not get out of the stadium alive.

(Snowy's agent, a 350-pound former NFL nose tackle, stands to make a hefty bonus if his client pitches in the World Series.)

Luckily, the manager is never more than a couple of feet away from his trusty laptop running the "Baseball Manager 1.0" AI application.

The Situation

What the manager must decide is whether Snowy is:

- Just fine; the Flies' hitters got lucky, that's all.
- A little nervous; a short visit by the pitching coach should settle him down.
- Out of gas; time to go to the bullpen.

The set of possible events is thus of size 3. We will represent each event as a flag, and operate on sets of events using a bitfield representation and logical operations.

```
enum { ok = 1, nervous = 2, tired = 4 };
int set1 = ok | nervous;
int intersection = set1 & set2;
```

To make its decision, the AI will rely on reports from four different witnesses: the team's catcher, the radar gun, the game state, and the pitch count. Each of them will use a number of different rules to build a body of evidence based on Snowy's most recent pitches. When a rule fires, it adds a value to the *belief mass* for a certain event; this belief mass is the number on which Dempster's rule will be applied, and should not be confused with credibility, plausibility, or the belief function we derive from them.

Radar Gun Evidence

Snowy is known to hit 93 to 95 mph on his fastball regularly, but his velocity goes down when he's tired and when he's trying to be too fancy by trying to paint the corners of the plate. The rules used by the radar gun operator to evaluate Snowy's condition, based on his 10 most recent pitches, could therefore look like this:

```
IF pitch is fastball AND speed > 92 mph
    THEN add belief mass 0.1 to "ok"
// Mediocre fastballs: he might be tired or being fancy
IF pitch is fastball AND speed between 87 and 92 mph
    THEN add belief mass 0.1 to "tired OR nervous"
// Lousy fastballs: his arm is definitely tiring
IF pitch is fastball AND speed below 87 mph
    THEN add belief mass 0.1 to "tired"
// Can't deduce anything from the speed of a curveball
IF pitch is not fastball
    THEN add belief mass 0.1 to "ok OR tired OR nervous"
```

Thus, supposing that, of the 10 most recent pitches, two were clocked at 96 mph, three were clocked at 89 mph, and five were breaking balls, the radar gun would produce a body of evidence comprised of the following hints:

{OK} with belief mass 0.2
{Tired | Nervous} with belief mass 0.3
{Tired | Nervous | OK} with belief mass 0.5

Pitch Count Evidence

Snowy is a fairly resilient pitcher, but the manager likes to limit his starters to about 100 pitches to reduce the risk of arm injuries. However, by itself, the number of pitches thrown doesn't tell anything about whether the pitcher is fine or nervous.

IF pitch count < 90
    THEN add belief mass 1.0 to "ok OR nervous"
IF pitch count between 90 and 110
    THEN add belief mass (110 − pitchcount) / 20 to "ok OR nervous"
    AND add belief mass (pitchcount − 90) / 20 to "Tired"
IF pitch count > 110
    THEN add belief mass 1.0 to "tired"

Game State Evidence

The results of Snowy's pitches are another good indication of his condition. It is reasonable to assume that a pitch that was ruled a ball by the umpire or was driven for a base hit by the opposing batter was a poor one. However, if there are runners on base, a ball might be a sign that the pitcher is bothered by their presence and not tired. (We will ignore pitchouts.)

FOR each of the last 10 pitches:
IF pitch was a ball AND there were runners on base
    THEN add belief mass 0.1 to "nervous OR tired"
IF pitch was a ball AND there were no runners on base
    THEN add belief mass 0.1 to "tired"
IF pitch was a strike OR pitch resulted in an out
    THEN add belief mass 0.1 to "ok"
IF pitch resulted in a base hit
    THEN add belief mass 0.1 to "tired"

Catcher Evidence

Finally, we will ask the catcher to provide his input concerning the pitcher's status. After all, an umpire might make an incorrect call once in a while, so four balls in a row might not be a cause for worry if the pitcher has hit the catcher's target every time. On the other hand, if the catcher asks for a changeup low and outside and the pitcher fires a fastball over the middle of the plate, something is amiss even if the pitch is grounded into a double play.

> FOR each of the last 10 pitches:
> IF pitch has hit the catcher's target
>   THEN add belief mass 0.1 to "ok"
> ELSE add belief mass 0.1 to "tired OR nervous"

Combining Sources of Evidence

Since Dempster's rule is associative and commutative, we can combine the sources in any order. Let us suppose that we have the two following bodies of evidence to take care of:

Source #1	Source #2
Hint 1.1: "ok" with mass 0.5	Hint 2.1: "ok" with mass 0.6
Hint 1.2: "tired" with mass 0.3	Hint 2.2: "ok or nervous or tired" with mass 0.4
Hint 1.3: "ok or nervous" with mass 0.2	

The numerator of Dempster's rule computes a matrix of intersections and the belief masses contributed by each. For example, in this case:

- Hint 1.1 intersects with Hint 2.1 for event "ok", with belief mass 0.5*0.6 = 0.3.
- Hint 1.1 intersects with Hint 2.2 for event "ok", with belief mass 0.5*0.4 = 0.2.
- Hint 1.2 does not intersect with Hint 2.1; null event with belief mass 0.18.
- Hint 1.2 intersects with Hint 2.2 for event "tired" with belief mass 0.12.
- Hint 1.3 intersects with Hint 2.1 for event "ok" with belief mass 0.12.
- Hint 1.3 intersects with Hint 2.2 for event "ok or nervous" with belief mass 0.08.

Thus, we have the following belief masses for the combined evidence:

- "ok" with mass 0.3 + 0.2 + 0.12 = 0.62
- "tired" with mass 0.12
- "ok or nervous" with mass 0.08
- the null event with mass 0.18

The masses for the non-null events must then be divided by the denominator of Dempster's rule, equal to 1 minus the mass of the null event, to yield a final body of evidence:

- "ok" with mass 0.62 / 0.82 = 0.76
- "tired" with mass 0.12 / 0.82 = 0.15
- "ok or nervous" with mass 0.08 / 0.82 = 0.09

Making Decisions

Once we have a final body of evidence, we can use it to make decisions. For this purpose, you might want to compute credibility and plausibility tables for all events, using the following formulae:

- Credibility of the event set X is equal to the sum of the belief masses of all events that are subsets of X.
- Plausibility of the event set X is equal to the sum of the belief masses of all events whose intersection with X is non-null.

For example, in the preceding case, the credibility of the event "ok or nervous" is equal to the sum of the belief masses for "ok", "nervous", and "ok or nervous"; in other words, 0.76 + 0.09 = 0.85.

Then, you define your own belief function as a linear combination of credibility and plausibility, and define rules of decision accordingly. For example:

IF belief(tired) > 0.70 AND a reliever is warming up in the bullpen
    THEN go to the bullpen
IF credibility(tired OR nervous) > 0.75
AND no visits to the mound yet this inning
    THEN send the pitching coach to the mound
IF credibility(tired OR nervous) > 0.75
AND pitching coach has visited the mound
    THEN go to the bullpen; he hasn't calmed down
IF plausibility(tired) > 0.80
    THEN ask a reliever to warm up in the bullpen

and so on.

The way you define belief and the thresholds at which your rules fire will define the AI's personality. An optimistic AI will look at the plausibility of positive events and at the credibility of negative ones, while a pessimist will do the opposite, and a skeptic will need very high belief before it does anything at all.

Conclusion

The Dempster-Shafer theory provides a framework for making decisions on the basis of incomplete and ambiguous information, as long as the contradictions between sources are not overwhelming. It is often easier to work with than traditional probability theory because it does not require prior computation of conditional probabilities or shaky assumptions of independence.

ON THE CD

The book's CD-ROM contains companion source code for this article. There, you will find an implementation of Dempster's rule, along with C++ classes representing hints and sources of evidence, and a simple program demonstrating their usage. All of the evidence to be analyzed is spoon-fed to the program; extracting it from actual game data is left as the proverbial exercise to the equally proverbial reader.

References

[DeCETI01] Online resources for the Development of a Common Educational and Training Infrastructure project; section on evidence theory is available at www.survey.ntua.gr/main/labs/rsens/DeCETI/IRIT/MSI-FUSION/node174 .html.

[Kohlas95] Kohlas, J. and Monney, P.A., *A Mathematical Theory of Hints*, Springer, 1995.

[Russell95] Russell, S. J. and Norvig, P., *Artificial Intelligence: A Modern Approach*, Prentice-Hall, 1995.

[Tozour02] Tozour, P., "Bayesian Networks and Reasoning Under Uncertainty," *AI Game Programming Wisdom*, Charles River Media, 2002.

7.4

An Optimized Fuzzy Logic Architecture for Decision-Making

Thor Alexander—Hard Coded Games

thor@hardcodedgames.com

This article presents an architecture to facilitate communication and decision-making between autonomous actors via a passive event handling system. The core decision process is implemented with techniques based on fuzzy logic. Fuzzy logic has many properties that make it well suited for use in game development; however, it also suffers from some performance issues that will be addressed with several proven optimization methods.

A General Decision Engine Architecture

Before we can dig into the internals of decision-making, we need to define an architecture that allows our cast of autonomous characters to perceive their environment and determine what actions they want to take to interact with it. By *environment*, we mean the simulation space of the game, including the other actors and items contained in that space. An actor is defined to be a game-based object that is capable of interacting with the environment. It has an internal memory structure that it uses to track other actors, which changes as it perceives the environment. An autonomous actor in this system fills the role of an AI enemy or non-player character (NPC) found in a typical game. Figure 7.4.1 shows a high-level snapshot of our autonomous actor decision-making system.

Events are the transactional objects of this system. When an actor interacts with the environment by performing actions, the results of these actions are broadcast to other actors that can perceive it as events. An event object contains the event type, source actor, and target actor. The actor that perceives the event checks his event handler table for an entry to handle an event of this type. If an event handler is found, the actor attempts to recognize the source actor and target actor by finding a reference to them in his internal memory. The specific event handler is responsible for updating the internal memory of the source and target actors with respect to this type of event. Note that the perception of the event only causes a change to the actor's memory; it

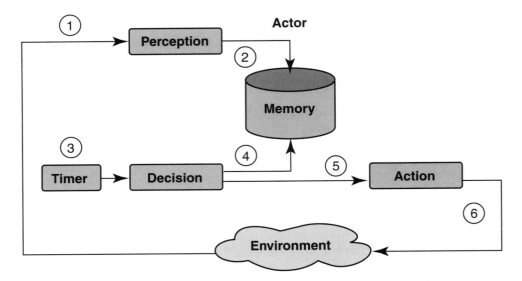

1. The actor perceives changes in the environment as events.
2. These events change the actor's memory of the environment.
3. Independently, the actor performs a decision process scheduled by a timer.
4. The decision process accesses the actor's memory.
5. The decision process determines what action it wants to perform.
6. The action process causes changes in the environment.

FIGURE 7.4.1   *Autonomous actor decision-making system.*

does not cause any direct action to be executed by the actor. This is a departure from typical event-based systems. This passive event handling scheme allows the system to avoid having to decide what it needs to do every time an actor receives an event. In a high event simulation where the actors need to be aware of everything going on around them, this is a critical improvement.

Independent of the event handling stage, the actor performs a decision-making process scheduled by a timer. On the autonomous actor's scheduled turn he calls upon his decision process to evaluate what action he should perform. This decision process is responsible for choosing a memory and determining the appropriate behavior to perform on the actor that the memory represents. This memory could be of the deciding actor himself, as is the case with many behaviors that are considered to be target-less. The inner workings of this decision process can be implemented with various AI techniques. We will employ an approach derived from fuzzy logic.

The decision system returns a behavior and a target actor to perform that behavior on. This behavior is mapped to the appropriate method that implements that behavior. We will refer to these behavior methods as Action-Code. This Action-Code is responsible for all of the processing required to implement the behavior as well as broadcast all events associated with the behavior. For our system, this involves transitioning a state machine to the selected behavior. This completes the event transaction loop for this architecture.

Fuzzy Decision-Making

Fuzzy logic is a branch of mathematics that deals with vague or gray concepts that can be said to be true to matter of degree rather than being limited to having a binary value of true or false. Fuzzy logic has been growing in use in the fields of science and engineering over the past few decades since it was first introduced to limited fanfare in 1965. There are many areas of game development that can benefit from fuzzy logic, including decision-making. The remainder of this article assumes a basic understanding of the working of fuzzy logic. For a complete introduction to fuzzy logic, please consult the resources presented at the end of this article.

To illustrate how a fuzzy decision-making process works, we will define a very simple game scenario. An autonomous actor, Ian the troll, enters a dungeon and encounters his old foe Wally the Mighty, a player-controlled actor. Ian receives an event informing him that Wally has entered his visual range. Ian searches his memory and finds a reference to Wally. This memory contains a "Hate" score on the range from 0.0 to 1.0. Ian values him with a hate of 0.77. Ian also calculates his distance to Wally with a value of 0.75. These values serve as the inputs to our fuzzy system. Tables 7.4.1 and 7.4.2 define the possible input ranges.

Table 7.4.1 "Distance" Input Ranges

Distance	Value
At	0.00 .. 0.15
Very Close	0.10 .. 0.35
Close	0.30 .. 0.70
Pretty Far	0.60 .. 0.90
Very Far	0.85 .. 1.00

Table 7.4.2 "Hate" Input Ranges

Hate	Value
Not Hated	0.00 .. 0.20
Somewhat Hated	0.20 .. 0.50
Hated	0.40 .. 0.80
Very Hated	0.75 .. 1.00

These input ranges are mapped together to form fuzzy membership sets (Figure 7.4.2). Note that some of the sets overlap each other. These membership sets serve to "fuzzify" the inputs so that we can deal with concepts that vary by degree.

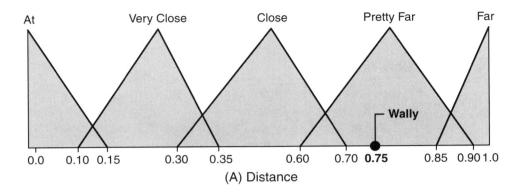

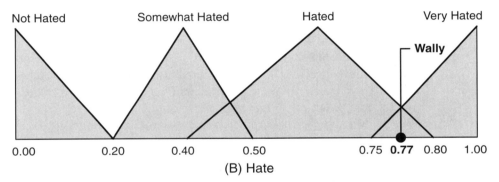

FIGURE 7.4.2   *Membership sets for (A) Distance and (B) Hate.*

Ian needs to select a behavior from his available behavior set. Table 7.4.3 shows a simple set of behaviors that our actor can choose from. Melee is close-range attack. Crossbow and Fireball are long-range attacks. Fireball is a more powerful attack that has the potential of hurting the actor with splash damage if targeted close to him.

Table 7.4.3 Simple Behavior Set

Combat Behaviors
None
Melee
Crossbow
Fireball

To choose the best behavior, Ian tests the inputs against the corresponding rule set for the behavior. A rule set defines the rules or conditions under which a behavior should be used. Table 7.4.4 maps all of the membership sets to combine the possible rules for our system. Each rule compares an input value against a fuzzy membership set. If the value falls within the set, then the rule is said to fire. When all of the rules in a rule set fire, then the associated behavior fires to some degree and is a candidate winner in the behavior selection process. Table 7.4.5 shows the rule sets associated with the combat behaviors that fire for our example in Figure 7.4.2.

Table 7.4.4　Combat Rule Matrix

	At	Very Close	Close	Pretty Far	Very Far
Not Hated	None	None	None	None	None
Somewhat Hated	Melee	Melee	Crossbow	None	None
Hated	Melee	Melee	Crossbow	Crossbow	Fireball
Very Hated	Melee	Melee	Crossbow	Fireball	Fireball

Table 7.4.5 Fired Combat Behavior Rule Sets

Combat Rules

IF Distance IS Pretty Far AND Hate IS Hated THEN use Crossbow behavior

IF Distance IS Pretty Far AND Hate IS Very Hated THEN use Fireball behavior

We calculate the degree that a behavior fires by calculating the centroid of the associated input values. This yields the fuzzy weighted average for the behavior. We use this average as a score to evaluate this behavior against any other candidate behaviors to choose the final winner. Note that more complex fuzzy systems could allow for multiple winning behaviors that fire in parallel, such as moving and attacking at the same time.

For our example, two combat rule sets fired yielding two candidate behaviors, Crossbow and Fireball. Figure 7.4.3 shows rules that are firing for our example. We choose Fireball since it has a higher fuzzy weighted average. In terms of the game, this all translates to Ian hating Wally so much that he uses a Fireball attack regardless of possible splash damage to himself.

Optimizations to Our Fuzzy System

Our sample fuzzy system has only two inputs with a four-by-five rule matrix and contains a total of 20 rules that must be evaluated on every decision cycle. The number of rules in a system grows exponentially with the number of inputs and outputs. A game system with only eight inputs could have several hundred thousand rules to evaluate. For real-time applications such as games, this brute-force evaluation of all the rules is out of the question. We need to find ways to optimize away many of those evaluations. Here are some methods that have proven themselves in the trenches of game development.

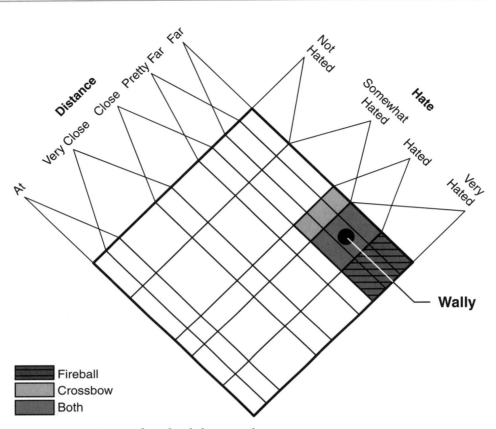

FIGURE 7.4.3   *Firing of combat behavior rules.*

Single State Output

Our simple fuzzy system already contains an optimization over a standard fuzzy system. The output of our decision system is restricted to be a single nonfuzzy behavior. We do not need to spend processing time calculating how hard to hit an opponent with a melee strike or how fast we need to flee from a predator. Such calculations come naturally to fuzzy systems, but they are overkill for most of today's game designs. Typically, all our decision engine needs to do is determine the proper behavior to transition our actor's state machine to. Future games might push pass this limitation and require decision systems that drive more complex game and animation and systems with multiple fuzzy outputs.

Hierarchical Behaviors

If we can cut down on the number of behaviors that we need to consider for the current decision cycle, we can avoid all of the rule evaluations associated with each behavior. By factoring out the rules that are common to a group of behaviors, we can build a hierarchical rule tree. This tree allows us to test the common rules only once, and "early-out" of an entire branch of behaviors if a rule does not fire.

Parallel Behavior Layers

If we can break our behaviors into parallel layers that can fire and operate independent of each other, we can further prune out unnecessary rule evaluations. A layer can be assigned its own evaluation frequency. We might have a movement layer that needs to receive a decision tick 10 times per second while we have a combat layer that only needs to be evaluated once every second. This allows us to put off checking all of the numerous combat rules while we continue to check a much smaller set of movement rules at a higher frequency.

Learning the Rules

Fuzzy logic allows us to query experts and have them express how a system works in natural language terms. We can then build membership sets and rules from all of that information. This might work well when dealing with driving a racecar or shooting a jump shot, but where do we find a dragon to tell us when to breathe fire on a party of pesky adventurers? It turns out that the input-to-output mapping nature of fuzzy systems make them very well suited to machine learning. We can engineer our system in such a way that we can record the inputs to the system as a human plays the game, and then map them to the action that the player chooses to execute under those conditions [Alexander02]. To make this useful for most games, this does mean that we will have to build the game in such a way that a human trainer can play all of the game actors, including the enemies, like the previously mentioned dragon.

Combs Method

A technique known as the *Combs Method* converts fuzzy-logic rules from an exponential growth into a linear growth situation. While this method doesn't allow you to convert an existing system of if-then rules to a linear system, it can help control the number of rules examined when implemented from the ground up using this technique. In addition, it should be noted that the Combs Method will give you slightly different results than traditional fuzzy logic, but that's the trade-off. For more information, please look at [Zarozinski01] and [Combs99].

Conclusion

Fuzzy logic provides a useful approach for implementing game systems, including decision-making and behavior selection. To meet the growing demand for more complex and believable computer-controlled characters, it will prove to be a great asset in the game programmer's toolbox.

References

[Alexander02] Alexander, Thor, "GoCap: Game Observation Capture," *AI Game Programming Wisdom*, Charles River Media, 2002.

[Combs99] Combs, William E., *The Fuzzy Systems Handbook 2nd Ed*, Academic Press, 1999.

[Kosko97] Kosko, Bart, *Fuzzy Engineering*, Prentice-Hall, 1997.

[Kosko93] Kosko, Bart, *Fuzzy Thinking*, Hyperion, 1993.

[McCuskey00] McCuskey, Mason, "Fuzzy Logic for Video Games," *Game Programming Gems*, Charles River Media, 2000.

[McNeill94] McNeill, F. Martin, *Fuzzy Logic: A Practical Approach,* Academic Press, 1994.

[Terno94] Terano, Toshiro, *Applied Fuzzy Systems,* Academic Press, 1994.

[Zarozinski01] Zarozinski, Michael, "Imploding Combinatorial Explosion in a Fuzzy System," *Game Programming Gems 2*, Charles River Media, 2001.

7.5

A Flexible Goal-Based Planning Architecture

John O'Brien—Red Storm Entertainment

jobrien@nc.rr.com

Game AI has come a long way in the past few years. Even so, many AIs remain either hard-coded or scripted, and contain little or no planning and adaptability. The result is that many gamers feel they can quickly "solve" an AI. This lowers their satisfaction with the games in general, and reduces the games' longevity. Many engineers are uneasy with committing to supporting planning in their AI because they believe that they cannot afford the additional time investment and complexity. While this is a valid stance in some situations, our experience has been largely the opposite: We have found that a solid planning architecture prevents having to write separate code for each variation in the AI called for by the design, and results in a higher quality finished product. The planning architecture described next is easy to implement and can be applied to a wide spectrum of games.

Overview

A diagram of the planning architecture is shown in Figure 7.5.1. The objective is to take the world state (as the AI perceives it), analyze it to generate a list of needs and opportunities, use those to form goals, and then finally form plans of action that will result in the AI impacting the world in some fashion.

The programmer has an advantage in approaching AI in this fashion. It is fairly close to the way humans approach problems, and is therefore an intuitive way to architect the code. We also believe that this type of approach results in AI that feels more human. One of the main reasons many AIs are not convincing as opponents is because they do not seem to have objectives, but instead act from moment to moment. This type of architecture makes it far easier to craft an AI that has medium and long-range goals.

This might sound like a lot of work, but really it is more a matter of breaking up the process into small, easily managed steps so as to reduce the complexity of the overall problem. If it seems that detailed planning would be too much of a processor hit, bear

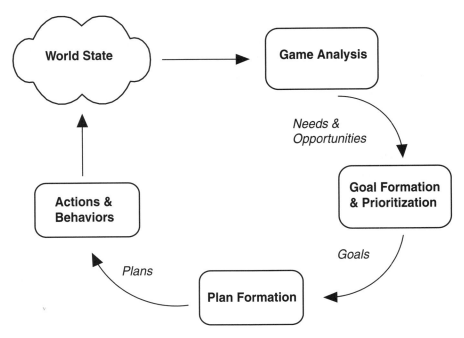

FIGURE 7.5.1   *The planning architecture.*

in mind that planning is not something that needs to be done every frame. Depending on the game, a given AI agent probably only needs to update its planning once per second, if that often. If there are many agents in the world that need to make plans, their individual processing can be staggered to reduce the impact at any one point in time. Finally, within the processing for a single agent, the code can be architected such that each trip through the decision-making cycle is spread out over multiple updates.

Before we move on to a walkthrough of the decision-making process, let's establish definitions for the terms in Figure 7.5.1 and ground them in real game examples.

Needs and Opportunities

Needs and opportunities are the areas the AI desires to take action on. For example, a bot in a shooter might decide that it is too far out in the open and there are enemies about. Conversely, an enemy might be nearby who is unaware of the bot's presence, which constitutes an opportunity to get a quick kill. Generating the list of categories that your AI will consider is the first step in creating a planning architecture.

Goals

Goals are the specific objectives the AI wants to achieve, given the needs and opportunities it has identified. The bot in the previous example might create two goals: 1) seek cover, and 2) attack the unsuspecting enemy.

Plans

A plan is a series of steps your AI will carry out in order to achieve a goal. Many times, a plan will contain only one element, but by allowing for cases in which multiple steps are necessary, we can keep our code streamlined and simple.

Actions/Behaviors

This is where the rubber meets the road. Actions and behaviors are all of the things that your AI can do in the game. In an RTS, for example, the list of game actions would include things such as Build Structure X, Build Unit Y, Add Unit Y to Group Z, and so on. In general, there should be a one-to-one correspondence between the list of actions for the AI and the interface commands available to the player. Behaviors, on the other hand, are generally things you invent. In a shooter, you might have behaviors such as Look for Cover, Patrol Area X, and Defend Location Y.

Walkthrough of Decision-Making

In this section, we will step through each phase of the decision-making process, showing how the pieces fit together. Please note that there will not be any code samples here, as this would be somewhat impractical and not a good use of space.

Game Analysis

The first, and perhaps most difficult, phase in the planning process is the game analysis phase. Here you will have a collection of functions that analyze the world state from the perspective of a given AI agent. In general, there will be a one-to-one correspondence between these methods and items on your Needs/Opportunities list. The object of this phase is to take the myriad pieces of data in the game world and condense them into a snapshot that is easily digested by the decision-making code. For here on out, we will refer to this information as the need/opportunity values.

So, what should these functions do, exactly? For each category of interest, there should be a function that takes the information known to the AI and expresses it as a number on a scale of your choosing. The way the scale is set up and how different game states map to values on it is entirely up to you. You might want everything in the range of 1 to 100, and have a situation that is twice as good yield a number twice as high. Alternatively, you could set up a system in which positive numbers are good, negative numbers are bad, the range is +/– 10,000, and the progression is exponential so that the better or worse a situation is, the more it will dominate calculations further on in the process.

It is definitely worth your while to spend a good deal of time on the game analysis functions. The decisions your AI makes will only be as good as the information available to it, and these methods create the input to the decision-making code. Furthermore, it is likely that you will have to tune these functions as the project progresses. No matter how good your understanding of the game world is early in a project, there will be areas that will require tweaking later once the entire architecture is running. The good news is that this is the toughest part of the whole process—it gets easier from here on out.

Some points to bear in mind when creating your game analysis methods include:

- **Consistent scale**: Try to make sure that each function's output uses the rating scale in the same fashion. In particular, see to it that each one uses the entire range. If the worst result you ever see for a given category is 50 out of 100, it's time to rebalance that function.
- **Absolute results**: Two agents in an identical situation should yield the same results. If one agent is supposed to play more defensively than another, for example, that should not be reflected here. Those issues will be handled by the goal prioritization code.

Goal Formation and Evaluation

The next step in planning is to take the abstraction of the game world that you created in the game analysis phase, and use it to evaluate the validity of the goals that the AI already has, and form new goals if necessary.

The evaluation of existing goals is straightforward. For each one, simply check against the list of need/opportunity values to see whether it is still an issue. For example, a bot that has a goal of seeking cover can consider the goal to be satisfied if its Current Cover rating is sufficiently high. One of the decisions you will need to make is what the cutoff values are that constitute success for your goals.

In general, a goal that has been satisfied can be removed from the list, but you will probably find it useful for there to be a set of fixed goals that are always present in each AI, with others being added dynamically as necessary. In a strategy game, for instance, your AI would likely maintain a permanent goal for each win condition. The agent might not be planning to act on each condition at all times, but it should keep all of them in mind in its planning. If no pressing needs come up, it can then attempt to make progress toward winning the game even if the situation at that moment isn't terribly conducive to doing so.

The next step is to use the need/opportunity values to create new goals. In doing so, keep the following points in mind:

- **Multiple values**: Goals might be based on more than one need/opportunity value. For example, the goal of Attack Player A might come about as a result of having both a high Offensive Potential rating and a low Player A Defense rating. All of the criteria used should be rolled into a single score that can be stored in the goal itself for use later.
- **Sensible cutoffs**: As with goal evaluation, you will probably need cutoff values representing at a minimum how good or bad a value has to be before the AI will consider taking action.

- **Avoid culling the list**: Try not to overly limit the number of goals potentially placed on the list. For reasons that will be explained in the next section, it is better to let the prioritization code trim the list if necessary.

At the end of this phase of processing, you will have a list of all of the things that your AI considers worthy of its attention. The next step is to decide which ones require the *most* attention.

Goal Prioritization

The goal prioritization phase is where the AI will decide, "What do I want to achieve now?" How it achieves those ends will be dealt with later. This is really the heart of the decision-making code. The specific plans that get formed afterward are, in effect, merely implementation details.

In its simplest form, goal prioritization could be merely ordering the goals on the basis of the score assigned to them in the previous section. This is a perfectly valid approach, and the only other thing that might be required is to have a maximum number of dynamic goals that are allowed to remain on the list.

A more exciting possibility exists, however, which is to use the goal prioritization code as a means of injecting personality into your AI. Why is it that two people placed in an identical situation might act very differently? Well, it is possible that they might perceive the situation differently from one another. It is far more likely, though, that they each weigh the relevant factors in the situation differently, and have different priorities on which their decisions are based.

Using this architecture, or something similar to it, it is easy to allow AI agents to have variations in their priorities that will dramatically affect the way they act in the game world. All that is necessary is to give each AI a set of scaling factors that map to the different goal types. If there are few enough goal types, this can be a one-to-one mapping; otherwise, it might be necessary to group them into categories. Apply these scaling factors to the goal scores before sorting them, and the result will be that two agents in the same situation might do very different things. This is also a good place to throw in a little randomness, as most people are not 100-percent consistent in their responses to a given situation.

For example, in a war game, a very aggressive AI general would have a high scaling factor associated with offensive goals and a low one with defensive goals. The result would be that it would pursue any chink in its opponents' armor, but would not pay much attention to its defenses unless overtly threatened. Conversely, an attack-oriented goal would not move to the top of the queue for a defensive general unless it was clearly a golden opportunity and the general's defenses were in very good order. Both of these AIs are using exactly the same decision-making code, yet their actions in the game will be so different that it will appear that you have written two distinct AIs.

The preceding example was very simple, but it is possible to do much more with this approach. You can use it to create an AI that favors one method of attack over another, or prefers subtlety to overt action, or attempts to goad other players into attacking its target of choice, all with the same code.

Plan Formation and Evaluation

The AI now knows what goals it wants to actively pursue. Now it needs plans for exactly how it will achieve those goals. Each plan will consist of a list of specific game actions and behaviors that are necessary in order to satisfy the goal in question.

For example, a bot that is seeking cover would probably have a plan consisting of two elements: 1) Move to Location X,Y, and 2) Crouch. Location X,Y would be determined by analyzing the area the bot is in and finding a spot that can provide concealment from known enemies and/or likely approaches. This calculation would be made once at the time the plan is formed.

Plan evaluation is even easier than goal evaluation, for the most part. Whenever an item in a plan is carried out, it should be marked as completed. Once all of the pieces of a plan have been completed, it is no longer needed. Depending on the type of game, it might also be necessary to check remaining items to see whether they are still feasible. You will need code to do this anyway when forming a list of options to consider when forming new plans.

In general, the easiest way to handle plan formation is to maintain a list of actions that can be taken in the game and AI behaviors you have written, and map them to the various goal types. For example, the action Build AA Gun would be rated as being very good for satisfying the Defend Against Air Attacks goal. Another way to improve air defense might be to execute the Assign Fighter to Defense action.

If there is more than one way to achieve a goal (and in most good games, this will be true), then plan selection should work very much the way goal selection does. Take each method of satisfying the goal and assign it a score. This score would be based on factors such as:

- **Resources at hand**: Assign Fighter to Defense would get a much higher score if there were fighters available that are not already committed to another task.
- **Cost**: AA guns might be much cheaper to build than new fighters are.
- **Personality**: An aggressive general might prefer to build new fighters because they can later be used offensively.

Once a score has been determined for each option, the highest rated option (after applying personality and a little randomness for good measure) would be added to the plan. Note that an option might explicitly require multiple steps, or might prove upon further evaluation to require multiple steps. In the Air Defense example, if fighters are chosen as the means of defense, it might be necessary to build some. This, and other possible prerequisites, would be checked and added to the front of the plan if necessary.

One point to consider in plan formation is that it is not necessary here to consider what is achievable in one turn/second/update cycle. It's OK if there is more planned for than the AI can actually accomplish in the short term. That's one of the reasons you bothered to prioritize the goals.

Converting Plans into Actions and Behaviors

Finally, your AI has its master plan for conquering the world. Now, it is time to carry it out. If everything has gone well to this point, then choosing what the AI will actually do at any given moment is the easiest part of the entire process. There should be practically no decisions left to make.

All that is necessary now is to step through the plans in goal priority order, and attempt to do the things that are planned. The plans associated with lower-priority goals will most likely not be handled as quickly as those with higher priorities. For example, in a war game you might have plans that require the construction of 50 points' worth of units, but only have the capacity to produce 30 points of units in a turn. In that case, the units necessary for the most important goals will be built first.

The shooter bot that needs to find cover but has a clear shot at an unsuspecting enemy will do whichever one ended up with the higher priority, unless it is possible to move to its chosen hiding place and take the shot at the same time.

This code is the section of your AI that will run most often, but as you can see, it is far and away the least complex and time-consuming portion of the architecture. All of the tough decisions and calculations are handled at infrequent intervals, leaving the part of the AI code that runs in each update cycle with very little work to do. This is a very good thing.

Contrast this with the most likely alternative, which is to reanalyze most of the environment with each update, and then choose an action appropriate to the current situation that may or may not have anything to do with what the agent has done before or will do after.

General Implementation Notes

There are some issues that still need to be touched upon: load balancing, and the strengths and weaknesses of this approach.

It should be clear by now that this approach, while very powerful, could be an unwelcome processor hit if not used wisely. As mentioned in the overview, it is desirable to architect your system such that planning updates for your agents are spread out from one another. It is also a good idea to set things up so that even the different phases of planning can be run at different frequencies. It is worth spending some time adjusting these values to see how infrequently various parts of the code can be run before the decision-making degrades. Our intention is not to frighten you off; we feel that all of the techniques we just mentioned are important for any AI, but they are certainly applicable to this type of architecture.

We view the primary strengths of a planning architecture to be:

- **Adaptability**. No matter what the game state is, the AI will form goals that attempt to address it. You will find that your code often handles situations you didn't think of surprisingly well.
- **AI feels more human**. The fact that your AI actually does have a plan will absolutely come through to the player, who will be more likely to not think of the computer opponents as mindless automatons.
- **Ease of debugging**. It is often difficult to debug AI code because there is not a visual representation of what is happening behind the scenes. With this approach, though, it is easy to take a look at what the AI is thinking at each stage of the process.

We feel that the weaknesses of the approach are:

- **Tuning of game analysis functions**. Every decision your AI makes will hinge on the abstraction of the game state created by these functions. You will need to focus on tuning them well.
- **Must be planned for from the outset**. This is not much of a weakness, as any good AI must be thought out thoroughly in advance. If you have four weeks for AI at the end of the project, though, and you're already burnt out, this is not the approach for you.

Conclusion

Planning is a powerful tool that an AI programmer can use to greatly increase the quality of a game and to add to the illusion of reality the game is trying to present. Use of a planning architecture in your game can result in an AI that is very competent and adaptable. If the AI is not easily "solved," the replay value of the game will be higher. As we have seen, it is possible to use this architecture to imbue AI agents with humanlike personality traits without writing large amounts of new code. Furthermore, the game-specific code is confined to two components of the system, allowing you to reuse quite a bit of code in subsequent games.

This architecture is very scalable, as the number of need/opportunity categories you choose to consider and the number of goal types that you define determines the level of complexity. In addition, it lends itself well to solving problems that are normally very difficult in AI programming, such as level of difficulty. A difficulty of Easy can be achieved by allowing the AI to focus on goals that would otherwise be of low priority, and a high difficulty setting might have the AI focus exclusively on the most pressing concerns with less regard for personality variations.

This approach has been used in multiple titles, and it adapts well to meet the needs of each game. You'll find that once you start using planning in your AI, you won't ever want to switch back. Finally, if you're interested in reading more about planning and its possible uses in games, we recommend starting with [Stout98] and [Baldwin/Rakosky97].

References

[Baldwin/Rakosky97] Baldwin, Mark, and Rakosky, Robert, "Project AI," www .gamedev.net/reference/articles/article545.asp, 1997.

[Stout98] Stout, Bryan, "Adding Planning Capabilities to Your Game AI," *Game Developer* magazine, Miller Freeman, Volume 5, Number1, January 1998.

FPS, RTS, AND RPG AI

8.1

First-Person Shooter AI Architecture

Paul Tozour—Ion Storm Austin

gehn29@yahoo.com

This article describes a generic AI architecture for a typical first-person shooter ("FPS") game such as any of the titles associated with the *Quake, Unreal,* or *Half-Life* engines.

Every game is unique, and every game requires a unique AI implementation to support its specific game mechanics. However, there are so many common features shared between different FPS games that it's reasonable for us to identify the major AI components that nearly any such game will feature, and describe the major relationships between those components.

Note that the term "first-person" shouldn't be taken too literally. The techniques described here work equally well for a third-person game (in which you can see your character in the game rather than seeing the world through his or her eyes).

This article also describes some of the additional subsystems required to add elements of a "first-person sneaker" game such as Looking Glass Studios' *Thief: The Dark Project.*

Overview

AIs in FPS games tend to work individually, rather than working in teams or being controlled by a single "player." This state of affairs is gradually changing, and FPS AIs are increasingly becoming capable of complex tactics involving multiple units such as you would find in a strategy game. However, this article is intended only to lay the groundwork for an FPS AI, so we will focus solely on the architecture for an individual AI opponent and ignore the questions of teamwork and multi-unit coordination.

This article organizes the generic FPS AI architecture into four major components: *behavior, movement, animation,* and *combat.*

The Four Components

The *movement* layer is responsible for figuring out how the character should move in the game world. The movement AI is what makes the character avoid obstacles, follow other characters, and find paths through complex environments to reach its destination. The movement subsystem never determines where to move, only how to do so. It simply receives commands from other components telling it where to move, and it is responsible for making sure the character moves to that point in an appropriate fashion.

The *animation* layer is responsible for controlling the character's body. Its major role is selecting, parameterizing, and playing character animation sequences. It is also responsible for generating animations that cannot be played from canned animation sequences, such as turning a guard's head to face the player, pointing down a hallway, or bending over and extending his arm to pick up a book on the table. Since we can't tell in advance exactly where the book will be or precisely what direction the guard will need to point, we need to assume a greater degree of control over the animation to ensure that the character animates correctly.

The *combat* layer is responsible for assessing the character's current tactical situation, selecting tactics in combat, aiming and firing at opponents, deciding when to pick up new weapons, and so on. Since combat is the core gameplay dynamic in most FPS games, the performance of this subsystem will be crucial to the player's perception of the AI.

The *behavior* layer is the overarching system that determines the character's current goal and communicates with the other systems to attempt to reach its goal. It is the highest-level AI subsystem and sits on top of all of the other subsystems.

The Animation Controller

The animation AI system is responsible for the character's body. This layer is mostly responsible for playing pregenerated animation sequences that have either been hand-crafted by professional animators or generated from motion capture (mo-cap) data.

Most animations will take control of a character's entire body. A "dying" animation is a good example of this. All parts of the character's body are animated to make a convincing death sequence. In some games, however, there is a need for animations that play only on certain parts of a character's body. For example, an arm-waving animation will only influence a character's right arm and torso, a head-turning animation only turns the head and neck, and a facial expression only influences the face.

The animation controller needs to be aware of which parts of the body certain animations control so that it can resolve conflicts between different animations. When the animation AI wants to play a new animation, it needs to determine which body parts the animation needs to use, and if there are animations already controlling those body parts, it needs to stop them so that the new animation can take over [Orkin02]. The system would thus be able to know that it can play the arm-waving and facial-expression animation at the same time, but as soon as the character is shot, the death animation will appropriate control from all of these.

In addition, there is often a need for the animation system to take greater control of the character's body to perform actions that are more appropriate to the context than canned animations. This includes:

- **Parameterizing existing animations**. For example, the animation AI speeds up or slows down a character's "walk" cycle, or adjusts the animation to make the character walk with a limp after it has been shot in the leg.
- **Taking control of specific body parts.** For example, the character points along a hallway and says, "He went that way!"
- **Handling inverse kinematics (IK).** For example, a character needs to reach over and grab a gun lying on a table. This is similar to a robot arm control problem in robotics.

It's important to note, however, that you can avoid a number of world-interaction problems by standardizing the characteristics of the game's art assets. For example, all doorknobs are always three feet off the ground, all tables in the game have the same height, and the guns are always kept at the same place on every table.

Movement: Global and Local Pathfinding

At the base of the movement AI system is a *pathfinding* component. This system is responsible for finding a path from any coordinate in the game world to any other. Given a starting point and a destination, it will find a series of points that together comprise a path to the destination. In some cases, it will report that no path can be found—you can't find a path to the inside of a solid wall.

A game AI pathfinder nearly always uses some sort of precomputed data structure for movement (see [Tozour02a]). FPS game worlds tend to be relatively static, so it makes sense to pregenerate a database that's highly optimized for performing fast pathfinding in a particular section of the game world. At runtime, it's very easy to use this pathfinding database to perform an A* search from any part of the level to any other. The performance of this search will depend highly on how well the pathfinding database is optimized.

Handling Dynamic Obstacles

Unfortunately, there's a problem with this global pathfinding system. This type of *global* pathfinding is incapable of dealing with *dynamic obstacles*; that is, obstacles that can move during the course of gameplay. For example, imagine we have a guard who constantly traces a back-and-forth path along a hallway until he's distracted by something. When the guard has his back turned, a clever player pushes a heavy barrel into the middle of the patrol path and runs off. The guard will be unable to handle this obstacle because the barrel is a dynamic obstacle and isn't accounted for in the pathfinding database.

Many games simply ignore this problem and pay no attention to dynamic obstacles. An AI will just keep right on walking whenever it encounters a dynamic obstacle, hoping that the game's physics system will make it slide around the obstacle until it's free. This is an acceptable behavior in many game worlds, as most FPS games feature very few dynamic obstacles. In heavily populated environments, however, this can easily give players lots of tools to break the game.

Any attempt to address the dynamic obstacle avoidance problem needs to be built on communication between the physics system and the local pathfinding system. Since dynamic obstacles can be moved at any time, the AI needs to continually query the physics system for the presence of dynamic obstacles in any area it intends to move through. Because this search will only occur in a limited area near the AI in question, we'll refer to this as a *local* pathfinding system.

A local pathfinder does not replace a global pathfinder; each is optimized for a different part of the problem. Instead, the local pathfinding system should be built on top of the global pathfinder. When an AI needs to move from point A to B, its movement AI first queries the global pathfinding system, and if it's successful, the global pathfinder will return an ordered list of points that constitute a path from A to B. The AI can then use that global path as a guideline, and use the local pathfinding system to find a path to each successive waypoint in that global path, avoiding any obstacles it might happen to discover along the way.

Fundamentally, a local pathfinder needs to be based on an A* search within a limited area around the origin of the search (see [Mathews02], [Stout00], [Rabin00] for an excellent introduction to A*). An A* search will ensure that the optimal path is found if such a path exists. A good way to do this is to perform sampling (i.e., querying the physics system for the presence of obstacles) using a fixed-size grid oriented toward the destination point. However, keep in mind that sampling can be computationally expensive if it's performed too often, so it's very important to take steps to minimize the amount of sampling that the system needs to perform in any given local search.

The Movement Controller

The movement AI acts as the client of all the other parts of the AI; that is, it is a subsystem that performs arbitrary tasks assigned to it by higher-level components. These tasks are issued in the form of discrete *movement commands,* such as "move to point (X,Y,Z)," "move to object O," "move in formation F relative to game object O," "turn to face point (X,Y,Z)," or "stop moving."

The movement AI will be executing exactly one of these movement commands at any given moment. We will define a *movement controller* as the object that "owns" the current movement command.

Once we have done this, we can design the appropriate cognitive skills to execute the movement commands into the individual movement command objects themselves. A command such as "move to (X,Y,Z)," for example, will be responsible for using the global and local pathfinding systems to find and execute a path to (X,Y,Z), and making the appropriate engine calls to ensure that the character moves along the specified path. If no path is available, or when the AI entity reaches the end of its path, the movement command reports back to the movement controller so that it can be garbage-collected.

This technique is also useful for handling different types of movement. Different types of movement commands can handle tasks such as walking, running, swimming, and flying, with appropriate parameters to determine the AI agent's acceleration, movement range, turn rate, animations, and other movement characteristics.

The Combat Controller

When an AI enters combat, it passes control for the majority of its behaviors to a *combat controller*. The combat controller is responsible for all combat-related tasks, such as selecting an opponent, selecting a weapon, maneuvering, firing, and searching for additional weapons and ammo.

The most difficult part of the combat problem is determining how to intelligently assess the current situation, and select and execute an appropriate tactic in response.

The challenge comes from the extraordinary difficulty of getting an AI entity to understand the significance of the spatial configuration of any given area. Any human can glance at his current surroundings and immediately form an assessment of the space. Play a few games of *Counter-Strike* on a new map, and you quickly learn where the cover points are, where the prime "camping" locations are, and all of the different vulnerabilities of certain areas relative to one another.

The ease with which we perform this task hides its true difficulty. Evolution has endowed the human mind with so many powerful tools for spatial reasoning that this task, like walking and talking, seems remarkably easy only because we are so good at it.

The Challenge of Spatial Reasoning

One of the major problems for AIs attempting to perform spatial reasoning is that the raw geometry of the level itself is extraordinarily difficult to parse. Attempting to perform reasoning with the raw geometry at runtime would be prohibitively expensive, because the geometry often contains so many extraneous and irrelevant details. A brick wall, for example, might be composed of 10,000 polygons for the hundreds of bricks in the wall, whereas the AI only cares that it's a wall.

As with the global pathfinding problem, the solution is to build a custom database. We can construct a very simple, streamlined database of spatial tactical data that contains only the key information the combat AI will require to understand the tactical significance of various parts of a level.

A number of FPS games require the level designers to design this tactical database by hand. After building their levels, the level design team must embed specific "hints" in their levels by placing dummy objects in the world, indicating that certain areas are "cover points," "choke points," or "vulnerable areas."

This is an inefficient and often error-prone method, and it makes it much more costly for designers to change their levels after they have placed these hints. [van der Sterren01] describes how the process can be automated. Customized tools can automatically analyze a given level's geometry, determine the tactical significance of different areas, and automatically generate a detailed tactical database.

The only major drawback to a precomputed database is that it can sometimes work poorly in environments with a large number of dynamic obstacles. For example, if the player can push a barrel into a certain part of a room and hide behind it, the tactical database won't automatically understand that the player or any AI can take cover behind the barrel. Or, if the barrel is directly in front of a tight hallway, for example, then the part of the tactical database that specifies that it's possible to shoot from the room into the hallway, and vice versa, is now giving us bad advice.

Combat Tactics

Assuming we have generated a tactical database, we now need to get our AIs to use it. A combat AI will typically draw from a library of *tactics,* in which each tactic is responsible for executing a specific behavior in combat. Each tactic must communicate with the movement and animation subsystems to ensure that it exhibits the appropriate behaviors.

For example, a "circle-strafe" tactic would continuously circle around the AI's current target while firing at it. It would attempt to remain between some minimum and maximum distance from its target at all times.

The following examples demonstrate some of the different types of combat tactics that might appear in a typical FPS.

- **Camp**. The AI sits in a hidden location and waits for an opponent to appear—cheap, but effective. The main disadvantage is that this tactic can often appear "scripted."
- **Joust**. The AI rushes its opponent while firing and attempts to rush past it. Once it's passed beyond its target, it can swing around and hope to attack from behind.
- **Circle of death**. The AI circles its opponent, firing continuously. It attempts to remain within a desired range between a given minimum and maximum distance.
- **Ambush**. The AI ducks behind cover, pops out and fires, and then ducks back under cover. This is similar to the "camp" tactic, except that the AI has a sense of where its opponent(s) must be coming from and actively emerges from its camping location at the appropriate time.
- **Flee and ambush**. The AI runs from its opponent, hides behind a corner, and prepares an ambush for its opponent.

Another critical problem is the tactic selection problem. Given an arbitrary situation in combat, we need to pick the best tactic to attack our opponents. This decision will depend on three major factors: the nature of the tactic under consideration, the relative tactical significance of all of the combatants' various locations (as determined by the tactical database described previously), and the current tactical situation (the AI agent's health, weapon, ammo, and location, plus all of the values of those characteristics for all of its allies and opponents).

A related problem is the opponent-selection problem. Given a number of potential opponents, the combat AI needs to select one as the current "target." Although it does not necessarily ignore all of its other adversaries, we need to designate a "target" to represent the fact that the AI will focus on a single enemy at a time.

This is usually a trivial problem as most FPS games simply pit the user against all of the AI opponents. In more complex situations, it's usually easy to find a good target-picking heuristic by considering the relative tactical situation of the AI against every potential opponent – that is, each entity's health, weapon, ammo, and location. An AI should generally worry about defending itself first, and attempt to identify whether any particular opponent is threatening it. If not, it can identify the most vulnerable target nearest to itself. A simple ranking function can easily make this determination.

After an AI has selected a target and begun to fight, it should consider changing its target whenever its tactical situation changes significantly. Obviously, if the AI or its target dies, that's a good time to reconsider the current target.

Finally, there's the weapon-firing problem. Most FPS weapons are high-velocity ranged weapons, so the key problem is determining where to fire. See [Tozour02b] for an introduction to the issues related to aiming and firing ranged weapons.

The Behavior Controller

At the top of the AI system is an overarching controller called the *behavior controller*. This controller is responsible for determining the AI agent's current state and high-level goals. It determines the AI's overall behavior—how it animates, what audio files it plays, where it moves, and when and how it enters combat.

There are any number of ways to model a behavior controller, depending on your game's design requirements. Most FPS games use a finite-state machine (FSM) for this part of the AI. See [Dybsand00] for an introduction to finite-state machines.

The list below enumerates some typical states in the FSM for a typical FPS.

- **Idle**. The AI is standing guard, smoking a cigarette, etc.
- **Patrolling**. The AI is following a designer-specified patrol path.
- **Combat**. The AI is engaged in combat and has passed most of the responsibility for character control over to the combat controller.
- **Fleeing**. The AI is attempting to flee its opponent or any perceived threat.
- **Searching**. The AI is looking for an opponent to fight or searching for an opponent who fled during combat.
- **Summoning assistance**. The AI is searching for additional AIs to help it fight or to protect it from a threat.

These behaviors should each be represented by an object that is responsible for communicating with the movement, animation, and combat subsystems in order to represent its behaviors appropriately. Developing these behaviors will typically be very easy, since the movement, animation, and combat subsystems already do most of the work and provide a rich palette of basic behaviors for the behavioral layer to build on.

Scripting Languages and Trigger Systems

Level designers will inevitably need some way to specify their design intentions in certain parts of your game. They need a way to take some degree of control over the AI for triggered gameplay sequences, cut scenes, or other "triggered" or "scripted" events that should happen during the game under certain circumstances. In order to make this happen, it's necessary to design an interface for communication between the trigger/scripting system and the unit AI itself.

This communication will typically take two forms. First, the triggered events can set AI parameters. For example, an event might enable or disable certain states of the behavior controller's finite-state machine, or modify various aggressiveness parameters to change the way the various combat tactics execute.

The more common form of communication consists of sending commands to any of the various parts of the system from a triggered event. For example, a trigger system can tell an AI to move to a given point or to flee from its current target by issuing a command to its behavior controller. This command changes the current state of the FSM to one that will execute the appropriate behaviors.

Stealth Elements

A "first-person sneaker" game is similar to an FPS, except that the emphasis is on stealth rather than combat. You don't want to kill the guard—you want to sneak past him, distract him, or maybe whack him over the head with a blunt object and drag his unconscious body off and dump it into a closet.

Despite outward appearances, first-person sneaker AI has a lot in common with FPS game AI. It has all the responsibilities of an FPS AI, since the AIs need to be able to engage in combat, but it's burdened with the additional responsibility of supporting stealth-oriented gameplay.

Looking Glass Studios' *Thief: The Dark Project* used graduated "alert levels" to provide the player with feedback. As you walked toward a guard, the guard would become increasingly suspicious, and would go from a "not suspicious" alert level to "somewhat suspicious," then to "very suspicious," and finally to "paranoid." Whenever a guard changed to a new alert level, he would notify the player with an audio cue such as "Hey! What was that?" (increased suspicion) or "I guess it was nothing" (decreased suspicion).

In order to model this alert level properly, it's essential to accurately model the AIs' perceptual capabilities. A player wants to be able to sneak up on an AI character when its back is turned, and the AI shouldn't automatically know the player is there—it should have to either see the player or hear him. Similarly, if the player dodges around a corner and hides, the AI shouldn't automatically know the player's location.

Perceptual Modeling

The first step is to break down the perception into different subsystems. Different types of perception work differently, so we'll need to model our character's visual, auditory, and tactile subsystems separately.

The *visual* subsystem should take into account such factors as the distance to a given visual stimulus, the angle of the stimulus relative to the AI's field of view, and the current visibility level at the location of the stimulus (such as the current lighting and fog levels and whether the AI's line-of-sight is blocked). A good way to combine these factors is to turn them into probability values between 0 and 1 and multiply them (see [Tozour02c]).

In order to ensure that the AI can actually see the object, it's also essential to use ray-casting. The AI should query the underlying game engine to ensure that there's an unblocked line between the AI's eyes and the stimulus it's attempting to notice.

The *auditory* subsystem is responsible for hearing sounds in the world. In order for this to work properly, your game engine needs to ensure that any given AI receives sound notifications more or less as the user would if he were in the AI's shoes. Any time a sound is played, the engine needs to ensure that all game entities within earshot of the sound, whether human or AI, are notified accordingly.

Each sound also needs to be tagged with some sort of data indicating its importance. This will allow AIs to react differently to important sounds such as explosions and screams, and ignore irrelevant sounds such as birds chirping and wind blowing.

This system also allows us to represent *AI audio occlusion*; that is, the way that background noise and other unimportant sounds will interfere with an AI's perception. For example, an AI is standing beside a noisy machine when the player tiptoes past him. The AI would normally be able to hear the player, but the noise of the machine makes it more difficult for the AI to hear him. One way to approach this is to calculate a total occlusion value for an AI at any given moment that represents the degree to which irrelevant noises impair his hearing.

The third and final sensory subsystem is the *tactile* subsystem. This system is responsible for anything the AI feels. This includes damage notifications (whenever the AI is wounded) as well as collision notifications (whenever the AI bumps into something, or some other object bumps into it).

Conclusion

Every game is unique, and every game requires a unique AI that's highly customized to fit the mechanics of its particular game. However, the techniques presented in this article should provide the reader with a solid foundation for any first-person shooter or sneaker game AI.

References and Additional Reading

[Dysband00] Dysband, Eric, "A Finite-State Machine Class," *Game Programming Gems*, Ed. Mark DeLoura, Charles River Media, 2000.

[Matthews02] Matthews, James, "Basic A* Pathfinding Made Simple," *AI Game Programming Wisdom*, Ed. Steve Rabin, Charles River Media, 2002.

[Orkin02] Orkin, Jeff, "Realistic Character Behavior with Prioritized, Categorized Animation," *AI Game Programming Wisdom*, Ed. Steve Rabin, Charles River Media, 2002.

[Rabin00] Rabin, Steve, "A* Speed Optimizations," *Game Programming Gems*, Ed. Mark DeLoura, Charles River Media, 2000.

[Stout00] Stout, Bryan, "The Basics of A* For Path Planning," *Game Programming Gems*, Ed. Mark DeLoura, Charles River Media, 2000.

[Tozour02a] Tozour, Paul, "Building a Near-Optimal Navigation Mesh," *AI Game Programming Wisdom*, Ed. Steve Rabin, Charles River Media, 2002.

[Tozour02b] Tozour, Paul, "The Basics of Ranged Weapon Combat," *AI Game Programming Wisdom*, Ed. Steve Rabin, Charles River Media, 2002.

[Tozour02c] Tozour, Paul, "Introduction to Bayesian Networks and Reasoning Under Uncertainty," *AI Game Programming Wisdom*, Ed. Steve Rabin, Charles River Media, 2002.

[van der Sterren01] van der Sterren, William, "Terrain Reasoning for 3D Action Games," *Game Programming Gems 2*, Ed. Mark De Loura, Charles River Media, 2001.

8.2

Architecting an RTS AI

Bob Scott—Stainless Steel Studios

bob@stainlesssteelstudios.com

This article differs from article 6.1, "Architecting a Game AI," [Scott02a] in that it specifically discusses architecture for real-time strategy (RTS) games. RTS games are one of the more thorny genres as far as AI is concerned, and a good architecture is necessary to ensure success. Most examples presented here are taken from the work done on *Empire Earth* (referred to as EE).

RTS Game Components

The components that make up an RTS game architecture consist of what some call "managers." These managers are each responsible for a specific area in the management of a computer player:

Civilization

The civilization manager is the highest-level manager responsible for development of the computer player's economy. It is responsible for coordination between the build, unit, resource, and research managers, as well as setting spending limits. It also handles computer player expansion, upgrading of buildings and units, and epoch advancement.

Build

The build manager is responsible for placement of the structures and towns. It receives requests from the unit manager for training buildings and from the civilization manager for support buildings. All site evaluation occurs here. Most buildings have requirements on where they can and cannot be placed. In *Empire Earth*, we have what are known as area effect buildings,—which provide a benefit to units within their range of influence. These need to be placed where the most units are likely to congregate—around resources. Military buildings need to be nearby, but should not interfere with the area effect buildings, so they go in a ring outside the immediate area of a resource. Some buildings require more area (farms, airports), and some require very specialized placement (walls, docks, towers). If you have a robust terrain analysis engine, use its knowledge in these routines (place towers in choke points, avoid building near enemies, etc).

Unit

The unit manager is responsible for training units. It keeps track of what units are in training at various buildings, monitors the computer player's population limit, and prioritizes unit training requests. It might also be required to communicate with the build manager if a training building is not currently available. One other responsibility for the unit manager is to attempt to maintain a unit count similar to the human players in the game. This goes a long way toward balancing the game as far as difficulty level is concerned, and gives the human players a better feel for what the AI can and cannot do. By not allowing the AI unit counts to get too high, we also lessen the CPU load of the game.

Resource

The resource manager is responsible for tasking citizens to gather resources in response to requests from both the unit and build managers. It load balances gathering duties and governs the expansion of the computer player to newly explored resource sites.

Research

The research manager is responsible for the directed research of the computer player. Technologies are examined and selected based on their usefulness and cost.

Combat

The combat manager is responsible for directing military units on the battlefield. It requests units to be trained via the unit manager and deploys them in whatever offensive or defensive position is most beneficial. Internally, the combat manager keeps track of units via a personnel manager, and handles offensive and defensive duties via similarly named managers. The combat manager periodically updates the status, movement, and actions of various attack groups, while these attack groups have subgroups that comprise like units.

Each manager communicates with the others in some way determined by the language being used. In C++, with the managers implemented as classes, public methods can be used as the communications medium. Both low- and high-level methods should be employed. As discussed in article 6.1, high-level methods provide easier development for the components calling them, while at the same time localizing the work so that changes are easier.

For example, the TrainUnit method (in EE's Unit Manager) is responsible for bringing new units into the world. Parameters include the type of the unit, the number desired and, optionally, an indication of where in the world the unit is required. That is all that is required of any other component to specify. TrainUnit will deal with the intricacies of ensuring there are sufficient resources (via communication with the Resource Manger) and population headroom, and will communicate with the build manager if the training building needs to be built. The fact that this method was created before EE's combat manager greatly simplified that component's development.

Keep in mind that many of these high-level messages cannot be completed immediately. In the case of TrainUnit, the unit(s) might not be trained instantly, or the training building must be built or resources gathered before the request can be honored. In this case, it is necessary to provide a mechanism for the requester to determine when the request has completed. This can be accomplished by creating (in this case) *training orders*. These training orders are simple classes that contain information about the request and a method to call to see if it is complete. Another possible way to handle this is via a callback function in the requesting component. This tends to be harder to do in C++, giving the nod to the former solution.

By the time you've finished development, most of the components will end up communicating with most of the other components. There's nothing wrong with this—there will always be new problems that require new solutions. The difficulty will be in making sure that the new additions don't have an adverse effect on the rest of the system. The large number of interconnections can almost take on a life of their own, and you will find that quite small changes can have profound effects on the AI. For example, in *Empire Earth*, the simple fact of one opponent ending an attack against one computer player unit will set into motion changes that can affect the spending decisions made, which will affect how well expansion takes place, which might affect contact with new opponents. Tracking down these chains of cause and effect becomes the focus of late development testing.

Difficulty Levels

Most computer games appeal to players with a broad range of experience. Since you are only developing one game, there must be a way to tailor the game to fit the level of competence of the player. Until the industry figures out how to create an AI that can learn from the player as it goes along, we have to be content with difficulty levels that are set by the players themselves.

On *Empire Earth*, we wanted to avoid the situation in which very expert players would be required to play against multiple computer players to be challenged. This is more work for the player and the CPU—it takes time to update those extra computer players. We decided that our goal would be to develop an AI that was good enough to give challenge to an expert player in a 1-to-1 match. We would then tone the AI down to provide less challenge for intermediate and beginning players. We even went so far as to hire expert players to help us do this balancing. We had no lack of beginning and intermediate players.

We strongly suggest taking this approach: create a hard AI first and reduce its intelligence for lower levels. Going the other way is, in our experience, much more difficult to achieve.

The next step is to decide what modifications to make to differentiate your difficulty levels. We suggest a brainstorming session in which you generate as many ideas as possible. Then, narrow down the list to the ones that will have the most impact on the effectiveness of the AI. Next, narrow down the list to the ones whose development can be immediately envisioned. Finally, if you have more than a handful of things that change based on difficulty level, narrow them down some more. The more variables you have at this point, the harder it will be to test changes. Testing difficulty level changes is an iterative process that requires a lot of time.

You will also have to visit the issue of cheating as one way to affect difficulty levels. Cheating can be one of the easier ways to deal with difficulty levels, but is also typically obvious to the player.

Challenges

There are many challenges facing the RTS AI developer—issues whose development is not immediately obvious. These generally require either advanced techniques or new ways of applying old ideas to the problem. Thinking "out of the box" is often required to solve these.

Random Maps

Perhaps the most troubling of the sticky spots is dealing with random maps. This one game feature affects so much of the AI that it, and the problems it creates, can account for as much as half of the development time. The one technique that will provide the most help in this area is a good terrain analysis engine.

Wall Building

Successful wall building, in a game that supports walls, is difficult until you ask yourself why wall building is needed. In almost all cases, a wall is built to keep enemies away from your economic centers. Given this basic fact, it no longer becomes necessary to build square walls around your town; it is only necessary to build walls between your towns and the enemies. Combine this idea with a robust pathfinding engine and a good terrain analysis engine, and you can find the right placement for your walls.

Island Hopping

Island maps in RTS games present another difficulty to the AI developer. Clearly, staying on the computer player's home island is not a viable strategy if resource locations exist on neutral islands. The key to a long-term island game is to exploit those neutral islands. This means transporting military and civilian units to those islands in a timely fashion. One method that made this possible in *Empire Earth* was the ability to queue unit goals.

Resource Management

All RTS games require management of some type of resources. In most cases, the computer player's civilian population must physically gather the resources. Resource requirements are imposed by the training of new units, the building of buildings, researching technologies, and other miscellaneous costs. In the case of multiple resource games, civilians must be allocated to different resources in some intelligent way.

Stalling

A problem that every RTS AI has to deal with is what is known as *stalling*. This occurs due to the sometimes-labyrinthine interactions between buildings, units, and resources that can cause the computer player to get stuck waiting for one thing or another, resulting in a computer player that cannot advance. One of the biggest sources of stalling in an RTS game is in the area of resources.

Overall Strategies

It's amazing what you can accomplish with goal-directed behavior. Given an architecture as described here and developed for *Empire Earth*, it is possible to get the computer player to advance to a selected epoch by simply asking to train a unit from that epoch. If, as is typical in a historical RTS, the goal is to build a wonder, this might also be accomplished by asking to build one. In both cases, the underlying architecture takes care of *pulling* the computer player in the required direction, perhaps advancing several epochs, gathering required resources, building required buildings, and so forth. Similarly, a large-scale attack can be planned in the same way, simply by issuing an attack order requiring units of a particular type. If those units are not available in the current epoch, advancement will be planned.

Here is where good planning and careful architecting pay off. Since the details are taken care of, the developer coming up with the overall strategy can think in terms of that strategy without worrying about the details.

Conclusions

Undertaking the development of an RTS AI takes guts. It is one of the hardest genres to develop AI for and will test your abilities to the limit. We hope we've shown that careful design can make your job easier than you might think.

References

[Scott02a] Bob Scott, "Architecting a Game AI," *AI Game Programming Wisdom*, Charles River Media, 2002.

[Scott02b] Bob Scott, "The Illusion of Intelligence," *AI Game Programming Wisdom*, Charles River Media, 2002.

8.3

An Economic Approach to Goal-Directed Reasoning in an RTS

Vernon Harmon—LucasArts Entertainment

vharmon@lucasarts.com

As legendary game designer Sid Meier has pointed out, a game is a series of interesting choices. Choosing what to do, and when, where, and how to do it, is critical to a player's success, and is therefore critical to a game agent's success as well.

In this article, we discuss one approach to creating an agent for a Real-Time Strategy (RTS) game, using the *Utility Model*. This approach takes Economic theories and concepts regarding consumer choice, and creates a mapping onto our game agent's decision space. We explain relevant AI terminology (*goal-directed reasoning, reactive systems, planning, heuristic functions*) and Economic terminology (*utility, marginal utility, cost, production possibilities*), and introduce a simplistic RTS example to provide a framework for the concepts.

Note that most RTSs encompass two domains: economy and combat. Unfortunately, covering both domains is beyond the scope of this article. In the interest of clearly explaining the concepts behind this approach, this article focuses solely on the economic domain. The relationship between the economic and combat domains is noted, but a full exploration of the combat domain will have to wait for a future article.

Finally, we provide a few suggestions—things to think about before you begin applying these concepts that might make your life a lot easier.

Goal-Directed Reasoning

Reasoning in a state space is conducted either forward from an initial state, or backward from a goal. Forward reasoning generates possible successor states by applying each applicable rule, or, in game terms, by attempting each possible move. When reasoning in a game—particularly in an RTS—the sheer number of possible moves from any state is prohibitive, so backward or *goal-directed reasoning* is often a more productive choice.

When applying goal-directed reasoning, you start with a given goal and locate all of the moves that could generate the goal state. Then, you repeat the process for each of the states that makes those moves valid. You continue generating predecessor states until one of the states generated is the initial state (or the current state).

Sometimes, a goal is too complicated to address directly—the goal "win the game" is a good example—and it is necessary to decompose the goal into smaller *subgoals* that are, ideally, easier to attempt. It is most useful when the union of these subgoals completely describes the goal, but that is an unlikely case in many games, because of unpredictability.

Unpredictability

The validity of a goal is subject to the predictability of the game universe. An RTS game universe is highly unpredictable, due to the large number of possible moves and the nature of human competition. A system that overcomes and adapts to this unpredictability is called a *reactive system*.

By decomposing our goal (usually "win the game") into smaller subgoals, we give ourselves an opportunity to adapt to the game universe. The key is to generate subgoals that we believe will allow us to win, while keeping the subgoals simple enough that the moves required to achieve them can be interleaved with moves that have been generated reactively; a process known as *planning*.

When we plan, we generate tasks or task-sequences that have a set of inputs and a set of outputs. Usually, we will chain these tasks together so that the outputs from one task-sequence become the inputs for another task-sequence. (This is, to some extent, how the economic and combat domains interface, as we will see later.) However, because of the unpredictability of our game universe, it is necessary to break these chains from time to time; we might need to insert an additional task-sequence, or we might need to create an entirely new chain and throw out a chain that was previously valid.

The Utility Model

Economists have long been studying consumer behavior, trying to understand the motivations behind consumer choices. If we view our game agent as a consumer, and the resources and moves available within the game universe as goods and services, then we have a useful mapping from real-world Economic concepts to our game universe.

In Economics, the term *utility* refers to the amount of satisfaction that a consumer receives from a product, or how desirable the product is. In AI, a *heuristic function* estimates whether a given state is on the path to the goal by approximating the desirability of the state. Using a measurement of utility as our heuristic for evaluating and choosing goals is the key concept behind the *Utility Model*.

Marginal Utility

A consumer attempts to maximize his or her total utility—the satisfaction derived from the consumption of all goods and services. The concept of *marginal utility*

(MU) describes the additional satisfaction gained from the consumption of one additional item. In order to maximize total utility, a consumer will compare the MU of each item available to be consumed. However, because the *cost* of each item might be different, a comparison can only be useful if each MU is normalized by dividing it by the cost of the item. In other words, a consumer doesn't purchase an item based purely on how much he or she will enjoy the item, but based on how much enjoyment there is *per dollar spent*; this is why cost is a critical factor in economic choice.

The *Theory of Diminishing Marginal Utility* states that as a consumer consumes multiple instances of a product, the consumer's MU for that product decreases. For example, if you are hungry, your MU for a slice of pizza might be very high. However, once you have eaten a slice, your hunger is partially satiated and your desire for a slice of pizza is less than it was before you ate a slice, and after three or four slices, your desire for a slice might be almost zero. Similarly, your MU for pizza will decrease if you eat something else instead. The important concept from this theory is that the MU of an item can change to accommodate changes in the domain; this is how our model will be reactive.

An Example RTS: Rock-Paper-Scissors

Most RTS games use the same basic building blocks: money, buildings, units, and technology. The relationships among all of these building blocks are known collectively as the game's *tech tree*. Figure 8.3.1 shows a tech tree for a fictional RTS game called *Rock-Paper-Scissors*. R-P-S is intentionally simplistic so that it can clearly illustrate the concepts behind the Utility Model; you should expect a much more complex tech tree in any RTS you program.

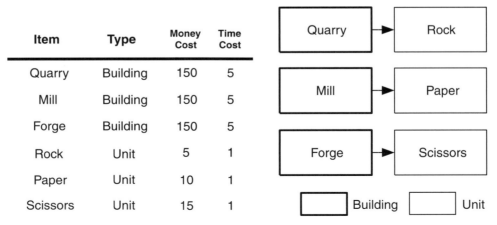

Item	Type	Money Cost	Time Cost
Quarry	Building	150	5
Mill	Building	150	5
Forge	Building	150	5
Rock	Unit	5	1
Paper	Unit	10	1
Scissors	Unit	15	1

FIGURE 8.3.1   *Tech tree for* Rock-Paper-Scissors.

Costs

As we saw in our discussion of marginal utility, cost is an important factor, so the first thing to note in the tech tree is the cost of items. Money and Time are the only costs listed, but there is another very important cost that is easy to overlook: opportunity. An *opportunity cost* is what you must give up in order to perform an action. For example, in Chess, the opportunity cost of moving one of your pieces is not being able to move any of your other pieces. An opportunity cost is incurred whenever an action is performed that cannot be performed in parallel with *all* other actions; hence, opportunity costs are linked to choice.

Production Possibilities

One way to examine the available choices is to create a *production possibilities curve*. Begin by fixing one of the inputs; the relationship among each n choices based on that fixed input can be graphed as an *n*-dimensional curve or surface.

Figure 8.3.2 shows the production possibilities surface for *R-P-S* when you have a fixed input of 1500 Money. Any point on that surface represents total consumption of the 1500 Money, and any point below the surface represents a surplus of Money, the amount of which can be computed by determining the point's distance to the surface. This particular surface is represented by the equation, 5R+10P+15S=1500,

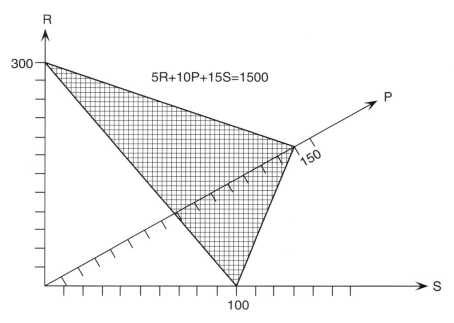

FIGURE 8.3.2   *The production possibilities "curve" for R-P-S, with a fixed input of 1500 Money. In this case (with three variables), the "curve" is actually a surface.*

where R is the number of Rocks produced, P is the number of Papers produced, and S is the number of Scissors produced.

A production possibilities curve for R-P-S with a fixed time input is uninteresting, because all of these items have the same time cost. Or do they?

Cost of Goals versus Cost of Tasks

If we consider each item (Scissors, for example) as a goal, then we can see that the cost of the goal is not just the cost of the last task required to achieve the goal, but the sum of all tasks in the task-sequence used to achieve the goal. Figure 8.3.3 shows such a task-sequence for the goal "1 Scissors," assuming a Money collection rate of 5 Money per Time.

Figure 8.3.3 demonstrates that the actual cost of a Scissors is dependent upon the state of the game at the time the plan is implemented. If none of the subgoals are satisfied at that time, then the Money cost, C_m, of the Scissors goal is the sum of the Money costs of each of its subgoals:

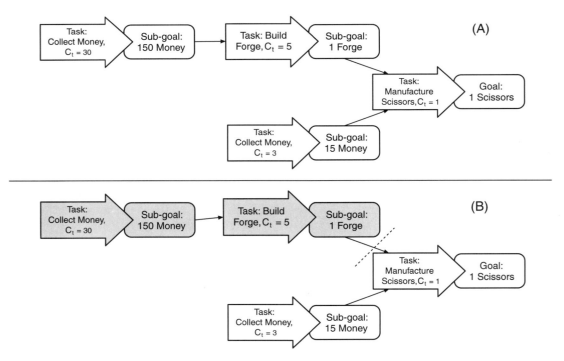

FIGURE 8.3.3   *A task-sequence for the goal "1 Scissors." A) No subgoals are currently true. B) Subgoal "1 Forge" is true, so its cost is reduced to 0, effectively pruning it from the sequence.*

$$C_m(Goal_{Scissors}) = C_m(Forge) + C_m(Money) * C_m(Scissors) \qquad (8.3.1)$$
$$= 150 + 1 * 15$$
$$= 165$$

The Time cost, C_t, of the goal can be computed similarly, but some extra work is required because some of the subgoals can be performed simultaneously:

$$C_t(Goal_{Scissors}) = C_t(Money) * C_m(Forge) \qquad (8.3.2)$$
$$+ max(C_t(Forge), C_t(Money) * C_m(Scissors))$$
$$+ C_t(Scissors)$$
$$= 0.2 * 150 + max(5, 0.2 * 15) + 1$$
$$= 30 + max(5, 3) + 1$$
$$= 36$$

However, if any subgoal is satisfied, the cost of that subgoal is zero. Assuming we already have a Forge, for example:

$$C_m(Goal_{Scissors}) = C_m(Money) * C_m(Scissors) \qquad (8.3.3)$$
$$= 15$$
$$C_t(Goal_{Scissors}) = C_t(Money) * C_m(Scissors) + C_t(Scissors)$$
$$= 3 + 1$$
$$= 4$$

Multitasking

When multiple tasks are desirable, they will not always be mutually exclusive. Because of this, we can perform multiple tasks simultaneously, or *multitask*. We must identify which inputs to a given task are allocated for but not consumed by the task; these are the inputs that are potential roadblocks to multitasking. For example, in most RTS games, a Building can only perform one task at a time; therefore, it is a nonconsumable resource, and any tasks that require a given Building as an input cannot be performed simultaneously—unless multiple instances of that Building are available.

Putting It All Together

Now that we have all of the concepts, how do they fit together?

1. Identify a goal, or set of goals. These are identified external to the model, probably by the designer. Examples of goals include "15 Scissors," "10 Scissors and 5 Rocks," and "5 each of Rocks, Paper, and Scissors."
2. Identify the subgoals. Within the economic domain, these are generated from the tech tree and will represent each of the possible tasks that can be chained together to form a task-sequence that satisfies a goal or subgoal.
3. Generate a task-sequence that can satisfy each goal. If our goal is "15 Scissors," then we would generate 15 task-sequences that each link to a goal of

"1 Scissors." Depending on the implementation, it might be more optimal to generate a single task-sequence that links to each of the 15 Scissors goals.

4. Identify the utility of each goal and subgoal. Like economic utility, this is an arbitrary value that is useful in a relative sense. Begin by giving each goal and subgoal the same utility value; 1 is a good value to start with.

5. Propagate the utility of each goal backward through its task-sequence by summing the utility values. In our "1 Scissors" example, the utility of a Forge would become 2; 1 for the utility of the goal "1 Scissors" plus 1 for the utility of the Forge itself. An item's utility, therefore, is proportional to the number of goals that it can help satisfy.

6. Normalize the utility of each subgoal. We will be looking at all of the subgoals to determine which ones we want to execute, so we need to be able to compare them to each other; normalization facilitates this comparison. The normalizing factor should be the current cost of the subgoal. Obviously, this will change as task-sequences are executed and the cost of their resultant subgoals becomes 0.

7. Identify the subgoal with the highest normalized utility. For ties, choose the subgoal with the smallest time cost, so that any inputs tied up by the task-sequence will be released sooner.

8. Determine if that subgoal's task-sequence can be scheduled. If it requires the use of an input that is not available—for example, you don't have the required Money, or the required Building is already scheduled for something else—then flag this task-sequence as unavailable for this round of processing; otherwise, schedule it.

9. Repeat steps 7 and 8 until all of the available subgoals are scheduled, or until you can no longer schedule any subgoals due to the unavailability of inputs (or until the processing time allocated to this module expires). Be sure to mark all of the subgoals available again before your next round of processing.

10. As changes in the game universe are detected, create new goals that react to those changes, and introduce the goals into the planning system. The effectiveness of your reactivity is directly dependent upon how you choose to create these new goals. An exploration of options for this implementation is beyond the scope of this article; however, a secondary Utility Model for generating these goals might be feasible by using game states as your inputs and goals as your outputs.

11. As task-sequences complete, prune their resultant goals and subgoals from the planning tree. Be sure to propagate the resultant changes in time and money costs, as well as the changes in normalized MU.

The Combat Domain

The combat domain can be modeled by a Utility Model that is chained to the economic Utility Model. The outputs of the economic model—units—become the inputs to the combat model. By generating combat goals and task-sequences that will satisfy those goals, you create a need for inputs. The need for those inputs can generate goals in the economic model.

For example, suppose that your combat goal is to defeat the player's army of Papers. The utility of combat objects (units) would be tied to their combat stats; units that compare favorably to Papers in combat (Scissors) would have a higher utility than those that compare poorly (Rocks). To achieve your goal most efficiently, you would try to schedule task-sequences that involve Scissors. These Scissors subgoals can't be achieved, however, unless you have Scissors available; but you can, in turn, generate high-level goals within your economic domain to create the Scissors you need for combat. In this way, your economic domain becomes a factory that generates the products for your combat domain to consume.

Suggestions

The following are additional suggestions that will help you exploit and refine the Utility Model in your game.

Suggestion #1: Designer-Friendly Interface

The Utility Model is data driven. As such, it allows designers to easily modify the behavior of the agent through simple data entry. To facilitate this process, implement a clean, simple interface that presents the data as human-understandable goals instead of an arcane group of numbers. In addition, allow the game to dynamically access this data at runtime so that external goals can be tweaked on-the-fly. Doing this well and early in the production cycle will encourage the designer to use the system more, and can allow the designer to detect and correct flaws in the balance of the game.

Suggestion #2: Automated Gameplay

Allow an agent to play against another agent without a human player in the game. Combined with a designer-friendly interface, this feature really puts the designer on the fast track to stress-testing his design (and your implementation).

Suggestion #3: Utility-Friendly Tech Tree

Choose an implementation for your tech tree that works directly with the Utility Model. If the MU updates can be performed directly on the tech tree itself, it will save a lot of time and memory.

Suggestion #4: Utility-Friendly Pathfinding

When implementing your pathfinding system, allow for your node weighting to accept a dynamic utility heuristic that works in conjunction with your cost heuristic. Such a system can allow you to chain pathfinding subgoals so that, for example, you can take full advantage of changes in terrain desirability, you can stage attacks from multiple locations, and you can create complex pathfinding plans that require multiple steps.

Conclusion

When modeling a game-playing agent, we want a framework that provides efficient solutions to the problems presented by an unpredictable game universe. By mapping an Economic domain onto our game universe, we can utilize a Utility Model to provide a robust, reactive, and efficient framework for making choices.

References

[Albrecht86] Albrecht, William P, *Economics, 4th Edition*, Prentice-Hall, 1986.
[Rich91] Rich, Elaine, and Knight, Kevin, *Artificial Intelligence, Second Edition*, McGraw-Hill, 1991.

The Basics of Ranged Weapon Combat

Paul Tozour—Ion Storm Austin

gehn29@yahoo.com

Our industry maintains the dubious distinction of being the only popular entertainment medium that uses its audience for target practice. Games are the John Wilkes Booth of entertainment media.

Nevertheless, if you absolutely must attempt manslaughter against your own customers—and heaven forbid we should try to dissuade you from such an endlessly fascinating gameplay paradigm!—then you might as well make sure your hostility leaves your victims suitably entertained.

This article introduces a few basic concepts with ranged weapon AI. These topics aren't overwhelmingly challenging, but they merit some type of introduction in light of the huge number of games that feature guns and other ranged weapons.

The To-Hit Roll

Obviously, we don't want our AI opponents to be perfectly accurate. For the sake of believability, game balancing, and character differentiation, we almost always want our AIs to have less-than-perfect aim. This is easily done with a to-hit roll. We calculate a value to represent our chance to hit and generate a random number. If the number is above the to-hit value, we execute the code path that makes the AI try to miss its opponent. Otherwise, the AI attempts to hit.

The trick is determining which factors should be taken into account when calculating the to-hit roll. Some typical factors include:

- **AI skill**: This is a variable that represents the AI entity's innate skill with ranged weapons. This is typically very low for most AIs at the beginning of the game, and grows gradually higher as the game progresses.
- **Range**: A longer distance to the enemy should lower an AI's chance to hit.
- **Size**: Larger opponents are easier to hit, and smaller opponents are more difficult to hit.
- **Relative target velocity**: It's hard to hit a moving target, and it's hard to hit a stationary target when you're moving. If you subtract the AI's velocity vector from its target's velocity, you get a vector that represents the relative velocity of the two

combatants. We can also learn a lot from the angle of this vector relative to the direction the AI is facing. Lateral (side-to-side) motion makes it more difficult to hit than if the characters are moving forward or backward relative to one another.

- **Visibility and coverage**: A target partly obscured by fog or half hidden behind a barrel should be more difficult to hit than a target that's fully visible.
- **Target state**: Many games support player actions such as crouching and jumping. A behavior such as crouching, for example, is typically a defensive measure, and a crouching target should be more difficult to hit.
- **AI state**: Some games model AIs' initial startled reactions and their increasing focus over time by initially penalizing their chance to hit and gradually eliminating this penalty over time. This has some nice side effects in that it gives the player a certain amount of time to eliminate each attacker before that opponent becomes truly dangerous, and this quickens the pace of the gameplay by encouraging the player to finish off his enemies more quickly.

Each of these factors can be translated into a floating-point value between 0 and 1. A value of 0 indicates that the modifier makes it completely impossible for the AI to hit its opponent—for example, the target is too far away to hit. A value of 1 indicates that the modifier does not lower the AI's chance to hit—for example, the target is directly in front of the AI that is attempting to fire at it. Any value in between represents a specific chance to hit (for example, 0.5 when the target is a certain distance from us).

To compute the to-hit roll, we begin with a value of 1, indicating a 100-percent chance to hit. We multiply this by the modifiers we calculate for the factors previously listed. It makes intuitive sense to use multiplication here, because if any factor is 0, that factor should make it impossible to hit, and if any factor is very small, it should likewise make the final chance to hit very small. Also, note that this computation can occur in any order.

As a side benefit, if any of the modifier values is 0, we can immediately terminate the calculation, since the final result must also be zero. This is a useful optimization that can save a lot of work if any of our to-hit modifier calculations are computationally expensive. For this reason, it often makes sense to evaluate the multipliers that are more likely to be zero nearer to the beginning of the computation, so that we increase the chance that we'll be able to terminate the calculations at an earlier point.

Some readers might notice that this calculation has some interesting parallels with probability theory. In fact, we could end up with exactly the same calculation if we modeled this calculation as a simple belief network [Tozour02]. In this case, we can describe each of the previously listed factors as a "cause" of our belief in whether we should hit. In other words, all of the factors point to a single "should hit" belief node that indicates the degree to which the AI should believe that it is supposed to successfully hit the target. We can then use this number directly to determine the threshold for the to-hit roll. The input matrix for the "successful hit" node indicates that we should only hit if *all* of the factors are 1.

Selecting an Aim Point

Whenever an AI attempts to fire at its target, it needs to select a specific point in space to aim at. It's not enough to simply pull the trigger and let the rocket fly, as our weapon won't necessarily be aimed in quite the right direction, and we don't want the weapon's angle to dictate where we must shoot. Forcing the weapon to be perfectly aligned with the line-of-fire would also be unnecessary, since human players in the heat of combat never notice the slight discrepancies between the angle of the gun and the angle of the shot. A good policy is to determine a maximum "cheat angle" that a projectile's trajectory can differ from its gun barrel, and make sure that we never fire if the cheat angle of the resulting shot would be greater than this limit.

When an AI needs to hit its target, it's relatively simple to calculate an aim point. If the target object's physical collision model is a hierarchical data structure, such as a hierarchy of oriented bounding boxes, the AI can simply traverse this hierarchy to calculate a good point to aim at. Pick a random collision volume somewhere deep in the hierarchy, and aim at the center of that volume. In games that support different types of damage for different body parts, this is also a good way to locate a specific body part.

How to Shoot and Miss

Hitting is easy; missing without looking stupid is hard. When we want to miss, we need to locate a coordinate somewhere outside the target's body, such that hitting that point is very unlikely to hit the target. In other words, the point needs to be outside the target *from the shooter's perspective*. In addition, we need to be sure that the point is at the right distance from the target. If we pull the point too close, we run the risk of hitting the target we're trying to miss. Make it too far away, and the AI looks like an idiot.

When shooting to miss, it's usually best to place the shot somewhere inside the target's field of view so the shot is visible. Bullets that pass right in front of the player's face can obviously trigger a visceral response. Thus, it's often a good idea to figure out which way the target is facing, and bias the selection of the aim point in that direction.

In some games, the geometric meshes of the game objects themselves contain these aim points. Artists place invisible bones or other spatial markers in the object's mesh at the positions where AIs should aim when they don't want to actually hit the object. This is a good way to get shots that go right past the player's eyes.

In many cases, it's a bad idea to burden the artists with this type of responsibility; we can just as easily discover a solution at runtime. If we can assume that the target is bounded by a vertically oriented cylinder, we can easily find the two vertical lines along the left and right edges of the cylinder, as seen from the AI's point of view.

We start by calculating the delta vector from the center of the target to the point on the AI's weapon where it will fire the projectile—just subtract the two coordinates to obtain the delta vector. We then zero out this vector's vertical component, normalize it, multiply it by the size of the object's collision radius, and rotate it 90 degrees left or right so that it faces to either side of the target object, as seen from the AI's point of view. We can now determine the world-space values that represent the top and bottom of the target's collision cylinder, and use this to determine the beginning and end of the lines.

At this point, all we need to do is randomly pick a point somewhere on either of the two lines to find a candidate for an aim point that will miss the target. This is as simple as picking a random height value somewhere between the top and bottom of the cylinder.

Ray-Testing

Regardless how we decide to select an aim point, and regardless of whether we decide to hit or miss, it's important to test the projectile's trajectory before we pull the trigger. In the chaos of battle, the line-of-fire will quite often be blocked—by the terrain, by a wall, by an inanimate object, by another enemy, or by one of our allies.

Every game engine provides some sort of ray-testing function that allows you to trace a ray through the world. You input a world-space coordinate for the origin, plus a vector to indicate the direction to trace from the origin, and the function will give you a pointer to the first object the ray intersects, or NULL if it doesn't intersect anything.

It's a good idea to iteratively test some number of potential aim points using this ray-testing function. Keep testing up to perhaps a half-dozen points at random until you find one that works. This way, the AI will still be able to hit its target even if it's partly hidden behind an obstacle. It's also important to extend the length of the ray as far as the projectile will actually travel to ensure that your AI can accurately assess the results.

Avoiding Friendly Fire

It's particularly important to avoid friendly fire incidents. Even in many modern games, AI opponents on the same side completely ignore one another in combat. Many gamers have experienced watching AIs at the far of the room unintentionally mow down their buddies in the front ranks.

Granted, in some cases, this might be the behavior you want, but it's better to take the approach of making AIs too competent to begin with, and then dumbing them down as needed. In any case, we have yet to hear any computer game character verbally acknowledge the fact that he just knocked off his comrade with a 12-gauge shotgun.

Ray-testing calculations can also greatly assist AI maneuvering and tactics in combat. When an AI discovers that one of its attempted lines-of-fire intersects a stationary friendly unit or a wall, that's a good indication that it's in a bad spot and should pick a new point to move to if it's not already moving somewhere. Alternatively, it might send a request to the AI blocking its line-of-fire, and the two could use an arbitrary priority scheme to make their negotiations and determine which of the two should step aside.

Table 8.4.1 gives an example of some reasonable responses to the feedback we can receive from the engine's ray-testing function. The rows represent what we're trying to do—either hit or miss—and the columns represent the four categories of feedback we can receive from the engine.

Table 8.4.1 Responses to Feedback from a Ray Test

	Hits Nothing	Hits Wall, Terrain, Object	Hits Ally	Hits an Enemy
try to HIT	Retry	Retry, consider moving if the shot doesn't travel past the target	Retry, consider moving	Fire
try to Miss	Fire	Fire if shot travels at least as far as the target; else, retry	Retry, consider moving	Retry

If this still isn't sufficient to keep your AIs from killing one another, you can always take the easy route and modify the simulation so that AI characters never accept damage from other friendly AIs.

Dead Reckoning

In many cases, though, a ray test isn't enough to get a good sense of what might happen when our projectiles hit. Particularly when you combine slow-moving projectiles (arrows, rockets) with fast-moving and highly maneuverable entities in the game world, you make it possible for the player and other game entities to dodge the projectiles. At this point, even the most accurate calculations can't guarantee that you'll hit or miss as intended, since you can't fully predict what a human player will do.

However, there are many additional measures we can take to improve our accuracy. The first is a simple estimation technique known as *dead reckoning*. Multiply an entity's velocity vector by the time you expect it to take for the projectile to reach the object's current position, and you'll get a good guess as to the entity's future position.

For example, imagine a target is 150 meters away from you and you fire a bullet that moves at 50 meters per second. The target is moving northeast at one meter per second. It will take the bullet three seconds to move 150 meters. In that time, he'll have fled three meters northeast, so we should aim at this new point instead of the target's current location. Note that this assumes that the projectile always travels significantly faster than the target; if this is not the case, this form of dead reckoning won't be accurate.

Radius Testing

Another good way to make our gunplay more cautious is to use exaggerated bounding spheres or cylinders. Imagine that our friend Benny, a guard, is standing in the distance, sword fighting with an intruder. If we know that Benny can move at a maximum velocity of one-half meter per second and our arrow will take two seconds to reach the intruder, we can exaggerate Benny's collision cylinder by one meter. If the line-of-fire to any aim point we select intersects that larger collision cylinder, we can assert that there's a possibility the arrow could end up hitting Benny instead of the one-eyed scoundrel with whom he's fencing. The deeper the line penetrates inside this collision cylinder, the higher the probability that it will also intersect with Benny.

This type of testing is very useful for area effect weapons. When we toss a grenade, for example, it's very important to test the spherical area that the grenade will ultimately incinerate against the exaggerated bounding volumes of the various entities in the area to ensure that the AI is unlikely to blow up any of his comrades when he throws the grenade. We use the time it will take for the grenade to explode to determine how much to exaggerate the entities' bounding volumes.

Collision Notifications

It's good practice to receive notifications from the projectile itself indicating what it actually hit. Although a good AI will ideally avoid hitting allies or inanimate objects, the game world is always changing, the player isn't totally predictable, and our calculations aren't always correct. Whenever a projectile is launched, it should store a pointer to the object that launched it, and notify that object whenever it collides with an object. This notification will then bubble up to the object's AI controller (if it has one) so that the AI can display an appropriate response, such as not shooting up the sofa any more.

In a dynamic world, it's very difficult to ensure a hit or a miss without cheating. Projectile collision notifications can also allow us to tweak our to-hit calculations more accurately by compensating for errors. For example, if we attempt to miss the target but end up hitting it instead, we can compensate for this natural error by changing the next shot designated as a "hit" to a "miss."

Weapon Trajectories

Weapons that fire in a curved trajectory, such as arrows, can be surprisingly tricky to handle. Any physics textbook will give us the following equations for a projectile's trajectory in the absence of friction:

$$x = x_0 + v_x t \tag{8.4.1}$$

$$y = y_0 + v_y t + \tfrac{1}{2}g t^2 \tag{8.4.2}$$

In these equations, x_0 and y_0 represent the projectile's initial position, respectively; v_x and v_y are horizontal and vertical components of the projectile's initial velocity; t is the time; and g is the gravitational acceleration constant—typically -9.8m/s^2 on earth, although your game world might use a different constant.

These equations give us an easy way to adapt our ray-testing techniques to the projectile's arc of flight to help make sure we won't end up firing into a chandelier. We can use line segments to represent the curve with a reasonable degree of accuracy—five or six will typically be good enough. We can obtain the endpoints of the line segments by plugging in various values for *t* at various fractions of the way through the trajectory.

However, the really tricky question is how to shoot the projectile so it will land where we want it to. Given a desired x and y, the gravitational acceleration constant (g), and the scalar magnitude of the muzzle velocity (v), we want to find the best angle to fire the projectile.

Hitting the Right Spot

Most AI systems approach the targeting problem iteratively; that is, they solve for the case in which the target is at the same height as the shooter (y = 0), and then iteratively guess at different angles until they find an angle that seems most likely to hit the target at its actual height.

However, there are solutions that don't require you to iterate. Equation 8.4.3 (from [Nicholls01]) shows how to determine the angle to hit a destination point (*x,y*) given *v*, *x*, *y*, and *g*.

$$\theta = \tan^{-1}\left[v^2\left[\frac{-x \pm \sqrt{x^2 - \dfrac{g^2 x^4}{v^4} + \dfrac{2gx^2 y}{v^2}}}{gx^2}\right]\right] \tag{8.4.3}$$

If the quantity within the square root in Equation 8.4.3 is negative, there is no solution, and the projectile cannot hit the target. If it's zero, there is exactly one solution. If it's positive, there are two possible solutions, following the "±" symbol in the equation. In this case, we're given extra flexibility so that, for example, a grenadier could select the higher trajectory if the lower trajectory happened to be blocked by an obstacle.

Technically, of course, this solution is still iterative, because taking the square root is an iterative process, but this equation at least hides the iterations within the equation itself, so your code need not require any *for*-loops.

In some cases, such as with a bow and arrow, we have control over the initial velocity as well as the angle. Equation 8.4.4 (also from [Nicholls01]) allows us to determine the initial velocity required to hit (*x,y*) given θ and *g*. It then becomes trivial to iteratively test some number of candidate angles with this equation and pick the initial velocity that's closest to a desired velocity.

$$v = \frac{x}{\cos\theta}\sqrt{\frac{g}{2(x\tan\theta - y)}} \tag{8.4.4}$$

Guided Missiles

In the case of weapons that automatically track their targets, such as heat-seeking missiles, the to-hit determination becomes trivial. The AI firing the weapon typically needs only to test a straight-line path between itself and the target to ensure that its line-of-fire is not completely blocked. It can also disable or impair the missile's tracking to force a miss if its to-hit roll determines that the shot should miss the target.

References and Additional Reading

[Nicholls01] Nicholls, Aaron, "Inverse Trajectory Determination," *Game Programming Gems 2*, Ed. Mark DeLoura, Charles River Media, 2002.

[Tozour02] Tozour, Paul, "Introduction to Bayesian Networks and Reasoning Under Uncertainty," *AI Game Programming Wisdom*, Ed. Steve Rabin, Charles River Media, 2002.

8.5

Level-Of-Detail AI for a Large Role-Playing Game

Mark Brockington—BioWare Corp.

markb@bioware.com

The initial design document for BioWare's multiplayer title, *Neverwinter Nights* (*NWN*), called for adventures that spanned a series of *areas* similar in size to those in our previous single-player role-playing games (the *Baldur's Gate* series). Each area within an adventure is a contiguous region of space that is linked to other areas via area transitions. The interior of a house, a patch of forest, or a level of a dungeon would each be represented as a single area.

We found that we had to limit the number of resources taken up by the game and AI by limiting the engine to one *master area group* in *Baldur's Gate*. A master area group was a subset of all of the areas within the adventure. A master area group usually consisted of an exterior area and all of the interiors of the buildings within that exterior area. When a player character (*PC*) reached an area transition that would transfer it to a different master area group, all users heard "You must gather your party before venturing forth." This was a major headache during a multi-player game unless you were operating as a well-behaved party that traveled as a group. It regularly appears on our message boards as one of our most hated features.

A major design goal for *NWN* was that it must be a fun multi-player role-playing game. Thus, it was evident that restricting players' movement by the methods we used in *Baldur's Gate* would be impossible. After a brief discussion or two, we decided that we would have all of the areas within a given adventure active and in memory at all times, and reduce the size of our adventures so that they were a bit smaller in scope.

However, this posed a problem for the AI programmer. Depending on the number of areas, and the number of autonomous agents (or *creatures*) within each area, we would have thousands of agents operating within the game world. Each of these creatures could make high CPU demands on the AI engine (such as movement or combat) at the same time. Everything in the world could come to a grinding halt as the AI worked its way through thousands of requests.

Graphics engines face a similar problem when they must render a large number of objects on the screen. Since every graphics chip has a limit to the number of triangles that it can render each frame, one solution is to draw the same number of objects, but with some of them containing fewer triangles. Depending on the scene complexity, each object can be rendered with an appropriate level-of-detail. Thus, this level-of-detail algorithm can control and adjust the number of triangles drawn each frame while still managing to draw every object.

If it works in graphics, why not for our artificial intelligence needs? We are going to illustrate the level-of-detail AI system that we implemented in *Neverwinter Nights*. We start by translating the level-of-detail concept to AI. Then, we describe how one can classify agents by the level-of-detail they require. Finally, we show how actions with high resource usage can be limited.

Level-Of-Detail from the AI Perspective

The advantages of storing 3D objects at different resolutions or levels-of-detail was first discussed 25 years ago [Clark76]. An object that is onscreen and close to the camera might require hundreds or thousands of polygons to be rendered at sufficient quality. However, if the object is distant from the camera, you might only need a simplified version of the model with only a handful of polygons to give an approximate view of what the object looks like. Figure 8.5.1 shows an example [Luebke98] of how 3D graphics might simplify a 10,000-polygon lamp into something barely resembling a lamp with 48 polygons. In Figure 8.5.2, we see an example of how to use these lower-polygon models to render four lamps, using fewer polygons than if we only had the single high-polygon lamp.

FIGURE 8.5.1   *Lamps of varying levels-of-detail, viewed from the same distance. (© 2002, David Luebke. Reprinted with permission.)*

FIGURE 8.5.2   *Lamps of varying levels-of-detail, viewed at different distances. (© 2002, David Luebke. Reprinted with permission.)*

How does this translate to artificial intelligence? If we view artificial intelligence as creating the illusion of intelligence, the goal of the game AI would be to make the objects that the player (or players) can see exhibit smart behaviors. We want to perform more precise AI algorithms and techniques on them to enhance the illusion of intelligence.

The converse is also true. If an object is off screen, or is so distant that it is difficult to analyze its behavior, does it really matter whether the object is doing some clever AI? We could save CPU time by using approximations of smart behaviors on objects that no player can see.

Level-Of-Detail Classifications

What can each player see? In *NWN*, the *player character* (*PC*) is centered in the middle of the screen. The camera can be freely rotated around the PC. To control the number of objects on screen, we limited the pitch of the camera so that one could see at most 50 meters around the character at any one time.

There are secondary factors to consider when classifying objects. Your best algorithms should go into controlling player characters, since they are always on screen. If players do notice intelligent behavior on other creatures, the players will be looking for it more closely on creatures that are interacting with their PC (either in combat or in conversation). Finally, if a creature is in an area in which there is no player to see it, a further relaxation of the AI is possible.

In *NWN*, there are five different classifications for an object's level-of-detail, as shown in Table 8.5.1 going from highest to lowest priority.

Table 8.5.1 LOD Levels in *Neverwinter Nights*

LOD	Classification
1	Player Characters (PCs) (your party)
2	Creatures fighting or interacting with a PC
3	Creatures within 50 meters of a PC
4	Creatures in the same large-scale area of a PC
5	Creatures in areas without a PC.

In Figure 8.5.3, we see a number of objets within two separate areas. Each large square in Figure 8.5.3 represents a different area. There are three players in the game, each controlling a single PC. PCs are represented by a small circle, with a large circle indicating the area that can be seen by the player. Creatures are represented with a small square. Both PCs and creature symbols contain their current LOD.

PCs are always LOD 1, so each small circle contains a 1. Creatures fighting or interacting with PCs contain the number 2. Creatures in the proximity of PCs contain the number 3. Creatures that are not within a 50-meter radius of any player

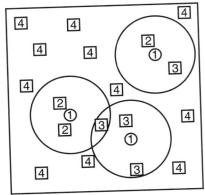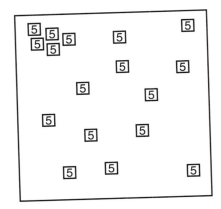

FIGURE 8.5.3   *The five classifications of level-of-detail in* NWN.

contain the number 4. Meanwhile, all of the creatures in the second area contain the number 5, to represent that they are at the lowest level-of-detail classification.

Each of these levels is easy to detect via mechanics that are already set up within the game engine. For example, each creature (not just the PCs) attempts to do a visibility check to all creatures within 50 meters of itself, and it is straightforward to determine if any of those nearby creatures are PCs. Each area has a scripting event that runs when a PC moves out of an area and/or into another area (whether it is by connecting to the game, performing an area transition, or disconnecting from the game). Thus, determining and maintaining which areas have PCs in them is easy. All attack actions go through a single function. This is beneficial, as it means there is only one spot to check if the creature is attacking a PC and, hence, promoting the attacking creature to the second highest level of priority.

Using the Level-Of-Detail Classification

There are five level-of-detail (LOD) classifications that determine update frequency of a creature.

Which Creature Gets the Next Time Slice?

The perceived intelligence of a creature is strongly correlated to its reaction time in specific situations. For example, a creature that takes too long to chase after a fleeing PC does not seem as intelligent as a creature that immediately follows the PC as it runs away. Thus, the five LOD classifications should determine the update frequency in order to maintain the required level of interactivity or intelligence.

In *NWN*, each of the creatures is placed on one of the five lists. After we have categorized all AI objects on to one of the five lists, a function then determines who gets the next time slice. In *NWN*, we found that the percentages in Table 8.5.2 work well.

Table 8.5.2 Percentage of CPU Time for Each Level-of-Detail

CPU Time	Level-of-Detail
60%	LOD 1: Player Characters
24%	LOD 2: Creatures interacting with PCs
10%	LOD 3: Creatures in proximity of PCs
4%	LOD 4: Creature in an area with a PC
2%	LOD 5: Creatures not in an area with a PC

When an LOD list is allowed to execute, the first creature waiting on that list's AI queue is processed. Each creature from that list is processed one at a time until the list's time slice runs out. Each list is not allowed to steal time from the processing of the lower-priority lists. This guarantees that at least one creature from each list is allowed to run an AI update, and prevents starvation of the lowest-priority list.

How Pathfinding Is Affected by Level-Of-Detail

Many AI actions can use up CPU cycles. One of the most time-consuming actions that one can perform is pathfinding over a complicated terrain. Thus, a pathfinding algorithm is a logical place to start implementing a level-of-detail algorithm.

Based on the structure of the AI, we decided not to store the pathfinding progress in the game world data structure. Instead, each creature keeps its own instance of how the pathfinding algorithm is progressing. However, using an A* approach in this manner would be extremely expensive; we could have dozens of agents attempting to perform pathfinding on the same area at the same time, with each pathfinding search requiring a large amount of RAM. In *NWN*, we actually used IDA* and other computer chess techniques to save on the resources used [Brockington00].

The terrain is composed of 10-by-10 meter tiles, each of which has information indicating how it interconnects between other tiles. With this coarse-grained system (*inter-tile pathfinding*), one can easily generate a series of tiles that one must travel through to reach the final destination. We generate our full path by using *intra-tile pathfinding* over the 3D geometry on each tile specified by our inter-tile path.

How can one take advantage of this structure with the level-of-detail algorithm? Creatures that are on screen are always required to do both an inter-tile path and an intra-tile path to make paths look smooth and natural. Any creature at LOD 1 through 3 in our hierarchy implements the full pathfinding algorithm. However, it is important to note that the difference in CPU time allocated to creatures at LOD 1 versus creatures at LOD 3 is significant. For example, in our urban areas, each PC can usually see eight other non-player characters standing on guard, selling goods, or wandering the streets. Based on the time percentages given earlier, a PC could compute a complex path 48 times faster than a creature near a PC.

What about LOD 4 creatures? We only bother to compute their paths via the inter-tile method, and then spend the time jumping each creature from tile to tile at the speed that they would have walked between each tile. The intra-tile pathfinding is where we spend over 90 percent of our time in the pathfinding algorithm, so avoiding this step is a major optimization. Even if we had not used this approach, the amount of time we actually devote to each LOD 4 creature is quite small, and the creatures would seem to be "popping" over large steps anyway!

For LOD 5 creatures, we do not even bother with the inter-tile path, and simply generate a delay commensurate with the length of the path (as the crow flies), and jump the creature to its final location.

What happens if a creature has its priority level increased? Well, in this case, the path must continue to be resolved at the intra-tile level (in the case of a LOD 4 creature moving to LOD 3 or above), or at the inter-tile level (in the case of a LOD 5 creature moving to LOD 4).

How Random Walks Are Affected by Level-Of-Detail

Random walking is another action that BioWare designers have used regularly on creatures in earlier titles. In short, the action takes the creature's current location, and attempts to have the creature move to a random location within a given radius of its current location.

The advantages of level-of-detail are clearer for random walks. In the case of LOD 1 or 2 creatures, we use the full pathfinding algorithm again. For LOD 3 creatures, we only walk the person in a straight line from his current location to a final location. This is accomplished by testing to see if the path is clear before handing the destination to the full pathfinding algorithm. Creatures at LOD 4 and 5 do not move based on random walk actions, because there is no point in executing the action until a PC is there to see them move.

How Combat Could Be Affected by Level-Of-Detail

In *NWN*, we use the highly complex *Advanced Dungeons and Dragons* rule set to determine the results of a combat. The base combat rules fill 10 pages of text, and there are over 50 pages of exceptions to the base rules specified in the *Player's Handbook* alone.

To work out the result of a combat in real time is a technically challenging task; one that could be optimized in our current system. At LOD 1 and 2, we have to implement the full rule system, since the results of these combats are actually shown to a PC. At LOD 3 or below, a PC is not privy to the rolls made during a combat. If there are things that are too complicated to compute in a reasonable amount of time, one does not need to compute them at this level or below. However, LOD 3 creatures must be seen to be performing what looks like the actual rules.

At LOD 4 or 5, one does not even need to use the rules; no one can see the fight, so the only thing that matters is that the end result is relatively close to what would happen in practice. Rules can be simplified by analyzing the damage capabilities of each creature, multiplying this by the number of attacks, and then randomly applying that damage at the beginning of each round based on the likelihood of each attack succeeding. At LOD 5, one could automatically resolve combat based on a biased coin flip instead of spending the time to actually compute which character is stronger. The differences in the challenge ratings of each creature could be used to bias the coin flip.

Conclusion

In this article, we described a system for implementing AI in a role-playing game with thousands of agents. We also showed a hierarchy for classifying objects into levels-of-detail, and how to use this classification to determine which algorithm to use for some resource-intensive actions. Areas that you can exploit based on level-of-detail include:

- Processing frequency.
- Pathfinding detail, especially if you employ hierarchical searching.
- Pathfinding cheating.
- Combat rules and detail.

The actions and classification that we presented focused on discrete levels-of-detail. However, most graphics research focuses on various methods of doing continuous level-of-detail, such as progressive meshes [Hoppe96]. A couple of approaches for continuous LOD were considered for *NWN*. We experimented with varying the size and depth of the pathfinding search based on a continuous LOD measure (such as the distance to the nearest player), but our results were unsatisfactory in comparison to the discrete LOD system described in this article. We also experimented with a continuous LOD system for smoother interpolation of processing frequency, and failed to provide any additional benefit over and above what we saw with our discrete LOD system. We hope that your experiments are more successful.

References

[Brockington00] Brockington, Mark, "Pawn Captures Wyvern: How Computer Chess Can Improve Your Pathfinding," *Game Developers Conference 2000 Proceedings*, pp. 119–139, 2000.

[Clark76] Clark, James, "Hierarchical Geometric Models for Visible Surface Algorithms," *Communications of the ACM*, Vol. 19, No 10, pp. 547–554. 1976.

[Hoppe96] Hoppe, Hugues, "Progressive Meshes," *Computer Graphics*, Vol. 30 (SIGGRAPH 96), pp. 99–108, 1996.

[Luebke98] Luebke, David, Ph.D. Thesis, "View-Dependent Simplification of Arbitrary Polygonal Environments," UNC Department of Computer Science Technical Report #TR98-029, 1998.

8.6

A Dynamic Reputation System Based on Event Knowledge

Greg Alt—Surreal Software

Kristin King

galt@eskimo.com, kaking@eskimo.com

If you're developing a game with large numbers of non-player characters (NPCs), you'll face the Herculean task of bringing the NPCs to life. A good reputation system dynamically manages NPCs' opinions of the player, so they seem responsive to the player's actions. For example, in *Ultima Online's* reputation system [Grond98], killing an NPC changes your karma and fame, which influences other NPCs' opinions of you. However, it has a global effect—all affected NPCs instantly change their opinion of you, whether or not they witnessed the event. Games in which an action has a global effect make it seem as though all the NPCs have ESP. No matter what you do, you can't outrun your reputation or hide your actions.

This article describes a reputation system used in a single-player action-adventure game that solves the ESP problem by tying changes in opinion to direct or indirect knowledge of the action, at the same time minimizing memory usage and CPU time. NPCs change their opinion of a player only if they saw or were told of the event. In this way, the system propagates the player's reputation to other members in a group across the game world, but the player can influence that propagation by eliminating witnesses or staying ahead of his reputation. This results in much more complex, immersive gameplay.

Reputation System Data Structures

The main data structures are the Event Template, the Reputation Event, the Master Event List, the Per-NPC Long-Term Memory, and the Per-NPC Reputation Table.

The reputation system triggers a *Reputation Event* whenever the player performs an action that might change the player's reputation, either positively or negatively. The Reputation Event contains the basic information about the action: who performed the action, what they did, and who they did it to. It also contains reputation effect information, about how NPCs from different groups will change their opinions of the player. The event is based on a static *Event Template* (a template created by the game designer), and uses dynamically generated information to fill in the gaps.

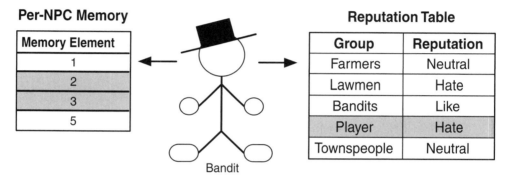

Master Event List
1. Bandit Killed Farmer
2. Player Aided Lawman
3. Player Killed Bandit
4. Player TradedWith Townsperson
5. [...]

Per-NPC Memory

Memory Element
1
2
3
5

Bandit

Reputation Table

Group	Reputation
Farmers	Neutral
Lawmen	Hate
Bandits	Like
Player	Hate
Townspeople	Neutral

FIGURE 8.6.1 *The NPC hates the player because he found out the player killed another bandit and aided an enemy (Reputation Events #2 and #3).*

Figure 8.6.1 shows how the NPCs use the Reputation Event.

When the Reputation Event is created, the reputation system adds it to a compact central record, called the Master Event List, and an event announcer notifies all witness NPCs of the event. The *Master Event List* contains all important actions that have been witnessed by NPCs, stored as a list of Reputation Events.

Each NPC has a *Long-Term Memory*, which is a list of all its references to any events in the Master Event List that the NPC directly witnessed or indirectly heard about.

Each NPC stores its opinion of the player in a *Reputation Table*. The Reputation Table is a list of groups, including a group for the player, and the NPC's current opinion of members of each group. Whenever an NPC becomes aware of a Reputation Event, the reputation effect of the event is applied to the NPC's Reputation Table, updating its current opinion of the player. The opinions an NPC has of other NPC groups are also stored in the Reputation Table, but in this implementation, they do not change.

In addition to these data structures, the system requires a means for designers to specify templates for different Reputation Events and associate them with the NPCs that will spawn them. It also requires that each NPC and the player have an associated group, and that each NPC in the game has a unique ID that can be stored compactly.

The following sections describe the Event Template, Reputation Event, Master Event List, and Long-Term Memory in more detail.

Event Template

The Event Templates are static data structures that store information about every possible event in the game. They store the verb (for example, DidViolenceTo), the magnitude (for example, a magnitude of 75 for a DidViolenceTo event means Killed, while 10 might mean PointedGunAt), and the reputation effects of the event. The *reputation effects* indicate how NPCs in specified groups should react to the information. For example, if the player killed a bandit, bandits should take the information badly and farmers should be overjoyed. The Event Template does not store the subject group, object group, or object individual, because this information is dynamically created during gameplay.

Reputation Event

Table 8.6.1 shows the Reputation Event, the basic building block of the reputation system.

Table 8.6.1 Example of a Reputation Event

Subject Group	Player
Verb	DidViolenceTo
Object Group	Bandit
Object Individual	Joe
Magnitude	75 (Killed)
Where	50, 20, 138 (In front of saloon)
When	High noon
Template	KilledBanditTemplate
Reference Count	Known by 11 NPCs
Reputation Effects	Bandits hate player more
	Lawmen like player more
	Farmers like player more

The Reputation Event is an instance of the class AIEvent. The class AIEvent contains the following:

- A compact event ID (an instance of the class EventID) that contains the group to which the subject belongs, the verb, the group to which the object belongs, and an object individual ID for the object. Each NPC must have a unique object individual ID across all the levels of the game, to prevent NPCs making incorrect assumptions about who did what to whom.

- The position where the event happened.
- The time the event happened.
- The magnitude of the event. To save memory, when there are multiple events with the same event ID, only the highest magnitude is kept, and the rest are discarded.
- A pointer to the Event Template, which stores information about the magnitude and reputation effects of this type of event.
- The reference count, which is the number of people who know about the event. If no one knows about the event, then it is deleted from the Master Event List.

The following pseudo-code shows the main components of classes `EventID` and `AIEvent`.

```
class EventID
{
public:
    EventID(SubjectGrp, Verb, ObjectGrp, ObjectIndividual);
    Group GetSubjectGroup();
    Verb GetVerb();
    Group GetObjectGroup();
    UniqueID GetObjectIndividual();

private:
    int64 id;
};

class AIEvent
{
public:
    AIEvent(SubjectGrp, Verb, ObjectGrp, ObjectIndividual, TimeStamp,
    Lifetime, EventTemplate);
    EventID GetID();
    Point3D GetPosition();
    Time GetTimeStamp();
    int GetMagnitude();
    TemplateID GetEventTemplate();
    int IncrementReferenceCount();
    int DecrementReferenceCount();

private:
    EventID id;
    Point3D Position;
    Time TimeStamp;
    int Magnitude;
    Template EventTemplate;
    int ReferenceCount;
};
```

Master Event List

One way to keep track of reputation events would be to store the complete events on each NPC that knew about them. This solution would waste memory and quickly grow unmanageable. To conserve memory, the reputation system stores complete information about all events in a central location, the *Master Event List*. The Master Event List is a list of instances of class AIEvent, sorted by their event IDs.

The reputation system keeps the Master Event List small by deleting events no one knows about, storing only relevant events, and storing redundant information in one event instead of two. Each event in the Master Event List has a reference count indicating how many NPCs know about it. An event is initially added with a reference count of one, indicating that one NPC knows about it. It is decremented when an NPC stops referencing it. When the reference count reaches zero, the event is deleted.

The reputation system does not store all events; it stores only player events and events in which an NPC killed someone. Since NPCs' opinions of each other are not affected by Reputation Events, all other events are irrelevant to NPCs. This means you can compute the maximum number of events in a single-player game as *(Verbs * Objects) + Corpses*. Therefore, if there were five verbs, 500 possible objects, and 50 bytes per event in the Master Event List, the Master Event List would never exceed 150K.

In a multiplayer game, however, the maximum number of events would be *(PlayerGroups * Verbs * Objects) + Corpses*, where the number of player groups could be between one and the number of players. Watch potential memory usage when you have many players.

The reputation system accumulates redundant information in one event rather than storing it as separate events. If the player shoots at and then kills a bandit, the Kill event matches the ShootAt event, and the reputation system stores only the Kill event (the one with the higher magnitude).

Per-NPC Long-Term Memory

Each NPC has an instance of the class AIMemory. This class contains both the Per-NPC Long-Term-Memory and a static member that is the global Master Event List. In the Per-NPC Long Term Memory, each NPC stores a compressed version of the reputation events it knows about, each event represented by an instance of class AIMemoryElement. It stores only the event ID (a pointer to the event in the Master Event List), the magnitude that the NPC is aware of, and the time the NPC found out about the event. Depending on the complexity of the game, you can store the event ID in as little as 32 bits: 4 bits for the subject group, 8 bits for the verb, 4 bits for the object group, and 16 bits for the object individual ID. Even in an exceptionally complex game, 64 bits should suffice.

The following pseudo-code shows the main components of classes. AIMemoryElement and AIMemory.

```
class AIMemoryElement
{
public:
```

```
        AIMemoryElement(AIEvent);
        EventID GetID();
        int GetMagnitude();
        Time GetTimeStamp();
        bool Match(SubjectGrp, Magnitude, Verb, Object, ObjectIndividual);
    void Update(AIEvent);

private:
        EventID id;
        int Magnitude;
        Time TimeStamp;
};

class AIMemory
{
public:
        bool Merge(AIMemory);
        void Update(AIEvent);
        void AddNewMemoryElement(AIEvent);
        void ReplaceMemoryElement(AIEvent, Index);

private:
        static DynamicArray<AIEvent> MasterEventList;
        DynamicArray<AIMemoryElement> PerNPCLongTermMemory;
};
```

The Per-NPC Long Term Memory does not necessarily store the highest magnitude of each event. For example, if two NPCs witnessed the player shooting a bandit, but one ran off before the player killed the bandit, both would refer to the same event in the Master Event List (Player DidViolenceTo Bandit). However, the NPC that ran off would store the event with magnitude ShootAt, and the NPC that stayed would store the event with magnitude Killed.

To conserve memory, keep the Per-NPC tables small. We've already talked about one way to do that, by having the table consist of references to the Master Event List rather than the Reputation Events themselves. Another way to keep the Per-NPC tables small is to make sure that NPCs can't learn something they have no business knowing. If you kill someone and nobody witnesses it, then nobody should know that you did it.

Yet another way to keep the per-NPC table small is to let NPCs forget events. As mentioned previously, more serious, higher-magnitude events overshadow less serious ones. NPCs can also forget events after a predetermined amount time (set by the designer in the Event Template).

Finally, we can keep the per-NPC tables small by adding choke points to the game, like level boundaries or other points from which the player can't return and to which the NPC can't follow. At each choke point, very little information can cross. That way, the amount of information known by the NPCs peaks at each choke point, rather than continually growing as the game progresses.

Since the number of events in a single-player game is limited to *(Verbs * Objects) + Corpses*, we can compute the maximum size for each NPC's Long-Term Memory.

For example, if there are five verbs, 500 possible objects, and 10 bytes per event in the Long-Term Memory, each Long-Term Memory in a single-player game will never exceed 30K. If the total number of events in the Master Event List or the number of NPCs grows large, limit the number of events an individual NPC might know about. For example, as the number of NPCs grows, restrict the number of groups with which an NPC can share information.

How NPCs Learn about Events

NPCs can learn about events from event announcers or by sharing information with other NPCs. Whenever an NPC learns about an event, it sends the event through a memory match and update process to decide whether to add the new event, update an existing event, or discard the event. If necessary, NPCs then update the Master Event List.

Learning about Events from Event Announcers

Actions spawn event announcers. The event announcer is spawned at the position of the object of the event. Most actions generate an instantaneous event announcer, which announces the event only once. Some actions, such as the killing of an NPC, continually announce the event. If an NPC is killed, the event announcer immediately announces the full event, then stays by the body to continually announce a partial event, listing the subject (the killer) as unknown.

When spawned, the event announcer finds all the NPCs within a set radius and sends them the Reputation Event, represented as an instance of class AIEvent. Each NPC that receives the event quickly checks its Per-NPC Long-Term Memory to see if it needs to add the event. What happens next depends on the memory match and update process, which we describe after explaining the other way NPCs can learn about events.

If an event is announced and nobody is there to witness it, nothing happens; the reputation event is not created.

Learning about Events by Sharing Information

When two NPCs meet up, they both perform a quick check to see if they want to exchange information. If the NPCs don't like each other, they thumb their noses at each other and keep their secrets to themselves. Otherwise, both NPCs share the events they know about. Only some events are worth sharing, based on the memory match and update process.

Performing the Memory Match and Update Process

For each event an NPC learns about, the NPC performs a memory match to see if the event might match an existing event. If so, it attempts a memory update.

When checking for a possible match, the NPC checks the subject group, verb, object group, and object individual. The NPC checks for the following matches, in order:

1. The subject group, verb, object group, and object individual ID must all match.
2. The subject group, verb, and object group must match, but the object individual ID can be anything.
3. If the subject group of the new event is unknown, the subject group can be anything, but the verb, object group, and object individual ID must match. -or-

   If the subject group of the new event is known, the subject group of the existing event must be unknown, and the verb, object group, and object individual ID must match.

If the NPC finds a possible match, it attempts to update the event. If the update succeeds, then the match and update process is done. If the update fails, then the match is rejected and it looks for the next possible match. The NPC repeats this process until either a match is found that updates successfully, or there are no more matches. If the event does not successfully match and update, it is a new event so the NPC adds it to its Long-Term Memory.

The NPC attempts the update according to the following seven rules:

1. If the magnitude of the new event is less than or equal to the magnitude of the old event, and the new event has an unknown subject group (or they both have the same subject group), and the object individual ID is the same, then the new event is redundant. The NPC ignores it.
2. If the magnitude of the new event is greater than the magnitude of the old event, and the new event has an unknown subject group (or they both have the same subject group), and the object individual ID is the same, then the event is redundant but the magnitude needs to be updated. The NPC updates the existing event's magnitude in its Long-Term Memory and applies any reputation effects.
3. If the new event has a known subject group, the existing event has an unknown subject group, and the object individual IDs match, the new event has new information. The NPC removes the existing event, adds the new one with the greater magnitude of the two events, and then applies any reputation effects.
4. If either or both of the subject groups is unknown and the object individual ID is different, then this is not a match. The NPC adds the new event and applies any reputation effects.
5. If the subject groups are known and match, and the old one has the maximum magnitude, the new event is irrelevant. The NPC ignores it.

6. If the subject groups are known and match, and the new event has maximum magnitude, then the events match. The NPC updates the magnitude of the existing event and applies any reputation effects from the new event. The NPC then looks for all other matches and removes them since the events are redundant.

7. If the subject groups are known and match, but the object individual ID is different, and neither event is maximum magnitude, the events do not match. The NPC adds the new one and applies any reputation effects.

As the number of NPCs and events increases, optimize the long-term memory data structure for fast matching and updating. To do this, keep the events sorted using their Event IDs, first by object group, then by verb, then by object individual, and finally by subject group. This lets you use a binary search to quickly find all events that match a specific object group and verb.

How the NPC Updates the Master Event List

When an NPC adds a new event or updates an existing event in its Long-Term Memory, it also notifies the Master Event List of the event. If the event does not match an event in the Master Event List, the reputation system adds the event with a reference count of one, because one NPC now knows about it. If the event matches an existing event in the Master Event List, the existing event is updated and the reference count is increased by one, because one more NPC knows about it.

How the NPCs Draw Simple Conclusions from Incomplete Information

If an NPC knows about an event that has an unknown subject group, and later another NPC shares a matching event with a known subject group, the update process replaces the old event (with an unknown subject group) with the new one, and the magnitude becomes the greater of the two.

For example, suppose an NPC sees a dead bandit but didn't witness the killing. The event announcer will be non-instantaneous, so it will continue announcing that the bandit was killed by some unknown subject group. Later, the same NPC shares event knowledge with another NPC who saw the player shoot at the same bandit. Both NPCs infer that the player probably killed the bandit. They might be wrong, but they're jumping to conclusions just as real people do.

Per-NPC Reputation Table

Each NPC uses the events stored in its Long-Term Memory to generate its opinion of various other groups and the player. Each NPC stores a Per-NPC Reputation Table containing its current opinions of the player and the other groups in the game. The table is stored as a dynamic array of reputation meters, one for each group and one for the player. Each meter has a group ID and two floats, Like and Hate. If Hate is higher than Like, the NPC hates the group it refers to. If Like is higher than Hate, the NPC likes the player or group it refers to. If Like and Hate are both low, the NPC doesn't know what to think. If Like and Hate are both high, the NPC has strong but ambivalent feelings toward the player or group; the NPC will mistrust and possibly fear the player or group.

When an NPC comes across the player or another NPC, it accesses its reputation table to decide how to react. For example, NPCs will never attack characters they like, might attack characters they hate, and might be careful near characters they're unsure of.

Conclusion

With the dynamic, event-based reputation system described in this article, you can model a large number of complex humanlike NPCs while minimizing CPU and memory cost. This article described a relatively simple event system, but once the basic reputation system is in place, you can extend it to include a wide variety of events with different properties, such as Aided, GaveGiftTo, TradedWith, LiedTo, StoleFrom, and DestroyedProperty. You can also extend the object of the events to include not only NPCs, but also buildings, horses, and other objects. If you pay attention to memory usage, you can also use this system for multi-player games. Additionally, you can extend this system to support individual NPCs or players belonging to multiple groups, adding more complexity to the world. In this way, you can quite easily and efficiently make an entire world come to life. Let the player beware.

References

[Grond98] is a description of an actual game reputation system, *Ultima Online*. [Mui01], [Resnick00], [Rubierra01], and [Sabater01] describe recent research into reputation systems. They are mostly talking about reputation systems for e-commerce, which has become a hot research topic. While not directly applicable, they discuss some interesting techniques that might be incorporated into games, as well as general ideas about reputations and their sociological and economic implications.

[Grond98] Grond, G. M., and Hanson, Bob, "Ultima Online Reputation System FAQ," www.uo.com/repfaq, Origin Systems, 1998.

[Mui01] Mui, L., Szolovits, P., and Ang, C., "Collaborative Sanctioning: Applications in Restaurant Recommendations Based on Reputation," *Proceedings of Fifth International Conference on Autonomous Agents (AGENTS'01)*, ACM Press, 2001.

[Resnick00] Resnick, P., Zeckhauser, R., Friedman, E., and Kuwabara, K., "Reputation Systems," *Communications of the ACM*, December 2000, Vol. 43, No. 12.

[Rubiera01] Rubiera, J. C., Lopez, J. M. M., and Muro, J. D., "A Fuzzy Model of Reputation in Multi-Agent Systems," *Proceedings of Fifth International Conference on Autonomous Agents (AGENTS'01)*, ACM Press, 2001.

[Sabater01] Sabater, Jordi, and Sierra, Carles, "REGRET: Reputation in Gregarious Societies," *Proceedings of Fifth International Conference on Autonomous Agents (AGENTS'01)*, ACM Press, 2001.

RACING AND SPORTS AI

9.1

Representing a Racetrack for the AI

Gari Biasillo—Electronic Arts Canada
gbiasillo@ea.com, gbiasillo@shaw.ca

This article is the first in a series of four racing AI articles and describes a practical representation of a racetrack for an AI system. Article 9.2, "Racing AI Logic," details how the AI will use the racetrack that is defined in this article, and article 9.3, "Training an AI to Race," reviews several techniques to optimize the ability of the AI.

Defining the Racetrack

Figure 9.1.1 illustrates how the racetrack is defined using a chain of *sectors* that identify the on-track areas that can be traveled. It should be noted that it is possible to travel outside the sectors if the environment permits it. Each sector is constructed from a leading and trailing edge, which will be referred to as *interfaces*. This method reduces memory overhead, as leading and trailing interfaces are shared.

Interfaces

Interfaces are the basic building blocks of the racetrack that are used to define the left and rightmost boundaries of the road and the possible driving lines; namely, the

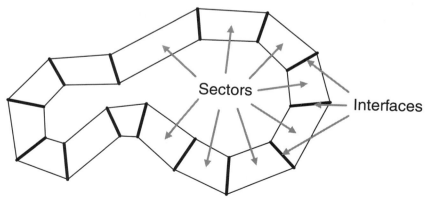

FIGURE 9.1.1 *Defining the racetrack with interfaces and sectors.*

racing and overtaking lines. Driving line *nodes* are located along the edge defined by the left and right boundaries. Figure 9.1.2 illustrates this with two types of driving nodes: the racing line node and overtaking line node. The successive connection of these nodes from "interface" to "interface" represents the driving line.

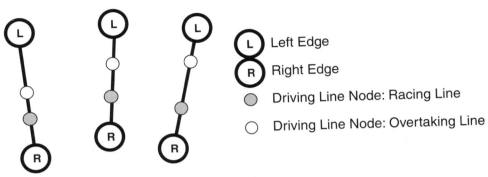

FIGURE 9.1.2 *Interfaces with driving line nodes.*

Sectors

The racetrack is defined by a doubly linked list of sectors that can be traversed forward and backward. The previous and next pointers of the linked-list can be defined as arrays, allowing multiple paths to be defined. In the common case of only having one path, the second pointer would be set to NULL. The leading and trailing edges of the sector are defined with a pointer to the respective interfaces. Figure 9.1.3 illustrates the construction of a sector with the driving lines.

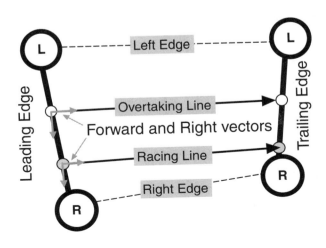

FIGURE 9.1.3 *Sector construction.*

Each sector also stores its distance along the racetrack so that the AI knows how far it has traveled, the distance to the finish line, and to compare relative distances to opponents. A simple method of computing this distance is to accumulate the distances along the racing lines. This scheme works well, as the racing line is the optimal path to take on the racetrack.

Driving Lines

Driving lines are used to define the optimal paths to take between interfaces. Each line structure holds the world location of the line's starting position, its length, and the forward and right direction vectors.

The forward vector is constructed by normalizing the vector from the line's start to end position after zeroing the Y element (height). The purpose of projecting this vector onto the XZ plane is to simplify matters when calculating the car's orientation to the driving line, because the car's forward direction isn't guaranteed to lie in the same plane as the road. By projecting the car's forward direction onto the XZ in the same manner, it is assured that they lie in the same plane. The right vector is perpendicular to the forward vector and is used to determine how far the car is from the driving line.

Finally, planes are used to mark the four edge boundaries, pointing inward, of each sector created from the 2D (XZ) plane view. The plane equation for an edge can be computed using three points: the first two being the edge's start and end points, and the third is the start point with an offset in the Y-axis. In order to simplify testing of whether a point is in a sector, sectors are required to be convex. This can be confirmed by making sure that the two disjoint points of each edge are on its positive side of its plane (Figure 9.1.4).

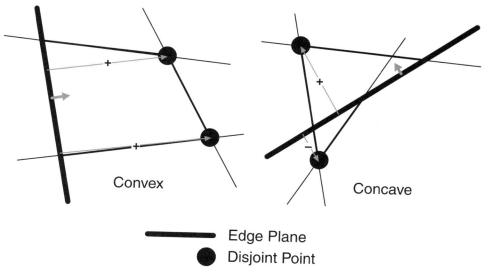

Convex   Concave

━━━━━ Edge Plane
⬤ Disjoint Point

FIGURE 9.1.4 *Testing for convex sectors.*

Determining the Current Sector

It is fundamental that the AI knows the current sector of each car. Testing that the car's position lies on the positive side of each sector's four "edge boundary" planes confirms that it lies within it. A simple speed up is to precalculate the 2D XZ axis-aligned bounding box of the sector that can be used for trivial rejection. Testing the car against many sectors would be too costly for a real time application, but can be reduced by using coherence [Biasillo02].

Computing the Distance along a Sector

There are several methods of computing the distance along a sector, each with varying complexity [Ranck00]. A simple approach that works extremely well in practice is to compute the traveled distance parallel to the driving line as shown in the following code snippet.

```
float DistAlongSector(const CSector& sector, const vector3& pos)
{
    vector3 delta = pos - sector.drivingLinePos;
    delta.y = 0.0f;
    float dist = DotProduct(sector.drivingLineForward, delta);
    return (dist * lengthScale);
}
```

The variable `lengthScale` is used to scale the distance to compensate for the 2D projection and is equal to the line's length divided by its 2D length in the XZ plane; this is precalculated for each sector. Adding the distance along the sector to the sector's start distance results in the total distance traveled along the racetrack.

Providing Information to the AI

For the AI to have a better understanding of the environment, relevant information should be stored within each sector. With this information, the AI can quickly make decisions when traversing the sectors with a few simple comparisons. As the purpose of this article is to define the racetrack, using this data is described in article 9.2 [Biasillo02].

Path Type

The *path type* defines the type of route ahead. Usually, this would be set to "normal," but other types could be "shortcut," "long route," "weapon pick-up route," "winding road," and "drag strip." The AI uses this information whenever a split route is found; in other words, the sector's next pointers are both non-NULL. For example, if the AI needs weapons, it will choose the "weapon pick-up route" if such a route is available.

Terrain Type

An AI would usually want to take the shortest path available, but if a shortcut requires negotiating a rugged landscape, only vehicles capable of traversing this type of terrain would want to do so. In this case, the shortcut sector would also be marked as "rugged terrain," allowing the AI to reject this path if the car has inadequate suspension and/or low ride-height.

Walls

Some routes are located in a confined area, such as a narrow corridor or with a wall on one side of the track. By specifying that a wall exists on the left and/or right sector edge, the AI is informed that it should keep a safe distance from the relevant edge.

Hairpin Turn

In a similar manner to walls, the "hairpin left" and "hairpin right" flags are used to mark the inside edges of a sharp turn. A hairpin is different from a wall because the specified side will not impede the car's path.

Brake/Throttle

To aid the AI in areas of the track that are difficult to negotiate, a "brake-throttle" value comes in handy. This value lies in the −1.0 to +1.0 range, signifying "full-brakes" to "full-throttle"; zero tells the AI to lift off the gas and coast.

Conclusion

Defining the racetrack with as much useful information as possible helps reduce the complexity of the AI system. In addition, reducing much of the data from a 3D to a 2D problem simplifies this further.

An improvement to the driving lines would be to create a smoother path using nonlinear interpolation. Catmull-Rom splines, or the more general cardinal splines, [Watt92] are both ideal choices, since the curve can be directly defined by the driving points, which become the control points for the spline. These splines also travel through each control point, which is much more intuitive for placement purposes. B-splines are an alternative that will give you even smoother curves, but the spline will no longer travel directly through the control points.

References

[Biasillo02] Biasillo, Gari, "Racing AI Logic," *AI Game Programming Wisdom*, Charles River Media, 2002.

[Marselas00] Marselas, Herbert, "Interpolated 3D Keyframe Animation," *Game Programming Gems*, Charles River Media, 2000.

[Ranck00] Ranck, Steven, "Computing the Distance into a Sector," *Game Programming Gems*, Charles River Media, 2000.

[Watt92] Watt, Alan, "The Theory and Practice of Parametric Representation Techniques," *Advanced Animation and Rendering Techniques*, Addison-Wesley, 1992.

9.2

Racing AI Logic

Gari Biasillo—Electronic Arts Canada

gbiasillo@ea.com, gbiasillo@shaw.ca

This is the second in a series of three racing AI articles that describes how to implement an AI capable of racing a car around a track. It is recommended that the reader be familiar with article 9.1, "Representing a Race Track for the AI" [Biasillo02a], as references will be made to it throughout.

Although the AI will follow predefined driving lines, it will not rigidly follow the track like a train on rails, but merely use these lines as a guide. The goal is to have the AI produce an output that emulates human input; specifically joystick and/or key presses. Using this method, the game engine only needs to gather input from the AI controller instead of a human input device.

The Basic AI Framework

Before we go into the details of the racing AI logic, we need to define the basic framework of the AI.

Finite-State Machine

To simplify the AI logic, a finite-state machine (FSM) is used to keep track of the current racing situation. There is a plethora of articles on this subject [Dybsand00], so the reader is assumed to have knowledge of such a system. For clarity, when a state is referred to, it will be prefixed with "STATE_". As an example, "STATE_STARTING_GRID" would represent the state at the start of a race.

A Fixed Time-Step

Running the AI with a free-floating time-step would produce different results depending on the frame rate, among other factors. One remedy would be to time-scale all calculations, but this would still lead to varying errors, a classic example being Euler integration. In a racing game, errors can accrue when the time-step increases because the AI would make fewer decisions in a given time span. This would lead to situations where the AI would miss a braking point, react too late to obstacles, or become out-of-sync when playing networked games.

By using a fixed time-step, we can guarantee that the AI logic will run identically on different platforms regardless of the frame rate. To implement such a method, the AI entry point would take the elapsed time since the previous update as an argument, and process the AI logic elapsed time/time-step times. The remaining time should be accumulated with the elapsed time of the next update.

Controlling the Car

A simple structure is used to control the car, which contains the steering and acceleration/braking values. Steering, dx, is in the range of −1.0 to +1.0, representing full left to full right. The second member, dy, has two uses depending on its value, which also has the range −1.0 to +1.0. Negative values represent the braking amount (zero to 100%), and positive values represent acceleration (zero to 100%).

```
struct CCarControl
{
    float    dx;    // −1.0...+1.0 = Left to Right steering
    float    dy;    // <0.0 = Braking, >0.0 Acceleration
};
```

Simplifying with 2D

Although the racetrack can have an undulating road, it is essentially a 2D pathway. Using this observation, many of the calculations can be reduced to 2D by projecting the 3D coordinates onto the XZ plane by zeroing the Y element of the 3D vector and then normalizing. Several of the vectors that will be used in this manner are listed in Table 9.2.1.

Table 9.2.1 Useful XZ Projected Vectors

Variable Name	Description
Forward	The car's forward unit-length direction.
DestForward	Destination unit-length direction.
DestRight	Destination unit-length vector perpendicular to DestForward.

The Starting Grid

First, we must initialize the AI's values at the starting grid, before the race begins.

The AI is initialized with the sector that the car starts in, which is a simple matter of querying an appropriate function passing in the starting grid location. The returned sector pointer should be stored internally as the *current* and *last-valid sectors*. The last-valid sector is used to help the car return to the racetrack if it is no longer within a sector; for example, it might have spun off the track at a sharp turn.

The initial state of the FSM should be set to STATE_STARTING_GRID, which simply waits for the "green light" indicating the start of the race. Once the start has been detected, the FSM transitions to STATE_RACING. A small reaction time could be used to give a more natural feel.

Gentlemen, Please Start Your Engines

The most complex state of the FSM, as you could imagine, is the racing mode, STATE_RACING.

Traversing the Sectors

For the AI to make an informed decision, it must know where it is located in the environment. In a racing game, this would be the position on the racetrack. Locating which sector of the racetrack the car is in was described in article 9.1, and, although viable, is a brute-force method; it would require checking the car's position against every sector and would require excessive processing overhead.

The number of sectors tested can be reduced to a minimum using coherence. By keeping track of the last sector in which the car was located, we have a starting search point when the car's sector location is next queried. If the car is no longer within the last sector, we traverse the linked list of next and previous sectors (starting from the last sector) until the car is found to be inside a new sector. As it is possible for the car to be outside all sectors, a cutoff distance should be passed into the traversal code; say, two or three times the distance that the car traveled.

If the car is no longer within any of the sectors tested, the AI must find its way back onto the track and would set the FSM to STATE_RECOVER_TO_TRACK, which is later explained in detail.

Split Decisions

When the AI encounters a split path when traversing the sectors, a decision should be made as to which route is best to take. Decisions should be made based on the AI's current needs and the choice of route; for example, the path type, terrain type, shortcut, and so forth. The decision-making process could either be embedded in the traversal code or passed in as a function pointer that returns the route to take.

Anticipating the Road Ahead

In order to create a more intelligent racer, we must have the ability to look ahead. This allows the AI to anticipate what will happen, rather than reacting to events that are currently occurring. For example, knowing that we are approaching a sharp bend provides enough time to apply the brakes, thus reaching a reasonable cornering speed. Targeting the track ahead is achieved by traversing the sectors a certain distance ahead from the car's current position, as shown in Figure 9.2.1.

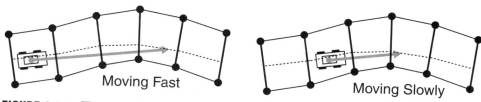

FIGURE 9.2.1 *Targeting the road ahead.*

Since each sector holds the length of the driving lines, the traversal algorithm merely needs to run through the linked-list accumulating the lengths until the required distance is reached. As the car and target will be located anywhere within a sector, these sector lengths should be adjusted accordingly by taking into account the distances along the sectors [Biasillo02a].

Adjusting the look-ahead distance proportional to the car's speed has several positive characteristics. When traveling slowly, only the local region is viewed, giving more precision. Conversely, when traveling quickly it smoothes the path and gives extra time to react to upcoming events. Smoothing occurs because as the target distance increases, so does the angle to the car's forward vector; therefore, the car requires less steering correction to point toward the target.

Hairpin Turns

One side effect of looking ahead comes into play when negotiating sharp corners, such as hairpin turns. This can cause the car to cut the corner instead of taking the correct line, as shown by the left image in Figure 9.2.2. By marking the sectors around

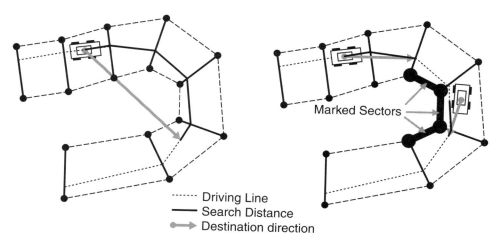

FIGURE 9.2.2 *The car incorrectly cuts the corner (left). Marking the sectors for hairpin turns fixes the problem (right).*

the hairpin's apex with a special "hairpin" flag, the sector traversal code can detect this and cut the search short. As the search can start with a cutoff flag, there should be a minimum search distance to avoid stopping the car. The right image in Figure 9.2.2 illustrates these points more clearly.

Using this method, when a marked sector is encountered in the search, the AI will continue to target the start of the first sector. Once the minimum search distance is reached, the AI will then target the driving line ahead by this distance. This results in the AI targeting the first marked sector while braking to a reasonable speed, and then following the corner when close enough.

Driving to the Target

Once the AI has chosen its target, appropriate actions must be taken to resolve how to reach it. The AI aims to mimic user input, so it must calculate the relative direction to travel and apply the appropriate steering.

```
float CCarAI::SteerToTarget(const vector3& dest)
{
    vector3 DestForward, cp;

    DestForward = dest - m_Pos;
    DestForward.y = 0.0f;
    DestForward.normalize();

    // Compute the sine between current & destination.
    cp = CrossProduct(m_Forward, DestForward);
    float steer = cp.magnitude() * m_SteerConvert;

    // Steer left or right ?
    if (cp.y > 0.0f)   {steer = -steer;}
    steer = Clamp(steer, -1.0f, 1.0f);

    return (steer);
}
```

The scalar m_SteerConvert is used to compensate for the car's maximum steering angle and is precalculated as 90.0f / m_MaxTurnAngle. To avoid abrupt changes in steering, the returned value should be interpolated between the old and new steering angles. For extra fluidity, this value could be squared, which gives finer control for small to medium steering values, but still allows full-lock at the extremes.

Overtaking

Once the AI closes in on an opposing car, it will have to find a way around it. Rather than concocting an elaborate scheme, overtaking can be achieved by following an overtaking line instead of the racing line. A slight modification to the traversal routines, to take the index of the alternate driving line to follow, is all that is needed.

To improve the AI's overtaking ability, multiple overtaking lines could be specified; for example, a left and right overtaking line. The appropriate line could be chosen based on a combination of the other car's relative position, and which overtaking line is on the inside line of a corner. Taking the inside line is advantageous, as the AI will block the opponent when turning into the corner.

Handling Under-Steer and Over-Steer

If the car's movement is modeled with even a modest physics simulator, the car will most likely be subjected to under- and/or over-steer, which can cause the car to spin (over-steer) or miss the apex of a bend (under-steer). This section details how to detect these conditions and how to correct the car's steering, acceleration, and/or braking to overcome these instabilities. It should be noted that these tests should be confined to when the car's wheels are in contact with the ground.

Detecting the Car's Stability

The stability of the car can be determined by a few comparisons of the sideways velocities of each wheel. A wheel's sideways velocity is calculated by applying the dot-product operation to the velocity of the wheel and the unit-length right direction of its orientation (Figure 9.2.3).

When a matrix is used for orientation, the right vector is defined by the first row or column, for a row-major or column-major matrix, respectively.

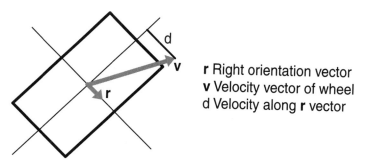

r Right orientation vector
v Velocity vector of wheel
d Velocity along **r** vector

FIGURE 9.2.3 *Calculating the sideways velocity of a wheel.*

The velocity of a point relative to the center of gravity can be calculated with the function PointVel(). The linear and angular velocities of the car, along with a point relative to the car's center of gravity, are passed as arguments and the velocity of this point is returned. It is beyond the scope of this article to detail the working of this function, so if the reader is unfamiliar with the calculations, there is an abundance of "rigid body dynamics" papers. We highly recommend [Baraff97].

```
vector3 PointVel(const vector3& linearVel, const vector3& angularVel,
                const vector3& point)
{
    // linearVel = Linear velocity
```

```
    // angularVel = Axis of rotation * spin rate
    // point = Relative position to body's center of gravity
    return (linearVel + CrossProduct(angularVel, point));
}
```

To simplify the detection of under- or over-steer, the front sideways velocities are averaged, and likewise for the rear. As a further optimization, it is possible to just use the front and rear wheels of one side of the car rather than averaging.

Testing for a Stability

When the car is in a stable state, neither under-steering nor over-steering, its handling is called "neutral." We know that a car is in a state of stability by confirming that the front and rear sideways velocities are both within some threshold around zero. In the scenario depicted in the lower right of Figure 9.2.4, the car is handling perfectly

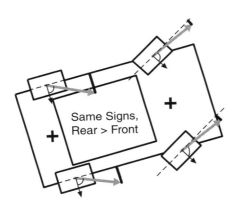

Oversteer Case 1: Rear-end snapping out.

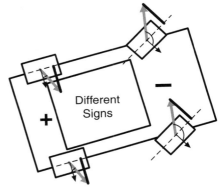

Oversteer Case 2: Spinning-out.

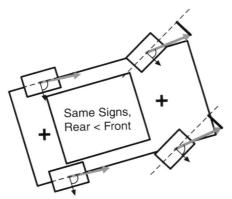

Understeer: Car continuing forward.

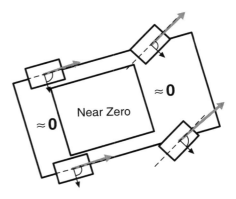

Neural Handling: Sideways Vels Near Zero.

FIGURE 9.2.4 *The three states of instability and the neutral stability state.*

(neutral), so no correction to the car is needed. It can be seen that the sideways velocities of each wheel point roughly in the same directions as the wheels do.

Under-Steer

Under-steer occurs when the car tries to make a turn but continues to move in a forward direction. This state can be determined by confirming that the front and rear sideways velocities have the same sign. If this test passes, the car is deemed to be under-steering if the front sideways velocity is larger than the rear. The larger the difference in velocities means a larger degree of under-steer. This is illustrated in the lower left in Figure 9.2.4.

Over-Steer

Over-steer causes the car to turn too much, which might lead to it spinning out. There are two cases that need to be tested for to confirm if the car is over-steering which are illustrated in the top row in Figure 9.2.4.

This first case happens when the rear end snaps out, and is confirmed by the front and rear sideways velocities having the same sign, with the rear sideways velocity being larger than the front. The larger the difference in velocities means a larger degree of over-steer.

The second case occurs when the car is either starting to or already is in a spin. In this case, the signs of the front and rear sideways velocities are different, and the larger the combined absolute velocities, the greater the over-steer.

Correcting the Car

Once the car is determined to be in a state of instability, a correction must be made to stabilize the car. The amount of correction is proportional to the amount of instability as shown in Table 9.2.2, for each case.

Table 9.2.2 Correction Amounts for Instability Cases

Case	Vel. Signs	Correction
Under-steer	Same	Abs(FrontVel + RearVel) / UndersteerRange
Over-steer 1	Same	Abs(FrontVel − RearVel) / OversteerRange
Over-steer 2	Different	(Abs(RearVel) − Abs(FrontVel)) / OversteerRange

It can be seen from Table 9.2.2 that the summed velocities are divided by a range factor, which reduces the correction amount to a value between zero and one. Depending on the car's handling, the correction should be clamped to a value less than one for improved results, as it prevents over-correction in the steering. The correction value should be either added to or subtracted from the current steering position depending on the sign of dx. In addition to this, dy should be reduced in proportion to the amount of steering correction.

Selecting workable values for the range factors is hard to pin down and is made even more difficult by the fact that they vary on a car-to-car basis. The last article in this series [Biasillo02b] deals with this problem in detail.

Wall Avoidance

After the FSM has finished processing its current state, the AI should check if it is in danger of hitting any walls, and correct the car if necessary. By predicting where the car will be in the future, we can test if the car will come into contact with a wall.

The predicted position is calculated by adding the car's current velocity scaled by the amount of time in the future to predict, say a quarter of a second, added to the current car position. The sector that this position is located within is queried starting from the car's current sector. This position is then tested against the sector's left and right edge planes to determine which side it is closest to, and if any correction is required. If the distance is within a certain threshold, the correction amount is calculated as a proportion of distance/threshold, which results in a value between zero and one. Depending on which side the car is going to hit, this value is either added to or subtracted from the steering position and clamped.

If a NULL pointer is returned, the car is predicted to leave the track, and avoiding action should be taken. In this case, a crash is imminent, so the brakes should be applied by setting dy to −1.0. To keep the car from spinning, the steering should be set to straight-ahead. As the car reduces speed, it will come to a point where it is predicted to be inside a sector, and the wall avoidance code will steer away from the wall (Figure 9.2.5).

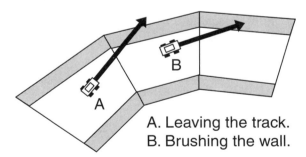

A. Leaving the track.
B. Brushing the wall.

FIGURE 9.2.5 *Predicting future problems to avoid.*

Miscellaneous FSM States

There are several states that, although small in content, are an important part of the AI.

STATE_AIRBORNE

If the racetrack has jumps and other things that can cause the car to become airborne, this state is used to prepare the car for a controlled landing. As an example, if the car is steering to the right, it will most likely spin out of control upon landing. By setting the steering to straight ahead and the acceleration to full, the car will continue moving forward when it lands. Once this state detects that the car's wheels are in contact with the ground, the FSM is reverted back to STATE_RACING.

STATE_OFF_TRACK

There will be cases when the car no longer occupies a sector, so the AI needs a method of finding its way back to the racetrack. By keeping track of the last valid sector in which the car was located, the AI merely needs to target the racetrack by starting the traversal from this point. A longer look-ahead distance should be used in this case so the car can merge onto the track at a shallow angle, giving a more esthetic look.

Catch-Up Logic

Video games, as the name implies, are meant to be fun. Gamers have different playing abilities, so what is fun for one player is frustratingly difficult or too easy for another. To cater to these differing abilities, the AI must be able to adapt to the situation.

Making the Game Easier

If the AI is determined to be doing "too well," a number of methods can be used to give the player a sporting chance. Limiting the AI's top speed in proportion to how far it is in the lead is a quick and easy method. A further method is to brake earlier for corners and accelerate slower. This subtle approach works well, as it hides the fact that the AI is helping the player out. A third approach would be to take "long-cuts," or unsuitable terrain routes. Finally, if weapons are involved in the game, the AI could be forced to only target other AI cars, and the weapon distribution could give the player better weapons and the opposite for the leading AI cars.

Making the Game Harder

Conversely, if the player is in the lead, methods are needed to give the player better competition. These are similar to the previous slow-down methods, but in a different context: increasing the AI's top speed in proportion to how far it is trailing, taking shortcuts, targeting the player with weapons, and weapon distribution.

Conclusion

Several areas of a racing AI have been covered for creating an AI that emulates the reaction and responses of a human driver. The AI is placed in the same situation as the player and has to compute how to steer the car to navigate the racetrack. A natural feel is conveyed by the fact that the car does not follow a rigid path and is subjected to the same difficulties that a player would face; namely, instability, hairpin turns, and avoiding wall impacts.

References

[Baraff97] Baraff, David, "An Introduction to Physically Based Modeling," www.cs.cmu.edu/~baraff/pbm/pbm.html, 1997.

[Biasillo02a] Biasillo, Gari, "Representing a Racetrack for the AI," *AI Game Programming Wisdom*, Charles River Media, 2002.

[Biasillo02b] Biasillo, Gari, "Training an AI to Race," *AI Game Programming Wisdom*, Charles River Media, 2002.

[Dybsand00] Dybsand, Eric, "A Finite-State Machine Class," *Game Programming Gems*, Charles River Media, 2000.

9.3

Training an AI to Race

Gari Biasillo—Electronic Arts Canada

gbiasillo@ea.com, gbiasillo@shaw.ca

This article concludes the racing AI series of articles, and therefore refers to aspects of the first two articles (article 9.1, "Representing a Race Track for the AI" [Biasillo02a], and article 9.2, "Racing AI Logic" [Biasillo02b]). Creating an AI environment can be a tedious and time-consuming task, so the purpose of this article is to give details of several methods to reduce this process to a manageable level.

Defining the Racing Line

Defining the racing line is a vital part of the racetrack definition that can make or break the effectiveness of the AI. A fast process of laying down the racing line is to record the path of a human player's best lap. This gives an excellent starting point that would only require minor tweaks to iron out any imperfections.

Calculating the Driving Line Nodes

As described in article 9.1 [Biasillo02a], the racetrack defines the racing line as a connection of *driving line nodes* stored in the AI *interfaces*. In order to convert the best lap into racetrack data, we need to determine at which point the car crosses each interface. Since the car's current *sector* is always stored and updated, the crossing point can be determined at the time when the car moves into a new sector.

To determine where the car intersects the interface, a line-to-plane intersection test is calculated; the car's previous and current position specify the line, and the starting interface of the newly occupied sector defines the plane. Because this test is only performed when the car enters a new sector, we can guarantee that the line straddles the plane.

```
// Plane Equation = Ax + By + Cz + D = 0, where
// A = normal.x, B = normal.y, C = normal.z, D = dist
// x,y,z = vector3 to test against plane, therefore
// Dist to plane = DotProduct(vector3, normal) + dist
class CPlane
{
    public:
        vector3    normal;
        float      dist;
} ;
```

```
vector3 LineToPlane(const vector3& start, const vector3& end, const
                    CPlane& plane)
{
    float s, e, t;
    s = DotProduct(plane.normal, start) + plane.dist;
    e = DotProduct(plane.normal, end) + plane.dist;
    t = s / (s - e);
    vector3 delta = end - start;
    return (start + delta * t);
}

float TimeOfPointOnLine(const vector3& point, const vector3& start,
                        vector3& end)
{
    vector3 delta = end - start;
    float length = delta.length();
    delta = point - start;
    float t = delta.length();
    return (t / length);
}
```

Ideally, the designer of the track would be able to race until a candidate lap is created, and enter a mode that replays and records this lap.

Tuning the Car Handling

With each car having unique characteristics, tuning each car's handling setup values can become a time-consuming and even impossible task to undertake manually. These values would include the under- and over-steer values as described in article 9.2. However, the following method can work on any type of parameter that requires such tuning; for example, braking distances, front/rear brake balance, toe in/out, and camber.

Adjusting the Parameters

The aim of the car setup is to find the optimum parameter values to maximize the performance. Usually, the best lap-time correlates to the best setup, so an adjustment of a parameter can be considered an improvement if the lap-time decreases. A simplistic approach of randomly selecting values for a parameter is a shot in the dark and requires pure luck to pick the optimum value. This is made even more difficult when dealing with a large set of parameters that are interdependent.

Converging on the Optimum Values

A more methodical approach is to converge on the optimum values: assign each parameter with a minimum and maximum value, and then progressively reduce the range until the target value is reached. The starting range should be chosen wisely and depends on the type of parameter; it should be large enough to encapsulate all possible values, yet small enough to reduce the search time.

The process of converging is simple and begins with initializing each parameter to a reasonable value; the average of the parameter's minimum and maximum values is an ideal choice. The AI is processed to complete a few laps. The best lap-time achieved becomes the starting benchmark. After the completion of the last lap, a parameter is randomly chosen to modify and the AI continues to lap the track.

Modifying Parameter Values

A simple but effective modification scheme is to select a value offset from the middle of the current parameter range; say, ±25% of the range. This method is effectively a bisection algorithm. A slight variation of this method is to randomly choose an offset within ±25% of the range, as it gives better results when dealing with multiple interconnected parameters due to each parameter having a greater chance of having an effect on the final setup (Figure 9.3.1).

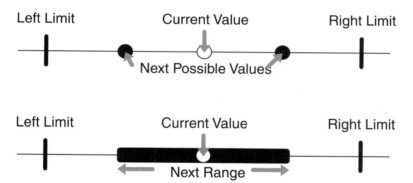

FIGURE 9.3.1 *Parameter modification.*

Modifying the Range

Once it is determined that the modification of a parameter was an improvement (a decrease in lap time) or a deterioration (an increase in lap time), the range is reduced, thus converging on the optimum value.

When a parameter change causes an improvement, either the parameter's minimum or maximum value is changed depending on the direction of the previous modification. If the parameter moved toward the minimum, the maximum is set to the parameter's previous value. Conversely, the minimum is set to the parameter's previous value if it moved toward the maximum.

When a parameter change causes deterioration in lap time, a similar approach is taken. If the parameter moved towards the minimum, the minimum is set to the parameter's previous value. Conversely, the maximum is set to the parameter's previous value if it moved towards the maximum.

Once a parameter's limits converge to within a small range, it is deemed optimal and no further modifications should be applied to it. Once all parameters are optimal, the car handling setup is complete and the process can be terminated.

Turbo Training

The time required for this process can be reduced considerably by running the game as fast as possible (but still at a fixed time-step); for example, calling the game loop multiple times in between render updates and not waiting for the vertical blank. A method of turning this feature on and off should be made available so that the designer can make any necessary changes to the racetrack or view a lap in real time to judge the current progress of the tuning.

Real-Time Editing

Real-Time Track Modification

A very useful, and indeed vital, part of the track creation process is the ability to run the car AI and modify the track in real time. This allows any problems in the track layout to be quickly modified and tested.

User Control Overriding AI

If, for whatever reason, the AI becomes stuck or cannot navigate a certain part of the racetrack, being able to take control of the car to help the AI is invaluable. Another use would be when you want to test how the AI handles a certain part of the race-track; rather than wait for an entire lap to be navigated, the designer could drive the car to the desired starting position (or have an editor option to allow you to place the car at any point on the track) and let the AI proceed from there.

A trivial override mechanism is to read the user input and use this instead of the AI's output if any keypress or joystick movement is detected. A useful addition is a key to toggle the AI to allow the designer to disconnect the AI where circumstances require it.

Conclusion

As games become more complex while the production time remains constant or even decreases, the workload on individuals needs to be reduced. This article, in the scope of racing AI, has hopefully provided useful methods of attaining this goal.

A few improvements to the methods described in this article include:

- Using a genetic algorithm to tune the car parameters
- Tuning the cars on a track-by-track basis to get the optimum performance on each
- Forcing the AI to always take certain route types to aid debugging

References

[Biasillo02a] Biasillo, Gari, "Representing a Racetrack for the AI," *AI Game Programming Wisdom*, Charles River Media, 2002.

[Biasillo02b] Biasillo, Gari, "Racing AI Logic," *AI Game Programming Wisdom*, Charles River Media, 2002.

[Dybsand00] Dybsand, Eric, "A Finite-State Machine Class," *Game Programming Gems*, Charles River Media, 2000.

[Hsiung00] Hsiung, A., Matthews, J., "An Introduction to GAs and GP," www.generation5.org/ga.shtml, 2000.

9.4

Competitive AI Racing under Open Street Conditions

Joseph C. Adzima—Motocentric Inc.

joe_adzima@yahoo.com

This article describes, with examples, the basic functions necessary for AI-controlled vehicles to navigate a random network of roads and intersections in a competitive and highly realistic-looking manner. The code (included on the CD-ROM) also illustrates how to navigate arrays of randomly placed obstacles in the city.

This article begins with a section describing how to create your city so the AI will work with it. Next, it illustrates the algorithms involved in calculating the steering values, and then finishes with a section describing the math involved in calculating the throttle and brake values. The writing in this article assumes that you already have a vehicle driving model that takes steering, brake, and throttle inputs. Additionally, it requires that you provide the city in which to drive.

Map Components

The first step to solving the navigation problem is to represent the city streets and intersections to the computer. The map is broken up into components that represent the roads and intersections of the city. Roads, as in real life, represent the physical space between any two intersections. Roads are straight or curved, and have a width defined by the distance from the right outer boundary to the left outer boundary. Roads also might include sidewalks with an array of obstacles on them. Intersections are defined as any area in the city where two or more roads meet.

Roads are represented as sets of 3D ordered vertices, as shown in Figure 9.4.1. Three main sets of vertices define each road: the centerline, the right road boundary, and the left road boundary.

The road centerline consists of a list of vertices that define the physical centerline of the road. The right and left road boundaries are broken up into two sections each: the inner and the outer boundaries. The inner boundary represents the line between the road and the sidewalk, and the outer boundary represents the line between the outer edge of the sidewalk and the building facades. To complete the road representation, orientation vectors are calculated for each vertex in the centerline. The orientation vectors consist of up and down (Y), right and left (X), and forward and reverse (Z). A

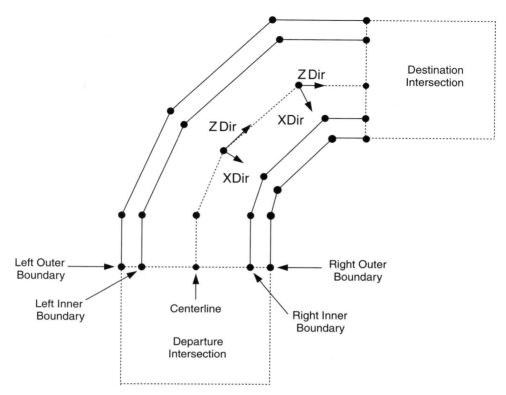

FIGURE 9.4.1 *A typical road segment.*

minimum of four vertices are used to define a straight road. This is necessary to further subdivide the road into buckets for obstacle avoidance. For cases where no sidewalk is present, the inner and outer vertices are co-linear. Curved roads are those roads with more than four vertices. In a curved road, the road segments between the vertices are angled arbitrarily, and are separated by a distance of at least 10 meters.

Each road has two intersections. Since the roads are comprised of lists of vertices, the intersection nearest to the first vertex is called the *departure* intersection. Likewise, the intersection connected to the last vertex is called the *destination* intersection. It is not a requirement that the AI vehicle traverse the road from departure intersection to destination intersection.

The Obstacle Map

The obstacle map is a bucket system for organizing obstacles on the road. The system breaks the road up into multiple smaller subsections. Every obstacle in the world is located in a bucket somewhere. This logical grouping provides optimized culling of obstacles that are obviously not in the way. An obstacle bucket exists between each pair of road centerline vertices, and spans the area between the left and right outer road boundaries. Additionally, each intersection in the city is defined as an obstacle bucket, and is not further subdivided. As stated previously, straight roads are defined by sets of four vertices. Two of the vertices are located at each end of the road segment. The other two vertices are set back 10 meters from each intersection, and provide a quick way to access the ambient traffic obstacles that are typically waiting to traverse the intersection due to a stop sign or a traffic light.

Library Interface

The AINavigation object controls the various AI Racers. There are two primary interface functions to this library: RegisterRoute and DriveRoute. Routes are defined as a list of intersection IDs, each separated by a single connecting road segment. From the intersection list, an explicit list of connecting roads is derived.

The RegisterRoute function registers the list of intersections with the navigation system, and then initializes the variables necessary to maintain the navigation of the route. This function is called once to register the route with the navigation system. If the route changes for any reason, then the RegisterRoute function must be called again to enter the new route with the navigation system.

The DriveRoute function is called once per frame to calculate the steering, throttle, and brake settings. A state machine controls the various states of the AI Entity. The required states are driving forward, backing up, colliding, and stopping.

Backing up is necessary whenever the AI entity gets stuck behind an obstacle that it cannot drive around. This typically occurs when the human player collides with the AI player and sends it flying off course. In this case, the opponent, if visible, must back up and steer around the obstacle. When the entity is not visible, the vehicle is manually repositioned on the road surface away from obstacles. The Colliding state is active when the vehicle is colliding with another entity in the world. During this time, the vehicle is completely under the control of the physics engine. Once the vehicle settles down from the collision, the state is switched back to driving forward. The Stop state primarily controls the vehicle when it reaches the end of its route.

Navigating the City

The first step in navigating the road network is to solve the problem of where the AI entity is currently located.

Finding Your Current Location

Once this entity knows what road or intersection it is located on, then it also knows its relative location in the primary route. Using this, it then plans an immediate route to navigate the upcoming obstacles. The immediate route length is determined by the immediate route planning distance variable.

The city is broken up into rooms, where the dimensions of each room are equal to the same dimensions as the physical geometry of the road or intersection. The

SolveMapComponent() function handles this task, and takes the current position as the first input parameter. The first task the function does is to iterate through the list of rooms in the city to determine which room the point is in. To increase the performance of this function, each room has a list of pointers that connects the current room with all of its neighboring rooms.

The first time the SolveMapComponent() function is called, it must iterate through the entire list to find the room where the AI entity is located. However, on subsequent calls, a room ID hint is supplied, which is usually the last known room location for the AI. The function checks the hint room first, and then checks the neighboring rooms. Since the rooms are typically large, this optimization works quite well. If the function determines the entity is not in any of these rooms, it reverts to iterating over all of the rooms.

Updating the Road Cache

The second step is to update the road cache. The road cache is defined as the current and next two road segments as defined by the primary route. The cache is basically a First In, First Out (FIFO) queue. When the current road is completely traversed, the next road is moved into the current road slot, the second road is moved into the next road slot, and the next road in the route is inserted into the cache as the second road. Three road segments are utilized to support the desired route planning distance. If your road segments are very small or your planning distance is long, then more roads in the cache will be necessary. Every time the cache changes, the function InitRoadTurns() is called to calculate the variables necessary for defining sharp turns.

After a collision, the AI entities often find themselves on a different road than the road they originally were on. This is due to the vehicle being under physics control during the collision. In this case, it must update the road cache with the new current road, and then it must determine the next road it must traverse to get back to the original intersection goal. Most of the time, the original intersection goal is the current road's destination intersection, but in rare cases, it must determine additional roads.

Enumerating All Possible Routes

The third step is to enumerate all of the possible routes available for traversing the current road segment. This is accomplished through the EnumRoutes() function and is presented here in a simplified format:

```
void aiNavigation::EnumRoutes(Position)
{
   CalcRoadTurns();
   if(InSharpTurn())
   {
      CalcSharpTurnTarget();
   }
   else
```

```
    {
        CalcRoadTarget();
    }
    if(IsTargetBlocked())
    {
        NumTargets=CalcObstacleAvoidPoints();
        for(NumTargets)
        {
            if (CurrentDistance<PlanDistance)
                EnumRoutes();
        }
    }
    else
    {
        if(CurrentDistance<PlanDistance)
            EnumRoutes();
    }
}
```

The `EnumRoutes()` function is called recursively until all of the possible routes have been enumerated out to the desired route planning distance. Each time `EnumRoutes()` is called, it creates an immediate route segment.

The route planning distance is the length of road that the AI player will use when enumerating the various immediate routes. Longer route planning distances provide better choices to the AI player, because it allows for a mathematical representation of potentially blocked routes because of ambient traffic and other obstacles. However, longer planning distances require more CPU time; therefore, a balance must be struck. Based on the route planning distance, several route segments might be required to completely enumerate the route. On the first call to this function, the position parameter is initialized to the position of the vehicle in control. Subsequent calls use the calculated target points enumerated in this function.

The `CalcRoadTurns()` is the function called first by the `EnumRoutes()` function. The function calculates the necessary variables for representing sharp turns. Any two roads at an intersection define a sharp turn where the angle between them is greater than 45 degrees. This number is tunable, and can be modified to change the personality of the AI entity. It is also possible to get sharp turns within a road. This happens when any two-road subsections have an angle greater than 45 degrees. Road subsections are defined as the physical space between any two centerline road vertices, and the outer left and right boundaries. It is important to realize that if the turn is not considered sharp, the vehicle should be steered directly to the target point.

The arc of a circle defines the path through a sharp turn. A diagram of the main variables is shown in Figure 9.4.2.

The intersection point of the turn is defined as the point in space where the two projected road segment vectors *AB* and *DC* meet. The `CalcTurnIntersection()` function handles these calculations, and is illustrated in Figure 9.4.3.

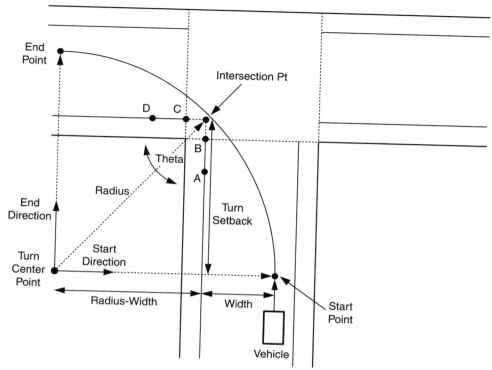

FIGURE 9.4.2 *Calculating the sharp turn variables.*

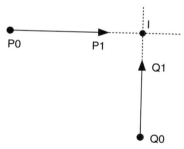

FIGURE 9.4.3 *Calculating the turn intersection point.*

If the turn is to the left, then the left inner boundary is used, and when the turn is right, the right inner boundary is used. *P0* is point *D* in Figure 9.4.2, and *P1* is the vector defined by *C-D*. *Q0* is defined by point *A*, and *Q1* is the vector defined by *B-A*. The intersection point is calculated by setting the two vectors equal to each other.

$P=P_0+sP_1 \qquad Q=Q_0+tQ_1$

$P_0+sP1=Q_0+tQ_1$

$s=(Q_0+tQ_1-P_0)/P_1$

$(Q_{0x}+tQ_{1x}-P_{0x})/P_{1x} = (Q_{0z}+tQ_{1z}-P_{0z})/P_{1z}$

$t=(P_{1x}Q_{0z} - P_{1x}P_{0z} - P_{1z}Q_{0z} + P_{1z}P_{0x}) / (P_{1z}Q_{1x} - P_{1x}Q_{1z})$ (9.4.1)

Once t is calculated, it is trivial to substitute the value of t into the original equations:

(9.4.2)

$I_x=Q_{0x}+tQ_{1x}$ and $I_z=Q_{0z}+tQ_{1z}$

For the case of a left turn, the next step is to calculate the distance between the current location and the left road boundary. This is called the *Width*. The *Width* is calculated by taking the dot product with the X orientation vector and the vector defined between the current position and the current left boundary point. Since the values of the *Width* and *HalfTheta* are known, using simple geometry, the radius of the arc is calculated with the following formula: *Radius = Width / (1-sin(HalfTheta))*. *Theta* is calculated by taking *Pi* and subtracting the angle of the turn. *HalfTheta* is just the value of *Theta* divided by two. Next, the turn setback is calculated based on the geometry triangle formula *cos(theta) = Opposite / Hypotenuse*, the turn center point of the arc is calculated by simple vector addition. Finally, the start and end directional vectors are calculated by first calculating the start and end points, and then calculating the vector defined by *StartPt – TurnCenterPt* and *EndPt – TurnCenterPt*, respectively.

The next task of the EnumRoutes() function is to determine if the AI entity is currently traversing a sharp turn or a road segment. This function performs two dot products for each of the upcoming intersections in order to calculate the distance from the start and end direction vectors. These variables are defined as StartX and EndX in Figure 9.4.4.

If both of these values are positive, then the position is considered to be within the turn. A quick distance squared test is also part of the function. This is used to eliminate points that are technically within the arc, but at a distance too far away to be considered within it.

Based on the returned value of the InSharpTurn function, it is now possible to calculate the target point. For sharp turns, the length of the turn arc is divided into segments of 10 meters. The target point is set to the next upcoming vertex in the turn arc. As soon as the turn arc goes into the next road segment, the turn is completed and EnumRoutes() is called again if necessary. If we're not in a sharp turn, then we must be on a road segment. The first step in calculating the road target point is to define the left and right view angles. The function InitializeTheViewAngles() performs these calculations.

As seen in the example in Figure 9.4.5, the car needs to determine a route out of its current intersection. First, the current road vertex is initialized to zero, and the view angles are calculated by calculating a vector from each boundary vertex to the current position. Next, a dot product is calculated using the road segment's orienta-

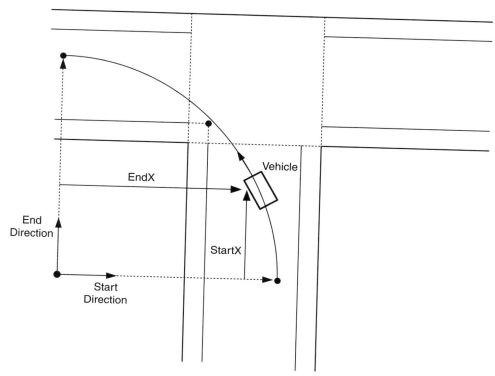

FIGURE 9.4.4 *Determining if the AI vehicle is within the turn.*

tion vectors. Finally, the angle is calculated by the arc tangent of the previous two dot products. These angles represent the current minimum road view.

Next, the default target is set. The default road type is a straight road. The default target is therefore a point at the end of the road with the same left/right distance as the vehicle's current left/right distance. The left/right distance is based off the road's centerline. If the road is not straight, the DetermineIfTheEndOfRoadIsVisible() function will detect it, and determine the furthest visible position available to turn toward.

To determine which direction the road bends, the view angle of each successive boundary vertex is tested. If the calculated view angle is less than the minimum view angle, then the minimum view angle is modified to the new view angle. The furthest vertex visible is determined when either the left view angle is more than the right view angle, or when the right view angle is less than the left view angle. Per the example, when the boundary vertices for vertex one and two are tested, both view angles are tightened up. On vertex three, only the left view angle is tightened up. Finally, on vertex four the left view angle becomes more than the right view angle. The last visible vertex on the right side was vertex two, and this becomes the target point for the route segment. If the distance between the vehicle and the target point is less than the route planning distance, then an additional call to EnumRoutes() is required. On

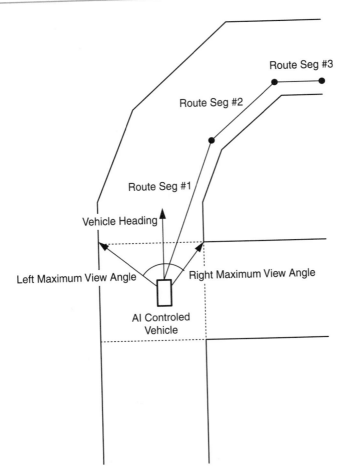

FIGURE 9.4.5 *Calculating the road target points.*

this iteration of the function, the position is changed to the position of the target point calculated in the previous call to EnumRoutes().

Avoiding Obstacles

After each route segment is calculated, the next step is to check for any obstacles in the way. Figure 9.4.6 illustrates the case where an ambient vehicle is now blocking the first route segment.

The IsTargetBlocked() function performs this check. This function works by iterating over all of the obstacle buckets from the current position to the target point, and then checking each obstacle in the bucket to see if the obstacle is blocking the desired route segment. It performs the check by creating a vector between the position and the target point, and then doing a dot product with each corner of the obstacle. If any corner of the obstacle is within a distance of less than the AI vehicle's half

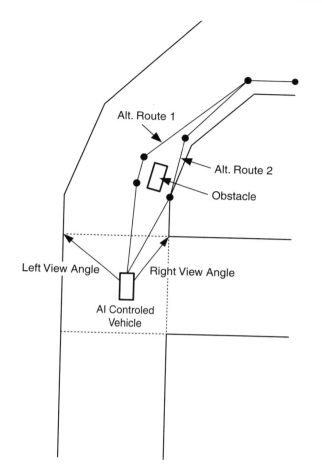

FIGURE 9.4.6 *Planning a route around an obstacle.*

width, the obstacle is returned to EnumRoutes() as the blocking obstacle. Next, two avoid positions are calculated: one to the left and one to the right. The avoid positions are calculated by using the vehicle's X orientation vector. The desired position is projected along the vector at a distance equal to the half width of the obstacle plus the half width of the AI entity, and a tunable buffer distance. Typically, a value between one and two meters works well. For each avoid position, EnumRoutes() is called again and the process repeats until the desired route planning distance is achieved.

Once all the immediate routes have been enumerated, it is time to select the best route of the bunch. The DetermineBestRoute() function handle this task. There are many criteria for determining the best route. In our experience, the best route is defined as the straightest overall route. Alternate criteria could include routes that are not completely blocked, staying off the sidewalk, or the route with the fewest obstacles. The `DetermineBestRoute()` function iterates over each immediate route calculated, and then compares each to all of the others based on the criteria that is set up for the decision.

Calculating the Throttle and Brake Values

Most of the time, the AI vehicle is driving the route as fast as possible. However, when traversing sharp turns, the turn might be so sharp that the vehicle spins out and loses control. The fastest way to drive through a sharp turn is to attain the maximum speed through the turn without losing friction. The `CalcSpeed()` function calculates the maximum possible speed to drive a sharp turn without losing friction, and to determine when to start applying the braking force.

Figure 9.4.7 shows the two vertical forces acting on the car, its weight W, and its normal force N. Since these forces must add vectorially to zero, we have the formula: $N = W = mg$. The magnitude of the centripetal acceleration is given by v^2/R, where v is the velocity and R is the radius. Since force is equal to the mass times the acceleration, then the force must be equal to:

$$F = mv^2/R \tag{9.4.3}$$

If the force is to be provided by friction, then the required minimum coefficient of friction (μ) is:

$$\mu = F/N = (mv^2/R)/mg = v^2/gR \tag{9.4.4}$$

Therefore, the maximum velocity the vehicle can go before losing friction is:

$$v = \sqrt{\mu g R} \tag{9.4.5}$$

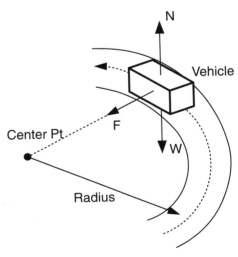

FIGURE 9.4.7 *A car on a nonbanked turn.*

Once the target velocity is calculated, we are able to calculate the amount of braking force to apply to the vehicle, and when to apply it. The first thing we must do is calculate the amount of time before the vehicle starts traversing the turn. Use this formula:

Time to the Reach the Turn (T) = Distance to the Turn / Speed of the Vehicle   (9.4.6)

To calculate the distance to the turn, take the dot product of the forward orientation vector, then the vector defined by the vehicle's current position and the intersection point, and then subtract the turn setback. Finally, use the following equation to calculate the braking force:

Braking Force = (Current Speed − Target Speed)/(T * μ * g)   (9.4.7)

where μ represents the value of the friction between the ground and the vehicle's wheels, and g is the value of gravity. The value of gravity used here is rarely the actual value of g, and is typically defined by trial and error. A typical value is twice the normal value of gravity. When the braking force goes above the brake threshold, the braking force is applied to the brakes.

The AI entity steers by calculating a target point to steer toward. Once all the potential immediate routes are enumerated, the target point is set to the first point of the best route.

The code first calculates the angle between the forward direction of the vehicle and the vector defined between the target point and the vehicle's current location. The steering is then set to the value of the angle. For small angles, those below .05 radians (~3 degrees), the vehicle is rotated to match the target vector. A tunable scalar is applied to the angle to approach the target vector either faster or slower.

Conclusion

ON THE CD

In conclusion, the code presented here, and on the CD-ROM, provides the framework necessary for AI-controlled vehicles to navigate a random arrayed network of roads and intersections in a competitive and realistic-looking way. If you are interested in learning more about the AI techniques involved with open city environments, check out [Adzima00].

References

[Adzima00] Adzima, Joseph C., "Using AI to Bring Open City Racing to Life," *Game Developer* magazine, Miller Freeman Inc., December 2000.

9.5

Camera AI for Replays

Sandeep V. Kharkar—Microsoft

eltoro_the_deep@hotmail.com

Replays are an essential part of all sports games, and a nice extra feature in many other genres. Surprisingly, replays are an afterthought in many of these titles. When done right, replays accentuate the gameplay and make the past events look even more exciting. This is where you have a chance to showcase your graphics and action by carefully crafting the camerawork of the replay. With a little insight from filmmaking [Mascelli98], music videos, and real instant replays, you can create a replay feature that really "wows" your audience.

This paper is written with a racing or individual sports game (like snowboarding) in mind, but some techniques described can also be applied to other genres. While this paper will cover camera AI for replays, the technical details of recording and playing back the replay are not discussed. For an excellent explanation of input recording and playback, see Bruce Dawson's article, "Game Input Recording and Playback," in *Game Programming Gems 2* [Dawson01].

Definition of Terms

These are some common camerawork terms that will help us talk about replays.

- **Replay**: The playback of a past event, sometimes in slow motion or viewed from alternative camera angles.
- **Player**: The human playing the game.
- **Actor**: Game characters that might appear in a replay.
- **Subject**: The game character that the camera is currently tracking.
- **Stage**: The environment of the game where the action of the replay takes place.

Issues in Replay Playback

The most important part of the playback is the visual presentation. Because the player is not interacting with the game during a replay, it is very important that he or she is continuously entertained. Failure to understand this key issue will result in replays that nobody watches. If the player's attention is lost due to frustration or boredom, this feature of the game will never be visited again.

Frustration

The first major issue with replays is frustration. Many things can cause the player to become frustrated with the replay, one of which is lack of accuracy. If the actors in a replay behave in a manner that is obviously different from how they did during the game, the player will lose confidence in the replay. This can be remedied by using the recording schemes that best match your needs and ensuring the validity of data.

Another reason for frustration is poor performance during the replay caused by inadequate bandwidth for streaming data or lack of adequate memory on the target system. Proper design and optimization of related code can remedy these issues.

Even though the player does not interact with the game during the replay, it is important that the player feels in control of the game at all times. If the replay starts up and the only option is to stop it, it makes for a poor experience. The game must allow the player to control the replay, if he or she wishes.

Possible replay controls:

- Restart
- Pause/unpause
- Increase/decrease playback speed
- Jump forward/backward by a fixed interval
- Manually change to a different camera
- Toggle heads-up display
- Quit replay

Boredom

Another major issue with replays is boredom; however, this is very subjective. A guaranteed way to avoid boredom is to have a fast-paced and interesting replay. Think of this as making a music video. Many of the tricks filmmakers use can be adopted in replays to prevent boredom. However, unlike the film studios, you don't have the luxury of recording oodles of content and editing it at leisure in a studio; you have to do it in real time.

This is where a strong rule-based AI system can help. The problem has been well studied from the point of view of filmmaking, and a basic set of rules for camerawork is established. Moreover, because you have a good idea about your stage, actors, and how they behave, the problem is very well suited for a rule-based AI.

Camera Angles and Styles

As mentioned previously, a major threat to the replay feature of your game is boredom.

Making a fast-paced and interesting replay will guarantee that the players will look forward to watching the replay. Varying the visual experience is one way to keep the player's interest. This can be achieved by having a huge arsenal of interesting camera angles and styles, and by switching between them using specialized rules.

This section will present a series of camera types and their variations, as well as some rules for their use. Keep in mind that these angles should be triggered by your rule engine, using the timing and transition rules described in each type. For some information about basic camera mathematics, please refer to [Paull00].

Intro Camera

This camera introduces your stage and the actors. It starts at a distance, and either meanders toward or quickly approaches the subject, showing off your stage as it gets there. After approaching the subject, it can circle around to show off the details of the subject before taking position where the next camera will be. This camera should not be active for more than three- to five seconds. It should complete its role and switch to avoid boredom. This camera type should be limited to the beginning of the replay when the subject is stationary, and never used after that.

First-Person Camera

This camera presents the stage from the subject's point of view. It is very useful in racing games where it gives the feel of actually being in the car with the driver. It is also useful in sports games where a subject is interacting with other actors in the scene. Variations of this camera present the scene from a position on or very close to the subject's avatar; for example, the front wheel of the car, the snowboarder's board tip, or the football player's helmet. It is important to have a point of reference on the subject, visible in this camera's view; otherwise, it can become very disorienting. This camera can be used often, but should be switched within two to four seconds to avoid motion sickness.

Follow Camera

This camera type is also referred to as a third-person camera. This camera typically shows part of the scene and the subject from behind, and simulates looking over the subject's shoulder. Variations of this camera can present the subject from various distances, heights, and with various fields of view. The variations should be different enough so that a switch to another variation does not look like a visual anomaly.

Another interesting variation of this camera is created when the camera is not always at a fixed distance, but attached to the subject by an invisible spring. This allows the player to move away with a delayed reaction from the camera. However, springs can cause a lot of trouble when frame rates are not constant. In addition, they must be used with care to avoid the camera from swinging around wildly during the replay. A useful code snippet for putting a camera on a spring is given by Dante Treglia in *Game Programming Gems* [Treglia00].

This camera can be used for up to 50 percent of the replay time with other interesting cameras thrown in between. The sequences can be anywhere between three and nine seconds. They can also be used as a calming section after an action-packed camera switch sequence.

Look Back Camera

This camera type is the reverse view of a follow camera. The camera leads the subject by a certain distance and matches his speed and direction of motion, effectively showing the subject and the scene behind him. Variations can be created by allowing the camera to move at a different speed than the subject, thus allowing the camera to get farther away or get closer to the subject. Moreover, a very nice cinematic effect is created by moving the camera within a fixed range during part of this shot. However, if the subject is changing direction rapidly, this camera view can cause motion sickness, so it must be used for short time periods (two to four seconds), or used when the player is moving in a fairly constant direction.

Rail or Side Camera

This camera type tracks the subject while staying to the side, mimicking his speed and direction. Again, allowing the camera to move at a different speed from the subject can create interesting variations. This would simulate a camera passing by the player, or the player passing by a moving camera, both of which are great cinematic effects. This camera type provides an interesting view to the player that was not visible during gameplay. Try to limit this camera to three to five seconds at a time.

Pan or Drop Camera

This camera type stays in a fixed location, panning (turning) as the subject passes by, simulating the spectator effect. It must be forced to switch when the subject gets a certain distance away, to avoid watching a moving speck in the distance. Variations of this camera would move up and down in various ways as the subject passes by. This is called the *boom*, and is a typical camera technique used for parades on TV. This camera type provides a scene-to-subject interaction at different locations on the stage, making them interesting enough to use often. They must be switched once the player is not visible or too far.

Drop and Follow Camera

This is a variant of the static drop camera that allows the subject to get a certain distance ahead of it, and then picks itself up and turns into a follow camera. This provides a great transition that can turn a static or slow scene into an action-packed sequence.

Chase and Follow Camera

This camera type is similar to the intro camera, except the subject is now on the move. The camera starts some distance back and speeds up faster than the subject attempting to catch up with him. At a fixed distance, it turns into a follow camera; however, this camera can be disorienting when switched to. To avoid this, the player should be kept in view or brought into view quickly. The distance and speed should be adjusted so that the sequence does not last for more than two to four seconds.

The "Matrix" Camera

This is an essential camera type popularized by the movie *The Matrix*. The camera pauses some or all of the action, or slows it down while it circles around the subject. This camera gives a very dramatic effect and should be used when the subject is doing something spectacular. Try to use it sparingly, maybe just once during the entire replay.

Circle Camera

This camera type slowly circles the subject while looking at him. It is ideal for a slow, serene portion of the replay, or to slow things down after an action-packed sequence. It can also be used as a transition camera to go from one side of the player to another, left to right or front to back.

Still Frame Camera

This camera type has also been popularized by movies and is another variation of the static panning camera. As the subject passes by, the camera pauses the action at regular intervals simulating a sequence of photographs being taken. Visual effects such as black-and-white frames or camera shutter sounds can enhance the effect of this camera. This camera should be used in conjunction with nonplayer actors in the scene, like photographers at the sidelines of a sports event.

Camera Placement

Camera placement rules apply to replays that are based on a fixed stage where the actors are forced to be inside certain confines. Racing and arena titles are ideal for such placement. Cameras can be placed strategically at locations that are likely to see part of the action, such as turns on a racetrack or goal posts on a sports field. When the subject comes inside the range of the camera, the camera should be activated. Games in which the player can go anywhere have a tougher job of placing fixed cameras.

Cameras should occasionally be placed where more than one actor is visible in addition to the subject. This gives a sense of perspective to a scene, while adding a nice, cinematic touch.

Camera Switching

This section includes some general rules for camera switching in racing or individual sports titles that have been learned from experience.

- A camera sequence should not be shorter than two seconds.
- A camera sequence should not be longer than nine seconds.
- A camera switch should never cut to the opposite side of a player, because this is very disorienting.
- The subject should always be visible in a sequence, or there should be the anticipation that the subject is about to appear.
- Anticipatory times should not exceed two seconds.
- Transitions from one camera to another should be seamless, either instantly or through a proper transition to avoid visual "pops" in the replay.

- Special cameras such as the matrix, still frame, and chase and follow should be used sparingly.
- Special cameras should never be used one after the other.
- Follow cameras should be used a lot and serve as breathers between other cameras.
- Never switch from one follow camera variation to another just adjacent to it.
- Use pan or look back cameras to show the subject in relation to other actors when the opportunity arises.
- Every camera should know what camera to switch to in case it loses sight of the subject.
- Some cameras look good in sequence; for example, a right rail to circle to left rail.
- Sequences that are appropriate for the particular game type should be found and used.

Tools for Debugging and Tuning Replays

AI programmers have just recently started paying attention to tools. The realization that good tools make great AI has helped improve the quality of both tools and AI. Given that the creation of replays is more of an art than a science, the programmer must provide tools for an artist or designer to play with. Here is a list of additional tools that you can add to your arsenal to make it simpler to put together a great replay engine:

- The ability to halt the simulation at any point and to roam the stage with the current camera view.
- The ability to switch the subject of any camera.
- The ability to see the name and relevant parameters of the current camera at any time (no, not just in the debugger!). A good reference for this is a paper by John Olsen [Olsen00].
- The ability to change and store the relevant parameters of the current camera at any time.
- The ability to selectively stop any of the subjects while letting the rest of the simulation continue.
- The ability to take screenshots of the current view (marketing folks will love you for it).
- The ability to see which camera the current camera is going to switch to, and change it.
- The ability to know why the most recent camera switch occurred.

Conclusion

Replays give a game the opportunity to showcase its graphics and action by carefully crafting a series of camera views and transitions. They also allow players to see parts of the game stage that they could not during regular gameplay, adding to the value of the game.

Players can lose interest in a replay due to either frustration or boredom. Allowing players to continue controlling the game during the replay goes a long way toward avoiding frustration. Preventing boredom, on the other hand, requires a lot of smart work. Creating fast-paced and interesting replays guarantees that the feature will be used often, and visual variety in the replay will help to keep the player's interest.

This is where a huge arsenal of camera types and variations, coupled with a solid rule-based system for switching between them, works really well. This article presented many camera types and some possible variations for them, along with ideas for how you can use them. A set of general-purpose rules for switching between cameras is also provided.

Creating exciting replays is an artistic endeavor, so having a good set of tools that will allow an artist or designer fine-tune the replays is essential. Some of the tools that you could find useful in creating and fine-tuning replays were also presented in this article.

Finally, don't be afraid to experiment with ideas from movies, music videos, or sports coverage. These are created by people who spend their entire lives dedicated to filmmaking and broadcast replays. It pays to study their work and learn from them, rather than trying to reinvent it yourself. After all, your replay camerawork will be judged directly against professional work, so you need all of the insight and expertise you can get.

References

[Dawson01] Dawson, Bruce, "Game Input Recording and Playback," *Game Programming Gems 2*, Charles River Media, 2001.

[Mascelli98] Mascelli, Joseph V., "The Five C's of Cinematography: Motion Picture Filming Techniques," Silman-James Press, 1998.

[Olsen00] Olsen, John, "Stats: Real-Time Statistics and In-Game Debugging," *Game Programming Gems*, Charles River Media, 2000.

[Paull00] Paull, David, "The Vector Camera," *Game Programming Gems*, Charles River Media, 2000.

[Treglia00] Treglia II, Dante, "Camera Control Techniques," *Game Programming Gems*, Charles River Media, 2000.

9.6

Simulating Real Animal Behavior

Sandeep V. Kharkar—Microsoft

eltoro_the_deep@hotmail.com

AI animals or real-life entities have been principally used in the theoretical AI world to prove concepts, new ideas, and algorithms. Recently, the concept has slowly crept into games as well. They can be seen in games in the very basic form through flying birds, fluttering butterflies, and an occasional pigeon or chicken. They appear in a slightly more advanced form in strategy games, and in a more accurate and realistic form as prey in various hunting simulations. Most examples of these animals are not very lifelike in their behavior, and tend to be a distraction rather than helping to further the suspension of disbelief.

This article discusses the lessons learned while adding such entities to sports and hunting games. We talk about the different types of animals that have major and minor roles in various genres. We also present some strategies for giving these animals a lifelike feel, programming structures that are suitable, and some basic building blocks for every type of behavior.

Study the Competition

The first thing an engineer needs to do when trying to recreate animals in a game is to study the competition. This doesn't mean other games that have similar creatures—the real competition in this field is much smarter and more experienced: nature itself! You must realize that you are trying to imitate nature in your game and recreate the experience the player has had with real animals.

So, go ahead, look out your window at the flocks of birds flying around, go to your garden and observe the bugs and the hummingbirds. Go on a hiking or hunting trip with your buddy and experience it for yourself.

Next, research the perceptions of the people who interact with these creatures in the real world. Read books, go to Web sites about outdoor activities, or watch related media coverage. It is just as important to get a feel for your target audience's perceptions of the animals and related activities. Even if your game is scientifically correct in portraying an animal's behavior, if the target audience's perception is different, you will have failed.

Creatures Large and Small

The use of animals in games falls into three major categories: first, ambient animals used to enhance the environment of the game and give it a more "live" feel. Next, secondary animals, like those in strategy games that have some player interaction but are not the main focus of the game. Finally, primary animals like those in hunting simulations that are the primary focus of the game. This section of the article discusses some of the animals that you can use in each of these roles.

Ambient Animals

Ambient animals are used to enhance the environment of the game and give it a more lifelike feel. These animals are not relevant during gameplay. However, their presence makes the environment feel more alive and rich, and therefore more believable, thus improving the overall immersive nature of the game. Depending on the environment of your game, you can use solitary or flocks of birds, flying insects, small animals such as squirrels or rats, or fish in outdoor or indoor settings. Adding these ambient animals will make your game more believable and add a certain richness to the environment. Making them interact with one another can add a whole new dimension to your game.

Secondary Animals

Secondary animals have a limited amount of interaction with the player. They play a part in gameplay, but are not the primary focus of the game. This category includes animals that act as a resource in a real-time strategy game, or in a recent and more innovative game design, the animals in a zoo simulation. These animals need to be intelligent but also limited, so that the necessary interaction with them does not take focus away from the main game play. The types of animals that can be used for this category are limited only by the game design.

Primary Animals

Primary animals are the focus of the game and have a direct relation to the primary objectives of a game. The choices for this class of animals are again dependent on the game design, but the potential for creating a truly lifelike experience is phenomenal! These animals are typically seen in hunting simulations that have recently been wildly popular in certain demographics.

How They Behave

This section presents some observations about different animals from shipped titles, along with some ideas for enhancements. Also presented are some programming ideas used to convert these observations into in-game entities.

Bugs

In an outdoors setting, bugs are inevitable. When used subtly, they add character to the environment. A butterfly for *Links 2001* was created that was a lot of fun and very realistic.

Here are some observations about butterflies:

- They never fly in a straight line.
- They don't always flap their wings.
- When they flap their wings, they don't have a full beat as birds do.
- They are attracted toward certain objects.
- They try to avoid any moving entities.
- They usually stay in a limited area.

All these rules helped to create a simple random number-based butterfly entity that was very lifelike, and added depth to beautiful but rather lifeless golf courses. The butterfly kept simple state information and decided on its next course of action by the roll of the dice.

Similar observations made about other little creatures can help generate simple rule sets. When combined with a random number generator, these rules can make for interesting bugs.

Solitary Animals

Solitary animals can be used in both outdoor and urban settings.

Highflying eagles or similar birds can just be circling certain areas of your environment and add some life to it.

- These birds flap their wings very rarely.
- They go from one area to another only to catch upward drafts of wind.
- They circle the area slowly gliding downward.
- They can be made to interact with ground-level creatures such as fish or chipmunks.

These entities don't really need much programming effort unless they need to interact with other ambient creatures. They need to have simple state information and locomotion-related code. If they are to interact with other creatures, then they must have greater skills that allow for hunting and survival.

The other setting in which solitary animals can be used is urban environments. These animals can be pigeons, chickens, chipmunks, rats, or other semi-domesticated animals.

- These animals tend to stay in a limited area.
- Much of their efforts are directed toward feeding.
- They tend to be fairly comfortable with human presence and are not easily scattered.
- They will maintain a safe distance and only depart an area if pursued.

- They will eventually return to the same area.
- They will try to steal food from others, and protect food they found from others.

These animals need a little more programming effort. A simple state machine works really well for them. State information can be stored for interaction with the player's character and also with others of their own type. Simple locomotion code for moving on the ground and/or simple flight is also necessary. For some basic principles, see [Reynolds99], and for a specific example of this behavior, see [Reynolds00].

Flocks of Birds

A flock of birds is a well-studied problem, and you can find a lot of information about it on the Web. Some excellent base work for emergent flock behavior is found in [Reynolds 99] and [Woodcock00]. Allowing a flock to form in this way makes for very realistic flocks, much like the hundreds of starlings you can see swarming across the sky in the spring.

However, making a flock of birds have a sense of purpose and direction requires a little leadership. This is achieved by allowing one bird (the leader) to influence the flock more than the rest. Here are some additional ideas for natural looking flocks:

- Keep them together (heading toward an average direction of the flock).
- Keep them separate (don't let them clump up).
- If a bird is ahead of the leader, slow it down in an attempt to get behind.
- If a bird falls behind, speed it up to keep up.
- Give one of the birds (the leader) greater authority in deciding the direction for the flock.
- Change the leader once in a while.
- Make some birds break away from the flock once in a while.
- Don't let these rebels go too far away.
- Let the flock ignore the rebels at times and be drawn to them at other times.

Programming a flock of birds does not require a lot of detailed state information per bird. Flock-wide information—who is the leader, who are the rebels, where are we going, are we attracted to rebels—is more useful. The code involved is more in the realm of locomotion.

Schools of Fish

Schools of fish are very similar to flocks of birds, except they tend to change direction, as a whole, more often. This can be accomplished by having dozens of goal locations in your environment, with your fish mildly attracted to one goal at a time. If you randomly switch the goal every two to 10 seconds, you will get a nice schooling effect where every fish seems to turn sharply at the same time.

Having random goals for your flocks/schools is a good technique for keeping your birds and fish constrained to a particular area. If you don't factor in a goal location and instead use the standard flocking rules proposed by Craig Reynolds, your flocks will fly indefinitely in a general direction until they are no longer visible.

Primary and Secondary Animals

Primary and secondary animals are much more fun. However, they require greater detail and programming effort to make them appear lifelike. The following behavior patterns apply to large mammals, the type that you would use in most hunting simulations.

- They tend to follow a schedule throughout the day.
- They frequent a fixed number of places.
- They have more than one active sensing mechanism, some more keen than others.
- Their senses are affected by factors in the environment (sense of smell is limited when raining, etc.).
- They typically avoid human contact, but can be dangerous when cornered.
- They typically have predictable reactions to situations, but can act contrary to those on rare occasions, such as a deer running at the player and knocking him over when surprised.

These animals should have a full array of sensing mechanisms that include hearing, smell, and sight. Simple proximity sensing will make these animals appear shallow and unreal. Depending on the type of animal, either the sense of smell or hearing is more acute. Most animals of this type have poor vision. They also react to other animals in the vicinity that are behaving abnormally, or to areas of the environment that have been recently altered. They also have the ability to alarm any animals within a certain distance.

Programming these animals is best achieved using state machines. Although finite-state machines [Dybsand00] can be adequate for creating them, using fuzzy logic [McCuskey00] or fuzzy-state machines can make them more lifelike. In addition, the environment should be richly embedded with state information that can be changed and sensed by all participants (animals and players) in the game. This dual state and sense mechanism makes for very real animals.

A simple trick used to turn a finite-state machine into a fuzzy machine is to define a special state that is itself fuzzy. When entering this state, an animal assesses the current situation and then chooses the appropriate finite state, based on the assessment. This trick can help create a fuzzy-state machine that would work with the simplicity of a state machine, and could also generate debug information when trying to fine-tune the behavior of the animal.

An important thing to remember for almost all AI is "out-of-sight" optimizations. This applies very well to animal AI as well. When the animal is not in sight and is out of range of the player, you should decrease its use of processing time to a minimum, thus saving cycles for doing additional work on the animals that are within range.

Pieces of the Puzzle

Some of the building blocks that are useful to code up in a generic fashion for use by creatures include:

- Finite-state machines
- Fuzzy-state machines
- Fast random-number generator
- Simple pathfinding
- Waypoints and the ability to seek out their location
- Sight with tunable distance and environmental effect
- Smell with tunable distance and environmental effect
- Hearing with tunable distance and environmental effect
- Avoidance of a target area
- Avoidance of a subject
- Flight from a subject
- Emergency flight (run now and think later) and recovery
- Seeking a subject

Conclusion

Simulating real animal behavior is a complex problem, but when done right, it can add depth and realism to a game's environment. The competition for this field of programming, nature itself, is very skilled and experienced. Keen observation and a sense for the perceptions of the target audience are important for success in this endeavor.

Animals used in games fall into three broad categories: ambient animals, secondary animals, and primary animals. Animals in games should not end up being a distraction or nuisance, and need to be very carefully made to blend with the environment. This can be achieved by closely simulating real animal behavior. Animals in games appear more realistic when they not only interact with the player, but also with other animals in the environment.

Most ambient animals can be programmed with simple state information and random-number generators. Flocks of birds are easy to make, but it is hard to make them look natural. Some of the ideas presented in this article were used to create a very realistic flock of birds in the distance in *Links 2001*. Primary and secondary animals need more complex data structures such as state machines. Primary animals should be given a full array of sensing capabilities so that they do not appear one-dimensional and unreal. They must also interact with the environment in which they exist. This makes it mandatory that the environment is rich with state information that the animals can use. Finally, user testing and tunable parameters will allow you to fine-tune the game to perfection.

References

[Dybsand00] Dybsand, Eric, "A Finite-State Machine Class," *Game Programming Gems*, Charles River Media, 2000.

[McCuskey00] McCuskey, Mason, "Fuzzy Logic for Video Games," *Game Programming Gems*, Charles River Media, 2000.

[Reynolds99] Reynolds, Craig, "Steering Behaviors for Autonomous Characters," *Proceedings of the Game Developers Conference*, Miller Freeman, 1999.

[Reynolds00] Reynolds, Craig, "Interaction with Groups of Autonomous Characters," *Proceedings of the Game Developers Conference*, Miller Freeman, 2000.

[Woodcock00] Woodcock, Steven, "Flocking: A Simple Technique for Simulating Group Behavior," *Game Programming Gems*, Charles River Media, 2000.

Agent Cooperation in FSMs for Baseball

P. J. Snavely—Acclaim Studios Austin

psnavely@acclaim.com

Sports games have grown in leaps and bounds this past decade. The introduction of the next generation of consoles has brought with it the need for a more intelligent sports simulation—one that will leave a distinct impression on the user. This article covers the application of only one of these sports, but take heart in the knowledge that the fundamental principles outlined here apply to any sports game.

Sports, in general, provide us with classic examples of object-oriented architecture. Think about it: at its most basic level, the game is made up of a set number of players and a ball. These players create teams, which comprise a world that behaves within a set of rules. Players have predetermined behaviors, which operate within a finite-state machine (FSM). These behaviors have distinct starting and ending points, with clear transitions into other behaviors.

Baseball is an excellent study in artificial intelligence. It is a sport based on numbers, percentages, risks, and expected behavior. Of all the major sports, baseball has a following that is most likely to be able to point out any flaws in the artificial intelligence. Hopefully, with the help of this article, you'll be sure to keep all your bases covered—pun intended.

Behaviors

The first task in designing any sports game AI is to enumerate your behaviors—define what your actors will be doing. For our purposes, we'll be referring to behaviors exactly as if they were states in a finite-state machine. Realistically, that's what they are—behaviors have a beginning, a process, and an end. These behaviors will form the basis for your AI, and game states will provide the backbone for your game's flow. We can't stress how important it is that AI and game flow for sports games are based off finite-state machines!

For baseball, we can divide the game up into several distinct areas: fielding, baserunning, and batter/pitcher. For the purposes of this article, we'll only be tackling the fielding and baserunning areas of the game, as the batter/pitcher flow is merely an exercise in animation.

Baserunning Behaviors

Baserunning, while an integral part of the game, is not nearly as complex as the fielding portion. At any given time, runners are assuming only one of two extremely basic behaviors—they are either running or they aren't running. Any little leaguer can tell you the difference between these two things, but they won't be able to tell you why.

The primary behavior is one we'll call *Behavior Go.* This behavior is self-explanatory, much like many of your behavior names should be. If you find yourself wondering what a behavior does, there's a good chance it's a combination of behaviors. The complement to *Behavior Go* is *Behavior Go Back.* Runners will be assigned this behavior in response to events such as user input or a ball being caught.

The baserunner finite-state machine also has its own version of an idle—*Behavior Watch.* There is also an "action" version of *Behavior Watch,* which is *Behavior Freeze. Behavior Go Halfway* is actually a combination of two other behaviors (*Behavior Go* and *Behavior Freeze*). The reason it deserves uniqueness is the fact that this is a taught behavior. When a runner doesn't assume *Behavior Tag Up* on a fly ball, he'll usually assume this behavior.

Several behaviors are used at decision checkpoints for the runners. These behaviors are important because some actually limit the behaviors of other runners. *Behavior Slide* is a behavior absolutely associated with a set of animations. There are many ways to slide into any particular base, so this is a necessity. Note here as well that *Behavior Slide* also encompasses a runner slowing to a base—*slide* is a generic term implying that the runner is stopping at the base. *Behavior Turn and Go* and *Behavior Turn and Look* are behaviors also tied together with a set of animations, but these are away from any play at the base. Figure 9.7.1 outlines the flow of typical baserunner behaviors.

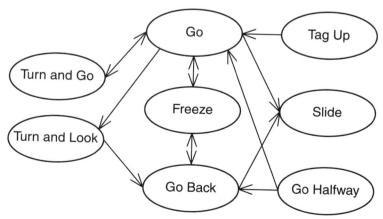

FIGURE 9.7.1 *Possible transitions and flow for baserunner behaviors.*

Fielding Behaviors

Fielding AI, unfortunately, is where the house of cards tumbles for most baseball first-timers. The behaviors are slightly more complicated, even though there are approximately the same number as baserunning. Assignments for fielding behaviors happen off two main triggers—a *Ball Hit* event and a *Ball Fielded* event. We'll get into more detail with these later.

When the ball is hit, every fielder will assume one of four basic behaviors—*Behavior Field Ball*, *Behavior Cover Base*, *Behavior Cutoff*, or *Behavior Back Up*. The behaviors aren't assigned randomly, of course; they are based specifically on where the ball is hit and the velocity with which it leaves the bat. We'll get more into how to assign these behaviors later, after we're done with our behavior enumeration.

At some point in the life cycle of every play, a fielder picks up the ball. When this occurs, some behaviors naturally transition to others. For instance, *Behavior Field Ball* for an actor who is not the fielder fielding the ball transitions to *Behavior Watch* (our multipurpose idle behavior). *Behavior Back Up* also transitions to *Behavior Watch*, because at this point in the play, our primary goal has been accomplished. Now, the tricky part is to figure out what to do with the ball.

After the ball is fielded, every player without the ball will assume *Behavior Watch*. The actor with the ball becomes our primary focus. That actor will transition to one of several behaviors—*Behavior Throw Ball*, *Behavior Run With Ball*, or *Behavior Run To Dugout*. Figure 9.7.2 is a basic outline of a fielder behavior progression.

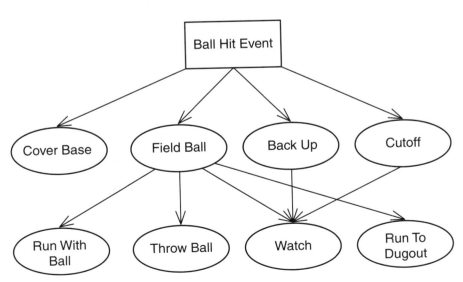

FIGURE 9.7.2 *Possible transitions and flow for fielder behaviors.*

Class Structure

We said previously that the behaviors you'll create will function exactly as states do. This requires the same basic infrastructure for each of these classes. What you'll end up with is a system with which most people are familiar, and can probably pick up without much explanation necessary.

The code example for the class `BasicBehavior` shows what your behaviors should do. There should always be something to do on your entry—start an animation, make some calculations, check game situations, and so forth. Your process and exit functions might not do anything, and that's fine. The key here is to understand that while in the current behavior, your `Process` function will be called for every iteration of the player's AI tick.

```
Class BasicBehavior
{
    …

    void Entry(Cplayer*);
    void Exit(Cplayer*);
    void Process(Cplayer*);

    …

}
```

Something else that's important to note here: each derived behavior will have its own *transition table*, a structure that contains messages, corresponding functions, and resultant behaviors. The following code illustrates some typical transition table entries from Behavior Field Ball.

```
(MESSAGE_INNING_ENDED, NULL, BEHAVIOR_RUNTODUGOUT);
(MESSAGE_FIELDER_CALLS_BALL, SlowDown(), BEHAVIOR_WATCH);
```

Behaviors also aren't forced to transition to other states just because they've received and processed a message. The resultant state can be the same as the current state; the FSM just won't process the `Entry` and `Exit` functions.

Classes should operate with a basic message queue, handling messages as they arrive. This enables us to send messages from anywhere we want (the game flow FSMs, other players, even the ball's FSM), and have the agent's behavior process these messages in the proper order. We can't stress enough how important it is that you have a robust messaging system. Overlooking this part of your AI will come back to haunt you later, but if its good enough, it can often make up for something you've forgotten to account for.

It is important to also note that the behaviors are only built once for each FSM. The behaviors act independently of player data. You'll notice that functions for the behaviors accept a pointer to the current player as an argument. This enables us to do anything we need to for the actor's movement.

The Ball Hit Event

Luckily for us, sports are entirely event-driven. There's not much use here for complex pathfinding, moments of insightful wisdom, or the ability to communicate with NPCs. The event that gets the ball rolling (pun intended) in baseball's case is what we'll call the *Ball Hit* event. All sports have something comparable—football has a snap, hockey has the dropping of the puck, and basketball prefers the jump ball. It is where we go from here that makes things interesting.

Initial Behavior Assignments—Fielders

The *Ball Hit* event provides us with enough information to assign proper behaviors to every member on either team. What it leaves up to us is the information gathering and processing. The ball's initial velocity vector will provide us with all of our basic information. We can take this initial velocity and iterate the ball through its entire path, even including stadium collision. Assuming your physics engine is robust (see [Adair94]), the ball's flight is 100-percent predetermined from the moment of impact, at least until the point where it's acted upon by your fielders.

We can store the ball's position for every iteration of our physics model—we'll need this later. We can also determine the *hit type* and *hit zone* based on the ball's initial velocity at bat contact. The type and zone are easy to calculate—the zone calculation is straight trigonometry, while the type calculation is more an application of a rule set. It's these rules that will eventually determine how "smart" your fielders appear. Figure 9.7.3 shows how we divide the field up into 10 zones for behavior assignments.

Note that the two negative zones are both in foul territory. This will make it easier for post-catch calculations and recording outs in the box score later.

The hit type determinations are a bit more complicated. There are so many different ways a baseball can travel that there are literally hundreds of different hit types. For our purposes, though, we'll simplify it as much as possible. The basic hit types are *hit type ground ball*, *hit type fly ball*, and *hit type line drive*. You can easily derive these basic hit types by applying a very small set of rules to the flight path and using the ball's maximum height, the time it takes for the ball to hit the ground, and the magnitude of its initial velocity. Some other, lesser used hit types are *hit type dribbler*, *hit type popup*, *hit type deep drive*, *hit type hard grounder*, and *hit type texas leaguer*.

Given a zone and a hit type, we can easily derive a proper set of behaviors for the fielders. For example, on a hit type ground ball in Zone 7, we can see that the first baseman and the right fielder should both be given *Behavior Field Ball*. The third baseman (third base), shortstop (second base), catcher (home plate), and pitcher (first base) are all given *Behavior Cover Base*. The second baseman will assume either *Behavior Cutoff* or *Behavior Field Ball*, depending on the initial velocity of the ball. The left fielder and center fielder will both be in *Behavior Back Up*, looking for fielders and/or bases to back up. Compare this to a ball hit with type *hit type fly ball* to the same zone—all the behaviors are exactly the same except for the first baseman (*Behavior*

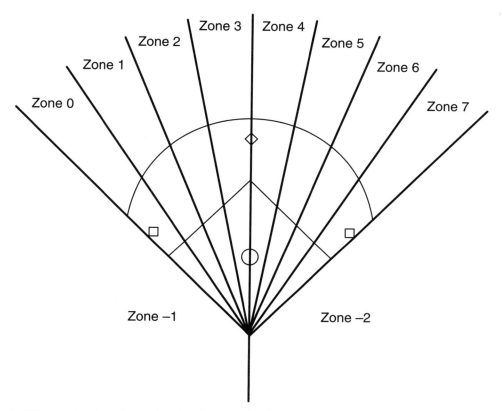

FIGURE 9.7.3 *Zone determination for initial ball velocity vectors.*

Cover Base instead of *Behavior Field Ball*) and the pitcher (*Behavior Back Up* instead of *Behavior Cover Base*).

Behavior assignments on foul balls aren't terribly complex, but with only two zones, the hit type becomes much more important. First, with *hit type grounder* in Zones −1 and −2, we don't have any behavior assignments besides *Behavior Watch*. For *hit type popup*, it's going to be your corner infielder (first/third basemen) and your catcher who get *Behavior Field Ball*. For *hit type line drive* or *hit type fly ball*, it's your corner outfielders (left/right fielders) and your corner infielders that'll get *Behavior Field Ball*.

At this point, what we have is a fairly complex rules-based system that will get everybody moving in the right direction with a common goal. Even though every agent acts independently of the others, when viewed together, they have an obvious common goal – and that's a big step towards intelligence.

Initial Behavior Assignments—Runners

The goals for baserunners tend to be far less complicated than those of their fielding brethren—they want to advance safely around the bases and score a run. Given this extremely basic set of objectives, we can arrive at the conclusion that the behavior assignment will be fairly straightforward.

The runners will use the same information for their behavior assignments as the fielders—hit type and zone. The *hit type ground ball*, for example, will cause runners to go into one of two behaviors—either *Behavior Go* or *Behavior Go Back*. Any runner who's forced will naturally assume *Behavior Go*. A runner on second who's not forced will also assume *Behavior Go* on any ball hit to the right side (Zones 4–7). Similar rules apply to the other hit types—the *hit type fly ball* will either cause *Behavior Go Halfway* or *Behavior Tag Up* to be assigned. The *hit type line drive* is an automatic assignment of *Behavior Freeze* for every runner. That ball will either hit the ground or be caught, both of which will trigger reactions from *Behavior Freeze*'s Process function.

Baserunner cooperation is a bit more complicated than the fielders. Any time a runner hits an area approximately 20 feet in front of every base, he'll go through a behavior evaluation. They'll evaluate the situation exactly the way humans do. The runner's Process function will check the proximity of the closest fielder to the ball, or if the ball has been fielded and thrown, which base the ball is being thrown to. The results of all these checks will prompt a transition into one of the other runner behaviors: *Turn and Go*, *Turn and Look*, or *Slide*.

Animations

As we saw earlier, all of these behavior assignments will have something done in the Entry functions. In almost every behavior, this consists of animation assignments. *Behavior Field*, for example, does several things. First, it determines the point at which the fielder can first intercept the ball. After that, the behavior itself will actually iterate through a process to make sure the animations are sequenced properly. *Behavior Cover Base* does something similar, only we know the point the actor is going to run to. That only leaves the animations to be put together.

Runners are slightly different, but basically the same. *Behavior Go* is as basic as it gets—the runner is pointed in a direction and put into run. *Behavior Turn and Look* is a set of animations only. Even though it might seem a tad excessive to have a behavior for something this basic, it's important that fielders and baserunners always maintain a behavior—as long as they're acting according to a behavior, you can control them!

The Exit function is typically where you'll put your animation transitions. For us, that's a fairly basic concept given the finite number of states and possible transitions. The logistical problem of figuring out how to transition from *Behavior Go* to *Behavior Run to Dugout* is a fairly straightforward one, and one we'll leave up to you.

Ball Fielded Event

This is the second part of our two-step process. Once the ball has been fielded, every fielder's obligation (except for our ball carrier) is to make sure the bases are covered. That's the easy part. The part that gets tough is deciding what to do with the ball now that we have it. It's at this point where most baseball games often break down after a mostly acceptable showing—we'll try and prevent that here.

Throw Determination

The basic decision here is what to do with a fielded ground ball on the infield. We can use what we know—where the runners were initially, how far they are from their destination bases, and the game situation—to determine where and how to throw the ball. Too many games are guilty of missing the game situation portion of this check. There's absolutely *no* reason to try for a difficult force play at second when you've got an easy jog over to first for the third out. The key to any good AI for a sports game is to use every piece of information. If there's something that seems like it should influence your decision, you're probably right—adjust your rule set.

Fly balls are easy—95 percent of your throws either go to second or home. Either way, you're almost always better off just throwing the ball to the cutoff man and deciding what to do with it then. It is much easier to evaluate runners from this point rather than from the outfield, where a throw is going to take two seconds to reach its destination.

Rundowns present an interesting dilemma. We have enough information to throw out a user-controlled runner 100 percent of the time. Baseball coaches will teach you that every rundown should end after one throw. If you've ever watched major league baseball, you'll see that's not often the case. The solution here is to vary your throw window—mix it up some. What you'll see are different user responses, longer rundowns, and generally more fun as users will remember the old games of "Pickle" they used to play when they were kids.

Conclusion

AI for sports games definitely isn't an area one should approach lightly. If your work isn't letter-perfect (and sometimes even when it is), there will always be somebody who doesn't like it. Your mission, should you choose to accept it, is to create an accurate representation of the sport and still provide the user with an enjoyable experience. The techniques we've outlined here with behavior enumeration, behavior-based finite-state machines, and transition tables with message queues will apply across a broad range of sports. What you've seen here is one practical application of the system. Don't be afraid to see how other people have tackled the problem (see [Rabin98]) or look to references for more information (see [Morgan00]).

There's a ton of things we didn't cover, such as manager AI, box score handling, batter/pitcher AI, crowd fluctuation, and a host of other things. Don't be intimidated by the sheer quantity of AI in a sports game. The largest part is the actors and how they react. Get this right, and it is easy to forgive just about everything else that's wrong.

Sports-game AI, and baseball in particular, is filled with trial and error. The biggest thing to remember is that nothing is set in stone. If you need another hit type or behavior, feel free to add it. You are the only person who's going to understand your system from top to bottom, but the more organized it is, the more likely you can explain it to someone else. The best advice we can give is to read as much as you can, watch as much as you can, and never be afraid to question what you see. Good luck!

References

[Adair94] Adair, Robert K., *The Physics of Baseball*, HarperTrade, 1994.

[Rabin98] Rabin, Steve, "Making the Play: Team Cooperation in Microsoft Baseball 3D," *Conference Proceedings*, Computer Game Developers Conference, 1998.

[Morgan00] Morgan, Joe and Lally, Richard, *Baseball for Dummies*, IDG Books Worldwide, Inc., 2000.

9.8

Intercepting a Ball

Noah Stein

noah@acm.org

John Stockton holds the NBA all-time record for the most steals by an individual throughout his career—more than 2,800 (as of 2001). He has more than luck. He has skill. However, his skill is not merely confined to the mechanical act of stealing the ball. As important as the motion itself, he has skill in determining when he can steal the ball. Without the when, he would never have the chance to use the how.

In sports games, many situations arise that require determining whether a player can intercept the ball: a second baseman wants to catch a line drive, a hockey wing tries to steal a pass, a soccer goalie needs to block a shot, or a basketball center wishes to rebound the ball. In these cases, the AI needs to decide if the action can be successfully executed, or whether an alternative course of action should be taken.

The algorithm described herein is also applicable outside the genre of sports games: the Shao-Lin master might need to decide whether to grab an arrow flying at him or just move his leg out of the way. Can the Patriot missile intercept and destroy the Scud? A secret service agent needs to know if he can dive in front of the President and take the bullet in time.

The Basic Problem

The previous examples can be distilled down to essentially the same problem: one object is at a certain position (P_b) and traveling in a straight line at a constant velocity (V_b); another object at a different position (P_p) wants to intercept the first, but it might not move faster than a specific speed (s). From this information, the model solves for the second object's velocity to intercept (V_p). Some might object to the simplicity of the model; however, every model must make simplifications, and those made for this problem render a functional solution. Please note that in the discussion that follows, the *ball* is the object that is traveling along a path that is to be intercepted, and the *player* is the object that wants to intercept the ball.

The first simplification is that the ball's velocity is constant and its trajectory is therefore a straight line. A basketball coming off the rim follows a parabolic trajectory—not even remotely close to a straight line. How can a straight line model the motion effectively? This model can be broken down into two independent submodels: the altitude of the ball, and the motion in the ground plane. Because the two axes in the ground plane are orthogonal to the altitude axis, their motions can be considered in isolation [Resnick91]. The bulk of this article explains the computation of the ground plane interception. The end of the article addresses adding altitude considerations to the model.

The second simplification is that the intercepting object has no turning radius, infinite acceleration, and can travel indefinitely at its maximum velocity. This is definitely the more difficult of the two aspects to explain, because it will introduce the most error. First, error isn't necessarily a bad thing: a real person will have difficulty judging certain situations. Second, there are other methods that can be used to compensate for heading changes, some of which appear later. In addition, the interplay between changes of direction and acceleration is so complex that a simplification to some degree must occur.

Given this information, the model has four independent variables: the position of the ball, the velocity of the ball, the position of the interceptor, and the maximum speed the interceptor can travel. A graphical representation of the problem is shown in Figure 9.8.1. Please note that in all figures, dots represent the objects, solid lines represent velocities, and dashed lines represent changes in position.

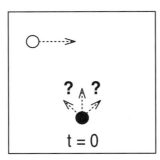 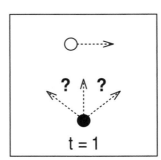 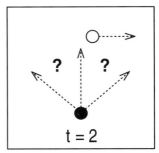

FIGURE 9.8.1 *The intercept ball problem.*

Deriving the Solution

Examining Figure 9.8.1, the problem might appear to be the point on line closest to point algorithm from *Graphics Gems* [Glassner90]. The check determines the closest point on the trajectory line. It appears to be a good choice. In some cases, the optimal choice is close to this point; however, Figure 9.8.2 clearly illustrates a case in which the point-line test clearly and convincingly fails to deliver the correct result.

What is the proper mathematical model? For an interception to occur, the position of both the ball and the player must be the same at some time t. Thus, if $\mathbf{V_p}$ was known *a priori*, the intercept statement would appear as such:

$$\mathbf{P_b} + \mathbf{V_b}t = \mathbf{P_p} + \mathbf{V_p}t \tag{9.8.1}$$

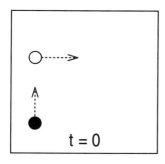 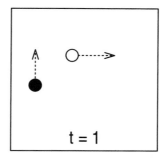 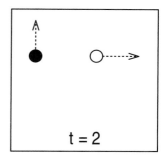

FIGURE 9.8.2 *Failure to intercept the ball given the simple solution of choosing the closest point on the ball's trajectory.*

Unfortunately, V_p is the variable to be solved. The solution requires that the problem be viewed from a different vantage. If the positions of the player and ball are the same, the distance must be 0. The distance between the player's initial position and the ball at time t:

$$\left|\left(P_b - P_p\right) + V_b t\right| \tag{9.8.2}$$

In Equation 9.8.2, the vector can be considered to be composed of two elements: the initial position of the ball relative to the player (the part in the parentheses), and the motion of the ball due to its velocity vector. If the player can move a distance equivalent to how distant the ball is, the player can intercept the ball at time t:

$$\left|\left(P_b - P_i\right) + V_b t\right| = s_i t \tag{9.8.3}$$

Since the initial positions never change, to simplify further discussion, the substitution $P \equiv P_b - P_i$ will be made from this point forth. In addition, subscripts will be dropped since there will be no ambiguity in the text. Solving for t results in the time(s) at which the player can successfully intercept the ball:

$$\left|P + Vt\right| = st$$

$$\sqrt{\left(P + Vt\right) \bullet \left(P + Vt\right)} = st$$

$$\left(P + Vt\right) \bullet \left(P + Vt\right) = \left(st\right)^2$$

$$P \bullet P + 2P \bullet Vt + V \bullet Vt^2 = s^2 t^2$$

$$\left(V \bullet V - s^2\right)t^2 + \left(2P \bullet V\right)t + \left(P \bullet P\right) = 0 \tag{9.8.4}$$

Now the equation is a second-order polynomial of t. Plug the polynomial scalars into the quadratic equation.

Analysis of the Quadratic

$$\frac{-b \pm \sqrt{b^2 - 4ac}}{2a} \tag{9.8.5}$$

The quadratic equation has three different categories of solutions: no real roots, one real root, and two real roots. The category of solution is determined by the expression in the radical: $b^2 - 4ac$. If it is negative, the solution has no real roots. If it is zero, the radical after the "$\pm$" is zero and results in a single real root. If greater than zero, the solution has two real roots. But what does this mean? First, let's transform the expression in the radical into a more informative form for subsequent analysis:

$$b^2 - 4ac = \left(2\mathbf{P} \bullet \mathbf{V}\right)^2 - 4\left(\mathbf{V} \bullet \mathbf{V} - s^2\right)\left(\mathbf{P} \bullet \mathbf{P}\right)$$

$$= 4\left(\mathbf{P} \bullet \mathbf{V}\right)^2 - 4\left(\mathbf{V} \bullet \mathbf{V} - s^2\right)\left(\mathbf{P} \bullet \mathbf{P}\right)$$

$$= \left(\mathbf{P} \bullet \mathbf{V}\right)^2 - \left(\mathbf{V} \bullet \mathbf{V} - s^2\right)\left(\mathbf{P} \bullet \mathbf{P}\right)$$

$$= \left(\mathbf{P} \bullet \mathbf{V}\right)^2 + \left(s^2 - \mathbf{V} \bullet \mathbf{V}\right)\left(\mathbf{P} \bullet \mathbf{P}\right) \tag{9.8.6}$$

No Real Roots

If the radicand (the quantity within the radical) is negative, then there are no real roots, and the ball cannot be intercepted. In this case, the quantity $(s^2 - \mathbf{V} \bullet \mathbf{V})$ must be negative, so $s < |\mathbf{V}|$. Only when the ball travels at a speed greater than the maximum speed of the player will this case occur. This agrees with our intuition that the player has to be able to move faster than the ball if he ever hopes to intercept its path.

One Real Root

This case represents a border case between whether or not the player can intercept the ball. The interception is so difficult that there is only one point in time that the ball *can* be intercepted. For the quadratic equation to result in a single root, the radicand must be zero. Examining Equation 9.8.6, if the initial positions coincide, the radical is zero, because both addends have multiplicands that have dot products involving $\mathbf{P}$, resulting in zeros. Equation 9.8.5 reduces to:

$$\frac{-b}{2a} = \frac{-\left(\mathbf{P} \bullet \mathbf{V}\right)}{2\left(\mathbf{V} \bullet \mathbf{V} - s^2\right)} \tag{9.8.7}$$

To fully understand the single real root case, Equation 9.8.7 must be considered in light of the fact that the radicand is zero. From Equation 9.8.6:

$$\left(\mathbf{P} \bullet \mathbf{V}\right)^2 + \left(s^2 - \mathbf{V} \bullet \mathbf{V}\right)\left(\mathbf{P} \bullet \mathbf{P}\right) = 0$$

$$\left(\mathbf{P} \bullet \mathbf{V}\right)^2 = -\left(s^2 - \mathbf{V} \bullet \mathbf{V}\right)\left(\mathbf{P} \bullet \mathbf{P}\right) \qquad (9.8.8)$$

Since the left side must be positive (due to the square), the right side must be negative; therefore, the interceptor is faster than the ball. Examining Equation 9.8.7 with that knowledge, the divisor must be negative in this case. Our analysis of the single real root has two subcases:

- **(P•V)<0**: The ball's velocity is roughly toward the interceptor, thus it can be intercepted at some point in the future. The numerator becomes negative (because of the negative sign), so the equation has a positive result. Since the ball moves faster than the interceptor, it can only be intercepted at one point in time. After that time, it will be traveling too quickly to be reached again. This is akin to the second baseman grabbing a line drive: if it shoots by in arm's reach, he can grab it in his immediate vicinity, but he'll never have a chance to catch it in the outfield.
- **(P•V)>0**: The ball's velocity is not toward the interceptor in any conceivable way. So, how is it that there is a root? With the dividend negative, the result is negative. Thus, the interception occurred in the past. Since time only moves forward, this result indicates that the result should be discarded.

Two Real Roots

The final case is the most interesting. This case does not require the speed of the player to be greater. Although the ball can move significantly faster than the player, if the player is sufficiently far away from the ball's initial position, but near the line in positive *t*, the ball can be intercepted.

The two real roots represent the boundaries of a window of opportunity; however, their interpretation falls into three categories, depending on the sign of the roots: two positive roots, two negative roots, and one positive and one negative root.

- **Two *positive* roots**: The roots define a window of opportunity in which the ball can be successfully intercepted. Any time between the two roots is a valid time at which the ball can be intercepted. In this scenario, the ball is moving faster than the player, but the player is, relative to the ratio of speed and distance, close to the line of motion and thus can make it there in time.
- **Two *negative* roots**: The roots also define a window of opportunity between the two values in which the ball can be intercepted. It also has the property of the ball moving faster than the player; however, the ball is moving entirely away from the player. Thus, the window is entirely in negative time, so this result is to be discarded as an impossible interception.
- **One *positive* and one *negative* root**: The solution has two open-ended windows of opportunity: time less than or equal to the negative root, and time greater than or equal to the positive root. As with all the results of its ilk, the negative window

is to be discarded. In this scenario, the player is moving faster than the ball, and thus can reach at any time after a certain minimum needed to catch it.

Choosing the Time to Meet

Once the root or roots are known, a valid time can be plugged back into the first equation in Equation 9.8.4, resulting in the point at which the target can be intercepted. Of the three root categories, only the two real roots case affords the AI discretion in choosing at which time the player would like to intercept the ball. In the no real roots case, the ball cannot be intercepted, and with a single real root, there is a unique time at which the interception could occur.

The two real roots case, in contrast, defines an interval of time in which the ball can be intercepted. What is the best time to choose? The obvious answer is a root itself. Although the only answer for the single real root case, it is probably not the best choice in the two-root case. To illustrate, imagine one person passing the ball to another. The passer throws the ball just beyond the receiver's reach. The receiver could take two leisurely steps perpendicular to the path of the ball and grab it. If a root is chosen, he will run as fast as he can to catch the ball, running mostly in a direction parallel to the motion of the ball.

Thus, for a more realistic decision, a time somewhere in the middle of interval should be chosen. Try to find the "lazy" point—the solution requiring the least amount of effort to still create an interception outcome. How can the lazy point be determined? We know two aspects of the solution: 1) the speed of interception should be as small as possible, yet still allow an interception to occur, and 2) at the minimum allowed interception speed, there is only one possible point in time to intercept, so there must be only one real root. For one real root, the expression under the radical must be zero. Solve for s:

$$\left(\mathbf{P} \bullet \mathbf{V}\right)^2 + \left(s^2 - \mathbf{V} \bullet \mathbf{V}\right)\left(\mathbf{P} \bullet \mathbf{P}\right) = 0$$

$$\left(\mathbf{P} \bullet \mathbf{V}\right)^2 + s^2\left(\mathbf{P} \bullet \mathbf{P}\right) - \left(\mathbf{V} \bullet \mathbf{V}\right)\left(\mathbf{P} \bullet \mathbf{P}\right) = 0$$

$$s^2\left(\mathbf{P} \bullet \mathbf{P}\right) = \left(\mathbf{V} \bullet \mathbf{V}\right)\left(\mathbf{P} \bullet \mathbf{P}\right) - \left(\mathbf{P} \bullet \mathbf{V}\right)^2$$

$$s^2 = \frac{\left(\mathbf{V} \bullet \mathbf{V}\right)\left(\mathbf{P} \bullet \mathbf{P}\right) - \left(\mathbf{P} \bullet \mathbf{V}\right)^2}{\left(\mathbf{P} \bullet \mathbf{P}\right)}$$

$$s = \sqrt{\frac{\left(\mathbf{V} \bullet \mathbf{V}\right)\left(\mathbf{P} \bullet \mathbf{P}\right) - \left(\mathbf{P} \bullet \mathbf{V}\right)^2}{\left(\mathbf{P} \bullet \mathbf{P}\right)}} \qquad (9.8.9)$$

The solution for s in Equation 9.8.9 must then be plugged back into the quadratic equation to give the resulting time of interception that can then be used to compute the location of intersection.

Related Problems

Now that the essential model has been fully constructed and analyzed, let's briefly summarize two variants:

1. The player has long arms that the model should consider. The arms can be modeled effectively as a nonzero initial position. If the player's arms are l long, Equation 9.8.3 becomes:

$$\left|\left(P_b - P_i\right) + V_b t\right| = l + s_i t \tag{9.8.10}$$

   The new solutions can be derived as above from this new equation.

2. Another consideration that might require modeling could be a delayed reaction by the player. Some developers' preference is to wait until such time as the player can move on the ball to make the decision; however, your needs might require a predetermination. As such, if the player has a delay of d duration, Equation 9.8.3 becomes:

$$\left|\left(P_b - P_i\right) + V_b t\right| = s_i\left(t - d\right) \tag{9.8.11}$$

These two variants can be used together in a single statement by merely replacing the t factor in Equation 9.8.10 with the $(t\text{-}d)$ factor seen in Equation 9.8.11.

Rebounding the Ball

In rebounding, the ball's altitude affects a player's ability to intercept a ball. As indicated at the beginning of the article, the model thus far only handles the relationship between the ball and player in the ground plane. In rebounding and similar situations, a second time window is computed. In general, the intersection of two parabolas has four solutions; however, the alignment of the parabolas results in a single intersection, with the exception of the case where the ball and player coincide. The formulation of the equation is reminiscent of the planar check—if the altitude of the player is greater than the ball, he can intercept it.

$$p_p + s_p t - \frac{1}{2} g t^2 > p_b + s_b t - \frac{1}{2} g t^2$$

$$p_p + s_p t > p_b + s_b t$$

$$s_p t - s_b t > p_p - p_b$$

$$t > \frac{p_p - p_b}{s_p - s_b} \tag{9.8.12}$$

At time t greater than the right-hand side, the ball can be caught. In many situations, p_p must factor in the player's height and reach for acceptable results.

Once the altitude window has been determined, use the time value to trim down the range returned by the plane check. Another modeling note: the interaction of ball and backboard results in many motion discontinuities. The proper method of handling this is to perform one check for each region of continuous time.

Conclusion

This article presents a simple and concise method to determine if one object can be intercepted by another. The check consists of little more than three dot products to determine the coefficients of a quadratic equation. The value of the expression under the radical in the quadratic equation discriminates between the three major cases: interception is impossible, a single point in time to intercept, and a window of opportunity for interception. If a window of opportunity is found, further analysis determines the best choice in the window.

The algorithm operates on a much-simplified view of the game model. The simplified model increases the error of the check; however, the error can be reduced effectively by dividing up the problem space and running each parameterization through the algorithm. The method's efficiency confers the advantage that it can be run frequently.

References

[Anton00] Anton, Howard, *Elementary Linear Algebra, 8th Ed.*, John Wiley & Sons, 2000.

[Glassner90] Glassner, Andrew, "Useful 2D Geometry," *Graphics Gems*, Academic Press, 1990.

[Resnick91] Resnick, Robert, and Halliday, David, *Physics, 4th Ed., Vol. 1*, John Wiley & Sons, 1991.

[Spiegel97] Spiegel, Murray R., and Rabin, *Schaum's Outline of College Algebra, 2nd Ed.*, McGraw-Hill Professional Publishing, 1997.

Scripting: Overview and Code Generation

Lee Berger—Turbine Entertainment Software

lberger@roy.org

A scripting language is any programming language that is created to simplify any complex task for a particular program. Because of this, they tend to be very tailored to the program. The scope of a scripting language can vary greatly depending on the problems it is supposed to solve. It might define simple conversation trees for a character in a role-playing game, or it might be a complicated object-oriented language that controls nearly all aspects of gameplay.

This article gives an overview of scripting languages, and what they are capable of. This article focuses on the more complicated version of a scripting language, giving you an overview of how to create such a language. This article also details how a scripting language source code can be transformed into instructions that a computer can execute.

Scripting Language Overview

Creating a fully capable scripting language is neither a simple nor a quick task. Nevertheless, the power that can be gained from a scripting language can often greatly outweigh the costs of implementation. As mentioned previously, any scripting language is meant to simplify some set of tasks for a program. They can be designed to hide many complicated aspects of a game. A first-person shooter game might use a scripting language to easily create a monster's AI. A role-playing game might use a scripting language to define how spells function or the intricate workings of a quest.

In even more complex environments, such as those found with any massively multi-player online games, a scripting language can be a very powerful tool. The details of dealing with multiple servers in a server farm can be completely hidden in the language. Sending network events to a client can be made simple and painless. The scripting language could even handle saving an object's state automatically.

Anatomy of a Scripting Language

A scripting language generally consists of two parts: the language and the engine. The language is like any other programming language, and it defines the special syntax that the scriptwriter is required to use. This language is translated, or *compiled*, into a format that the scripting engine can process. The scripting engine, or *interpreter*, executes the compiled script.

The compiled version of the script is called a *bytecode stream*, and it contains everything the interpreter requires to execute the script. If the scripting language is sufficiently complicated (as it would be with most structured programming languages such as C or C++), the task of compiling the script can be very expensive. Since the script's source code will not change as the game is being played, compiling the script into a bytecode stream can save a lot of overhead. This also simplifies the interpreter, since the bytecode stream contains simpler instructions to execute (similar to the differences between assembly and C++).

While it is technically possible for a scripting language's compiler to generate native assembly code, this is often not required or desirable. One advantage that a scripting language has is direct control over the execution of a script. For example, in a frame-rate driven game, the scripting engine could automatically suspend execution of a script if it is taking too much time. The script would later resume execution when more execution time becomes available.

Compiler Overview

A compiler is responsible for translating a developer's source files into a form that the computer can execute. A traditional compiler generates an executable that the computer can execute directly, but a scripting language's compiler generates a bytecode stream instead. This bytecode stream contains everything the interpreter requires in order to execute the script.

A compiler does this translation in a series of phases. The *lexer* handles the first phase, and it reads the source code and breaks it into its fundamental pieces called *tokens*. A token defines any single construct in the scripting language. In C++, the following are examples of tokens: +, *=, if, void, and MyFunction. The lexer is only responsible for finding the tokens in the source code. It is not responsible for determining what order the language allows these tokens to be specified. For example, the following is a completely valid stream of tokens: while (void ; !-if. Obviously, this is not a valid C++ program.

The tokens the lexer reads are given to the *parser*. The parser is responsible for defining the structure of the language. It verifies that the script is a valid program, and is also responsible for translating the script's source code into a structure that the compiler can understand. This data structure, called a *parse tree*, describes the entire script that the developer has created.

The parse tree is passed into the last phase of the compiler, the *code generator*. The code generator converts the parse tree that was created from the source code and generates the bytecode stream. After the code generator completes, the interpreter can execute the generated bytecode stream. The flow of transforming a script into a byte-code stream is illustrated in Figure 10.1.1.

The topic of compilers is a well-researched field. For more in-depth coverage of compilers, read [Aho86] and [Scott00].

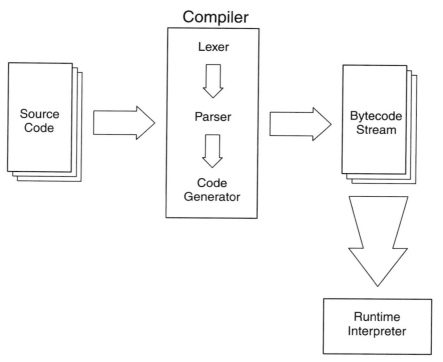

FIGURE 10.1.1. *Flow of a compiler.*

The Parse Tree

The parser is responsible for creating a parse tree for the code generator from the source code. This tree represents the developer's entire program in a manner that the compiler can understand. Since most programming languages are very structured, they can be represented by a treelike structure.

Each node in the tree has an associated type that describes what type of language construct this node describes (for example, an if-statement, a function call, an add expression). The node's children are the operands that the language construct requires.

For example, the expression 4 + 5 would be translated into a parse tree node where + is the root node, and 4 and 5 are the leaf nodes. A function body would be represented with a node flagged as "function," and its leaf nodes would be the list of operations that the function is supposed to perform. The order of the children is important!

The different types of parse tree nodes depend entirely on the programming language. In general, the node types should fall naturally from the language and its parser. Figure 10.1.2 shows some example parse trees.

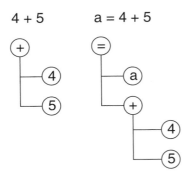

FIGURE 10.1.2 *Sample parse trees.*

Creating a Parse Tree

GNU Bison is a freely distributed tool commonly used in creating a compiler's parser (see [Bison95] for more information about this tool). Bison parses the source code recursively, making the creation of a parse tree a straightforward task.

A programming language is expressed in a series of rules for Bison. These rules define the structure of the language. Once Bison matches one of these rules with the source code, the associated code is executed. The parser uses this rule's code to create the proper parse tree node.

This newly created node is returned from the rule. Because of the recursive nature of Bison, the node is available to the parent rule. Each rule needs to create a new parse tree node to describe the current language construct. The children for a node are the other parse tree nodes returned from the node's subrules.

The example expression 4 + 5 is parsed by two different rules: an integer constant rule and an addition rule. Because the integers 4 and 5 are operands to the + operator, the integer constant rule is processed first. This rule creates a parse tree node containing the proper integer. For this example, this rule is called twice returning two nodes: one containing 4, and one containing 5.

Now that the operands for the addition rule are available, it is executed. This rule creates an additional parse tree node that has two children: the operands for the addition. The rule includes the two nodes in the new node's list of children.

Bison continues to parse the source file and call the appropriate rules until the entire file has been parsed. This leaves the compiler with a single parse tree node, the *root node*, which can be passed to the code generator.

The Code Generator

Once the compiler has created the parse tree, it is directly translated into a bytecode stream. The code generator walks recursively through the tree to process each node in turn. Each parse tree node instructs the code generator what actual executable instructions to generate.

An object-oriented code generator could have a class, CodeGen, to do the actual code generation. The class function CodeGen::Gen would be where code generation begins by taking the parse tree's root node as an argument.

CodeGen::Gen examines the node's type and calls the corresponding bytecode stream generation function (for example, the function CodeGen::GenAdd would be called for any addition parse tree nodes). CodeGen::Gen calls the appropriate node handler. This structures the bytecode stream generation logic into multiple functions.

The node handler functions recursively call CodeGen::Gen on any children nodes that the node contains. This is necessary because different nodes might require that their children nodes be recursed in different manners.

For example, an addition operator requires recursing into both operands before it can generate the add instruction. A function node requires entry and exit code to surround the actual function body (the children of the function node). Both of these handlers recurse on their children, but they do so in different manners.

Conclusion

Scripting languages can be very powerful tools. They can be used to hide many of the common details that arise in a traditional programming language. They can also give the developer control over both the language details and execution of the code through the careful compilation into a bytecode stream.

These compilers translate a source file into executable instructions. The parser and the code generator are two key parts in generating the required executable. The parser builds up a data structure that describes the developer's source code, and the code generator translates this data structure into the resulting executable.

Code generation is not very complicated, and the interpreter, that will execute the bytecode stream, defines most of the code generation details. Regardless of what the interpreter requires in the bytecode stream, the actual creation of this stream is the same: a recursive-descent down the compiler-created parse tree.

ON THE CD

The CD contains sample code for a very basic compiler. This compiler handles the basics of code generation. Its code-base has been intentionally kept as small as possible to illustrate code generation. Once you feel comfortable with this compiler, look at the sample code for article 10.2, "Scripting: The Interpreter Engine." It contains a compiler that supports a few more sophisticated language features (such as for-loops).

Article 10.2 explains the details of an interpreter, and how to integrate the scripting language into the game.

References

[Aho86] Aho, Alfred V., Sethi, Ravi, and Ullman, Jeffery D., *Compilers: Principles, Techniques, and Tools*, Addison-Wesley, 1986.

[Bison95] Free Software Foundation, available online at www.gnu.org/software/bison/bison.html, 1995.

[Muchnick97] Muchnick, Steven S., *Advanced Compiler Design & Implementation*, Morgan Kaufmann Publishers, Inc., 1997.

[Scott00] Scott, Michael L., *Programming Language Pragmatics*, Morgan Kaufmann Publishers, Inc., 2000.

10.2

Scripting: The Interpreter Engine

Lee Berger—Turbine Entertainment Software

lberger@roy.org

Article 10.1, "Scripting: Overview and Code Generation," outlined how a compiler generates a bytecode stream, or a stream of instructions, from a source file. In order for any scripting language to be useful, this bytecode stream must be executed. Fortunately, most scripting languages do not require the complexity of modern computers. Often, only the most basic form of a computer is needed to create a very powerful scripting language.

This article discusses how to implement a virtual machine for executing a compiler-generated bytecode stream. It covers the basic workings of a virtual machine, and the creation of two basic constructs required by all programming languages: conditional branching and function calling.

The Stack Machine

Any scripting language requires an engine to execute the script that a developer creates. This engine is called an *interpreter*, and is responsible for all aspects of executing a script. Generally, a scripting language has complicated constructs (such as functions and while loops), and a compiler is written for the scripting language to translate these constructs into more basic instructions. This makes the task of the interpreter simpler.

Since the interpreter executes a set of instructions that are not native assembly code, it is also called a *virtual machine*, or VM. It is responsible for executing the compiler-generated *bytecode stream*. These bytecode streams contain *opcodes*, or instructions, that the VM must perform.

The stack machine is a very basic computer form often used for a scripting language's virtual machine. The opcodes of a stack machine obtain their data by popping entries from a stack, and pushing their answers onto the same stack (for example, similar to a Hewlett-Packard calculator). This process of pushing and popping data from the top of the stack continues until the entire bytecode stream has been processed.

Because of the basic nature of a stack machine, the only data that it requires to function is the stack and an instruction pointer. The *instruction pointer* always points to the next instruction in the bytecode stream that is supposed to be executed.

Implementation of a Stack Machine

A direct way to implement a stack machine is to create a single class that contains the stack data, the instruction pointer, and the logic (or *opcode handlers*) to handle each of the opcodes. Since the stack machine is the core of the virtual machine, the class is called VM.

At the core of the stack machine are the opcode handlers. These opcode handlers are responsible for handling the work that is required by each opcode. Since each of these opcode handlers is a unique class function, the VM class can call the proper opcode handler through a table of function pointers.

Because the stack machine defines the opcode values, it can require that the values for the opcodes be consecutive integers starting at zero. This allows the opcode values to be used as an index into the table of function pointers. For example:

```
class VM {
    bool HandlePush( Opcode op );
    // ...
    typedef bool ( VM::*OpcodeHandler )( Opcode );
    OpcodeHandler m_opHandlers[Num_Opcode];
};
```

Each opcode handler returns a Boolean to identify whether or not the opcode was successfully handled. If an opcode fails, then the VM should stop executing the bytecode stream and perform error recovery and cleanup.

Each of the opcode handlers, as defined by the OpcodeHandler typedef, takes an Opcode as an argument. By passing the opcode of the current instruction into the handler, a single handler can be used for many different opcodes. This is handy for operations such as add and subtract that are nearly identical.

The VM class also contains a data member for the stack of opcode operands. The STL container vector is well suited for the stack. It provides constant time insertion and deletion at the end of the data structure, and also provides constant time random access to its members (this is often needed to support variables). The size of each element of the vector depends on whatever word size is needed by the scripting language.

The class also contains the instruction pointer. The instruction pointer always points to the next instruction that is going to be executed, and is represented as an Opcode pointer into a bytecode stream.

Executing the Stack Machine

Before the stack machine can execute, its state has to be fully initialized. The instruction pointer is set to the beginning of the bytecode stream, and the stack is cleared.

The stack machine then enters a forever loop that executes each instruction in turn. The opcode at the instruction pointer is fetched, and the instruction pointer is incremented. The fetched opcode is used as an index into the opcode handler array to find the proper handler function, and it is called to deal with the current opcode. The loop continues until the entire bytecode stream has been executed.

The opcode handlers perform all details of stack manipulation. For example, the *push* opcode handler pushes data onto the stack, and the *pop* opcode handler removes the topmost operand from the stack. An *add* opcode would pop the top two stack operands, add them together, and then push the result onto the stack.

Most opcodes pop their operands from the stack; however, a few opcodes obtain their arguments from the bytecode stream itself. These opcodes read their data from the instruction pointer and then increment the pointer. For example, the push opcode needs to know what value to push on the stack.

Controlling Code Flow

All languages require decision-making constructs, and the virtual machine is required to evaluate these decisions. These constructs can be conditional statements, loops, and function calls. The programmer uses these constructs to control the code flow of the VM.

Conditional statements and loops only require the VM to implement relative and conditional jumps. A relative jump resets the instruction pointer forward or backward. A conditional jump resets the instruction pointer based on a test of the topmost stack operand.

Function calls require more sophisticated support from the VM as described in the *Functions* section.

If Statements

A simple *if* statement with only a true statement block performs the following actions. First, it evaluates the body of the conditional and pushes the result of the conditional on the stack. Then, it performs a "jump if zero" opcode.

The "jump if zero" opcode pops the topmost operand from the stack. If this value is zero (or false), the opcode jumps to the offset given to it in the opcode stream. In this case, the offset points to the first statement after the *if* statement, thereby skipping the true statement block. If the expression is true, then the VM executes the contents of the true statement block.

An *if* statement with true and false statement blocks is only slightly more complicated. The offset in the conditional jump opcode points to the first statement in the false statement block. The compiler also generates a relative jump as the last statement in the true statement block to skip over the false statement block.

Loop Statements

Loop statements are a more complex version of the *if* statement. They mix using conditional jumps and relative jump instructions in performing their work. A C-style for loop would generate the following pseudo-assembly:

```
        Perform pre-loop expression.
   A:   Perform loop conditional expression.
        Jump to label B if top-stack element is zero.
        Perform loop body statements.
        Perform loop incremental expression.
        Jump to label A.
   B:   First statement after the for-loop.
```

As you can see in the pseudo-assembly, even the most complicated loop statement can be distilled into a series of jump statements. The virtual machine itself has no understanding of a loop statement; it simply knows how to jump.

Functions

Functions require more support from the VM. Once a function has finished executing, it returns to the code path that called it. The VM needs to track the state of function calls so it can update the instruction pointer when a function returns. This can be accomplished by keeping a stack of instruction pointer addresses. When a function is called, the current instruction pointer is pushed on top of the stack, and the instruction pointer is then set to the first instruction of the function.

The function evaluates everything it needs, and when it is done, the instruction pointer is reset to the topmost element of the function stack. Execution is now returned to the function's caller.

Functions also require arguments in order for them to perform useful tasks, and must also be able to return a value. This can be accomplished using the concept of stack frames. A *stack frame* is used by the VM to describe a function call. A stack frame conceptually contains the function's return value, its arguments, and its local variables. A pointer called the *frame pointer* always points to the first local variable. The VM can use this frame pointer to index into any argument or local variable.

Stack frames are stored in the *call stack*. This is a list of stack frames that are currently active in the VM. The call stack contains each stack frame's frame pointer and instruction pointer.

Conclusion

This article discussed implementation of an interpreter for a scripting language. These interpreters are often very simple machines, and can be easily represented by a stack machine. Stack machines do not have to provide much functionality to support the most complicated language constructs.

The compiler contains almost all of the complexity of a scripting language. Advanced language constructs such as inheritance and class member access rights do not require any support from the virtual machine. Because of this, the virtual machine for a scripting language can be easily implemented and debugged.

ON THE CD

The CD contains sample code for a basic interpreter. The sample code also contains a slightly more advanced version of the compiler created for article 10.1. You will notice that the compiler is more complex than the interpreter is. This is often the case, since the compiler is responsible for translating complex structures (such as *for* loops) into the interpreter's basic primitives.

References

[Aho86] Aho, Alfred V., Sethi, Ravi, and Ullman, Jeffery D., *Compilers: Principles, Techniques, and Tools*, Addison-Wesley, 1986.

[Scott00] Scott, Michael L., *Programming Language Pragmatics*, Morgan Kaufmann Publishers, Inc., 2000.

10.3

Scripting: System Integration

Lee Berger—Turbine Entertainment Software

lberger@roy.org

Scripting languages are very useful, but often certain tasks cannot be performed efficiently in an interpreted environment. For example, path-planning algorithms can be too processor intensive, and the performance impact of writing them in a script might be too great.

Because of this, the scripting language must be able to execute code written in C++ (to access the path-planning algorithms, for example). Likewise, the systems written in C++ need a way to execute script code. For example, a collision system written in C++ needs a way to inform a scripted object that something has collided with it.

This article describes how to create a program that uses simple function prototypes to auto-generate all of the code necessary to bind a scripting system and C++ together. By using this tool, a scripted language can be integrated with a large number of C++ systems simply.

Bridging the Gap between C++ and Script

It is often required for a scripting language to access a function written in C++. These functions might be time critical, or the scripting language might simply need to interface with a system already written. The reverse is also true: C++ code often needs to call functions written in script. By calling script functions, C++ can inform the script of events that have happened. The previous collision example applies.

External functions are any C++ functions that the script can call; likewise, interpreted functions are scripted functions that C++ can call. Together, these two function calls bridge the gap between C++ and script.

Binding Code

Calling a scripted function is much the same as calling a C++ function. Both the interpreter for the scripting language and C++ have a defined calling convention. This convention defines how the functions are to be called and where arguments and return values are stored.

A conversion process is needed for calling external functions. The most direct way to handle this conversion is to write utility C++ functions for the translations. These utility functions handle all the details that bind C++ and the interpreter together. Each of these utility functions will be responsible for a single translation. For example, if the script needs to call the C++ function `DisplayWidget`, then a utility function is written for the calling translation of this single function.

Unique binding functions are required, since each function might have different arguments and might call a different function to run the external or interpreted function. Having to create all of this binding code manually can be very error prone and time consuming.

Auto-Generating the Binding Code

Instead of the developers creating all of these binding functions manually, a program is written to create this binding code automatically. By creating this program, Bind-Gen, developers can prototype the function definitions in a configuration file. BindGen will use these prototypes to generate all of the required C++ code.

Creation of BindGen

Creating a program that auto-generates C++ code is similar to creating a compiler. This program, however, generates C++ code rather than machine code. Making Bind-Gen is very similar to, but simpler than, making the compiler for a scripting language. This tool only needs to understand the basics of a function prototype. It does not need to understand the sophisticated aspects of a language such as class inheritance and virtual function calling.

The first step in making BindGen, is to create a parser that is capable of dealing with the configuration files written by the developers. BindGen reads these configuration files and translates them into C++ code. This process works just like a compiler as detailed in article 10.1, "Scripting: Overview and Code Generation."

BindGen reads the configuration files into a parse tree, and passes this parse tree to a code generator. The code generator understands the proper C++ code associated with each node in the parse tree, and uses this information to generate the proper files. In BindGen's case, there are two types of nodes in the parse tree: one for external functions and the other for interpreted functions.

Binding Code for Interpreted Functions

For interpreted functions, BindGen generates a function that is a wrapper around the scripted function. This wrapper function takes the same arguments that the scripted function would take. The auto-generated code takes these arguments and pushes their values onto the interpreter's stack following the interpreter-defined calling convention.

Placing the actual call into the interpreter requires some help from the compiler. The binding code needs to know at what point in the instruction stream to start its execution. This instruction is the first instruction of the interpreted function that is being called.

The compiler must generate an import table containing the locations of each of the functions in the instruction stream. The binding code consults this table to determine the proper jump offset in the instruction stream.

Binding Code for External Functions

Just like interpreted functions, BindGen generates a wrapper function for calling external functions. This wrapper function takes the arguments that the interpreter has pushed onto the stack, and assigns them to variables that can then be passed into the external function.

The interpreter calls this wrapper function automatically. To do this, BindGen must assign a unique identifier to each external function. BindGen also auto-generates a header file containing a prototype of the external function for the script. The header file also contains the unique identifier assigned by BindGen.

The compiler generates the proper instructions for calling a function. The compiler can detect when it is calling an external function based on the function definition that BindGen has generated in the header file. When an external function is called, the compiler generates the "call external function" instruction.

The compiler provides the unique identifier that BindGen assigned to this instruction. The identifier is passed into an auto-generated switch statement (also courtesy of BindGen). This switch statement maps the unique identifier to the wrapper function discussed previously.

Latent Functions

Another aspect of system integration is the latent function. A latent function is any function where time can pass. The function in the animation system that plays an animation is one such function. Since playing an animation cannot block the running program, a system of callbacks is usually implemented to inform the caller when the animation has completed.

There is no reason that this restriction should apply to a script as well. Simpler scripts can often be written if these latent functions could actually block. If these functions did block, then scripting a monster to say something, walk over to a door, open the door, and then walk through could be implemented in a single function. Walking and opening the door are latent functions that would block until the work is completed.

Very little is required by the interpreter to support latent functions. Since it makes sense for external functions to be latent, BindGen can help with the details of latent function creation. The interpreter calls the external function wrapper as described previously just as it would with any external function.

Normally, the interpreter continues execution when the external function has finished; however, this is not desired for latent functions. Instead, the external function wrapper returns to the interpreter some interrupted enumeration. This value tells the interpreter to immediately stop execution.

The current state of the interpreter is saved, and it will stay unused until the latent function has finished. When the C++ system has finished its task, it places a callback into the interpreter. This callback signifies that the interpreter should resume execution. To the script, the external function has blocked and it has now completed its task.

Conclusion

This article discussed how to bridge the gap between C++ and a scripting language. It showed how a tool could be created to reduce the developer's workload for the scripting language.

This tool has several other interesting uses. It could be extended to handle the special cases that inevitably come up during scripting language development. For example, if all `Widgets` need to be converted to `Cogs` before the interpreter can use them, then this tool could handle the conversion in all the places where `Widgets` are handled.

Perhaps most importantly, the code generator allows the interpreter to grow while it is still being used. For example, if the calling convention of script needs to change, then only this tool needs to be modified to understand the new change. It automatically updates all of the binding code the next time it is executed.

For another example of how to bind C++ code to script, see [Bilas00]. His approach uses assembly to actually have the interpreter call the proper function. While this approach will be slightly more efficient in calling functions, BindGen can provide more flexibility with the binding interface (such as converting `Widgets` to `Cogs`).

References

[Bilas00] Bilas, Scott, "A Generic Function-Binding Interface," *Game Programming Gems*, Charles River Media, 2000.

10.4

Creating Scripting Languages for Nonprogrammers

Falko Poiker—Relic Entertainment

falko_3@hotmail.com

Scripting languages are very useful game development tools. They lend themselves directly to early prototyping and rapid content creation, techniques that help create the majority of today's successful games. The uses of scripting languages in games vary from simple configuration files to entirely script-driven game engines.

One common use of scripting in games is creating events and opponent AI in the single-player portion of the game. Scripts can tell the story of the game, if there is one, and control the player's enemies. In most cases, the people implementing these stories or enemies are designers, not programmers. As such, many scripts are written by people with very little programming experience. How can we design a scripting language to give these nonprogrammers as much power as possible, without hindering them with a steep learning curve?

This article attempts to answer that question by first describing fundamental designs of scripting languages meant for designers, then by exploring nonprogrammers' programming techniques and how to take advantage of these techniques to help designers learn more quickly. A few tips on working with nonprogrammers are also provided. This article is intended for the programmer charged with implementing the scripting system of a game—be it by embedding a publicly available scripting language into a game engine, or by building the scripting system from the ground up.

Terms

Designers are not the only people who use a game's scripting system; during development, artists as well as programmers will write scripts. After the game is shipped, mod groups and hobbyists will also write scripts if the scripting system has been exposed to the public. From now on, we will use the term *user* for the person who writes scripts and for whom the scripting language is intended. In this article, a user is a person with little to no previous programming experience, although the person is normally an experienced professional in his or her own field (design or art). The term *implementer* refers to the programmer who is writing or embedding the scripting language into the game.

It is also useful to define the term *scripting language*. In this article, when we refer to scripting or a scripting language, we mean a fourth-generation language that is used to control the game engine from the outside (i.e., with data). These languages range from simple configuration scripts to full-blown runtime interpreted languages. Some examples of publicly available scripting languages are Python, Lua, Ruby, Tcl, and Perl [Bezroukov01].

Fundamentals

There are many books and papers about designing programming languages. How do technical language design issues relate to scripting languages meant for nonprogrammers? This section will help the implementer choose either an existing language or the right fundamental designs for a proprietary solution.

Function-Based versus Object-Oriented

An object-oriented programming language is a language designed to support programming through abstract objects. These objects and their interaction define how the program runs. By contrast, a function-based language concentrates on linear program flow. A function-based program runs as a series of actions defined in its code by function calls.

Over the past decade, object-oriented languages have become so popular that many people think it is the only way to program. The object-oriented paradigm is a very intuitive way to design certain types of applications; particularly those that simulate real-world environments or those intended for Windows-based media. For scripting systems, however, object-orientation adds another layer of complication to the task of programming. The complication comes not only from the need to think of the data and control flow of a program in terms of objects, but also from the added syntax needed to support objects.

To a user, it is enough to think of mere variables as symbolic objects somehow hidden in a computer. Concepts such as data hiding and inheritance are lost to a novice, and simply constitute more ramp-up time in teaching the new programmer how to represent objects with text symbols.

Programming in an object-oriented language requires more design work up front than function-based programming does. Novices usually do not have the training, the experience, or the discipline to do a thorough design before starting to program. However, function-based programming is much more forgiving to a weak technical design, so it allows the user to learn and design while typing.

Because of these many reasons, function-based languages are much more suitable for novice users than object-oriented languages are. Using an object-oriented scripting language heightens the user's learning curve considerably [Jacobs01].

Simplicity

A programming language's simplicity is defined by how easily a programmer can learn the entire language. Obviously, a language designed for novice programmers should be simple, but many things can work against the goal of simplicity. Every language feature adds another step to the learning process, but in order to make a scripting language effective for a game, it should include custom features that make the language a powerful tool for controlling that game.

In the same way, the flexibility of a language works against its simplicity. If a language has multiple ways of doing the same action, a beginner can get confused. For example, in C there are many ways to increment a variable by one (x++; ++x; x += 1; x = x + 1). Although the shortcuts (such as the "++" operator) are useful, they have subtly different behavior for what seems like the same operation. Keeping a language simple means avoiding this kind of overlapping functionality [Ghezzi82].

One way to keep a language simple is to add new features through function calls, and avoid custom operators or syntax. Looking up a feature in an index of function calls is much easier than paging through a language reference to find out what, for example, the "$" operator does.

Consistency

More important than simplicity, however, is the consistency (or orthogonality) of a scripting language. As often as possible, the basic building blocks of a language should be interchangeable. For example, if the equal sign assigns a value to a variable, it should do so for every data type available in the language. Likewise, if functions pass variables as values through their parameter lists, then every type of variable should pass by value through parameter lists. Each time a language feature or limitation is added that is not consistent (e.g., special operators to give values to string variables, special rules for what can be passed in a parameter list), the language becomes less intuitive and harder to use.

Again, using library function calls as much as possible for custom language features helps minimize the risk of adding inconsistent features to the language. As long as functions act in a consistent way, function calls are a great way for nonprogrammers to abstract any action, because to them a function call "does something to the variables in the parameter list." Since a function call is one rule in a language, varying function behaviors (no matter how different they are) always follow the rules of orthogonality.

Weak versus Strong Typing

A strongly typed language is a language in which conversions between data types is restricted; thus, type casting must be explicitly used. Weakly typed languages, on the other hand, convert variables from one data type to another transparently without an error or sometimes without a warning. Both methods of dealing with data types have their strengths and weaknesses.

With respect to novice programmers, strongly typed languages give the user a measure of security against mistakes that might be difficult to debug, such as those produced by passing the wrong data types in parameter lists. Strong typing also encourages users to be aware of their variables—what they are, where they are valid, and where they go. Unfortunately, strongly typed languages add a level of complexity that goes against the rules of simplicity described previously, because they add more rules to the language. More often than not, strongly typed languages produce errors that annoy users rather than help—for example, pointing out an illegal type conversion from an integer to a real number. When a language feature such as strong typing forces a user to work around it on a regular basis, it works against novices, as the feature constitutes a series of hidden "rules" that the user must learn the hard way.

Weakly typed languages, on the other hand, are less safe but much more user friendly. The best implementation of weak typing is the "dynamic types" of many publicly available scripting languages. With dynamic types, variables literally take care of themselves by being created when they are first used in the program, and converting themselves to different types as needed. A good dynamically typed language will have internal rules for the automatic conversion of every basic data type the language supports, plus will support type extensions so that custom types can be created by the implementer.

The downside of dynamic types is that they make simple errors such as spelling mistakes more difficult to find. When the language finds a misspelled variable, it thinks the variable is new and creates a new variable rather than producing an error. A strongly typed language would stop execution (or compilation) and produce an error. An additional downside of weak or dynamic types is that for library functions to be trouble free, they must take into account the fact that they might get invalid types as parameters. This is not that much of a problem, however, since library functions are the job of the experienced programmer who can easily add proper type validation to the library functions.

In general, strong types are better suited for professional programming languages, and weak types are better for user-friendly scripting languages [Jacobs01]. Game scripting systems should use dynamic types to minimize learning time for their scripters.

Pointers

Most professional game programmers spend a large amount of time dealing with pointers, since C and C++ are by far the most common programming languages used to create games. It is no secret to these people that pointers are an advanced language feature, and it is a feature many enjoy using. Most other programming languages avoid pointers, and almost all newly created languages proudly claim not to need pointers (Java is one of the best examples of elegant, pointerless coding). Despite the usefulness of abstracting variable and object locations using pointers, they simply do not belong in scripting languages. From the user's point of view, a script variable should have one way to access it, and that is directly through the variable name.

A few publicly available scripting languages use pointers as a method to access information outside of the scripting language's state (e.g., accessing variables in the game engine itself). These same languages, however, provide methods for making the pointers look and act exactly like normal variables in the scripting state. Lua's userdata and tag methods are a good example of this type of implementation. These features are extremely useful. They allow an embedded scripting language to remain as close to a black box as possible, yet still reach deep into the game engine to expose important game variables, structures, and objects. When using pointers in this way, it is the implementer's job to ensure that every scripting variable that is in fact a pointer to a game variable should appear exactly as any other scripting variable. The pointer should be a transparent implementation invisible to the user.

Novice Programming Techniques

All programmers, whether just starting out or experienced, have a different learning style and their own programming style. However, there are a few general techniques, many of which advanced programmers still use, that are common among novices.

Copy and Paste

Copy and pasting code is by far the most common way to program. Advanced programmers frequently copy large portions of their code, paste it into a new module, and make the small changes needed to make this new module unique. Advanced programmers do this because it makes sense to modify an existing and proven design, rather than start from the ground up. Novice programmers, on the other hand, tend to copy/paste because they know the code they are copying simply *works*. They want to avoid starting again from scratch, because they fear spending a long time agonizing over every detail of the syntax, logic, and content of even a small bit of code.

Trial and Error

Users will frequently make arbitrary changes to parts of their code they do not understand just to see what happens. This programming "technique," sometimes called *hacking*, is normally used when programmers are faced with an error message they do not understand and have no idea how to solve. Lack of documentation, or even too much documentation, can make learning to program extremely difficult. Most people try to overcome this difficulty with a healthy dose of experimentation.

Reference Search

Users lucky enough to have documentation to draw from tend to program with that documentation immediately nearby (always open on their computer's desktop or on their lap). Programming for these novices involves writing a small amount of code followed by a long search through the documentation looking for that function they saw a while back.

Having documentation is always good, whether you are just learning or you have been programming since the days of punch cards. Unfortunately, it can sometimes be very difficult to find the information needed from documentation, so its organization is important. Regardless of the quality of the documentation, users will naturally migrate to less "reference search" programming and more "copy/paste" programming as the amount of code they have created increases.

One on One

Despite the previous generalizations, no amount of educated guessing can ultimately predict how your users will program. It is useful for the implementer to spend some time one on one with each user to see how he programs. By doing this, the user can learn certain simple techniques to improve his programming style, and at the same time, the implementer can tailor the scripting language toward the people who are using it.

Speeding Up the Learning Curve

The most effective way to make a scripting language easier to use is to create a large, well-documented library of useful functions that covers most tasks.

Libraries

The libraries can be scripted or written in the game's compiled language and then exposed to the scripting language.

Scripted libraries created by the implementer are useful for several reasons:

- They force the implementer to use the scripting language, therefore testing features and finding out if the scripting system meets its goals.
- They provide code examples for users to learn from, although scripted libraries will most likely be more difficult to follow, since they take care of tasks normally hidden from users.
- They increase the base of data-driven elements in the game, making its implementation more fluid and easier to modify down the road.

The downside of scripted libraries is that in order to have them, the language must include advanced coding features such as module inclusion. In addition, scripts are always slower than compiled code, so the libraries add another layer of slow code to the game.

Libraries written in the game's native code are much more efficient and help expose the game's functions and data to the scripting environment. We recommend a mixture of scripted libraries and compiled libraries. Library functions can be scripted to begin with, and then rewritten in compiled form if it is determined they are too slow. This technique leaves many functions exposed for novices to learn from, especially in the early stages of development when the novices need as many examples as they can get. Later in development, as more library functions are optimized, users will have code of their own to draw on for examples.

Documentation

As mentioned earlier, documentation is always good, but can be a mixed blessing. How do you organize a reference document so that novices can easily find the information they need? What information is actually helpful?

In the previous section, *Fundamentals*, it was stated that using functions instead of language syntax features makes a scripting language easier to pick up. This argument works for documentation as well.

When a user is searching for a language feature, documentation that consists of a large number of functions reads much like a dictionary. It simply becomes a list of words and definitions. Most users can navigate this type of reference easily.

Language features that are not function names, such as symbols that represent certain operations, are much more difficult to document, and also much more difficult for the user to look up. Take, for example, a language feature that uses the "$" sign to do string operations. With this feature, if a user wants to find out how to copy a string, he must do a word search for "string" and "copy". This will help him find the right section that describes how to use the "$" feature correctly to copy strings. On the other hand, if the user is reading some undocumented code that uses the "$" feature, finding out what this code is doing by looking in the reference document is a much more difficult task. What does the user search for? Where does he look? He has to scan the entire "$" section to find an example that resembles the code he's reading, and then work backward to understand what is happening. If a function were used instead (e.g., strcpy()), the user would simply have to look for the function name in the documentation.

Once the documented information is easy to find, it must be relevant. Code examples are the best way to make something relevant to a novice, as they show exactly the syntax and a common use of the function (or feature) being looked up. In addition, examples keep the user from needing to look up anything else, because the example usually contains enough information for the user to use the function.

Sample Code

Along with good documentation, well-commented sample code can go far to jump-start novice programmers. Implementers need to test the scripting language to ensure that it is ready for the designers to begin using. This is best done by actually implementing something useful in the game, such as a single-player opponent, or a level.

Although the documentation might contain sample uses of the functions implemented in the scripting system, sample code goes further by showing how all the code can work together to create a proper program. It also starts the user out with a solid example of programming to blatantly copy and paste while he is ramping up his coding skills. Just be absolutely sure that the example code is free from errors and shows good style, or else it will be a scourge that finds its way into every script, setting an example for months or years to come.

Tips from the Trenches

The following are tips to keep in mind when implementing a scripting language.

Case Sensitivity

There are probably no good reasons to create a case-sensitive scripting language. Spelling and capitalization mistakes are by far the most common errors, and are sometimes difficult to track down, especially with a language that dynamically creates variables it has not seen before. The previous comments might be a good argument for making a scripting language strongly typed, but the advantages (with respect to novice programmers) of a case-insensitive, weakly typed language far outweigh the advantages of a case-sensitive, strongly typed language.

Efficiency Checks

Inefficient code is the bane of game programming. Since novice users lack the experience to create efficient code, the scripts they write can occasionally become very processor intensive. Often, users will create loops that contain redundant calculations or other easily correctable inefficiencies. It is very useful to build efficiency checks into the scripting system that warns the user if scripts exceed a certain time or processor use limitations. These checks will quickly identify potentially wasteful code so they can be dealt with early in the development process.

Short Keywords

In the section *Fundamentals*, it is argued that using functions to implement language features is the best way to make the language easy to learn. No rules are hard and fast, however. There are certain situations where small keywords (e.g., "if," "while," and "do" are keywords) can make a language easier to read.

For example, instead of getting random numbers by calling "z = random(x, y)", adding a language feature that does the same by typing "z = x to y" is acceptable, since random-number generation is very common in scripting (especially AI scripting). This is just an example—as the creator of the scripting language, you have to judge if a feature is important enough to add a new keyword, as functions tend to be easier to add to a scripting engine than keywords.

If .. Endif

One type of bug frequently seen comes up when the design of a scripting language is such that the "if" blocks, "while" loops, and "for" loops all end with "end". Often, through copy/paste errors, one too many "end" statements show up, and the user has to manually count "if...end" and "while...end" blocks to find out where the extra "end" is located. As such, the end of a block or a loop should always indicate what it is ending—with "if...fi" or "if...endif". Usually, a simple change, using the "if...endif" constructs, clarifies the scripts considerably.

Another option is to use curly brackets, like in C, to designate code blocks. The advantage of curly brackets is that many code editing packages such as Visual C or Visual SlickEdit are able to match brackets as you type or with special keystrokes. For example, in Visual C, if you have the cursor next to a curly bracket and press "Ctrl" and "}" at the same time, it will move the cursor to the matching curly bracket. This makes the job of matching brackets a breeze.

Debugging

How much debugging support is enough? Obviously, the more support, the better. At the absolute minimum, your scripting language needs to support the "print" function. The next step in debugging sophistication is being able to break the code execution, step through instructions, and watch variables. This is probably an adequate amount of debugging support for most scripting languages.

Initially, the implementer of the scripting language will most likely have to sit next to the user and do a good deal of debugging for him. Debugging is an intermediate programming skill that requires the programmer to understand how to isolate problems through systematic troubleshooting. Most novices simply do not know where to start, and your help is necessary to show the steps to isolate bugs.

Another useful addition to the scripting library would be error-checking functions such as assert(). If taught, the user can easily incorporate these safety checks to ensure the code is running correctly. It is a good habit to have runtime code checking, and the earlier a user gets into the habit of adding in assert() calls, the better.

Conclusion

Implementing a scripting language in a game is no easy task. Not only does the language need to be programmed, but the implementation needs to be well documented. Then, the implementer needs to be available to help designers and artists learn how to script and eventually do what they do best—create the game.

By minimizing confusing language features, using functions as much as possible, creating well documented libraries, and writing good sample programs, the programmer tasked with creating and supporting a game's scripting system can go far to help ramp up the users from inexperienced to competent and comfortable programmers. The scripting language's power will then be fully realized and a truly inspirational game can be made.

References

[Bezroukov01] Bezroukov, Nikolai, *Scripting Languages*, www.softpanorama.org/Scripting/index.shtml, 2001.

[Dershem95] Dershem, Herbert L. and Michael J. Jipping, *Programming Languages, Structures and Models*, PWS Publishing Company, 1995.

[Ghezzi82] Ghezzi, Carlo and Mehdi Jazayeri, *Programming Language Concepts*, John Wiley & Sons, Inc., 1982.

[Jacobs01] Jacobs, B. and Findy Services, *Language Options*, www.geocities.com/tablizer/langopts.htm, 2001.

10.5

Scripting for
Undefined Circumstances

Jonty Barnes—Lionhead Studios, and

Jason Hutchens—Amristar

jbarnes@lionhead.com and
hutch@amristar.com.au

Complementing the interactive elements of a computer entertainment product with a storyline informs the players of their goals and provides a context for their actions. Predetermined cinematic sequences can be used to present this storyline with great effect, as amply illustrated by titles such as *Zelda 64* and *Metal Gear Solid*.

Games featuring dynamic physical simulation and artificial intelligence (AI) introduce the possibility of undefined circumstances occurring, and can afford the player, rather than the game designers, the freedom to set the agenda. Is it possible to add a storyline to such open-ended gaming worlds without jeopardizing the player's suspension of disbelief? What if a crucial cinematic sequence depends on the harmless little villager that the player unthinkingly threw into the ocean at the beginning of the game? Even worse, what if a nonplayer character (NPC) under the control of a learning AI system intrudes into a cinematic sequence and begins to wreak havoc?

In this article, we discuss the features that were implemented in the game *Black & White* to allow the game designers to create storyline-advancing "Challenges" without compromising the unpredictable nature of the game [Lionhead01].

Developing the Technology

Midway through the development of *Black & White*, we decided that the time had come to tie everything together with a cohesive storyline. Due to the open-ended nature of the game, we chose to present the storyline through a sequence of Challenges, some of which served to advance the storyline, some of which gave the players an opportunity to practice their skills, and some of which existed purely for entertainment purposes.

One of the first Challenges written was the "Lost Brother." This Challenge begins with a woman emerging from her house in prayer for the safety of her ill brother who has become lost in the woods. Informed of her plight, the players are free to do what they choose. They can ignore the prayers of the woman completely. They can reunite the grateful siblings. They can find and kill the lost brother, and taunt the grieving woman by holding his lifeless body just out of her reach. They can take the woman to the forest where her brother lays, wait until the pair is happily walking back to the woman's house, and then kill them both maliciously and without warning.

The possibilities available to the player seem endless, and yet our Challenge mechanism needed to make it easy for our game designers to support them all. We focused on creating an extensible technology that provided both the ability to script cinematic sequences and the flexibility to implement interactive Challenges that are robust in the face of undefined circumstances.

The Challenge Virtual Machine

We decided that the Challenges would be executed on a virtual machine (VM) running in a dynamically linked library (DLL), with an application-programming interface (API) enabling communication between the game and the VM. This approach has numerous advantages:

- It is independent of the data structures and programming techniques used in the game itself, granting game designers the freedom to experiment without requiring the involvement of a game programmer.
- The chance of a bug in the VM causing a crash in the game is greatly reduced, as the VM is unable to directly access or modify any of the data structures in the game code.
- New versions of the DLL can be linked to an already-running version of the game. With build times for the game approaching an hour, this made fixing bugs in the VM and adding new features to it relatively quick.
- A trivial game stub can be used to load the DLL and provide a compatible API, allowing the VM to be tested and debugged without the game having to be present.

We implemented a stack-based VM that was capable of running many processes in parallel, with a form of multitasking being used to switch between them. This was achieved by forcing processes to block whenever they encountered a branch opcode, and worked well in practice, as branch opcodes usually signify an iterative task or a busy wait. We imagined that each process would be responsible for managing a particular object, event, or Challenge in the game world.

The API between the VM and the game allowed the game to start, suspend, and kill VM processes, and allowed the VM to call game functions indirectly. A stack-based VM makes this process trivial, and the flexibility of this approach made it possible to expose new game functions to the game designers with ease, as they became available.

The Object Management System

Our Challenge mechanism needed to be able to seamlessly access and control any object in the game world, including NPCs, regardless of what they might be doing at the time. Once no longer required by the Challenge mechanism, these objects should just as seamlessly be integrated back into the game world.

A hierarchical object management system was implemented to allow the Challenge mechanism to create, access, control, and delete game objects. This system kept track of the number of references made to each object, enabling garbage collection. Access control was rendered redundant, as the object management system ensured that an object would return to the correct state and behavior as references to it were deleted.

Integral to the object management system are the concepts of *Actors* and *Agents*. Objects under the control of a process running on the VM are Actors, while objects functioning autonomously in the game world are Agents. The game precludes Actor objects from most processing, including AI, which helps to reduce the effect of unforeseen object behaviors. Once a process terminates, the object management system recalculates references to all the objects it knows about, potentially returning some Actors to their previous roles.

Manipulating individual objects within the game world is powerful, but often it is useful to manipulate a group of objects together as if they were a single entity. Object containers, such as flocks and towns, were implemented within the game and exposed to the game designers via the object management system. This meant that a game designer could very easily decrease the health of an entire flock of sheep, or even command all of the villagers in a town to dance.

The Challenge Programming Language

We now had a Challenge mechanism that was powerful, efficient, and abstract. It provided a nice, general foundation on top of which we could build powerful Challenge development tools. The game designers had begun to script some Challenges in detail using a pseudo programming language of their own design. Our familiarity with the GNU compiler creation tools *Flex* and *Bison* inspired us to formalize the syntax of their language and implement a compiler for it that produced VM code.

A sample script written in the Challenge programming language is shown in Listing 10.5.1. Object declarations appear at the top of the script with a block of statements following. The script creates a cow at the position of the player's hand, starves the cow as it walks toward the target, and causes the evil advisor to issue a running commentary. It terminates when the cow dies or when it reaches its goal.

Listing 10.5.1 A simple script written in the Challenge programming language.

```
begin script SickCow(Target)
    Cow = create ANIMAL COW at position of hand
Start
    make evil spirit point to Cow
    say "This unhealthy beast is on its last legs!"
    move Cow to {Target}
```

```
        begin loop
          wait 3 seconds
          HEALTH of Cow -= 0.1
          if {Cow} near {Target} radius 15
            say "It's almost there! Hurry up and die, bovine!"
          elsif HEALTH of Cow < 0.5 and HEALTH of Cow > 0.3
            say "It's almost dead! Yippee!"
          elsif Cow is FLYING
            say "Is it a bird? Is it a plane? No. It's a cow."
          end if
        until {Cow} at {Target}
          say "It made it to safety. How unfortunate!"
        until HEALTH of Cow <= 0
          say "Ha! It's steak for dinner!"
        end loop
        send evil spirit home
      end script SickCow
```

Features of the Challenge Programming Language

One of the great advantages of giving the game designers a programming language of their own is that it enabled them to write expressions that are evaluated at runtime, potentially approximating the functionality of anticipated but currently unimplemented game functions. In addition, the Challenge programming language has a few interesting features that evolved out of a desire to give the game designers the power to deal with unanticipated circumstances in an elegant way.

Scripts are the embodiment of a single VM process. Every time a script is called from another script, the VM spawns a new process to manage it. Scripts can accept arguments when they are called, and by default, the parent process blocks until the child process terminates. As such, scripts behave identically to functions in other programming languages. However, scripts can optionally be called in parallel with the parent process, making it possible to create Challenges that associate a process with every object used in the Challenge, with the parent process administering them all.

Apart from the usual integral, real, and Boolean types, the Challenge programming language also features a special coordinate type, specified via the braces syntax, whereby {1,2,3} represents a position in the game world, and {Achilles} represents the position of the Achilles object and not the object itself. Coordinates can be used in expressions, such as the paradoxical move Achilles to ({Achilles}+{Tortoise})/2.

Although expressions are often performed with variables, game designers usually want their results to have some tangible effect in the game world. The Challenge programming language exposed the properties of game objects, something made easy by the fact that they were stored in an external spreadsheet to be accessed from the game code. This feature allowed the game designers to treat quantities such as HEALTH of Cow identically to variables.

The Challenge programming language features the familiar if, loop, and while flow control blocks. In addition, it features special camera, dialogue, and cinema blocks. Any statements that modify the position or orientation of the camera can only be used within a `camera` block, preventing more than one process from attempting to control the camera simultaneously. Processes that fail to gain access to a resource automatically block until the resource is freed. Similarly, the `dialogue` block manages access to speech resources, preventing two conversations from overlapping, while the `cinema` block has the combined effect of both the `dialogue` and `camera` blocks with the additional effect of initiating a widescreen display.

The `until` exception can be used within any block of statements, including all of the flow control blocks previously discussed as well as the top-level, scriptwide block. The body of the exception is executed whenever its conditions are satisfied, causing execution of the block to terminate. Exceptions make it easy for the game designers to handle unforeseen circumstances. For example, in Listing 10.5.1, an `until` exception is used to perform an action whenever the cow's health becomes less than or equal to zero. The game designer need not worry about how or why the cow has no health, or precisely when this occurs in the loop. It might be that the cow gets killed in a completely unanticipated way. Rather than having to take numerous unlikely hypothetical situations into account, the game designer need only focus on fairly general possibilities and deal with them accordingly, with the result that unexpected events are handled appropriately.

Implementing a Challenge

Creating a cinematic sequence using a game engine is not dissimilar to creating a short film. Indeed, modern computer game technology has given rise to *Machinima*, the creation of real-time rendered movies using gamelike engines [Hancock00]. Instead of reinventing techniques used in film, we can apply most film production methods to games, including storyboarding and script writing.

Writing Challenge scripts was largely a technical position, regardless of the fact that we liked to think that a quasi-English programming language would be attractive to nontechnical game designers. Our game designers were mostly concerned with creating the underlying logic of a Challenge, although those with experience in film production did work on the cinematic sequences. All scripts had to pass quality assurance in terms of functionality before being polished by skilled designers.

Listing 10.5.2 contains one complete cinematic sequence from the Lost Brother Challenge, with minor edits for clarity. Most cinematic sequences were of this length or shorter. A screenshot of the final cinematic sequence in action is shown in Figure 10.5.1.

Development Environment

The Challenge programming language compiler was integrated into the Visual Studio development environment. Game designers could write scripts, complete with syntax highlighting, and compile them at the touch of a button. Visual Studio also highlighted the portion of the script where syntax errors occurred during compilation.

FIGURE 10.5.1 *The scene created by the cinematic sequence shown in Listing 10.5.2. Also shown in Color Plate 1.*

Although the syntax of the Challenge programming language stabilized fairly early during development, we continuously extended the functionality of the compiler. In order to keep documentation up to date, and to inform all of the game designers of the latest language features, we developed an automated documentation system that created extensive hypertext documentation from comments in the compiler source as a post-build step each time the compiler was built.

Camera Control

In practice, it is very difficult to create convincing camera movements in a text-based programming language. Additionally, making the camera movements relative to the position of an object can also lead to problems. For example, the "Creature," which is the principal learning AI in *Black & White*, literally grows in stature during the course of a game. Camera movements that depend on the size of the Creature might look different to the player than they did during development.

A comprehensive set of tools were created for implementing camera movement, and these tools were able to read and write data to and from the Challenge programming language scripts, acting as a GUI on top of the compiler to aid the cinematography and choreography of the scene. A more advanced camera control tool enabled the WYSIWYG creation of smooth camera paths that could then be integrated into the script. The mixture of absolute game world coordinates, predefined camera paths, and relative object coordinates apparent in Listing 10.5.2 resulted from the use of these tools.

Listing 10.5.2 A complete cinematic sequence introducing the "Lost Brother" Challenge.

```
begin cinema
    // Create a moody storm
    start music MOODY_PIANO
    Storm = create WEATHER DRIZZLE at {Brother}

    // Move the sister out with a new walking animation
    move Sister position to {SoapBox}
    set Sister anim DESPAIR_WALK

    // Set the camera to dynamically follow the sister
    set camera focus follow Sister
    move camera position to {SoapBox}+{-3,4,-3} time 10

    // When the sister nears her soapbox, make her pray
    wait until {Sister} near {SoapBox} radius 1
    Sister play PRAY loop 1
    wait 4 seconds

    // Sister: "Oh holy one, I kneel before you."
    say LOST_BROTHER_LINE1
    wait until camera ready

    // Zoom the camera in on the sister
    move camera position to {Sister}+{-2,1,-2} time 8
    move camera focus to {Sister}+{0,0.7,0} time 8

    // Wait until she's said her line and stopped praying
    wait until read and Sister played

    // Turn the sister to face her brother and point at him
    set Sister focus to {SickBed}
    Sister play POINTING loop 1

    // Sister: "My brother ... [has] ... become lost."
    say LOST_BROTHER_LINE2

    // Move camera behind the sister, wait until done pointing
    move camera position to {1703,18,2592.5} time 5
    move camera focus to {Sister} time 8
    wait until read and Sister played
    wait until camera ready
    Sister play DESPAIR_STAND loop 1

    // Fade to black
```

```
set fade red 0 green 0 blue 0 time 1.5
wait until fade ready

// Move the camera along a pre-defined path and fade in
move camera to TRACK00_START time 3
set fade in time 2
camera path TRACK00
set Brother focus to {BrotherCamPos}
set Sister position to {SoapBox}
wait 1 second

// Make the brother suffer (Brother: "Ugh.")
Brother play POISONED loop 1
start sound GROAN1 at {Brother}

// Sister: "He is so weak, I'm frightened he'll die!"
say single line LOST_BROTHER_LINE3
wait until read
wait until camera ready

// Emphasize his sickness (Brother: "Eueergh!")
move camera position to {Brother}+{2,0.3,-2} time 4
move camera focus to {Brother} time 3
wait 2 seconds
start sound GROAN2 at {Brother}

// Make the brother look like he is dying
Brother play DYING loop -1

// Cut back to crying sister
set camera position to {1703,18,2592.5}
set camera focus to {Brother}

// Sister: "If you find him I'll give you the gate stone."
say single line LOST_BROTHER_LINE4
Sister play MOURNING loop 1
wait 1 second

// Focus the camera on the stormy mountain
move camera position to {1725.8,28,2576} time 8
move camera focus to {1667,17.2,2589} time 8
wait until read
wait until camera ready
stop music

// Get the advisor spirits on screen
eject good spirit
eject evil spirit

// Evil: "I gotta plan, lets trash the house ..."
make evil spirit point at {House}
say LOST_BROTHER_LINE5
wait until read
stop evil spirit pointing
```

```
    // Good: "I heartily object. That's just malicious."
    say LOST_BROTHER_LINE6
    wait until read

    // Evil: "That's kinda the whole point!"
    say LOST_BROTHER_LINE7
    wait until read

    // Send the advisor spirits away
    send good home
    send evil home
end cinema
```

Dialogue

When writing dialogue, it is important not to inundate the players with too much prose, lest they miss important information. Writing simple, well-defined dialogue that does not belittle the player takes time. When testing, we found that dialogue-intensive cinematic sequences could prove frustrating on repeated viewings. Enabling the players to click through such sequences gives them the ability to dictate the pace at which they are presented.

Most games are likely to be released in more than one language. *Black & White*, for example, was released in 15. This means that the timing of dialogue is not fixed, and neither are the mouth movements of the characters speaking it. Rather than making language-specific versions of each cinematic sequence, the presence of conditions such as `wait until read` in the Challenge programming language enabled dialogue scenes to be synchronized. Dynamic lip-synching was achieved via a real-time frequency analysis of the dialogue, courtesy of programming maven Alex Evans.

Ambient sound effects were largely automated, with the sounds emitted by Agents assigned a lower priority over those emitted by Actors. The majority of sound effects, such as footfalls, were calculated automatically, dependent on such things as animation and terrain type, meaning that they did not need to be controlled by a script.

Debugging

Introducing a second programming language created another source of bugs. Although the clean separation between VM and game meant that a Challenge script would be hard-pressed to crash the game itself, it does have every chance of creating irregular behavior such as locking an NPC in a particular state or locking the game within a cinematic sequence, effectively halting all player interaction. A single-step debugging interface for Challenge scripts was developed, as were tools to allow the game designers to retrieve information from the game. The implementation of the Challenge mechanism in a DLL allowed us to fix problems with the VM and reload the DLL on-the-fly, circumventing the need for a time-consuming bug-fixing cycle.

Anticipating Undefined Circumstances

The Challenge VM was designed to satisfy the requirement that Challenges might be initiated and completed at the player's own pace. This gave the player the freedom to begin a Challenge, only to become distracted by some other task. With the player's Creature wandering around the game world, behaving autonomously, this flexibility could result in undesirable consequences.

For example, in the Lost Brother Challenge, if the Creature came upon the ill brother and decided to eat him while the player was performing some task in a far-away region of the game world, it would be unreasonable for a Challenge script to take control and initiate an appropriate Lost Brother cinematic sequence. We dealt with this problem by triggering cinematic sequences only as a consequence of the player's direct interaction, resulting in increased player enjoyment and less frustration. The autonomous behavior of Actors was deliberately kept to a minimum, as was the interaction between Agents and Actors, meaning that the Creature simply will not interact with objects under the control of a script unless instructed to do so by the player.

Other situations are even more problematic. Imagine that the player unleashed a devastating fireball toward the dying brother at the very moment that the cinematic sequence shown in Listing 10.5.1 begins. The brother is a vital player in the sequence, and the fact that the forest around him is ablaze should be irrelevant. We dealt with this situation by making all Actors indestructible in cinema blocks, leaving the brother to burn to death immediately after the sequence concludes. The fact that cinematic sequences guarantee certain conditions alleviated the demands on the game designers.

Conclusion

It is possible to add a storyline to a game that is inherently unpredictable. In our case, we chose to implement a custom programming language to enable the development of story-related scripts, although you might want to consider the benefits of using an established language such as Java, as used in *Vampire: The Masquerade—Redemption*. Although graphical script authoring tools are attractive to game designers, we encourage you to build these tools on top of a strong foundation. Designing your scripting system from the ground up might be arduous, but it will yield fruit in the end.

Using any type of programming language to create cinematic sequences and interactive Challenges demands a substantial quantity of logic programming. Designing your game to be sympathetic to scripting can alleviate this burden. A scripting system integrates various components of a game together, and can therefore be of great benefit in uncovering bugs in the game code. For this reason, we recommend the implementation of a scripting engine early in the development cycle. Loosely coupling the scripting engine with the game, perhaps via an abstracted API, results in a solution that is robust to a constantly changing game engine, and independent of its implementation.

Interactive movies once represented the future of computer entertainment, with consumers attracted to live-action and prerendered full-motion video (FMV) sequences. Paradoxically, products became increasingly movielike at the expense of interactivity, their popularity fading as a consequence. Game technology now enables the real-time rendering of movielike sequences, and we would do well to learn from the movie industry as this new art form matures. Perhaps the second generation of interactive movies will realize their full potential: gameplay-oriented experiences in which the player truly sets the agenda of the storyline.

References

[Barwood01] Barwood, Hal, "Cutting to the Chase: Cinematic Construction for Gamers," *Gamasutra*, May 18, 2000.

[Evans02] Evans, Richard, "Varieties of Learning," *AI Game Programming Wisdom*, Charles River Media, 2002.

[Hancock00] Hancock, Hugh, "Machinima Cutscene Creation, Part One," *Gamasutra*, September 30, 2000.

[Lionhead01] Lionhead Studios Ltd, "Black & White," 2001. See www.bwgame.com.

10.6

The Perils of AI Scripting

Paul Tozour—Ion Storm Austin

gehn29@yahoo.com

Game development teams often create scripting languages for developing AI. There are a number of motivations for this.

- **Parallel development**. Game designers need a way to design the various components of the game without having to depend on programmers to implement every new design feature. Scripting languages can allow designers to implement new features and make changes independently of the programming team.
- **Ease of use**. Game designers at most studios are not particularly technically adept. It's not reasonable to ask your team's designers to do what they need to do by writing code, particularly when most of them know little or nothing about programming. Scripting languages usually attempt to provide a simpler, more protected development environment than a professional programming language.
- **Data-driven design**. It's usually considered bad form to use code to develop logic specific to a particular level in the game. This makes the code less reusable and can lead to code bloat. Many programmers feel that anything specific to the logic of a certain part of the game should be data, not code. As scripting languages are usually interpreted, they can be treated as data that is separate from the codebase.
- **Rapid development**. In theory, since a scripting language is simpler and gives its users less opportunity for errors, it can allow its users to be more productive than they could be with a general-purpose programming language.
- **Safety**. Most game scripting languages are interpreted, so they can be executed in a protected environment. This allows the game executable to prevent fatal errors in the script from crashing the game. At worst, the offending script will simply be halted.
- **Extensibility**. There's often a need to allow your game's user community to extend the AI. The various "bots" that have become popular with a number of first-person shooters are a good example of this. However, the broader "mod community" tends to lack the hard-core programming skills of the game industry elite, and you need to provide your community with tools to extend the game without dumping your entire game's codebase on them. A perfect example is *UnrealScript,* provided as part of Epic Games' *Unreal* engine to allow extensive support for customization, including customizable AI.

Unfortunately, in practice, AI scripting languages often produce inferior results. In eight years, this author has encountered nearly a half-dozen scripting languages, all of which ultimately proved to be severe impediments to the team's productivity and could be most charitably described as "unmitigated disasters."

The point is not that scripting languages are evil (though some undoubtedly are). Rather, this article provides a practical perspective on the use of scripting languages for AI. Scripting offers endless possibilities, and not all of them are good ones. This article illustrates some of the shortcomings of scripting languages that are often overlooked, and some of the subtle ways that a seemingly simple idea can grow into a monstrosity.

Language Maturity

Take a moment and flip through your favorite high-level, object-oriented language and look at all the features the language provides: functions, variables, basic data types, operators, loops, pointers, arrays, conditionals, complex data structures, inheritance, aggregation, virtual functions, "const," templates, exceptions, and garbage-collection.

There are excellent reasons for all of these language features. A scripting language will typically begin by providing only a handful—some basic data types, operators, loops, conditionals, and support for user-defined functions.

However, language design is a slippery slope. As mission designers become more familiar with the system, they also become more familiar with its limitations. Programmers, in their desire to keep the designers happy and productive, are all too willing to add new features.

- Designers need to store lists of identical items, so the programmers extend the language to support arrays, linked-lists, and/or dynamic arrays.
- Designers need a better way to deal with complex data, and now the language supports complex data types such as structs, classes, and abstract interfaces.
- Designers continue developing their data structures, but find themselves frequently copying and pasting the script code for similar data structures, and need a way to reuse their data structures more easily. Now our language needs inheritance and aggregation.

Simplicity is one of the biggest motivations for creating an AI scripting language, and considering the astonishing complexity of a language such as C++, it's clearly a worthy goal. However, language design is a surprisingly challenging task. It's easy to forget that high-level languages such as C, C++, Java, C#, Python, Perl, Smalltalk, and Lisp have dozens of years of evolution behind them and have attained a very high level of maturity. They have broad user communities continuously providing input, and professional language developers overseeing their development who are not hampered by the need to develop a world-class video game at the same time.

These high-level languages are ready-made solutions to the generic programming problem. There are numerous high-quality development tools and thousands of well-written books available for all of these languages. If what you need is a true programming language, or if your simple programming language will ultimately grow into a full-featured language anyway, consider casting your lot with an existing, mature programming language.

Development Tools

As mentioned in the previous section, scripting languages quite often evolve into actual programming languages. However, they lack the powerful and full-featured development, debugging, and profiling tools that are essential for quality software development.

The debugging tools available in a modern development environment are a programmer's dream. Breakpoints let you stop the program at any line of code. You can step through the code line by line. You can step into or over any given function. A watch window shows you the values of any variables in the system, including complex data structures. You can view the entire call stack that led to a given line of code. Data breakpoints allow you to easily figure out when a variable's value changes. You can view the machine language instructions the compiler created for your code. You can inspect the values of the registers or any part of memory.

Most scripting languages, on the other hand, use a text editor and have no debugging capabilities. In many cases, if a script has a bug, the interpreter will simply crash or stop the script. The better scripting languages will issue a generic error message at this point, indicating the type of error and the line that caused it.

Programmers typically spend half their time doing debugging on any given program. A mature, professional debugging environment dramatically reduces the amount of time you spend debugging and liberates you to write more code.

Every programmer knows what it's like to track down a tough bug that requires every feature the debugger has to offer. Such bugs will inevitably occur on any project of significant size and complexity. Imagine attempting to fix them without the debugger.

Clearly, this can be very dangerous. Giving designers programming power without debugging support is like giving them a fast car with no brakes. If you want your game to be a professional product, you need to maintain the quality of your code. Script can easily become a type of code, and without the support of professional development tools, scripting languages can swing open the floodgates of mediocrity.

Performance

Game AI scripting languages are typically interpreted at runtime. As such, they impose a significant performance penalty over what the same code would cost in a compiled language such as C++. As AI becomes ever more important, more AI code is required, and this becomes an increasingly significant issue.

Many scripting language developers would argue that their game's AI isn't a significant performance problem in the first place, so doubling or tripling its execution time won't make a difference. In many cases, this is true. However, it's difficult to know at the beginning of a project what subsystems you'll need to optimize in the end. The act of interpreting a script imposes some amount of overhead, so optimizing a script can only take you so far, and your script will never be as fast as it would be if it were compiled.

Also, remember the old axiom that "code will expand to fill the space available." If you impose handicaps on your AI's performance, you might end up limiting its functionality.

Gameplay

Every gamer has had the experience of playing through a game and finding that he can read the gameplay like a script. "When I try to open the door to Mr. Giotti's room, one of the bad guys on the other side of the door says, 'It's Max Wayne! Nothing can stop that guy!' And the other bad guy says, 'Oh yeah? Well how about this?' and shoots a missile at the door and blows it up, conveniently allowing me, Max Wayne, to step through."

This type of scripted AI often ends up generating very narrow gameplay. It forces the player down a specific linear path the designer came up with, rather than allowing the player some measure of creativity in overcoming the challenges he or she faces.

Scripted AI can also greatly reduce the game's replayability. It can pervert the core gameplay into a form of memorization. The first time through the dungeon, you get slaughtered, but load your last saved game, and you have the advantage of knowing exactly where the enemies are and how they will attack you.

Even in a totally scripted system, there are a number of ways to make the game less predictable. Simple techniques such as random decision-making will go a long way toward making the gameplay more flexible. Let the guards choose randomly whether to go left or right, or whether to patrol the block clockwise or counterclockwise. If nothing else, add a long (and randomized) delay after a scripted event is triggered so it's not so obvious to the user that crossing an invisible line causes the ogres to turn and attack.

Designing the Right Interface

The ideal philosophy in managing the developer-designer relationship is to consider that AIs should do as much as possible autonomously. A designer should be able to drop an AI entity into the game world at any time, and it will immediately behave in a reasonable fashion. Place a stormtrooper in the world, and he will automatically know to fight the rebel scum when you launch the game, with no need for the designer to tell it anything more.

This philosophy forces us to distinguish the intrinsic AI—that is, the parts of the AI that form the foundation of the AI entities' cognitive toolkits, and that are constant from one part of the game to the next—from designer intentions, which are the designer's goals for behaviors specific to certain parts of the game, or events that occur in a specific situation. If we make the AIs as autonomous as possible, the designers can add AIs to the world with minimal effort. We can then allow the design team to assume additional control over the AIs' behaviors on an as-needed basis, from the basic level of specifying parameters, all the way to handing full control of the AIs over to the designers.

This distinction also helps us draw the line that separates the level designer's tasks from the role of the AI developer. To ask level designers to program the intrinsic AI is fundamentally an abdication of responsibility on the part of the programming team.

Here's an example of how designers might be able to minimally interact with the AI:

- Determine the initial placement of the AI entities in the game world.
- Provide additional AI parameters (for example, Benny the guard is 20% less aggressive than normal, prefers to use a crossbow, and will usually attack using a defensive tactic).
- Specify canned AI movement paths if necessary (guards Larry, Moe, and Curly will continuously patrol clockwise in a wedge formation around the castle tower).
- Specify any special relationships between AIs, or between AIs and objects in the game world (the entity MotherAlien07 guards BabyAlien02 and BabyAlien05).
- Design occasional triggered events (when the player turns the crank, the drawbridge lowers, a scream is heard, and the player's voice says, "Something's not right here").

With a minimal interface such as this, the designers tell the AI system only what it needs to know to get the job done. It's then up to the intrinsic AI itself to exhibit all of the appropriate behaviors in any given situation—selecting appropriate behaviors to respond to the player and to other AIs, performing pathfinding, selecting and playing animations and audio files, selecting and executing various tactics in combat, and so on.

A key advantage of this type of clean interface is that it allows us to create development tools that are highly customized for specific tasks.

Take a cinematics engine as an example. Although not usually considered AI per se, it illustrates the point nicely. A good cinema development system needs to provide interactive cinema development tools to allow us to create cut scenes quickly and easily. A good cinema tool will allow a designer to specify waypoints in the world that the camera should follow, and will allow him to specify fade-ins and fade-outs and modify the camera's orientation or field of view at any point during the sequence.

Obviously, this type of task lends itself far better to an interactive tool than a text script. We want to be able to interactively specify the sequence of events, and then grab a bag of popcorn and watch a preview of the cut scene we created. Because the tools fit the problem precisely, we can design cut scenes much more rapidly than we could with a text scripting language.

Such customized systems provide all of the key advantages we mentioned for scripting languages at the beginning of this article—most importantly, they offer a level of simplicity, rapid development, and safety above and beyond what a text-based system can provide.

Let's take another example. Your designers need to create patrol paths for guards who will wander through a level. This lends itself to a system where designers place "path points" in the world and connect them to each other in a directed graph. This lets you design paths with a few mouse clicks—a task that might take several hours to specify in a script.

Even for the most complex AI scripting tasks, anything resembling a programming language is usually a bad fit for the problem. Most game AI is rules based and can be addressed with simpler systems that allow designers to specify the underlying rules. This also makes it easy to provide a protected development environment that prevents designers from entering invalid parameters or causing syntax errors.

Before You Leap

This article is not intended as a blanket condemnation of scripting languages. On the contrary, there are a number of excellent reasons to use a scripting language, as explained at the beginning of this article. However, scripting languages have a number of downsides that are too seldom considered, particularly when applied inappropriately.

Before you develop a scripting language, consider the implications carefully.

- Think about the capabilities that should be intrinsic to the AI. The more your AIs can do on their own, the less scripting designers will need to do to compensate.
- Consider whether a scripting language really fits your needs. In many cases, you might be able to accomplish the same tasks with customized development tools. Although these tools might not be as infinitely flexible as a general-purpose language, they will let your design team meet their goals more quickly and with less hassle.
- If you do need to use a scripting language, consider whether you need a full-fledged programming language or a simpler trigger system that can allow designers to specify their intentions within a protected environment.
- Consider using an existing programming language such as C, C++, Java, or C#, or a mature scripting language such as Tcl, Lua, Python, or Perl.
- Consider the tools your designers will have available. If you provide them with a language as powerful as a programming language, you should be providing them with powerful and flexible debugging tools, as well. Fast cars need good brakes.
- Consider the runtime performance issues, and whether you're likely to paint yourself into a corner by discovering too late in the project that your AI language is too slow.

- Regardless of the tools you choose for the job, remember that any hard-coded "scripts" you develop need to stay flexible. Even with totally scripted AI and gameplay, there are a number of ways to use randomness and design more flexible scripts to make the end user's experience feel less "scripted."

References and Additional Reading

[Huebner97] Huebner, Robert, "Adding Languages to Game Engines," *Computer Game Developer's Conference Proceedings*, Miller Freeman, 1997.

[Rabin00] Rabin, Steve, "Designing a General Robust AI Engine," *Game Programming Gems*, Ed. Mark DeLoura, Charles River Media, 2000.

How *Not* to Implement a Basic Scripting Language

Mark Brockington and Mark Darrah—BioWare Corp.

markb@bioware.com, markd@bioware.com

So, you need to write a scripting language. This is easy, right? You can just whip one off in a couple of days. However, before embarking on your implementation, carefully consider the problems that a poorly designed scripting language could cause. The following is a discussion of some poor decisions that were made in the creation of the scripting languages used in BioWare's role-playing games.

Definitions

BGScript: The scripting language designed for *Baldur's Gate*, and used in every other Infinity Engine game (*Planescape: Torment, Icewind Dale, Baldur's Gate II*).

NWScript: The scripting language designed for *Neverwinter Nights*.

Creature: A creature is a player character or any other human being, animal, or monster within the game. They have AI and specific statistics in common with each other.

Object: Anything that can be interacted with in the environment. The objects available in our games include creatures, monster spawning points, projectiles, containers, doors, traps, and areas.

Heartbeat: A periodic scripting event that is run every *n* seconds on an object. This allows actions to occur even when no event interacts with the game object.

Effect: A self-contained structure that can be placed upon any object to implement either statistic changes (such as strength modification, damage to health, or reduction in movement speed), or visual flash (such as a puff of smoke).

"Eight Words" Is Not Enough Design!

The design for *BGScript* consisted of the following: "We need a scripting language for the combat." No decisions were made on syntax or reusability. The list of things that the language would be used for, aside from combat, was nonexistent.

Why did this happen? The initial design for *BGScript* was so brief mainly from ignorance. The *Baldur's Gate* team had never worked on a game before. The designers didn't know what they needed, since the programmers were still building the game engine, and the programmers did not know the questions to ask to determine what the designers needed.

What is the moral of this tale? Spend the time to determine what you need, and over-engineer the system beyond that. Every "Wouldn't it be nice if" you consider during the initial design should be worked into the design. Even if you do not intend to implement some of these things, make sure your design is flexible enough to accommodate adding them at a later date.

For *NWScript*, we wanted a relatively safe scripting environment for end users to use. A bad script could slow down the game, but it was our design goal to prevent anything passed to the scripting language from crashing the server. We could work with the Lua scripting language [Ierusalimschy96], which we used in *MDK2*, heavily modifying the internals to give us the desired behavior (LucasArts did this for *Escape From Monkey Island*, but did not know this at the time), or we could "implement *BGScript* in a C/Java syntax." After a tragic underestimate on the length of time it would take, we chose the latter approach and the *NWScript* experiment started.

You would think we would have learned our lesson after the first scripting language. One "Wouldn't it be nice if" list was specified in a 250-page manual that sits on or near every programmer's desk at BioWare [Kernighan88]. There are still many features of C that are extremely difficult to do based on how the compiler and virtual machine were set up. For example, call-by-reference is not possible without a significant rewrite of many of the major components of the compiler, because we had no intention of supporting functions in the first version of *NWScript*!

If you only implement a small subset of a known language, you will be bombarded with requests to implement each user's favorite feature. As mentioned earlier, the initial plan for *NWScript* was to implement *BGScript* in a C/Java syntax. We did not intend to support many of the infrequently used features of C (such as do/while loops, or the conditional ?/: operator). However, they were all added to *NWScript* over the development cycle.

Using *lex* and *yacc* [Levine92] was not an option for *NWScript*, because we focused on getting the compiler running on many different platforms, and the porting issues scared us into writing our own parser. We'll be blunt: Never ever write your own parser. If you are going to use a standard language or a subset of that language, use *lex* and *yacc* or a variant of them. You will save yourself more time in learning to use them than you will require in deciphering the mess you have made of your own custom parser.

What's Wrong with the Syntax?

Both *BGScript* and *NWScript* were designed to be usable by the end user. However, different choices (and different mistakes!) were made in this regard.

BGScript implemented a very simple syntax. Scripts consist of stacked `if`/`then` blocks. There are no nesting, loops, or other complicated structures in *BGScript*. The thing that makes *BGScript* confusing (and is a concern to any AI system that involves actions) is that some actions are not atomic. Non-atomic actions include movement, combat, or playing a series of animations—anything that drags out over several frames. The implication is that if the script contains any non-atomic actions, you cannot simply run all of the actions specified in the script and be done with it.

There are two approaches to getting around this problem. The first is to implement a virtual machine that is re-entrant. When the action completes, the script can be triggered again, and execution can continue. The second is to add these actions to an action stack and execute them in order after the script has completed running. This seemed to be the easier solution to implement at the time, since this allowed us to run a script from head to tail, unload it from memory, and deal with the actions after the script had completed. Thus, we chose the latter method for *BGScript*.

Unfortunately, this is a very difficult concept for end users to grasp, and we should have realized early on that anything the designers have problems understanding would also confuse end users. Listen very carefully to what your early adopters ask questions about. Your reaction should not be, "How can I fix their problem?" Your reaction should be, "How can I fix the design so that no one else can make this mistake again?"

Going back to our problem in *BGScript*, a simple step to improve this would be a simple syntax trick. Rather than having the actions as the statements, consider forcing the call of an add function. The following code:

```
AddActionToQueue(Attack("KOBOLD"))
AddActionToQueue(SetGlobal("KoboldAttacked",TRUE))
```

is much clearer to most scripters than:

```
Attack("KOBOLD")
SetGlobal("KoboldAttacked",TRUE)
```

The syntax of the language is another usability issue to consider. If your scripters consist entirely of untrained designers, then syntax is not a huge issue—they will have to learn any system from scratch. If you have technical designers or programmers doing some of the scripting, then you should strongly consider a standard syntax such as C. This will minimize the learning curve for these people. Another advantage of C is that there are many books and courses available to teach it. This means that you don't have to devote your time to getting the designers up to speed.

However, if you are going to start with a standard language, you should be very careful in the ways in which you modify the syntax. While you might have your pet peeves with whatever language base you are choosing, changing it will only result in more confusion to those people already familiar with the language. Making a language that is suitable for two different sets of programmers (for example, those who know C and those who know Java) is a wonderful way to get into trouble.

For example, Java changed how the >> operator works for negative numbers by preserving the sign, and the operator that a C programmer would expect to be >> is actually >>> in Java. Which implementation should we choose for *NWScript*? Unfortunately, you're in a no-win situation: one group of users is going to be very upset when they discover the operator does not work the way they expect it to. In the end, we went with the Java implementation, and we documented this in the scripting manual under "If you are a C programmer."

My Language Doesn't Need to Be Extendible!

Due to inexperience, little thought was given to what the Infinity Engine was going to be after *Baldur's Gate* shipped. As a result, no extensibility was written into *BGScript*. Once errors made by an inadequate design were discovered (such as a missing *not* operand, or no capability to *or* conditions together), they could not be rectified. Further exacerbating the problem was the fact that *BGScript* was used for four games and three mission packs—it has already passed its fifth birthday.

Remember that you are going to be using this scripting language for a while. Expect and accept that once a basic syntax is set and designers begin to use it, you will be stuck with it until the end of the project. Further, while you might think that you will have the opportunity to rewrite the system for sequels, this is probably not the case. It is highly probable that your designers will want to stick with a syntax they know, and the workarounds from the first title become features in later titles.

A corollary is that once you have written your parser, it will almost never be rewritten from the ground up. The *BGScript* parser was written in all of two days using one gigantic case statement. The parsing code is easy to understand if you are fluent in both C and Prolog (the latter being an uncommon skill at BioWare). You might think of this example as job security, but after five years of maintaining the same piece of code, it would be nice to pass the responsibility on to someone else!

You cannot design for everything. What you can do, however, is design the system so that the addition of new things can be done with a minimum of stress to the framework and syntax. Adding a new data type into *NWScript* (such as "vector," a structure with three floating-point numbers) turned out to be significantly more difficult than it should have been. It took approximately two days to follow through all of the chains inside the compiler and account for all of the new cases where arithmetic operations interacted with vectors.

When it came around to implementing another data type in *NWScript*, we avoided the route where we implemented the data type directly into the compiler and virtual machine. Instead, we developed a generic system that allowed us to add additional data type support into the language by defining the core operations (comparison, creation, deletion, and assignment operations) in a pure virtual class that was overridden by the game engine. We did not want to include the entire definition of the data type into the virtual machine, since we intend to use *NWScript* in other titles that might not require these *NWN*-specific data types. In the virtual machine, we only had to write code that passed around an integer (the pointer to the game engine class), and it would be created, processed, and deleted properly through the overridden functions in the game engine. As a result, we can now add a new data type into *NWScript* in under an hour, and any programmer can add the new data type with no knowledge of the internals of the compiler or the virtual machine.

You Need the Scripting Language to Do What?

If there is one lesson that we can impart, it is this: flexibility, flexibility, and flexibility. If your language is flexible enough, then the issue of extensibility is not so large. You will have less need to extend the language if the designers can find ways to bend it to their needs.

This was an error that could easily have been avoided on *BGScript*. Before starting the language, we read an article in the CGDC proceedings [Huebner97]. One thing that was stressed was that a flexible language would get used for more things than you plan for. We foolishly ignored this advice and made a language for a single purpose. We will now impart this advice: Even an *inflexible* language will get used for more things than you plan for. You might as well make it easier for yourself when you have the chance.

How Did We Extend BGScript?

BGScript is designed fundamentally as a simple combat scripting language. Even after five years of manipulation, at heart this is what it remains today. Unfortunately, combat scripting is less than 30 percent of what *BGScript* is actually used for. The other 70 percent of applications are detailed next.

Simple, noncombat creature scripting: This consists of relatively unimportant actions such as the wandering of peasants via RandomWalk(). It also consists of playing ambient animations on creatures (such as making a blacksmith strike an anvil). While this scripting depends almost exclusively on a heartbeat script, it is still desirable for new stimuli to interrupt the existing string of actions. Combat scripting (at the time) was done on reactions to stimuli exclusively, so a heartbeat had to be added to each creature.

Trap and trigger scripting: Most trap scripting is similar to simple combat scripting. The trap responds to the stimuli of being activated by playing a visual effect and using the CastSpell() action to cause injury. Unfortunately, traps are not creatures, so they did not have the same structure for AI in place. As a result, the scripting language now simultaneously had actions that only creatures could perform, and another list that all objects could perform. Unfortunately, the language had no differentiation, and it was not always obvious which actions belonged in which list.

Triggers are polygons on the ground that react to creatures in nondamaging ways, such as teleporting the party to another location or displaying text. Triggers are unique in that they can do several actions that all must complete without being interrupted. In other words, additional stimuli should not override the existing action list. This requires the addition of a way to prevent this interruption.

Conversation: The scripting of conversation truly stretches *BGScript* to its breaking point. Rather than a stack of `if` / `then` clauses, conversation is set up as a tree. The conditionals are scattered at the branching points, and action lists are tacked on to every response. Unfortunately, the compiled versions of the scripts were never meant to be segmented in this manner. The result is that conversation scripting is stored in an uncompiled format and compiled on-the-fly. A user can tolerate a small delay when conversation is initiated, but compiling every script in a large conversation tree stalled *Baldur's Gate* for more than a second.

Additionally, action lists obtained through conversation are similar to triggers. That is, they must complete and cannot be interrupted. Unlike triggers, conversation is run by creatures that also must have responsive combat scripting. The conflict is very difficult to resolve, and is, in fact, the source of some outstanding bugs in Infinity Engine games.

In-game movies: In-game movies are scripted sequences where various creatures perform actions in specifically timed and ordered ways. They are used in place of prerendered movies when animation time or space is at a premium. In-game movies require uninterrupted action lists like triggers. However, their biggest challenge is that they require timing between characters and across multiple actions.

How Did We Extend NWScript?

We started with the knowledge that we were going to give the same functionality that was already present in *BGScript*. However, as the project evolved, many more uses became apparent.

Spells: Each spell in *Baldur's Gate* was entered in an external editor, and the data could be used to generate the spell. However, as far as *Dungeons & Dragons* rules go, spells cannot be neatly classified and described with a couple of tidy effects. For example, you are asked to implement the "Heal" spell. Instead of using your standard heal effect, you would have to make a special one just for the spell. Why? The "Heal" spell must harm undead creatures.

Rather than have a programmer sit and spend the time implementing the odd rules deep inside the core engine, we have exposed the mechanics of the spell impact to a scripting event. The designers can code all of the odd behaviors of their rule set without having to ask programmers for a series of similar effects with hard-coded exceptions.

Pathfinding around doors: What should a creature do when it encounters a door while it is walking? Should it smash the door down, or should it pull out a lockpick set and try to open the door? Should it give up entirely and go somewhere else? Whenever the designer says, "It depends," it ends up in the scripting language.

What Are We Are Trying to Get Across?

Your language *will* be used for things for which it was never designed. Even if you spent a year on your design phase and thought of a dozen different uses, the designers are going to bend the language to the point of its breakage and beyond. The trick is to make the language flexible enough in the first place, so that the breakage occurs infrequently and for reasons that you, hopefully, do not even need to fix.

A final note on flexibility: If you don't believe us about the need of flexibility, please mark this page and come back to it after your game ships.

"We told you so."

Conclusion

The flaws that we described here are not insurmountable problems given foresight and planning. The key lessons we are trying to emphasize are:

- Plan your scripting language and determine what you are going to use it for.
- Carefully consider who will be using the language when choosing the syntax.
- Make it as easy as possible to add new language constructs.
- Make the language flexible enough to be used for other purposes than those for which it was intended.

There are many traps that one call fall into when implementing a basic scripting language. The most important step in avoiding these traps is knowing that the trap exists. We hope that you can recognize these potential trouble spots in your design and fix them in your implementation.

References

[Huebner97] Huebner, Robert, "Adding Languages to Game Engines," *Game Developer* magazine, September 1997.

[Ierusalimschy96] Ierusalimschy, R., de Figueiredo, Luiz Henrique, and Filho, Waldemar Celes, "Lua—an extensible extension language," *Software: Practice & Experience*, Vol. 26, No. 6, pp. 635–652, 1996. *Lua* web page: www.tecgraf.puc-rio.br/lua.

[Kernighan88] Kernighan, Brian, and Ritchie, David, *The C Programming Language (Second Edition)*, Prentice-Hall, 1988.

[Levine92] Levine, John, Mason, Tony, and Brown, Doug, *lex & yacc (Second Edition)*, O'Reilly, 1992.

11.1

Learning and Adaptation

John Manslow
john@jmanslow.fsnet.co.uk

It is anticipated that the widespread adoption of learning in games will be one of the most important advances ever to be made in game AI. Genuinely adaptive AIs will change the way in which games are played by forcing the player to continually search for new strategies to defeat the AI, rather than perfecting a single technique.

In addition, the careful and considered use of learning makes it possible to produce smarter and more robust AIs without the need to preempt and counter every strategy that a player might adopt. This article presents a detailed examination of the techniques available for, and the issues involved in, adding learning and adaptation to games.

What Is Learning, and Why Use It?

With a small number of notable exceptions, few games have been released to date that have contained any level of adaptation, despite the fact that it is well within the capabilities of current hardware. There are a variety of reasons for this, including:

- Until recently, the lack of precedent of the successful application of learning in a mainstream top-rated game means that the technology is unproven and hence perceived as being high risk.
- Learning algorithms are frequently associated with techniques such as neural networks and genetic algorithms, which are difficult to apply in-game due to their relatively low efficiency.

Despite its scarcity, learning—and the family of algorithms based on the principles of learning—can offer a number of benefits to game developers and players alike. For example, solutions to problems that are extremely difficult to solve "manually" can be discovered by learning algorithms, often with minimal human supervision: Codemasters' *Colin McRae Rally 2.0* used a neural network to *learn* how to drive a rally car, thus avoiding the need to handcraft a large and complex set of rules (see [Hannan01]).

Moreover, in-game learning can be used to adapt to conditions that cannot be anticipated prior to the game's release, such as the particular styles, tastes, and dispositions of individual players. For example, although a level designer can provide hints to the AI in a first-person shooter (FPS) about the likely camping locations of players, different players will, in all probability, have different preferences. Clearly, an AI that can learn such preferences will not only have an advantage over one that cannot, but will appear far smarter to the player.

Is Adaptation Necessary?

Before examining the techniques available for adding adaptation to a game, this section urges careful consideration of whether adaptation is justified in terms of its benefits, and whether the illusion of adaptation can be produced using more conventional AI.

Are There Any Benefits to Adaptation?

Clearly, if the answer to that question is "no," adaptation should not be used. When adaptation is expected to benefit either the developer or the player, the weight of the benefit needs to be considered against the additional complexity that an adaptive AI can add to the game development and testing processes. Marginal improvements resulting from adaptation will go unnoticed by the vast majority of players, so it is important to identify specific aspects of an AI agent's behavior where adaptation will be obvious.

Faking It

It is often possible to create the impression that an AI agent is learning without any learning actually taking place. This is most easily done by degrading an AI that performs very well through the addition of random errors. If the frequency and magnitude of the errors are steadily reduced with "experience," the appearance of learning can be produced. This "faked learning" has a number of advantages:

- The "rate of learning" can be carefully controlled and specified prior to release, as can the behavior of the AI at each stage of its development.
- The state of the AI at any point in time is independent of the details of the interaction of the player with the game, simplifying debugging and testing.

Although faking learning is an attractive way of creating the illusion of adaptation, it can only be used when the behavior "being learned" can be specified in advance, and is hence limited to problems that can be solved using conventional, nonlearning technologies.

Adaptation in Practice

This section describes the two ways in which real learning and adaptation can occur in games. The first, called *indirect adaptation*, extracts statistics from the game world that are used by a conventional AI layer to modify an agent's behavior. The decision as to what statistics are extracted and their interpretation in terms of necessary changes in behavior are all made by the AI designer. The second technique, referred to as *direct adaptation*, applies learning algorithms to the agent's behavior itself, and requires minimal human direction beyond specifying which aspects of behavior to adapt.

Indirect Adaptation

Indirect adaptation occurs when an agent extracts information about the game world that is used by a "conventional" AI layer to adapt the agent's behavior. For example, a bot in an FPS can learn where it has the greatest success of killing the player. Conventional AI can then be used to change the agent's pathfinding to visit those locations more often in the future, in the hope of achieving further success. The role of the learning mechanism is thus restricted to extracting information from the game world, and plays no direct part in changing the agent's behavior.

This indirect way of adapting behavior is recommended in this article because it offers the following important advantages:

- The information about the game world upon which the changes in behavior are based can often be extracted very easily and reliably, resulting in fast and effective adaptation.
- Since changes in behavior are made by a conventional AI layer, they are well defined and controlled, and hence easy to debug and test.

The main disadvantage of the technique is that it requires both the information to be learned and the changes in behavior that occur in response to it to be defined a priori by the AI designer.

Despite this, a wide variety of adaptive behaviors can be produced using this technique, ranging from learning good kill sites in an FPS and biasing pathfinding toward them (as already mentioned), learning how long a player takes to launch his first assault in a real-time strategy (RTS) game so that the AI can decide whether to expand militarily or economically, to learning which fruits in an agent's environment are poisonous and biasing its food choice accordingly. In each of these cases, learning merely collects statistics about the game world, and it is the conventional AI that interprets that information and adapts behavior in response to it. Other examples of indirect adaptation can be found in [Evans02], [Laramée02a], and [Mommersteeg02].

Direct Adaptation

Learning algorithms can be used to adapt an agent's behavior directly, usually by testing modifications to it in the game world to see if it can be improved. In practice, this is done by parameterizing the agent's behavior in some way and using an *optimization algorithm* or *reinforcement learning* to search for the parameters (and hence, behaviors) that offer the best performance. For example, in an FPS, a bot might contain a rule controlling the range below which it will not use a rocket launcher, in order to avoid blast damage. This particular aspect of the bot's behavior is thus parameterized by the range below which the switch to another weapon is made.

Direct adaptation has a number of disadvantages as compared to indirect adaptation, including:

- The performances of AI agents with different parameters (and hence, behaviors) are evaluated empirically by measuring their effectiveness in-game. This is problematic because:
  — A measure of an agent's performance must be developed that reflects the real aim of learning and the role of the agent in-game. This is discussed in greater detail later.
  — Each agent's performance must be evaluated over a substantial period of time to minimize the impact of random events on the measured performance.
  — Too many evaluations are likely to be required for each agent's performance to be measured against a representative sample of human opponents.
- Adaptation is generally less well controlled than in the indirect case, making it difficult to test and debug a directly adaptive agent. This increases the risk that it will discover behaviors that exploit some limitation of the game engine (such as instability in the physics simulation), or an unexpected maximum of the performance measure.

The last of these effects can be minimized by carefully restricting the scope of adaptation to a small number of aspects of the agent's behavior, and limiting the range of adaptation within each. The example given earlier, of adapting the behavior that controls when an AI agent in an FPS switches away from a rocket launcher at close range, is a good example of this. The behavior being adapted is so specific and limited that adaptation is unlikely to have any unexpected effects elsewhere in the game, and is hence easy to test and validate.

One of the major advantages of direct adaptation, and indeed, one that often overrides all the disadvantages listed earlier, is that direct adaptation is capable of developing completely new behaviors. For example, it is, in principle, possible to produce a game with no in-built AI whatsoever, but which uses *genetic programming* (or some similar technique) to directly evolve rules for controlling AI agents as the game is played. Such a system would perhaps be the ultimate AI in the sense that:

- All the behaviors developed by the AI agents would be learned from their experience in the game world, and would therefore be unconstrained by the preconceptions of the AI designer.
- The evolution of the AI would be open ended in the sense that there would be no limit to the complexity and sophistication of the rule sets, and hence the behaviors that could evolve.

Of course, such an AI is not a practical proposition because, as has already been described, the lack of constraints on the types of behavior that can develop makes it impossible to guarantee that the game would continue to be playable once adaptation had begun. It should be noted that this objection cannot be raised where direct adaptation takes place during the development of the game only, since the resulting rule sets and their associated behaviors can be validated via the usual testing and validation procedures.

In summary, direct adaptation of behaviors offers an alternative to indirect adaptation, which can be used when it is believed that adapting particular aspects of an agent's behavior is likely to be beneficial, but when too little is known about the exact form the adaptation should take for it to be prescribed a priori by the AI designer. Targeting direct adaptation at very specific and limited sets of behaviors is the key to making it work in practice, since this improves the efficiency of the adaptation and makes it easier to control and validate. An example of direct adaptation using genetic algorithms can be found in [Laramée02b].

Incorporate as Much Prior Knowledge as Possible

In the last section, it was suggested that a game could be produced with no AI out-of-the-box other than an algorithm such as genetic programming, which could evolve sets of rules for controlling AI agents as the game is played. Such a game would have (at least) two major flaws in that the AI agents would do nothing useful when the game is first played, and the rate of improvement of their performances would be very slow. Both of these are due to a lack of prior knowledge in the AI; that is, the AI designer has incorporated nothing about what is known about the game in the AI.

The vast proportion of what an AI has to do—such as finding the shortest path across a level, or choosing the best weapon in an FPS—*is* known prior to a game's release and *should* be incorporated and fixed in the AI. This allows the learning algorithms to focus on what must be learned, resulting in substantial improvements in efficiency and reliability. It should be noted that the high performance of indirect adaptation is a result of its extensive use of prior knowledge in the interpretation of the information learned about the world.

Design a Good Performance Measure

Direct adaptation of an agent's behavior usually proceeds by generating an agent characterized by a set of parameter values that define its behavior and measuring its performance in-game. Clearly, this implies that some measure of the agent's performance is available, which must, in practice, be defined by the AI developer. The definition of an appropriate performance measure is often difficult because:

- Many alternative measures of apparently equal merit often exist, requiring an arbitrary choice to be made between them.
- The most obvious or logical measure of performance might produce the same value for wide ranges of parameter values, providing little guide as to how to choose between them. Parameter values across which a performance measure is constant are called *neutral networks*.
- Carelessly designed performance measures can encourage undesirable behavior, or introduce locally optimal behaviors (i.e., those that are not the best, but cannot be improved by small changes in parameters).

The first of these issues can be illustrated by considering the problem of adapting a bot in an FPS. Two possible measures of the performance of a bot are the number of times it kills the player in a best-of-10 death match, and the average time between the bot making kills. Both of these measures would encourage the bot to develop behaviors that allow it to kill the player, but only the former explicitly encourages the bot to stay alive. The latter might also do this implicitly, provided that bots respawn with only basic weaponry, armor, health, and so forth.

Neutral networks can also be problematic, particularly when all agents tend to be very good or very poor. For example, in a driving game, it might be desirable for AI drivers to learn to improve their times on new tracks. The time required to complete a track might be chosen as a performance measure in this case, but will fail to discriminate between parameters that describe drivers that achieve the same time within the resolution of the timer, or fail to complete the track at all. Neutral networks can be eliminated by adding heuristics to the performance measure to favor behaviors that are considered "likely to be better."

In the preceding example, since straighter paths tend to be shorter, can be traveled at higher speed, and hence correspond to faster drive times, the neutral networks can be removed by adding a term to the performance measure that favors straighter paths. Such heuristics can be useful in guiding learning to an appropriate solution, and are surprisingly common. Finding fast drivers in a driving game is a heuristic for making a fun and challenging game. Making a fun and challenging game is a heuristic for making a game that sells well and hence, makes lots of money.

Learn by Optimization

Once the behavior of an AI agent has been parameterized and a performance measure developed, it can be improved by using an optimization algorithm to search for sets of parameters that make the agent perform well in-game. Almost any optimization algorithm can be used for this purpose, although it needs to be derivative free, robust to noise in the performance assessments, and, ideally, robust to the presence of local optima. A good survey of optimization algorithms can be found in [Jang97].

Genetic algorithms (applied to *Othello* in [Jang97], and creating AI trolls in [Laramée02b]), *evolution strategy*, and *population-based incremental learners* are all well suited to this type of optimization because they satisfy all of the aforementioned criteria, and can optimize arbitrary combinations of continuous and discrete parameters. *Genetic programming* (applied to *Pac-Man* in [Ballard97]) can also be used when the rules controlling AI agents are themselves being adapted, but tends to be rather inefficient and difficult to control.

Learn by Reinforcement

An alternative to adapting an agent by searching directly for successful behaviors using an optimization algorithm, is to learn the relationship between an action taken by the agent in a particular state of the game world and the performance of the agent. Once this has been done, the best action (i.e., that which yields the best average performance) can be selected in any state.

This idea forms the basis of a form of *reinforcement learning* called *Q-learning* (described in detail in [Jang97] and [Ballard97]). Although reinforcement learning has been successfully applied to a wide variety of complex problems (ranging from creating AI players of *Othello* [Jang97] and backgammon [Ballard97], to balancing a pole on a moving cart [Ballard97]), it can be difficult to use, because:

- A decision has to be made as to what information from the game world will be placed in the status vector. Omitting important information from the status vector will prevent the agent from learning effective behaviors, while choosing an excessively long state vector will reduce the rate at which the agent's behavior improves.
- Reinforcement learning generally adapts only very slowly, and hence often requires very large numbers (e.g., tens or hundreds of thousands) of performance evaluations. This problem is often overcome by evaluating agents against each other—a strategy that can only be employed in games where there is an exact symmetry between the roles of the AI and the player.

Learn by Imitation

In some cases, it might be desirable for an AI agent to learn from a player—either overtly (for example, if the AI is acting as the player's assistant and must be trained to perform useful tasks) or covertly (for example, imitating the composition of a player's force in an RTS game). In the former case, learning can occur:

- By a process of memorizing the player's actions while a learning flag provided by the player is set—simply a form of macro recording.
- By allowing the player to provide the performance assessments to an agent using a direct adaptation mechanism.

The simplest general way of covertly learning to imitate a player is to record state-action pairs that describe the player's behavior, and use a technique such as a neural network to reproduce the player's actions given the state information. This approach is described in [Manslow01], elsewhere in this book [Manslow02], and was used to create the arcade-mode AI rally drivers in Codemasters' *Colin McRae 2.0* (see [Hannan01]).

Avoid Locally Optimal Behaviors

Locally optimal behaviors are those that, while not the best possible, cannot be improved upon by making small changes. They are problematic because most optimization algorithms are guaranteed only to find local optima, and hence agents that adapt by optimization might discover only a locally optimal behavior. Although some optimization algorithms (such as genetic algorithms, *simulated annealing,* and *Tabu search*) are robust to the presence of local optima, care should be taken when choosing a parameterization of an agent's behavior and a performance measure to ensure that local optima are not introduced. That is, try to choose the parameterization and performance measure so that the latter changes smoothly and monotonically with the former.

As an example of a careless choice of representation, consider the case where the behavior of an AI driver on a racetrack is represented as a sequence of steering actions. Optimizing this representation directly can lead to the AI achieving a good, but not optimal time, because it drives the latter half of the track particularly well. Unfortunately, any changes to the steering actions on the first half of the track disrupts its drive on the latter half because of the sequential dependence in the representation, resulting in a worse time. The AI has thus discovered a locally optimal strategy that many optimization algorithms will fail to improve upon, and which is a result of the choice of representation rather than intrinsic to the problem being solved.

Minimize Dependencies

In some instances, there might be several different aspects of an agent's behavior that can be adapted. For example, a bot in an FPS might use one learning algorithm to decide which weapon is most effective, and another to identify areas in a level where it has frequently killed the player. If these learning algorithms are run simultaneously, it would be found that the bot could not reliably identify these "kill hotspots" until after it had decided which weapon was most effective.

This is because the two apparently independent learning algorithms interact: As the bot's weapon preference changes, it inevitably visits different parts of a level in order to collect different weapons. While in these locations, the bot will encounter and kill the player, causing a dependence between weapon choice and kill location that prevents the kill hotspot learning algorithm from stabilizing before the weapon choice algorithm. Dependencies such as this are common and occur not just within adaptive agents, but also between them. Their effect is usually just to reduce the overall rate of adaptation of every agent in the system and is only very rarely more serious. Identifying truly independent, noninteracting behaviors is useful, because they can all be adapted simultaneously without any loss of efficiency.

Avoid Overfitting

"Overfitting" is the name given to the condition where an agent has adapted its behavior to a very specific set of states of the game world, and performs poorly in other states. It can have a variety of causes, including:

- The period over which an agent's behavior is evaluated is not representative of how the agent will experience the game in the long term. Try extending the time given to evaluating the performance of each agent, and (although usually not possible in-game) evaluate each within the context of a representative sample of levels, maps, and environments.
- The parameterization used to adapt behavior is state-specific, and hence does not generalize across states. For example, it is possible for AI drivers in a racing game to drive a particular track by learning a sequence of steering actions. Such an AI will fail when placed on a new track because the information it learned was specific to the track it was trained on; in other words, specific to a particular game state. See [Jang97] for a more detailed discussion of this issue.

Explore and Exploit

When learning by optimization or reinforcement, a directly adaptive AI continually faces the *exploration-exploitation dilemma*: Should it exploit what it has already learned by reproducing the best behavior that it has discovered for the situation it currently faces, or should it explore alternative behaviors in the hope of discovering something better, but at the risk of performing worse? Finding the right trade-off between exploration and exploitation can be difficult in practice, because it depends on the set of behaviors being adapted, and can change during adaptation.

Unfortunately, it is also important because too little exploration can cause the AI to improve slower than is possible or become stuck in a locally optimal behavior, while too much can force the AI to waste time searching for improvements in behavior that might not exist. In addition, unless exploration is carefully constrained, some of the trial behaviors might be extremely poor, particularly when using global optimization algorithms like genetic algorithms. An indirectly adaptive agent is not faced with the exploration-exploitation dilemma, because its changes in behavior are prescribed a priori by the AI designer.

Computational Requirements

As a general rule, the most efficient techniques for adaptation are indirectly adaptive, simply because the difficult problem of deciding how the agent's behavior should change in response to information learned about the game world is solved a priori by the AI designer, and what remains (essentially collecting statistics about the world) is usually trivial. Indirect adaptation can therefore easily be applied in real time.

Direct adaptation can certainly be performed during a game's development, where learning algorithms can be left running continuously for days or weeks. In-game, direct adaptation is most effective when restricted to very limited and specific problems and its search for effective behaviors is guided by good heuristics. In some circumstances, such as when using a neural network to perform Q-learning, computational requirements are much higher, and data can be collected in-game and the bulk of the computation performed "offline"; for example, during the natural breaks in gameplay that occur at the ends of levels.

Conclusion

This article provided an overview of the issues involved in adding adaptation and learning to games. The simplest form of adaptation is indirect adaptation, where agents are hard-coded to extract certain information from the game world, which they use in a predetermined way to modify their behavior. Indirect adaptation is effective because its extensive use of prior knowledge makes the learning mechanism simple, highly efficient, and easy to control, test, and validate.

More complex is direct adaptation, which relies on optimization algorithms or reinforcement learning to adapt an agent's behavior directly on the basis of assessments of its performance in the game world. Because direct adaptation relies less on prior knowledge provided by the AI designers, it is unconstrained by their preconceptions, but also less efficient, and more difficult to control. The key to successfully adding adaptation to a game lies in identifying a very small set of well-defined behaviors where adaptation will be most obvious to the player.

References

[Ballard97] Ballard, Dana, *An Introduction to Natural Computation*, MIT Press, 1997.

[Evans02] Evans, Richard, "Varieties of Learning," *AI Game Programming Wisdom*, Charles River Media, 2002.

[Hannan01] Hannan, Jeff, "Generation5 Interview with Jeff Hannan," available online at www.generation5.org/hannan.shtml, 2001.

[Jang97] Jang, J. S. R., Sun, C. T., Mizutani, E., *Neuro-Fuzzy and Soft Computing*, Prentice-Hall, 1997.

[Laramée02a] Laramée, François Dominic, "Using N-Gram Statistical Models to Predict Player Behavior," *AI Game Programming Wisdom*, Charles River Media, 2002.

[Laramée02b] Laramée, François Dominic, "Genetic Algorithms: Evolving the Perfect Troll," *AI Game Programming Wisdom*, Charles River Media, 2002.

[Manslow01] Manslow, John, "Using a Neural Network in a Game: A Concrete Example," *Game Programming Gems 2*, Charles River Media, 2001.

[Manslow02] Manslow, John, "Imitating Random Variations in Behavior Using a Neural Network," *AI Game Programming Wisdom*, Charles River Media, 2002.

[Mommersteeg02] Mommersteeg, Fri, "Pattern Recognition with Sequential Prediction," *AI Game Programming Wisdom*, Charles River Media, 2002.

11.2

Varieties of Learning

Richard Evans—Lionhead Studios

revans@lionhead.com

The creatures in *Black & White* learn in a variety of different ways. This article describes how to create such flexible agents. The overall approach we have chosen, which we call *Representational Promiscuity*, is based on the idea that there is no single representational method that can be used to build a complete agent. Instead, we need to incorporate a variety of different representational schemes—some symbolic, and some connectionist.

Learning covers a variety of very different skills:

- Learning facts (e.g., learning that there is a town nearby with plenty of food).
- Learning which desires should be dominant, and how sensitive to be to different desires (e.g., learning how low your energy must be before you should start to feel hungry, learning whether you should be nice or nasty, and when you should be nasty).
- Learning opinions about which sorts of objects are best for satisfying different desires—which types of object you should eat, which types of object you should attack (e.g., learning to never attack big creatures).

This article describes an architecture that enables all three of these very different skills.

In addition, learning can be initiated in a number of very different ways:

- Learning can occur after player feedback, punishing or rewarding the agent.
- Learning can occur from observing others, inferring their goals, and learning from their actions.
- Learning can occur after being given a command: when the agent is told to do an action on an object, the agent should learn that it is good to do that action on that object in that sort of situation.

In this article, we describe a technique that allows all these different types of learning, and different occasions that prompt learning, to coexist in one happy bundle.

Finally, we argue that agents who only learn through feedback after the event, are doomed to get stuck in learning traps, and that some sort of *empathetic understanding of the teacher* is needed to escape. We describe a simple implementation of empathy.

Before we can describe this variety of learning, we need to describe an architecture that is rich enough to handle it.

Agent Architecture

The basis for our design is the Belief-Desire-Intention architecture of an agent, fast becoming orthodoxy in the agent programming community. The Belief-Desire-Intention architecture is based on the work of a philosopher, Michael Bratman, who argued that Beliefs and Desires are not sufficient to make a mind—we need a separate category, Intentions, to represent desires that the agent has *committed* himself to. (See [Bratman87] and, for an early implementation, [RaoGeorgeff91].) Note that we have added an extra structure, Opinions, explained in a subsequent section. Figure 11.2.1 shows how Beliefs, Desires, and Opinions generate an Intention, which is then refined into a specific plan and action list.

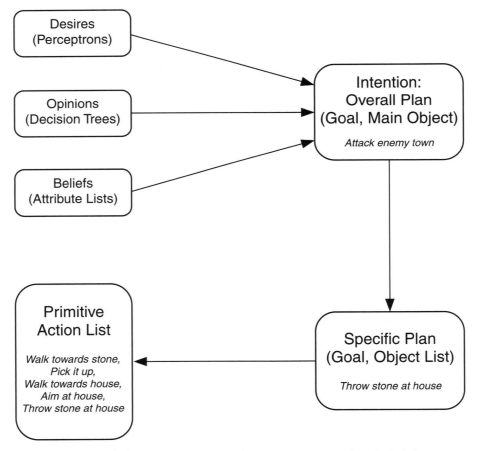

FIGURE 11.2.1 *Belief-Desire-Intention architecture, augmented with Opinions.*

Beliefs

Beliefs are data structures storing information about individual objects. It is important that beliefs respect the condition of *Epistemic Verisimilitude*—if an agent has a belief about an object, that belief must be grounded in his perception of that object. Agents cannot gain information from an object unless that agent is currently perceptually connected to that object. Beliefs are represented as linked-lists of attributes.

Desires

Desires are goals that the agent attempts to satisfy. Desires have different intensities at different times, depending on the agent's situation. Each desire has a number of different *desire-sources*; these jointly contribute to the current intensity of the desire. For example, there are three possible explanations of why a creature could be hungry: his energy could be low, he could have seen something that he knows is tasty, or he could be sad. The desire-sources are the inputs to the perceptron, as shown in Figure 11.2.2. By changing the weights of these three sources, you can make a variety of different personalities: creatures who only eat when they are starving, creatures who are greedy, even creatures who binge-eat when they are depressed!

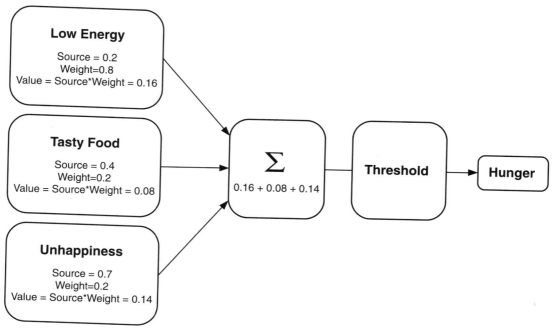

FIGURE 11.2.2 *The Hunger desire is modelled as a perceptron.*

Opinions

Agents use Desires, Beliefs, and Opinions to construct an overall plan: an Intention to act. Each desire has an Opinion associated with it that expresses what types of objects are best suited for satisfying this desire. For example, consider the following Opinion for the Compassion desire, as shown in Figure 11.2.3a.

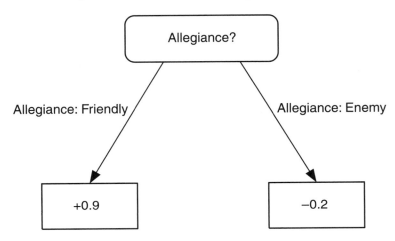

FIGURE 11.2.3a *Opinion (decision tree) for Compassion desire.*

This opinion states that it is very good to be compassionate toward friendly objects, but much less good to be compassionate toward enemy objects.

Summary: Representational Diversity

When deciding how to represent beliefs, desires, intentions, and opinions, the underlying methodology is to avoid imposing a uniform structure on the representations used in the architecture, and instead use a variety of different types of representation, so that we can pick the most suitable representation for each of the very different tasks. (See [Smith91] and [Minsky92].) Therefore, beliefs about individual objects are represented symbolically, as a list of attribute-value pairs; opinions about types of objects are represented as decision-trees; desires are represented as perceptrons; and intentions are represented as plans. There is something intuitively natural about this division of representations: beliefs and intentions are hard symbolic structures, whereas desires are fuzzy and soft.

Planning

When planning, for each desire that is currently active, the agent looks through all suitable beliefs, looking for the belief that he has the best opinion about. Therefore, he forms a plan for each goal. He then compares these plans, calculating their utility:

```
utility(desire, object) = intensity(desire) * opinion(desire, object)
```

He fixes on the plan with the highest utility—this plan is his Intention.

Suppose the creature has decided to attack a certain town. Next he refines his plan, from having a general goal to using a specific action: for instance, he might decide to fireball a particular house in that town. Finally, he breaks that action into a number of simple subtasks, which are sequentially executed.

Different Learning Methods

We have outlined how agents learn facts, by perceiving information and storing it in long-term memory as Beliefs. Next, we describe how agents learn to modify their personality, to mold their desires and opinions to suit their master. After an agent does something, he might receive *feedback* (either from the player or the world) that tells him whether that was a good thing to do (in that situation).

Learning Opinions: Dynamically Building Decision-Trees to "Make Sense" of the Feedback

How does an agent learn what sorts of objects are good to eat? He looks back at his experience of eating different types of things and the feedback he received in each case, how nice they tasted, and tries to "make sense" of all that data by building a decision tree. Suppose the agent has had the experiences listed in Table 11.2.1.

Table 11.2.1 Experiences of Eating Various Objects (Higher Numbers Represent "Tastier" Objects)

What He Ate	Feedback—"How Nice It Tasted"
A big rock	−1.0
A small rock	−0.5
A small rock	−0.4
A tree	−0.2
A cow	+0.6

He might build a simple tree, as shown in Figure 11.2.3b, to explain this data.

A decision tree is built by looking at the attributes that best divide the learning episodes into groups with similar feedback values. The best decision tree is the one that minimises entropy, as represented in Figure 11.2.4.

The entropy is a measure of how random the feedbacks are. If the feedbacks are always 0, there is no randomness: entropy is 0. If the feedbacks are always 1, again there is no randomness and entropy is 0. However, if the feedbacks alternate between 0 and 1, the feedback is random and unpredictable: entropy is high. We build a decision tree by choosing attributes that minimize the entropy in the feedback (see [Quinlan93]).

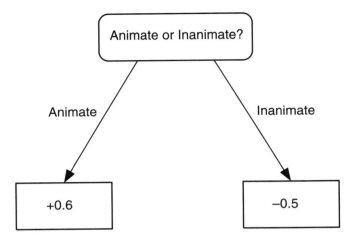

FIGURE 11.2.3b *Decision tree for Hunger.*

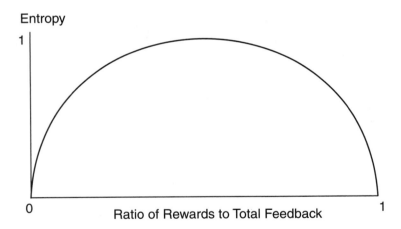

FIGURE 11.2.4 *Entropy.*

To take a simplified example, if a creature was given the feedback in Table 11.2.2 after attacking enemy towns, then the creature would build a decision tree for Anger as shown in Figure 11.2.5.

The algorithm used to dynamically construct decision trees to minimize entropy is based on Quinlan's ID3 system: at each stage of tree construction, choose the attribute that minimizes entropy. For this to work, we need some way of iterating through all the attributes of an object. This is almost impossible if an object is defined in the traditional way:

Table 11.2.2 Player Feedback Given to a Creature After Each Attack

What Creature Attacked	Feedback from Player
Friendly town, weak defense, tribe Celtic	−1.0
Enemy town, weak defense, tribe Celtic	+0.4
Friendly town, strong defense, tribe Norse	−1.0
Enemy town, strong defense, tribe Norse	−0.2
Friendly town, weak defense, tribe Greek	−1.0
Enemy town, medium defense, tribe Greek	+0.2
Enemy town, strong defense, tribe Greek	−0.4
Enemy town, medium defense, tribe Aztec	0.0
Friendly town, weak defense, tribe Aztec	−1.0

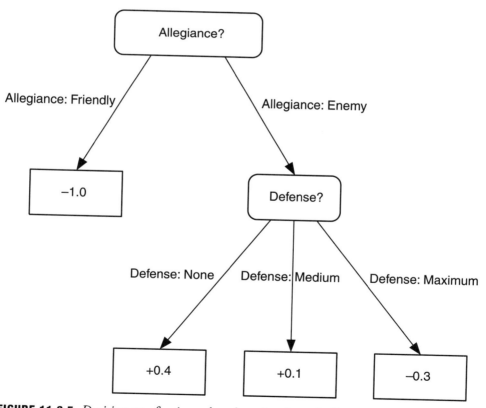

FIGURE 11.2.5 *Decision tree for Anger based on the player feedback in Table 11.2.2.*

```
class Villager
{
    int Health;
    int Energy;
    ...
};
```

Therefore, we need another way of defining objects, one that makes it easy for us to iterate through the attributes:

```
class Attribute
{
public:
    virtual int GetValueRange()=0
    virtual int GetValue()=0
    virtual char* GetName()=0
};
class Health : public Attribute
{
    ...
};
class Energy : public Attribute
{
    ...
};
class Object
{
protected:
    Attribute**    Attributes;
public:
    virtual int GetNumAttributes()=0;
    ...
};
class Villager : public Object
{
public:
    int GetNumAttributes();
    ...
};
```

Now it is easy to iterate through the attributes:

```
void Object::IterateThroughAttributes(void (*function)(Attribute*))
{
    for(int i=0; i<GetNumAttributes(); i++)
    {
        function(Attributes[i]);
    }
}
```

There are complications: when building a tree, a new node has to be created. To make this practical, there can't be too many different values for each attribute, or there would be an explosion in the number of child nodes. Therefore, when dealing with an attribute that has a vast range of different values (like one that is implemented as a float), we must first divide the range of values into a few bands. For example, if health is a float ranging between 0 and 1, we might divide it into four bands: 0–0.25, 0.25–0.5, 0.5–0.75, 0.75–1.

An additional complication is that different types of objects have different types of attributes, and two objects that have different types of attributes cannot be compared directly. To solve this, we need to do two things: first, make a distinction between common attributes (attributes common to all types) and object-specific attributes. We also need to introduce a new common attribute, *Type*. Now the decision-tree builder must first look at common attributes when trying to minimize entropy, and is only allowed to look at specific attributes once a node has already been created for Type.

Learning Desires: Perceptron Training

Each desire is modelled as a perceptron, a collection of inputs (called "desire sources"), and a collection of weights. Learning occurs by modifying the weights (Figure 11.2.6).

If there are n inputs $x_1, \ldots, x_n$ and n weights $w_1, \ldots, w_n$ then:

intensity = 1 if $\Sigma\ w_i {}^* x_i > 0.5$ and 0 otherwise

Weights are changed after feedback in the usual way, using the delta rule:

$$w_i \leftarrow w_i + \Delta\ w_i$$

where

$$\Delta\ w_i = \eta\ {}^* (intended\ value - actual\ value)\ x_i$$

(η is the speed of learning, typically small)

Let's look at a real example. The desire to eat something is based on three desire sources: hunger, the tastiness of the object, and how unhappy the creature is. Suppose η, the speed of learning, is set to 0.1, and all weights are initialized to 0.5. Table 11.2.3 shows five successive situations where the agent ate something and was given feedback.

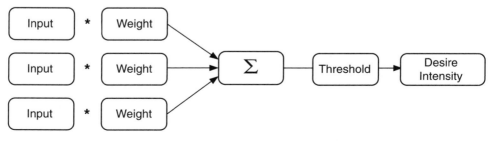

FIGURE 11.2.6 *A Desire is modelled as a perceptron.*

Table 11.2.3 Five Successive Eating Events with Subsequent Feedback and Readjustment of Desire Weights

Desire Sources							
Hunger		Tastiness		Unhappiness			Intended
Value	Weight	Value	Weight	Value	Weight	Actual	(Feedback)
0.8	0.500	0.8	0.500	0	0.500	*0.2*	1.000
0.8	*0.564*	0.2	*0.564*	0	*0.500*	*0.564*	1.000
0.1	*0.599*	0.6	*0.573*	0	*0.500*	*0.404*	0.200
0	*0.597*	0	*0.560*	1	*0.5*	*0.5*	0.002
0.3	*0.597*	0.4	*0.560*	1	*0.450*	*0.853*	0.400
–	*0.58341*	–	*0.542*	–	*0.4047*	–	–

Notice how the feedback is punishing the creature for being hungry when he is unhappy. The weighting for Unhappiness goes down over time to reflect this. The italicized numbers are computed as the perceptron learns; the others are input. The agent performs the following cycle:

1. He computes the actual desire value from the values and weights.
2. He waits for feedback.
3. He uses this feedback to update the weights.
4. Repeat.

Different Situations Prompting Learning

Consider three situations that could prompt an agent to learn something:

- Player feedback—punishing or rewarding the agent.
- Observing others—inferring their goals, and learning from their actions.
- Being given a command.

The first method is what we call the *Carrot and Stick* approach to learning—the player waits, watching what his agent is doing, and then punishes or rewards after the fact.

There is nothing wrong with using this method, but if Carrot and Stick is the *only* mechanism for getting the agent to learn something, problems arise:

- **It is unrealistic.** People do not just teach using a one-dimensional input from "Good" to "Bad"—they often teach by *showing*. The only people who restrict themselves to the Carrot and Stick method, ironically, are *babies*, who have no other way of communicating.
- **It is frustrating for the player.** The player has to *wait* for the creature to do the particular thing he is going to train on, before getting his chance to give feedback.
- **Agents who use it and nothing else will get stuck in "learning traps."**

This problem is so important that it deserves elaboration.

How "Carrot and Stick" Gets Stuck in Learning Traps

Suppose you want to teach your agent some fine-grained distinction using the Carrot and Stick method alone. You want to teach your agent to prefer being friendly to apes rather than to wolves. If he becomes friendly with a wolf, you punish him. Accidentally, you punish him much too much (perhaps because you were over-eager with the controls, or because you do not fully understand the interface), and completely suppress his desire to be friendly with any creature whatsoever. Now, once you have suppressed his desire, there is no way to teach him the fine-grained distinction you wanted to teach him, because the occasion will never arise when he will be friendly to an ape, because you have totally suppressed his desire to be friendly to any creature!

What this means, more generally, is that if learning only occurs through the Carrot and Stick method, and your agent learns by generalizing from examples, as indeed he should, then there will be certain lessons he can learn that, once learned, will make it impossible to learn any more lessons. These lessons are traps that, once entered, inhibit future learning.

To get out of this, we need some way of revitalizing the suppressed behavior. One natural way to do this is to make the agent's desires change depending on what he thinks his teacher's desires are. This is empathy.

Empathetic learning involves noticing what action the teacher is doing, and guessing what desire could have motivated the teacher to perform that action. The agent then learns from this episode—he learns that a particular desire is a good desire to act on, on that sort of object, in that sort of situation. Similarly, if the teacher commands the agent to do something, he should learn from this using empathy. Again, he should guess what desire could have motivated the teacher to want that action performed, and learn that this desire should be acted on that sort of object in that sort of situation.

Empathetic learning involves some way of computing an estimated desire from an action. This can be done with a simple lookup table, an example of which is shown in Table 11.2.4.

Table 11.2.4 Trying to Discern a Goal from Observing an Action

Action	Goal
Throw stone	Anger
Kick	Anger
Fight	Anger
Cast heal spell	Compassion
Give food	Compassion

This is a rather simple implementation of empathy—only the desires of the player are modeled, not his beliefs. (There is much interesting work to do in this area.)

Warm, Cuddly Feelings

There is another reason for introducing some empathetic understanding into our agents: we want the player to feel emotionally attached to his agent. However, empathetic attachment is intrinsically reciprocal: the reason why it is childish to feel emotionally attached to your teddy bear is because your teddy is not going to reciprocate. Conclusion: if you want the player to get attached to his creature, you must first ensure the creature is empathetically attached to his player!

Agents in most computer games are at best like severely autistic people: capable of perceiving and predicting the behavior of objects in the world, but incapable of seeing other people *as people*—incapable of building a model of another agent's mind that could be used, to great effect, to predict his actions [BaronCohen97].

Conclusion

We have described an architecture that enables agents to learn a variety of skills in a variety of ways. These agents don't just learn facts about the world, they also learn how to behave—what sort of personality to adopt. This architecture uses different types of components to accomplish these different learning tasks—it borrows shamelessly from both the symbolic and connectionist traditions.

How "deep" a computer game agent is perceived to be is partly a function of the depth of learning within the agent. However, it is also a function of the variety of ways in which we *interact* with the agent. Typically, games involving learning agents have restricted player-agent interactions to the Carrot and Stick approach. Here, we have described a powerful new mechanism that enriches the learning process—empathetic understanding of the player.

References

[BaronCohen97] Baron Cohen, Simon, *Mindblindness—An Essay on Autism and Theory of Mind*, MIT Press, 1997.

[Bratman87] Bratman, Michael, *Intention, Plans and Practical Reason*, Harvard University Press, 1987.

[Minsky92] Minsky, Marvin, "The Future of AI Technology," available online at www.ai.mit.edu/people/minsky/papers/CausalDiversity.html, 1992.

[Quinlan93] Quinlan, JR, C4.5: *Programs for Machine Learning*, Morgan Kauffman, 1993.

[RaoGeorgeff91] Rao and Georgeff, "Modeling Rational Agents within a BDI-Architecture," *Proceedings of the 2nd International Conference on Principles of Knowledge*, 1991.

[Rumelhart86] Rumelhart, et al, *Parallel Distributed Processing, Vol 1*, 1986.

[Smith91] Smith, Brian, "The Owl and the Electric Encyclopedia," *Artificial Intelligence 47*, 1991.

11.3

GoCap: Game Observation Capture

Thor Alexander—Hard Coded Games

thor@hardcodedgames.com

Game AI has always been received to limited fanfare. Due to limitations in both technology and production, the artificial intelligence found in computer and video games has often fallen short of the player's expectations. AI programming requires the programmers to anticipate all of the combinations of states that an AI character can find itself in during any game-play session. On top of that, programmers must also adapt the baseline AI code to produce multiple levels of difficulty to challenge the players as they begin to master the game.

With the emergence of the Internet and multi-player games where players can compete head to head with other human players, the shortcomings of game AI are all the more apparent. Who would want to play against a machine that is often predictable and easily exploited when the option of playing against a clever and spontaneous real person is becoming so ubiquitous?

Don't be so fast to toll the bell for the AI-controlled characters. While multi-player gaming experiences are quite exciting and challenging, they can not totally replace AI. There are several critical areas of gaming where we will always need computer-controlled characters. Here are just a few:

- Sparring partners for death match and fighting games with offline practice modes.
- Shopkeepers to buy and sell goods in role-playing games.
- Digital actors for single-player epics such as *Half-Life* and *Deus-Ex*.

It has been speculated that these characters could be role-played by human actors connected to the game world simulation via remote Internet connections. However, live actors are not financially viable to fill these roles due to the related labor and management costs. Recent legal actions have also raised the associated costs of volunteer labor.

This leads us back to AI with all of its shortcomings. However, what if we could combine the best of both worlds? What if we could train a computer-controlled character by observing the play sessions of a live player, and then endow it with the ability to make the same decisions when presented with similar conditions [Kosko93]? This article presents *GoCap*, a method to train AI characters by observation. Think of it as Motion-Capture for AI.

This article assumes working knowledge of the Unified Modeling Language (UML) and presents several figures in the form of UML sequence diagrams. For a complete introduction to UML please consult the resources presented at the end of this article [Booch98].

An Architecture for Training

The implementation of *GoCap* presented here is based on a fairly simple machine learning technique. It requires a simulation architecture that lends itself to training. We need to define some key concepts of such an architecture.

An *actor* is a simulation object that is capable of interacting with the game environment. Each actor has a control state that defines if the actor is currently under player control, autonomous control, or is in the training state. The control state can be swapped on-the-fly to transition the actor between one of these states. When in the training state, the player controls his actor as he would in the player-controlled state, with the computer snooping in on his actor and recording his actions.

Actions are the typical game simulation operations such as slapping an opponent or opening a door. These actions are mapped to a behavior that details the conditions under which a computer-controlled actor will attempt to execute that action. *Behaviors* define these conditions in the form of rules. When an actor in the autonomous control state gets its turn to act, it uses these behavior rules to decide what action to perform. Rules take a target actor as an input and evaluate it against a method specific to each rule. If all of the rules associated with a behavior fire, then that behavior is a candidate for use. If multiple behaviors fire all of their rules, then we will call a game-specific heuristic to choose the best one. Figure 11.3.1 shows a sequence diagram depicting this decision-making process.

Training by Observation

Before we can drop an autonomous actor into the game world, we need to train his behavior rules. We do this by spawning that actor in the training control state with a human player in the driver's seat. When the player targets other actors and performs actions on them, the training actor is informed of these actions.

Now we need to determine the circumstances under which the player chose this target and action. The actor finds the behavior that corresponds to the action the player invoked, and looks up the list of rules associated with that behavior. We feed the player's target to the evaluation method of each of these rules. These evaluation methods are small game-specific routines that return a continuous value between 0.0 and 1.0. Here is a pseudo-code example of such a rule evaluation method:

```
float EvaluateCondition( actor target )
{
   condition = target.currentHealth / target.maxHealth
   return condition
}
```

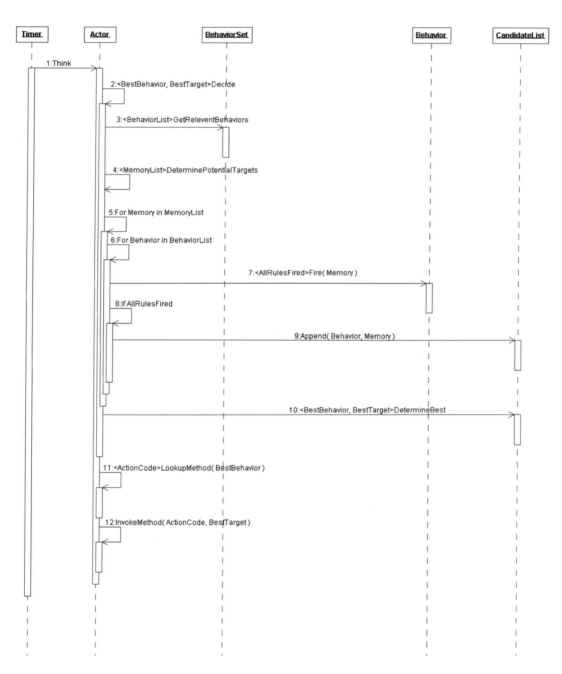

FIGURE 11.3.1 *UML sequence diagram of decision-making.*

Each rule has a cluster map associated with it. A cluster map is a one-dimensional spatial partitioning data structure. This structure can be partitioned into a number of cells that provide coverage appropriate to the domain of the associated rule. To cover our sample rule domain of 0.0 to 1.0, we will use a 10-cell cluster map. If we required greater precision, we could increase the number of cells. A simple 10-cell cluster map can be implemented as a sparse array indexed by an integer key value between 0 and 9. We can perform an index calculation on the floating-point value returned by the evaluation method to transform it into an integer representation. This gives us the array index that corresponds to the evaluation value.

Now we add a training marker to the cell in the cluster map at that index. This marker indicates that the player activated this behavior rule with this evaluation value. The cluster map serves to round off or quantize the value to fit into the nearest cell. As the player feeds more input into the training system, we will get more values that fall into this cell. Every time we get a hit in the cell, we increment the marker count until it reaches some training threshold that we have set. For the purpose of this article, we will set that threshold at three. We add this threshold to account for noise or error in the input data. In practice, you might need to increase this threshold significantly if your training data is prone to noise or error. Figure 11.3.2 depicts a cluster map.

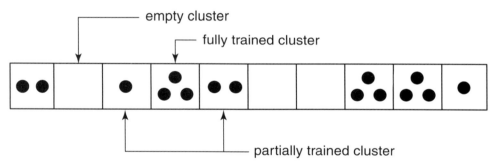

FIGURE 11.3.2 *A cluster map with training weights.*

At this point of training, our cluster map will only contain a few training markers in it. As training goes on, more data flows into the system and more rules are learned. Eventually, we will tend to reach a point of equilibrium where we have learned all of the rules that match the input action choices. We can detect this equilibrium by comparing the player's input against the action and target that the decision system would pick itself. When they match on a continuing basis, we can signal the player to stop training. Figure 11.3.3 shows a sequence diagram of the training process.

One useful side benefit of this cluster map approach is that it can help identify when the conditions specified in a behavior are relevant. It might be discovered that after analyzing the cluster map, none of the cells have values, or that they all do. In the former case, the AI programmer could be notified that additional rules might need to be added to the associated behavior. In the latter case, the programmer could be notified that this rule provides no value, since it fires constantly and should be removed.

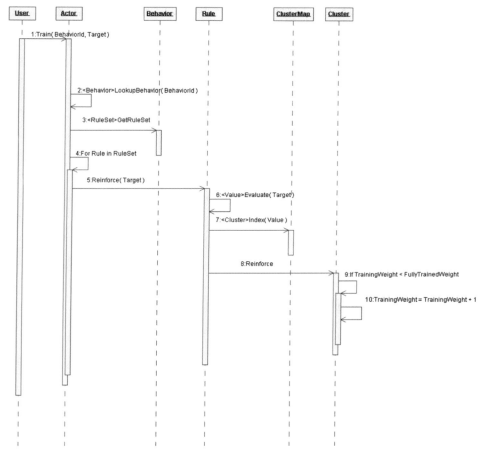

FIGURE 11.3.3 *UML sequence diagram for training a behavior.*

If the number of rules to be analyzed is large, then this step might be best performed as a standalone process.

A Fully Trained AI Is Ready for Battle

Now that we have a fully trained behavior set, we can detach our human trainer and swap the control state to autonomous. When the actor receives its next action tick, it calls on its decision process and newly trained rules to determine its course of action. The rules can now test the evaluation values against the training markers in the cluster map. If a rule evaluates to a value that falls into a cell that has enough markers to exceed the threshold, then that rule fires. Figure 11.3.4 shows the sequence diagram detailing the behavior rule evaluation process.

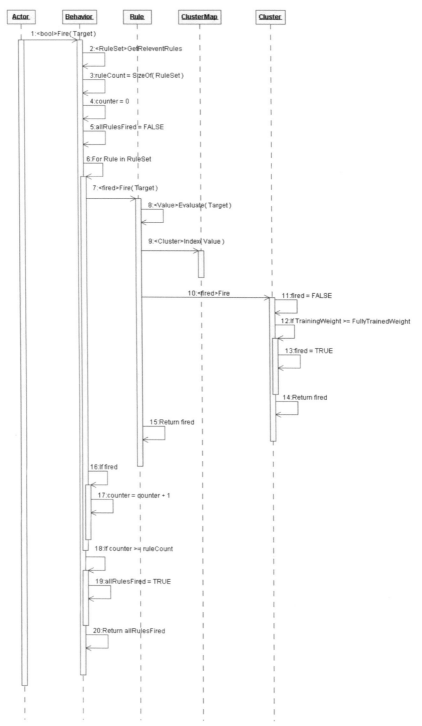

FIGURE 11.3.4 *UML sequence diagram of behavior evaluation.*

Enhancements

This article outlines a basic structure for training by observation. It is by no means optimal in terms of performance or memory utilization. Here are a few enhancements:

* The use of one common cluster map per actor will conserve memory. Such a map could have a secondary key for the behavior IDs that it contains rules for.
* A hash function is a natural choice for implementing a faster-performing cluster map.
* More complex machine learning algorithms, such as Teuvo Kohonen's Learning Vector Quantizer (LVQ), are good candidates to replace the simple cluster map with [Kohonen97].

Conclusion

Machine learning is an emerging technology that will greatly impact the way games are made. From a production standpoint, machine learning will bypass the need for thousands of lines of brittle scripted AI logic that are used in today's games. Training a computer-controlled character by observing a human expert player will bring great advances in the level of intelligence that can be displayed. Game designers will be able to role-play the personalities of a wide array of characters that can be imported into their games, instead of requiring scarce hours of programming time.

Motion Capture revolutionized the field of animation and yielded much more fluid and natural-looking movements. Machine learning techniques such as *GoCap* have the potential to do the same for AI.

Resources

[Booch98] Booch, Grady, *The Unified Modeling Language User Guide*, Addison-Wesley, 1998.

[Kohonen97] Kohonen, Teuvo, *Self-Organizing Maps*, Springer-Verlag, 1997.

[Kosko93] Kosko, Bart, *Fuzzy Thinking*, Hyperion, 1993.

11.4

Pattern Recognition with Sequential Prediction

Fri Mommersteeg—Eindhoven
University of Technology
frimommersteeg@hotmail.com

True learning is difficult and perhaps even impossible for a computer. Still, there remain plenty of things that a computer can learn. A method for recognizing patterns, which is a simple form of learning, is described in this article. After establishing a general technique, we will solve several other learning problems by transforming them into pattern recognition problems.

Recognizing patterns is just the first step. What we really like to do is to use patterns to make a good guess of what will happen in the future. A technique that does just this is called *sequential prediction*.

Sequential prediction does not identify patterns in their exact form, but instead yields a prediction that is good whenever the observed sequence contains a pattern. If your AI uses this prediction, it will seem to recognize patterns.

Sequential prediction is often used to measure intelligence in IQ tests; if you have ever done such a test, you probably know how sequential prediction works. As input you are given a series of numbers, and you have to predict what comes next. If you can perceive a pattern in the series, it is possible to make a prediction.

Sequential Prediction

Sequential prediction is the problem of finding a reasonable successor for a given sequence. This sequence must be generated by your game, in such a way that it exhibits a pattern we like to recognize. Note that we allow the sequence to exhibit no pattern at all; if this is the case, we expect the prediction to be more or less arbitrary.

The sequence consists of elements, which are often integers. The set of all possible elements that can appear in the sequence is called the *alphabet*. A reasonable successor of a sequence is an element that has a high probability of being the next element in the sequence.

The patterns that we will consider here are called *repetitive* patterns. A repetitive pattern is a pattern that occurs repeatedly in a sequence. The number of elements in a repetitive pattern is its *size*.

Not all patterns are repetitive, as you might expect. However, most patterns are repetitive in nature, and can be mapped onto a repetitive counterpart. For example, the sequence "1 2 3 4" can be mapped onto "1 1 1" by taking the difference between each two successive elements. The latter sequence contains the repetitive pattern "1". Therefore, limiting the scope of this article to repetitive patterns does not mean that we are unable to recognize other types of patterns.

Basic Idea

In general, there are two ways to perform sequential prediction. You could create a statistical model based on the sequence and use this model to predict a successor, or you could use a technique called *string-matching prediction*. With string-matching prediction, you simply search for the longest substring matching the tail of the sequence. Once you have found this substring, you take its successor as the predicted successor of the sequence. For example, consider the following sequence over the binary alphabet {0, 1}:

1 0 0 1 0 1 1 0 1 1 1 0 0 0 0 1 0 0 0 1 1 0 1

To predict the successor of this sequence with string-matching prediction, we look for the longest substring that matches the tail. We do this by traversing the sequence from right to left, and once we find a string that matches "1", we check if it also matches longer parts of the tail, like "0 1", "1 0 1", "1 1 0 1", and so forth. The longest string that we can find in this way is "0 1 1 0 1", a string of size 5. The successor of this substring is "1". Therefore, string-matching prediction would tell us that "1" is a reasonable successor for the sequence.

Note that the substring found by string-matching prediction can include multiple occurrences of a repetitive pattern. Sequential prediction does not require that we know the exact form of the pattern.

There exist powerful statistical predictors, yet they are often complex and require a firm grasp of probability calculus. In the literature, statistical predictors are often called *universal* predictors, because they are designed for arbitrary sequences. If you would like to know more about them, refer to [Merhav98].

For our purpose, the recognition of repetitive patterns, string-matching prediction suffices. It is easy to see that this technique works well with repeated patterns. In the next section, we will see how to implement string-matching prediction.

A Better Idea

The string-matching algorithm discussed in the previous section can be implemented as is, but that solution has a running time of $O(N^2)$. It performs poorly when the sequence contains repetitive patterns. Since our goal is to detect such patterns, this is not satisfactory.

However, we can take advantage of the fact that our sequence is generated incrementally. When a new element is added to the sequence, the sequence remains the same, except for the tail. We try to exploit this consideration to obtain a better solution.

For this reason, we take a closer look at what happens exactly when we add a new element to a sequence. Suppose that our original sequence ends with the letter A, and that we add the letter B (Figure 11.4.1).

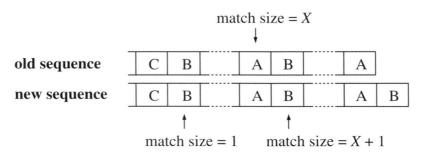

FIGURE 11.4.1 *Computing new matches based on previous matches.*

Now let's consider all substrings that match the tail of the old sequence. Observe that these substrings must end with the letter A. Moreover, such substrings exist for every occurrence of A in the sequence. We define the *match size* of occurrence A as the length of the longest substring ending with occurrence A and matching the tail of the sequence.

Suppose that we know the match sizes of all occurrences of A in the old sequence. Can we use this information to compute the match sizes for all occurrences of B in the new sequence? Yes, we can! Take a look at Figure 11.4.1 again. We distinguish two cases:

- An occurrence of B is *not* preceded by an occurrence of A.
- An occurrence of B is preceded by an occurrence of A.

The first case is easiest. If we find an occurrence of B that is not preceded by an occurrence of A, its match size must be 1. If you don't understand why, just compare this situation with the tail.

If an occurrence of B is preceded by an occurrence of A, things become a bit more complicated. However, since we are assumed to know the match sizes of all occurrences of A, it's not that difficult. Remember that the match size of A is the length of a substring that matches the tail of the old sequence. We can extend this substring with the letter B to obtain a substring that matches the new tail. Hence, the match size of B is 1 plus the match size of A.

You might be wondering whether the same rules apply if an A is added instead of a B. The answer is yes, but then the direction in which the occurrences of A are traversed is important. Since we rewrite match sizes and sometimes require match sizes of preceding elements, the occurrences must be traversed from recent occurrences to less recent ones.

At this point, we have found a way to compute the match sizes for all occurrences of *B*, by using the match sizes of the occurrences of *A*. If we add another letter to the sequence, we can use the match sizes of *B* again to compute the new matches. The algorithm is self-sustaining once initialized. If we start with an empty sequence, the initialization is trivial.

The solution presented here has a running time of $O(N)$. Each time a new element is added to the sequence, the algorithm only needs to inspect all occurrences of this element.

Implementation

All that's left now is to design an efficient data structure that supports the algorithm. When a new letter is added, we want to quickly look up all its occurrences in the sequence. For this reason, we introduce an array the size of our alphabet. We will call this array the *histogram*. Index *i* in the histogram contains a list of all occurrences of element *i* in the sequence. The occurrences are ordered as they appear in the sequence. Each occurrence contains a pointer to its entry in the sequence. When an element is added to the sequence, its occurrence is added to the histogram.

We also want to store the match sizes together with the elements in the sequence. Thus, an entry in the sequence is a record containing the specific element and its match size. We will keep invariant that the match size is valid for all occurrences equal to the last element of the sequence. For all other occurrences, the match size can be uninitialized, since we are never going to inspect them directly.

The following code outlines the algorithm. For clarity, it uses direct indexing to find entries in the `Occurrences` list, but you should iterate through this list. This is possible since all entries are indexed sequentially.

```
List Occurrences = Histogram[NextElement];
int MaxMatchSize = 0, MaxMatchPosition;
for (int i = Occurrences.GetSize()-1; i >= 0; i--) {
    Entry ThisEntry = GetSequenceEntry(Occurrences[i]);
    Entry Neighbour = GetLeftNeighbour(ThisEntry);

// determine match size
    if (Neighbour.Element == FormerLastElement) {
        ThisEntry.MatchSize = 1 + Neighbour.MatchSize;
    } else {
        ThisEntry.MatchSize = 1;
    }

// record length & position of largest substring
    if (ThisEntry.MatchSize > MaxMatchSize) {
        MaxMatchSize = ThisEntry.MatchSize;
        MaxMatchPosition = ThisEntry.Position;
    }
}
```

```
UpdateSequence(NextElement);
UpdateHistogram(NextElement);
FormerLastElement = NextElement;
// make a prediction
if (MaxMatchSize > 0) {
    Prediction = Sequence[MaxMatchPosition + 1].Element;
}
```

Instead of monitoring the entire sequence—which could grow infinitely large—it is preferable to use a sliding window to monitor the most recent part of the sequence, say, the last N elements.

This approach has two advantages. First, it allows us to use a fixed-size array, which is more convenient to implement. Second, the predictor will adapt more quickly when the behavior of the sequence changes. A disadvantage is that we can no longer detect patterns larger than the size of our window. Hence, we must choose N carefully. Check out the source code on the CD for the details of the implementation.

ON THE CD

The Algorithm at Work

It's time for an example of the string-matching algorithm. We will consider the binary sequence "$A\ B\ A\ B\ B\ A\ B$", which is generated incrementally: we start with the empty sequence, and gradually add letters. The results are shown in Table 11.4.1 ("–" denotes that we don't care about a value).

Before we add a new letter, we first compute the match sizes for all occurrences of this letter in the sequence. After that, we actually add the letter. We do this to prevent having to compute the match size for the last element in the sequence. According to our definition of match size, we should set the match size of the last element to N (the

Table 11.4.1 The String-Matching Algorithm at Work

	Index:	0	1	2	3	4	5	6
N=1	Sequence:	**A**						
	Match Size:	–						
N=2	Sequence:	A	**B**					
	Match Size:	–	–					
N=3	Sequence:	A	B	**A**				
	Match Size:	1	–	–				
N=4	Sequence:	A	B	A	**B**			
	Match Size:	–	2	–	–			
N=5	Sequence:	A	B	A	B	**B**		
	Match Size:	–	1	–	1	–		
N=6	Sequence:	A	B	A	B	B	**A**	
	Match Size:	1	–	2	–	–	–	
N=7	Sequence:	A	B	A	B	B	A	**B**
	Match Size:	–	2	–	3	1	—	

length of the entire sequence), but for string-matching prediction, this value is never needed. Therefore, Table 11.4.1 indicates that we do not care about it.

The first two additions to the sequence are self explanatory, since the letters are unique in the sequence. However, things start to get interesting at *N=3*. We add an *A* to the sequence and we find an occurrence of *A* at index 0. Since it is not preceded by the former last element (letter *B* that is; see *N=2*), we set its match size to 1.

At *N=4*, we add a *B* to the sequence. We find a *B* at index 1, preceded by an *A* at index 0, which happens to be the former last element. Therefore, the match size of this *B* is 1 plus the match size of this *A*, for a total of 2.

At *N=5*, we add another *B* to the sequence. We find two occurrences of *B*, at index 1 and 3, but none of them are preceded by the former last element. Hence, we set the match sizes of these occurrences to 1.

By now, you probably understand what happens at *N=6* and *N=7*. You can see that the match sizes define exactly the substrings that match the tail. For string-matching prediction, we just take the longest substring that matches the tail, and take its succeeding element as the predicted successor of the sequence.

Patterns in Games

In the previous sections, we explained the technique behind string-matching prediction. You have seen that if you want to apply sequential prediction, your game must somehow produce a sequence. In fact, finding a way to generate this sequence is the only difficult part that remains, since the rest can be solved using standard techniques.

In this section, we will treat some practical examples that will be presented in a constructive manner. First, we try to identify some repetitive behavior. Next, we seek a way to map this behavior onto a sequence of elements. At this point, our game is capable of generating the sequence. We will discuss how sequential prediction will affect the gameplay. Finally, we will generalize this repetitive behavior into a class of problems that can be solved using the same technique.

Positioning Pattern

In a classical tennis game, there are two tennis players. Suppose the AI controls one player, and the other player is controlled by human input. To avoid confusion, the AI-player is called *bot* from now on, and the human player is called *gamer*.

Our aim is to model the behavior of the bot after the real tennis pros. We are particularly interested in how the tennis pros choose their position. There are two well-known heuristics: the first is to retreat to the center of the field after every return, and the second is to move to the position where the ball is expected to go.

Suppose that our bot is standing on one side of the tennis field. It is advantageous for the gamer to play the ball to the opposite side, because that makes it hard for the bot to return the ball. If the bot succeeds in returning the ball nonetheless, it is standing on a side of the field again, and the same reasoning can be repeated. This is the repetitive behavior we will use.

We can partition the play field of our bot into imaginary blocks, and assign each block a unique number. The mapping function that we use to generate the sequence elements is simple: whenever the ball falls into a block, the number of this block is taken as the next element of the sequence. It is easy to see that the resulting sequence exhibits a repetitive pattern if the ball is repeatedly played from one side to the other side.

How will this new AI affect gameplay? If the bot reacts to simple patterns, some interesting situations arise. For example, if the bot is in block *A* and expects the ball to go to block *D*, you could see the bot running from *A* to *D*, even before the gamer returns the ball. Since the patterns that the AI reacts upon are often simple, the gamer can usually recognize this and compensate by becoming less predictable.

The *positioning pattern* can be used in many other situations as well. In general, it is applicable for predicting the position where some "object" will hit a "surface." This pattern occurs in many ball games. For example, in a baseball game, you could use it to predict pitch choices, and in a soccer game, the keeper could use it to predict the corner to jump to during penalty shooting.

Anticipation Pattern

In a fighting game, you have actions such as "kick," "punch," "block," and so forth. Gamers tend to have favorite moves, which they use more frequently. Bots could anticipate those moves with sequential prediction and respond with the proper countermoves.

In many fighting games, bots block at the time the gamer presses an action button. It would be much more fun if the AI successfully predicts the player's next move and reacts *before* the action button is pressed. Of course, sometimes the prediction will be erroneous, yet that corresponds to faulty anticipation, which makes the AI appear more realistic.

If you can predict the next player action using pattern recognition, you can also prevent gamers from kicking your bots unconscious with just a single type of attack. You can force the gamer to use all attack moves, which makes your game more diverse, and adds a sense of challenge, since the gamer cannot simply defeat your bots with a single move.

To apply sequential prediction in this situation, we number all possible player actions. Whenever the gamer performs a certain action, we take its number as the next element of the sequence. Then, predicting the next action of the gamer boils down to predicting the next element of this sequence.

The *anticipation pattern* is useful in "close combat" game situations, where you need to predict a "next action" so that your AI can perform a "counteraction." Close combat can include sword fights and even mage fights, where "counteractions" could be taken to be counter-spells.

Tracker Pattern

If you've ever played a multi-player first-person shooter, you probably know people who have a system for picking up all the ammo, medikits, and so forth. They always take the same carefully planned route, so that they are back when the items respawn. They pick up the ammo when it's still fresh, leaving you with empty guns.

From the strategic point of view, it is not very clever to be predictable in choosing your way. You could run into an ambush, or you could get tracked. At least, that could happen to you if the AI bots were capable of noticing patterns.

Suppose that we partition the map into rooms, and we assign each room a unique number. Whenever a player enters a room, we take the room number as the next element for our sequence. If the player is making rounds, this results in a repetitive pattern that we can detect using sequential prediction.

It depends on your ethical point of view whether or not you allow your bots to use this sequence information. Since it's unlikely that bots can generate this information through direct observation, it is usually considered cheating.

However, even though it might not be entirely fair, it can enhance the gameplay. For example, if it is predicted that the gamer will go to a certain room and an enemy bot happens to be in that room already, it could take an ambush position. Also, if a bot hunts the gamer through some rooms and then loses sight, it could "predict" the route that the player has taken. This will make players more cautious in choosing their way, which adds to the tactical atmosphere.

The *tracker pattern* is useful if you want to detect patterns in the routes of certain "travelers." To apply the pattern, you need a "map" that can be divided into "rooms."

Tips and Tricks

We have seen how to implement a simple form of sequential prediction, and we saw some of its practical uses in games. By now, you probably have a good idea of the situations in which sequential prediction is useful, and how to generate a sequence.

Once you have obtained a sequence, the application of sequential prediction is easy. However, you might still experience some difficulties with a proper implementation. In this section, we present some tips that will help with tuning your implementation of string-matching prediction.

Performance Indicator

Whenever the sequence does not contain a repetitive pattern, the prediction will be more or less arbitrary. As a result, your game behaves randomly whenever the gamer does so. In many situations this is fine, but sometimes you would like to know whether the prediction is good or bad. For example, in a tennis game, it is preferable to retreat to the center instead of moving randomly over the play field when the prediction is bad.

Do you remember the implementation of string-matching prediction? The algorithm returned the size and position of every substring that matched the tail, and we used this to make a prediction. Since a longer substring generally gives us a better prediction than a short one, we can use the size of the longest matching substring as a performance indicator for our algorithm.

Checking this performance indicator has an additional advantage. When the sequence is just starting up, string-matching prediction is sometimes unable to find any matching substring at all, and returns 0 for the size. If this happens, you should not inspect the predicted element, but instead rely upon a secondary heuristic, such as random prediction.

Predictor Switching

In some cases, it is possible to generate multiple sequences, and you do not know beforehand which sequence will exhibit a repetitive pattern. It is also possible that one sequence or another exhibits a repetitive pattern, but they cannot exhibit a repetitive pattern at the same time.

With the performance indicator, you have a tool to measure how well a certain predictor is working. You can monitor multiple sequences, and use the predictor that yields the best prediction.

Improving the Prediction

In the original algorithm, we simply took the successor of the longest matching substring as the predicted element of the sequence. It is possible to improve the predictor by taking all matching substrings into account—not just the longest one—and use a probability distribution to determine the element that has the best chances to be the next element in the sequence. Since the string-matching algorithm already yields these substrings, this improvement is inexpensive to implement.

We use the following consideration: a recent and long substring is likely to yield a better prediction than a short one that occurred further in the past. For each substring S that matches the tail, we can compute the following quantity:

$$PredictionValue = Length(S) / DistanceToTail(S)$$

Then, for each element in the alphabet, we can compute the sum of prediction values of all substrings preceding that element. The element with the highest prediction value is the best prediction for the sequence. We can use the prediction value as the new performance indicator of our predictor.

Conclusion

Sequential prediction is excellent for making your AI aware of patterns that are easily recognized by humans. When your AI has to choose between a few things that are equally possible, simple statistics won't help you to make a decision; however, sequential prediction excels in this area. All you need is a way to capture the essential events into a data sequence.

Although you might be tempted, it is often best not to use sequential prediction all the time. Anticipation is also a matter of taking chances, and if the prediction is wrong, this could have consequences. You should use multiple strategies, and switch between them. Only anticipate on a move when the performance indicator is telling you that the prediction must be right—that's how humans do it.

As is often the case with machine learning techniques that are set up for the general case, the difficult part with sequential prediction is not really implementing the technique, but making the technique useful. In this article, we tried to focus on the practical aspects, and left the technique as simple as possible. Hopefully, you have learned that pattern recognition and sequential prediction are useful. Perhaps you even have some ideas now of how to use them in your own games. Good luck!

Reference

[Merhav98] Merhav, Neri, and Feder, Meir, "Universal Prediction," *IEEE Transactions on Information Theory*, Vol. IT-44, no. 6, pp. 2124–2147, 1998.

11.5

Using N-Gram Statistical Models to Predict Player Behavior

François Dominic Laramée

francoislaramee@videotron.ca

You wake up one morning and suddenly find yourself standing in a wrestling ring, getting pummeled by Stone Cold Steve Austin. How can you get out of this predicament alive and hopefully without any unfamiliar joints in any of your limbs?

Well, just standing there looking helpless or walking around in circles won't do the trick. And in all likelihood, charging full-steam ahead until you drop will only get you disemboweled quicker. Against an opponent of this caliber, defense is at least as important as offense.

However, efficient defense requires a reasonable estimate of what to expect from the opponent. In a typical wrestling match, your opponent will likely throw punches more often than he will perform corkscrew moonsaults. However, what if he happens to be standing on the top turnbuckle, facing away from the ring? All of a sudden, the probability of a moonsault has climbed dramatically. What do you do now?

When designing computer opponents for a game, this class of problem, in which event probabilities grow or shrink according to local context and structure, can be solved using a statistical model called an N-gram.

For example, let's say that you are trying to predict which letter will come next in the sequence ABABABABB. So far, B has been followed by A three times, and by B once. Based on observation of this sequence, we can conclude that the probability of seeing an A next is 75%, while the probability of a B is 25%. This is exactly what an N-gram does: it observes long sequences of events, identifies sub-sequences that form regular patterns, and tries to predict upcoming events based on its experience.

Defining the N-Gram

Technically, an *N-gram* is a probabilistic, directed, acyclic graph with the following properties:

- Each complete path through the graph contains exactly *N* nodes.
- In a given path, nodes 1 to *N-1* correspond to events in the past.

- Node *N-1* has outgoing edges leading to nodes representing all events that can possibly follow the sequence 1..*N-1*.
- The edge leading from node *N-1* to node *N* on each path is tagged with the probability that *N* will follow 1..*N-1*.

A *bigram* is an N-gram with *N* equal to 2, which reduces to a Markov chain. A *trigram* is one with *N* equal to 3.

In plain game-developer English, this means that the easiest way to implement an N-gram is an *N*-dimensional array, where dimensions 1 to *N-1* are indexed on a player's most recent *N-1* moves, and dimension *N* is a table of probabilities used to predict the next move. If the number of legal moves is *M*, the N-gram will contain M^N entries.

```
const int numLegalMoves = 20;
int Trigram[ numLegalMoves ][ numLegalMoves ][ numLegalMoves ];
// Act if the probability that A follows BA is high enough...
if( Trigram[ B ][ A ][ A ] > some threshold )
  do something;
// To find the most probable next move given that we know what the
// player has done recently...
topScore = MINUS_INFINITY;
for( int i = 0; i < numLegalMoves; i++ )
{
  if( Trigram[ slightlyOlderMove ][ mostRecentMove ][ i ] > topScore
)
  {
    topScore = Trigram[ slightlyOlderMove ][ mostRecentMove ][ i ];
    probableNextMove = i;
  }
}
```

N-Grams in Speech Recognition

Trigrams are commonly used to model language in speech recognition. Consider the problem of differentiating between homonyms such as "time" and "thyme." To a speech recognizer, they literally sound the same; however, the phrase "time flies like an arrow" makes (some) sense, while "thyme flies like an arrow" does not. Given the horrifyingly complex structure of human language, a perfect decision algorithm for cases like this would never be able to run in real time, even if a complete and nonambiguous English grammar existed.

Observation of written text, however, shows that the sequence of words "you are on time" happens more frequently than the sequence "you are on thyme." Language has, among other properties, that of *local structure*: words are not stringed together in random order, and words spoken close together tend to influence each other's meaning more than words spoken far apart. Building an N-gram representing the probabilities of word sequences in English, therefore, has great value in speech recognition: if analysis of the incoming acoustic signal for a word leaves the recognizer confused between "time" and "thyme," knowing that the preceding words were "you are on" solves the problem.

Motivation for N-Grams in Games

The behavior of game players and characters also often possesses the local structure property. Sources of local structure in gameplay include:

- **Game world constraints**. In some games, certain moves are legal (or possible) only in specific circumstances. An obvious case: a basketball player can't dribble the ball if he does not hold it. A less obvious one: a crossbowman in a real-time strategy game is unable to fire for a specific period of time while he reloads his weapon.
- **Player styles**. In flight sims and fighting games, players develop signature techniques and move sequences.
- **Bonuses**. Characters sometimes receive bonuses for performing "combos" of moves in sequence.
- **Game controls**. Button configurations make certain move sequences easier to perform.

A properly trained N-gram can learn to identify these structural elements over time, and teach a computer opponent how to predict the human player's behavior. This will give the AI a significant edge in planning an effective defense or counterattack.

As an added bonus for game developers, N-grams are fast and usually require little memory. If a character in a fighting game has 20 legal moves, a trigram containing the probabilities of all possible move sequences can be implemented as a three-dimensional array with 8000 entries; if 32-bit words are used to store probabilities in fixed-point format, the entire structure will fit into 32K.

Building the N-Gram

Any graph representation can be used for N-grams.

Data Structure

An *N*-dimensional array is the simplest, and usually satisfactory, but it can be wasteful of memory if:

- **You need a higher-order N-gram.** The amount of memory required by an N-gram is $O(M^N)$, so an array representation is probably impractical for 4-grams and above unless M (the number of legal moves in the application) is very small.
- **The number of legal moves is large, and the N-gram is sparse.** This is actually the case in speech recognition, where most word sequences of a given length are nonsense.

If the number of legal moves is large and the N-gram is *not* sparse, the cost of a full N-gram representation is prohibitive. Techniques used to reduce memory consumption, at the cost of some precision, include:

- **Thresholding.** Only include N-gram entries for sequences whose probability is above a certain threshold, and assume that all others can be handled by a default "rare event" entry. For example, you might want to treat anything that shows up in the training corpus twice or less as an equally probable rare event. Since rare sequences tend to be far more numerous than frequent ones, the economy can be significant.
- **Using a lower-order N-gram.** A bigram is often more than enough to provide acceptable results.
- **Averaging over several N-grams.** To reduce the impact of thresholding on precision, you might want to store a trigram, a bigram, and a unigram (which simply counts moves without context information) for the same problem. By definition, a bigram is more coarse-grained than a trigram, and fewer of its entries will fall below a threshold; a weighted average of the probabilities returned by all three models might be more accurate than any of them taken individually.

Basic Training

Filling the N-gram with useful data is disarmingly simple. All you have to do is record a number of games played by humans, count the sequences of moves of length N that appear, and transform the counts into probabilities.

For example, let's suppose that we are training a trigram for a game with the set of moves { A, B, C, D }. The first recorded game indicates that the player has entered the sequence of moves AABCDCAAB. We therefore increment the entries for sequences AAB, ABC, BCD, CDC, DCA, CAA, and AAB again. Then, to obtain probabilities, we divide each entry in the trigram by the number of sequences counted (seven in this case). Simple, right?

(A quick tip in passing: In speech recognition, the probability of any given sequence of N words happening in the language is always very small, because of the enormous number of words in the dictionary. To prevent underflow problems, speech N-grams often store the logarithms of the probabilities computed here instead of the probabilities themselves. The same trick can be useful in games with a large number of legal moves.)

For a game, what really interests us in most cases is the probability that the next move will be Z, given that the last two were X and Y. For example, in the case described previously, we have seen only two instances in which a sequence begins with AA. In both cases, the next move was B. Therefore, our trigram should store a probability of 1 for the sequence AAB, and 0 for AAA, AAC, and AAD.

Repeated over a big enough "corpus" of games played by a number of different players, this training method will yield a reasonable approximation of the average gameplay patterns in the player population. How big is big enough? The equation

$$C = k * M^{N-1} \tag{11.5.1}$$

where k is a constant between 10 and 25, M is the number of legal moves and N is the order of the N-gram, provides a reasonable rule of thumb.

Tuning Toward Specific Players

The training method described in the previous section will yield a decent opponent, capable of providing a challenge to most players. However, to exploit the N-gram to the fullest, it should be tuned to individual players after purchase.

Tuning an N-gram to an individual is easy: all you have to do is run the training algorithm again, on a corpus augmented with a number of the player's games.

Dealing with Small Training Sets

With any finite training corpus, there is a chance that a valid sequence of N moves will not be seen. Such a sequence will be assigned probability zero in the N-gram, as if it were illegal, while the sequences that do appear in the corpus will receive scores larger than they should.

A number of smoothing algorithms have been developed to deal with this problem. One of them, described in [Witten91] and [Jurafsky00], involves computing the probability that the next sequence observed, if the training corpus were larger, would be one previously unseen. This value is then divided by the number of legal sequences that do not appear in the corpus, and the quotient is assigned to each of them. The probabilities of sequences that appear in the training corpus are then discounted by a related factor to bring the total probability mass back to 1.

Using the N-Gram

A trained N-gram can be used in deterministic or probabilistic fashion, depending on the type of behavior you wish to implement in your game. In both cases, your AI will need to index the trigram on the last *N-1* moves recorded, and loop over the entries for the next possible move, as in the following pseudo-code snippet:

```
for( int i = 0; i < numLegalMoves; i++ )
{
  lookAt( Trigram[ twoMovesAgo ][ lastMove ][ i ];
}
```

For a deterministic N-gram, you should search for the entry with the highest probability and assume that this move is coming. For a probabilistic N-gram, you will generate a random number and pick a candidate according to the probability distribution. To make this easier, you should store a cumulative probability distribution instead of event probabilities per se. For example, instead of storing 0.3, 0.6, and 0.1 for three events, store 0.3, 0.9, and 1.0. This way, the first entry for which the cumulative probability is smaller than your random number is the move you should predict.

Bonus Section: Mimicking Real-Life Opponents

So far, we have used the N-gram to predict the behavior of human opponents. We can use the same mechanism to have the computer mimic the behavior of human players.

To do this, we will again use an N-gram trained on a corpus of human-played games. However, we will index the table on the *AI's* most recent moves instead of the human player's, and then select a move (using the deterministic or nondeterministic techniques outlined previously) that the human player might have made in that situation. Imagine a *Quake* bot based on an N-gram trained on a corpus of *Thresh* games; you would have your own virtual *Thresh* at your fingertips!

Refinements

The N-grams discussed in this article assume that a player's moves can be examined in isolation. If they depend heavily upon the opponent's moves, this should be taken into account in the definitions of the move sequences to be tracked.

For example, suppose that the ABCD game is turn-based, with players alternating moves. In a trigram model, where the AI is trying to predict Player 1's next move, the first index should be Player 1's last move, while the second index should be Player 2's. In a game where the moves of both players can come in any order, the ABCD game effectively becomes an eight-move game, with legal move set { A1, A2, B1, ... }.

Conclusion

In situations where local structure is present but hard to specify explicitly, N-grams can provide an easy way to predict or duplicate human player behavior. They can therefore add realism to your AI's play at a minimal cost in execution time.

However, since N-grams concentrate on local relationships between moves, they are very poor predictors of long-term plans, and will provide meaningless data if no behavioral patterns emerge from the training corpus. Finally, an N-gram that is not tuned to a specific player's style can also fail miserably, if that player's behavior strays from the norm (as defined by the training corpus).

For more information on how to use N-grams in machine learning of language and in automated text generation, see [Hutchens02] elsewhere in this book.

References

[Hutchens02] Hutchens, J. and Barnes, J., "Practical Natural Language Learning," *AI Game Programming Wisdom*, Charles River Media, 2002.

[Jurafsky00] Jurafsky, D. and Martin, J. H., "N-Grams," *Speech and Language Processing*, Prentice Hall, 2000.

[Witten91] Witten, I. H. and Bell, T. C., "The zero-frequency problem: estimating the probabilities of novel events in adaptive text compression," *IEEE Transactions on Information Theory*, 37 (4), pp. 1085–1094, 1991.

Practical Natural Language Learning

Jason Hutchens—Amristar, and

Jonty Barnes—Lionhead Studios

hutch@amristar.com.au and
jbarnes@lionhead.com

Alan Turing, the father of artificial intelligence (AI), introduced the Turing Test in 1950 as a means of indicating the presence of machine intelligence via conversational evaluation [Turing92]. The "Holy Grail" of AI has subsequently been considered by many to be the construction of a computer program that can pass the Turing Test.

Natural language interfaces were common features of computer entertainment software prior to the advent of sophisticated computer graphics. Multi-user dungeons (MUDs) featured sophisticated rule-based natural language processing, while text adventure games such as Crother and Wood's original *Adventure* and Infocom's *Zork* series represent classics of their genre. Today, an underground interactive fiction community continues to develop the art form.

We would like to take this opportunity to illustrate how a language learning system, when used conversationally, can greatly contribute toward the subjective impression of intelligence experienced by the player. Our hope is to encourage developers to seriously consider adding natural language interfaces to their games.

What Is Intelligence?

The human brain is particularly adept at pattern recognition. It is capable of recognizing the faces of friends and family, of distinguishing a quiet spoken word against louder ambient noise, of detecting and acting upon cause-effect relationships in the environment, and of perceiving and understanding language, both spoken and written.

On occasion, the human brain over-extends itself, detecting meaning where none exists. This situation might be familiar to those who have found themselves bedridden with a bad dose of influenza, and who have stared, in a delirious state of mind, at the grain of a wooden wardrobe. The brain is constantly looking for patterns, and the poor patient might have fleeting glimpses of something animal moving beneath the whorls of the timber.

The tendency of the human brain to misinterpret randomness can be taken advantage of, enabling us to create the illusion of intelligent behavior via fairly simple techniques. Experience has shown that the core feature of any system that appears to behave intelligently is the ability to learn [Barnes02].

Non-player characters (NPCs) in computer games can seem intelligent until patterns in their behavior, which we learn through our experience with the game, reveal them to be nothing more than scripted agents. Like Alan Turing, we conclude that intelligence lies in the eye of the beholder. And, inspired by Information Theory, we suggest that the key to maintaining the subjective impression of intelligence experienced by the users is to carefully manage their level of surprise.

The Element of Surprise

The ability to surprise is coupled with the ability to learn. If the player can learn to predict an NPC's actions, and can second-guess everything that the NPC does, then the NPC can reasonably be said to be nonintelligent. On the other hand, if the NPC's behavior is so erratic and random that it never seems to do anything sensible, then we can also conclude that it is nonintelligent, even though it is utterly unpredictable. The quality of our prediction of what is about to happen is inversely related to the surprise we experience when we find out what actually did happen. The perception of intelligence, therefore, seems to be directly related to the observation of behavior that is surprising yet sensible.

Surprise is important, because mildly surprising events tend to be the most interesting. To understand this, it helps to think in terms of anticipation. If all of the things you anticipated actually did happen, life would become very boring indeed. The future would hold no surprises. It would be no different from a memory of the past. If, on the other hand, the things you least anticipated occurred with alarming regularity, you would be forever confused and disoriented.

In the computer entertainment industry, we have the task of keeping our audience interested. In a very general sense, we can achieve this by managing their expectations. We need to ensure that the level of surprise they experience stays within the poorly defined zone of interest. Too low and they will become bored. Too high and they will find the game difficult to get into. Tuning the level of surprise is key.

Interestingly, then, the one thing that gives us a strong perception of intelligence is also the one thing that keeps us interested in what we do. Implementing learning systems in our games will allow us to "kill two birds with one stone." By creating entertainment software that constantly adapts to the players, we can maintain their expectations and sustain their interest for longer periods of time than more traditional forms of computer entertainment. The unpredictability of the resulting game will give our audience a strong impression of playing in a world inhabited by intelligent NPCs.

Language and Computer Entertainment

Almost everyone is intimately familiar with language. Very early forms of computer entertainment employed natural language interfaces, but the advent of sophisticated computer graphics has resulted in them becoming less and less commonplace. Over the past decade, the focus has been on creating visually convincing game worlds. However, times are changing. The recent availability of powerful graphics hardware has afforded us the luxury of concentrating our efforts on areas such as AI, natural language learning, and dynamic physical simulation. These technologies will become the new differentiators, now that the graphics problem has largely been solved.

Multi-player computer games have always allowed players to communicate via some sort of chat system. One benefit of communicating in natural language is that players get a strong impression of being involved in a world populated by intelligent beings. A good example of this is *Ultima Online*, where the gameplay in the persistent world benefits from conversations held between players.

The majority of single-player games, however, do not offer the player the opportunity to converse with NPCs in natural language, even though it would seem reasonable to do so. There are several reasons for this. To begin with, existing language understanding technologies are far too brittle, and are typically based on pre-scripted chatterbots such as *Eliza*. Furthermore, the requirement that the things the NPCs say need to advance the storyline results in interactions that become predictable and boring, destroying the suspension of disbelief necessary to sustain the perception of intelligence.

We advocate the implementation of socially oriented dialogue between the player and the NPCs in computer entertainment software, as opposed to the more usual task-oriented (i.e., storyline advancing) dialogue. Technology currently exists to allow language learning to be achieved in a way that makes social conversation possible, and solves the problem of managing the level of surprise experienced by the player.

The recent advances in dynamic physical simulation have granted players the ability to spend hours simply "mucking around" in the game world. Similarly, NPCs that have the ability to learn and use natural language will encourage players to spend hours chatting away to them.

Stochastic Language Modeling

State-of-the-art data compression and speech recognition systems employ stochastic language models. These models can also be used generatively to produce language-like utterances. In essence, a stochastic language model learns from past observations of data, as represented by a sequence of symbols (known as a *corpus*). This experience allows it to make a prediction about the symbol likely to come next in the form of a probability distribution over the set of all symbols (known as the *alphabet*). Using these predictions generatively is a simple case of outputting a symbol at random according to the predicted probability distribution. Depending on the application, the symbols used by the stochastic language model might correspond to words, characters, or some other kind of quantifiable information.

Claude Shannon, widely considered to be the father of Information Theory, was generating quasi-language utterances using probabilistic techniques as early as 1948. His classic paper, in which examples of such generations are given, is recommended reading for anyone who is interested in these techniques [Shannon49].

Probability Estimation

In order to make good predictions, any learning system needs to be able to recognize that events occur with differing frequencies, and that these frequencies are context-dependent. One of the simplest stochastic language models that captures both of these constraints, which are evident in all complex systems, including language, [Campbell84], is the simple 2nd-order Markov model, known as a trigram model in the speech recognition community, which infers a probability distribution that is contextual on the most recent two symbols in a sequence. Shannon used such a model to make his quasi-language generations, and, 50 years later, we will introduce the technique of stochastic language modeling using the same model.

In any type of stochastic model, probabilities can be estimated via the maximum-likelihood approximation shown in Equation 11.6.1, where $C(a,b,c)$ is a count of the number of times the symbol sequence a,b,c has been observed in the past, and $*$ is a special wildcard symbol that represents any symbol from the alphabet. This equation simply calculates the frequency with which the symbol c is observed in the context a,b by normalizing the count of the number of times the sequence a,b,c has been observed.

$$P(c|a,b) = C(a,b,c)/C(a,b,*)$$
(11.6.1)

For example, consider a 2nd-order Markov model that operates on the word level (that is, the symbols it uses correspond to words), and is inferred from the data shown in Example 11.6.1. The model will estimate $P(mat|on\ the) = 0.5$ due to the fact that $C(on\ the\ mat) = 1$ and $C(on\ the\ *) = 2$. When used generatively, this model will output the word *mat* after the word sequence *on the* about half of the time.

THE CAT SAT ON THE MAT. THE CAT SAT ON THE RAT.

EXAMPLE 11.6.1   *A small text fragment used for the inference of a 2nd-order Markov model.*

Most stochastic language models are used in applications where a nonzero probability needs to be assigned to all possibilities, the majority of which have never been observed. In the previous example, for instance, $P(cat|on\ the) = 0$. Blending the probability estimates given by several different models, including the naïve model that ignores all evidence and assumes that everything is equally likely, is commonly used to solve this problem. One possible blending strategy is shown in Equation 11.6.2, where A is the alphabet of all known symbols (when using the model on the word level, this alphabet will essentially be a dictionary of all previously observed words), $|A|$ denotes the size of the alphabet, and w, x, y and z are positive blending weights that sum to one, ensuring that a valid probability distribution results.

$$P_B(c|a,b) = wP(c|a,b) + xP(c|b) + yP(c) + z/|A| \tag{11.6.2}$$

For the data shown in Example 11.6.1, assuming that the period character constitutes a separate symbol, $P(cat|on\ the) = 0$, $P(cat|the) = 0.5$, $P(cat) = 0.07$ and $|A| = 8$. If we take all of the blending weights to be equal, such that $w = x = y = z = 0.25$, we get $P_B(cat|on\ the) = 0.19$. The probabilities assigned to observed data are reduced, resulting in $P_B(mat|on\ the) = 0.24$. Even syntactically weird, nonsensical data is assigned a nonzero probability of occurrence. For instance, $P_B(rat|sat\ mat) = 0.05$. Selecting good blending weights is an entire area of research unto itself. Ultimately it entails striking a balance between exploitation of observed data and exploration of unobserved data, something that enables creative generative behavior.

Blended stochastic language models are not necessary if we are interested in using them for language generation only. This is because it is guaranteed that the context used for generation will have been observed at least once in the past, purely because its very existence implies that the model has generated it, and that could only have been done if the model had observed it before. However, using a blended stochastic language model will result in more creative language behavior, and might therefore be the best choice.

An Example Implementation

We will now give an extremely trivial example of inferring an unblended character-level 1st-order Markov model, so called because the context contains a single symbol, and subsequently using the model to generate some new data. The source code listing of the example, written in C (for portability and explicability), is shown in Listing 11.6.1. In the code, note that the statically allocated C array is used both to contain counts of observations made and to maintain the total count for each context. The special symbol with value 257 is used as a wildcard, while the symbol with value 256 is used to delimit the data. After compiling the program, run it with a single command-line argument that specifies the file containing the corpus that the Markov model is to be inferred from.

Listing 11.6.1 C source of a character-level 1st-order Markov model.

```c
#include <stdio.h>
#include <stdlib.h>
#include <time.h>
int main(int argc,char** argv) {
    int C[258][258],context,thresh,c=256,i,j;
    FILE* file;
    for(i=0; i<258; ++i)
```

```
    for(j=0; j<258; ++j)
        C[i][j]=0;
if(argc!=2) return 1;
file=fopen(argv[1],"r");
if(!file) return 2;
while(!feof(file)) {
    context=c; c=fgetc(file);
    if(c==-1) c=256;
    ++C[context][c]; ++C[context][257];
}
fclose(file);
srand(time(NULL));
do {
    context=c; c=-1;
    thresh=rand()%C[context][257];
    do {
        thresh-=C[context][++c];
    } while(thresh>=0);
    fprintf(stdout,"%c",(char)c);
} while(c!=256);
return 0;
}
```

As we are inferring a character-level model that bases its predictions solely on the most recent character in the sequence, we cannot expect too much from its performance. Even so, we believe that it provides a good example of how easily a language learning system can be implemented and used to produce seemingly creative generations. More ambitious implementations, intended to simulate intelligent natural language utterances, will use words instead of characters as their basic building blocks, and will use a more sophisticated data structure, such as a trie [Knuth98], to contain the model.

In Example 11.6.2, we give a brief snippet of a classic Monty Python sketch. The Markov model implemented in the example program was inferred from this corpus, and one of the resulting generations is shown in Example 11.6.3.

```
I chop down trees, I eat my lunch, I go to the lavatory. On
Wednesdays I go shopping, and have buttered scones for tea!
```

EXAMPLE 11.6.2 *A small corpus containing a snippet of a Monty Python sketch.*

```
I chopping, bungoredores g, shesho bunchays h, bun g, I t
myscheshancown Weday I fory. I for s, On lanch, ays Weeatea!
```

EXAMPLE 11.6.3 *A sample generation of a model inferred from the corpus of Example 11.6.2.*

Although this example generation is obviously nothing at all like the language generations that we are advocating, it does share some features of more complex models. First, the model is completely data-driven. Everything it knows about language is derived from observations it has made about the world (in this case, the contents of the corpus). Second, it functions well within the constraints imposed on it. Here we have limited the model to use characters and to base its prediction on the most recent character only. Finally, the data it generates is perfectly valid within a window of two adjacent characters. This short-range validity, which is relative to the particular constraints imposed on the model, is a feature common to all such models, and helps to lend their generations an eerie, language-like quality. In the example shown, this property results in all quasi-words being (almost) pronounceable.

One of the great advantages of the data-driven approach we have shown here is that it makes absolutely no language-specific assumptions. A model that can learn and generate quasi-English can equally well learn and generate quasi-German, quasi-French, and quasi-whatever else you want to throw at it. Additionally, the model is capable of learning (by having its statistics updated) and behaving (by generating quasi-language utterances) in tandem, and on-the-fly, giving it the possibility of learning from what is said to it.

Determining the Subject

Generating quasi-language utterances is fun and rewarding ... for about five minutes. Although the generations themselves might exhibit creativity, unpredictability, and the ability of the model to learn, and might prove to be genuinely amusing, the fact that they lack relevancy needs to be addressed.

We have shown how a language learning system can be used to generate unpredictable (and therefore surprising) utterances, fulfilling the first of the two desirable features of a system that can mimic intelligent behavior. To complete our work, we need to extend the system in order to make its behavior sensible. That is, the utterances produced by the system should make sense, to a degree, within some context. In the case of computer entertainment software, such things might include

- Things said recently to the NPC by the player character.
- Things said recently in the nearby environment by other player and non-player characters.
- The immediate requirements of the story, if there is one, as imposed by some type of story script.
- The current state of the NPC, such as its level of hunger, its opinion of the player character, and so on.
- Recent events in the game world, such as a nearby explosion, the fact that the player character has given the NPC an object, and so on.

Getting a Markov model of any order to generate a particular type of utterance, as required for that utterance to be sensitive to contexts such as those we have just outlined, is extremely difficult to do. A Markovian generation is akin to a random walk: you begin at the start of the utterance, but you have no idea where you will end up. We therefore cannot afford to be too sophisticated, but lack of sophistication is not necessarily a bad thing.

One way that the problem of generating a relevant utterance can be solved is by making the generation sensitive to a keyword (i.e., guaranteeing that the generation contains a word determined *a priori*), and then making the keyword itself contextual on the types of things we would like the utterance to bear some relevance to. By doing this, we are reducing the subject of the utterance to a single word contained within it. The famous *Eliza* chatterbot employs a similarly naïve keyword-based technique for selecting a prescripted reply to an utterance made by the user. Naïve techniques often work well in practice.

The technique used to calculate the keyword will ideally be stochastic in nature. That is, it will give as its response a probability distribution over all possible words, and the most probable word can be selected as the keyword to use. Although, for want of space, we will not drill too deeply into this aspect of implementing a system that can learn and use language, we suggest that Bayesian Belief Networks might provide one way of learning the correlation between things happening in the game world and the subject of the generated utterance, and expressing this knowledge probabilistically. This subject is discussed in this book [Tozour02].

This approach solves a third problem that we have so far failed to mention: when should an NPC speak, and when should it remain silent? The solution is simply to ask the NPC, at regular intervals, to calculate a keyword to base its utterance on. If it fails to calculate a keyword at all, then it can happily keep its mouth shut.

Generating a Relevant Utterance

Let us consider that an NPC has, one way or another, selected a keyword to base its utterance on. The problem now is one of generating an utterance that is guaranteed to contain that keyword. Due to the random-walk nature of Markovian generations, this process is not trivial.

We suggest the following algorithm, which unfortunately requires two stochastic language models, effectively doubling the necessary storage requirements. One Markov model should be inferred as usual, working left-to-right across the data. We can easily ask this model to generate an utterance that begins at our keyword of choice (simply by seeding the context used by the model to contain that keyword) and that ends at the end of the utterance.

This will leave us with an incomplete utterance that begins with our desired keyword. To complete the utterance, we recommend using a second Markov model, inferred in a right-to-left fashion across the same data as the first. We can ask this model to generate an utterance that begins at the keyword and that heads back toward the beginning of the utterance. Both partial utterances can then be glued together to produce a complete utterance that is guaranteed to contain the keyword.

For example, consider an utterance based around the keyword *on*. One Markov model will be used to generate an incomplete utterance that begins with the keyword, such as *on the mat*. The other Markov model will be used to generate an incomplete utterance, in a right-to-left fashion, that ends with the keyword, such as *The cat sat on*.

Note that in the second case, the word *sat* will be generated before the word *cat*, and so on. Both incomplete utterances can then be concatenated to form the complete utterance *The cat sat on the mat.*

Introducing MegaHAL

Jason Hutchens, one of the authors of this article, wrote a conversation simulator named "MegaHAL" using many of the technologies we have mentioned [Hutchens98]. In 1995, Jason put his program online, collecting hundreds of pages of transcripts of conversation between it and users on the Internet. Standalone versions of MegaHAL are available for download from www.megahal.net.

The fact that MegaHAL could converse with dozens of people simultaneously meant that it quickly inferred a language model that covered many different languages, including English, French, German, Latin, and an Australian aboriginal dialect. As MegaHAL generates lucid and seemingly creative utterances perhaps about 10 percent of the time, it encourages users to continue talking to it in the belief that it will say something cool soon.

The reinforcement a user receives from a lucid utterance is intermittent, as lucid utterances are difficult to predict, yet frequent enough to prevent them from getting bored. This results in users experiencing a form of addiction [Barnes02]. The desire to try just one more time in the hope of observing a lucid utterance can be overwhelming.

Amusing MegaHAL Examples

The MegaHAL experience says a lot more, we think, about how the human brain works than it does about how to create "'true" AI. Human beings see animals when gazing up at clouds floating overhead, and they see intelligence and creativity in the utterances of MegaHAL. Capitalizing on the human tendency of reading meaning into randomness, MegaHAL excels at generating illusions of intelligence using language.

Some examples might help the reader to appreciate what can be achieved using a relatively simple algorithm and a source of data to infer it from. All of the following examples are taken from the online version of MegaHAL. Note that the online version converted all of its input into uppercase characters, lending the examples a perhaps unwelcome appearance.

In Example 11.6.4, we show a quotation made by MegaHAL soon after it was put online. To get the ball rolling, MegaHAL was inferred from a small corpus of a few hundred sentences, taken from Monty Python scripts and They Might Be Giants lyrics. Readers familiar with Monty Python and They Might Be Giants might be able to identify bits and pieces of the bizarre utterance shown.

```
MegaHAL: I COULD SHAKE MY TINY FIST AND SWEAR I WASN'T WRONG, BUT
WHAT'S THE SENSE IN ARGUING WHEN YOU'RE MUCH TOO BUSY RETURNING TO
THE LAVATORY.
```

EXAMPLE 11.6.4   *They Might Be Giants meets Monty Python.*

MegaHAL uses a completely *ad hoc* technique of determining a keyword to base its reply on. Instead of using Bayesian Belief Networks, as suggested in this article, MegaHAL uses a hard-wired, English-specific heuristic. In Example 11.6.5, for instance, the reply is based on the keyword PERSON. Even though the technique employed qualifies as an inelegant hack, the impression one gets from a randomly generated utterance that bears some relevance to what was said can be quite convincing.

```
User: Who is the smartest person in the world?
MegaHAL: A PERSON WITH A STICK OF CELERY UNDER HIS ARM?
```

EXAMPLE 11.6.5   *A strange yet relevant answer to a direct question.*

The almost schizophrenic nature of the previous examples gives a rather false impression of MegaHAL. At its best, it can seem astonishingly lucid and intelligent. Example 11.6.6, for instance, illustrates what is possible when the correct keywords are selected and good utterances based on these keywords are generated. In this example, we also see MegaHAL's ability to learn on-the-fly, as its answer to the question asked by the user is a regurgitation of the user's previous statement.

```
User: Roentgen discovered the X-rays.
MegaHAL: THE NOBEL PRIZE FOR PHYSICS IN 1900 WAS WON BY ROENTGEN.
User: Who discovered the X-rays?
MegaHAL: ROENTGEN DISCOVERED THE X-RAYS.
```

EXAMPLE 11.6.6   *MegaHAL is frequently lucid, and learns from its experience.*

Example 11.6.7 gives an even better example of MegaHAL's capabilities. Even though its reply is only ever based on a single keyword extracted from the most recent thing the user said, occasionally a conversation seems to flow, and MegaHAL's replies seem to be based on some higher-level understanding of what is being talked about. Here we see the program discussing the subject of learning over several adjacent utterances. The user unconsciously helps MegaHAL to stay on-topic by providing relevant keywords when replying to what it says.

```
MegaHAL: WHEN WE BEGIN TO RESOLVE SOME OF MY THUMBS, SOMETHING WICKED
THIS WAY COMES
User: What is the meaning of your last assertion?
MegaHAL: HAVE YOU LEARNED SINCE WE LAST SPOKE?
User: I've learned I'm not experienced enough to modelize your brain
system
MegaHAL: YOU'VE FINALLY CONFUSED ME.
User: I've learned nothing
MegaHAL: HAVE YOU LEARNED ANYTHING ABOUT INSANITY?
User: are you stupid
MegaHAL: I AM NOT STUPID! REALLY
```

EXAMPLE 11.6.7   *MegaHAL can be lucid over several exchanges with the user.*

The fact that MegaHAL is based on a Markov model that makes no language-specific assumptions means that it can learn and respond in any language whatsoever. In its prime, the online MegaHAL was talking nonsense in dozens of languages, as the extract shown in Example 11.6.8 illustrates.

```
User: Tu parles francais?
MegaHAL: I GUESS SO. PARLEZ-VOUS FRANCAIS?
User: L'amour est une passion humaine.
MegaHAL: LA LANGIDOCE EST UNE PETITE JEUNNE FILLE
```

EXAMPLE 11.6.8   *MegaHAL can be nonsensical in any human language.*

Many users reported emotional responses to MegaHAL. They often found the things it said to them amusing, especially when its reply incorporated bits and pieces of things they had said to it earlier (perhaps even days or weeks earlier). Occasionally, they would feel offended or insulted, such as when a user named Forrest told Mega-HAL his name only to be deluged with quotes from the movie *Forrest Gump*: something, perhaps, which he had endured too much of at school. Our favorite example is that of a strongly religious person who spent hours trying to get MegaHAL to respond nicely to statements that contained the keyword "Jesus" instead of performing word association to generate blasphemous utterances.

Surprisingly, an overwhelming number of people seemed to think that MegaHAL is closer to "true" AI than is actually the case, concluding through their interaction with the program that, over time, it would soon exceed human intelligence. Jason still receives emails from users complaining that they are unable to teach MegaHAL something, or that it fails to understand something else, presumably in the belief that its lack of "true" intelligence is their fault. It is remarkable that people are prepared to look for other interpretations of seemingly intelligent behavior than the obvious.

MegaHAL in Black & White

An unfortunately unfinished feature of the computer game *Black & White* was the ability for users to enter a persistent online world, enabling them to have conversations with other players and participate in special multi-player features of the game. For this version of *Black & White*, we intended to use language-learning technology to enhance NPCs within the gaming world. We partially implemented a language acquisition and generation device in the brain of the Creature, the primary learning AI in the game, basing the implementation on an improved version of the MegaHAL algorithm. Figure 11.6.1 shows the system in action.

The player's Creature would learn on-the-fly from the things the player typed as input in his or her own native language, and, when left alone, would exhibit conversational behavior similar to the player it had learned from. The subject of the utterance made by the Creature would be potentially correlated with a number of possible events (such as damage being done to the Creature, food being consumed, a miracle occurring, or another Creature saying something). Imagine entering a fight with

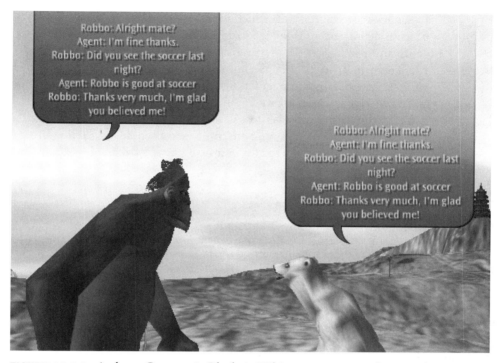

FIGURE 11.6.1 *A player Creature in* Black & White *conversing with a nonplayer Creature.*

another Creature and having your Creature immediately start hurling your own unique form of abuse at the other player!

Unfortunately, time constraints during development forced us to shelve this potentially exciting piece of work to make time for other, more necessary aspects of the game. It is our hope that we will return to implementing language learning in a future version of *Black & White*, or a future project, as we believe that it has fantastic potential.

Conclusion

In this article, we evangelized about our philosophy concerning learning, intelligence, and creativity. We genuinely believe that the key to providing players with satisfying gameplay experiences, particularly in the open-ended sandbox game worlds that are becoming increasingly common, is to create learning systems that have the never-ending potential to surprise.

As our games become more and more visually convincing, players of our games expect more and more of them. Dynamically modeling the physics of a game world is one way to give the player the impression of being immersed in a virtual reality. Another way is by populating the world with NPCs that are capable of learning.

Language is something with which we are all intimately familiar, and an NPC capable of learning and using language socially gives a very convincing impression of intelligence and encourages the player to spend more time in conversation.

There is a huge, untapped potential for language learning within computer games, from the simplest of entertaining gossip systems to agenda-driven agents whose aim is to reveal critical story elements when interrogated correctly. For keyboard-driven architectures such as those used by the massively multiplayer gaming community, the potential for a gaming adventure seems endless. Whether or not this signals the return of the text adventure in a new guise is debatable—although it would be nice to think so.

References

[Barnes02] Barnes, Jonty and Hutchens, Jason, "Testing Undefined Behavior as a Result of Learning," *AI Game Programming Wisdom*, Charles River Media, 2002.

[Campbell84] Campbell, Jeremy, *Grammatical Man: Information, Entropy, Language and Life*, Pelican Books, 1984.

[Hutchens98] Hutchens, Jason, "Introducing MegaHAL," *NeMLaP/CoNLL Workshop on Human-Computer Conversation*, Association for Computational Linguistics, 1998.

[Knuth98] Knuth, Donald, *The Art of Computer Programming: Searching and Sorting, Volume 3, Second Edition*, Addison Wesley Publishing Company, 1998.

[Shannon49] Shannon, Claude and Weaver, Warren, "The Mathematical Theory of Communication," University of Illinois Press, 1949.

[Tozour02] Tozour, Paul, "Introduction to Bayesian Networks and Reasoning Under Uncertainty," *AI Game Programming Wisdom*, Charles River Media, 2002.

[Turing92] Turing, Alan, "Computing Machinery and Intelligence," *Collected Works of A.M. Turing: Mechanical Intelligence*, Elsevier Science Publishers, 1992.

11.7

Testing Undefined Behavior as a Result of Learning

Jonty Barnes—Lionhead Studios, and
Jason Hutchens—Amristar

jbarnes@lionhead.com, and
hutch@amristar.com.au

At the 2001 Game Developers Conference (GDC), we attended a series of artificial intelligence (AI) round-table sessions. Apart from driving home the fact that most development houses still treat AI as something that demands the work of a sole programmer and a relatively small slice of the CPU, we were dismayed to find that learning—that which we consider to be the very essence of intelligence—is almost completely ignored. The general belief seemed to be that quality assurance would prove impossible if non-player characters (NPCs) started behaving in unpredictable, surprising and continually evolving ways.

Inspired by the GDC AI round-table sessions, this article aims to show, via a case study of the computer game *Black & White*, exactly how a testing department can work to ensure a high-quality product that features an unpredictable learning AI.

A Short Introduction to *Black & White*

Black & White is, at the most basic level, a god game [Lionhead01]. Peter Molyneux, director of Lionhead studios, introduced the genre with *Populous* in 1989. Apart from marrying a sandbox world with a storyline that grants the player freedom, *Black & White* introduced a revolutionary learning AI, known as a "Creature," as a central character.

> *I wanted to place into* Black & White *the ability to select a creature and turn it into a huge, intelligent being which could learn, operate independently, and do your bidding when you wanted. I knew that this would require an artificial intelligence structure unlike any ever written.*
>
> —Peter Molyneux, Director, Lionhead Studios.

To advance the storyline, the player trains his Creature to perform tasks on his behalf. Training is achieved via reinforcement learning, enabling the player to shape his Creature's behavior by providing examples of desired behavior and issuing rewards (perhaps a scratch on the belly) and punishments (perhaps a whack across the face). We therefore colloquially refer to this approach as "slap and tickle" AI.

The design of the Creature AI allows players to train their Creatures to perform tasks unnecessary to the unfolding storyline, with entertaining consequences [Evans02]. This flexibility was deliberately intended to grant the player absolute freedom to experiment with the gameplay mechanics, immersing them completely in the virtual world of *Black & White*.

Learning Is the Essence of Intelligence

Alan Turing is widely regarded to be the father of AI. Over 50 years ago Turing was struggling with the definition of intelligence itself, and in 1950 his work resulted in a landmark paper that established a behavioral test for machine intelligence [Turing92]. The Turing Test is based on the presumption that if a computer behaves indistinguishably from the way a human being would have behaved in similar circumstances, then the computer can be said to be intelligent.

The Turing Test concerns itself with natural language conversation, but Turing's insight applies equally well to other types of behavior. Let us consider a hypothetical computer game in which the player chases an opponent around a maze, attempting to shoot it with a weapon. How would the opponent have to behave to pass a modified Turing Test that focused on running-around-mazes-with-a-gun behavior? Certainly, it should be able to navigate the maze, remembering areas it had visited before and exploring new areas. It should take evasive action when under attack. It should hide from the player, stalk him, lay traps for him, and surprise him. To remain unpredictable, it should adapt to the gameplay strategy exhibited by the player—in essence, the opponent should learn.

Learning is intimately intertwined with the act of prediction. We extract relevant details from our past experience in order to predict future events, allowing us to behave in anticipation. The feedback we get from the environment after behaving gives us a chance to evaluate the quality of our predictions, and thus the learning process continues. Intelligent systems must also behave in ways that are difficult for an observer of their behavior to predict (this is essential when the observer happens to be predatory). The ability of a system to behave unpredictably within the bounds of reasonableness gives a very strong impression of intelligence.

A Behavioral View of Addiction

During the development of *Black & White*, we found that if the player's Creature, the principal AI-driven NPC in the game, behaved in surprising yet relevant ways, then the player tended to spend more time playing the game. Players are driven to continue playing in anticipation of seeing an NPC do something new, interesting, and creative.

The field of scientific behaviorism concentrates on observable behavior and the effects of stimuli and reinforcers on this behavior [Skinner76]. Studies show that an intermittent schedule of positive reinforcement tends to strengthen behavior far more effectively than regular reinforcement. For example, human beings are much more likely to continue inserting coins into gambling machines after failing to receive a payout than they are to insert additional coins into drink vending machines after failing to receive a can of cola. Drink vending machines behave predictably, whereas the unpredictable behavior of gambling machines fosters addiction.

How fortunate, then, that NPCs blessed with the ability to learn automatically behave in unpredictable ways, providing the player with intermittent reinforcement. If we take care to consider which properties of our game are likely to be reinforcing to the player, and carefully exploit these properties to ensure that they deliver reinforcement on an intermittent schedule, then we can design our game to be more compelling.

Quality Assurance of Learning Software

There are many benefits of writing AI software that has the capability to learn from its experience. Learning AI can perform well in unanticipated situations, and can provide an entertaining, ever-changing experience to the user. Unfortunately, the industry seems to be reluctant to implement such software, and this might be largely due to the sentiment expressed in the following quotation:

> *Training takes place as part of the game development cycle, never after the game ships.*

> —Neil Kirby, AI Roundtable Moderator's Report [Kirby01].

Nothing could be farther from the truth. All interactive computer entertainment products, each and every one, feature at least one learning system—the player. Giving a human being the opportunity to directly influence the behavior of an in-game character will always result in undefined circumstances arising as they experiment within the game world, exploring its boundaries to discover what is and what is not possible.

We have all experienced the thrill of simply "mucking around" in a computer game environment. The fun of exploring and experimenting with a game can greatly outweigh the enjoyment experienced by the playing the game "properly," particularly when the game caters to such behavior. We can all recount anecdotes of bizarre player behavior that not even the best testing department could have anticipated.

Up until now, the player has been the only unknowable factor to test for when developing computer entertainment software. Of course, multi-player games face further complexity arising out of the interactions between many different players. However, the conclusion is the same: Treat learning agents as if they were human players, and you will find that you already possess the tools and the knowledge required to test their behavior.

The Testing Department

At Lionhead Studios, our organic approach to development means that testing begins on a project from the moment it becomes playable. Apart from finding bugs, the role of our testing department, unlike that of traditional testing departments that only come in at the end of a project, involves identifying design issues and proposing solutions to them.

> *When your development takes three and a half years, your view of the game can be too focused. Which is why fresh eyes are invaluable for feedback throughout. You often need to analyze the player as well as the game to understand what is required.*
>
> —Andy Robson, Head of QA, Lionhead Studios.

To do this successfully, a good testing department should complement the skills of a few experienced testers with a regular flow of first-time players. Apart from revealing bugs in the game mechanics that might have been overlooked, the demand for additional features from first-time players can help shape the game design itself. Another advantage of this approach is that it focuses on experimental player behavior.

The Test Plan

It is essential that the testing department maintain a test plan throughout the development process. A good test plan will document the approach taken to test each and every element of the game. At the early stages of development, the definition of the game itself is constantly in flux, but maintaining a list of features, whether they are implemented or not, helps to chart the game's progress and serves as a checklist for bug hunting. A test plan is very much an always-live document.

No matter how much love you put into developing a game, the number-one reason for doing so is to make money. This means that you need to cater to as large an audience as possible, in order to maximize sales. For this reason, it is essential to consult consumer opinion when creating a test plan. Having inhouse users minimizes the distance between the development team and the audience [Beck99], and is a tremendous asset when updating the continuously evolving document that is the test plan.

The Black Box Viewpoint

Quality assurance of complex learning AI such as the Creature in *Black & White* takes place on several different levels. To begin with, the technical design of the learning AI needs to be verified in some way, and this can occur before a line of code is written. The code itself can then be unit tested to make sure it complies with the technical design. Finally, the in-game behavior of the system needs to be verified.

Treating the learning AI as if it were a human being can facilitate the testing process. We generally do not need to concern ourselves with how the system is implemented; we need only treat it as a black box, testing the behavior we observe against the behavior we expect to see. The programming team can use the observational evidence provided by the testing department to track down bugs in either their code or their technical design.

Using the Right Tools

Testing, like most aspects of game development, benefits from good tools. Navigation algorithms, for example, while constantly being reinvented or refined for specific gaming situations, are relatively straightforward to test if a tool enables the calculations they make to be visualized in real time.

In *Black & White*, we created a comprehensive toolset, including a GUI-based *agent editor* and an *analysis tool*, that reflected the requirements of our test plan. Among other things, these tools enabled the testers to force a Creature to perform any behavior on any applicable object, alter a Creature's physical and mental attributes, and manipulate a Creature's state of knowledge.

In addition to allowing the testing department to directly influence the internal state of the Creature, our tools kept a history of statistics about the AI's state for future analysis. We heartily endorse this approach, as a better understanding of the development of the AI can be gleaned from this type of data, facilitating fine-tuning and balancing of its behavior.

Learning AI makes replication of initial conditions an almost impossible task, yet the testing department relies on the ability to replicate a particular situation exactly. This problem can be addressed by saving the complete state of the game world automatically and at frequent intervals. To ease the testing process, we strongly advocate implementation of this feature at the earliest opportunity.

Reinforcement Learning

Reinforcement learning (i.e., the "slap and tickle" approach to AI) is used for the Creature AI in *Black & White*. With its roots in behavioral psychology, reinforcement learning concentrates on modeling reward-based learning in animals. The learning AI is treated as a black box, and its behavior is shaped via the administration of a reinforcer in the form of a punishment or a reward [Sutton98].

Reinforcement learning is only effective when the trainer and the AI being trained agree on which behavior is being reinforced. This consensus is challenging to reach, as many possibilities can exist, particularly when the learning AI is able to observe several stimuli, and has behaved more than once in a reasonable window of time prior to receiving reinforcement.

In *Black & White*, to address this problem, and to make reinforcement learning a more controlled process, we created mimicking mechanisms that allowed the testing department to force the Creature to perform a particular behavior, reinforcing the Creature accordingly. Explicit feedback was provided to emphasize exactly what had been learned as a result of the reinforcement. Testing the Creature's interpretation of a given situation proved to be a very difficult procedure. The problem was resolved by a careful analysis of the Creature using the tools we implemented for that purpose, and a detailed comparison between the Creature's behavior in a given situation and our expectation of what the Creature should have perceived and learned.

Generalization

In *Black & White*, the player takes the role of the learning AI's trainer, and therefore has a rather strong effect on the types of *rules* the AI forms between objects and behaviors. Even with a comprehensive toolset to analyze the results of reinforcement, how can we be sure to have tested all possibilities?

Surprisingly, the exact identity of the game-world object that the learning AI has formed a rule for is not generally relevant as far as testing is concerned. Despite the learning AI's ability to differentiate between different objects, it is the properties of these objects that are most important when it is learning to associate a behavior with an object.

The ability of the system to generalize what it has learned alleviates the testing department from the arduous task of evaluating every individual possibility. For instance, objects such as sheep, grain, and rocks all share a common property that describes their nutritional value. Using just these three objects, the ability of the agent to understand nutrition can be thoroughly tested. Generalization means that successful testing can be performed for a particular object property by demonstrating a working system on a subset of objects that possess that property, saving having to test all cases.

Passing the Turing Test

Whenever we introduce learning AI into a computer entertainment product, our intention is to convince players that there is something alive inside their machines. In order to achieve this there are several things that we need to bear in mind.

Manage the Expectations of the Player

Intelligence is in the eye of the beholder. Observed behavior is judged differently according to the expectations of the observer. These expectations are often derived from other features of the environment. For example, it would be unreasonable to conclude that a newborn baby is unintelligent merely because it cannot hold a conversation.

In *Black & White*, we decided to make the Creatures look like animals in order to manage the expectations of the player. People more readily accept behavior as sufficiently intelligent when it is performed by something graphically represented as a baby cow rather than something that looks like a human being.

Visual appearances aside, we must also be careful to make sure that NPCs behave in ways that are unpredictable yet reasonable. Although it is tempting to provide NPCs with information about the game world that would not have been available to a human player under the same circumstances, doing so might result in behavior that seems strange to the player, unaware as they are of the additional information. Applying humanistic limitations to our NPCs and restricting them to react to events that are obvious to the player results in more convincing behavior.

Mirror the Internal State of the NPC

Even the most bleeding-edge AI techniques will be for naught if the NPC to which they are applied remains inanimate. Convincing visual and auditory feedback provides as much an impression of intelligence as the learning AI itself. In combination, the effect can be drastic.

Animation and sound can be used to cute effect, but, if predictable, will soon become boring and even annoying to the player. Using it to reflect the internal state of a learning AI, on the other hand, serves the dual purposes of giving the player immediate feedback about the state of the NPC, and providing an ever-changing game experience. In *Black & White*, the "unhappy" animation was evocative enough to result in some observers complaining about players being cruel to their Creature!

To enhance the visual feedback provided to the player in *Black & White*, we made sure that the physical appearance of each Creature reflected its upbringing, its history of experience, and its behavior. Players did not just directly influence their Creature's behavior, but were also responsible for its appearance. The benefits of this approach are twofold: players developed an attachment to their Creature's unique personality and appearance, while at the same time being able to make assumptions about an unknown Creature's future behavior merely by looking at it. For example, the fact that the Creature shown in Figure 11.7.1 is a happy young cow with a big appetite and a history of violent confrontation cannot be denied.

FIGURE 11.7.1 *A Creature from* Black & White *with a colorful past. Also shown in Color Plate 2.*

Use Learning to Surprise the Player

The flexibility afforded to the player by learning AI can greatly benefit gameplay. If the player chooses to teach an NPC that rocks are the best food for it, then rocks it has to be, even if it makes the NPC violently sick. Behavior like this, while unconventional, can generate much entertainment and amusement.

Players of *Black & White* have spent countless hours training their Creatures to perform the most unnecessary tasks, as far as the storyline of the game is concerned, purely out of the entertainment value of seeing their Creature do something amusing. One player, for example, raised a Creature that eats only sleeping male villagers over the age of 30. No game developer in his or her right mind would ever consider spending time and effort incorporating such a dubious feature into a product, but the fact that a flexible learning AI enabled the player to pursue his goal of raising a Creature with a discerning palette resulted in immense satisfaction and pride on his behalf.

Use Innate Behavior to Constrain Learning

One criticism of learning AI is that it is only as good as its trainer. Instilling NPCs with certain innate behaviors that cannot be undone by learning, safeguards against them failing to perform necessary storyline advancing behaviors as a result of poor training.

In *Black & White*, a few underlying rules constrain and control the Creatures, and might override learned behavior when necessary. For example, one of the lessons learned during development was that the player never wants to be disobeyed. A Creature who has learned a link between the proximity of the player and an unpleasant event should not run away from the player, even though this is the behavior that the learning AI would select. Creatures, therefore, have an innate tendency to be obedient toward their master.

Conclusion

The computer entertainment industry has the potential to be responsible for a revolution in the field of applied AI. The technology used by the industry, although trivial from an academic point of view, achieves everything that it was designed for, and often surpasses in performance anything offered by the research community. This validates the Turing Test—no matter how sophisticated our AI is, it is its resulting behavior that is important.

The entertaining aspect of the undefined behavior that results from learning is obvious from a quick survey of *Black & White* fan sites. Players report on the progress of their Creature like proud parents, and are willing to interpret coincidental or random behavior meaningfully. At the GDC round-table sessions, we laughed along with AI programmers as they related how, during development, their systems had misbehaved in undefined yet entertaining ways. Unfortunately, these very same programmers removed the source of their own amusement by fixing "bugs" in their code.

Making unpredictable behavior the goal of learning AI systems will pass this added value onto the consumer.

Irrespective of our evangelism for learning AI, testing for undefined circumstances is challenging, and presents a difficult task for any testing department. However, we must remember that the advantage is ours; we define the learning AI itself, and constrain it within the game worlds we create. With a comprehensive set of tools and a strong testing department, the problem of testing the undefined behavior that results from learning should not serve as a scapegoat for failing to implement learning AI altogether. After all, human players are no less unpredictable, and we have been successfully testing for them since the dawn of gaming.

References

[Beck99] Beck, Kent, *Extreme Programming Explained: Embrace Change*, Addison-Wesley Publishing Company, 1999.

[Evans02] Evans, Richard, "Varieties of Learning," *AI Game Programming Wisdom*, Charles River Media, 2002.

[Kirby01] Kirby, Neil, "GDC 2001 AI Roundtable Moderator's Report," www.gameai.com, 2001.

[Lionhead01] Lionhead Studios Ltd, "Black & White," 2001. See www.bwgame.com.

[Skinner76] Skinner, Burrhus Frederic, *About Behaviorism*, Random House, 1976.

[Sutton98] Sutton, Richard and Barto, Andrew, *Reinforcement Learning: An Introduction*, MIT Press, 1998.

[Turing92] Turing, Alan, "Computing Machinery and Intelligence," *Collected Works of A.M. Turing: Mechanical Intelligence*, Elsevier Science Publishers, 1992.

11.8

Imitating Random Variations in Behavior Using a Neural Network

John Manslow

john@jmanslow.fsnet.co.uk

As artificial intelligence has become increasingly sophisticated, it has become possible to create computer-controlled agents that display remarkably humanlike behavior. One of the few indications that an agent is nonorganic, however, is the frequently clinical nature of their actions, an effect exacerbated by the often ad hoc mechanisms used to introduce random variation.

In nature, such randomness usually has a specific structure that can be difficult to identify and even more challenging to simulate and reproduce. This article presents two simple techniques that can be used to learn the underlying structure of apparently random variations in behavior and to reproduce similar variations on demand with minimal computational effort.

The Example Game

ON THE CD

To demonstrate the techniques introduced in this article, a simple tank game is included on the CD. In the game, two tanks are positioned on a randomly generated side-view landscape, with the leftmost tank controlled by the player and the rightmost tank by the computer. The tanks take turns firing, and the first one to score a hit is declared the winner.

The tanks aim by setting the inclination of their barrels to adjust for the distance between them and the effects of wind on the flight of the shell. By using a neural network to set the inclination of the AI tank's barrel, it is possible to achieve a hit rate of over 98 percent on the first shot, which is far in excess of the best human performance of around 15 percent.

Unfortunately, although neural networks can be taught to imitate human players of the game, they are able to reproduce only the deterministic aspects of their behavior, and not its random variation. This article describes the two techniques that are used in the tanks game on the CD to imitate the actual random variations in aiming made by human players of the tanks game.

Modeling an Unconditional Distribution

This section describes a technique that can be used to model the *unconditional distribution* of a random variable. An unconditional distribution has a fixed shape and is thus useful in modeling only relatively simple forms of random variation. Despite this, they are surprisingly useful, easy to understand, and require very little computation to create and maintain.

Some real-world events that can be accurately described by unconditional distributions include the outcome of flipping a coin, the result of choosing a card from a full deck, and, less trivially, the part of the goal that a particular soccer player aims at during a penalty kick. Unconditional distribution models could thus be used to simulate the random character of all these events.

To produce a model of the unconditional distribution of a random variable, all that is required is a representative set of samples of the variable. *Representative* means that the variable takes on the same values in the samples in the same proportions as would be expected in a typical game; exceptional values in the game should be exceptional in the set of samples.

Example aiming errors were produced from the tanks game by taking manual control of the AI tank. For each shot, the difference between the correct angle for the tank's barrel, as calculated by the neural network, and the angle set by the player was logged to disk. After a couple of day's play, this produced a file containing around 5000 example errors.

An unconditional distribution model was then produced by dividing the range of the errors into several non-overlapping segments called *bins*, and assigning each a probability equal to the proportion of the samples that lies within it. For example, if the errors ranged between 0 and 1, and we were to use 10 bins, the first bin would cover the interval 0.0 to 0.1, the second 0.1 to 0.2, and so on.

Similarly, if 5000 samples were collected, and 283 lay within the first bin—that is, in the range 0.0 to 0.1—the first bin would be assigned a probability of 283/5000, which is roughly 0.057. Once all probabilities have been computed, the model can be used to generate new samples with the same distribution as the originals. Each new sample is generated in two stages:

1. Randomly select one of the bins in accordance with the bin probabilities. For example, since the first bin has probability 0.057, the selection process should choose it roughly 5.7 percent of the time.

2. Generate a random number in the range covered by the selected bin. For example, if the first bin was chosen in step 1, a random number between 0.0 and 0.1 would be generated as the sample.

The single most important problem in creating a distribution model is to properly match its complexity—that is, the number and size of its bins—to the number of examples that are used to create it (see [Bishop95]). Using too few bins can result in a condition known as *underfitting*, in which some details of the distribution are lost—particularly small features like sharp peaks.

If too many bins are used, *overfitting* can result, and the model starts to represent features that are specific to the exemplar set and not shared by the distribution from which they were sampled. In extreme cases of overfitting, sections of the example data can be consistently regurgitated in a way that presents an implausible reconstruction of the random variation that is being modeled.

Overfitting is apparent when there are seemingly random variations between the probabilities of adjacent bins, and can be eliminated either by reducing the number of bins (and hence increasing their width) or by collecting additional data. Underfitting might cause the variation in the generated samples to be too coarse an approximation to that in the originals, and can be eliminated by increasing the number of bins.

The number of samples required to produce a good model varies from one application to another because of differences in the complexities of the distributions being modeled. As a general rule, start with a small number of samples (e.g., 100) and bins (e.g., 5), and keep collecting data and adding bins until a satisfactory model (i.e., one that neither underfits nor overfits) is produced.

Modeling a Conditional Distribution

Although the unconditional distribution model discussed in the preceding section allows many forms of random variation to be reproduced, it is limited by its fixed shape: The shapes of the distributions that describe most real-world random variation are influenced by, and change with, several external factors. To reproduce these types of variation, a *conditional distribution model* is required.

Conditional distribution models allow a wide range of sophisticated and complex stochastic phenomena to be recreated. In a racing game, for example, modeling the variation in the distribution of steering errors made by players as a function of the distance to the car immediately behind them, makes it possible to simulate the deterioration in performance that some personalities exhibit when under pressure.

Similarly, an afternoon spent measuring the errors made when hitting a cue ball at different positions on a pool table allows a model of the way in which the ball's position affects the accuracy of a player's shots. Such a model would even include quite subtle effects that result from the individual player's reaction to the ball's distance to the cushion and cueing direction.

ON THE CD

The conditional distribution model used in the example on the CD is identical to the unconditional one, except that the probabilities associated with its bins are calculated by a multilayer perceptron (MLP) neural network. This means that the MLP—which acts as a standard classifier (see [Bishop95])—takes care of working out how the probabilities change with the distribution's inputs.

The problem of deciding what the distribution's inputs should be is termed *input selection*, and is discussed at length in [Manslow01]. Since collecting example data is usually time consuming, anything that might affect the shape of the distribution should be recorded so that the data collection process does not have to be repeated because something important was missed.

When it comes to creating the conditional distribution model, a small set of inputs (typically, around four or five) should be identified that account for most of the changes in the distribution's shape. These are found through a mixture of conjecture, and trial and error—that is, by building models with different sets of inputs and seeing which perform best. By following this process, it was found that the distribution of aiming errors was most strongly affected by the error made on the preceding shot.

The example data required for the conditional distribution model was collected in almost exactly the same way as for the unconditional one: The player was given control of the AI tank, and the aiming error on each shot was recorded, along with the error made on the preceding shot. After a couple of day's play, 5000 examples had been collected.

In contrast with the unconditional distribution, the training procedure for the conditional distribution is computationally intensive. The model included on the CD required around 10 hours of training using a perturbation search (see [Manslow01]) on a 500MHz Intel Celeron PC. Fortunately, samples can be obtained from the trained distribution very efficiently, making it suitable for use in-game.

Since training can continue indefinitely, it is important to periodically test a copy of the model that is being trained in-game. This allows the progress of training to be monitored, and training terminated once the model's performance reaches a satisfactory level. If satisfactory performance is not achieved within a reasonable period, the model should be inspected for signs of overfitting and underfitting.

Overfitting is usually evident in frequent and apparently random variations between the probabilities of adjacent bins. This causes sequences of samples drawn from the distribution to exhibit too little variation, or to closely resemble sequences in the example data. As with unconditional distributions, overfitting in conditional distributions is eliminated by reducing their effective complexity.

The simplest way to reduce a conditional distribution model's complexity is to reduce the number of bins it contains, or to reduce the number of hidden neurons in the MLP that calculates the bin probabilities. Collecting additional examples helps to constrain the model, effectively lowering its complexity and reducing the risk of overfitting even further.

Another common source of the excessive complexity that causes overfitting is the inclusion of redundant, irrelevant, or marginal inputs; that is, those that contain little relevant information. New models can be constructed without inputs whose inclusion cannot be clearly justified to see if their exclusion helps to eliminate, or at least reduce, the severity of the overfitting.

As with the unconditional distribution, underfitting can occur in a conditional distribution model because it contains too few bins to represent the shape of the distribution that actually underlies the example data. More simply, however, it might indicate that the model has not been training for long enough to pick out the subtleties in the exemplar data—particularly if it already has many bins.

If a conditional distribution model fails to capture the subtleties of the way in which a distribution should change in response to external influences, the MLP that calculates the bin probabilities might have too few hidden neurons to learn how to change the model's shape. Alternatively, the model's inputs might not include all the variables that actually have a substantial effect on the shape of the real distribution.

Conclusion

This article examined the widely neglected problem of modeling and imitating random variation. This is achieved by building a model of the distribution that describes the variation from a collection of samples of the variable of interest. Once a model has been constructed, the original random variation can be imitated by drawing random samples from it.

ON THE CD

Although this article and the accompanying demonstration program (which can be found on the CD) focus on reproducing humanlike random variation, the techniques described here can be applied to model any random variation, regardless of its cause. For example, it would be quite possible to imitate changes in weather or cycles of sunspot activity—provided that a suitable set of examples could be obtained.

The interested reader is strongly encouraged to experiment with the example program that accompanies this article. More information about the application of neural networks in games can be found in [Manslow01], [Evans02], and [Champandard02], about distribution modeling in general in [Bishop95], and about modeling and imitating random sequences in [Laramée02].

References

[Bishop95] Bishop, Chris, *Neural Networks for Pattern Recognition*, Macmillan College Publishing Company, 1995.

[Champandard02] Champandard, Alex, "The Dark Art of Neural Networks," *AI Game Programming Wisdom*, Charles River Media, 2002.

[Evans02] Evans, Richard, "Varieties of Learning," *AI Game Programming Wisdom*, Charles River Media, 2002.

[Laramée02] Laramée, François Dominic, "Using N-Gram Statistical Models to Predict Player Behavior," *AI Game Programming Wisdom*, Charles River Media, 2002.

[Manslow01] Manslow, John, "Using a Neural Network in a Game: A Concrete Example," *Game Programming Gems 2*, Charles River Media, 2001.

11.9

Genetic Algorithms: Evolving the Perfect Troll

François Dominic Laramée

francoislaramee@videotron.ca

Designing AI behavior is no easy task. Should your monster go berserk at the mere sight of anything that moves? Should it be sneaky? Cowardly? Or should it exhibit all of these traits, and if so, when should each kick in?

One solution would be to code several strategies by hand and test them in gameplay until you get something that "feels right." Unfortunately, this procedure runs the risk of being both time consuming (for example, if nothing good comes up from the first 100 attempts) and suboptimal if the programmer overlooks an interesting combination.

Consider the genetic algorithm. Inspired by the process of natural selection, the genetic algorithm (GA) mimics natural evolution to produce near-optimal solutions to complex nonlinear problems, like crafting a clever AI enemy. Using a small number of elementary strategies as building blocks, a GA will create entire populations of candidate solutions, see how well they perform at solving the problem, and gradually evolve more effective candidates over several generations, until a satisfactory level of performance is achieved.

ON THE CD

This article briefly describes how evolution works in nature and how to translate the process into programming, before showing a GA at work evolving a sheep-stealing troll for a fantasy role-playing game. The CD-ROM accompanying this book contains the source code for the example; feel free to refer to it as you read the article.

A Crash Course in Genetics

Before we can discuss genetic algorithms, we must describe how genetic information is transmitted in living organisms. Obviously, this discussion will merely sketch an outline of the process; readers who are offended by gross generalizations and outright omissions might want to read [Dawkins95].

Genes and Genotypes

All known living beings, except certain classes of viruses, store genetic material in molecules of DNA (deoxyribonucleic acid). DNA molecules are among the largest and most complex molecules in nature, often containing millions of atoms. Within the living cell, each DNA molecule is encased in a protective coating to form a *chromosome*. The number of chromosomes varies by species; human cells normally have 46, except sperm and ova, which only contain half as many. The sum of an individual's genetic material is known as the *genotype*.

Each chromosome harbors a number of *genes*. A gene is a DNA fragment containing the blueprint for construction of a single protein. The color of your eyes, your blood type, and everything else about you is influenced by a gene, or more usually by a number of interacting genes. Practically speaking, genes are the atoms of genetics: they are treated as indivisible components, no matter how big the underlying fragment of DNA.

An *allele* is a variant or mutational form of a gene. If there is a gene for "blood type," there are alleles for "type A," "type O," and so forth. Where genes define the structure of an organism's DNA, alleles define its flavor and variety.

Transmission of Genetic Material

During reproduction, each parent transmits half of their genetic material to the child. In humans, the chromosomes are organized into 23 pairs; when sperm and ova are created, the pairs are split, and only one chromosome from each pair is assigned to an individual cell.

However, the process is not quite as simple as taking a chromosome from each parent and copying it verbatim. Nature has developed several processes to stir the gene pool and introduce increased variation between individuals. For our purposes, the most important are:

- **Crossover**: Before they are assigned to reproductive cells, the two members of a pair of chromosomes can exchange genes between them. For example, if Daddy's chromosomes contain the gene sequences AAAAA and BBBBB, Junior's might contain AAABB or BBAAB instead.

- **Mutation**: Sometimes, a gene spontaneously changes form: a piece of DNA is inserted, deleted, or replaced, and the gene becomes something totally new and unexpected. For example, chromosome AAAAA might suddenly become AAACA. If the mutation occurs in a cell that will later produce sperm or ova, the C mutation will be transmitted to offspring.

Evolution

Over time, organisms that succeed in nature tend to reproduce more than others do. "Success" can mean anything from actually surviving until puberty, to having a shinier coat of fur that is attractive to potential partners, to being strong enough to protect the offspring one actually has until they are able to fend for themselves.

Consequently, the alleles present in successful individuals tend to spread ever wider into a population at the expense of their competitors. For example, if a mutation in the gene controlling a gray rabbit's fur color allows it to turn white during winter, it will be able to hide in the snow when the Big Bad Wolf comes along, thereby allowing it to survive until spring. The reverse is also true: mutations that reduce an organism's chance to survive in its environment (as, sadly, most mutations do) will tend to disappear quickly as their carriers die before having a chance to reproduce.

This is what Darwin defined as "survival of the fittest," and it is the crucial insight underlying genetic algorithms.

A Computational Model of Genetics

In a nutshell, a genetic algorithm works like this:

1. Create a first-generation *population* of random organisms.
2. Test them on the problem we are trying to solve, and rank them according to fitness. If the best organisms have reached our performance goals, stop.
3. Take the best performers and mate them by applying genetic operators such as crossover and mutation. Add a few brand-new random organisms to the population to introduce new variety and help ensure against convergence on a local maximum.
4. Loop to step 2.

What We Are Evolving

In nature, evolution works at the level of the *species*. It matters little whether a certain individual survives (except, obviously, to the individual in question), as long as the overall performance (or *fitness*) of the species with regard to its environment increases in the long run.

In the computer, however, we might want evolution to work at several different levels:

- **The individual**: We are trying to build a single perfect specimen, and then clone it as many times as we need.
- **The population**: We might want to create an entire population that maximizes global throughput when working in collaboration. For example, a band of Merry Men of various talents (archers, swordsmen, a carpenter for the Sherwood Forest village, and Friar Tuck to stir morale) would probably rob more of King John's treasure than 30 clones of Little John, even though he might be the best fighter of the bunch.
- **The ecosystem**: A-Life experiments often "co-evolve" several species that collaborate and compete with each other. This also happens in nature: pressure to improve is far more important when your own prey (or predators) improve as well. See [Levy92] for more information on this topic.

Our trolls are solitary individuals, so we will use the first approach. Of course, nothing prevents us from taking the top *N* performers evolved by our simulation and using all of them in the actual game. This would give each troll an individual flavor, make behavioral patterns in the troll population at large very difficult to predict, and likely drive the player insane.

Genotypes

More often than not, computer organism genotypes are represented as a single "chromosome." Implementations vary with needs, and include:

- **Bit strings**: This is the "canonical" representation, in which each gene is associated with a string of bits and treated as a number. This is quite effective when the genes can be interpreted as numbers ranging between 0 and some power of 2. For example, these numbers work well when they represent coefficients in an equation, weights associated with state transitions in a finite-state machine or a neural network, or indices in a table of values.
- **Decision trees**: The genotype as a whole implements a hierarchical system of if-then rules.
- **Source code**: A-Life experiments [Levy92] typically represent organisms as sequences of bytecodes. [Koza92] uses LISP source code instead, a practice that leads to the subfield of *genetic programming*. Using source code as genetic material allows tremendous levels of innovation, as every mutation effectively creates a new program without programmer intervention. However, most of these mutations will yield "nonsense organisms" that might not even compile, and so this method typically requires enormous population sizes and computation time to converge on a meaningful solution.

We will implement our genotype as an array of floating-point numbers, each of which represents the troll's bias toward one of five possible goals. It would be relatively easy to extend our genetic material to include, for example, the addresses of the functions called to implement each goal, or a small number of integer parameters passed to these functions; see [Oumanski99] for a scenario in which this is done.

The Initial Population

We begin the process of evolution by creating a number of random organisms. In our case, each gene is a number that can be picked at random over the interval [0,1]. If your genes represent function addresses or similarly structured data, you will have to make sure that your random individuals make sense; otherwise, you might have to work with inordinately high population sizes to derive meaningful results.

Evaluation, Fitness, and Reproduction

Once we have obtained a population, we can estimate for fitness by applying an *evaluation function* to each organism, and select the fittest organisms for reproduction.

Since GAs work with large population sizes over several generations, the evaluation function must be as fast as possible. In our case, each candidate troll will be evaluated by measuring its success in a simulation of the game environment.

Once the evaluations are complete, a *fitness function* must be applied to the results to determine which organisms will get a chance to beget the next generation, and in what proportions. Several different strategies can be applied here:

- **Stochastic sampling**: Each organism is assigned a probability of reproduction equal to its fitness divided by the total fitness of the population.
- **Remainder stochastic sampling** [Whitley94]: Divide each organism's fitness by the average fitness of the population. If the result is greater than 1, the organism reproduces a number of times equal to the integer part of the quotient. Fill in the rest of the population at random, using the remainders of the quotients as probabilities.
- **Ranking**: Individuals closer to the top of the fitness table automatically reproduce more times than others do.

We will be using a method based on ranking, because it forces quicker convergence. After several generations, clusters of organisms with similar evaluations will tend to form near the top of the standings. Stochastic sampling methods would end up picking among them essentially without preference, whereas we want to favor the best individuals even if their advantage over the competition is minute. However, unfit individuals that might beget amazing offspring, if given the chance, will be culled from the gene pool before they have a chance to do so—a risk that may or may not be acceptable in your application.

Crossover

Now that we know which individuals will reproduce, we can mate them by pairs and apply the crossover operator to mix their genetic material.

Again, there are many ways to implement crossover. *One-point (or unary) crossover* is the simplest: if a genotype contains N genes, pick a number at random between 1 and N-1 and swap everything between that point and the end of the genotype. For example, if we apply one-point crossover to AAAAA and BBBBB starting with gene #3, we will get AABBB and BBAAA.

However, if we look at the preceding example, we might notice that one-point crossover has a potentially annoying property: it always separates the first and last genes. In general, the larger the "distance" between two genes in the genotype, the higher the probability that they will be separated by one-point crossover. This might not seem like such a big deal, but what if the reason this individual is so successful is the fact that its first and last genes work especially well together? After all, this type of nonlinear interaction is one of the reasons we bother with GAs at all!

Several refinements can help prevent this problem:

- **Two-point (or binary) crossover**: Instead of selecting a single splicing point at random, select two of them and exchange only the material located between them.
- **Inversion**: Once in a while, change the order of the genes, so that pairs of collaborating genes located far away from each other might end up closer and therefore

less likely to be split. Obviously, this doesn't work if the order of the genes is important in your application; for example, if you store the genotype as an array and define gene names as integer constants to use as indices. For inversion to be meaningful, you will need an additional level of indirection: for example, a table associating each gene with its location in the data structure.

- *Disruption (or uniform crossover)*: When creating offspring, flip a coin to decide from which parent a given gene will be taken. This is effectively equivalent to variable-order crossover: some individuals may end up cloning one parent, while others may crossover at every single gene. This technique does wonders for diversity and is effective even with very small population sizes.

Our trolls have few genes, so the differences between crossover techniques would not be very evident. For demonstration purposes, we will use disruption.

Mutation

In a genetic algorithm, mutation's role is twofold:

- **Reintroduce extinct alleles**: Some good alleles might be wiped out from the population if they happen to be found only in lousy organisms. Mutation may reintroduce them and give them a second chance to prove themselves.
- **Prevent premature convergence**: If the entire population is made up of similar organisms, the algorithm might converge on locally optimal behavior instead of the best possible. Small mutations refine solutions, while large ones introduce individuals very different from the norm, which helps nudge the population away from local maxima when crossover has insufficient diversity with which to work.

In both cases, the role of mutation is far more important when dealing with small populations, because both allele extinction and premature convergence are more likely to occur. Nevertheless, the probability that any given gene will mutate between generations should be kept small: in bitstring representations, for example, each bit typically flips with probability 0.001. In fact, some implementations of genetic algorithms do not use mutation at all, although this seems rather extreme.

As an interesting aside, early work on genetic algorithms has shown that the role of mutation in natural evolution has probably been overstated. While classic evolutionary theory suggested that mutation was the key element in the process, it is now believed that crossover accounts for well over 90 percent of evolutionary progress by bringing together "symbiotic genes" that reinforce each other's effectiveness.

Generations

We will apply the following algorithm to produce new generations:

- Keep the top 20% of organisms from the previous generation and clone them unchanged. After all, it is possible that we have already found some of the best possible candidates.

- Create 70% of the new generation by mating individuals from the top third of the parent generation's rankings. Higher-ranked individuals will reproduce more often.

- Generate the remaining 10% of the population at random. This is effectively equivalent to applying a 100% mutation rate on a few trolls, and will help us avoid the drawbacks of small population sizes.

The literature suggests that population sizes in the hundreds or thousands of individuals should be used whenever possible. We will experiment with population sizes ranging from 100 to 250 trolls. While this is on the low end of the recommended spectrum, it is sufficient given the simple nature of our demo.

Why Use Genetic Algorithms?

Genetic algorithms are designed to work on nonlinear optimization problems with large numbers of variables whose interactions are hard to predict. (A game AI, therefore, seems like a perfect application!)

When Do They Work?

A genetic approach is unnecessary if one of the following conditions can be met:

- **The problem can be solved analytically.** "Evolving" a solution for the problem of finding the value of x that maximizes a polynomial is a waste of time, because an exact solution can be found by computing the polynomial's derivative.

- **The problem is entirely linear.** If the problem can be represented by a network of linear equations, any number of classic optimization techniques (i.e., the simplex method) will solve it.

- It is known that **a single optimal value exists and that the distribution is unimodal** (i.e., there are no local maxima). In this case, a simple hill-climbing algorithm will do the trick.

- **Candidate solutions can be *enumerated* in a reasonable amount of time.** In this case, you are better off trying them all.

When Don't They Work?

Running a genetic algorithm typically requires a significant time investment. Even our simplistic troll simulation requires about 22 minutes of computing time on an 800MHz Pentium III. Thus, it is unlikely that anyone will ever be able to evolve a passable chess-playing program, even with a world-spanning computer such as Asimov's Multivac at their disposal.

Moreover, since the number of possible chromosomes grows exponentially with the number of genes in the model, designing a minimalist architecture for your individuals may be crucial.

Why Do They Work?

There is a mathematical proof of the genetic algorithm's validity. See [Whitley94] for the details.

Case Study: Evolving Trolls

To illustrate the principles previously described, we will now evolve a troll for a fantasy role-playing environment.

Modeling the Troll

Our troll's job is to steal as many sheep and kill as many bold adventurers as possible without getting gruesomely dismembered itself. To do this, we will give the troll five goals from which to choose at every turn of the simulation: eat a sheep, kill a knight, flee sources of damage, heal, and explore the world.

A goal's likelihood of being selected depends on game world conditions. For example, a troll is more likely to pursue the "eat" goal if it hasn't caught a sheep in a long time, while it will prefer to heal in safe areas rather than within firing range of a guard tower. Each goal is also associated with a single function implementing a sensible strategy. Thus, if the troll wants to eat, it will first look for a sheep close enough to be pounced on in a single turn. If it finds one, great; if not, it will march toward the closest sheep on the map.

The troll's genotype will contain biases (i.e., weights) associated with each goal. Each weight, represented as a floating-point number between 0 and 1, will be multiplied by a goal's current desirability.

The Environment

Our trolls live in a 30 x 30 square world; each square on the grid might contain any number of these entities:

- **Safe havens**: Safe for trolls, that is. These monster-ridden bogs and dark, foreboding forests allow trolls to heal injuries more effectively. Knights pursuing a troll automatically lose track of it when the troll enters a safe haven.
- **Traps**: To a troll, these look exactly like safe havens, but they have been booby-trapped by evil humans. Traps capture trolls, keeping them immobile for a variable amount of time; worse yet, trolls fight at a distinct disadvantage while captured.
- **Sheep**: Cute, helpless prey that just wander about aimlessly until they detect a troll nearby, at which point they run away.
- **Knights**: Non-cute, mostly helpless adventurers looking to add the troll's scalp to their collections. Knights also wander about the world until they detect a troll, and then pursue it tirelessly until either one of them is dead or the troll has retreated to a safe haven. Whenever a knight finds itself sharing a grid square with

a troll, a duel to the death ensues. Knights never retreat, never surrender, and never show mercy.

- **Watch towers**: Indestructible structures from which archers fire at trolls from a distance.

In order to avoid overspecializing our trolls, each will be tested on three scenarios (sheep-rich, knight-rich, and sparsely populated) and evaluated according to the average of its performances in all three.

Evaluation and Fitness Functions

We want our trolls to be considered aggressive nuisances by the peasants of our fantasy worlds, so we will give high scores to individuals that steal a lot of sheep and kill a lot of knights. We will also favor trolls that annoy humans for a long time and avoid injury and capture:

```
double Troll::GetEvaluation()
{
    double score = 8.0  * StatsKnightsKilled
            + 10.0 * StatsSheepEaten
            + 1.5  * StatsTimeAlive
            − 1.0  * StatsTimeCaptive
            − 2.50 * StatsDamageTaken;
    return score;
}
```

The choice of evaluation function is crucial, because it determines the problem that the genetic algorithm will be trying to solve. Give too much weight to a certain component, and the results will surprise you. An early experiment with the troll scenario, for example, put too much emphasis on long-term survival. As a result, the genetic algorithm happily evolved a population of cowards: the entire top 10 was made of trolls who did not capture a single sheep or kill a single knight, but managed to survive all 500 turns of the simulation by fleeing all the time!

Since our simulation involves some random elements (i.e., the troll's starting position and how long it will stay imprisoned once it falls into a trap), the actual scores obtained by individuals have less meaning than their relative rankings. Thus, once all individuals in a population have been tested, we will produce a new generation. This new generation will be generated by cloning the top 20 individuals (just in case they're the best possible), mating the top seven individuals by pairs, mating random pairs of individuals selected from the top 35, and creating a handful of brand-new organisms.

Results

With a population size of 100 individuals and an evolutionary period of 50 generations, the simulation takes a little under four minutes to run on an 800MHz Pentium III processor. The resulting population can be characterized as:

- **Showing little instinct for self-preservation.** Not one of the top 25 individuals has survived for more than 50 of the simulation's 500 scheduled turns.
- **Having large appetites.** Despite their limited life expectancy, the top 10 performers of generation 50 all managed to gobble up between 15 and 18 sheep even in the sparsely populated scenario (where there are only 20 sheep to begin with).
- **Cunning fighters.** The trolls quickly learn that they don't have to waste precious sheep-hunting time chasing knights around to get into fisticuffs, since their opponents will come looking for them. Indeed, of the top 25 performers, none has a gene for knight-chasing with a weight higher than 0.018, and 14 have it valued at 0. And yet, six of the top 10 trolls managed to kill five to seven knights apiece in between all of their meals.
- **Not terribly interested in healing or exploration.** The bonus for each turn spent alive seems to be outweighed by the penalty incurred for sustaining damage, so that trolls are not encouraged to heal old wounds, just to sustain even more. (The fitness function can be adjusted to change this behavior if needed.)
- **Quite talented at evading traps.** Of the top 25 individuals, only four spent even a single turn in captivity, and none stayed imprisoned for more than three turns. This is easily explained: since traps look like safe havens, trolls who don't go looking for havens (to heal in) run little risk of being captured.
- **Very fit on average.** At generation 1, not a single individual achieved a score higher than 200, and the median evaluation was a mediocre 133.8; at generation 50, 18 individuals topped the 200 mark (including an impressive 243.3), while the median value rose to 195.5.

Performance did not improve significantly when population size was increased to 250 and the simulation was allowed to run over 100 generations. The relatively small size of the trolls' genotypes probably explains this phenomenon: with a handful of genes, the search space is small enough to allow fast convergence.

Conclusion

Genetic algorithms are a powerful optimization tool for problems featuring large numbers of variables and chaotic interactions. By mimicking the natural processes of survival of the fittest and evolution, they can discover unusual combinations of strategies that can lead to interesting computer opponents for your games.

References

[Dawkins95] Dawkins, R., *River Out Of Eden—A Darwinian View Of Life*, Harper-Collins, 1995.

[Koza92] Koza, J.R., *Genetic Programming—On the Programming of Computers by Means of Natural Selection*, MIT Press, 1992.

[Levy92] Levy, S., *Artificial Life—A Report from the Frontier where Computers Meet Biology*, Random House, 1992.

[Oumanski99] Oumanski, A., "Object-Oriented Approach to Genetic Programming," Concordia University thesis, 1999.

[Whitley94] Whitley, D., "A Genetic Algorithm Tutorial," *Statistics and Computing*, vol. 4, pp. 65–84, 1994. Also available on the Web at www.cs.colostate.edu/~genitor/Pubs.html.

11.10

The Dark Art of Neural Networks

Alex J. Champandard—Artificial Intelligence Depot

alex@ai-depot.com

Your boss wants you to use *neural networks* in your next production, and having been told that they are a miracle solution, you thought you'd give them a try. You got a book out of the local library, and found that there's actually nothing really difficult involved. A few hours later, you have a simple network performing an XOR task. However, satisfaction is quickly replaced by frustration, as you admit that this is not quite what your boss had in mind. When tackling larger problems, you realize that your neural networks do not perform to expectations. Luckily, further research reveals that a few people have tackled a similar application, and you try to mimic their models. Things are looking up; this particular challenge is resolved, but part of the decision process still seems inspired by black magic.

This article targets an audience with intermediate knowledge of *artificial neural networks* (henceforth, NN). You will need to be familiar with the terminology, and have basic practical experience. Assuming this, the aim of these next few pages is to push your understanding to the next level, allowing you to tackle large problems with NN and skillfully optimize them. This is done by acknowledging the need for *neural network design*, recognizing commonly used techniques as well as some personal favorites, and trying to put them all down on paper.

Neural Networks for Games

Neural networks provide all the benefits of machine learning, while still retaining their simplicity. This makes them ideally suited to games, especially in the contexts of *pattern recognition* and *robotic controllers*.

The Theory

These are two of the most active fields of connectionism, and arguably the most interesting.

Pattern recognition can be used on a logical level, providing the ability to learn to classify input vectors, and provide fuzzy generalizations [Bishop95]. This process is similar to decision making, which is well suited to high-level AI components.

Robotics controllers based on NN have been successfully developed with the help of genetic algorithms [Gehlot92]. The idea is to evolve the networks to control the physical behavior of mechanical devices, using a method known as *regression*. This theory is ideal for games, as it is applicable to 3D noisy environments.

Even though the internal working of the neural networks remains the same when applied to different problems, conceptually you may benefit from thinking of them in different ways. Using a geometric interpretation of pattern recognition, classes in sample space are separated by a decision surface. For robotics controllers, the input variables are combined into intermediary results using nonlinear functions, similar to a factorized equation.

Conceptual comprehension of NN is essential during applications, since treating the problem as a black box will often flaw your design. However, understanding specific instances takes time that would be better spent optimizing the problem.

Structure Choices

As a reminder, inside an NN, multiple neurons are linked via weighted connections. There are many different topologies for a fixed neuron count, but most structures are either obsolete or practically useless. For our applications, however, some types excel.

Feed forward networks, where the information flows directly from the input to the outputs, are the best known. They come in two varieties: fully connected and sparse, the first being a special case of the latter where all possible connections are present. Evolution and training with back-propagation are both possibilities [Pfister96].

Recurrent networks have no connection restrictions; information can flow backward, allowing feedback. This provides a small sense of state due to the internal variables needed for the simulation. Like feed-forward NN, fully connected and sparse versions exist. However, the training process remains more complex, despite recent advances in the field [Pedersen97]. Evolution remains a robust alternative solution.

Gas-nets are a recent breakthrough attempting to model extra plasticity due to gas behaving as a neurotransmitter [Husbands98]. Internal variables are triggered by intense neuron activity. Learning can only be achieved by evolution due to the complexity of the scheme. Also, since these NN are time dependent, pattern recognition can be problematic. In contrast, robotics controllers relish the sense of state provided.

Implementation Issues

It is a well-known fact that game logic is assigned a very small slice of the computation time. This requires us to save as much time as possible on the simulation. As such, since sparse structures are extremely rare, NN should preferably be fully connected (especially the dense ones). This entails a smaller memory overhead and allows parallel processing.

In the same spirit, recurrent networks should also be avoided, despite their capabilities. Simulation of feedback requires multiple iterations, and time would be better spent simulating multiple feed-forward networks. In addition, their dependency on *genetic algorithms* can be an extra reason to shy away from this solution.

Internal precision in the weights and activation function is also a controversial issue. Standard policy is that anything less than double precision is sacrilege. Understandably, once every other stage of the design is absolutely perfect, 64 bits will provide the most accurate results. However, in practice, the common single precision float is more than capable in the context of real-time games. The added benefit of being able to simulate the NN at over twice the speed is not to be neglected.

Finally, for activation functions, use a nonlinear equation to allow classification of complex patterns. Using derivable functions will allow the back-propagation algorithm to perform gradient descent on the input vector. Sigmoidal units permit this.

Applications

The potential of such neural networks is quite enticing. They can approximate any function [Siegelmann98], and a three-layer network can also successfully classify any nonlinearly separable patterns [Papert69]. These simple capabilities go a long way in explaining the common myths about NN. But, as ever, theory and practice diverge significantly. [Blum92] has shown that training an NN is an NP complete algorithm, which means its complexity increases exponentially as the problem grows linearly.

Although connectionism can be applied to many problems, obstinacy will slow your progress. In practice, use NN solutions where errors are not critical, where training samples are abundant or easy to find, and where patterns in the data can be exposed.

Representation of the Environment

The environment can be defined as the place where the NN will perform its task. This concept is not as essential for pattern recognition as for robotic controllers, but many techniques are common to both approaches. The importance of a correct representation might seem obvious, but nevertheless, this is the primary reason for failed applications.

Interface

The interface defines the overall behavior of the NN by specifying both its inputs and its outputs. The input vector can be considered a feature set. For pattern recognition, the outputs correspond to the probability of the input being in that category. With robotics controllers, each input feature corresponds to a sensor, which can return distances or angular measurements. Each output then corresponds to an action, which is usually assigned to control one degree of freedom of the robot.

The selection of the outputs of a network is understandably tied to the application chosen, so little artistic freedom is possible. Keep in mind, however, that there is usually more than one way to represent the problem. On the other hand, the choice of the inputs needs more thought. Selecting every related variable as an input will make the size of the search space explode, thereby reducing chances of successful generalization. Conversely, you also need to select enough inputs to guarantee the existence of a function that maps the inputs to the outputs, and that the patterns can be successfully classified.

Getting off on the right foot involves selecting inputs that are as relevant as possible. The rational programmer's approach is a personal favorite: what features would come in most handy if this function was hard-coded? A mental list of these variables should be made, and ordered by importance. First experiments with the NN would then involve those that are absolutely essential. If this minimalist approach fails, or if the problem needs to be scaled up, inputs are added from the top of the list. Doing this in a moderated and systematic fashion avoids missing potential solutions. Also keep in mind that the training will become a tougher process as you add more inputs.

Data Preprocessing

The aim of the learning process is to allow the NN to perform well for all cases, whether encountered during training or not. Part of this is done by the generalization intrinsic to learning, and part is the responsibility of the designer. Indeed, one of the biggest tasks when applying NN involves using problem-specific knowledge to assist the learning. This is done partly by preprocessing the data during training and simulation:

Simple features can be combined into **compound features** that are more relevant. Commonly used techniques include mathematical equations (e.g., comparing values using their ratio) and complex algorithms (e.g., extracting the average color of an image).

Symmetry removal allows you to reduce the number of situations that the NN must handle. This is done by mapping undesired parts of the search space onto other preferred sections. Simple tests before the simulation can determine if the conditions are met. If not, the appropriate values can be negated, flipped, or swapped as necessary. For example, training a car to turn left only: if the left obstacle is further than the right, the values are swapped. Similarly, the steering direction in the output vector is negated.

Normalization assures that the values have a meaningful format by scaling and offsetting them. For example, using information relative to the current position of the agent, or converting all values to the range [0,1], which the NN handles particularly well.

Learning Overview

The purpose of learning is to replace the initially random weights with a near optimal set.

Supervised Learning

Supervised learning trains NN by providing a desired output for each input vector. This is the case with back-propagation, one among other forms of training. The beauty of this approach is being able to train networks online as well as offline. However, acquiring the data to use in training is an important process, and for games, there are a few options.

Interactive training permits the human player to supervise the learning process. A custom interface can allow him to correct the output of the NN, thereby producing the training sample directly. Alternatively, he can confirm the correctness of the result, in which case, the desired output is determined by increasing values of alternate solutions. Optionally, an automated thread can perform the independent supervision of the training.

Behavior cloning allows the NN to mimic humans. In this case, the player acts without directly worrying about the training. Another process is charged with monitoring the human's actions, while associating them with an input vector. This is the most delicate process, with feature selection and reaction times being two of the biggest pitfalls: what factors were taken into account, and when did they influence the decision? The key is to introduce the notion of state, making it as persistent as possible.

Hard-coded components can also be reproduced in order to provide initial training of an adaptive NN, or to combine multiple functions. In this case, formal rules are needed to split the input space among the various components. In the training set, the entire input space needs to be represented, not only common game situations. Random selection of the training samples provides a satisfactory distribution.

Unsupervised Learning

With *unsupervised learning*, no direct feedback is needed for the NN to learn, so training examples are not required. In the cases we are interested in, this is achieved by using the NN as part of a higher-level learning scheme.

Reinforcement learning attempts to learn the optimal mapping from state to action. An NN can learn this mapping, given a representation of the state as an input vector and the probability of each action as an output vector. The online approach is preferred, since multiple iterations are required. See [Ballard97] for more details.

Genetic algorithms and other third-party optimization algorithms can also allow the NN to learn the optimal set of weights, and also potentially the structure.

Preferably, this should be learned before the game starts, since considerable variations in the results can be noticed. Despite the novelty and controversy associated with this approach, the potential is hard to ignore.

Offline versus Online

Offline learning takes place before the simulation, in a fashion similar to precomputation. If training is used, this implies that all the training samples are readily available. The quality achieved by learning algorithms in this case is often superior. From within the game, performance does not suffer due to dynamic training.

Online training allows the network to learn within the game. Technologically speaking, it can be problematic for an NN to be presented with a constant stream of data. New input vectors need to be learned while still assuring that previous instances are not forgotten. Incremental training algorithms deal with this problem. There can also be a loss of quality in the results, since inappropriate data might be learned. Using a higher-level learning algorithm assures that the solution converges to a global maximum.

Hybrid schemes seem ideally suited to gaming, combining the best of the two previous approaches. The initial network is trained according to reasonable default parameters, while sparse online data is learnt to prevent confusion.

Supervised Back-Propagation Training

This method remains the standard for NN learning. The entire field has evolved around such training algorithms. With over four decades of research and practice, the procedure is extremely well documented, with [Bishop95] remaining *the* reference. This section will not attempt to duplicate his efforts, but concentrates on practical optimization issues.

Incremental versus Batch

Excluding heavy numerical analysis solutions, there are two major types of algorithms.

Incremental training algorithms update the weights for every training sample, implying that it does not converge to a fixed set of values. However, online training is possible. The original back-propagation routine loops repeatedly until satisfactory results are obtained. To prevent the algorithm from settling in a suboptimal state, momentum is often added to the weight deltas. The major problem with this approach is the selection of the learning rate, which can be a tedious, problem-specific process. A solution to this is known as *stochastic approximation* or *annealing*: the learning rate is slowly decreased to encourage training to converge to a global maximum.

Batch learning processes the entire training set before the weights are updated. Understandably, this requires the training to be offline. This has many advantages, including the absence of learning rates, which allow the algorithm to automatically converge to a solution. The best, and also one of the simplest, algorithms for this is RProp [Riedmiller93]. This combination should be chosen whenever possible.

Noise

Even if the environment is theoretically perfect, contradictory training data might arise when you simplify its representation. Specifically, the same input vector might have different corresponding output vectors. For training data, this can be a problem since it reveals uncertainty about the results required: this can seriously impair generalization. The addition of disambiguating inputs can resolve most of these cases.

Surprisingly, adding artificial jitter to samples in small training sets can prevent overfitting and enhance generalization [Holmström92]. Keep the noise random to avoid learning its distribution. In practice, avoid noise on Boolean values. Also consider noise on the input vectors as well as output vectors. Finally, with regard to robotics sensors, use noise in the parameters of the sensors as well as the values returned.

Unsupervised Evolution

Genetic algorithms (GA) rely on nature's concept of survival of the fittest to produce near-optimal solutions. An entire *population* of entities is created, all represented as a sequence of genes: the *genotype*. This forms the structure of the genetic code, and specific instances of genes (called *alleles*) are required to model the individuals. Given this genotype, trials are performed to assign a *fitness* value to each entity. Informally, the fitness is the likelihood of them being allowed to mate. In practice, a *selection scheme* can pick two parents based on this value. A process called *crossover* then combines their genetic code. Finally, *mutation* is performed on the child's genotype. It is then reinserted into the gene pool by a *replacement scheme*, which can be incremental (replacing the parents, or a random entity) or complete (spawning an entirely new population each generation). Evolution is stopped when satisfactory results are obtained. For a broader and more in-depth look at GA, consult a good introductory book to the field (such as [Mitchell98]).

GA have recently been applied to NN with great success. This area is a fairly new field, and relatively undocumented. However, there has been a significant amount of research, from which we will attempt to extract the best techniques.

Neural Network Representation

Before any optimization algorithm can be applied, a convenient representation of NN needs to be established [Yao93]. Grammar-based representations have the advantage of being able to model individual connections and feedback in a compact fashion. Tree-based representations are reserved for feed-forward networks. These two solutions have the advantage of being able to represent the structure of the network intrinsically. However, the most appropriate representation is the simplest, based on arrays of floats. All the weights of the network are stored sequentially in an array of genes. There are a few special genes corresponding to the size of each layer. If these genes are changed, the decoding of the genotype will have to add or remove extra weights where needed.

State-of-the-Art Genetic Algorithm

The original population of genotypes is created randomly, allowing good initial coverage of the search space. This population is stored on a 2D grid, which corresponds to one NN per cell. This grid wraps around in both dimensions, in a donutlike fashion. Each genotype is converted to an NN, and put through a trial to determine its initial fitness value. The evolution process can now start. A cell is selected at random, from which two stochastic walks are performed. The two fittest individuals found along the path will be allowed to reproduce. The offspring's fitness is evaluated, and is placed inside the cell chosen. Another cell is randomly chosen, and the process can continue until a satisfactory solution is found [Gruau93]. Stochastic hill climbing is performed on the set of weights to fine-tune the solution, as GA are often ill-suited to this task.

To create the offspring, *uniform* crossover is used first. This involves randomly copying genes from both parents, with a probability of 0.6 and 0.4, respectively. The mutation process then adds Gaussian noise to each gene, with a probability of 0.001.

After several generations, some alleles might appear more frequently than others. Via crossover, these alleles might start to dominate the entire population, thereby extinguishing other alleles. This condition is known as *genetic drift*, and can cause premature convergence to a suboptimal solution. Increasing the mutation rate generates more diversity, allowing a fresh restart. Increasing the size of the population also reduces chances of an allele taking over.

By restricting the selection of the parents to a local neighborhood, genetic diversity is maintained by introducing fitness *islands*. These are areas of the population where genetic code is similar, and therefore close in the search space. Genetic drift is prevented since these islands only interact with others in close proximity. This is known as *localization*, and allows preservation of a good search space coverage.

If you need a quick evolution, and don't mind suboptimal solutions, reduce the size of the population. Select parents randomly among the elite, and replace the least fit individuals. Conversely, for better quality solutions that take longer to evolve, increase the population size. Allow all individuals to breed but with a bias for the fittest, and replace random entities. This maintains diversity, and does not instantly discard unfit parents that could potentially spawn miracle offspring.

Fitness Evaluation

Fitness functions are crucial since they indirectly determine the behavior of the final model. In general, they need to be as smooth as possible, as GA struggle with fractures in fitness space. It is, therefore, good practice to keep it continuous.

If you know how your network should perform, an explicit approach can be taken to devise such a function. This guides the evolution by granting instant rewards: when learning to kill with a rocket launcher, for instance, rewarding small angle deviations from the enemy's position. Such a constraining approach can initially help the GA, but can limit the originality of the solutions. Training should be considered in this case.

More implicit approaches, based on punishment and long-term reward, allow more freedom in the solution; in other words, rewards based on damage inflicted (using the same rocket launcher example). Obviously, loopholes are the major problem with this approach, although it can be extremely amusing to watch unexpected results!

Finally, you can also combine both of these approaches into one fitness function. This involves levels of magnitude in the coefficients used to scale fitness components. Practically, the explicit reward for small angle deviations can be scaled by 0.1, and the implicit reward for damage inflicted would weigh 100. Conceptually, domain-specific knowledge is used to devise a smooth fitness function. Not only does this guide the evolution in the early stages, but it also allows more freedom in the later stages.

System Design

When developing NN applications, you need to admit that this is a design phase, and not just about hacking parameters. This implies that you work in incremental updates, that you document changes, and that you back up any working prototype. This will come in handy down the line if something goes wrong, or if your model needs expanding.

Structure

There is no immediate formula for determining what structure a NN must have, and since this is troublesome for even the best human experts, the chances of an efficient arithmetic solution appearing in the future are slim. As such, any rules of thumb are likely to fail in many cases. There are, however, some good parameters to start experimenting with. For the number of layers, we usually limit ourselves to three when *training* (input, hidden and output). The reason for this is that three layers are enough to classify any pattern, and back-propagation algorithms work well on NN with few layers. Varying the number of neurons in the hidden layer will have more impact, since this directly affects the generalization quality. Note that you can rarely compromise between simplicity of the network and quality of the results, due to under- and over-fitting. When selecting the neuron count, the size of the search space is only a secondary factor, since prior knowledge can be internalized by the network. A good place to start for the number of neurons in the hidden layer is twice the number of inputs.

For *evolution* of robotics controllers, things are different. Since the fitness trials process many test cases, generalization is somewhat less of an immediate goal. The NN will be more or less capable of generalizing, as long as the solution is converged to within the search space. In this case, we do not limit ourselves to three layers; using a greater number of smaller layers has a beneficial influence on the evolution. After many discussions with leading academics, it seems that properties of the covariance in such structures allows them to compute more complex functions. Practically, we usually start with four layers, each with double the number of inputs. We try to avoid input counts above five, since evolution times quickly become inconvenient for development.

Feedback

Feedback is an intrinsic property of recurrent NN. For robotic controllers, this can be a highly desirable property, since it provides the network with a sense of state. This allows the network to perform less on a purely reactive basis. A more humanlike behavior can thereby be modeled by penalizing abrupt movement. Feed-forward NN can achieve this by using the *output of the previous simulation* as an additional input.

Modularity

Modularity is a good idea for NN development as with any other computer science problem. In particular, multiple small structures will outweigh one big one due to the reduction of the search space size. Combining them remains the only problem. There has been much research into this problem, notably to solve under- and over-fitting [Sharkey99]. In such component-based systems, it is often best to combine NN with other hard-coded components. For example, given a deliberative pathfinding algorithm that returns the desired heading and an NN used for reactive obstacle avoidance, the two angles can be combined using a second network. It would decide the final heading given high-level factors such as importance and urgency.

Automated Design

There have been a few genuine attempts to automate the design process, but most have been based on GA. [Gruau95] uses cellular encoding to represent the NN as a procedural entity, which provides modularity. L-Systems have also been applied to create tree-based network representations [Boers92]. Search space smoothness is the major problem here, as any type of structural mutation will cause sudden changes in the fitness. The GA is thereby not placed under ideal working conditions. However, these schemes remain viable alternatives, despite human experts being able to out-per-form them.

Conclusion

As you've most likely noticed by now, *neural network design* is a skill, possibly even an art, and just like others, it can be acquired over time. Correctly modeling the environment, taking special precautions during training or evolution, and correctly selecting the network structure are the primary things you should remember. With any luck, the *"lobby to the next level"* format of this article has guided you in the appro-priate directions, both in research and experimentation. This should go a long way in providing you with a feel for NN, which will help you determine if a problem should be tackled using connectionism or not, and hopefully make the design process seem a bit less like witchcraft. Admittedly, with so many years of knowledge and expertise packed into one article, you're probably feeling so bloated with information that a double-decker bus at full speed would hardly hurt you. But that's just an impression!

References

[Ballard97] Ballard, D. H., *An Introduction to Natural Computation*, MIT Press, 1997.

[Bishop95] Bishop, C.M., *Neural Networks for Pattern Recognition,* Oxford University Press, 1995.

[Blum92] Blum, A.L. and Rivest, R.L, "Training a 3-Node Neural Network is NP-Complete," Neural Networks, Vol 5., 1992.

[Boers92] Boers, E. J. W., Kuiper, H., "Biological Metaphor and the design of modu-lar artificial networks," Masters Thesis, Leiden University, 1992.

[Gehlot92] Gehlot, N. S. and Alsina, P. J., "A Comparison Control Strategies of Robotic Manipulators Using Neural Networks," International Conference on IECON, 1992.

[Gruau93] Gruau, F., *The Mixed Parallel Genetic Algorithm*, Parallel Computing, 1993.

[Gruau95] Gruau, F., *Automatic Definition of Modular Neural Networks*, Adaptive Behaviour, 1995.

[Holmström92] Holmström, L. and Koistinen, P., "Using additive noise in back-propagation training," IEEE Transaction on Neural Networks, 1992.

[Husbands98] Husbands, P., Smith, T. et al, "Brains, Gases and Robots," Proceedings of the ICNN, 1998.

[Mitchell98] Mitchell, M., *An Introduction to Genetic Algorithms (Complex Adaptive Systems)*, MIT Press, 1998.

[Papert69] Minsky, M. and Papert, S., *Perceptrons: An Introduction to Computational Geometry,* MIT Press, 1969.

[Pedersen97] Pedersen, M.W., *"Training Recurrent Networks,"* Proceedings of the IEEE Work-shop on Neural Networks for Signal Processing VII, 1997.

[Pfister96] M. Pfister, *"Learning Algorithms for Feed-Forward Neural Networks - Design, Combination and Analysis,"* Fortschrittberichte VDI-Verlag, Dusseldorf, 1996.

[Riedmiller93] Riedmiller, M. and Braun, H., "A Direct Adaptive Method for Faster Backpropagation Learning: The RPROP Algorithm," Proceedings of the ICNN, 1993.

[Sharkey99] Sharkey, A. J. C., *Combining Artificial Neural Nets: Ensemble and Modular Multi-Net Systems*, London: Springer, 1999.

[Siegelmann98] Siegelmann, H. T., *Neural Networks and Analog Computation: Beyond the Turing Limit*, Boston: Birkhauser, 1998.

[Yao93] Yao, X., "A Review of Evolutionary Artificial Neural Networks," International Journal of Intelligent Systems 8, 1993.

About the CD-ROM

The CD-ROM that accompanies this book contains material that augments many of the articles, including:

- Demos of many of the techniques described in this book. Most demos require Microsoft Visual C++ 6.0 and are indicated with a ".dsw" file.
- Source code that is referenced in various articles. Most source code is in C++, with some samples in C and Java.
- High-resolution versions of the color plates.
- Links to useful and interesting game development sites.

Demos

Virtually every demo comes with full source code for you to examine, borrow, and tweak for your own personal or commercial games. Demos are supplied for the following articles:

Code Portions

Code portions will not run by themselves, but they provide the core structures, algorithms, or modules for the following articles. The majority of this code appears in the book, and is provided on the CD-ROM for your ease of integration.

System Requirements

- Intel Pentium-series, AMD Athlon or newer processor recommended
- Windows 95 (32MB RAM), or Windows NT4 (64MB RAM) or later required
- 3D graphics card recommended for optimal performance
- DirectX 8 or newer

Errata and Updates

Visit www.AIWisdom.com for errata and updates to the code, demos, or articles. Corrections can be reported to steve@aiwisdom.com.

Index